THE

STATE

OF THE

INTERIOR

DESIGN

PROFESSION

fb

THE
STATE
OF THE
INTERIOR
DESIGN
PROFESSION

EDITED BY

CAREN S. MARTIN&
PhD, CID-MN, FASID, IDEC, IES, IIDA
DENISE A. GUERIN
PhD, FIDEC, FASID, IIDA

UNIVERSITY OF MINNESOTA

FAIRCHILD BOOKS
NEW YORK

Vice President & General Manager, Education &
    Conference Division: Elizabeth Tighe
Executive Editor: Olga T. Kontzias
Assistant Acquisitions Editor: Amanda Breccia
Editorial Development Director: Jennifer Crane
Senior Development Editor: Joseph Miranda
Associate Art Director: Erin Fitzsimmons
Production Director: Ginger Hillman
Associate Production Editor: Andrew Fargnoli
Copyeditor: Susan Hobbs
Ancillaries Editor: Noah Schwartzberg
Cover Design: Erin Fitzsimmons
Text Design: Tom Helleberg
Director, Sales & Marketing: Brian Normoyle

Library of Congress Catalog Card Number:
2009931526
ISBN: 978-1-56367-920-9
GST R 133004424

Printed in the United States of America

TP09

To my kids,
Julia, Nate, and Lucas,
for sharing me,
and to my loving husband, Jeff,
I dedicate this book.
Technical support was the least of it.

—CSM

To my children, Amy, Nora, and Jay,
and their father, Patrick, my late husband,
who taught us to cherish one another.

—DAG

Together, we dedicate this book to
the interior design profession—
and interior designers of the future.
We hope it helps in some small way.

—CSM & DAG

CONTENTS

① VALUE OF INTERIOR DESIGN

5 FACTORS INFLUENCING PRACTICE

6 ETHICS AND LEGALITY

7 REGULATION OF PRACTICE

8 DIVERSITY

(11) PERCEIVED IDENTITY

(12) CHALLENGES

LIST OF ACRONYMS AND ABBREVIATIONS

AAHID	American Academy of Healthcare Interior Designers
ABC	Associated Builders and Contractors
ACHA	American College of Healthcare Architects (FACHA, Fellow of ACHA)
ACSA	Association of Collegiate Schools of Architecture
ADA	Americans with Disabilities Act
ADPSR	Architects, Designers, Planners for Social Responsibility
AERA	American Educational Research Association
AIA	American Institute of Architects (FAIA, Fellow of AIA)
AICP	American Institute of Certified Planners
AID	American Institute of Interior Decorators
AIGA	American Institute of Graphic Arts
ANSI	American National Standards Institute
APA	American Psychological Association
APS	American Physical Society
ARIDNB	Association of Registered Interior Designers of New Brunswick
ARIDO	Association of Registered Interior Designers of Ontario
ASAE	American Society of Association Executives
ASID	American Society of Interior Designers (FASID, Fellow of ASID)
ASLA	American Society of Landscape Architects
AUID	Association of University Interior Designers
BAAID	Bachelor of Applied Arts in Interior Design
BID	Bachelor of Interior Design
BOCA	Building Officials and Code Administrators International
BOMA	Building Owners and Managers Association International
BIFMA	Business and Institutional Furniture Manufacturers Association
CABO	Council of American Building Officials
CEU	Continuing Education Unit

CID	Certified Interior Designer (e.g., CID-MN, CID-NJ)
CIDA	Council for Interior Design Accreditation (formerly known as FIDER)
CLARB	Council of Landscape Architectural Registration Boards
CPE	Certified Professional Ergonomist
CSI	Construction Specifications Institute
CQRID	Council for Qualification of Residential Interior Designers
EDRA	Environmental Design Research Association
HFES	Human Factors and Ergonomics Society (FHFES, Fellow of HFES)
HSW	Health, Safety, and Welfare
ICBO	International Conference of Building Officials
IDC	Interior Designers of Canada
IDCA	Interior Design Coalition of Arizona
IDCEC	Interior Design Continuing Education Council
IDEC	Interior Design Educators Council (FIDEC, Fellow of IDEC)
IDEP	Interior Design Experience Program
IDA	International Design Alliance
IDS	Interior Design Society
IES	Illuminating Engineering Society (IESNA, of North America)
IFMA	International Facilities Managers Association
IFI	International Federation of Interior Architects and Designers
IIDA	International Interior Design Association (FIIDA, Fellow of IIDA)
IIDEX®	NeoCon Canada
ISID	International Society of Interior Designers
KYCID	CID-KY
MARCH	Master of Architecture
MID	Master of Interior Design
MIDLAC	Minnesota Interior Design Legislative Action Committee
LEED® AP	Leadership in Energy and Environmental Design Accredited Professional
LEED® CI	LEED® for Commercial Interiors
NABAR	National Administration Board of Architectural Registration (China)
NARI	National Association for the Remodeling Industry
NCARB	National Council of Architectural Registration Boards
NCEES	National Council of Examiners for Engineering and Surveying
NCIDQ	National Council for Interior Design Qualification
NCQLP	National Council on Qualifications for the Lighting Profession
NCSL	National Conference of State Legislatures
NEOCON®	Trade Fair for Interior Design & Facilities Management
NFPA	National Fire Protection Association
NHFA	National Home Furnishings Association
NKBA	National Kitchen and Bath Association
NLCID	National Legislative Coalition for Interior Design
NOCA	National Organization for Competency Assurance
NOMA	National Organization of Minority Architects
NSPE	National Society of Professional Engineers
RDI	Retail Design Institute

RID	Registered Interior Designer
RSA	Royal Society for the Encouragement of Arts, Manufactures and Commerce
SIOP	Society for Industrial & Organizational Psychology, Inc.
USGBC	United States Green Building Council

FOREWORD

The role of interior designers is rapidly changing. We are long past the narrow view of equating interior design with decoration or surviving on space planning for a "buck a square foot." Our professional responses are based on strategic intelligence from observed trends, market drivers, and *wildcards* that unexpectedly surface and influence our course. The maturation of the profession has spun varied opinions and issues specific to each interior designer and market sector, demanding a closer look at the role and responsibility of interior designers and our value to society. Thus, it is very timely and appropriate that a book collecting the thoughts of many leading design visionaries be compiled now, when the profession is at a crossroads.

The State of the Interior Design Profession is a compilation of 76 essays written by the best interior design thinkers in North America. They are members or associates of the interior design profession; they are the visionaries, leaders, and emerging leaders, and doers that use design practice or research to solve problems between people and their interior environments; and they each present their ideas about how the interior design profession moves forward from this crossroads. The diversity of viewpoints put forth by the authors in *The State of the Interior Design Profession* will make you think. They will ask you to consider their opinions and expect you to interpret their approaches to problem resolution—whether design solution- or society-specific.

These enlightening perspectives will give you an enhanced understanding of the many issues that face the interior design profession at this crucial time of growth and development. There are many interior designers who know a limited amount about a large part of the interior design profession; conversely, there are many who know much about a limited aspect. Gaining an understanding of the background of the numerous issues the interior design profession faces will make us all more conscious of our reasons for doing things and better able to understand the reasons behind the actions taken by others, thus developing a level of awareness that has eluded the profession as a whole.

The diverse views and experiences shared here illustrate the necessity for interior designers to begin the dialogue around future demands, research studies, and organizational learning—issues that are affecting both our own and our clients' environments, families, businesses, practices, professions, and lives—their worlds. *The State of the Interior Profession* helps us identify and embrace complexity and uncertainty and the sometimes contradictory demands on individual interior designers, as well as our profession's leaders, educators, researchers, design teams, and clients.

Newcomers to the profession and design world veterans alike can use these perspectives to better identify issues that face the individual and the profession. *The State of the Interior Design Profession* provides us with new knowledge that allows us to go beyond the surface issues and contribute to shaping the interior design profession. This new knowledge will allow us to join the dialogue and raise important questions at critical moments. This book provides us with relevant knowledge; we must simply use it. Through this process, we can become more effective members of the profession and better interior designers.

Today, interior designers working across the globe are focused on a diversity of design values for clients: addressing needs, designing for operational payback, and creating a new and evolving sustainable aesthetic. We are resetting our profession with interior design actions that engage culture, values, experiences, metrics, functional disciplines, and more. We are establishing a *new* interior design profession to meet the desires and needs of our future. This crossroads in the profession's development requires truth-searching! We must expand our design response to be ahead of the game, to lead and respond to future demands, to be technically sophisticated, to create the experiences that our clients need for success, and to be the design consultant that the client and the world's societies respect for the value we bring.

The State of the Interior Design Profession presents new and diverse points of view of the many design opportunities on our horizon and from the many design thinkers of today. You will be enlightened as you search for truths that will guide the profession into this century. We can affect and change lives through good design. Let the dialogue begin!

EVA L. MADDOX, FIIDA, Assoc. AIA, LEED® AP

Design Principal, Perkins+Will | Eva Maddox *Branded Environments*
Cofounder *Archeworks*

CAREN S. MARTIN &
DENISE A. GUERIN

PREFACE

WHY THIS BOOK?

In January 2008, as we were sitting around with little to do but feel our hands thaw from exposure to the frozen tundra that is Minnesota, we discussed the recent events in the interior design profession. This is an ongoing topic for us, though at times a stressful one. Rattling off the current issues, primarily focused upon the students returning to classes in a few days, publication deadlines for IDEC's narratives, keeping InformeDesign® running, and the stress of the interior design licensure hearing in our state, we said—"let's write a book about it!" We decided that although we know much about what is happening and could certainly frame the issues, you would benefit more from reading the thoughts of many smart, engaging leaders from all segments of the profession instead of just our thoughts. We accosted Olga Kontzias, executive editor of Fairchild Books, with our "great idea" in the lobby of the IDEC conference hotel in Montreal in March, 2008. She enthusiastically agreed with the timeliness of this book and helped us frame the issues. We sincerely hope we were on target with this idea and the dialogue we hope it initiates.

We developed *The State of the Interior Design Profession* to provide you with an informed view of the interior design profession as it stands today and as the basis of purposeful, exciting discourse that will inspire you to consider your role and responsibility in developing the profession's future.

The profession faces many interrelated challenges comprised of significant internal and external issues influenced by today's professional, social, cultural, and economic environments. We identified 12 issues as integral to the future development of the interior design profession. We then invited renowned and emerging interior design thinkers (authors), who represent complementary and conflicting viewpoints on the same issue, to write their opinions (essays) on each issue. Their experiences are diverse; they have contributed to practice, industry, publication, research, education, engagement, and service—and many to several of these. Their responses reflect the currency of their opinions, thoughts, and research on the issue.

Each chapter begins with our brief introduction to the issue. By identifying the underlying theme and criticality of each chapter's issue, we attempt to create context as well as a bridge among essays, chapters, and to the whole. Each essay begins with the question(s) posed to the author(s) and their biographies so you can see their experience and investments in the profession, which provided the impetus for our invitation to them to write.

The State of the Interior Design Profession's voice is aimed at practitioners, educators, and students. It is our goal that you will find it to be interesting, pithy, and thought provoking. Specifically, we attempted to:

1. Identify, create, and assemble dialogue about issues that are currently shaping the interior design profession and influencing its future;
2. Discuss the issues and their influence on the state of the profession; their immediacy becomes evident when presented as a "whole" (i.e., a body of thought);
3. Highlight critical junctures that require decision-making by the profession; and
4. Illustrate a critical mass of issues for discussion and debate by practitioners, graduate students, educators/researchers, allied professionals, and the public.

WHY SHOULD YOU READ THIS BOOK?

At this point in the maturation of the interior design profession, unique events, actions, and positioning are happening that have different degrees of impact—individually and cumulatively, on the profession. It is important to *take stock*; that is, determine what the state of the profession is at this point in time. These important issues will ultimately drive decisions of stakeholders within the interior design profession, and legislators, regulators, and the public as they ponder the profession via their perceptions, beliefs, and actions. Some issues may appear peripheral when taken individually, but when viewed in context of related issues, their meaning and value become imperative or central to the future of the interior design profession.

It's important to note that these issues are not apparent or well understood by all members of the interior design profession. Each stakeholder of the profession sees one part of the profession. This means that there is a gap in understanding all issues among members of the profession. It means that some may know small parts of several issues, a larger part of one or two issues, or a significant amount about a few larger issues. But few people all have the same level of understanding of the major issues that are subtly or drastically shaping our profession. Nor do we!

But we have listened and talked with colleagues, friends, and peers during our national and international experiences; our leadership positions; and over years of practice, teaching, and research. And, now, we have been substantially informed by authors of essays in this book, who freely gave of their time, energies, and intellect.

Members of the interior design profession are primed to take a worldview of themselves including the broader environmental and philosophical influences. Experienced interior design leaders, practitioners who are moving into leadership positions in the profession, younger members who are emerging leaders, and informed interior designers need current knowledge about these challenging global, professional issues to form their own, broader perspectives. There is also a need for this type of stimulation and dialogue for the increasing number of graduate students who are practitioners of interior design. All of these designers need to be prepared to shape the future.

Assembly of these well-constructed viewpoints provides a foundation for critical dialogue for all to consider, perhaps for the first time. Dialogue resulting from this assemblage of viewpoints will strengthen the profession by enabling a more thorough exploration of the meaning of the issues. This consideration will ensure that the direction taken by the interior design profession in the future is a meaningful and informed proposition for those in the profession and especially those served by it.

It is our intent that this book will create a current map of the playing field. It will establish a baseline of information about key issues, setting the foundation from which substantive dialogue will occur. This book will provide the profession with context, knowledge, and interrelationships among the issues.

HOW DID THIS BOOK GET WRITTEN?

We initially identified 12 issues that we felt *must* be addressed as integral (past, present, or future) to the development of the interior design profession. The selection of authors in many cases was intrinsically tied to specific issues. For example, we recognized that *identity* of the interior design profession is a crucial and much-debated issue; we also had been informed about that issue by several authors who have outspoken opinions on the issue. Therefore, in many cases we identified the issue and the authors simultaneously.

We then invited authors to submit 50-word abstracts focusing on the direction and key points they would make in their full essay in response to one or two questions that we posed about the issue. These questions are placed at the beginning of each essay. Authors were limited to 2,000 words (a feat few achieved!), and the writing was to be their opinion or viewpoint, albeit referenced when appropriate or necessary. These essays are not academic pieces; their brevity allowed authors to hit only the main points of an issue; they beg for continued dialogue—a key goal of the book. Authors submitted their essays to us; and we reviewed, edited, and suggested revisions. They returned their revised essays to us with figures, tables, or images ready for us to "make a book"! In addition, they supplied brief biographies to add context and background for you to understand why their viewpoints were chosen. For many of you, these authors will be well-known or familiar, if not by biography, by photo.

The most difficult part of this process was narrowing down the field of potential authors. There are many excellent thinkers who are not included in *The State of the Interior Design Profession.* The only reason is simply the need to keep the focus on initiating a dialogue. It should be noted, too, that there were authors invited who, for reasons of work schedule or availability, were unable to contribute at this time. We miss their contributions. As you read these chapters and discuss issues among your colleagues, perhaps you'll consider being an author within the next edition!

Our perception is that these are times of turbulence and change for the interior design profession. There are many issues that could have been selected for exploration in the text of this book; however, we feel that none supersede the importance and/or potential impact of those that are included. Our contributing authors agreed, you'll find. Following is a brief introduction to the 12 issues.

CHAPTER 1. VALUE OF INTERIOR DESIGN

Overt and well-known or intrinsic and lesser-known values of interior design are addressed as perspectives of authors' value proposition of the profession. Specialization and an intensified focus on effects of interior design on human and environmental needs are explored and clarified.

CHAPTER 2. DESIGN THINKING

Stepping back—way back—to consider the influence of interior design as an outcome of the larger issue of *design thinking* is explored. What it means to the profession and the world is discussed by diverse authors.

CHAPTER 3. BODY OF KNOWLEDGE

Two studies by the editors of this book (2001, 2006) defined the interior design profession's body of knowledge (BOK) as required for the first stage of the practitioner's career. There has been some controversy about what value a BOK has to our profession and if it limits us in our practice. Where do we go from here, and how do we embrace the embedded knowledge possessed by practitioners? These questions are posed and answered in this chapter.

CHAPTER 4. EVIDENCE-BASED DESIGN

The entire *design discipline* (i.e., interior design, architecture, landscape architecture, and others) is exploring the idea that design decisions need to be based on evidence or research findings, not solely on normative practice. Interior design's consideration of evidence-based design (EBD) by practice, education, and industry are discussed relative to criteria, creativity, and prediction of outcomes.

CHAPTER 5. FACTORS INFLUENCING PRACTICE

Practice with a small "p" (i.e., ergonomics, work styles, technology) and with a capital "P" (i.e., *the* Practice) are considered in this chapter. What has influenced practice to get us to this point? What will influence practice to set the stage for the future? Are we too insular? What values direct the formation and structure of our decisions, and are they changing?

CHAPTER 6. ETHICS AND LEGALITY

A cornerstone of a profession is a code of ethics. The development of our ethics and the relationship between ethics and legal decisions are explored by the authors as well as our behaviors in these regards. Society is increasingly litigious—how will your practice fare and do you personally know enough?

CHAPTER 7. REGULATION OF PRACTICE

Licensure of interior design practice or title is one of the hottest issues in interior design practice in North America today, reflected by the media in an ongoing volley of positions and viewpoints. Opinions range widely among our authors too. Where does regulation stand today, how did we get *here*, and where is it headed? Authors discuss if we're on the right track.

CHAPTER 8. DIVERSITY

Interior designers pride themselves on understanding human behavior and designing for people's physical and psycho-social needs. If that is true, then are we limited in our understanding of diverse races, cultures, ethnic groups, and gender? Broadening the design profession by engaging minorities as practitioners and clients, dealing with gender bias in business, and creating methods to understand cultural diversity are all issues presented in this chapter.

CHAPTER 9. GLOBALISM

The world is getting smaller, and our practices are growing globally. We must understand the difference between designing for global clients from a North American viewpoint or designing from North American expertise. What is the difference and how can knowledge modify our perspective of what is "right"?

CHAPTER 10.
CONFRONTING EDUCATIONAL CHALLENGES

There is more knowledge to learn; there is more technology to use; and there are even more theories and approaches to try. How do these new pieces fit into the same mold of the four-year interior design degree—can they? Options for meeting the educational needs of future interior designers are discussed. And, with the aging population of educators, where will our new educators come from?

CHAPTER 11. PERCEIVED IDENTITY

Is perceived identity the *chicken* or the *egg*? Authors suggest ways to approach branding our profession first to illustrate and popularize our value, embrace others to be more integrative and inclusive, or call a halt to overlap and integration. Such a plethora of opinions!

CHAPTER 12. CHALLENGES

The last chapter highlights the viewpoints of different authors as they focus on the paramount challenges facing the profession each has identified. This is a stimulating look at what we need to attack now to secure our place in the design discipline in the future. It is a *call to arms* for our problem-solving abilities.

THE BIG PICTURE

The State of the Interior Design Profession is a treatise of issues, a *snapshot* in time. It is timely, temporary, and periodic. The essay authors are the top thinkers and doers in design practice, industry, publication, education, and research. They can serve your firm or your school as an elite, informal group of advisors. Discuss their viewpoints on issues that you question; consider their advice on the future of the profession; and use their words as guidance for the present and the future. Let their words *inspire dialogue and debate* among you and your peers or across peer groups.

Issues and subsequent dialogue could serve as the basis of a college course, a continuing education seminar, or a summit on the future of the profession. It can be the basis of discussion in undergraduate and graduate classes by presenting an engaging look at the profession as seen and perceived by those currently engaged in determining its future. Create a series of discussions based on each chapter for your local professional organization chapters. Develop a series of questions to be explored by teams of practitioners, educators, and students—enjoy the liveliness of interdisciplinary and intergenerational debate. This type of professional discourse is necessary for healthy development of the interior design profession.

Our greatest wish? By the time you finish reading these essays, even if you only read a few, you will find your passion; you will discover an issue about which you are stimulated, angered, intrigued, or soothed. Let your intellectual curiosity be piqued—join other good thinkers and get ready to make your mark on the interior design profession!

ACKNOWLEDGMENTS

We would like to express our sincere appreciation to the dozens of authors who contributed to *The State of the Interior Design Profession*. Their dedicated communication (nearly 1,000 e-mails were received from them during the process!), intellect, and timeliness made meeting our timeline possible. We also thank the hundreds of people we have had the opportunity to meet, talk with, and listen to at the University of Minnesota, around North America, and throughout the world, who continue to contribute to informing and challenging our thinking and scholarship on this and many other projects.

Specifically, we would like to thank Becky Yust, PhD, department head of Design, Housing, and Apparel, for her leadership, generosity, and support of our work and literary ambitions. Furthermore, we appreciate the considerable efforts of Jain Kwon, PhD, who was instrumental in the initial editing process of this book. We also wish to express our gratitude to Olga Kontzias, executive editor of Fairchild Books, for her enthusiastic support of our concept, for believing that this work was important, and that we would meet our deadlines!

—Caren S. Martin & Denise A. Guerin

I would like to acknowledge the extensive patience and contributions of Jeffrey Martin. Thank you for the endless conversations ("ad nauseam") about this book. And in fact, you could probably have written much of it after listening to me all these years about my scholarship, my practice, my students, my university, my colleagues, my presentations, my committees, my legislative efforts, my travels, and my InformeDesign!

—CSM

I, too, wish to acknowledge Jeff, who "let Caren come play with me" so many evenings and weekends and for those over-the-phone computer technology consults. We could not have done this without you!

—DAG

THE

STATE

OF THE

INTERIOR

DESIGN

PROFESSION

VALUE OF INTERIOR DESIGN

OVERVIEW The authors of this chapter hope to pique your interest in actively defining the worth interior design adds to occupants' lives. It seems there is a need in our profession to underpin our existence by denoting its relative, monetary, and intrinsic worth. If we are so certain that professional interior designers add value to environments designed by them, why are we unable to convince others? The authors exhort you to speak out about our value as loud leaders, not silent contributors. Several authors identify the design value of engaging in social responsibility, creative thinking, and strategic planning. The chapter ends with three essays that document four leaders' life-changing journeys in sustainable design in industry, education, and practice.

Suzan Globus asks us to create an "elevator definition" of interior design—one that truly defines the value of interior design. Katherine Ankerson and Betsy Gabb discuss the need for interior designers to let all know the value we bring to the design of built environments,

in fact, to the relevance of every situation and problem. The importance of creativity and creative thinking cannot be underestimated in the amount and type of value it adds to people's lives, suggests Brad Hokanson. Jill Pable defines socially beneficial design and challenges us to take a risk—search for ways to make a difference in our communities and, therefore, a little piece of the world. Gary Wheeler's approach rests with acknowledgement that interior design adds to clients' bottom lines in ways that are measurable; we just don't manage to get that information presented in thoughtful and timely ways.

The last part of the chapter chronicles the journeys into sustainable action by industrialist Ray Anderson, educator Lisa Tucker, and practitioners Rachelle Schoessler Lynn and David Loehr. These inspiring stories remind us that we, too, can make a difference by adding value to people's lives. What is your definition of the value interior design adds to people's lives—are you ready to speak out and contribute to change?

> What is interior design's "value proposition"?
What do interior designers know about it?
Why should the public care?

SUZAN GLOBUS

THE INTERIOR DESIGN VALUE PROPOSITION

Defining the value of interior design is like trying to answer the question about how many angels fit on the head of a pin. It is a vast and somewhat mysterious subject. The value of interior design is largely undocumented, unsubstantiated, and, yet, undeniable. We are talking more frequently about the value of interior design today than we did, say, 10 years ago, in an effort to define our profession, eliminate marketplace confusion, and, perhaps, to educate ourselves. As a comparatively new profession, interior design has evolved to the point where its practitioners and educators feel justifiably proud of it, and some have been working to attain a legislative definition of the profession and those who practice it. Others are beginning to question why, in an effort to define interior design, we are modeling it on architecture, yet saying interior design is different from architecture.

If we continue to follow the architect's path of regulating the profession by trying to prove interior design's effect on the health,

SUZAN GLOBUS, CID-NJ, LEED® AP, FASID, and past president of ASID, leads Globus Design Associates, Fair Haven, New Jersey, in the interior design of public, educational, and special libraries. The firm also includes municipal, residential, and veterinary projects in its award-winning, published portfolio. Globus was appointed by New Jersey's governor to serve as a charter member of the state's Interior Design Examination and Evaluation Committee. She is a member of the advisory committee to develop green remodeling guidelines for the New Jersey Center for Green Building at Edward J. Bloustein School of Planning and Public Policy at Rutgers University. Globus is a former interior design adjunct instructor for Brookdale Community College, Lincroft, New Jersey, and an advisory board member of InformeDesign®. Globus writes about sustainable business practices and green design, and presents at conferences across the country about sustainability, future trends in library design, and using research to achieve design solutions.

safety, and welfare of the public, we are doing ourselves a disservice because we risk limiting the discussion of the value of interior design. Interior design does so much more than protect the health, safety, and welfare of the public. The welfare of others is where interior design has the most to contribute. However, welfare, or well-being, is difficult to document, which brings us back to the head of the pin.

MY CLIENTS DON'T UNDERSTAND WHAT I DO

The discussion of the value of interior design is especially relevant at this time when the marketplace is flooded with an array of people and businesses offering interior design services. The public, understandably, is confused. "My clients don't understand what I do" is a frequent lament of interior designers. In my experience, consumers of interior design services speak about interior design differently from the way I think of it. They frequently talk in terms of aesthetics, such as making things look good or making the space work well. My firm's institutional clients have mentioned that they are motivated to hire an interior designer to make their organizations' spaces warm and welcoming or user friendly. I think they are on to something here because they are identifying the value they receive from interior design by describing how people feel as a result of it.

Our profession has grown beyond decorating, but unfortunately its representation has reinforced its perception as decoration. There are exceptions, but for the most part, interior design is captured in print, online, and in awards as uninhabited beautiful spaces with little to no explanation of what issues were addressed in the design program, and what outcomes resulted. Interior design is featured as fashion. It is fashion in the sense that it reflects the culture of the owner and, hopefully, users of the space at a point in time, but it is so much more. I was fortunate enough to understand the potential value of interior design after working with my first client, a young couple.

Their main living space contained kitchen and living/dining areas open to each other. They explained that their hectic professional schedules and attention to raising their children left them feeling tired, disconnected, and without "adult" space. For one part of the design solution, I placed two comfortable chairs facing each other with a common ottoman in front of the living room fireplace to encourage them to sit together and enjoy a conversation after the children were in bed. After the installation, the woman told me that she felt her husband had become a better listener, and the man told me his wife was paying more attention to him since the house was redesigned. My realization that interior design can change people's lives had a profound impact on me. I felt, and still feel, that it can change the world.

WHAT IS INTERIOR DESIGN?

It may be helpful to begin the discussion about the value of interior design with a definition of interior design—something that continues to be discussed among educators and practitioners. I have long been an advocate of an *elevator definition* of interior design. A brief, cohesive definition of interior design could create a much-needed tool to explain the value of interior design. Until interior designers can succinctly explain what we do, we shouldn't expect our clients to understand the profession, much less value it.

Definitions of interior design do exist. The National Council for Interior Design

Qualification (NCIDQ) begins its definition of interior design with "a multifaceted profession in which creative and technical solutions are applied within a structure to achieve a built interior environment. These solutions are functional, enhance the quality of life and culture of the occupants, and are aesthetically attractive" (2004).

NCIDQ's definition continues by addressing codes, sustainability, the process used to arrive at the creative and technical solutions, and so forth. It is a widely used definition that has been adopted by interior design regulatory agencies, professional associations, and academia, but it is by no means an elevator definition. When asked for an elevator definition during an interview by Susan Szenaszy, editor of *Metropolis* magazine, I responded by saying, "Interior design is the creation of environments that sustain and support human beings (to live) to the highest of their capabilities" (Szenasy, 2009). Although it is far from comprehensive, this definition will serve as the basis of this conversation.

THE TRIPLE BOTTOM LINE

If great interior design contributes to human beings living to the best of their capabilities, one can expect positive outcomes as a result. These outcomes are key to interior design's value statement. Interior design leaders are beginning to discuss value in terms of the *triple bottom line*, a term describing benefits to people, the planet, and profit popularized by Savitz and Weber (2006) in their book, *The Triple Bottom Line*. This approach is valuable because it establishes a broader context for the benefits of design. The triple bottom line conversation has caught the attention of businesses that are recognizing design as a tool to prosper.

Product designer Yves Behar (2007) said that those companies that do not recognize the value of design will not survive. "Over time, they will fail to connect to consumers in a relevant way and become obsolete" (p. 92). Businesses need proof of outcomes to justify investing in interior design, and evidence is being collected. The healthcare profession, steeped in a tradition of conducting research and documenting results, is leading the way in gathering research results that indicate the value of design. The practice of using such evidence to guide design decisions has been tagged evidence-based design (EBD) (The Center for Health Design, 2009) and is embraced by leaders of the design community.

CAPTURING EVIDENCE OF INTERIOR DESIGN'S VALUE

Evidence of the effectiveness of interior design is most easily captured when dealing with readily measurable outcomes such as patients' recovery time, increased sales, or employee productivity. These types of behavior changes can be documented. There is a strong financial incentive to conduct such research to prove that good design means good business. Linking interior design to corporate profit is welcome information in our capitalistic economy where a sound economy has far-reaching benefits to society.

Research suggests that patients in well-designed hospitals recover faster than those in poorly designed facilities (Walach et al., 2005; Watson, 2005; Schweitzer, Gilpin, & Frampton, 2004). Quicker recovery rates can translate into a higher volume of patients, resulting in increased profits for hospitals. In this case, the context of the value of interior design encompasses the increased profit of the hospitals and the rapidly cured patients.

These are measurable benefits. But the value doesn't stop there. When the interior design of the hospital is executed in an environmentally responsible manner, the planet is served. When the patient returns to being a contributing member of society and the economically viable hospital expands its contribution to the community through, for example, free blood pressure screenings, interior design has contributed to the triple bottom line. This value is more difficult to capture.

THE EMOTIONAL REACTION TO INTERIOR DESIGN

When evidence of the value of interior design is documented and disseminated, it will help to eliminate the confusion about interior design in the marketplace. Interior designers have made a good start, but we have much more to do. We have not yet delved into what I believe is a core benefit of interior design, which is the emotional response it evokes. There are a number of reasons for this. That powerful, visceral reaction to an environment may be difficult to identify, much less describe.

Practitioners may be reluctant to discuss emotional reactions to interior design when they are striving to be perceived as professionals. Emotions are fuzzy. Emotions are difficult to measure, and emotions cannot be directly linked to bottom lines. However, emotions are drivers of human behavior and have far-reaching effects. Using the example of the hospital, consider the role of the patient's family frantically trying to locate the room of their loved one who was admitted for a medical emergency. Unable to follow inadequate signage, or confused by similar visual signals, the family members' stress elevates to a level that renders them unable to express their love and reassurance to the patient upon arrival at the bedside. The emotions in this case resulted in behavior that does not support the patient's recovery. It would be difficult to capture this evidence.

I believe the best interior designers are especially sensitive to the emotional reactions to the spaces they design because they establish human beings as the basis of their approach to design. I have no data to support this belief. In fact, I haven't heard it discussed much among my colleagues. I feel interior designers so intuitively consider human emotions in their work that they may not be aware of it. If they are, they may not think in terms of how valuable a deliverable it is via their services.

However, some people beyond design practitioners are taking note of the value of emotions as a benefit of design. In *The Power of Design*, Farson (2008) states, "Designers can foster creativity, community, security, effectiveness, understanding, and affection" (p. 27). When talking about creating a high-performance workspace where people are emotionally connected to it, Jim Keane, president of Steelcase Group, said that the goal is to get people to feel they love to work there. "And that's the hardest to define because it's a softer kind of emotion, but it's an area where the design community excels" (Powell, 2009).

NEXT STEPS

Interior design educators and practitioners hold the keys to unlocking understanding about the value of interior design. Capturing the outcomes of interior design work is imperative to the growth of the profession, and it is not a solo task. The start of the path is clear.

EDUCATORS
➤ Help interior design students understand the greater context of every decision they make.
➤ Infuse students with the idea that they are connected to something larger than themselves.

PRACTITIONERS

> Conduct pre- and post-occupancy studies
> Invite environmental psychologists, social scientists, and others in the field of human behavior to document the emotional effects and related behavioral outcomes
> Team with educators and journalists to write case studies
> Share the information at conferences and with students and educators
> Collaborate with those who will use the space: clients, members of the building team, industry, scientists, and community leaders to create the best possible outcomes

Interior designers are able to create environments that make people feel secure, welcome, competent, engaged, and stimulated, to name just a few emotions. If people are living at their very best, they are capable of optimal behavior, whether they are loving, generous, respectful, productive, or innovative, and characterized by limitless achievements.

REFERENCES

The Center for Health Design. (2009). *Definition of evidence-based design.* Retrieved March 12, 2009, from http://healthdesign.org/about/us/mission/EBD_definition.php

Farson, R. (2008). *The power of design: A force for transforming everything.* City: Ostberg Library of Design Management, Greenway Communications.

Masters of design. (2007, October) All about Yves. *Fast Company,* 119, p. 92.

National Council for Interior Design Qualification. (2004). *NCIDQ definition of interior design.* Retrieved March 12, 2009, from http://ncidq.org/who/definition.htm

Powell, B. (2009, March 9). Steelcase's Jim Keane and design thinking. *officeinsight.* Retrieved March 12, 2009, from http://www.officeinsight.com

Savitz, A., & Weber, K. (2006). *The triple bottom line.* New York: John Wiley & Sons.

Schweitzer, M., Gilpin, L., & Frampton, S. (2004). *Healing spaces: Elements of environmental design that make an impact on health.* Retrieved February 15, 2009, from www.InformeDesign.umn.edu

Szenasy, S. (2009). Interview with Suzan Globus. *Metropolis.* Retrieved March 12, 2009, from http://www.metropolismag.com/multimedia/video/20090201/the-metropolis-conference-interview-with-suzan-globus

Walach, J., Rabin, B., Day, R., Williams, J., Choi, K., & Kang, J. (2005). The effect of sunlight on post-operative analgesic medication use: A prospective study of patients undergoing spinal surgery. *Psychosomatic Medicine, 67,* 156–163.

Watson, C. (2005). *Integration of technology and facility design.* Retrieved February 15, 2009, from www.InformeDesign.umn.edu

↘ What is social justice and
do interior designers have a role?

JILL B. PABLE

SOCIALLY BENEFICIAL DESIGN: WHAT CAN INTERIOR DESIGNERS DO?

THE PROBLEM OF SOCIAL ISSUES AND THE DESIGN RESPONSE THUS FAR

Although an exact percentage is difficult to confirm, many sources suggest that architects and interior designers currently provide services for less than 10% of the world's population, and do so nearly exclusively for those who are able to pay for their efforts (Fisher, 2009; Wilson, 2009). This state of affairs presents an irony: The majority of the world's population does not benefit from design, yet it is this group that could thoroughly gain the most from appropriate shelter, transport, health, and education facilities (Bleby, 2007). The statistics of the world population's problems are daunting and urgent. More than one billion people (one-sixth of the world's population) dwell in extreme poverty and lack safe water, food, basic healthcare, and social services. In many of the poorest countries, life

JILL B. PABLE, PhD, IDEC, IIDA, is an associate professor in the Department of Interior Design at Florida State University, and an NCIDQ-certificate holder. She has BS and MFA degrees in interior design and a doctoral degree in instructional technology with specialization in architecture. Her professional work includes residential, hospitality, healthcare, and office projects completed within her own firm as well as with Universal Studios Florida theme parks. She is the past chair of IDCEC and is serving as the 2009 president of IDEC. Pable's service and research focuses on design education and social justice, and she believes passionately that design holds great potential to help make the world a better place. Her educational papers and creative works have six times been awarded Best Presentation at international and regional educational conferences. She has authored *Interior Design: Practical Strategies for Teaching and Learning* (with Katherine Ankerson) and *Sketching Interiors at the Speed of Thought*.

expectancy is 40 years old—about half of that in the high-income world (UN Millennium Project, 2009). This grinding poverty is viewed as a major reason behind many other world challenges. For example, disease and inequality are prominent reasons for violence, war, and state failures.

The design fields, including interior design, graphic design, and architecture, have largely been silent in their response to these issues. Bryan Bell (2009) notes, "Designers have let . . . market forces alone determine whom we serve, what issues we address, and the shape of all our design professions" (p. 15). More condemning yet, we designers "have limited our potential by seeing most major human concerns as unrelated to our work" (p. 15). Although protection of the public's health, safety, and welfare has been the bedrock for designers' stated existence legally and otherwise, some suggest these professional licensure standards should not serve to limit a professional's role (Maurice Cox, as cited in Wilson, 2009). The changing fashion of architectural theory has similarly reflected designers' indifference to world problems, and many have preferred to only rarely engage the political realm and remain "out of touch with reality" (Gamez & Rogers, 2009, p. 20). If it is said that a civilization may be measured by how it treats its most vulnerable members, it is likely that designers as a group have not held up their end of the bargain in their service to broader humanity. In defense of designers, however, it is not always easy to know the nature of the problem, nor how to best contribute to its solution.

WHAT IS SOCIALLY BENEFICIAL DESIGN?

A review of recent literature on design and social responsibility suggests socially beneficial design is an emerging but currently vague concept, not only in name but in terms of engagement. Most documented work thus far has emerged from architecture and less so from interior design, though lack of written documentation may distort the extent of engagement by interior designers.[1] Terms for the concept include public interest design, socially responsible design, socially just design, and community design. Here, however, the term *socially beneficial design* will be used.[2] By whatever name one chooses, there is a growing sense that labeling a project *socially responsible* may needlessly compartmentalize an idea that should be universally pervasive. Some interior designers advocate that "we pull it out of being a project type and make it just part of a design ethos" (*Contract's* Design Forum, 2008). What would this new ethos look like?

First, tenets of social responsibility may be found in all project types. In this way, socially beneficial design likely mirrors the journeys of sustainable design and universal design into their current places as necessary hallmarks of everyday, good design practice. Second, socially beneficial design embodies how a problem and need are defined, how a solution is developed, and how that solution is implemented. It will require empathetic thinking and prioritization, exceeding the self-centric thinking that currently drives most programming decisions. For example, an interior designer who seeks to provide socially beneficial services might work with a client to determine how a retail environment may reduce its need for shopping bags, thus reducing the human chlorine exposure required in those bags' fabrication. Similarly, an interior designer may integrate physical features that permit a bakery to make day-old products easily available to the hungry or develop a homeless shelter from a programmatic base of psychological wellness theory.

WHY SHOULD INTERIOR DESIGNERS ENGAGE IN SOCIALLY BENEFICIAL PRACTICE?

Whereas it is easy to feel intimidated by the breadth and depth of social issues currently besetting human populations, the need for interior designers' engagement is great. Sources suggest that world conditions are not improving, and many calamities produce needs for physical environments that interior designers are prepared to offer. For example, although one in seven people live in slum settlements in 2009, by 2020 this number will be one in three (Architecture for Humanity, 2009). World problems are also increasingly coming home: in even the most affluent areas such as the United States, economic conditions have transfigured homelessness from an isolated problem for single males to a crisis-level condition afflicting families with children in the last 20 years (Roman, 1999).

Beyond need, interior designers are now beginning to recognize their collective obligation to contribute skills that transcend beauty and function, recognizing that "it's time to set aside the superficial benefits of design and embrace a culture where design's true worth is measured by the problems it solves . . . and the lives and activities it enhances" (Busch, 2008, p. 18). Simply put, socially beneficial engagement is the right thing to do. The zeitgeist of these economically troubled times may partially be responsible for recent increased interest in design's social sensitivity—faced with uncertain futures themselves, interior designers may realize they now have both the time and skill to contribute to collective betterment (Bleby, 2007). This new interest in volunteerism is reflected also in the broader public spirit and has garnered renewed support in the Obama administration, which has promised increased funding to public service organizations.

SOCIAL ISSUES ENGAGEMENT PATTERNS AND TRENDS

Although the specifics of what a socially beneficial design ethos looks like are yet to be defined, there appear to be many different ways to positively engage in social issues as interior designers. For example, they may be involved in completing projects for little or no compensation, or monitoring how one's actions impact others' existence, such as in manufacturing processes and transport of the products one specifies are beneficial activities.[3] One designer has pursued this latter goal to admirable lengths. Struck by the tragedy of human trafficking she observed while designing projects in the Far East, Gensler interior designer Eve Blossom started Lulan Artisans, a global-scope organization dedicated to making international, high-quality, traditionally produced interiors textile fabric available to western markets. In doing so, she has ensured 650 individuals in Laos and Taiwan a fair wage and also averted numerous weavers from entering prostitution to make a living (Blossom, 2009).

Eve Blossom's global initiative likely represents the exception rather than the rule for interior designers' engagement with social issues. A review of documented projects suggests that interior designers are primarily engaged at the local and regional levels at this point in time. Table 1.1 provides a partial listing of interior design organizations active in attending to social issues. Typically, these organizations assist targeted groups such as nonprofit organizations or the homeless within a specific geographical area. Professional organizations including the American Society of Interior Designers (ASID) and the International Interior Design Association (IIDA) also provide admirable services to others in need through coalitions within their memberships (Jones, 2009). Whereas little hard data exist to confirm percentages of all firms, many interior design and architectural firms with interior design departments describe their social outreach activities in their promotional materials, and an Internet

TABLE 1.1

INTERIOR DESIGN–ORIENTED ORGANIZATIONS AND INITIATIVES AT THE REGIONAL AND NATIONAL LEVELS WITH A PRIMARY MISSION OF SOCIALLY RESPONSIBLE DESIGN

ORGANIZATION OR INITIATIVE	DESCRIPTION OF ACTIVITIES/GOALS	WEB SITE ADDRESS
Design Response	Improves facilities for nonprofit agencies and schools in Silicon Valley, California.	www.designresponse.org
DIFFA (Design Industries Foundation Fighting AIDS)	Raises funds for people with AIDS. Fund-raising efforts include interior design and other types of nationwide events.	www.diffa.org
Furnish a Future	Provides formerly homeless families leaving city shelters with free furniture and household goods. Primarily benefits New York City residents.	www.partnershipfor thehomeless.org
Interior Design Educator's Council	Hosts yearly "Interior Design Student Make a Difference Project" through interior design educators in the Social Justice Network. Students define a local community issue and then use design to provide a solution.	www.idec.org/events/ mad.php
Philanthropy by Design	Renovates interior environments of community service organizations. Primarily benefits San Francisco Bay Area at-risk youth, seniors, AIDS patients, and the homeless.	www.pbd.org

search under the terms "interior designer" and "pro bono" yields thousands of hits. However, local and regional efforts may not always be sufficient to address global-scope problems. Some suggest because the problem is so vast, we "must find a way to be both unified and diverse" in our response (Gamez & Rogers, 2009, p. 22).

There is more to be done at the national and international levels. In general, the architecture profession has made more gains in public-interest design than has interior design to date. Table 1.2 summarizes a selected list of architecture-oriented organizations whose primary mission is social outreach.

The organization Public Architecture provides one example of a way that a national organization within design may benefit social causes (Public Architecture, 2009). Their 1% project challenges designers to devote 1% of their time to assist nonprofit organizations and also provides lists of organizations that need architectural and interior design services (http://www .theonepercent.org). Of 46 total projects posted at the site as of January 2009, 28 organizations list "interior design/brand integration" or "healthy and sustainable environments" among the requests—implying that there is much pro bono work available within the interiors realm.

TABLE 1.2

ARCHITECTURE-ORIENTED ORGANIZATIONS AND INITIATIVES AT THE REGIONAL, NATIONAL, AND INTERNATIONAL LEVELS WITH A PRIMARY MISSION OF SOCIALLY RESPONSIBLE DESIGN

ORGANIZATION OR INITIATIVE	DESCRIPTION OF ACTIVITIES/GOALS	WEB SITE ADDRESS
Architecture for Humanity	Provides professional design services to needy groups. Focuses efforts in disaster mitigation and reconstruction, poverty alleviation, design innovation for at-risk populations, and addressing climate change through sustainable design. Open Source Network permits sharing of plans for worldwide structures.	www.architectureforhumanity.org www.openarchitecturenetwork.org
Community Design Collaborative	Offers design services to nonprofit organizations through community-based design center that has a volunteer base of 300 designers who offer services, primarily in Pennsylvania region.	www.cdesignc.org
Design Corps	Provides architectural and planning services to communities in need. Places architecture and planning graduates who provide technical assistance to small rural communities. Design fellows participate in grant projects.	www.designcorps.org
Just Building Alliance	Seeks to monitor working conditions in the construction industry, promotes construction-related markets in developing regions to enhance the quality of life in the world's most disadvantaged communities, and lobbies for fair trade in the building industry.	www.justbuilding.org
Public Architecture	Matches architecture and design firms with nonprofit organizations in need through 1% solution initiative. Public-interest design initiatives include the scraphouse and the day laborer station.	www.publicarchitecture.org www.theonepercent.org
SEED Network (Social, Economic, and Environmental Design)	Seeks to create an evaluation system for socially responsible design similar to the LEED (Leadership in Energy and Environmental Design) system created by the U.S. Green Building Council.	N/A

In terms of its prominence and impact, socially beneficial design is largely in its infancy. There are many things to be done that will "move the movement" into an echelon of heightened awareness and committed wide-scope action:

1. *Codify socially beneficial design as a legitimate professional activity.*

   First, interior design organizations must raise the prominence of social responsibility by placing it within its code of ethics. The American Institute of Architects (AIA) has already done so, stating "members should render public interest professional services and encourage their employees to render such services" (AIA, 2009). Typically, interior design organizations' codes of ethics do not rise above the vague level of "responsibility to the public" in their verbiage. Second, continue the work of Social, Economic, and Environmental Design (SEED), an organization that seeks to create an evaluation system of socially responsible design (much like LEED® does for sustainable design) to establish guidelines for this type of work (Wilson, 2009) and expand its influence to interior design practice activities. Third, develop policies and standards that help designers manage liability concerns when they engage in socially beneficial projects.

2. *Develop incentives for socially beneficial practice.*

   Besides the positive press a firm can receive for engaging in socially beneficial design, connections should be established that make designers aware of private and public funds that can support their efforts. Similarly, an awards program that increases the awareness of socially responsible work can help prompt others to get involved.

3. *Build connections: create and build national and international databases to connect givers and receivers, and extend product availability through its life span.*

   Much like the problems of food distribution, part of the dilemma of delivering socially beneficial design services lies in the lack of information connecting givers and receivers. For interior designers, a database (much like eBay) of available overstocked furnishings and products from manufacturers that could be used in social projects at reduced costs would be helpful. Manufacturers, too, could use bar code identification to track their products from cradle to grave, assuming the responsibility to get products from one organization to a more needy one until those items reach the end of their useful life and then get disassembled for recycling.

4. *Engage design researchers to assess socially beneficial design activities and find the gaps in our knowledge.*

   For too long, interior design's outreach to others in need and respect for others' existence has been an afterthought. Active, timely research is needed to determine those processes that work and those that do not. For example, we know very little about the success of socially sensitive design projects after the ribbon-cutting ceremony has concluded. Further, research can help make clear the objective benefits of design to a public that has for some time been unaware of its virtues for healing and wellness.

5. *Specify responsibly.*

   Like sustainability, enduring change in attitude and perspective toward socially beneficial practices will likely happen from the grass roots up. Therefore, interior de-

TABLE 1.3

EDUCATIONAL INITIATIVES WITH A PRIMARY EMPHASIS IN SOCIALLY BENEFICIAL DESIGN

ORGANIZATION OR INITIATIVE	DESCRIPTION OF ACTIVITIES/GOALS	WEB SITE ADDRESS
Archeworks	An alternative design school where students work in multidisciplinary teams to form solutions for nonprofit partners. Founded by Stanley Tigerman and Eva Maddox.	www.archeworks.org
Institute without Boundaries at George Brown College	A center of research and learning focused on design innovation and interprofessional collaboration.	www.institutewithout boundaries.com
Project M	An intensive immersion program meant to inspire designers, writers, filmmakers, and photographers to use their work for impacting communities. Project M has taken place in cities around the world and now has a physical lab in Greensboro, Alabama.	Described in www .metropolismag.com/ story/20090130/project-m-thinking-wrong-doing-right

signers should demand accountability from manufacturers of the products they specify to determine provenance of their materials and labor practices.

6. *Instill change through education—and change the way education prepares tomorrow's designers.*

As socially responsible design will demand a holistic grasp of many related issues, teach interior design students how to collaborate not only with the architecture profession but also with social workers, anthropologists, and ethicists. A full awareness of social issues will likely imply getting students out of the classroom and into the life stories of the other 90% of the world's population through interviews, travel, or other means. Further, stop the students' preparation to exclusively create projects for those with substantial budgets. Table 1.3 describes a selection of educational initiatives that lead the way, placing socially beneficial design among their priorities.

Some writers have suggested that socially beneficial design should be developed as a separate learning track, much like law has a specialized learning experience for public defenders (Fisher, 2009). This specialization (perhaps at the master's level) may serve current interior design students who voice a desire to give back to society.

CONCLUSION AND CHARGE

It may be that the cost of engaging in socially beneficial design is high, but the ultimate cost of not doing so may be infinitely higher. The words of Le Corbusier spoken in 1923 still ring true: "It is a question of building which is at the root of the social unrest of today: architecture or revolution" (2007, p. x). Perhaps every age sees its own as the most critical, the most on the verge of collapse. This time, however, multiple crises such as global climate change, water scarcity, population growth, poverty, and financial collapse seem to be colluding, all angling for our immediate attention. In part the key to their resolution lies in our responsibility to be respectful of all persons and assistive to those who are less fortunate. There is cause for hope. In the words of John Bielenberg, design director of Project M,

> Everything is linked now. . . . You can either be pessimistic about the future or you can be optimistic. For me, an optimistic alternative includes ingenuity and creativity, and I package that under the big D: Design Thinking and how that can shape the future. (Dickinson, 2009, para 8)

At this time of many great challenges, it may be time for interior design to step up, putting its potential to the test to effect positive change in social sensitivities.

NOTES

1. The relative lack of published information on the interior design profession's engagement with socially responsible practices raises larger issues of the nature of its identity and that of architecture. That is, many interior design firms profess engagement with pro bono work in their promotional materials, but, in this author's assessment, have far less representation in the public dissemination of their efforts than their architectural counterparts. This issue is an interesting aside to the larger idea of architecture as a "hero" culture and the more modest nature of interior designers in general.

2. Here, the term *socially beneficial design* will be used. Socially responsible design and socially just design seem to impart a guilt-inducing flavor that may make the term tiresome over time. Public interest design and community design seem vague. They also limit the idea to certain project types and appear to omit the idea that socially aware design can occur in all project types, in this author's opinion.

3. Some manufacturers are beginning to add social-responsibility criteria to their product manufacturing. One such example is Steelcase, which is now tracing the provenance of source materials that are integrated into its entire product line. Additionally, Steelcase is also seeking to help its end users locate organizations for donation of their used products (Melissa DeSota, Steelcase, personal communication, January 15, 2009).

American Institute of Architects. (2009). *Code of ethics and professional conduct.* Retrieved January 28, 2009, from http://soloso.aia.org/eKnowledge/Resources/PDFS/AIAP017690?dvid=4294964840&recspec=fd268d6fb813bbdb142908d7c23e4a88

Architecture for Humanity. (2009). *Open architecture network.* Retrieved January 25, 2009, from http://www.openarchitecturenetwork.org/about

Bell, B. (2009). Expanding design toward greater relevance. In B. Bell and K. Wakeford (Eds.), *Expanding architecture: Design as activism* (pp. 14–16). Singapore: Metropolis Books.

Bleby, M. (2007, December 12). Designing an argument for architecture. *Business Day* (South Africa), p. 7.

Blossom, E. (January 19, 2009). Keynote address. *Art + design symposium for social justice.* Sponsored by Florida State University Departments of Interior Design and Art Education. Proceedings available at http://interiordesign.fsu.edu/symposium/

Busch, J. (December 2008). Be of good cheer. *Contract.* Retrieved January 30, 2009, from http://www.contractmagazine.com/contract/content_display/esearch/e3i686368ba4cd6a88c0d9677c652b0e2ca

Contract's Design Forum (advisory board meeting). (2008, January 1). Socially responsible design. *Contract.* Retrieved February 7, 2009, from http://www.contractmagazine.com/contract/esearch/article_display.jsp?vnu_content_id=1003699909

Dickinson, E. (2009, January 30). Project m: Thinking wrong, doing right. *Metropolis Urban Journal.* Retrieved February 5, 2009, from http://www.metropolismag.com/story/20090130/project-m-thinking-wrong-doing-right

Fisher, T. (2009). Public-interest architecture: A needed and inevitable change. In B. Bell & K. Wakeford (Eds.), *Expanding architecture: Design as activism* (pp. 8–13). Singapore: Metropolis Books.

Gamez, J., & Rogers, S. (2009). An architecture of change. In B. Bell & K. Wakeford (Eds.), *Expanding Architecture: Design as Activism* (pp. 18–25). Singapore: Metropolis Books.

Jones, T. (Winter, 2009). Design rebels. *Perspective.* pp. 30–37.

Le Corbusier. (1985). *Towards a new architecture.* Mineola, NY: Dover Publications.

Lulan Artisans. (2009). *About Lulan artisans.* Retrieved February 5, 2009, from www.lulan.com/lulan/about.php#materials

Public Architecture. (2009). *Public architecture.* Retrieved February 4, 2009, from http://www.publicarchitecture.org

Roman, N. (1999). Ending homelessness in America. In P. Brookman & J. Siena (Curators), *The way home: Ending homelessness in America* (pp. 142–145). NY: Harry N. Abrams.

U.N. Millennium Project. (2009). *About the UN millennium project.* Retrieved February 2, 2009, from http://www.unmillenniumproject.org/who/index.htm

Wilson, B. (2009). The architectural bat-signal: Exploring the relationship between justice and design. In B. Bell and K. Wakeford (Eds.), *Expanding architecture: Design as activism* (pp. 28–33). Singapore: Metropolis Books.

> What is the value of creativity?
Are there constraints to
using creative thinking?

BRAD HOKANSON

BEYOND FUNCTION: CREATIVITY IN INTERIOR DESIGN

Creativity is the ability to produce work that is novel, original, unexpected, and appropriate, i.e., useful, adaptive concerning task constraints (Lubart, 2001). It is central to design and to the life of the interior designer. Everyday interior designers are constrained and challenged, escaping only by creative ability.

A critical skill required in any discipline, creativity is the ability to generate new ideas. This skill is particularly essential in the discipline of interior design with its many challenges such as aesthetics, culture, technical capability, function, and safety. The value of creativity is seen on both small and large scales.

Creativity is not limited to any subset of professions; creativity is important in most disciplines in development of new products, solving of problems, and answering professional challenges. "Creativity is a topic of wide scope that is important at both the individual and societal levels for a wide range of task domains" (Sternberg & Lubart, 1999, p. 3).

BRAD HOKANSON, PhD, is an associate professor in the College of Design at the University of Minnesota. He teaches in the areas of interactive media, critical thinking, and creative problem solving. Hokanson won the College of Design's award for Outstanding Teaching in 2008. He has a diverse academic record, including degrees in art from Carleton College, architecture from the University of Minnesota, and urban design from Harvard. Hokanson received his doctoral degree in instructional technology from the University of Minnesota. His research focuses on creativity and the use of technology to aid cognition. Hokanson has published his research in *Computers in Human Behavior, Interactions with Media, Educational Technology,* and the *Handbook of Visual Languages in Instructional Design.* He is a registered architect with a number of award-winning projects, although is no longer in active practice. Frequent visits to Buenos Aires support his Argentine tango habit.

Recent popular books such as *The Rise of the Creative Class* (Florida, 2004) and *The World Is Flat* (Friedman, 2005) celebrate the global value of creativity. Many governments and corporations seek to encourage creativity among citizens and employees as a means to improve economic status; the development of new products is essential to business and to the health of a country. As an example, Lego®, the Danish toy company, is constantly engaged in creating new products and new ways of efficient production. In Denmark, Lego is viewed as essential to national economic health (A. Nielsen, Director of Communications, personal communication, March 16, 2004). Nationally, a similar viewpoint is evident in the Republic of China (Taiwan), which has instituted a nationwide program to develop creativity in all its schoolchildren. The United Kingdom and the People's Republic of China actively support the development of creativity and design disciplines such as product design, architecture, and interior design. Design is no longer viewed merely as part of the cultural expression of a country, but also as part of the economic capability of the country, as *creative industries* (see Cox, 2005; Tischler, 2006).

Many people think that creativity resides only in a few individuals, that is, brilliant artists such as Mozart or scientists such as Einstein. They contend creativity is present only in a genius that is recognized by society and not in the average individual. In contrast, for some time it has been generally understood that creativity is a broadly held cognitive and inventive ability (Torrance, 1972). Creativity is how we generate the new, the different, and how we solve problems in all disciplines: "Creativity is the generation of new ideas—either new ways of looking at existing problems, or of seeing new opportunities" (Cox, 2005, p. 8). "The creative process . . . refers to the sequence of thoughts and actions that leads to novel, adaptive productions" (Lubart, 2001, p. 295).

Creativity researcher Robert Epstein (2000) describes a creative lifestyle as essential to creativity. He contends we are creative because our lives are filled with practices that encourage creativity and creative results. His four central tenets of a creative lifestyle parallel the lives and habits of many interior designers. These tenets include:

- the omnipresent use of journals and other recording devices to capture creative thoughts and preserve new ideas
- the seeking out of challenges that require performance outside current levels of skill or knowledge
- the broadening of skills and knowledge through training or experience outside of one's expertise
- consistent changes to their current physical and social environment

By its very nature, the work of interior designers is this web of creative acts; it involves the direct production of completely new products, artifacts, environments, ideas, and experiences. The very practice of interior design involves the use of a high number of creative skills, from the fluidity of developing a large number of ideas to the originality of developing ideas that are innovative in society.

Within the discipline, the effective creativity of the individual design firm may be what distinguishes the firm from competitors, and that which leads to entrepreneurial success. This may involve finding and using materials in unique and effective ways, or overcoming challenges in processes, materials, regulations, or highly expressive aesthetics. All aspects of interior designers' work are involved with creativity: from winning the project to the initial project brief or program, to the resolution of post-occupancy problems. Creativity is what sets interior designers apart, and it also is the essence of why interior design work has value.

DEVELOPING CREATIVITY

Design is generally learned through the studio experience. This is true in the disciplines of architecture, fashion, graphic design, and interior design, among others. As opposed to learning the facts of interior design, one *becomes* an interior designer through studio-based practice, integrating the knowledge of the field directly into the work. Instructor-posed design projects are resolved, challenging newer designers to examine novel and unique resolutions. The difficulties posed as part of the design problem include the aesthetic and the mechanical, the structural and the environmental, and the regulatory and the administrative. In each aspect, the interior designer must find answers from outside inspiration and from within.

Failure comes through having too few ideas. The ability to generate new ideas, i.e., creativity, develops through repeated practice and effort. Within professional practice the raw number of creative ideas may decline, but through experience and knowledge of practice, a more targeted set of elite responses will be built on experience.

Experienced interior designers often have fewer ideas with greater inherent differences between concepts, that is, a broader range of focused ideas. Of course, good interior designers continue to increase their ideational skills through their own meta-cognitive challenges, i.e., they know to diversely conceptualize and when they need to seek more ideas.

Any design process has a series of different activities with attention to various different aspects of the work. A broad understanding of the project, as well as background in the field and ability in each aspect of the work, structure the nature of the project. In addition, time must be dedicated to the experimental aspects of the work, both on specific projects and to generally advance one's work. A rigorous understanding and evaluation of the discipline's body of knowledge must be applied, and ultimately, the project must be implemented with skill and a continuous improvement of the design, even after formal completion (Hokanson & Miller, 2009). All of these process stages lie within a broad definition of creativity.

PROCESSES FOR CREATIVITY

Many processes (including those within interior design) are often reduced to routinized procedures or algorithms for undertaking the work. Algorithms are step-by-step ways of producing generally reproducible results, which is a valued means of ensuring successful completion. The means of production are codified, as most algorithms seek an anticipated solution, a single answer that any interior designer could achieve, and one that is often independent of context or participants.

Within a knowledge-based society, algorithms have significant value. They are one reason, combined with technology of computing, for advances in 20th-century thought, according to Moldoveanu and Martin (2008):

The power of the algorithm lies precisely in the fact that it makes efficient the translation of knowledge into action. Knowledge structures progress in levels of precision and specificity, from pictures to heuristics to theories to models to algorithms. Algorithms also become more easily translatable into predictable, output-oriented behavioral patterns or routines. Not surprisingly, the development of algorithmic agents—both human and artificial—has been a natural outgrowth of the recognition of the power and use of the algorithm and a key driver of the decreasing marginal value of algorithmic tasks and skills. (p. 40)

Design, however, is not an algorithmic process, a following of a recipe for a standardized result. Complex tasks cannot be optimally resolved through a codified sequence of steps or sub-routines. Holistic and value-based guidelines, i.e., *heuristics*, must be utilized to analyze, understand, and solve such problems. Heuristics are a series of "informal judgmental rules" (Lenat, 1983, p. 243) and could be described as procedural guidelines. Heuristics are generalizable in their flexibility and recognition of the complexity of problems. Moreover, heuristics are often embedded in the values and experiences of designers as a tacit form of knowing (Cross, 1982; Lawson, 2004).

Design problems of the modern age have become more complex, and these are problems that cannot be resolved through algorithmic processes. They have moved from simple problems with clear solutions to what are described as complex or ill-structured problems, i.e., having unclear problem and solution states. Occasionally, interior designers are challenged by "wicked" problems that are similarly defined but are, in addition to the challenges of complex problems, contentious, contextual, subjective, and completion critical (Becker, 2007; Jonassen, 2006; Nelson & Stolterman 2003; Rittel & Webber, 1973; Simon, 1973). The interior designer of the future will face more such problems, with more problems definable at a higher level of complexity and challenge. Challenged with complex and wicked problems, the goal of the interior designer *cannot be* to produce consistent designs—particularly those that replicate previous work. The goal must be to produce better work, designs that are, as yet, unconceived. Inherent in this goal for the profession is one of constant improvement and innovation of the design process; there is an inherent need for creativity. The work must be resolved in a heuristic manner, one that encompasses the essence of the interior designer as creative; the first heuristic for the interior designer is creativity.

As we have seen, creativity is an essential element of any form of interior design. It addresses the functional aspects of design in the making of the built environment; it exists within the aesthetics of the work, in challenging the cognitive and visual limits of the viewer; and it exists within the very process of interior design practice, in being inventive in the way the work is done.

Design is a constant effort to overcome limits, challenges, and constraints; inherently, there is a need to be creative, to go beyond the functional completion of the project. Good design in any discipline involves much more than functional solutions. Creativity is how the interior designer extends the solution beyond an algorithmic, recipe-like solution. Design is what happens past done.

REFERENCES

Cox, G. (2005). *Cox review of creativity in business.* Retrieved February 26, 2006, from http://www.hm-treasury.gov.uk/cox

Cross, N. (1982). Designerly ways of knowing. *Design Studies, 3*(4), 221–227.

Epstein, R. (2000). *The big book of creativity games: Quick, fun activities for jumpstarting innovation.* New York: McGraw-Hill.

Florida, R. (2004). *The rise of the creative class: And how it's transforming work, leisure, community and everyday life.* New York: Basic Books.

Friedman, T. (2004). *The world is flat: A brief history of the twenty-first century.* New York: Farrar, Straus and Giroux.

Hokanson, B., & Miller, C. (2009). Role-based design: A contemporary framework for innovation and creativity in instructional design. *Educational Technology, 49*(2) 21–28.

Jonassen, D. (2006). A constructivist's perspective on functional contextualism. *Educational Technology: Research and Development, 54*(1), 43–47.

Lawson, B. (2004). *What designers know.* Oxford: Architectural Press.

Lenat, D. (1983). The role of heuristics in learning by discovery: Three case studies. In: R. Michalski, J. Carbonell, & T. Mitchell (Eds.), *Machine learning: An artificial intelligence approach.* Palo Alto, CA: Tioga, pp. 243–306.

Lubart, T. (2001). Models of the creative process: Past, present and future. *Creativity Research Journal, 13*(3 & 4), 295–308.

Moldoveanu, M., & Martin, R. (2008). *The future of the MBA.* New York: Oxford University Press.

Nelson, H., & Stolterman, E. (2003). *The design way: Intentional change in an unpredictable world: Foundations and fundamentals of design competence.* Englewood Cliffs, NJ: Educational Technology Publications.

Rittel, H., & Webber, M. (1973). Dilemmas in general theory of planning. *Policy Sciences, 4,* 155–169.

Simon, H. (1973). The structure of ill-structured problems. *Artificial Intelligence, 4*(3), 181–201.

Sternberg, R.J., & Lubart, T. (1999). The concept of creativity: Concepts and paradigms. In R. Sternberg. (Ed.), *Handbook of creativity.* Cambridge: Cambridge University Press.

Tischler, L. (2006). The Gucci Killers. *Fast Company,* [106] 42–48.

Torrance, E. (1972). Can we teach children to think creatively? *Journal of Creative Behavior, 6,* 114–143.

GARY E. WHEELER

HOLISTIC REVOLUTION: ELEVATING THE VALUE OF INTERIOR DESIGN

In a *Harvard Business Review* article entitled "The Human Moment at Work," the comments of psychiatrist Edward Hallowell from 1999 pointed out that the anxiety many people feel at work has a simple antidote: a personal moment between two individuals in the same place at the same time. This encounter may only take a few minutes, but "the positive effects of a human moment can last long after people have walked away," wrote Hallowell. "People begin to think in new creative ways; mental activity is stimulated." But, he warns, "I can tell you without a doubt that virtually everyone I see is experiencing some deficiency of human contact. . . . People feel lonely, isolated, or confused at work" (in Lawrence, 2007).

Ten years later, with our overdependence on technology and e-mail, the situation has not improved and may actually be worse. In today's work environment, the value of a company is the value of its people and not of the building or the cost of equipment therein. People sell, design, manufacture, and provide services.

GARY E. WHEELER, FASID, FIIDA, is a renowned professional with more than 30 years of interior design experience and a passion for creative excellence. A member of the *Interior Design* Hall of Fame, and a senior fellow and board member of the Design Futures Council, Wheeler is recognized internationally for his strategic leadership in workplace design and his advocacy for integrated design solutions. In 1978, he cofounded the Wheeler Group, which he sold to Perkins & Will in 1996 and remained the firm's managing partner of the headquarter office in Chicago. In 2004, Wheeler joined Gensler as the European director of interior design and in 2009 established Wheeler Kanik, a new agency headquartered in London, focusing on strategic business objectives specializing in the corporate, financial, media, and educational sectors.

When companies struggle or fail, it's usually because their people have failed to perform these functions as well as they could.

The challenge for interior designers, therefore, is how do we set about delivering holistic design solutions that encompass not only the strategic objectives of an organization but, equally, a platform to support an understanding of the interaction of its people with space, culture, and the workplace. Bottom line: what is the true value of interior design?

Today, the nature of work is changing. It's now more mobile, cognitively complex, team-based, and collaborative—and younger generations are entering the fold. These factors, combined with increasing demands to remain competitive and continually innovative while controlling ever escalating real estate and staff costs, tee up the workplace as the battleground among an organization's cost-saving strategy and its efforts to retain the status quo, to act as a facilitator of change, and to serve as the visual statement of the brand.

Why then, when workplace design can be used to support such key business efforts as enhancing existing structures, enabling organizational transformation, and creating an identity and brand (Levin, 2001), are the decisions surrounding workplace design often based on a combination of trends, entitlement, and more often than not, cost? Only when a more systematic approach to workplace design is recognized—one that encompasses human psychology, anthropology, work processes, and most importantly, long-term business strategies—will a holistic solution be realized.

ACHIEVING A HOLISTIC SOLUTION

Traditional workplace design is based upon corporate structure and hierarchy and dates back to when manufacturing was dominant. We again must ask why, in today's knowledge economy, have most organizations not changed the physical environment where their employees work? Bechky and Elsbach (2007) reported "less than 5% of U.S. corporations tie the workplace to corporate strategy or see it as a tool for improving organizational performance" (p. 9).

Kimberlee Burt, FCSD, director and founder of Original Creative Co-op B.V., says,

Too many clients still see strategy separate from design, and as a consequence, the interior designer is placed too far down the food chain to be able to create a holistic solution. The challenge, therefore, is to broaden our clients' viewpoint beyond a facilities management, cost-point orientation to see the added business value of strategic interior design. (Kimberlee Burt, personal communication, 2009)

I often joke that the modern interior designer should come equipped not only with an MBA but also master's degrees in human psychology and anthropology because holistic solutions will only be realized after addressing the complex relationship between office design and individual employee attitudes and behaviors. Research has provided evidence that office design influences individual identities, creativity, and mood, in addition to traditionally researched variables such as comfort, safety, and ergonomics.

Further still, a research project into gender in the workplace led by Nila Leiserowitz, co-managing director of Gensler's Los Angeles office, Barbara Annis of Barbara Annis & Associates, Inc., and me has shown that, over the past 20 years, the movement toward conferencing and team rooms has been driven by women due to their greater need to share ideas and receive validation versus the needs and wants of their male colleagues.

Another example of the need for interior designers to adopt a holistic approach comes from anthropologist Karen Stephenson, PhD, president of Netform and associate professor of management at the Rotterdam School of Management, Erasmus University, The Netherlands. Stevenson suggests that for clues to predicting the future of design, one must regard the last 300 to 400 years and the transformation from the simple concept of location in 17th-century physics to a fixed observable location in the 18th century (Bentham's panopticon), to the regulated workplace of the 19th century, to the virtual nomad in the 20th century. She continues with,

> And, what's even more remarkable is that we daily partake in the wisdom of those ages. Walk into any university and revisit the 18th century for the 19th-century look at manufacturing; Internet software firms for the 20th century, and what is still on the drawing board for the 21st century. (personal communication, March 26, 2009)

We've seen that adopting a strategic approach to workplace design creates a plan enabling the interior designer and client to focus on the real, long-term goals of the organization. Jay Galbraith (1995) uses the Star Model (see Figure 1.1) to illustrate five factors that entail organization-focused or strategy-focused design:

- Strategy determines direction of the organization
- Structure determines the location of decision-making power of the organization
- Process entails the flow of information, and work processes and methods of the organization
- Reward systems of the organization influence the motivation of people to perform and address organizational goals and their perception of the role of workplace assignments
- People, referring to the skills required of employees to execute their work processes along with the human resource policies of the organization toward employees (p. 12)

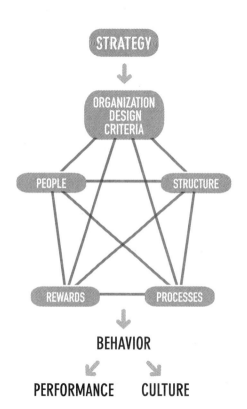

Different Strategies = Different Organizations
Organization Is More than Structure
Alignment = Effectiveness

FIGURE 1.1. The Star Model guides the assessment, planning, and implementation of holistic change to ensure sustainable performance improvement throughout the interior design process. (photo credit: J. Galbraith 1995)

FIGURE 1.2. Edelman's London headquarters. (photo credit: Gensler/Morley Von Sternberg)

Together, these five factors contained by the workplace determine the culture of an organization, and when each of them is aligned, only then can you begin to formulate a holistic design strategy. Without this alignment, and without due consideration linking design to business strategies and human needs, the workplace will fail to deliver its full potential.

My message to interior designers: take the holistic plunge and reap the benefits. We've seen that in 95% of U.S. businesses—and in the European Union we find similar statistics—workplace design is not linked to business strategy. What, then, is done by the remaining 5%?

An excellent example lies with Edelman, the world's largest independent public relations agency. Edelman's European CEO, Robert Phillips, identified office design as the key tool to help overcome certain cultural and structural problems within their European headquarters based in London. Driven by a vision of a workspace that would not only support the business but enhance it, Phillips demanded a powerfully evocative and highly productive work environment that would reduce costs, increase

productivity, unite a geographically fragmented workforce, and define a new company-wide cultural personality and working ethos (see Figure 1.2).

And, if that wasn't enough, another acute problem on the Edelman project faced by the design team led by London-based designer Grant Kanik and me was how to integrate three very different, dynamic, and culturally strong-minded brands and enable each to "work" alongside one another. The solution, billed as "the office of the future" by the *London Financial Times*, is a sprawling 38,000-square-foot single-floor plate enveloped by the theme of "inside media" defining the space for what Phillips calls the *Conversation Age*.

In the Edelman office, staff work in an open-plan, Velcro-like environment that's as flexible as a Swiss army knife. The directors' offices double as meeting rooms, adhering to the design team's strict "multifunctional" policy (see Figure 1.3). A unique, variable-density desking system that supports 260 people can accommodate an additional 110 people overnight. Robert Phillips, Edelman CEO, says productivity is up 60%, their win

FIGURE 1.3. Key to Edelman's success is the flexible "Velcro" working environment designed to support change, collaboration, and communication. (photo credit: Gensler/Morley Von Sternberg)

FIGURE 1.4. Staff choose to come to the office early and stay late. (photo credit: Gensler/Morley Von Sternberg)

rate on cross-practice pitches is up 30%, and absenteeism is all but a thing of the past (see Figure 1.4). The environment permits rapid alignment of resources, people, technology, and systems.

This focus on the workstation design and density achieves several aims. In contrast to the pre-assigned desks of the past, the new work style eradicates the *silo* mentality commented on by Phillips, and inherently promotes the Holy Grail of collaboration and communication. As Kanik explains,

> The entire approach was about creating synergy. A strict "multi-use" policy is evident throughout the entire space. The small number of directors' offices double up as meeting rooms; flexible-walled conference rooms expand and contract to accommodate an astonishing number of meetings and events. The reception area is a veritable chameleon of coffee bar, reference library, informal meeting space, creative hub, and breakfast area. (personal communication, November 17, 2008)

To achieve this, we developed a close partnership with Edelman very quickly and built a mutually trusting relationship. We explored Edelman's aspirations, technology, processes, and its people, their strengths and weaknesses. We worked together to understand the business, where they are today, and their goals for the future. Phillips is a busy man, but he made himself available 24/7—his decisiveness was critical to the project's success (Grant Kanik, Wheeler Kanik LLP, personal communication, November 19, 2008).

Nine months after occupancy, the direct and tangible results are evident, says Phillips.

> Our win rate on cross-practice pitches has gone up by 30% because people don't sit in silos. Staff churn is tracking 25% below this time last year, and sick days are all but a thing of the past. Another measurement is our quality of life survey where we've seen a 50–60% jump in approval ratings. (Robert Phillips, CEO, Edelman, personal communication, 2008)

Another textbook example of where a strategic approach has delivered holistic results is Gensler's New Line Learning Academy in Kent (UK). Led by Phillip Gillard, Gensler's global head of education design, and working with a cross-disciplinary team in parallel with a Yale University research study on emotional intelligence, the aim was to create an integrated, reengineered, high-tech model of learning (see Figure 1.5).

To accommodate this vision, a new spatial-use model was developed. As a *test bed*, the team designed a Plaza Prototype on site for 120, year-8 students (13 years old). The Plaza conveys the key attributes of the space on one level, utilizing technology such as 360-degree projection and large display areas, biometric lighting techniques to control and vary the ambience of individual spaces, and flexible and adaptable furniture to allow a variety of work mode settings

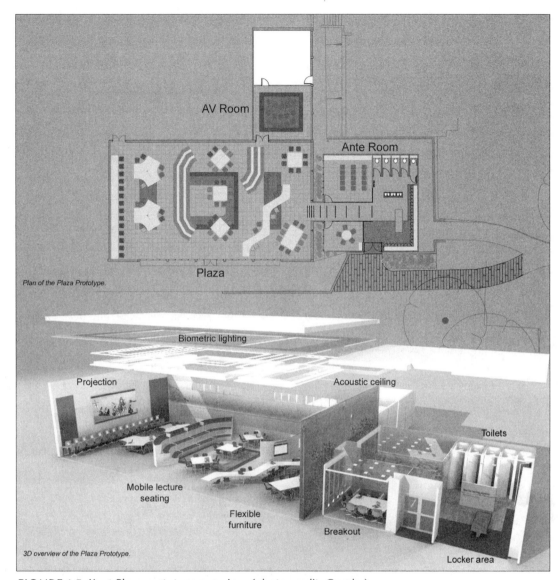

Plan of the Plaza Prototype.

3D overview of the Plaza Prototype.

FIGURE 1.5. Kent Plaza prototype overview. (photo credit: Gensler)

orientated around sizes of user groups and activities being undertaken. Gillard explains,

> The design brief was to look at a diverse range of spaces that allow you to have 90 people in a space because that's the type of space required for the learning activity that's taking place. But, also within that volume is a multi-layering of different levels of space that allows one-to-one, small groups, medium-sized groups, and larger groups to all learn at the same time. To have space working that hard, you need to think about how people use space, and how behavior changes when people sit next to each other. (Phillip Gillard, personal communication, March 24, 2009)

FIGURE 1.6. Kent work groups. The lighting helps divide the plaza into different zones: small group work, one-on-one tutoring, and self-study can happen at the same time. (photo credit: Gensler/Owen Raggett)

FIGURE 1.7. Southwest Washington Medical Center lobby. (photo credit: Benjamin Benschneider)

Designed to impact both mood and behavior, the prototype has already seen dramatic success with attendance levels up by 90% (see Figure 1.6).

In addition to strategic thinking, the changing demands and emerging research in many fields will impact the approach and value placed upon interior design. Many medical institutions, for example, now encourage family members to stay with patients in the medical center, which requires these centers to be much more home-like in design (Knackstedt, 2008).

Scott Wyatt, CEO of NBBJ explains, "Research has shown that the more you make people feel at ease (reducing stress), the better the outcome. The less institutionalized you make a hospital, the less anxious patients are and the quicker and better they recover. The same thinking applies to the caregivers. Less stress results in fewer errors and better care" (personal communication, March 27, 2009). (See Figure 1.7.)

Not only is this good for patients, but it also helps to drive down costs. In 2008, the former U.S. Treasury Secretary Paul O'Neill spoke about healthcare costs and claimed that up to 50% of the healthcare spending in the United States provides no medical value. O'Neill argues that a large percentage of that money is lost in process-related problems, citing situations in which nurses are spending half of their time searching for equipment or preparing equipment that should be ready. O'Neill said the goal of our medical system should be to identify how to improve processes and spread those practices to all providers (Boat, Chao, & O'Neill, 2008).

That's exactly what Wyatt and his NBBJ team are working toward. "Modern hospitals are adopting a lean, manufacturing-inspired process to deliver healthcare much more efficiently. Through modern approaches to interior design we're creating holistic change to the well-being and recovery process of patients" (S. Wyatt, personal communication, March 27, 2009).

As interior designers, we are constantly battling a barrage of challenges and obstacles—none more so than the spiraling cost of real estate, healthcare, and people. But what other, often more subtle, considerations do we need to think about? We've already touched on gender and the need to accommodate for both the needs of men and women along with human psychology and our attempt to understand the way people interact with one another.

What about how we communicate at work? In the 1960s, a researcher at MIT, Thomas Allen (1984), conducted a decade-long study of the ways in which we communicate within the workplace. Allen found that the likelihood that any two people will communicate drops off dramatically as the distance between desks increases. This, therefore, presents further considerations and further anthropological questions around networking, group behavior, and socializing that also need to be addressed.

Another step-change during the past decade, and now very much a corporate prerequisite, is the drive to deliver socially responsible design to all of our clients. While campaigning for the White House, President Barack Obama repeatedly warned America of the need for change and the importance of not getting left behind the rest of the world, echoing the sentiments spoken by Winston Churchill some 70 years before: "If we do not grasp change by the hand, it will grasp us by the throat" (in Knackstedt, 2008, p. 107). Interior designers need to embrace new trends and respond with agile and updated solutions. As the four horsemen of the financial apocalypse continue to gallop around the world laying waste to all before them, does this signal a new dawn of austerity and the end to the gratuitous corporate consumption to which we've become anesthetized? Is this recession a perfect storm of economic, environmental, and social crises leading to significant opportunity for innovation and change? The Eskimos have a proverb: "The storm is the time to fish." Our storm is upon us, and now is the time to innovate through design.

Over the past 50 years we've seen the workplace change drastically. The emergence of a global economy where culture, technology, and work modes collide necessitates a thorough understanding of business practice. To provide an effective design approach to support business, it is now critical that the interior design practitioner addresses the strategic needs and goals of the organization. Only when the whole structure is addressed, rather than the interdependence of parts, will a holistic solution be realized and the true value of interior design understood.

REFERENCES

Allen, T. (1984). *Managing the flow of technology: Technology transfer and the dissemination of technological information within the R&D organization.* Cambridge, MA: MIT Press.

Bechky, B., & Elsbach, K. (2007). It's more than a desk: Working smarter through leveraged office design. *California Management Review, 49*(2), p. 9.

Boat, T., Chao, S., & O'Neill, P. (2008). From waste to value in healthcare. *Journal of the American Medical Association, 299*(5), 568–571.

Galbraith, J. (1995). *Designing organizations: An executive briefing on strategy, structure + process.* San Francisco: Jossey-Bass.

Knackstedt, M. (2008). *The challenge of interior design.* New York: Allworth Press.

Lawrence, P. (2007). Enabling innovation through office design. *Business Week.* Retrieved March 26, 2009, from http://www.businessweek.com/innovate/content/oct2007/id20071015_340312.htm

Levin, A. (2001) *Workplace design: A component of organizational strategy.* MBA dissertation, Harrow Business School, University of Westminster, UK.

KATHERINE S. ANKERSON, MS, NCARB certified, IDEC, is associate dean and professor of interior design in the College of Architecture at the University of Nebraska–Lincoln where she has taught since 1996. Previous experience as a professor at both Radford University and Washington State University came following 15 years as an architecture and interior design practitioner. Ankerson's work lies in the areas of translation of research from medical and other professions as formative issues in design of the built environment, principally related to senior living environments (particularly adaptive environments that encourage aging-in-place); learning and teaching in the design disciplines, especially related to use of an interactive and integrated digital technology environment as interface for learning. She has written multiple books published by Fairchild Books and has authored multiple articles and presentations. Ankerson has served IDEC for many years as *Record* editor and board member.

BETSY S. GABB, EdD, FIDEC, IIDA, is a professor and program director in the interior design program in the College of Architecture at the University of Nebraska-Lincoln. She holds bachelor and master's degrees in interior design and a doctorate in education. Gabb has served on the board of directors for CIDA and is currently serving as chair of CIDA's Standards Committee. She is also currently serving on the editorial board of the *Journal of Interior Design*. In the past, she has served as the Midwest regional chair for IDEC. Gabb's research interests include teaching strategies for design, and the design of senior living environments. Her work has been published in a variety of publications including the *Journal of Interior Design* and IIDA's *Perspective*.

> What are some of the issues that interior design practitioners contribute to value for clients that the public, and many other designers, are unaware of? Can they be articulated clearly?

KATHERINE S. ANKERSON &
BETSY S. GABB

BENEFITS OF INTERIOR DESIGN FOR ALL

The value of design permeates the lives of all in sometimes unseen or unrecognized ways. Historically, design has been valued for its aesthetic and artistic contributions. Those contributions are not only viewed as important but as a "given" when considering the value of interior design. There are many great interior designers and design firms that have designed wonderful spaces created as art. But this cannot be communicated as the sole aim of interior designers.

Brand awareness increases the bottom line; workplace productivity is increased through reduced stress and injury; health costs diminish as appropriate healing environments are created; and natural resources are conserved through informed choices. There are many ways to express the value of design in our world. Whereas some may tout the advantages of a well-designed room or vehicle, others may seek to value the contribution of design in a much different way.

BRAND AWARENESS AND THE BOTTOM LINE

The most recent recognition related to design value occurs in brand awareness. In the last 10 to 20 years, a noteworthy company has been attempting to bridge the gap between good design and affordability for all. Target Corporation's philosophy is "good design for all," not "good design for the elite only." Their focus is to understand the client's needs, as well as introduce new design ideas to the public. They have enlisted talented designers and architects for developing new and improved product lines. By teaming up to provide affordable, innovative, and user-friendly products, Target has successfully helped educate and bring the value of good design to the forefront for the general public.

Various ads explain how Target feels about design with statements such as "design inspires, design shapes, design shines, design creates, design transforms, design moves, design fits, design protects, design comforts, design colors, and design unites" (Millman, 2005; Shapiro, 2005; Target Corporation, 2007). "Great design isn't reserved for the few. It's for everyone to enjoy, every day" is the prevailing motto on the Target Web site (see www.target.com).

"The philosophy of Target has helped educate the general public on the value of good design by introducing innovative, user-friendly product lines and services at affordable prices" (personal communication, Carissa Mullaney, graduate student comment from course assignment, University of Nebraska-Lincoln, 2007). Target recognizes that good design doesn't come easily, nor does it tend to be created by one person. Target Corporation is headquartered in Minneapolis, but this doesn't stop the company from expanding its outreach beyond Minnesota's borders to seek out highly talented designers such as Michael Graves, Isaac Mizrahi, and Sonia Kashuk.

> Great design is the essence of the Target brand. Target partners with world-class designers to offer amazing products at affordable prices. Since day one, our company founders recognized that the appeal of smart, stylish, well-designed products and stores would set Target apart. (Target Corporation, 2009a)

Target not only thinks about the product itself but good design is a value placed on their entire identity through marketing and advertising.

Because of the relationships between Target and these talented designers, common everyday items are being reevaluated and redesigned to make life easier and less confusing. For example, thanks to the design talents of Deborah Adler, Target has patented their redesigned Rx medicine bottles, which they call the "ClearRx system" (see Figure 1.8). The system is meant to reduce errors in dosage and misuse because it is considered to be easier to read due to a variety of graphic enhancements, including a magnifier. In addition, the packaging provides color-coding for each member of the household, and a new shape that can easily be gripped and opened (Bernard, 2005; Shapiro, 2005; Target Corporation, 2007; 2009b).

Gordon Segal, chairman of Crate and Barrel, also emphasizes the importance of the value of good design and brand awareness to his employees:

> Good design sells better in the world at large. Apple is the prime example we hold up to students. They not only have very good technology, but their products are customer-friendly and are simply beautiful. Everyone is wowed by them. . . . I teach our buyers at Crate and Barrel, "Look at a product, if it's really beautiful, get interested in it and understand the price. But at the end of the day, make sure it functions." (International Interior Design Association, 2009)

In other words, products should be able to improve the human condition.

WORKPLACE PRODUCTIVITY

Productivity in the workplace has long been of interest. "Businesses are waking up to the fact that the workplace is much more than just real estate and a means to house their people, they are embracing performance-focused workplace design as a strategic business initiative," states Diane Hoskins, an executive director at Gensler (O'Neil, 2006, p 34).

Because design plays an increasingly integral role in the business world, more companies should be aware of the direct relationship between the effective use of ergonomics and employee comfort and productivity. Buildings and interiors have a significant effect on worker productivity, establish environments that optimize workplace performance, and benefit companies by improving workplace design.

Tens of thousands of injuries each year are caused by repetitive motions. There are different ways injuries can happen, but all result from stress or strain imposed on some part of the body from a task's repetitive nature. Poor ergonomics and the injuries they cause represent significant drivers of business costs. Poor lighting can be a workplace hazard because it affects productivity, work accuracy, and quality of work. Alan Hedge, PhD, certified professional ergonomist, Cornell University (Hedge & Sakr, 2005), found a comfortable working environment can do more than make workers happy; it can improve productivity as well. Researchers have found that individual performance increases by 25% when employees use an ergonomically designed workstation (as reported in Croasmun, 2004).

In today's competitive business environment, companies challenge all aspects of their operations to continuously create more value for the company. Effective workplace design brings important benefits in several key areas—attracting and retaining employees, facilitating innovation, and promoting teamwork. A company's success is often related to the connection between building design and its impact on culture, creativity, and performance. As a result, people's inventiveness continues to emerge as a valuable business resource. Therefore, one of the primary challenges facing business leaders is to maximize the talents of the people they lead while recruiting and retaining good people in the tight labor market (Richter, 2001). Design plays a valuable role in these goals.

This premise is reinforced by John Lijewski, FIIDA, LEED® AP, senior vice president, interior design executive, Bank of America Corporate Workplace:

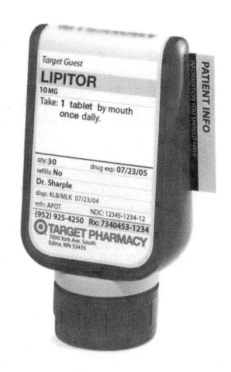

FIGURE 1.8. Target's flat-face medicine bottle.

At Bank of America, we understand the value of design and invest a great deal of time and money in our built environments. We believe that investment in "good design" will give us a competitive advantage and enhance our ability to attract and retain top talent to our company. (personal communication, February 18, 2009)

As indicated, there are many benefits a company should expect from a well-designed workplace. Good design in the workplace can elevate morale and improve productivity, promote the image, and help reinforce a corporate identity. It can also help to attract and retain a higher quality workforce by enhancing efficiency and employee satisfaction.

HEALING ENVIRONMENTS

Nowhere do we see a more direct impact of interior design on humans than in the healthcare arena. Research vividly illustrates reduced healing times and stress among patients, and increased accuracy and satisfaction among staff, as a result of interior design. An ever-rising population density, coupled with an aging populace and expanding environmental concerns, has forced a renewed interest in human health and well-being. This focus has brought with it an increasing awareness across many professional and academic domains concerning the impact the designed environment has on health, healthcare, and health outcomes. Evidence-based design (EBD) provides a quantifiable approach to communicating the effect of interior design decisions on the built environment, and certainly organizations such as The Center for Healthcare Design promote the value of this approach.

CONSERVATION OF NATURAL RESOURCES

The success of a project, its projected value, its effect on the community, and society's perception of interior designers and architects in the community often determine the public's view. Today's societal values differ from the values of earlier days. Earth-friendly strategies, a community-based focus, and a multifunctional space help interior design to be viewed as an invaluable asset to the community (Heywood, 2007). With growing waste and lack of natural resources, many communities are searching for designs that will assist in conserving resources while being an efficient design. The Johnson County Building, in Olathe, Kansas, does just that. Along with winning many awards for green design, the building is also known for its beneficial environment for its employees. The innovative use of natural light and biophilia-inspired workspace allows the county's employees to work in a "happier" environment. In addition to these environmentally friendly elements, a reduced level of taxpayers' dollars and a promise of $1.5 million a year in avoided future leases, the building is viewed as "community friendly" (personal communication, Meg Heywood, graduate student, comment from course assignment, University of Nebraska-Lincoln, 2007).

So, what is the value of interior design, and how do we communicate it? Graduate students in a University of Nebraska–Lincoln class, "Evolving Issues in Interior Design," were asked to evaluate how the value of interior design is expressed through the profession's Web sites. Their response was that value is often not defined at all. The class consisted of an on-line enrollment of widely diverse students from throughout North America. In another assignment, they were asked to discuss the "value of design" in general. They examined the Web sites of professional organizations: the International Interior Design Association (IIDA), the American Society of Interior Designers (ASID), the Interior Design Educators Council (IDEC), the Interior Designers of Canada (IDC), the Council for Interior Design Accreditation (CIDA), the National Council for Interior Design Qualification (NCIDQ), the American Institute of Architects (AIA), and the American Institute of Graphic Arts (AIGA). Several interesting trends emerged over all classes in the last three years. Students observed that the missions of the organizations were regularly provided on the Web sites; none of the interior design-related sites gave any explanation as to why interior design is of value. However, in reviewing the AIA Web site, the "value of an architect" can be found on the first page. Similar results concerning value were found on AIGA's Web site for graphic designers.

The students also found the Web sites for architecture and graphic design to be much easier to navigate and provided more insights as to what the professions entail. Examination of these Web sites caused one student to describe interior designers as *silent contributors*:

> Our contributions are not publicized, and neither is our value. I can remember when taking a tour of campus, many of the buildings had plaques on the sides that mentioned the donor, architect, engineer, and contractor. None recognized the interior designer. . . . I do not believe that our profession sufficiently explains the value of interior design to society. It is difficult to comprehend why the value of interior design is not understood, but I believe in many aspects interior design is a silent contributor to our world. Many of the benefits a well-designed space brings to clients are hard to, or not commonly, measured. Aspects related directly to interior design of spaces such as higher productivity, health/healing and monetary savings/gains to a client may be tracked but the results can be, and often are, attributed to other facets. A well-designed space disappears into the background. (personal communication, Jessica Kirk, graduate student, comment from course assignment, University of Nebraska–Lincoln, 2008)

The profession of interior design has come a long way over the last 50 years with the advent of the accreditation of education programs; the development of the Body of Knowledge (Martin & Guerin, 2006); the recognition of interior designers' contribution to the protection of the health, safety, and welfare of the public; and the initiation of legislative recognition. Yet there is much to be done. How can interior designers become more than *silent contributors*?

Leadership is one of the characteristics of the Interior Design Program at the University of Nebraska–Lincoln described in a portion of our Program's Mission Statement:

> More so than other fields, interior design is concerned with creating and forming the material world to reflect the ever-changing human condition. As educators for this field, our role is to respond to the needs of the profession, but to also respond to a higher calling. With ourselves as examples, we seek to foster among our students a responsibility to the profession itself, and to take a leadership role in the future direction it will take. In short, we seek to create a program that celebrates the potential power and diversity of the field of interior design. (Interior Design Program, 2007)

Leadership is also reflected in our educational goals:

> [O]ur students shall be prepared to lead and not merely follow innovations in design. Leadership can be achieved in many ways: through innovation in design, the power to motivate people, or simply the ability to inspire others with a quest for precision and excellence. (Interior Design Program, 2007)

Graduates sensitive to the issues related to healthy work and living conditions, in the near or global context, create communities that encourage livable rural and urban environments, and design buildings and environments that enhance and promote health and healthy lifestyles. They are poised to be excellent citizens and leaders.

Design, then, is a verb, a tool, a way of life. Its value to society is an advantage placed upon those who acknowledge interior design as a powerful tool that can be used to understand the relevance of every situation and problem. Design makes people proactive, forcing them to move in the direction they intend to lead (Fleming, 2007). One student best expressed our challenge this way: "As designers we really do have the unique opportunity to make an invaluable contribution to society by creating great design to make people's lives better. We are lucky to have this opportunity. Not many can say they have this wonderful chance to enhance people's daily environment, one that is going to affect them each and every day of their lives" (personal communication, Abbie Reece, fourth-year interior design student, University of Nebraska–Lincoln, 2008).

REFERENCES

Bernard, S. (2005). *The perfect prescription: How the pill bottle was remade—sensibly and beautifully.* Retrieved March 16, 2009, from http://nymag .com/nymetro/health/features/11700/

Croasmun, J. (2004, October 20). *Comfort means productivity for office workers.* Retrieved March 2, 2009, from http://www.ergoweb.com/news/ detail.cfm?id=1004

Hedge, A., & Sakr, W. (2005). Workplace effects on office productivity: A macroergonomic framework. *Proceedings of ODAM 20th Annual Meeting,* Maui, June 22–25: IEA Press, pp. 75–80.

Interior Design Program Analysis Report. (2007). Unpublished report for the Council for Interior Design Accreditation, University of Nebraska–Lincoln.

International Interior Design Association. (2009, Winter). In other words. *Perspective.* Retrieved May 21, 2009, from http://www.designmatters .net/pdfs/0109/0109otherwords.pdf

Martin, C., & Guerin, D. (2006). *The interior design profession's body of knowledge, 2005 edition.* Grand Rapids, MI: Council for Interior Design Accreditation, American Society of Interior Designers, Interior Designers of Canada, International Interior Design Association, and the National Council for Interior Design Qualification.

Millman, D. (2005). *Target: Design for all?* Retrieved March 16, 2007, from http://www.underconsid eration.com/speakup/archives/002200.html

O'Neil, M. (2006, October 5). Survey examines ergonomics in the workplace. *Interior Design,* pp. 34–35.

Richter, C. (2001, Summer). Workplace design: A laboratory for inventiveness. *Journal for Quality and Participation,* pp. 8–10.

Shapiro, E. (2005). Target: Design for all. *Communication Arts, 47*(5), 48–50.

Target Corporation. (2006). Growing by design. *Target Corporation Annual Report 2006,* 4–5. Minneapolis, MN: Target Corporation.

Target Corporation. (2007). *Questions and answers.* Retrieved March 16, 2007, from http://www .answers.com/ topic/target-corporation

Target Corporation. (2009a). *Press release.* Retrieved May 21, 2009, from http:// sites.target.com/site/en/company/page .jsp?contentId=WCMP04-031806

Target Corporation. (2009b). *Press release.* Retrieved May 27, 2009, from http://pressroom.target .com/pr/news/health-wellness/clearrx/ backgrounder.aspx

> What drives your manufacturing
approach to environmental responsibility?

RAY C. ANDERSON

THE POWER OF ONE GOOD QUESTION

Someone has said, "Everybody has just one story to tell, her or his own story." This is an excerpt from my story—one which I believe will define my legacy. It started with you, my customers, and one simple question. Let me explain.

In 1994, Interface's 22nd year, we experienced something totally unexpected and unprecedented. We began to hear a new and recurring question from our customers, especially architects and interior designers—a question we had never heard before: "What is your company doing for the environment?" Eight little words. To address this disturbing question, because we had no good answer, we formed a new environmental task force at Interface. Its purpose: to frame some answers; what were we doing for or to the environment? What were our environmental policies?

The organizers of the task force asked me to launch the new task force with a kickoff speech, to give the task force my environmental vision. I did not have an environmental vision. I did

RAY C. ANDERSON is chairman and founder of Interface, Inc. In 15 years of forging the company's environmental vision, Interface is more than halfway to its target of "Mission Zero." Anderson authored *Mid-Course Correction* (1998) and has a new book chronicling his journey, *Confessions of a Radical Industrialist* (2009, St. Martin's Press). He has become an unlikely screen hero in the 2004 Canadian documentary *The Corporation*. Anderson was named one of *TIME International's* "Heroes of the Environment" in 2007. He's a sought-after speaker and advisor on all issues eco, including a stint as co-chairman of the President's Council on Sustainable Development and as an architect of the Presidential Climate Action Plan, a 100-day action plan on climate that was presented to the Obama administration.

not want to make that speech. In all my working life, 38 years at that time, I had never given one thought to what we were taking from the Earth or doing to the biosphere in the making of our products, except to obey the law, to comply. So, I dragged my feet, but they stayed on my case. Finally, I relented and agreed to speak. The date was set, August 31, 1994. Come the middle of August, I was sweating. I had not a clue as to what to say. I could not get beyond obey the law, comply. Somehow, though, I knew "comply" was not a vision. It was a propitious moment.

At that very moment, by pure serendipity, a book landed on my desk. It was *The Ecology of Commerce* (HarperCollins, 1993) by Paul Hawken. I had never heard of him. I picked it up and began to thumb it. By page 19, I was reading. By page 25, it was a spear in my chest, an epiphanal experience. Hawken's central point was in three parts:

1. The living systems and life-support systems of Earth are in decline. We humans are degrading the biosphere. If that goes on and on unchecked we, that is our descendants, will *lose* the biosphere.

2. The biggest culprit in this decline is the industrial system, the linear take-make-waste industrial system, digging up the Earth, converting it to products that quickly end up as waste in a landfill or incinerator or greenhouse gases in the atmosphere.

3. The only institution on Earth that is large enough, wealthy enough, pervasive enough, and powerful enough, to lead humankind out of the mess it is making for itself is the same one doing the greatest damage—the institution of business and industry—my institution, perhaps your institution.

I was convicted there and then as a plunderer of the Earth, and I was struck by the thought: Someday people like me will go to jail for theft—theft of our grandchildren's future.

I took Hawken seriously, and I made that kickoff speech, using his material. I challenged that tiny task force to lead our company to sustainability and beyond—to make Interface restorative. I just stunned them, and amazed myself with this whole new challenge in my 61st year. I simply said, "If Hawken is right, and business and industry must lead, who will lead business and industry? Unless somebody leads, nobody will. Why not us?" They accepted the challenge and for 15 years now, I have been a recovering plunderer. The 3,100 people of Interface are a daily part of that recovery.

So, how are we, one petro-intensive company, climbing this huge "mountain," Mount Sustainability? I can tell you the first decision was mine: to determine that we *are* going to climb it and to articulate this BHAG—this big, hairy, audacious goal—as a vision for my company; and even when many people thought I had gone "round the bend," to stay on message, consistently, persistently, year after year. My second decision was to put the right people in the key roles and empower them to make it happen. But, the most important decision was made collectively by the people of Interface, *one mind at a time*, to embrace this challenging vision.

We began where we were in 1994 with a schematic showing all of the connections or linkages between Interface and the Earth—its lithosphere and its biosphere—directly, and through our people, our suppliers, our customers, and communities. Then we asked ourselves, "What is wrong with this picture?" We asked this when very few, if any, companies anywhere were asking such a question of themselves.

Out of that analysis came a plan, in terms of climbing the *seven* faces of Mount Sustainability, to meet at the top—that point at the summit symbolizing zero impact (zero footprint). This plan is the heart of the book I published in 1998, entitled *Mid-Course Correction*, and you can read more about the plan (and our progress) in my 2009 book, *Confessions of a Radical Industrialist*.

Today we find ourselves 15 years into our journey, demonstrating in very tangible and profitable ways the business case for sustainability. If our mountain climb has taught us anything, it is that sustainability doesn't cost, it pays; it has been amazingly good for business. Our costs are down, not up, dispelling a myth and exposing the false choice between economy and environment. Our products are the best they have ever been because sustainable design has provided an unexpected wellspring of innovation. Our people are galvanized around a shared higher purpose. Better people are applying to work with us, the best people are staying, and all are working with purpose. You cannot beat this for attracting and bringing people together. It is the pinnacle of Maslow's hierarchy of human needs—a higher purpose. And the goodwill in the marketplace generated by this initiative exceeds, by far, what any amount of advertising or clever marketing could have generated at any cost. We believe we have found a better way to more legitimate profits—a better business model. Even during the most trying days of recession and belt-tightening during the recession of 2000–2003, we had not one thought of turning back, not one. Here we are again in 2009 with a global recession and again, there is no thought of turning back.

So what does this mean to the interior design community? Let me share three stories of how sustainability has informed innovation at Interface.

David Oakey, our lead product designer, frustrated with lack of progress in implementing sustainable design, pleads, "Let's do something, anything!" So, a designer redesigns a typical product to have 4% less of its most expensive and energy-intensive material component (in this case, DuPont nylon). The redesigned product performs well in all the usual tests, so, for the moment, this is considered to be the "something" for which David was pleading.

But an engineer, thinking new kinds of thoughts, wonders about the effect upstream of this kind of design modification if it were made across our entire product line. So he asks DuPont a question that DuPont has never, ever been asked before: "How much energy did DuPont expend from well-head to my receiving dock in making and delivering that bit of nylon?" We now know to call this "embodied energy." The DuPont response is applied by the inquiring engineer, theoretically, across the hypothetically redesigned product line, and to his amazement and everyone else's, on an annualized basis this turns out to be enough energy *not used* by DuPont (call it "nega-energy") to run the engineer's entire factory for half a year!

Today, the average Interface product from this factory contains 17% less nylon than 15 years ago, and the off-set created upstream is equivalent to more than two years of nega-energy—to Earth's great benefit each year. We now call this approach "De-Materialization through Conscious Design." It is new thinking that considers upstream effects—whole system optimization, taking into account the entire supply chain. The new thinking reminds us that each of our companies or organizations *is* its entire supply chain. No one stands alone.

Another team of Interface engineers, production personnel, and product designers collaborate to find another way to create patterned carpet. The conventional way, employed for years by us and by our chief competitors, is to print patterns on a plain-colored carpet base. Printing is water- and energy-intensive, requiring an aqueous dye application, high-energy steaming to fix the dye to the fibers, washing to remove excess unfixed dye, and energy-intensive drying to remove the wash water. Excess wash water and dyes also require chemical treatment before release into the waterways.

But, new thinking suggests that the tufting machine that forms the pile face of the carpet in the first place has untapped potential to precisely place tufts of yarn of selected colors to form very intricate patterns. The bold decision is made to *burn the bridges* and abandon wet printing altogether, and to scrap the existing, stranded investment. Left with only one means of creating patterns—which the marketplace demands—development efforts resulted in entirely new families of *patented* inventions, giving us a proprietary edge, rather than handicap, in our marketplace.

One of those patented inventions arises from the outrageous assignment by David Oakey to his design team: to go into the forest and see how Nature would design a floor covering. "And don't come back with leaf designs," he says. "That's not what I mean. Come back with Nature's design principles." David had read *Biomimicry*, by Janine Benyus. (Biomimicry: Nature as teacher, Nature as inspiration, Nature as mentor and measure.)

So the design team spends a day studying the forest floor and the streambeds, and they come to realize there is total diversity, even chaos—no two things are alike, no two sticks, no two stones, no two leaves. Yet there is a very pleasant orderliness in this chaos. So the designers go back to the design studio and design a carpet tile such that the face designs of no two tiles are identical. All are similar, but every one is different. This is totally contrary to the prevailing industrial paradigm that every mass-produced item must be the *cookie-cutter* same—Six Sigma uniformity. Nature, the inspiration, is anything but perfect, yet she is very effective.

We introduced this new product to the market with the name *Entropy*® (a scientific term associated with "disorder"), and in 18 months it moved to the top of the best-seller list, faster than any other product ever had. The advantages of breaking the old paradigm, *insistence on perfection and sameness*, are surprisingly numerous:

- There is almost no waste and no off-quality in production; Inspectors cannot find defects among the deliberate "imperfection" of no-two-alike;
- The installer can install tiles very quickly without having to take the traditional care to get the pile nap running uniformly—the less uniform the installation, the better; so he can just take tiles out of the box the way they come and lay them randomly;
- There is almost no scrap during installation; even piece-tiles can find a place in the installation;
- The user can then replace an individual, damaged tile without creating the "sore thumb" effect of a new tile that so typically comes with precision perfection;
- Furthermore, there are no longer issues of dye lots; dye lots merge indistinguishably;
- The need for shelf stock (i.e., extra tiles) of the original dye lot, inventory on the shelf waiting to be used, is therefore obviated; and
- The user can even rotate the carpet tiles on the floor to equalize wear, the way we rotate tires on our cars, and make selective replacement of damaged areas to extend the overall useful life.

All of these innovations are good for the environment because they increase resource efficiency. *What is Interface doing for the environment?* I hope this helps you understand. We've experienced firsthand the power of that one question and the new course that it put us on, for Interface and, I daresay, for the entire commercial interiors industry. An industry has been forever changed by those eight words.

➤ What drives your educational approach to environmental responsibility?

LISA M. TUCKER

ENVIRONMENTAL RESPONSIBILITY AND INTERIOR DESIGN EDUCATION

PART 1: THE PAST

Optimism in the face of the need for revolutionary change in our approach to the built environment is the primary belief that drives my approach to environmental responsibility. Our students have the ability to change the world, and my job as an educator is to lead them to accurate information about the state of the world. We must also provide them with the tools they will need to be successful—most importantly, an ability to think and problem-solve.

For this essay, I was asked, what drives my educational approach to environmental responsibility. The personal answer is my desire to save the world for future generations, both human and other species, and a desire to redeem myself for past sins against the environment. We do not have a choice; we must change our ways both dramatically and quickly. When faced with the facts, people can see the reasons for change.

LISA M. TUCKER, PhD, CID, LEED® AP, has been a practicing interior designer and architect for 20 years with a specialization in historic preservation. She has owned her own firm since 1998. In addition to being a licensed architect and certified interior designer, Tucker is an assistant professor in the interior design program at Virginia Polytechnic Institute and State University where she teaches courses on lighting, building systems, and upper-level design studios. She holds degrees in architecture and architectural history from the University of Virginia and a PhD from the University of Missouri–Columbia in architectural studies. Tucker has recently completed a book entitled *Sustainable Building Systems and Construction for Designers*. She is active in both ASID (Virginia Chapter president 2009–2010) and IDEC (board of directors 2009–2010).

However, despite what we know, it is hard to change our ways, but we must because the world depends on every single one of us.

We Americans are at a critical crossroads; we must not only believe in the need for change, but we must also be willing to change ourselves—our habits, our beliefs, and dependence on the material wealth we have come to expect. As an interior design educator, I have a crucial role to play in this process.

PART 2: THE PRESENT

> Human beings and the natural world are on a collision course. Human activities inflict harsh and often irreversible damage on the environment and on critical resources. If not checked, many of our current practices put at serious risk the future that we wish for human society and the plant and animal kingdoms, and may so alter the living world that it will be unable to sustain life in the manner that we know. Fundamental changes are urgent if we are to avoid the collision our present course will bring about. (Union of Concerned Scientists, 1992a, p. 1)

When I stumbled across this message on the Internet in 1998, I was both scared and shocked. Then I got mad, wondering, "Why didn't anyone tell me?!" Then I realized that this was what I had been looking for—a way to justify my participation in a profession I viewed as inherently wasteful and had actually walked away from at one point because of that belief. What if it didn't have to be this way? What if I could make a difference through the act of environmentally responsible design, and by teaching my students about this type of design? I could ensure they were equipped to make decisions with a broader vision for humanity and our prolonged existence in mind. Now that I know the building industry significantly impacts the health of the planet, I believe I must do all I can to try to make some difference; this is no longer an option or choice.

The bad news is that, according to some scientists, we are at a critical juncture, if not already too far gone. According to *Thoreau's Legacy: American Stories about Global Warming*, an online anthology published by the Union of Concerned Scientists (1992b), "compelling new evidence demonstrates that global warming is already under way." The Intergovernmental Panel on Climate Change (2007) unequivocally concluded that our climate is warming, stating with at least 90% certainty that "the warming of the last several decades is primarily due to human activities" (p. 1). Mazria and Kershner's (2007) study, *Nation Under Siege: Sea Level Rise at Our Doorstep*, references a study completed by 47 scientists from NASA, the Berkeley National Laboratory, and other leading think tanks. They state that we are dangerously close to the tipping point that triggers dangerous climate change, including irreversible glacial melt and rapid sea level rise. Within their report, Mazria and Kershner provide images of all the coastal areas within the United States that would be underwater as a result of such changes. These include a large part of the states of Florida and California as well as Manhattan and most of Boston. Mazria is the founder of an organization called Architecture 2030, which calls for the immediate discontinuation of the use of coal. Yet, despite the negative impacts known, the federal government is currently constructing a new coal-powered plant intended to supply electricity to the government buildings in Washington, DC.

The World Watch Institute's "State of the World 2009 at a Glance" (2009) indicates that buildings use 41% of global energy, approximately two-thirds of which is wasted and released into the environment as heat. Meanwhile, arctic summer ice is diminishing at a rate of approximately 9% per year and the carbon

FIGURE 1.9. Student design solution for the first-floor restaurant and bar of the AD German Warehouse, Richland Center, Wisconsin, using sustainable materials including 3-form™, plaster, concrete flooring, and energy-efficient electric lighting integrated with daylighting provided by a skylight.

dioxide we release into the air today will still be there in 100 years or more (World Watch Institute, 2009). Species are going extinct at an alarming rate. According to *Scientific Daily* (2006, April 12), "The Earth could see massive waves of extinctions around the world if global warming continues unabated." Ben Block (2008), staff writer for the World Watch Institute, writes, "The world is on the brink of a massive extinction event, according to the United Nations." As of October 2008, 38% of the species studied by the International Union for the Conservation of Nature are threatened with extinction. Their Red List of Threatened Species shows 22% of mammals, 31% of amphibians, and 14% of birds are threatened or already extinct (Block, 2008). How did this happen?

As an interior design educator, it is imperative that my students are apprised of these harsh and rapidly changing environmental realities. A book I have students read at the beginning of this educational odyssey is Daniel Quinn's (1992) *Ishmael*. This book helps to explain and distinguish the worldview that has allowed much of the destruction to take place—a view of the world wherein humankind rules over all other life on planet Earth, by natural right. I intend for this book to provide a wakeup call to my students.

Through my teaching, I couple the bleak state of the world and humans' role in it with hope. My course assignments require students to design sustainably, as shown in Figures 1.9 and 1.10, as they use sustainable materials and daylighting.

FIGURE 1.10. Student design solution for the fourth-floor condominium of the AD German Ware-house, Richland Center, Wisconsin, illustrating sustainable materials including low-VOC paint, bamboo and concrete flooring, and plaster walls and ceilings. Partial-height walls permit natural light to pen-etrate into the interior kitchen space.

Several sources I have found inspiring and like to share with my students are *Biomimicry: Innovation Inspired by Nature* (Benyus, 1997), *Biophilic Design: The Theory, Science, and Practice of Bringing Buildings to Life* (Kellert, Heerwagen, & Mador, 2008), and any of the books on ecological design by Sym Van Der Ryn, such as *Ecological Design*. I have also had students read *Cradle to Cradle* (McDonough & Bruangart, 2002). Although I teach them about LEED® and I am myself a LEED® Accredited Professional, I fear that LEED exists within the same paradigm where the problem was created. To paraphrase McDonough, LEED® is "less bad," when what we need is "good." Still, isn't it better to do something than nothing at all?

PART 3: THE FUTURE

It is important to comprehend and digest the sheer devastation our species has wreaked on the world. Rather than adapt, as all other species are required to do, we chose to conquer, and the consequences are dire. We have no choice but to change or become extinct as have all the other plants and animals we have destroyed.

I hope this essay leaves you sober and contemplative. We will not solve our ecological problems in the way we worked to get here in the first place. Einstein is credited with saying, "We can't solve problems by using the same kind of thinking we used when we created them." After 10 years of teaching undergraduate students, it is clear to me that in many ways these students do not think the way I do or the way previous generations did. They have the ability to think in ways I cannot. As educators, we must arm them with good information, teach them to problem-solve, and most importantly instill a sense of personal responsibility; I am convinced they will create a new way of designing. A way in which the world is preserved, versus one in which conquering and destroying is an option. Many of them already are there.

REFERENCES

Benyus, J. (1997). *Biomimicry: Innovation inspired by nature*. New York: Quill.

Block, B. (2008). Coral reef loss suggests global extinction event. *World Watch Institute, Eye of the Earth, Energy and Climate*. Retrieved January 27, 2009, from http://www.worldwatch.org/node/5960

Intergovernmental Panel on Climate Change. (2007). *Panel report*. Retrieved April 10, 2009, from http://www.ipcc.ch/ipccreports/assessments-reports.htm

Kellert, S., Heerwagen, J., & Mador, M. (2008). *Biophilic design: The theory, science, and practice of bringing buildings to life*. Hoboken, NJ: Wiley & Sons.

Mazria, E., & Kershner, K. (2007) *Nation under siege: Sea level rise at our doorstep*. The 2030 Research Center.

McDonough, W., & Braungart, M. (2002). *Cradle to cradle: Rethinking the way we make things*. New York: North Point Press.

Quinn, D. (1992). *Ishmael: An adventure of the mind and spirit*. New York: Bantam Books.

Scientific Daily (2006, April 12). Retrieved April 1, 2009, from http://www.scientificdaily.com

Union of Concerned Scientists. (1992a). *1992 world scientists' warning to humanity*. Retrieved February 9, 2009, from http://www.ucsusa.org/americanstories/globalwarming.html

Union of Concerned Scientists. (1992b). *1992 world scientists' warning to humanity*. Retrieved February 9, 2009, from http://www.ucsusa.org/about/1992-world-scientists.html

Van Der Ryn, S., & Cowen, S. (1996). *Ecological design*. Washington, DC: Island Press.

World Watch Institute. (2009). State of the world at a glance. Retrieved April 3, 2009, from http://www.worldwatch.org

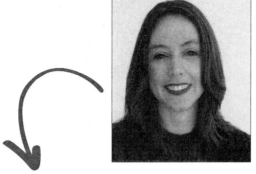

RACHELLE SCHOESSLER LYNN, CID-MN, LEED® AP, ASID, is a partner at Studio 2030, Inc., and has devoted her career to sustainable design. Before cofounding Studio 2030, she led the interior design practice for two major Minnesota design firms. She serves on the licensing board for the State of Minnesota and chairs ASID's National Sustainable Design Council. Schoessler Lynn is a frequent lecturer on sustainable design, indoor air quality, workplace issues, and material development. She is an adjunct faculty at the University of Minnesota and an advisory board member for Iowa State University's College of Design. Schoessler Lynn helped create Minnesota's current sustainable building design guidelines, *Buildings, Benchmarks, and Beyond*. Schoessler Lynn was awarded the 2004 "Designer of Distinction" award from the Minnesota chapter of ASID, and has most recently won the prestigious "40 Under 40 Business Leaders" award by the *Twin Cities Business Journal*.

DAVID LOEHR, AIA, AICP, LEED® AP, is a partner at Studio 2030, Inc., and has built a 21-year reputation of design integrity for complex, mixed-use, urban projects. His projects are acclaimed for their design statements, community contributions, innovative use of materials, and collaborative processes. Loehr's award-winning focus on design excellence and sustainable design creates projects embraced by their communities, including projects in 11 different countries. Prior to cofounding Studio 2030, he held significant leadership positions in two other design firms. Loehr's leadership in professional organizations builds relationships between design, construction, real estate, and policy professions. He is an adjunct faculty at the University of Minnesota and a registered architect in 29 jurisdictions. He has been recognized as a Minnesota Young Architect of the Year, and he won the 40 under 40 Business Leaders award from the *Twin Cities Business Journal*.

RACHELLE SCHOESSLER LYNN &
DAVID LOEHR

OUR DESIGN
RESPONSIBILITY FOR
PEOPLE AND PLANET

WHAT WE BELIEVE

We at Studio 2030 believe in the power of design. We believe that creative design solutions are transformative ideas that elevate the ordinary to the extraordinary. We believe design captures the imagination and engages the senses. We believe design helps meet economic objectives, solves social disparity, improves our health, and contributes to the well-being of our planet. We believe design inspires the soul and raises the human condition. And we at Studio 2030 believe that design must always embody environmental responsibility.

At Studio 2030, we use the design process to put forth our ideas of sustainability and environmental responsibility. We have witnessed a transformation within our profession. Environmental responsibility has always been a component of interior design, practiced passionately by a few, but largely not integrated into the mainstream. Sustainability gained momentum following the 1992 Earth Summit (United Nations Conference on Environment and Development). Now, clients, contractors, and suppliers have an emerging awareness and commitment to environmental responsibility. Our interior design profession is on the cusp of widespread leadership on sustainability issues. We are poised to embed environmental responsibility into our standard way of doing business. We have the skills, education, and understanding to present sustainable design solutions to our clients as the accepted norm and minimum baseline.

We founded Studio 2030 on the premise that environmental responsibility is the only way we practice. To us, it is only logical. Of course, we will design projects that sip energy. Naturally, we want our projects to improve the health of all occupants. Conversely, we will not create design solutions that waste energy or

49

FIGURE 1.11. The design team integrated this 40-kilowatt photovoltaic array to reduce annual carbon emissions by 30 metric tons for Quality Bicycle Products in Bloomington, Minnesota.

are unhealthy. To make this clear, we created goals and a point of view about design that is founded on our beliefs. We have invested in different tools in our quest for integrated, sustainable, creative design solutions. And we seek opportunities to integrate our design goals into all aspects of our projects. With 72% of the U.S. electrical consumption used by buildings, our design solutions transform spaces from consuming resources into spaces that contribute and produce resources for the broader benefit of everyone (see Figure 1.11). This essay summarizes our beliefs, goals, point of view, and approach to our design process.

DESIGN AND SOCIAL EQUITY

In Paul Hawken's *Blessed Unrest* (2007), the social justice movement is described as composed of many individual efforts working independently, but seemingly in harmony. According to Hawken, the harder we push environmental issues, the deeper we immerse in social justice issues. He stated, "Sustainability, ensuring the future of life on Earth, is an infinite game, the endless expression of generosity on behalf of all" (2007, p. 187). It is this sense of designing spaces on behalf of future generations that forms the core of Studio 2030's responsibility to the environment. As interior designers, we are expected, required, and obligated to create environments that ensure the health, safety, and welfare of occupants. To do less is not just unethical, but illegal.

So where do we draw the line? We know that it is healthier for occupants to breathe air not contaminated by volatile organic compounds (VOCs). And so, we must create spaces that purify the air and rejuvenate the soul through form, light, and composition. But let's not stop there; we should also design spaces that use less energy so that power plants have fewer emissions with cleaner air for everyone. Or, if we are really up to the challenge, we should design spaces that operate solely with renewable energy so that emissions are eliminated. Occupants expect that the structure, systems, and water used in the spaces we design are safe.

But as interior designers, we need to be obligated to conceive spaces that use water wisely and minimize its discharge so that a long-term, safe water supply remains intact for everyone. As interior designers, we create environments that foster the well-being of each occupant through views, daylight, and fresh air. We design spaces that are inspirational and fully accessible. We need to be equally responsible for maintaining biodiversity on our planet and limiting the amount of resource consumption as part of our obligation to the welfare of our broader community. With one-third of the world's population living in areas with stressed water conditions and limited access to safe drinking water, we must be responsible for designing environments that reduce water consumption. For Red Stag Supperclub in Minneapolis, Minnesota, our design solution reduced water usage by 70% as compared to similar restaurants (see Figure 1.12).

FIGURE 1.12. Unseen decisions, such as specifying low-flow aerators, high-efficiency toilet fixtures, and high-performance dish cleaning equipment, reduced water consumption for Red Stag Supperclub by 70% as compared to similar restaurants.

At Studio 2030, we approach our design process at this higher level of commitment to society. We believe that environmental responsibility and social justice are inseparable conditions of being interior designers. We must act in a leadership role to promote sustainability as a standard expectation of our design solutions.

Our understanding of environmental responsibility as an inherent element of design is derived from the core definition of sustainability: "[to meet] the needs of the present without compromising the ability of future generations to meet their own needs" (United Nations, 1987, p. 43). Since 1987, many suggestions have been made to change this definition to read, "[to meet] the needs of the present *while improving* the ability of future generations to meet their own needs." The design process itself has always included an element of looking forward and creating environments that anticipate the needs and functions of its occupants.

More importantly, at Studio 2030, we believe that interior design has a much richer context—it recognizes and reconciles the past, it uses the present as a compositional framework, and it aspires to meet future needs for a much broader community. We program and design spaces that not only anticipate the needs of today's occupants, but also so that future generations can meet their own needs.

DESIGN AND THE TRIPLE BOTTOM LINE

Green accounting has become a popular method for measuring the impact of a much wider spectrum of costs than just profitability. This was first articulated as the "Triple Bottom Line" by John Elkington (1997) in *Cannibals with Forks: The Triple Bottom Line of 21st-Century Business*. The Triple Bottom Line approach has become a cornerstone of sustainable design by maintaining the equal balance of economic prosperity, environmental quality, and social justice. It gives us, as interior designers, the ability to discuss environmental responsibility with the same vocabulary as our clients. It broadens the discussion of bottom-line results and places equal emphasis on all three elements.

For Studio 2030, we are able to translate our design goals as well as our commitment to environmental responsibility into a tangible, quantifiable return on investment. We approach all three elements—economic prosperity, environmental quality, and social justice—with an integrated mind-set. We utilize tools and techniques to embed our design ideas into a Triple Bottom Line framework.

STUDIO 2030'S DESIGN POINT OF VIEW

Studio 2030 was founded as an integrated design practice merging the art and science of architecture and interior design with the values of social and environmental responsibility. Our attitude about design is intentional and rooted in both the process of design as well as the final product of design. Design is broad and comprehensive. Design solves problems. Design rises far above formulaic responses and shuns attempts to be defined through checklists or overlays. From our founding, we continue to challenge ourselves about our own design point of view.

Design embodies environmental responsibility, which is an inherent attribute of our design process. It is part of the "genetic code"—the DNA of our design. Environmental responsibility helps solve design challenges and provides a strong foundation to support creative solutions. For example, by salvaging old fixtures and retrofitting with LED lamps, we were able to balance aesthetics, ambiance, reusability, and efficiency at the Red Stag Supperclub (see Figure 1.13). Today's design response demands social and environmental responsibility. Future generations must have the same ability to prosper unencumbered from missteps of our own generation.

Design is inclusive and integrated. The design of our environments reaches out to all who encounter them, directly and indirectly. It doesn't exclude anyone or any species. The design of our spaces draws people together, but cannot harm our planet in the process. Our interior spaces are interdependent with the outside environment. Building systems are fine-tuned to each space. Design breakthroughs come from all members of a design team working in a collaborative, integrated way.

Design makes you think; it inspires; it delights; it challenges; it provokes; and it is holistic. Our environments are not benign backdrops. Our spaces are more than just shelter. They interact with light and people and materials to create a dynamic three-dimensional experience. Our design solutions embrace safety, security, accessibility, flexibility, aesthetics, economics, productivity, and sustainability, as demonstrated with the "left-over" space between a parking structure and an office building that we converted into a light-filled amenity (see Figure 1.14). Our spaces are designed to be well planned from the first day and provide superior performance throughout occupancy.

Design makes you healthy. The inherent nature of design is to feed the mind, body, and soul. What if this were not true—that the design of our environments actually made you unhealthy? Yet sadly, all too often this occurs; spaces contribute to illness, the process of constructing our environments creates health hazards, and the manufacture of products used in our spaces makes people sick. We

FIGURE 1.13. At the Red Stag Supperclub, LED lamps comprise 100% of the lighting throughout the space and use daylighting strategies with integrated controls and new lighting technologies.

cannot compromise; we must design spaces that improve human health.

Design eliminates waste. Our programming process defines efficiency. Our design solutions eliminate excessiveness. Reuse and disassembly are intentionally part of our design process. We have a responsibility to reverse the trend of an end-of-life mind-set into a closed-loop, *cradle-to-cradle* (McDonough & Braungart, 2002) practice. For example, by salvaging furniture and specifying

FIGURE 1.14. The Norman Pointe II office building in Bloomington, Minnesota, was designed to capture natural light. We integrated a water feature, sculpture, seating, and textures to transform a "leftover" space into a public amenity.

waste reduction and diversion measures, we have been able to design highly innovative spaces that reduce landfill waste (see Figure 1.15).

Design is a powerful force for positive change. Studio 2030 continues to push the limits of design exploration. From its dynamic process, design draws upon existing knowledge and adds new knowledge as an outcome. Design relies on research as part of the process, while at the same time our spaces become vast sources of research opportunities. Studio 2030 continues to broaden our understanding of the world through a deeper commitment to environmental responsibility through the design process.

STUDIO 2030'S APPROACH

For us to achieve environmental responsibility, we must apply our convictions within the work we do every day. For each project, we aspire to reach the following six studio goals:

1. Become carbon neutral
2. Create net water producing projects
3. Implement net energy producing buildings
4. Eliminate waste
5. Improve human health
6. Design with intent

Studio 2030's design process is comprehensive, integrated, and holistic. We draw inspiration from nature through simple, elegant, and sustaining natural systems. We approach our design solutions from a long-term perspective through the use of life cycle assessments. We use evaluation tools and systems, such as EcotecTM, BEES®, and ATHENA® applications throughout our design process. (See Authors' Note for source of tools.)

We created and utilize an Environmental Impact Questionnaire to evaluate the life cycle impact of manufacturers and products. This allows us to prepare specifications that meet high environmental measurements and remain on the cutting edge of innovation. Our resource library and databases retain only those sources that meet our life cycle assessment standards. In addition, Studio 2030 has prepared carbon footprint measurements using the Greenhouse Gas Protocol (World Resources Institute & World Business Council for Sustainable Development, 2009) to help our clients make informed strategic business decisions. Our design decisions have a significant effect on global warming because buildings are responsible for 39% of U.S. carbon dioxide emissions. By measuring Red Stag Supperclub's carbon footprint, we have quantified direct and indirect emissions so that operational changes can be made to reduce its carbon footprint (see Figure 1.16).

An integrated and collaborative team process is the starting point for Studio 2030's projects. We allocate resources on the front end to exploit every advantage before major decisions are locked in. Throughout the process, we measure and analyze different strategies to understand the final impact of each decision.

Through this integrated process, we enhance the quality, depth, beauty, and performance of what we create. By tapping a wide spectrum of knowledge—of interior design, architecture, urban planning, energy modeling, engineering, landscape architecture, technology, and science, our clients receive the benefit of a broad range and depth of collective professional expertise. Because there is no predetermined outcome or prototypical concept, our process yields work of originality, crafted to the specific needs of the site, client, and circumstances.

Our firm is intentionally structured to be different. We invest in applied research to address today's rising challenges. We seek opportunities that showcase our integrated mind-set. We hire the best talent. We have established a partnership network of diverse and skilled professionals. We serve our profession through publications and conferences. And, we give back; we volunteer through committees, boards, and community forums.

FIGURE 1.15. At CB Richard Ellis's Bloomington offices, we reused 45% of the furniture and diverted 74% of construction waste from the landfill.

FIGURE 1.16. The carbon measurement of Red Stag Supperclub provides a comprehensive understanding of carbon emissions for total restaurant operations.

CONCLUSION

At the Technology, Entertainment, and Design (TED) Conference, Hans Rosling (2007) presented a remarkably crisp summary of the global dimensions of development. His conclusions placed culture, human rights, environment, and health at the top of the list of our long-term societal goals. His insight into what is important and what really matters provides a key lesson for our profession. We, as interior designers, play a pivotal role as caretakers of our culture, our human rights, our environment, and our health.

At Studio 2030, we approach environmental responsibility as an integral attribute of our design, a framework. We design every project with the vigor and enthusiasm of creating a lasting environment for future generations. We are different from a traditional design practice; we research, we teach, and we employ a wide range of tools to provide extraordinary environmental and design results. It is our commitment and our passion.

REFERENCES

Elkington, J. (1997). *Cannibals with forks: The triple bottom line of 21st-century business.* Oxford: Capstone Publishing.

Hawken, P. (2007). *Blessed unrest, how the largest movement in the world came into being and why no one saw it coming.* New York: Viking Penguin.

McDonough, W., & Braungart, M. (2002). *Cradle to cradle.* New York: North Point Press.

Rosling, H. (2007, June 25). *New insights on poverty and life around the world.* Paper presented at the annual conference of Technology, Entertainment, and Design (TED), Monterey, CA.

United Nations. (1987). *Report of the world commission on environment and development: Our common future.* [commonly referred to as the Brundtland commission's report: Our common future]. Oxford: Oxford University Press.

U.S. Green Building Council. (2009). *Green building facts.* Washington, DC: Author.

World Resources Institute & World Business Council for Sustainable Development. (2009). *Greenhouse gas protocol.* Washington, DC: Author.

AUTHORS' NOTE

Resources identified in the text:

Athena Sustainable Materials Institute. (2009). *ATHENA® Impact Estimator 4.0 and ATHENA® EcoCalculator* (whole building and assembly evaluation software). Merrickville, Ontario, Canada.

EcotecTM. (2008). *Comprehensive environmental design tool.* San Rafael, CA: Autodesk.

National Institute of Standards and Technology. (2007). *BEES® 4.0* (Building for Environmental and Economic Sustainability, software selection tool for cost-effective, environmentally preferable building products). Washington, DC.

Simply put, design thinking is focused on human beings; it is inspired by what people say and how they behave; and it results in telling the users' stories through the designed object, interior, structure, or place.

—Susan S. Szenasy

DESIGN THINKING

OVERVIEW The term *design thinking* is gaining recognition as a problem-solving process by business, industry, and government leaders. They have been unaware of the design studio's typical approach and are now touting it to resolve issues outside of design. It is possible that in some respects, interior designers are in the right place to become leaders in the design thinking movement, as viewed by many of the authors in this chapter.

Thomas Fisher clarifies the role and value of design thinking and its influence on the business world beyond design. He notes that many authors from varied disciplines are calling for their audiences to embrace design thinking. Joseph Connell echoes this viewpoint and notes its importance to the business world, as commissioners of design. He suggests a relationship among design "at its worst," design "at its best," and design thinking. Meanwhile, taking a complementary view of design thinking, Judith Heerwagen encourages interior designers to engage in design thinking by looking to nature for clues to design human habitat in ways formerly not considered.

The final two authors of the chapter challenge interior designers regarding their level of engagement with design. Susan Szenasy suggests that the staleness of interior design students' design solutions is the result of their interior design educators' thinking, contrasting them with examples of creative, futuristic problem-solving design thinking by students of architecture and graphic design. In contrast, the focus of Stephanie Clemons's concerns regard future interior designers and the youngest inhabitants of spaces—our children. She encourages interior designers to engage with students in the K–12 environment to bring interior design and design thinking into the curriculum. As a profession, can interior designers engage with design thinking in a more meaningful way within our practices; can children, fully engaged in their environment, consider what they experience in new ways through design thinking; and can the public begin to benefit more broadly from design thinking? Design thinking has much to offer.

> Design thinking is being considered
> a societal "tipping point." Based on your
> readings, discussions with others, and
> experiences, how do you anticipate
> design thinking will benefit the world?
> What role do interior designers play?

THOMAS FISHER

FUTURE SENSE: WHY DESIGN THINKING MATTERS

Design thinking remains one of the least understood and most valuable modes of thought. Given the fact that we spend most of our lives inside designed environments, it remains one of the paradoxes of our educational system that most people receive almost no instruction in design thinking and in how our designed environment comes to be: why some spaces work better than others and why some spaces affect us more than others. Indeed, most of us learn far more in school about the natural environment, which we can do relatively little to change, than we do about the designed environment, which we have a great capacity to improve.

The lack of schooling has led many laypeople to assume that design thinking is highly subjective, mainly involving matters of taste. That has created a real challenge for interior designers, whose years of education and long hours of hard work often go unappreciated and undervalued by many clients. It has also led many occupants to have an almost fatalistic

THOMAS FISHER is a professor and dean of the College of Design at the University of Minnesota. Educated at Cornell University in architecture and Case Western Reserve University in intellectual history, he previously served as the regional preservation officer at the Western Reserve Historical Society in Cleveland, the historical architect of the Connecticut State Historical Commission in Hartford, and the editorial director of *Progressive Architecture* magazine in Stamford, Connecticut. Fisher has lectured or juried at over 40 different schools of architecture and 60 professional societies and has published 35 book chapters and over 250 articles in various magazines and journals. He has published four books: *In the Scheme of Things; Alternative Thinking on the Practice of Architecture; Salmela Architect, Lake/Flato Buildings and Landscapes;* and *Architectural Design and Ethics, Tools for Survival.*

response to the interiors they encounter. The amount of poorly lit, inadequately ventilated, overly noisy, physically uncomfortable, and occupationally hazardous spaces many people inhabit and largely put up with in poorly designed interiors reveals the gap in the public's understanding of design and the harm to our health and happiness that bad design can cause.

Bad design also has real economic consequences. In a recent study of office environments in eight industry groups, the research group D/R Added Value (2006) estimated that poor design resulted in $330 billion in diminished worker productivity, with over one-third of those surveyed reporting that their offices did not enhance their health and well-being. Knowing how design happens has value not only to interior designers, but also to all who live in designed environments and with designed objects. Our health, well-being, and prosperity literally depend on it.

Design thinking has not received enough attention even in *design* schools. Too many schools remain so focused on students' work that too little attention gets paid to the thinking behind it, which, paradoxically, reinforces the common prejudice that design is more a matter of opinion than the result of a rigorous thought process. It also encourages a view of design as a somewhat mysterious activity, as something that a designer cannot explain but can only demonstrate for others to emulate, creating a culture of hero worship in which a relatively few star designers get a preponderance of the attention (Prak, 1984).

Although design stars may attract to the field students who hope that they might someday become stars themselves, this celebrity culture does design a disservice. We spend too much time in and money on designed environments to know so little about how they come about or to have such an idealized and intuitive view of them. The more we understand the process of design, the better we will be as consumers of design and as designers ourselves. We need fewer design epiphanies and more of a design epistemology: the study of what we know, how we think, and what value that has. And recent events have shown how necessary that is not only to the design community, but also to the larger world, as we shall see.

THINKING LIKE A DESIGNER

As far back as Aristotle, thinking has typically been divided into two types: inductive and deductive reasoning, with the former starting with specifics and moving toward general laws and the latter starting with principles and moving toward particular applications. But there exists a third type, what the philosopher Charles Sanders Peirce called "abductive" reasoning that involves making lateral connections among seemingly disconnected phenomena to see something new (Peirce, 1903). That abductive way of thinking underlies all creative ideas, and it defines designers' distinctive form of thinking.

Designers, of course, engage in inductive and deductive thinking every time they draw general conclusions about a project from the specific needs in a client's program, for example, or when they apply an overall theory of design to a particular project. But, design thinking has a "both-and" character, and it involves inductive, deductive, and abductive reasoning almost continuously and simultaneously. This, in turn, runs counter to the way most people think about thought itself, heavily influenced by Aristotle's "law of the excluded middle," which holds that something cannot be one thing and something else at the same time (Aristotle, 1952). Designers do not just take things apart and keep them distinct; they also put them back together and reconnect them in new ways, while accepting a high degree of ambiguity and simultaneity in the process.

Designers also project ideas forward in time and space. The humanities generally focus on the past, on what was, and the sciences and social sciences largely address the present, on what is. But very few fields direct their attention to the future, as designers mostly do. Designers, of course, also look to the past, to history for lessons and ideas, and to the present, to the sciences and social sciences for information and data. The distinguishing characteristic of design thinking, however, involves imagining the future, while accepting the fact that we can never know for certain what doesn't yet exist.

Certainty has long served as the holy grail of modern thought, with science becoming the standard against which we measured other disciplines, and so the inherent fluidity and uncertainty of design made it seem undisciplined as a result (Dewey, 1960). But with post-modern thought has come a much greater openness to the ambiguity and complexity of design, which has found itself much more in the center of intellectual life. Now embraced by fields as diverse as biology and business, design thinking has begun to be recognized for its ability to keep many, seemingly contradictory ideas in play at the same time as a way of finding the most creative solutions (Benyus, 1997; Martin, 2007).

Another aspect of design that distinguishes it from many other forms of thought involves its interweaving of thinking and making. Western thought has had a long-held suspicion of those who work with their hands, perhaps a reflection of the fact that the first academy that Plato founded in ancient Greece arose out of an aristocratic culture in which slaves did much of the hand labor. That first institution of higher education in the West instilled in academics a deep bias against the making of forms, as opposed to the thinking about form (Dancy, 2004). Here, too, design thinking flies in the face of that mind-body split. Design involves an iterative process of thinking in the act of making and of making as an act of thinking, and it encompasses both the making of things and the things themselves, both the environments of daily life as well as the ideas that underlie them.

That process of thinking and making also involves another skill: problem seeking. Other fields, such as literature and philosophy, have a history of envisioning utopias, idealized futures that overcome the perceived problems of the present. Most of those utopias, however, remain thought experiments, and in the rare instance where people have actually tried to put utopian ideas into practice, it has often turned into a nightmarish dystopia because of the lack of critical assessment of the possible problems and their potential downsides (Baker-Smith & Barfoot, 1987). Designers also envision idealized futures. But, along with that visioning comes a set of critical skills in how to assess the shortcomings and potential liabilities of every scenario we create. The often perceptive and sometimes picky criticism that occurs in design juries and journals can seem brutal to non-designers, but it is essential in ensuring the appropriateness and responsiveness of the solutions that designers devise.

Design, in short, involves a particular kind of lateral, expansive, speculative, iterative, and skeptical form of thinking that can handle high levels of ambiguity and uncertainty. But how, exactly, do designers think when they work? How do they come up with new ideas or imagine environments that don't yet exist? Most designers use analogies, looking for something new based on its similarities with what we already know. The analogies may be more visual than verbal, and more figural than literal in nature, and the connections may arise from within design or from other fields (Grudin, 1990). But designers get good at finding productive analogies and practical parallels.

Other forms of design thinking involve techniques common to all creative fields. These include:

- Transference: taking something from one context and applying it to another
- Rescaling: transforming something by interpreting it at a very different size
- Inversion: flipping something metaphorically on its head or turning it inside out
- Reassembly: chopping something up and rearranging it for a new purpose or potential

These and other tools enable designers to envision possibilities and alternative scenarios, seeing beyond what is to what could be (Grudin, 1990; Rowe, 1987).

The designer's skill in doing so has become particularly important in the world in which we find ourselves, where we need to create a greener economy, more resilient infrastructure, and a more adaptable physical environment if we are to accommodate the needs of a growing human population threatened by dwindling resources and a decaying natural environment. Never have the imagining and testing of alternative futures been more pressing than they are now.

DESIGN THINKING IN ACTION

Consider the global economic crisis that began in 2008. Although it may seem far removed from design, the financial collapse that began in the United States and spread across the world related to design in several ways. The downturn largely resulted from the over-building and over-inflating of residential and commercial real estate—designed environments whose actual functionality came to mean far less than their role as abstract commodities whose value many investors believed would never decline (Gallagher, 1992; Roberts, 2008). The excessive production of housing and commercial real estate, beyond what any reasonable assessment of the marketplace would support, represents a design failure: a breakdown in the relationship not only between supply and demand, but also between the form of our real estate investment system and its function in providing structures and spaces that people wanted or could possibly afford.

Had those investors had any exposure to design thinking, they might have predicted the possible negative consequences of their decisions, something that every good designer knows how to do. The financial industry created a number of new products that generated a lot of profit, but those products have been so incredibly destructive to the global economy that their initial design was obviously fatally flawed (Krugman, 2009). Had the creators of these financial instruments anticipated problems before they occurred by subjecting their ideas to the same critical evaluation that designers subject other products to, we might have averted the worst effects. If nothing else, the situation suggests that we can no longer continue to marginalize the mode of thought that would have helped prevent such irresponsible design.

The bursting of the global real-estate bubble has led to a tremendous amount of vacant space, both in the residential sector, with the large number of houses in foreclosure, and in the commercial sector, with millions of excess square footage in office and retail buildings left in the wake of layoffs and bankruptcies. In the short term, the financial crisis has idled many designers, but there remains a tremendous amount of work that interior designers, especially, need to do to help us all rethink possible uses for space whose initial purpose no longer has much market demand. How might high-rise office buildings be converted to rental housing? How might big-box stores become recreational or educational facilities? How might single-family houses accommodate multiple units or live-work programs?

Such questions, key to our economy's recovery and its adaptation to a standard of living more in line with the rest of the world, reveal the real value of design thinking. The ability to see what others have missed, to envision possibilities others can't imagine, and to show how out-of-the-box alternatives can work— this is the thinking that the world needs right now and for years to come. Although design thinking may not be valued nearly enough, we will never achieve a more sensible future without it.

REFERENCES

D/R Added Value. (2006). Poor workplace design could cost American businesses $330 billion annually in lost productivity" *Today's Facility Manager*, Facility Blog, July 24, 2006. Retrieved from http://todaysfacilitymanager.com/facility-blog/2006/07/poor-workplace-design-could-cost-american-businesses-330-billion-annually-in-lost-productivity.html

Aristotle (1952). Metaphysics (W. D. Ross, Trans.). *Great books of the western world, volume 8*, R. M. Hutchins (Ed.). Chicago: Encyclopedia Britannica.

Baker-Smith, D., & Barfoot, C. (1987). *Between dream and nature: Essays on utopia and dystopia.* Amsterdam: Rodopi.

Benyus, J. (1997). *Biomimicry: Innovation inspired by nature.* New York: William Morrow.

Dancy, R. (2004). *Plato's introduction of forms.* Cambridge, MA: Cambridge University Press.

Dewey, J. (1960). *The quest for certainty.* New York: Capricorn Books.

Gallagher, D. (1992). *Easy money: Reagan's roaring 80s and the overbuilding of America.* Hastings-on-Hudson, NY: Ultramarine Publishing.

Grudin, R. (1990). *The grace of great things: Creativity and innovation.* New York: Ticknor & Fields.

Krugman, P. (2009). *The return of depression economics and the crisis of 2008.* New York: W.W. Norton.

Martin, R. (2007). *The opposable mind: How successful leaders win through integrative thinking.* Boston: Harvard Business School Press.

Peirce, C. (1903). Harvard lectures on pragmatism, *Collected Papers of Charles Sanders Peirce, 5*, C. Hartshorne, & P. Weiss (Eds.). Boston: Harvard University Press.

Prak, N. (1984). *Architects: The noted and the ignored,* New York: John Wiley & Sons.

Roberts, L. (2008). *The great housing bubble: Why did house prices fall?* Monterey, CA: Monterey Cypress Press.

Rowe, P. G. (1987). *Design thinking.* Cambridge, MA: MIT Press.

> Is design thinking used to discriminate between precedent-based and thematic design approaches? Is vernacular design losing value in the face of thematic design? What are the challenges and opportunities?

JOSEPH T. CONNELL

WHAT IS DESIGN THINKING?

THE STATE OF DESIGN

Centuries before the poets, philosophers, authors, and architects sought to qualify and codify the means and methods of connecting built environments to their users, Vitruvius asserted that two of the three famous qualities a building must exhibit, *utilitas* and *venustas* (i.e., function and attractiveness), relate to the occupants' functional and emotional needs. Countless design models, curricula, symposia, and plenary sessions have resulted in numerous publications and modes to both expand and explain the design universe and directing processes to purportedly solve problems with more predictable and positive outcomes and relate to occupant needs.

Many influences and influencers are raising the consciousness and concern of designers of society's heightened design literacy. An appetite for good design is seemingly at an all-time

JOSEPH T. CONNELL, LEED® AP, IIDA, is a principal of Perkins+Will, a multidisciplinary firm providing services to clients worldwide. He has served on the IIDA Large Firm Round Table and the board of the first IIDA Research Summit. Connell has a BS in interior design and is an adjunct faculty advisory board member at Southern Illinois University, his alma mater. He is a frequent juror and speaker at Columbia College in Chicago, the University of Wisconsin, and The School of the Art Institute of Chicago. He served on the editorial advisory board for *Contract* magazine and is an ad hoc reviewer for the *Journal of Interior Design*. An advocate for use of environmental behavior and design research, Connell served on the technical review board for InformeDesign®. Connell's projects and interviews have been published in *Interior Design, Architectural Record, Contract, Effico, Interiors & Sources, Buildings,* and *officeinsight,* and his work has received awards from IIDA and AIA.

high, as is the misuse and misunderstanding of *design*. Popularly, design is often viewed as a styling exercise akin to fashion. As Carl Magnusson, former director of design for Knoll and founder of Carl Gustav Magnusson Design, New York, observes, design is perceived (by the client) as a process that adds cost and time.

When design results in ineffective, unwanted, unneeded, and unempathetic solutions, the design process and the designers have indeed failed—and the failed solution becomes the reality of the public's perception. Effective, efficient, empathetic, warranted, and desirous artifacts, places, and experiences are understood by most. But, how to achieve such outcomes is barely understood outside the design community.

Good design (architecture, engineering, interior design, product design, graphic design, interaction design, etc.) seeks to encompass an inclusive, comprehensive understanding of the problem to be solved; the creative process used in developing and testing a hypothesis; the critical judgment in deciding how to address the problem holistically; and responsibly implementing the solution within the means of the commissioner. However, many observe the typical design process as unsound, exclusive, not human-centered, not iterative, and not effectively implemented within means, and, therefore, it falls below expectations. At its worst, design is private and mysterious. At its worst, design eschews the goals and means of a business or organization. At its worst, design is narrow and minimizes societal needs and goals. So, what is design at its best?

DEFINING DESIGN THINKING

Design thinking is gaining traction through promulgation via conferences, blogs, the academy, and leading design strategists, which establish design intentions and outcomes based on business and/or organizational goals. The term carries great momentum at this time for entirely plausible reasons. Consider design thinking an earnest effort to restore the genuine purpose and purposefulness of interior designers and the design process. Design thinking is a method, a language, a protocol. It is a point of view accepted as a departure from the status quo design process that often limits the sphere of influence and outcomes of the design industry. Design thinking is distinctive from *design*, the *design process*, the *designer* because of its systematic priority of human-centeredness throughout an iterative design process and a maintained connection to a business's or organization's strategy.

Design thinking stewardship is advanced by, among others, IDEO president and CEO Tim Brown, who keeps the conversation alive and lively through his blog and assertive advocacy for design and innovation. Brown outlines attributes of design thinking with an emphasis on creative rather than analytical processes to solve problems; on human centeredness; on direct observations of behavior and culture; on the use of rapid prototypes to gain rapid insights; and on the use of meaningful narratives to capture the attention, inclusion, and imagination of the intended audiences. In his blog (http://design thinking.ideo.com), Brown defines design thinking as "a discipline that uses the designer's sensibility and methods to match people's needs with what is technologically feasible and what is a viable business strategy can convert into customer value and market opportunity." Brown invites readers to comment, refine, and otherwise challenge each other and the status quo.

So it is with many Web sites, publications, academic institutions, and organizations. Significantly, design thinking is gaining understanding—if not acceptance—in business schools and the business community because of its perceived value in integrating the design goals and process with the goals of the enterprise. As the meaning of design thinking is in its infancy, little is known at this time about its impact on the built environment. Some of the questions surrounding design thinking include:

> What are the advantages, disadvantages, and concerns related to design thinking?

> What is the role of ethics in design thinking?

> Does design thinking result in predictable outcomes, formally or thematically?

> Is design thinking used to discriminate between precedent-based and thematic design approaches? Will vernacular design lose value in the face of thematic design?

WHAT ARE THE ADVANTAGES, DISADVANTAGES, AND CONCERNS RELATED TO DESIGN THINKING?

The success of design thinking lies not in a predictable, broad-to-narrow, linear progression of the resolution of a problem, but in the interior designers' capacity to synthesize and create in a whirling, iterative test of contradictory and competing goals, objectives, and opportunities. This is not a process to think about the design, but a process to encourage thinking like a designer; weighing and refining the creative, practical, strategic, tactical, and pragmatic goals and the objectives presented by a problem or opportunity. These aptitudes and skills are not easily nor quickly developed in academic settings often aligned with professional prejudices—boundaries and definitions that partition both parts of a defined problem and parts of possible solutions—by discipline.

Turf wars, or narrowly defined areas of responsibility, inhibit, if not prevent, integrated design solutions from being considered and implemented. One does not experience a space, product, or interaction on trade-by-trade or expertise basis. As such, a design process that accommodates all senses of the user's experience with the intended behaviors and messaging of the commissioner should be integrated.

WHAT IS THE ROLE OF ETHICS IN DESIGN THINKING?

Made for the 1969 exhibition "What Is Design?" at the Musee des Arts Decoratifs in Paris, France, Charles Eames sketched a series of overlapping amoeba-like shapes, creating a famously Seussian Venn diagram (see Figure 2.1). He noted:

1. If this area represents the interest and concern of the design office
2. And, this is the area of genuine concern of the client
3. And, these are the concerns of society as a whole
4. Then, it is in this area of overlapping interest and concern that the designer can work with conviction and enthusiasm

These areas are not static; they grow and develop as each one influences the others. Putting more than one client in the model builds the relationship in a positive and constructive way.

It is easy to argue that there is always a need for good, if not great, interior design. There is no shortage of unmet needs, though it is apparent that human-centeredness and societal needs have been an inconsistent, if not inadequate, priority until sustainable building and climate change awareness emerged (thanks largely to the market acceptance of LEED® by the U.S. Green Building Council). Was design as a human-centered, iterative, empathetic, holistic process hijacked? Did the design

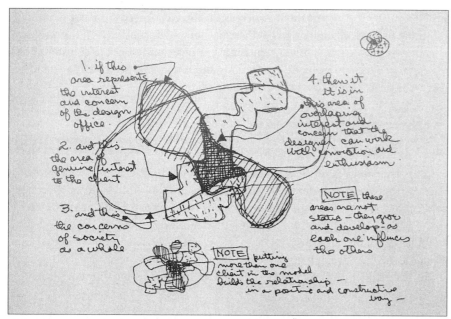

FIGURE 2.1 Charles Eames (1969) drew this diagram to explain the design process as achieving a point where the needs and interests of the client, the design office, and society as a whole can overlap. (©2006 Lucia Eames dba Eames Office)

industry lose its way, that is, if it ever had a "way"? It did have a way, and in fact, still does. As a result, design thinking may aid both the clients' and the designers' priorities because the best interior designers do their best work when tested by constraints and/or by taking an expansive view of the problem.

Common business and societal sentiment is that interior designers care only about aesthetics, thereby focusing narrowly on style, fashion, or self-interested form-making. The pejorative use of the term *aesthetics* is typically misplaced. The German Alexander Baumgarten (1758) used the term *aesthetics* in its modern philosophical context in his book *Aesthetica*. Prior to his publication, aesthetics was the contemplation of visual orders (Greeks and Romans used rule-based systems of order, proportion, balance, composition), cognition of nature (the golden mean and section), and the literacy of objects and artifacts—in short, the enjoyment of

seeing. The Vivtruvian quality *venustas*, meaning attractiveness or visual delight, ignores societal consideration whereas Baumgarten showed us that, perhaps for the first time, aesthetics is equal parts beauty and dignity. The coupling of these principles is powerfully relevant today and essential to framing an ethical and hopeful future.

Beyond the ubiquitous "paper or plastic?" question, many consumers consider the carbon footprint of goods, services, and even food prior to purchase. Not long ago, many may have viewed a fur coat as a beautiful and purposeful garment. But, many wonder if something can be beautiful if producing it is hurtful. Can something be beautiful if it is also harmful? The observer's perception of beauty, or even purposefulness, is informed by what we believe to be right or not right. It is formed and informed by morality, and morality is formed by culture. Cultural differences inform the morals and ethics of the observer and, thereby, one's sense of beauty or purposefulness.

Human-centeredness and altruism are connected in an inclusive design process, though success is not guaranteed by design thinking. Advocacy for all dimensions of the problem, including ethical and societal considerations, requires attention often perceived to be outside a project's scope.

IS DESIGN THINKING USED TO DISCRIMINATE BETWEEN PRECEDENT-BASED AND THEMATIC DESIGN APPROACHES?

Design thinking as a methodology and as a mind-set rightly oscillates between precedent-based, thematic, vernacular, and original design outcomes. The iterative nature of design thinking tests multiple hypotheses against an expansive definition of the problem by developing a solution appropriate to context, while fulfilling ethical and moral/societal responsibilities. In problems relating to the built environment, "appropriate to context" may include a literal, referential, suggestive, or juxtaposed relationship to context as judged by designer and commissioner. This is necessary, though not sufficient, to make great buildings or places.

IS VERNACULAR DESIGN LOSING VALUE IN THE FACE OF THEMATIC DESIGN?

Vernacular design is authentic, and this authenticity instills meaning and relevance to users and observers alike. Thematic design outcomes may be the architectural equivalent of the "Wal-Mart effect" (Fishman, 2006); that is, a franchise model that eschews local methods, materials, and meaning. Such solutions do not devalue vernacular design, but easily lessens its frequency. This approach to design is not insignificant as a reduction of vernacular places and loss of critical mass that further dilutes meaning and connection to place, erode expectations, reduce variety, and extend monotony. Thematic design solutions, while breeding familiarity and predictability—often considered a desired business and brand outcome—brings a loss of local input, meaning, connectedness, individuality, and regionalism. Thematic design crowds out innovation and failed attempts at innovation. Lessons from thematic, vernacular, and original design can inform us and expand the growing base of knowledge of how to best build environments to serve us for predictable and unpredictable needs.

DESIGN THINKING CHALLENGES AND OPPORTUNITIES

Design thinking relies on rapid input, but the synthesis and response is the responsibility of the designer. The sad, proverbial camel is the outcome of a design-by-committee intent to create a horse. Poor choices and compromised priorities predictably lead to such failures. Accordingly, design thinking's iterative nature is no guarantee of success or satisfaction. It is essential to distinguish between input and feedback from users and design by users. The discerning use of evidence (precedence combined with knowledge) and all elements and principles of design in service to individuals, commerce, and civil society by interior designers and design thinkers improves the likelihood of intended and reliable outcomes.

Must this be an either/or proposition? If so, the only place for innovation is to create new themes. The opportunity for designer and commissioner alike lies in the continuous challenge of the status quo, of untested assumptions and easy, ineffective outcomes. Innovation need not be attained only by establishing avant-garde forms and exclusivity. Innovation can be a process of inclusively illuminating the problem and the problem solver alike. This, then, is design at its best.

REFERENCES

Baumgarten, A. (1750). *Aesthetica. 3rd fascism. Traiecti cis Viadrum* [i.e., Frankfurt a d. Oder]: Impens. Ioannis Christiani Kleyb.

Brown, T. (2009). *Blog*. Retrieved April 14, 2009, from http://designthinking.ideo.com

Eames, C. (1969) Drawing from exhibit. *What is design?* Musee des Arts Decoratifs, Paris, France.

Fishman, C. (2006). *The Wal-Mart effect*. New York: The Penguin Press.

JUDITH H. HEERWAGEN

INTERIOR DESIGN MEETS THE ADAPTED MIND

When we walk into a building, we experience it through many filters. Personal history and culture certainly influence our response, from the sense of relief that comes when we enter our home at the end of a stressful day to the sense of serenity we feel in places that nourish our spirits. But, there is more. There is the tug of ancient memories that we are not even aware of. These ghosts from the past help us find hospitable places and keep us from harm. They intuitively guide us as we move in both new and familiar spaces.

The desire for refuge and protection, the lure of the lookout space with promises of panoramic views, the smile that naturally lights our face when we see spring flowers in bloom—all are the result of programs written in our genome and operating nonconsciously in our sensory systems and brains. They help us avoid hazards, make us apprehensive at night in strange places, turn our noses up at foul odors, and cause us to startle when we hear loud noises.

JUDITH H. HEERWAGEN, PhD, is an environmental psychologist whose work focuses on the social impacts of sustainable design and biophilia. Prior to starting her own business, she was a senior research scientist at the Pacific Northwest National Laboratory (PNNL) and a research faculty member at the University of Washington, College of Architecture and Urban Planning. Heerwagen's work at both PNNL and the University of Washington focused on the psychosocial impacts of buildings and the development of basic principles of human-centered sustainable design. She has written and lectured widely on natural aesthetics, sustainability, and habitability from a biobehavioral perspective. Heerwagen's most recent publication is *Biophilic Design: The Theory, Science and Practice of Bringing Buildings to Life* (Wiley, 2008, with S.R. Kellert and M. Mador). The book won the 2008 Publishers Award for Professional and Scholarly Excellence in architecture and urban planning.

What are these ghosts of the past, and what do they have to do with interior design? For answers, we turn to evolutionary psychology, which explores how mental modules, designed to solve consistent problems in ancestral natural habitats, continue to guide human behavior today. One such problem is finding a place to live. For most organisms, being in "the right place" is an important determinant of survival and well-being. There is no reason why this should be different for humans. If evolutionary theory has relevance to interior design, then the features and attributes of high-quality natural habitats should be revealed in today's built habitats. Furthermore, we should find that preferred building habitats—in contrast to less preferred buildings—should have beneficial outcomes.

BUILDINGS AS HABITATS FOR PEOPLE

If we think of a building as a habitat for people, what makes it a good habitat? What interior features and attributes signal safety, comfort, and pleasure? What features and qualities invite exploration and engagement with place? What aspects of the environment have the opposite effect? What do we dislike and avoid? What makes us hurry through a space rather than linger and enjoy it?

In nature, all organisms need to solve two fundamental, adaptive problems: protection and access to resources. Although a building by its very nature is meant to serve as a shelter and therefore provide protection, buildings and interiors vary considerably with respect to how they convey a sense of protection.

THE SAVANNAH THEORY

Habitat theory, as developed by Orians and Heerwagen (Heerwagen & Orians, 1993; Orians & Heerwagen, 1992), predicts that people will prefer environments that have the essential features of the natural habitats in which humans evolved and flourished: the African savannahs. Savannahs provided high-quality animal and plant foods and also afforded protection for sleeping (e.g., caves and trees) and high visual access for anticipating dangers. Design-relevant savannah features include:

- A rich diversity of plant and animal life for food and resources
- Clustered trees with spreading canopies for refuge and protection
- Open grassland that provides easy movement and clear views to the distance
- Topographic changes for strategic surveillance to aid long-distance movements and to provide early warning of approaching hazards

- Scattered bodies of water and rivers for food, drinking, and bathing
- A "big sky" with a wide, bright field of view

In addition to these landscape features, fire was also a critical element in ancestral environments. Konner (1982) describes the control of fire and its focal point in human social life as resulting in

a quantum advance in human communication: a lengthy, nightly discussion, perhaps of the day's events, of plans for the next day, of important occurrences in the lives of individuals and in the cultural past, and of long-term possibilities for the residence and activity of the band. (p. 50)

Research on landscape preferences shows strong cross-cultural preferences for savannah-like environments and especially for water

(Heerwagen, 2006; Ulrich, 1983). What are the implications for interior design?

First, our ancestors' immersion in a bio-centric world should have made humans especially attentive to living organisms and natural processes (e.g., weather, breezes, and sunlight). Wilson (1984) coined the term *biophilia* to describe this innate attraction to nature. *Biophilic design* is the application of natural elements and qualities in building and interior design (Kellert, Heerwagen, & Mador, 2008).

A second implication of the savannah theory and biophilia for interior design relates to the visual-spatial environment. As a species without natural defenses, humans need to anticipate and plan for dangers. High visual access to the surrounding landscape is critical for safe movement, whereas spaces that afford hiding keep one's presence unknown to others. Appleton (1975) refers to these features as "prospect" and "refuge." In *The Experience of Landscape*, he explores how variation in the provision of prospect and refuge influences aesthetic response to landscapes. The application of prospect and refuge theory to interior design is discussed in more detail later in this essay.

A third savannah factor relevant to interior design is the "big sky" effect with a bright, vertical, visual field and open landscape. In our evolutionary past, the important visual field was what we could see when moving through the environment. Visual focus was likely to have been on the intermediate and distant environment, with occasional attention to details near at hand and at the feet. Today, the functionally important visual field is the close horizontal work surface or the computer screen. Nonetheless, the important surfaces for aesthetic purposes remain the vertical fields of windows and walls and the ground surfaces that connect spaces. Just how are these characteristics of biophilia, lighting, and prospect/refuge serving as components of interior design?

THE BIOPHILIA FACTOR

Given our affinity for nature, it is hardly surprising that many large building complexes create indoor parks and outdoor nooks with large trees and plants, water features, daylight, multiple view corridors, an interior big sky, comfortable retreats, and varied sensory conditions. Builders and developers would be disinclined to invest in such costly aesthetic touches if they didn't believe such amenities had positive payoffs.

Evidence suggests that these design amenities do indeed have economic consequences (Heerwagen, 2006). Large trees and views of water and nature improve property values for both owned and rented properties. Daylit spaces are consistently preferred and rated as more psychologically beneficial than spaces with little or no daylight (Heerwagen & Heerwagen, 1986). There is also evidence that bright, daylit rooms in hospitals reduce pain perceptions, improve moods, and reduce the length of hospital stays (Beauchemin & Hayes, 1996; 1998; Walch et al., 2005).

From an interior design perspective, access to real nature may not always be possible. Thankfully, there are many other ways to convey the qualities and attributes of nature (Heerwagen & Gregory, 2008). Sensory variability, resilience, movement, variations on a theme, and serendipity characterize many natural environments. These qualities can be integrated into interior design with natural materials, changes in sensory conditions, interior views, and use of natural patterns and textures. A simple element, such as a ceiling fan or a wall mural, can greatly change the atmosphere of a room.

The sense of discovered complexity that occurs with close visual inspection of nature elements can also be experienced indoors through the use of biophilic patterns and textures. The U.S. Green Building Council (USGBC) used this strategy in its new headquarters in Washington, DC. High-resolution photos of vegetation, flowers, animal patterns, rocks, water, and sky were printed on translucent film and attached to glass panels in workstations throughout the office. From a distance, the design looks like a mosaic of colors and patterns; up close, each photo offers details and complexity that invites viewing and provides visual relief.

PROSPECT AND REFUGE: AESTHETICS OF PRIVACY AND PERCEIVED SAFETY

Appleton's (1975) prospect-refuge theory provides a conceptual framework for an analysis of how building features engage us in an intuitive assessment of safety and hazard. Beyond the simple fact that a building is a shelter and should thus provide a sense of safety and refuge from harm (both animate and inanimate), additional cues seem to enhance the feeling of protection.

Appleton argues that people should prefer to be in spaces that allow opportunities to see without being seen. If prospect and refuge behaviors have an evolutionary basis, people should behave "as if" they were conscious of what they were doing, yet unaware if asked. For example, people intuitively sense that having a surface at the back or overhead is protective and "enclosing" without being able to explain why (Thiel, Harrison, & Alden, 1986). Extensive studies of small urban spaces by Whyte (1980) also show that people seek out columns or edges while observing behavior in a more open space. If asked why they were doing so, people are not likely to say "I want to see into the space while not being seen easily by others."

Prospect and refuge are dominant themes in interior design. Changes in light levels, the use of screening materials to separate spaces, lowered ceilings to create a cozy feeling, mirrors, borrowed views, vistas to the outdoors, balconies with colonnades, wall-wash lighting, and viewing platforms are all part of the design palette used intuitively to create appealing interior spaces (Hildebrand, 1999). These features generally have positive effects and enhance satisfaction (Scott, 1992).

In contrast, spaces with an imbalance between prospect and refuge tend to have low satisfaction levels and to be perceived as bland and unappealing. Windowless rooms; blocked views; long, brightly lit interior hallways with little or no views to other spaces; and windows that provide little visual privacy—all are common examples of an imbalance between prospect and refuge. Yet, simple redesign can greatly enhance the psychological value of space through changes in visual access or sensory retreat. Hildebrand (2008) demonstrates how changes in sight lines, doorways, screening, and openings between spaces in an elderly housing complex can greatly alter the psychological comfort of space.

BENEFITS OF CONTACT WITH NATURE AND NATURE SURROGATES

The research on the benefits of nature in building design focuses almost exclusively on sunlight, water, and vegetation. Much less is known about the more abstract and evocative aspects of biophilia, such as use of natural materials, patterns, and textures or variations in prospect and refuge features.

The evidence, as a whole, shows that connection to daylight, sunlight, flowers, nature views, green plants, large trees, and water reduces stress, enhances emotional functioning, increases positive social interactions, and improves overall physiological functioning (see Kellert, Heerwagen, & Mador, 2008, for an overview of the research). In contrast, the environments that we avoid hold risks for our well-being. Polluted water, foul odors, unkempt spaces, dark pathways, and blocked views all signal potential dangers and tend to be avoided.

There is also growing evidence of links to cognitive functioning. For example, an experiment found that subjects working in a windowless room with plants worked more efficiently, had lower blood pressure readings, and felt more attentive than subjects working in the same room without plants (Lohr, Pearson-Mims, & Goodwin, 1996). Another study varied window views; Tennessen and Cimprich (1995) found that people whose view was predominantly natural (as opposed to built) scored better on tests of directed attention. Hartig, Mang, and Evans (1991) report similar results in a field experiment. People who went for a walk in a predominantly natural setting performed better on several attentional tasks than those who walked in a predominantly built setting or who quietly read a magazine indoors.

Although the research on the benefits of biophilia is convincing and continues to grow, the design applications are not keeping up. Many offices, hospitals, and schools—places where people spend significant amounts of time—are largely devoid of biophilic qualities and features. Simple applications could make a real difference in the psychological and health benefits of space, light at the end of a long hallway to provide prospect symbolism, open views to the outdoors rather than private offices along the window wall, vegetation used as visual screening in cafes and interior open spaces, carpet with nature-like patterns, indoor plants, landscape photos and paintings, changes in ceiling height, canopies with dappled light as transition spaces, fireplaces, window seats with pleasing views, sunlight patches, and natural artifacts. These applications are not expensive. They merely require a step back into nature for inspiration, whether it is a favorite garden with a rich diversity of color and pattern, the sunset over the ocean, a meadow with clustered trees and distant views, or a small pond at the edge of the woods. Nature is rich with possibilities.

The brief essay is only a glimpse into the many ways interior design can tap into humanity's deep connections to nature and to natural places. Using the broad umbrella of biophilic design, today's built spaces can tap into ancient memories and mental modules that evolved to keep us safe, happy, and healthy.

REFERENCES

Appleton, J. (1975). *The experience of landscape.* London: Wiley & Sons.

Beauchemin, K., & Hays, P. (1996). Sunny hospital rooms expedite recovery from severe and refractory depression. *Journal of Affective Disorders, 40*(1–2), 49–51.

Beauchemin, K., & Hays, P. (1998). Dying in the dark: Sunshine, gender and outcomes in myocardial infarction. *Journal of the Royal Society of Medicine, 91*(7), 352–354.

Hartig, T., Mang, M., & Evans, G. (1991). Restorative effects of natural environment experiences. *Environment and Behavior, 23*(1), 3–26.

Heerwagen, J. (1990). Affective functioning, "light hunger," and room brightness preferences. *Environment and Behavior, 22*(5), 608–635.

Heerwagen, J., & Gregory, B. (2008). Biophilia and sensory aesthetics. In S. Kellert, J. Heerwagen, & M. Mador (Eds.), *Biophilic design: The theory, science and practice of bringing buildings to life.* New York: Wiley & Sons.

Heerwagen, J., & Hase, B. (2001, March/April). Building biophilia: Connecting people to nature. *Environmental Design + Construction Magazine,* pp. 30–36.

Heerwagen, J., & Heerwagen, D. (1986). Lighting and psychological comfort. *Lighting Design and Application, 16*(4), 47–51.

Heerwagen, J., Loveland, J., & Diamond, R. (1992). *Post-occupancy evaluation of energy edge buildings.* Seattle: Center for Planning and Design, University of Washington.

Heerwagen, J., & Orians, G. (1986). Adaptations to windowlessness: A study of the use of visual décor in windowed and windowless offices. *Environment and Behavior, 18*(5), 623–639.

Heerwagen, J., & Orians, G. (1993). Humans, habitats and aesthetics. In S. Kellert & E. Wilson (Eds.), *The biophilia hypothesis.* Washington, DC: Island Press.

Heerwagen, J., & Orians, G. (2002). The ecological world of children. In P. Kahn & S. Kellert (Eds.), *Children and nature.* Cambridge, MA: MIT Press.

Hildebrand, G. (1999). *Origins of architectural pleasure.* Berkeley, CA: University of California Press.

Hildebrand, G. (2008). Biophilic architectural space. In S. Kellert, J. Heerwagen, & M. Mador (Eds.), *Biophilic design: The theory, science and practice of bringing buildings to life.* New York: Wiley & Sons.

Humphrey, N. (1975). Natural aesthetics. In B. Mikellides (Ed.), *Architecture for people.* London: Studio Vista.

Kellert, S., & Wilson, E. (1993). *The biophilia hypothesis.* Washington, DC: Island Press.

Kellert, S., Heerwagen, J., & Mador, M. (2008). *Biophilic design: The theory, science and practice of bringing buildings to life.* New York: Wiley & Sons.

Konner, M. (1982). *The tangled wing: Biological constraints on the human spirit.* New York: Holt, Rhinehart & Winston.

Lohr, V., Pearson-Mims, C., & Goodwin, G. (1996). Interior plants may improve worker productivity and reduce stress in a windowless environment. *Journal of Environmental Horticulture, 14*(2), 97–100.

Orians, G., & Heerwagen, J. (1992). Evolved responses to landscapes. In J. Barkow, L. Cosmides, & J. Tooby (Eds.), *The adapted mind: Evolutionary psychology and the generation of culture.* New York: Oxford University Press.

Scott, S. (1992). Visual attributes related to preferences in interior environments. *Journal of Interior Design, 18*(1–2), 7–16.

Tennessen, C., & Cimprich, B. (1995). Views to nature: Effects on attention. *Journal of Environmental Psychology, 15* (1), 77–85.

Thiel, P., Harrison, E., & Alden, R. (1986). The perception of spatial enclosure as a function of the position of architectural surfaces. *Environment and Behavior, 18*(2), 227–245.

Ulrich, R. (1983). Aesthetic and affective response to natural environment. In I. Altman & J. Wohlwil (Eds.), *Behavior and the environment (Vol. 6): Behavior and the natural environment,* pp. 85–125. New York: Plenum.

Ulrich, R. (1993). Biophilia, biophobia and natural landscapes. In S. Kellert & E. Wilson (Eds.), *The biophilia hypothesis.* Washington, DC: Island Press.

Ulrich, R. (2008). Biophilic theory and research for healthcare design. In S. Kellert, J. Heerwagen, & M. Mador (Eds.), *Biophilic design: The theory, research and practice of bringing buildings to life.* New York: Wiley & Sons.

Walch, J., Rabin, B., Day, R., Williams, J., Choi, K., & Kang, J. (2005). The effects of sunlight on postoperative analgesic medication use: A prospective study of patients undergoing spinal surgery. *Psychosomatic Medicine, 67,* 156–163.

Whyte, W. (1980). *The social life of small urban spaces.* New York: Project for Public Spaces.

Wilson, E. (1984). *Biophilia.* Cambridge, MA: Harvard University Press.

> How do you see design thinking manifested in design outcomes across disciplines? How can interior designers take on a leadership role in the promotion and execution of design thinking?

SUSAN S. SZENASY

THE GROWING NEED FOR CREATIVE PROBLEM SOLVING THROUGH DESIGN THINKING

It is late winter 2009, a season when the world as we knew it last fall has taken on a baffling look of uncertainty. It's hard to tell what the dramatic changes will bring, but there are clear signs pointing to an America in the process of refocusing. We are learning to be a sober, complex nation concerned with community, sustainability, accessibility, technology, research, rebuilding, innovation, and education, while holding on to our sense of fun. Health, safety, and well-being issues dominate the national discourse; this dialogue meshes neatly with the publicly pronounced mission of the interior design profession. But, are future interior design professionals preparing to embrace their ethical responsibilities? The signs are not altogether encouraging. Nevertheless, I remain hopeful. Design thinking has a lot to do with my optimism.

In the midst of writing, I click to entries in an interior design scholarship competition I'm asked to judge. The student work, submitted by

SUSAN S. SZENASY is editor in chief of *Metropolis*, the award-winning New York City–based magazine of architecture, culture, and design. Since 1986, she has led the magazine through years of landmark design journalism, achieving domestic and international recognition. Szenasy is internationally recognized as an authority on sustainability and design. She sits on the boards of CIDA, FIT Interior Design, the Center for Architecture Advisory Board, and the Landscape Architecture Foundation. Szenasy has been honored with two IIDA Presidential Commendations, is an honorary member of the ASLA, and the 2008 recipient of the ASID Patron's Prize and Presidential Citation. Along with *Metropolis* publisher Horace Havemeyer III, she was a 2007 recipient of the Civitas August Heckscher Award for Community Service and Excellence. Szenasy holds an MA in modern European history from Rutgers University, and honorary doctorates from Kendall College of Art and Design, the Art Center College of Design, and the Pacific Northwest College of Art.

schools from all over the United States, comes from as far afield as New York and Texas. What I see leaves me baffled. Why? In studying this sampling of projects, I realize that these particular future interior designers are stuck somewhere in the bygone days of the 20th century. Their focus is luxury. Their work presents the interior designer as a handmaiden to the moneyed classes. In loving details, and with materials boards arranged to showcase high-end products, they designed exclusive jewelry stores, hotels, skyboxes, and condos. Not a school, a hospital, a community clinic, or a library anywhere. Only a rare entry mentions green design or accessibility, and none of them even attempt to acknowledge social and environmental sustainability; yet these issues are increasingly folded into the designer's portfolio, regardless of specialization.

Across the country, in the cities where these interior design students go to school, discussions abound on how professionals, used to serving the upper 2%, can cultivate a broader client base. *Expanding Architecture: Design as Activism*, edited by Bryan Bell and Katie Wakeford (2008), has led to a series of public forums in Steelcase's showrooms in New York, Atlanta, Los Angeles, and Chicago. The gathered crowds examine local public initiatives that address each city's unique needs, and interior designers explore ways to engage in improving daily life for everyone in their communities. Many of the activists' work featured in *Expanding Architecture* were also shown in the U.S. Pavilion at the 2008 Venice Architecture Biennale, carrying abroad a very American message: Our physical environments can express our democratic ideals.

New Web sites, blogs, magazine and newspaper articles, books, even television shows such as the PBS series *design: e2* expand on the thought that designers have useful and necessary skills—notably their unique, hands-on methods—for fixing our neglected infrastructure, from outdated schools to crumbling bridges. School boards and governments are looking for smart, beautiful, sustainable, and accessible solutions. And, design thinking is being scrutinized by corporations in search of solving complex, global challenges by applying creativity, collaboration, and empathy—once considered "soft" skills by hard-nosed businesspeople. Simply put, design thinking is focused on human beings; it is inspired by what people say and how they behave; and it results in telling the users' stories through the designed object, interior, structure, or place.

The student work I'm examining shows something of that design thinking. I see evidence, for example, of observational research applied to define the problem at hand. The presentation boards are clearly illustrated with electronic images, photos, and graphics—creating a visual narrative of beautiful and functional spaces. Technically, however, the entries vary in sophistication. Even the best of them fall short of the kind of electronic wizardry that's now commonplace among architecture and industrial design students. And, whereas some of the projects are well researched, too many seem to take the easy way out and focus on the obvious as their inspiration.

No surprises, no significant discoveries. No recognition of the need to accommodate social interaction in a tech-crazy society. No reaching out to communities. No attempts at presenting interior furnishings and finishes that would create healthy, toxin-free rooms. No evidence of incorporating daylight into the design by carefully choosing and placing colors, textures, and furniture to take advantage of this varied source of illumination. It's as if this design thinking happened in the 1990s when the even light of 50 footcandles and the 24/7 air temperature of 70 degrees were considered the standards of interior comfort in sealed glass buildings occupied by the employees of the upper 2%.

The current design dialogue seems to have bypassed these interior design students. How is this possible? They are, after all, part of a generation that's famous for its heartfelt advocacy of community service and a clean environment. They navigate the world of electronic information with ease, instantly checking for facts even on the most arcane topics. Demographers see them as the most connected generation of all time. Their role in the success of Barack Obama's presidential campaign is often cited; and so they're familiar with the president's call for responsibility, service, rebuilding, innovation, and widened communication via our web of high-tech connections. So I conclude that the projects I see represent the standards of the educators rather than those of the students.

Just what are activist interior design students and young designers doing today? They tackle problems that relate to essential resources such as water and energy. Their stellar, often breakthrough work can be seen in a growing number of ideas competitions such as *Metropolis*'s annual Next Generation Design Prize or the Solar Decathlon. These collaborative groups represent every design discipline; only a rare interior designer appears on their lists. Here is a small and inspiring sampling of current design thinking.

Young architecture educators, working with their students and code writers, dig into the very DNA of structures. Their intimacy with their design tools helps them design buildings inspired by biological forms, such as spiderwebs and cocoons. Their experiments aren't meant to copy nature, but rather to learn from nature's supremely efficient processes. This tech-savvy, ecologically concerned approach puts the new generation at the leading edge of thinking about high-performance buildings, a preoccupation of architects and engineers of every age and in every size of practice. Furthermore, these young people, in life and in work, are natural collaborators; they call on biologists, psychologists, artists, engineers as well as other design specialists to help them define complex questions related to sustainable living.

Industrial designers, too, reach out beyond their profession's former comfort zones. No longer seeing themselves purely as servants of mass production, they invent objects and systems that are desperately needed by underserved populations, not just those who live in highly developed consumer societies. Thus, easy-to-use water gathering and transporting devices help people in arid climates purify brackish water, or transport it safely in higher volumes than the old bucket would allow. By employing their profession's well-tested skills in observational research, prototyping to test optimal forms and performance before committing to production, searching for the most appropriate material for the purpose as well as the environment, they are reaching people who have been ignored in the 20th century's rush to economic dominance. Here is design thinking in the service of saving lives; supporting the health, safety, and well-being of ever-increasing populations the world over.

Graphic designers, using communication skills that not long ago were in the service of the printing industry, work easily in the electronic media that is so familiar to them in their everyday interactions. They design Internet services to help citizens keep track of their energy use or trace where their food comes from. They build test sites and incorporate user feedback to refine their ideas. This work shows the new generation's belief in their ability to identify and connect with user groups, similar to the designers themselves, who search for reliable information on ways to live more sustainable lives. Here is design thinking in the service of everyday decision making.

Why is it so important to refine our understanding of design thinking now? The growing interest of corporations, manufacturers, and government in studying the ways designers solve problems provides one clue. The other clue can be found in the many interior decorating and home improvement shows that put a shorthand version of interior design thinking in front of a receptive public.

Tim Brown, CEO of IDEO, the interdisciplinary think tank, is a most credible source on the subject. His firm continues to be at the forefront of applying the process of research, prototyping, and conceptualizing to such diverse things as consumer and medical products, hospital and school interiors, and even urban planning. Brown himself likes to go back to the source of modern design thinking to Thomas Edison, the wizard of Menlo Park, New Jersey. In 2008, he reminded *Harvard Business Review* readers that Edison didn't just invent the lightbulb, but he also invented "an entire industry around it. . . . [He] understood that the bulb was little more than a parlor trick without a system of electric power generation to make it truly useful. So he created that, too." The key word here is *system.*

Looking at the big picture—the whole system—has become the assignment for the 21st century. Although small, simple fixes made by isolated professionals continue to have their place, there are much bigger problems to solve. These require unprecedented access to information from many different experts, interpreted by design teams that work together in seamless collaborations.

An interior designer's material choices, for example, have far-reaching implications. This seemingly simple act, in reality, is connected to a larger system of:

- Procurement (where the material comes from, what its extraction does to the environment, how it is replaced)
- Manufacturing (nontoxic methods, non-child labor, providing jobs for local communities)
- Distribution (how far the product needs to travel to reach its market, how much fuel is used in transporting it)
- Use (its fit to the varied ergonomic needs of at least four generations working together; how its exhalents interact with other products and surfaces in the room)
- Reuse (what happens to the material at the end of its useful life; can it be easily disassembled and quickly recycled)

Such robust analysis of a complete system assumes that designers at every stage of production, from the industrial designer to the interior designer, recognize the environmental and social implications of their decisions.

As Brown (2008) unravels Edison's design thinking, he calls it,

a methodology that imbues the full spectrum of innovation activities with a human-centered ethos. By this I mean that innovation is powered by a thorough understanding, through direct observation, of what people want and need in their lives and what they like or dislike about the way particular products are made, packaged, marketed, sold, and supported.

This "human-centered ethos" is in the DNA of designers who, when asked why they went into design in the first place, will often say that they wanted to make the world a better, more beautiful, more equitable place. Designers want to improve things.

Interior designers are intimately involved in the human condition—where we sit, how we find peace and quiet, how we socialize, how we work and love and eat and bathe and play. They have prided themselves on their intuitive, as well as learned, understanding of the human-centered ethos. Because that ethos has taken on a new complexity in response to global warming and exploding populations worldwide the purview of interior designers must expand similarly.

The best design thinker, as Brown (2008) says of Edison, is "a broad generalist." Interior designers have always fit this bill. The profession is made up of people who have a deep understanding of art, architecture, and human behavior, to which they now need to add a familiarity with biology, physics, material and political sciences, technology, and whatever new area of knowledge informs the human condition.

Like Edison, says Brown (2008), business managers need to surround themselves "with gifted thinkers, improvisers, and experimenters" if they are to embrace design thinking and benefit from it. Interior designers already have this down pat; they are natural collaborators who have made an art of getting along with extreme personalities. This skill is a solid foundation for the profession to take on the 21st century when more people than ever before are seeking to live happy and healthy lives.

REFERENCES

Bell, B., & Wakeford, K. (2008). *Expanding architecture: Design as activism.* New York: Metropolis Books.

Brown, T. (2008). Design thinking. *Harvard Business Review.* Retrieved May 29, 2009, from http://hbr.harvardbusiness.org/2008/06/design-thinking/ar/pr

> Is knowledge about interior design
important to K–12 students?
What is the importance of that knowledge
to the interior design profession, and could
that knowledge engage students in
design thinking for their lifetimes?

STEPHANIE A. CLEMONS

K–12 + INTERIOR DESIGN: A NATURAL, CRITICAL PARTNERSHIP

STEPHANIE A. CLEMONS, PhD, FASID, FIDEC, has been teaching interior design for over 20 years at Colorado State University (CSU), where she is a professor in the Department of Design & Merchandising. She has been the recipient of both the Outstanding Teacher and Advisor awards from her college and Best Teacher award from the Alumni Association. Clemons's research focus is related to infusing interior design content into elementary and secondary education levels (K–12). Clemons has held numerous leadership positions including president of both IDEC and the IDEC Foundation, and currently serves as chair of the *Journal of Interior Design*. Clemons also serves on the national board of directors for ASID. She has published numerous journal articles and, with colleagues, has received multiple "outstanding research paper/presentation" awards from IDEC.

With 90% of our time spent indoors, interior spaces provide a natural, easily accessible learning environment for youth (Guerin, 2004). From a very young age, children are introduced to concepts of design such as scale (e.g., *Goldilocks and the Three Bears*, "this chair is just right"), color (e.g., Dr. Seuss's *Red Fish/Blue Fish*), and proportion (e.g., *Alice in Wonderland*). Consciously or unconsciously, children evaluate good (and bad) design in their public and personal spaces. Their legs swing from chairs too large; they delight in playing in small, cozy alcoves rather than large vaulted spaces; and they are captivated by bright museum colors that invite discovery and manipulation.

As children enter school, standard academic units lend themselves to the study of the interior spaces they inhabit, inviting opportunities for design thinking. For example, in junior high schools, young teens study cultural spaces and sense of identity, which correlate to the study of personal spaces. While in high school, teens take specialized rather than general classes, such as American History that can be linked directly to the study of American interiors and cultural norms. Other topics elementary and secondary education (K–12) curriculum specialists indicate relate to interior design include math (e.g., fractals and geometry), science (e.g., sustainable design and textile chemistry), languages (e.g., written word concerning the design process), and social studies (e.g., cultural studies of place and people and economics of the marketplace). Given this feedback, this essay will explore a few questions. They include:

- How can interior design content in the K–12 environment enhance design thinking?
- What are the issues when teaching in the K–12 environment?
- Can interior design content fit with K–12 educational standards?
- What "voices" do youth hear about the profession of interior design?
- How can the profession and local designers help educate youth about interior design?

DESIGN THINKING ENHANCED THROUGH INTERIOR DESIGN

The interior environment is composed of procedures, processes, and products. Yet the critical element is the human being who inhabits the space. When a child is exposed to thinking about the design of spaces, and the people living and working within those spaces, they move from *manipulation to origination*. In other words, they shift from cognition that involves adapting to "bad design," or trying to fix things after the fact (manipulation), to designing better from the onset (origination).

In today's economy and throughout the world, design thinking is in high demand. Tim Brown, IDEO president, in a recent article in *Harvard Business Review* (2008) indicated that rather than a linear, business model it is better to use a design thinking model of inspiration, ideation, and implementation to create opportunities for innovative design solutions.

These steps are part of the process commonly used when designing interior environments. To foster design thinking in our society, it has to begin at the elementary school level. The study and analysis of the interiors in which children live, move, and dream can help encourage that type of thinking.

THE K–12 ENVIRONMENT + INTERIOR DESIGN

If the study of interior design would enhance design thinking, how would the curriculum fit into the current academic environment today? Youth are truly busy! They are learning the basics of "reading, writing, and arithmetic" amid the challenge of unlearning bad habits such as phonetic text message spelling and math-by-cell-phone calculations. Likewise, K–12 teachers are busy. They are challenged with the need to encourage student proficiency in the academics, yet prepare them for the annual "assessment exam" delivered by school districts. How can students be expected to find time in their education to learn about their interior spaces as well?

Thankfully, there is support for infusing interior design content into K–12 curriculum based on the results of a study (Clemons, 2007) with elementary and secondary teachers, curriculum specialists, and interior design professionals and educators. Findings revealed that teachers felt kindergarten was not too early to introduce concepts of interior design to children. However, they felt it was critical to "infuse" interior design content into existing curriculum rather than "add it on" to the teacher's responsibilities.

As this is done, there are several key issues the interior design profession must grapple with when infusing interior design into K–12 on both a national and local level:

- On a national level, the K–12 education standards are available to all states, yet each state shapes the standards to fit the needs of their constituency and communities.
- On a state level, K–12 standards may be administered in a centralized manner (e.g., Texas) and others in a decentralized manner (e.g., Colorado).

- On a local level, allocation of resources and technology usage is varied, even within the same school district.
- Teachers are overburdened with an increased demand for student performance concerning national standards and, at times, larger classroom enrollment.
- Due to the economy, school budgets are cutting art programs from the curriculum, which is where many administrators assume interior design content and thinking should go.
- Teachers are certified as generalists but many act in a "specialist" mode; teacher training and certification are additional issues.

THREE VOICES ABOUT INTERIOR DESIGN HEARD BY HIGH SCHOOL STUDENTS

Given the lack of standardization in K–12 schools nationally, is there an existing channel to use when infusing interior design into the K–12 environment? How do youth hear about interior design?

Since the mid-1990s there has been a clarion call for interior design professionals, both educators and practitioners, to become involved in teaching our youth about the career and subject matter of interior design (Clemons, 1999; Nussbaumer, 2002; Portillo & Rey-Barreau, 1995). As early as first grade, youth in elementary and secondary grade levels (K–12) are exposed to numerous careers such as teaching, law enforcement, and firefighting. Yet rarely are they exposed to the profession of interior design, and if they are, it is seldom by those who represent the profession accurately (Rey-Barreau & Portillo, 1996).

Currently, junior high and high school students hear about interior design from three different "voices"—none of which offer accurate information about the profession. The American Institute of Architects (AIA) discusses interior spaces as they relate to architecture; typically as an afterthought once the building shell is designed. Design reality shows (e.g., those on the HGTV network) put interior design in the context of decoration and sensationalistic entertainment (Waxman & Clemons, 2005). The third "voice" teens hear concerning interior design is in their local high schools.

In over half the states in the United States, anywhere from one to three semester classes in interior design courses are offered to youth based on standards published by the American Association of Family and Consumer Science (AAFCS), an organization formerly associated with home economics. Unfortunately, AAFCS's national standards do not accurately reflect the breadth of the profession as they primarily dwell on residential design. In addition, the Family and Consumer Science (FCS) teachers typically have little formal education or training in interior design as they are also responsible for teaching human growth and development, food and nutrition, apparel and textiles, and resource management as well as housing and interiors. Therefore, those teaching interior design in K–12 may not be the best prepared to accurately represent the profession.

Rather than developing a new channel of communication to junior high and high school students, in spring 2009 the American Society of Interior Designers (ASID), the Interior Design Educators Council (IDEC), and AAFCS (along with 27 states) developed a formal partnership to create a pre-professional assessment and certificate for interior design. The certificate will be awarded to high school students after completion of their design coursework and successful completion of an examination assessing their basic minimum competencies (appropriate to that level) in interior design. This examination will, hopefully, guide revisions of the national AAFCS standards that relate to interior design and shape what is taught by teachers in their school districts throughout the nation.

Several other steps have been taken in the past few years to accurately introduce youth to interior design. The Issues Forum, an informal association composed of six organizations: ASID, the Council for Interior Design Accreditation (CIDA), the Interior Designers of Canada (IDC), IDEC, the International Interior Design Association (IIDA), and the National Council for Interior Design Qualification (NCIDQ) collaborated to develop a Web site (www.careersininteriordesign.com) to inform high school and college students about the profession. This Web site is updated periodically by all organizations and continues to be an effective channel to inform students about the interior design profession. In addition, ASID and The Art Institutes (a system of for-profit schools of higher education) developed a DVD entitled "Careers in Interior Design" and distributed it to high school career counselors. This DVD serves as a great tool to discuss current trends in interior design as they relate to human behavior.

There are many other ways interior design practitioners can help infuse content into K–12. On a local level, assistance is needed from every sector of practice and education. Following are some ideas suggested by K–12 teachers and curriculum specialists (Clemons, 2007) that could be used when volunteering in community schools. Table 2.1 illustrates the suggestions provided by the curriculum specialists in terms of integrating interior design content into the curriculum. Table 2.2 contains activities for educators, student groups, or practitioners. Content for both tables was gleaned from the aforementioned study (Clemons, 2007). In addition, with the new pre-professional certificate in place by 2010, there will be many opportunities to serve in nearby schools both with the teachers and the youth.

TABLE 2.1
CURRICULUM SPECIALISTS' SUGGESTIONS
FOR INTEGRATING INTERIOR DESIGN CONTENT

STANDARD	INTERIOR DESIGN CONTENT AREA
Social Studies Curriculum Specialist	• Sustainable design; geography versus overpopulation • Teach youth about history using art; not art history • Cultural design; cultural connections between periods • Materials used to build buildings that were reflective of that geographical area
Visual Arts Curriculum Specialist	• Elements and principles of design • Use of interior design as a communication method to describe who you are • Design a business • Various historical/cultural traditions • History of interior design; how interior objects are organized to reflect the historical period • Aesthetics—good and bad design
Technology Curriculum Specialist	• Virtual tour of the town/city where the school district resides—interior and exterior spaces • 360 view of the way people lived and how they lived in different parts of the country
School to Career Curriculum Specialist	• Natural fit with family and consumer studies; interior design standards
Mathematics Curriculum Specialist	• Architectural principles; ratio/proportion • Relationship of art theory (Mondrian) with the golden ratio • Efficiency of space when teaching calculus • Composition and how parts fit together is mathematical • Networking
Science Curriculum Specialist	• Space and light; including natural light • Health and safety
Communication Curriculum Specialist	• Relationships and communication between interior designer and end user/client • Relationship between subcontractors
Staff Development Specialist	• Teachers need to constantly understand the reasons why they teach what they teach—exercise on classroom design • Teachers need to understand connections—between fifth and sixth grade learning and between interior design and the national standard; develop an exercise on how to help a teacher work

TABLE 2.2
EDUCATORS' AND PRACTITIONERS' SUGGESTED ACTIVITIES TO INTEGRATE INTERIOR DESIGN INTO THE NATIONAL EDUCATION STANDARDS

STANDARD	INTERIOR DESIGN CONTENT AREA	METHOD
Health	• Health, safety, and welfare of the public • Interior products that affect health (outgassing of materials, sick building syndrome) • Daylighting issues • Life cycle; generational changes • Designing for different user groups • Designing for people with different disabilities	• Analysis of town hall, library, hospital unit • Look at carpet on flooring and analyze recycled materials used • Study daylighting of room • Design for "grandma" • Evaluate needs of a fellow student in wheelchair
Civics	• Diversity of design and cultural issues • Health, safety, and welfare issues • Connection of sociology, art, and architecture • Sustainability issues	
Science	• Sustainability issues • Physics; lighting design • Anatomy; ergonomics, how people relate to furniture, how the eye is used for sight/light • Anthropometrics; relationships to space	• Learn design terminology • Measuring space, relationships • Using anatomy of the eye to teach lighting
History	• Future thinking; where we came from, where we are, where we are going • How people lived in the past • What their interior spaces looked like • Analysis of the architecture in that area to determine why it was developed the way it was to support the human living needs • Where are we going; future workstations	• Trip to a natural history museum • Project relative to current literature (e.g., American Girl dolls) • Field trip to a design center; field trip to workplaces
Social Studies	• Value systems of African Americans vs. Macaw Tribes vs. Caribbean . . . Motifs used, materials, philosophies captured • Why housing is designed the way it is	• Why does a house in Polynesia take a certain form (materials and motifs) compared to Native Americans • Use of interior space; different depending on culture (public vs. private)

TABLE 2.2 (*CONTINUED*)
**EDUCATORS' AND PRACTITIONERS' SUGGESTED ACTIVITIES TO
INTEGRATE INTERIOR DESIGN INTO THE NATIONAL EDUCATION STANDARDS.**

STANDARD	INTERIOR DESIGN CONTENT AREA	METHOD
Languages	• Symbolic design; imagery • Values communicated through design • Visual design is the language of design; visual literacy • Design is a universal language	• What do I want to say about who I am . . . as soon as you walk into my space. Sense of space
Math	• Proportion • Measurement of spaces, relationships • Construction; building, measuring, contracts, project timelines • Geometry with shapes	• 44-piece project
Visual Arts	• Multicultural color theories • Design criticism • Abstract to practical	• Take apart a small appliance, study the shapes, abstract them into a 3-D model, put the model on computer or draft it, use it to design a personal space • Concept statements, capture concept in dual pairs, design 12 concept squares from words • Design conceptual postcards with elements and principles of design used, send to relative
Geography	• Sustainability issues • Pick a country and study the interior materials made or used in the country • How environment and culture are shaped by available resources; sunlight, climate • Regional/cultural differences	• Study of different countries—how geography affects interior spaces; red clay in Oklahoma or breezes in the southern states that are encouraged by dogtrot-style homes • Cultural differences in materials • Study of different geographic style homes (tapestries)
English	• Study writers and the physical/interior environment they wrote in when composing their work • Interior environment (put writers' work in context)	• Go on a bus or tour around the exterior of the school in pairs; one is blindfolded; describe images/smells/light • Research where one parent works; look at context of work being done; use imagery evoking words • Analyze where students study best; do their own evaluation and analysis, design criticism

CONCLUSION

The interior design profession is grappling with many issues, such as the attack on interior design licensure by the Institute for Justice (IJ) or the untruths spread on a national level by the National Kitchen and Bath Association (NKBA) concerning the interior design profession as a whole. It would be easy to negate the need to spend time reflecting and placing priority on how to infuse interior design content and thinking into K–12. However, if this call had been heeded when issued 15 years ago, a new generation would be emerging from high schools today with a clear, distinct understanding of why interior design is critical to the health, safety, and welfare of the public and how its practitioners offer meaningful design in the development of fulfilling spaces. In addition, they would have been exposed to design thinking from a young age and be emerging into the higher educational realm with an understanding and ability to think differently, more holistically, and creatively.

Although minimum standards have been developed for entry-level interior designers (CIDA, 2009) and beyond (NCIDQ), a gap exists in the interior design education continuum from "kindergarten to career." Although interior design professional organizations have spent millions of dollars to market and educate the adult public about the career, few resources have been spent to educate youth. In part, this may be due to a lack of information concerning how to address this complex issue and diverse national audience.

Our youth offer an avenue and opportunity for education that is currently only minimally utilized. Each one of us is needed. Educating the youth is a critical key to the growth and maturation of the interior design profession as well as for the betterment of our society. If accurately taught, our youth will teach their parents, who not only are our consumers and potential future clients but our advocates and educators as well.

REFERENCES

Brown, T. (2008, June). Design thinking. *Harvard Business Review*, 84–94.

Clemons, S. (1999). Development of interior design career information for dissemination to students in grades six through eight. *Journal of Interior Design, 25*(2), 45–51.

Clemons, S. (2007). Interior design in K–12 curricula: Asking the experts. *Journal of Interior Design, 32*(3), 15–40.

Bunker-Hellmich, L. (2004). Design for development: The importance of children's environments. *Implications, 1*(2), 1–3. Retrieved December 13, 2004, from http://www.informedesign.umn.edu/_news/Children01_02.pdf

Nussbaumer, L. (2002). Interior design—An exciting career choice: A curriculum for high school students with an intergenerational approach.

Proceedings of the Interior Design Educators Council Conference, Santa Fe, NM, 56–57.

Portillo, M., & Rey-Barreau, J. (1995). The place of interior design in K–12 education and the built environment education movement. *Journal of Interior Design, 21*(1), 39–43.

Rey-Barreau, J., & Portillo, M. (1996). Enter the K–12 arena: A built environment education model. Proceedings of the Interior Design Educators Council Conference, Denver, CO, 175–177.

Waxman, L., & Clemons, S. (2005). Mixed messages: The impact of design-related television shows on student perceptions of the interior design profession [Abstract]. *Proceedings of the International Interior Design Educators Council Annual Conference*, Savannah, GA, 32–33.

The BOK allows us to operate with overarching purpose and expectations that can be maintained, adapted, or rejected as community building continues.

—Joy H. Dohr

3

THE BODY OF KNOWLEDGE

OVERVIEW A profession's body of knowledge is the compilation of its specialized knowledge that allows it to function as an informed group of individuals; it is the currency of a profession, that which gives it value to the public. Defining a body of knowledge for a profession can provide positive and negative boundaries; we've asked these authors to give their opinions about the value of delineating interior design's body of knowledge.

Joy Dohr provides an understanding of the value of identifying a professional body of knowledge and what it can do for a profession. She then challenges us to consider plans for moving forward as we build in this foundation through coalescing community and integrated understanding.

Anna Marshall-Baker provides a viewpoint on what a body of knowledge does and does not do for a profession. Insightful thinking about the fluidity of a body of knowledge and inherent issues involved in setting boundaries are the focus of her essay. She suggests that for the seasoned interior design practitioner, few boundaries exist, and we may not want to be limited by a defined body of knowledge.

Ernest Rhoads suggests a potential solution to the idea that embedded and interdisciplinary knowledge must be included in our body of knowledge. He develops a process to bridge the gap between explicit and tacit knowledge. Then, a method and rationale for adding to the body of knowledge by documenting embedded knowledge related to designing for people's welfare is offered by Denise Guerin and Jain Kwon. These are four different viewpoints on the importance of, limitations of, and continued development and expansion of the interior design profession's body of knowledge.

> What has this BOK done for the interior design profession? Where do we go from here?

JOY H. DOHR

BODY OF KNOWLEDGE: COALESCING COMMUNITY AND INTEGRATING UNDERSTANDING

BODY OF KNOWLEDGE AT WORK

At 8:00 AM this sunny, cold day, I wasn't taking up my pencil to begin writing; I was meeting future designers. I'd been invited to lecture on creativity and civility in design to 85 university students who were headed into interior design or other design-related fields. My primary question to them was, "How do you know creativity and civility in design when you see or experience it?" I shared definitions of design, creativity, and civility. I briefly introduced them to indices and results from studies, ideas from books, and theory. Students reflected on this material against their previous experience and learning.

Such steps are preparation, a base from which to focus thinking and ultimately to see new patterns and gain a deeper understanding. To delve into these abstract, complex concepts and truly make the topics come alive for these students, I tell them stories of four award-winning designers to demonstrate the realities of interior design.

JOY H. DOHR, PhD, FIDEC, is professor emeritus at the University of Wisconsin–Madison, where she also was chair of the design studies department and an associate dean for academic affairs. Dohr presents, writes, and consults on interior design education at undergraduate and graduate levels, the creative design process, design and civility, and environmental color. She serves community institutions and civil agencies in analysis of space, color, and the selection/installation of public art. Dohr is a past president of IDEC and has served on the boards of CIDA, the IIDA Foundation, and InformeDesign's® technical review board, among others. Recently, Dohr was named to the profession's work group for sustaining interior design education. She is recipient of numerous awards from her field and institution.

- Designer One, "A Best Model," is a story about giving vision, being down to earth, and being a clear communicator who refreshes, confirms, and challenges society and design.
- Designer Two, "Community Builder," and Designer Three, "Gallant, Progressive Presenter," act on knowledge and skill, and honor relationships over time. Tangible and intangible meanings in practice and education are evident.
- Designer Four, "Wise, Global Artistry," features integration of two cultures and balances the best from both to address sustainable environments while a recent master's student.

All stories contain dichotomies of professional struggles and success plus examples of actual work in different settings. The designers' own words voice insight to community-building versus self-interest; ordering environments and human behavior; acknowledging client roles and satisfaction; and accounting for natural environment, materials, and products as well as societal and economic conditions. All share worldviews. From general theory to concrete specifics, the information about creativity and civility in design is condensed, discussed, and remembered in image and word. Knowledge central to interior design works anew.

The lecture has parallels to this essay. You and I are asked, "What has the body of knowledge done for the interior design profession?" The question is about the body of knowledge (BOK) at work and the tangible and intangible results realized from its existence. As "what" we think about and the substance of solution, it is central to our organization and growth at all levels. This essay on the BOK fittingly falls between chapters on design thinking and evidence-based design. Content is held in thought and hand, which is seen and experienced by others. Likewise, given such a large topic to discuss in limited space, words must be condensed, yet come alive through compelling realities. Three realities of a body of knowledge are highlighted: (1) a dynamic energy is realized for coalescing professional community over time; (2) the asset of its interdisciplinary nature gives an interior design focus in a new landscape of integrated understandings; and (3) challenges are opportunities for education and practice in confirming, balancing, and invigorating the BOK to move forward. We must question the interior design BOK in context of these realities.

BOK: COALESCING PROFESSIONAL COMMUNITY

The term *body of knowledge* encapsulates a breadth and depth of information that interior designers learn, study, explore, research, apply, and communicate. The scope of its meaning can invigorate or discourage. We know its subject topics, content, skills, or scholarship; it is material we love. It is our grounding and is named in theory and in practice. We equally know designing architectural interiors is interactive and dynamic with external and internal influences. And, time hovers. Yet, ground can shift, or we decide to plow. No wonder raw emotions arise in debates over the state of interior design; such debates are healthy, though. With input from many constituents and engagement in numerous settings, a complex field evolves. Decisions in transforming places to improve the quality of human life rest in this know-how and our interpretations. Energy is expended and energy is gained through framing the BOK and through resulting dialogue about interpretations.

Interior design scholarship has been described as thought to action within a context (Dohr, 2007). Scholarship, a synonym for knowledge, assumes six critical components: a field, topic questions, purpose, methods of work, outcomes, and sharing results. The complexity of interior design scholarship was viewed from current vantages of creative performance, research-based practice (i.e., evidence-based design), and design research. Specific examples drew upon information key to interior design—the BOK (Dohr, 2007). While vantage points and cultural norms of those views may vary, and better articulation of evidence-based design was called for, the field and topics were not in question. Formalized work on the interior design profession's BOK was precedence. Interior design integrates knowledge of human environment needs, design, codes and regulations, products and materials, professional practice, and communication (Guerin & Martin, 2004; Guerin & Thompson, 2004; Martin & Guerin, 2006). The processes and nuances in content of these categories form the bases for further exploration and disclosure of the field's development.

The coalescing of information to build the profession has been addressed (Guerin & Thompson, 2004). However, coalescing community has a slightly different connotation. It is through community spirit that collective work of a BOK sustains and advances each of us. Its impact as dynamic energy concerns the usability, vitality, and accomplishments connected to it. One sees cohesive energy or lack thereof regarding practitioners' and academicians'

engagement with that knowledge. As examples, interior design educators and non-design colleagues discern performance and qualities of know-how within educational programs. Firms, organizations, practice groups, interests, or new services of expertise develop and change based upon the knowledge. The fact that interior designers have specialties in wayfinding, branding, sustainability, strategic planning, and design research (particularly in the last decade) are tangible results that add to expertise of traditional markets. Nonprofit organizations also tap the expertise of the profession (R. Sweet, personal communication, March, 2008).

Importantly, competency gained and attached to this knowledge base supports students, educators, researchers, practitioners, and, in turn, clients and users. A clearer perspective of one's place in the profession can now be attained. New directions for study and work may be based upon precedence within (i.e., BOK studies noted previously), as well as from without. Attending to the BOK inspires us to reinvent or to accomplish something new. The BOK allows us to operate with overarching purpose and expectations that can be maintained, adapted, or rejected as community building continues.

BOK: INTEGRATED UNDERSTANDINGS

Whereas individuals and groups enter and leave active design work, the BOK and its contributions to society extend, becoming a legacy. Design solutions and design literature communicate something all on their own. It is in this context that a judgment and understanding of the BOK are revealed and live. The very character of our knowledge poises the interior design profession to reach out with new, expanded, and deeper understandings and to continually refresh education and practice based on our observations of what is happening today in learning and work environments.

Whether in academics, practice, or industry, the *interdisciplinary movement* is changing the landscape of work and place and the profession's mind-set. Attitudes about knowledge and behaviors for generating knowledge are changing. We see growth of institutes, centers, and classes that bring different disciplines together to address societal or global issues. Those issues might be aging, health, sustainability, social justice, innovation, or global cultural design. Those centers require spatial designs where interdisciplinary work can be supported. Professionals join teams where interior design knowledge and expertise are valued and coalesce with disciplines and expertise of others committed to the project. Boundaries blur, and the interdisciplinary movement applauds. This process intends that new questions about human-environment relationships be asked, leading to new discoveries. In a common moment, interior designers are asked to be independent and interdependent in their work and knowledge simultaneously.

This process of creation demands that interior designers be well aware of their knowledge and skills as well as embody the skill to communicate with team members (Tharp, 2003). Openness to other perspectives is heightened. Revisiting and drawing upon our own interdisciplinary roots in art, humanities, and science seems prudent, and evidence of this grounding is in the BOK. Articulating where and when our intellectual and analytical knowledge is needed, as well as where and when our integrative and creative knowledge is required, seems advantageous and this flexibility beneficial (Dohr, 2007). Seeing patterns across seemingly disparate information, things, and space, then bringing them to a whole is the basis of each and every design decision as questions or problems of relationships from elemental ones to complex ones are addressed.

Yet, acknowledging interior design's grounding in interdisciplinary knowledge shouldn't lull us into overconfidence. Working across knowledge areas and integrating them through new visual, experiential, or written form can also be our nemesis. In the past, jabs were felt for *not* fitting neatly into one or another setting or discipline. Criticism was heard that our work was fuzzy. Our response of choice, "You don't understand my work or my field," was reflexive. Today, the BOK shows the depth and richness of specialized knowledge from areas coming together to form a new, respected, integrated landscape.

Interdisciplinary mind-set might suggest ability and evidence that individual designers use criteria from different perspectives of knowledge across planning and design. In creative speak, this is flexibility of thought. For example, evidence

exists that those interior designers knowledgeable in color use compositional, behavioral, symbolic/cultural, preferential, and pragmatic criteria in planning and decision making (Portillo, 2009). Another interdisciplinary mind-set is represented by practitioners who operate with both business minds and design minds. This can also occur within an interdisciplinary partnership or team. A project or study can be the catalyst to bring the group together and the know-how of each elevates the team, as well as the common work. The yield is great given creative tensions and challenges faced by team members to be clear in language and meaning.

Interdisciplinary also references a combination of disciplines where individuals seek to learn something to produce new integrations. One topic usually is central to this relationship. For example, an MBA class taught by both business faculty and a design practitioner has structure surrounding know-how about innovation. Business sought design. The class imitates or adapts design knowledge and skill from practice with intent that the business major forms innovative thinking, as well as understands benefits of design fields to their mission.

In other cases, individuals ask questions and search for answers in the *cracks* between two disciplines. It's the birth of a *tweener* particularly prior to emergence of a new area of study. Tweeners provide identity and describe where knowledge stands to peers firmly positioned in a disciplinary tradition.

Visual culture and material culture are examples of knowledge areas beyond tweener stage; therefore, new names were acquired. Individuals from architecture, interior design, art and design history, history, anthropology, and language studies formed new questions and put answers to work. The current problem for these evolved tweeners is the issue of who will hire them in academics or practice to do such work. Are those who serve the new and old perceived to be spread too thin? Usually, empathy comes from others with interdisciplinary mind-sets and background.

As discussed, posing and answering questions relative to the impact of the BOK are critical to energizing our community from within. This examination is also an asset as the interdisciplinary landscape is considered. Engaged interior designers address human conditions, approach planning and design from an interdisciplinary mind-set, understand values, and apply design theories and research findings in an innovative manner (Dohr, 2007). They filter and reflect the BOK to bring strength to a project, a study, and the field.

Although precedence is considered, professionals must ask new or expanded questions of literature and theory that comprise the BOK to respond to questions that reflect clients' experience and needs. This suggests maintaining efforts to read more rigorously and listen and write better, enhancing the creation of visual and experiential environments. A depth of knowledge in balance with our breadth of knowledge vitalizes focus while keeping collaborators and the public in perspective.

To further build and enhance the BOK, a greater attention by interior design practitioners to graduate education must be continued in light of knowledge development and opportunities for interdisciplinary work. To address interdisciplinary knowledge in today's terms, it begins with collaborators seeking interior designers' expertise and solid execution of design solutions. It means interior designers also seek to form new types of partnerships. New partnerships are readily found in academe, practice, and industry to further explore this phenomenon collectively. Lastly, the public (i.e., consumers, policymakers, media) will see qualities of the profession's work and form their own collective image, whether accurate or not. To be accurate, may our legacy demonstrate strength of community, deep understanding of interior design's integrated reality, and a literature in form and word to reflect upon a best model, universal truths, and wise global sensibilities.

REFERENCES

Dohr, J. (2007). Continuing the dialogue: Interior design graduate education inquiry and scholarly cultures. *Journal of Interior Design, 33*(1), v–xvi.

Guerin, D., & Martin, C. (2004). The career cycle approach to defining the interior design profession's body of knowledge. *Journal of Interior Design, 30*(2), 1–12.

Guerin, D., & Thompson, J. (2004). Interior design education in the 21st century: An educational transformation. *Journal of Interior Design, 30*(1)1–12.

Martin, C., & Guerin, D. (2006). The interior design profession's body of knowledge, 2005 edition. *Grand Rapids: Council for Interior Design Accreditation, American Society of Interior Designers, Interior Designers of Canada, International Interior Design Association, and the National Council for Interior Design Qualification.*

Portillo, M. B. (2009). *Color planning for interiors: An integrated approach to color in designed spaces.* New York: Wiley & Sons.

Tharp, T. (2003). *The creative habit.* New York: Simon & Schuster.

> What has this body of knowledge done
for the interior design profession? Is there
a benefit from documenting the body of
knowledge? Conversely, is there a risk from
documenting the body of knowledge?

ANNA MARSHALL-BAKER

REFLECTIONS ON THE INTERIOR DESIGN PROFESSION'S BODY OF KNOWLEDGE

The editors of this book invited me to comment on the effect of the body of knowledge of interior design on the interior design profession. Because my profession is teaching and not interior design praxis, I am not in a position to know the effect of the body of knowledge on the practice of interior design. I can, however, provide an academic's view of the body of knowledge.

CONTEXT

First, we need to recognize and honor Denise Guerin and Caren Martin for their pioneering efforts regarding documentation of a body of knowledge in interior design. They have single-handedly focused, if not begun, a dialogue regarding knowledge in interior design. This is critically important to the development of interior design education and praxis. Yet, documenting a body of knowledge in interior design is a daunting task, and one that continues to evolve.

ANNA MARSHALL-BAKER, PhD, FIDEC, is
an associate professor and coordinator of the
undergraduate program in the department of
interior architecture at the University of North
Carolina at Greensboro (UNCG). She focuses on
sustainable design and the reciprocal effects of
environments and human development, particularly in the newborn intensive care unit (NICU)
in healthcare facilities. In addition to her work in
academia, Marshall-Baker serves as a consultant
for NICU design and is engaged in the redesign
of furnishings typical of an NICU, including the
infant incubator. Marshall-Baker is past president of IDEC, coordinator of the Sustainability
Initiative at UNCG, a member of the system-
wide University of North Carolina Committee on
Sustainability, and serves on the Recommended
Standards Consensus Committee for Newborn
Intensive Care Unit Design.

Drs. Guerin and Martin and I have spoken with each other about a body of knowledge in interior design. We have all participated in a joint dialogue at a Body of Knowledge Conference in May 2003, and we have published our ideas (Guerin & Martin, 2001, 2004; Marshall-Baker, 2005; Martin & Guerin, 2006). The conversation is important because it is through dialogue that converging and diverging views are discovered, fledgling ideas become more certain when compared to contrasting views, and full exploration of ideas occurs.

Admittedly, I was not engaged in developing or even thinking about a body of knowledge in interior design when Drs. Guerin and Martin began to discuss their work. But, as I listened to what they were saying, read what they were writing, and reviewed requests for funding while serving on the executive board of the Interior Design Educators Council (IDEC), I realized that in many ways I, too, was a stakeholder in this endeavor.

A body of knowledge in interior design would define the boundaries of the profession—it would distinguish, for example, where architecture ends and interior design begins; it would provide the very foundation for education—it would inform our curriculum; it would influence research—we would differentiate interior design research from that of social scientists. In other words, a body of knowledge would separate interior design education and praxis from other fields such as psychology, sociology, engineering, architecture, history, art, and textiles.

Presently, no one claims this result. At best, we are still in the process of articulating that body of knowledge; i.e., we are still on the journey. My position is that because the *ultimate outcome is a product of the journey*, we have to be careful crafting the journey. Drs. Guerin and Martin have done this differently than I would.

KNOWLEDGE

Because I have written about knowledge in interior design (Marshall-Baker, 2005), I will not reiterate those thoughts here. To summarize, my understanding of knowledge is that it is "fluid, dynamic, evolving, emergent, contextual" (p. xiv), and informed by many sources across all time. Thus, attempts to "reflect one point in time" (Guerin & Martin, 2004, p. 19) even if through a "rearview mirror" (Martin & Guerin, 2006, p. x) are futile. I understand why we want to do so (see paragraph 4 in this essay), but I don't think it's possible. Further, because interior design is inherently multi-, inter-, and trans-disciplinary, the body of knowledge necessary for the practice of interior design is at once collectively enormous and individually distinct. Let me explain using my own work as an example, not because it is unique or special in any way, but because it is what I know best.

My particular interest in interior design is in healthcare, particularly newborn intensive care units (NICUs). This interest requires that I become knowledgeable about the development of preterm infants—about their fragilities and strengths, their vulnerabilities to an intensive environment, and about the environmental features necessary not only to support but *form* the very biology that will sustain them across their life spans, a formation that occurs within an extrauterine environment for which they are systematically unprepared.

Following graduate school in interior design, I was unprepared to provide an appropriate environment for neonates in an NICU—not because my education in interior design was deficient, but because the direction my interior design path was taking required knowledge of design as well as medicine and human development. Thus, the knowledge necessary for me to understand interior design in an NICU "wandered" (see Abbott, 2001, or Marshall-Baker, 2005) across other disciplines, including psychology (prenatal, neonatal, and infant development), sociology (mother/infant interaction), industrial engineering (ergonomics regarding the infant incubator), medicine (neonatology and nursing), and design (art, interior design, and architecture).

Collectively, these wanderings formed the knowledge base necessary for me to knowingly alter the NICU in effective ways. Thus, what I know about interior design varies from what a hospitality designer knows about interior design, and that varies from what a residential designer knows. But our individually distinct knowledge necessary for the design of healthcare, hospitality, and residential interior spaces collectively forms a larger body of knowledge in interior design. Drs. Guerin and Martin don't document this kind of knowledge in their work. I don't blame them. Who could do so?

Instead, the journey to document the body of knowledge in interior design began with available documents from education and practice (Guerin & Martin, 2001; 2004). Knowledge areas were discerned using the Foundation for Interior Design Education Research (FIDER; now the Council for Interior Design Accreditation) accreditation standards, the Interior Design Experience Program (IDEP) experience guidelines, the National Council for Interior Design Qualification (NCIDQ) examination content, and regulatory statutes. Each of these documents quantifies interior design education and practice. CIDA articulates the minimum requirements necessary for an academic program to be accredited, and NCIDQ tests the "minimum level of competency needed to practice interior design" (Guerin & Martin, 2004, p. 14). IDEP, a program developed by NCIDQ, articulates features of an internship program for entry-level interior designers.

Collectively, these documents represent a six-year period that begins in higher education and extends through the first two years of practical experience as an interior designer. These are valid documents and a logical place to begin documentation of interior design education and practice. Yet by definition and purpose, each represents a limited perspective. Regulatory statues are similarly restrictive. Knowledge areas that form the basis for the "interior design profession's body of knowledge" thus are products of documents that by definition reflect nascent stages in the career cycle.

The knowledge areas have been qualified by analysis, panel review, a review of the literature, and recently statistically weighted to "determine the level of importance each knowledge area has to the practice of interior design" (Martin & Guerin, 2006, p. viii). These various forms of analysis consistently reveal support for the knowledge areas. This is not surprising. Knowledge areas culled, extracted, or revealed from documents that describe the fundamentals, the underpinnings, for interior design education and practice should surface reliably in a content analysis, resonate with experts from the field, and emerge in a review of publications regarding interior design.

Knowledge areas formed from foundational documents will by definition be basic rather than multifarious. They will reflect the activities in which all interior design educators and practitioners engage, albeit at a fundamental rather than comprehensive level. For example, knowledge areas most heavily weighted in each of six categories distributed across three larger groups (Martin & Guerin, 2006) are:

- Programming (problem identification, requirements, p. 31)
- Building codes, laws, regulations; life safety standards (movement, stairs, corridors, ramps, exits) and requirements; welfare (p. 32)
- Interior components design and detailing (custom furniture, cabinetry, millwork, floor patterning, textiles, p. 32)
- Materials (products, sources, selection, cost, installation, maintenance, specifications, p. 33)
- Contract administration (bidding/negotiation, contract documents, p. 33)
- Oral, visual, and written communication (p. 33)

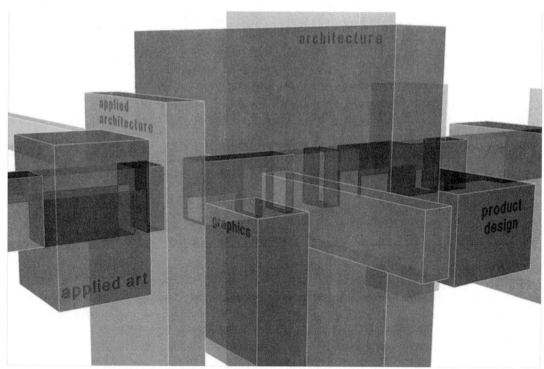

FIGURE 3.1. Local knowledges wandering in design.

"Theory" appears among the 96 knowledge areas on two occasions. It is #13 on an ordered list of 20 knowledge areas in the most heavily weighted group of three "human environment needs." Theory appears again in the lower of two categories in the middle group, "interior construction, codes, and regulations." Of 39 knowledge areas in two categories in this group, theory is #37.

The knowledge areas, then, reflect the fundamentals of what we do, not what we know. Documenting twice that I use theory doesn't reveal how I use theory or what I know. The knowledge areas don't articulate social learning theory, for example, in which I may design space that supports the social interaction of occupants in the space. They don't explain behavior-setting theories in which the setting (e.g., a church or courtroom) determines behavior. What I *know* about the design of interior space does not appear in the knowledge areas.

Consequently, the knowledge areas reflect the fundamentals of practice and thus also apply to other professions involved in the design of the built environment. Nothing on the list of knowledge areas is unique to interior design or distinct from architecture, for example. These conjoined fundamentals of practice not only are the consequence of process, but also reflect a different way to think about knowledge.

Abbott (2001) describes larger frameworks of knowledge upon which local knowledges "wander." In his example, sociology is a local knowledge that wanders across a larger framework of social science. As such, it wanders among other variants of sociology and other disciplines, such as psychology. Each local knowledge is influenced by others, and, collectively, they form the larger framework of social science. Similarly, we would expect a larger framework for "design" upon which local knowledges such as architecture and interior design wander, as shown in Figure 3.1.

Each would be informed by the other and also share knowledge inherent to the larger framework of universal knowledge of design. This could explain why the knowledge areas that comprise the interior design profession's BOK (Martin & Guerin, 2006) also apply to architecture. It's possible that the professions would diverge at the level of theory or, at least, at a level above the baseline; but at baseline, at the level of fundamentals of practice, architecture and interior design overlap completely.

EDUCATION AND PRACTICE

The complexity of knowledge is not only an intellectual exercise. Though originally contracted by the Association of Registered Interior Designers of Ontario (ARIDO) for legislative purposes, *The Interior Design Profession's Body of Knowledge: Its Definition and Documentation* (2001) also is promoted for its value as a "resource for individuals involved in writing, planning development, and evaluation of curriculum for interior design courses and programs" (inside ARIDO's order form). Brian Sinclair, dean of the faculty of environmental design at the University of Calgary, expresses concern about such a practice: "With the arrival of professions as self-regulating bodies established to guard and protect the public health, safety, and welfare, the education of such professionals [becomes] increasingly prescriptive and debatably rigid" (2003, n.p.). Sinclair goes on to say:

> New problems demand new approaches. It is my contention that such problems evade investigation, characterization and solution using the tools of a single field of study. Quite simply such problems fly under the radar of individual disciplines—disciplines whose boundaries arguably seem outdated, and whose continued existence seems more related to managing the academy than to handling problems or realizing significant change in the market. (2003, n.p.)

A significant change in "the market" that requires new thinking is sustainability. At the University of North Carolina at Greensboro, where I teach, we have developed a working definition of sustainability as

> the enduring interconnectedness of social equity, the environment, economics, and aesthetics. . . . The intent of sustainability is to instill values that promote justice, invent innovative approaches and solutions to environmental and economic challenges, and invest civility and grace into our communities. (UNCG, Sustainability Value Working Group of the Strategic Planning Committee, 2008)

The enormous challenges associated with environmental degradation are confounded by necessary, simultaneous considerations of economic, social, and aesthetic concerns. This constitutes what Rittel (in Buchanan, 1998) describes as "wicked problems." These challenges are so complex that determinate methods used on problems with definite conditions do not apply. Wicked problems require an indeterminate approach because they are universal in scope, they are continuous, there is more than one valid approach to the problem, and they are "higher level" challenges. Wicked problems thus are inherently multidisciplinary. Dean Sinclair believes that the role of design with its "innovative methodologies, inclusive approaches, and praxis orientation" (2003, n.p.) holds the key to making a difference in just such a wicked problem as sustainability. The challenge is gaining trust of the public to do so.

DEFINING A PROFESSION

Carol Burns (1997) writes that professions gain respect when the public recognizes that the service provided is valuable. In other words, despite what we say about ourselves, the public's confidence in the services we render as interior designers who protect health, safety, and welfare ultimately will legitimize the profession. There could not be a more opportune time than now for interior designers to rise to the occasion.

As we face challenges related to sustainability, we can develop a reputation among the public as the design professionals who create indoor environments that are not harmful to human or environmental health. To do so requires knowledge not only about interior design, but also about areas such as chemistry, biology, medicine, anthropology, sociology, business, geography, agriculture, psychology, and ecology. Educating interior designers beyond the confines of legislative parameters of a profession positions us to be recognized for our expertise, service to the common good, and stewardship of the public's health, safety, and welfare. Surely this would advance interior design education and praxis in ways that determinate efforts will not.

REFERENCES

Abbott, A. (2001). *Chaos of disciplines.* Chicago: University of Chicago Press.

Association of Registered Interior Designers of Ontario. (2001). *The interior design profession's body of knowledge: Its definition and documentation.* Toronto: ARIDO.

Buchanan, R. (1998). Wicked problems in design thinking. In V. Margolin & R. Buchanan (Eds.), *The idea of design: A design issues reader* (pp. 3–20). Cambridge: The MIT Press.

Burns, C. (1997). An approach to alignment: Professional education and professional practice in architecture. *Practices 5/6* (pp. 33–39). Cincinnati, OH: University of Cincinnati.

Guerin, D., & Martin, C. (2001). *The definition and documentation of the interior design profession's body of knowledge.* Association of Registered Interior Designers of Ontario: Toronto, CA.

Guerin, D., & Martin, C. (2004). The career cycle approach to defining the interior design profession's body of knowledge. *Journal of Interior Design, 30*(2), 1–22.

Marshall-Baker, A. (2005). Knowledge in interior design. *Journal of Interior Design, 31*(1), xiii–xxi.

Martin, C., & Guerin, D. (2006). *The interior design profession's body of knowledge: 2005 edition.* Retrieved December 22, 2008, from http://www.careersininteriordesign.com/idbok.pdf

Sinclair, B. (2003, November). A Canadian perspective on changing design education. *DesignIntelligence.* Retrieved February 16, 2009, from http://www.di.net/articles/archive/2223/

> Is it important to incorporate embedded knowledge (i.e., the knowledge a practitioner learns through experience) into the BOK? If so, how can that be done?

ERNEST (ERNIE) RHOADS

THE IMPORTANCE OF INCORPORATING EMBEDDED KNOWLEDGE INTO THE INTERIOR DESIGN BOK

A profession's body of knowledge (BOK) is the abstract knowledge needed by practitioners to perform the profession's work. Abstract knowledge is what an interior design practitioner knows and applies to a design project. This is not to be confused with the skills designers need to practice or tasks designers are required to perform. When we, as interior designers, identify the profession's abstract knowledge, we can communicate within and beyond our profession about our work (Guerin & Martin, 2001).

A BOK is more than simply a collection of terms, a professional reading list, a library, a Web site or a collection of Web sites, a description of professional functions, or even a collection of information. A BOK inherently contains explicit and tacit knowledge without much of a bridge to span the gap between the two.

Academics specialize in explicit knowledge—formalized knowledge that can be taught with words, symbols, and numbers. Practitioners, on the other hand, develop tacit knowledge that is personal, gained through action and experience, and often hard to communicate formally.

ERNEST (ERNIE) RHOADS, ASID, received his BFA in interior design from Seattle's Cornish College of the Arts. He holds an MBA with an emphasis in management and an MS in information systems management, both from Seattle Pacific University. Rhoads's professional experience includes restaurant and hotel design for U.S. Foodservice, Inc.; facilities design for Boeing's Commercial and Military Aircraft Divisions; space planning analysis for Safeco Insurance Company; and healthcare design for MultiCare Health System. Currently, he is a project manager for CB Richard Ellis-Global Corporate Services and enjoys teaching part-time when possible. He served as the 2008–2009 ASID Washington State chapter president and has chaired ASID's National Legislative & Codes Advisory Council. In 2008 Ernie sat on the NCIDQ board of directors and was a contributing member of the NCIDQ Examination/Practicum Committee from 2003–2008. He is a founding chairman and advisor to Washington State's Interior Design Coalition.

RATIONALE FOR A BODY OF KNOWLEDGE

Tacit knowledge is what takes practitioners beyond their education and gives them expertise to apply what they learned to the situations of individual design problems, but it is often ignored by academics because it is difficult to capture and pass on. Capturing this *embedded knowledge* as another part of the interior design BOK is very important to assure it is reflective of what interior designers do throughout their careers. What practitioners learn after their entry-level position is what becomes embedded in their own bodies of knowledge. And, this is where we must begin as it has not been captured.

DEFINING EMBEDDED KNOWLEDGE

Embedded knowledge is derived from extended experiences that cannot easily be expressed, articulated, or explicated (e.g., embodied knowledge, intuition). As Polanyi (1967) stated, "we know more than we can tell" (p. 44). Tacit knowledge itself is a quite fuzzy notion that is used to refer to:

> Knowledge embedded in skills, i.e., rules, procedures, and know-how, that may be difficult to verbally explicate (procedural skills)

> Informal knowledge that encapsulates theoretical knowledge organized around problems and cases, e.g., how to approach and solve problems

> Knowledge embedded in regular and predictable patterns of organizational activities (e.g., an intuitive grasp of the relevance of data that a company should focus on and provides a basis for an inimitable competitive advantage)

Embedded knowledge is a particular form of tacit knowledge that is essentially linked with tools and practices, rather than explicitly codified or represented. Human beings are able to overcome their cognitive processing limitations by utilizing knowledge embedded in the milieu of their activity.

It is important to acknowledge that essential embedded knowledge specifies:

> General material that is embodied in theory, principles, and practice

> Specific knowledge that is derived through the conscious and unconscious learning processes that lead to competence

What is specified as essential, embedded knowledge in the BOK can then be built into educational programs in the form of content and activities (Vorwerk, 2002). Thus in an inherent and circuitous way, embedded knowledge is a critical element to the interior design BOK and must be consciously incorporated into it in a way that bridges the gap between explicit and tacit knowledge.

MELDING EXPLICIT AND TACIT KNOWLEDGE

It is difficult to bridge the gap between academics' formal or explicit knowledge and the tacit knowledge of interior design practitioners. However, doing so is worth the effort because it can both enhance research and provide interior design practitioners with knowledge they find useful, can build upon, and document the value of their practice.

Academics and practitioners can benefit from correcting misconceptions of one another's work, creating social relationships, organizing joint discussion forums, developing a common language, and working in one another's environments.

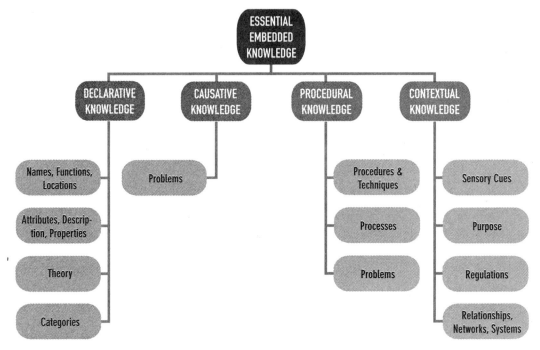

FIGURE 3.2. Taxonomy of interior design embedded knowledge.

Academics have traditionally tried to create context-free theories that can be generalized to suit most situations. But, this tends to make their work seem disconnected to practitioners, who are typically looking for practical information they can easily use in concrete ways for specific clients.

It's not easy, however, to move knowledge between the academic communities of interior design and the practitioner communities of interior designers. Academics worry practitioners' knowledge is not tested and could be biased. Practitioners feel that academics are not dealing with the issues presented by real clients and constant industry changes. Each group tends to take a simplified view of the knowledge of the other group, creating further barriers to knowledge transfer.

The language of researchers and practitioners can be quite different, so developing the ability to translate from one to the other is a key to getting the parties working together. It will be important to find a way to share tacit knowledge, but can be done by the two groups working closely together in one another's settings to develop an understanding of the context of each other's work. Assessing what specific informational outcomes are borne from a practitioner's embedded knowledge, and thereby added to the interior design BOK, may be one of the first collaborations that could meld explicit and tacit ideologies.

Specific outcomes and essential embedded knowledge would need to be assessed in relation to each other. If a practitioner is able to explain the essential embedded knowledge but is unable to perform the specific outcomes, they should not be assessed as competent. Similarly, if a practitioner is able to perform the specific outcomes but is unable to explain or justify their performance in terms of the essential embedded knowledge, they should not be assessed as competent.

A systematic analysis and capturing of the essential embedded knowledge related to a specific set of activities provides a platform to improve the linking of knowledge and action, to transform teaching and learning practices, and to improve the value of assessment while capturing the practitioner's tacit or embedded knowledge.

PROCESS TO DOCUMENT EMBEDDED KNOWLEDGE

To be systematic, the process used to capture and analyze embedded knowledge needs to be guided by a set of knowledge categories. It is useful to have a taxonomy (i.e., set of categories) of knowledge items that need to be considered during standard-setting while creating a BOK.

A taxonomy enables us to consistently determine what knowledge is required for a particular skill. This consistency makes it easier to develop learning programs, activities, and materials, as well as devise a more repeatable assessment process across different contexts. It would also help capture and categorize various aspects of embedded knowledge. The following categories could make up the taxonomy though the order of the categories is not particularly important. Figure 3.2 (opposite) shows a model of embedded knowledge, knowledge types, and knowledge categories. The four types of knowledge types are declarative, causative, procedural, and contextual. Within each of these knowledge types, there are one or more categories that reflect that knowledge type.

Box 3.1 shows some examples of the embedded knowledge within the categories.

BOX 3.1
EXAMPLES OF ESSENTIAL EMBEDDED KNOWLEDGE WITHIN CATEGORIES

DECLARATIVE KNOWLEDGE

- Names, functions, locations: objects, concepts or phenomena, entities, components
- Attributes, descriptions, characteristics, properties: features or qualities that characterize the objects or differentiate them from other similar ones
- Theory (rules, principles, laws): explanations or proposals that try to explain the physical or natural world
- Categories: ways of grouping, ordering, or classifying information

CAUSATIVE KNOWLEDGE

- Problems, causes and effects, implications: knowledge that underpins and derives from problem solving, responsibility, and accountability

PROCEDURAL KNOWLEDGE

- Procedures, techniques: formalized ways of carrying out tasks and activities; different methods of performing tasks and activities
- Processes, events, incidents: planned or structured ordering of activities, occurrences

CONTEXTUAL KNOWLEDGE

- Sensory cues: signals or signs relating to conditions or changes in the environment; seldom found in textbooks but passed on by experts or acquired through experience
- Purpose: meaning of or reason for objects, activities, etc.
- Relationships, networks, and systems: issues surrounding the project/problem
- Regulations, legislation, agreements, policies, standards: legal or agreed framework that guides or circumscribes what we do

To clarify this, the Theory category under the Declarative Knowledge type may focus on and include critical path analysis, diagramming methods or planning work, and constraints, principles, and laws. Surely these things might be mentioned in school, but it is only as the interior design practitioner matures and takes on additional responsibility that these categories of knowledge become embedded.

Under Causative Knowledge type, the Problems, Causes, Implications category might include practitioners' embedded knowledge about understanding customer motives, needs, and benefits as part of problem solving.

Under Procedural Knowledge type, the category of Procedures, Techniques might include embedded knowledge such as methods to develop project scopes and descriptions, methods to identify the skills required by the project, and methods to retain interior designers.

The Causative Knowledge type might include embedded knowledge about labor/employee regulations that come from exposure to and experience with regulations, legislation, and policies.

The interior design BOK should be developed with a combination of information from formal education and practical experience. Keep in mind that many contemporary problems and opportunities are occurring first in practice, where one encounters important professional frontiers (i.e., globalism, emerging technologies, sustainability, risk management). Cultivating these issues will have a positive, direct effect on academic programs and on the practice of interior design generally.

Related coordination with academic degree programs is also highly desirable. In particular, explicit linkage with "capstone" and other design, teamwork, and leadership activities within educational programs is warranted (Braun, Evans, Knight, & Ruehr, 2007). Similar synergies are desirable where issues are maturing in practice and deserving either research or conceptual development within the university. The twin themes of cooperation and leadership need to be embedded.

IMPLICATIONS AND CONCLUSION

It is clear that interior design is in a period of rapid change in which the professional role is changing in scope. As the potential and value of professional services evolve, so must the interior design BOK. Clearly, several dimensions of rapid change are being driven by practice, and it is important to accommodate that process in the BOK. To freeze the BOK would be to jeopardize the future of the profession.

In a period of rapid techno-social change, many items of professional importance are being recognized and distilled first in practice and only thereafter in more scholarly terms in universities. A profession's strategy that relies on infusing knowledge solely by academic preparation of entry-level recruits cannot keep pace with professional demands.

How will busy practitioners find time that is not considered "billable hours" to disseminate this useful information to the academic world? Will interior designers ever freely give what they may think of as proprietary information— information that may give them a business edge, as tacit knowledge to share with students and other interior designers?

It will take a sense of altruistic service to the interior design profession to move people to the point of freely collecting and adding their personal embedded knowledge to the interior design BOK. This is where the road forks for interior design as to whether or not it wants to claim being a profession or simply an array of occupational specialists. If interior design wishes to be considered a profession, there must be reasonable consensus on two overall defining characteristics. First, there is the cultivation of specialized, theoretical knowledge, and second, there is the direction of that knowledge toward the common good (Friedson, 1994).

The first item is often made synonymous with profession. The specialist relies only on a definable knowledge base; useful ways of asking and answering questions; and finding some kind of order in chaos. A profession is more. It must express how its distinctive knowledge serves the common good; and it must embody an institutional realization of this.

According to a study of responses by a group of recognized visionaries from interior design education, practice, and industry (Hassel & Scott, 1996), there are a number of trends important to the future of the practice of interior design. One of the most significant trends notes that future interior designers will need a broad-based liberal arts education complemented with specialized expertise to prepare them for new roles and responsibilities in an emerging global market. There is a need for new knowledge to be acquired, research to be undertaken, and new design business skills and methods to be developed that address these global markets.

The BOK is being called upon to serve rising expectations in terms of breadth, depth, and professionalism simultaneously. This is a tall order, and, among other things, it calls for a renewed concept of lifelong learning in terms of fulfilling an evolving BOK.

A dynamically evolving BOK will need to be fulfilled across the practicing profession. It will not do to have senior practitioners operating on a BOK whose scope is not equal to contemporary challenges.

So, it comes full circle—practitioners will be continually adding real-world knowledge to the BOK in turn only to be required, at some point in their career, to refer back to that BOK that they may have contributed to at one time or another.

In obtaining the BOK required for successful, meaningful practice, interior designers must acquire specialized knowledge that is fueled first by their formal education and after that, enhanced by interior design experiences with increasing levels of decision making and responsibility.

Orange (1995) sums up best why a body of knowledge is essential to interior design and any other newly formed profession when she wrote "history and memory thus become the unarticulated bases of all attempts at understanding" (p. 108.).

REFERENCES

Braun, D., Evans, E., Knight, R., & Ruehr, T. (2007). Integrating the development of teamwork, diversity, leadership, and communication skill development into a capstone design course. *Proceedings of the American Society of Engineering Education Annual Conference and Exposition,* Honolulu, HI.

Friedson, E. (1994). *Professionalism reborn: Theory, prophecy, and policy.* Chicago: University of Chicago.

Hassel, J., & Scott, S. (1996). Interior design visionaries' explorations of emerging trends. *Journal of Interior Design, 22*(2), 1–14.

Martin, C., & Guerin, D. (2006). The interior design profession's body of knowledge: 2005 edition.

Grand Rapids: Council for Interior Design Accreditation, American Society of Interior Designers, Interior Designers of Canada, International Interior Design Association, and the National Council for Interior Design Qualification.

Orange, D. (1995). *Emotional understanding: Studies in psychoanalytic epistemology.* Guilford Press, New York, NY.

Polanyi, M. (1967). *The tacit dimension.* Gloucester, MA: Peter Smith.

Vorwerk, C. (2002). *Contextual qualifications model: A new approach to designing national qualifications framework (NQF.) qualifications book 1: Skills development research series.* Pretoria, ZA: German Technical Cooperation.

DENISE A. GUERIN, PhD, FIDEC, FASID, IIDA, is a Morse-Alumni distinguished professor and director of interior design, University of Minnesota. She earned bachelor's, master's, and a PhD in interior design. She teaches undergraduate studios, ethics and professional practice, and interior design research methods and advises both master's and PhD students. Guerin's research focuses on post-occupancy evaluation in sustainable buildings and implementation of evidence-based design in practice. She has served as president and vice president of the IDEC Foundation, on several task forces for NCIDQ, and as editor of *JID*. Currently, she serves as a CIDA site visitor and actively participates in Minnesota's interior design practice legislation efforts. She is coauthor of *The Interior Design Profession's Body of Knowledge: Its Definition and Documentation, 2001 and 2006,* and is coordinator of InformeDesign®. Guerin is a recipient of IIDA's Michael Tatum Excellence in Education Award, NCIDQ's Louis Tregue Award, and ASID's Distinguished Educator for 2007.

JAIN KWON, PhD, is a professor of interior design at the Savannah College of Art and Design–Savannah. She earned her PhD in interior design from the University of Minnesota and her MA degree in interior design from Ewha Womans University, Seoul, Korea. Kwon's academic research focuses on the meaning of design and culture; health, safety, and welfare. She has investigated cultural meaning of color in healthcare environments based on the theoretical framework of symbolic interaction. Prior to studying at the University of Minnesota, Kwon taught as an adjunct faculty member and practiced as a certified designer in Korea. She holds a first grade engineer of interior architecture license from the Korea Ministry of Labor. Kwon received the Juran Doctoral Award in 2007 for her work on an integrative design approach to continuous quality development of healthcare environments.

> Is it possible to define *welfare*? Is it important for the interior design profession to define *welfare*?

DENISE A. GUERIN &
JAIN KWON

WELFARE: CAN YOU TALK ABOUT YOUR SPECIALIZED KNOWLEDGE?

Interior designers utilize a systematic, human-centric design process to identify and solve problems. This design process is well documented in the literature and focuses on interior designers' understanding of human behaviors and how people's physical, social, and psychological needs are met through design of interior environments. To do this, interior designers use specialized knowledge gained through education and experience and tested by examination. Use of this specialized knowledge, or their body of knowledge, prevents people from coming to harm in the interiors they design, that is, interior designers protect people's *health*, *safety*, and *welfare*.

This is an often-used phrase, but what does it really mean? The terms *health* and *safety* seem to be pretty straightforward and easy to understand. But, what does *welfare* mean? What is the specialized knowledge from the interior design profession's body of knowledge that is used to protect or enhance people's welfare or well-being? More importantly, can you easily discuss how your specific practice improves people's lives? Can you tell others—your clients, consultants, students, or legislators—what that specialized knowledge is and how you apply it? Finally, can you document success in supporting people's well-being?

HEALTH AND SAFETY

Let's take a quick look at the terms *health* and *safety* first; then we'll move on to *welfare* or *well-being*. The National Council for Interior Design Qualification (NCIDQ) (1999) addressed health and safety as one inseparable component and

defined them "as conforming to codes, regulations, and product performance standards to protect the public" (p. 22). A further look shows that *health* is defined by *Merriam-Webster* as "the condition of being sound in body, mind, or spirit; especially: freedom from physical disease or pain." *Safety* is defined by *Merriam-Webster* as "the condition of being safe from undergoing or causing hurt, injury, or loss." ＊

Health and safety are seen as protection from injury and illness caused by the building, i.e., safe exiting in a fire, use of nonflammable materials and products; and protection from the spread of medical disease (World Health Organization, 2006). We tend to consider that people's health and safety are protected by building codes, standards, and regulations. Additionally, most interior designers associate the term *safety* with specifying slip-resistant flooring, creating interior layouts that meet building and fire codes, and providing a safe place or sanctuary within an environment. For interior designers, the meaning of safety has changed since September 11, 2001. Today, a safe design now considers protection against a host of natural and unnatural hazards, including explosives and biological contaminants such as anthrax (Hoist, 2004).

Interior designers have expanded these basic interpretations of harm prevention and continually added to their own specialized knowledge to design in ways that support people's lives. For example, today most interior designers use sustainable design to reduce toxins and improve indoor air quality or use ergonomic standards to prevent back strain or repetitive

motion injury. And, they consider people's social and psychological needs; in fact, mental health is also a component of people's lives that needs protection.

> Mental health is sometimes thought of as simply the absence of a mental illness but is actually much broader. Mental health is a state of successful mental functioning, resulting in productive activities, fulfilling relationships, and the ability to adapt to change and cope with adversity. Mental health is indispensable to personal well-being, family and interpersonal relationships, and one's contribution to society. (U.S. Department of Health and Human Services, 2000, p. 37)

And, that's where the waters seem to get muddy. We can pretty easily tell others how we protect people's health and safety; we've even documented it pretty well. But, is human welfare, or well-being, separate or distinct from health or even from safety? Welfare is not so clearly defined; yet, we might argue that human well-being is the basis of the value interior designers provide to occupants in the spaces in which they live their lives. The issues, then, are to understand human welfare, determine how to document the application of specialized knowledge to provide it, and learn to tell others about this value we bring to people.

WELFARE

Welfare is a "flourishing condition; the state of doing well especially in relation to good fortune, well-being, or happiness." NCIDQ (1999) defines welfare as "the promotion of social, psychological, and physical well-being of individuals, the community, and the environment" (p. 22). The problem is, it's a difficult term to define explicitly, but we know, implicitly, when it's missing. Well-being is more difficult to document and measure because it's intrinsic. However, we are making progress in measuring some outcomes

of well-being such as employee productivity, workplace performance, and employee satisfaction. Other outcomes are more difficult to measure and relate to the designed environment such as comfort, identity, or stress. Box 3.2 presents a list of terms that can be considered outcomes of welfare or well-being and are part of the interior designer's specialized knowledge.

These terms are ones that interior designers are well acquainted with and recognize as often-stated design goals. Clients want "a workplace that reduces stress or increases sense of place or belonging for their employees." Interior designers have the knowledge with which to produce these outcomes, but we are not yet deft at producing them with regularity and predictability. For example, we know that good wayfinding can reduce people's confusion, increase their efficient movement through a building, and provide overall harmony—if done right. The difficulty is, depending on the user of the space, i.e., child, elder, patient, or shopper, the type of wayfinding cues that are appropriate to each user and building type vary, and the potential for achieving success is based on a myriad of factors.

The relationship between safe environments (good indoor air quality) and welfare (productivity, morale, and well-being) has been shown in numerous studies (Roberts & Guenther, 2006). A sense of identity and belonging can be supported by design features such as a separate, scaled-to-fit children's entrance in a healthcare facility (see Figure 3.3). Or, a feeling of danger and discomfort can be suggested by an unfortunate use of heavy materials on an inward sloping interior wall (see Figure 3.4.). This environment might be quite safe based on the construction method used, but there is a sense of danger or risk, thereby reducing any sense of well-being.

FIGURE 3.3. Entrance to the Children's Imaging and Sedation Center, University of Minnesota Children's Hospital, Minneapolis, Minnesota.

BOX 3.2
HUMAN OUTCOMES OF WELL-BEING

Adaptation	Identity	Refuge
Arousal	Meaning	Satisfaction
Beauty/aesthetics	Performance	Sense of place
Coherence	Personal space	Sense of security
Comfort	Personalization	Stimulation
Crowding	Place attachment	Stress
Cultural identity	Preference	Territory
Harmony	Privacy	Wayfinding
Hierarchy	Prospect	

FIGURE 3.4. Lobby of the McNamara Alumni Center showing historic brick gateway to demolished stadium used as a feature wall, University of Minnesota.

Well-being can be elusive such as confusion brought about by the lack of defined planes in afashion house VIP room (see Figure 3.5), or explicit in the lack of safety in the visual loss of edges on these stairs and landing (see Figure 3.6).

This difficulty is exacerbated by the lack of evaluation or testing of outcomes. We do have specialized knowledge of what provides certain emotional responses, but often the exact nature of the design components are not tested. For example, through research, we know that spaces with daylight and views of nature are healing, restful, and restorative. However, although we know that specific design elements support a sense of comfort, calmness, and security such as spaces whose scale, proportion, materials, and color are pleasing to the user, testing the outcomes remains limited and results are often inconclusive. Another link between the physical environment and human well-being is research that shows that the ability for people to maintain regular physical activity enhances their psychological well-being, may prevent their premature death by increasing health, and may even

FIGURE 3.5. VIP room in Balenciaga, Los Angeles, California. Source: Interior Design, April 2008, pp. 278–279; photo credit: Gregoire Vieille.

FIGURE 3.6. Stairs and landing in lobby area, Museum of Modern Art, New York City. Photo by Jain Kwon, 2008.

reduce their risk of developing depression (U.S. Department of Health and Human Services, 2000). Where climate prevents year-round outdoor activity, physical activity must be provided for within the interior, even a small home. Interior designers have the specialized knowledge to provide this type of space. How many of you have done that? How many of you have evaluated the outcome? Doing so will document the value you have added to people's well-being.

These outcomes of design are the human-centered or social science part of interior designers' specialized knowledge. Employee satisfaction can be supported by access to others, ease of communication, and functional space layout. Performance can be facilitated by appropriate social interaction and meaning can be enhanced by use of products to create boundaries and territories. This does not happen only in public or commercial environments, but residential as well. Residential space can be designed to facilitate family interaction, which is a critical component to healthy family functioning and children's psychological growth and emotional well-being.

The challenge is to be able to express ourselves about the heart of our work, people's well-being—how we support people as they live their lives, physically, socially, and psychologically. Interior designers research people's needs; become informed about codes and regulations; and work with space, light, color, products, finishes, materials, and furnishings to create environments. The depth and breadth of knowledge required to change people's lives is the specialized knowledge of the professional interior designer who contributes to wellness, performance, and productivity, that is, those things known as "welfare." The challenge is to talk about it in a coherent, informed way that educates your clients and other members of the design industry about the value you bring to the project.

You have been educated, gained experience, and then examined in ways that demonstrate your ability to prevent harm from coming to people in the way you design:

> Offices, shared workstations, banks
> Hospitals, assisted-care facilities, operatories
> Clinics, dental offices, emergency care facilities
> Hotels, motels, conference centers
> Restaurants, cafes, banquet facilities, coffee shops
> Casinos, spas, sports arenas, hockey locker rooms
> Classrooms, laboratories, administrative offices, advising centers
> Residences: single and multifamily, condominiums, townhouses, homeless shelters

The problem is, we inherently understand what we do, but we don't often have the opportunity to tell others, and when we do have the opportunity, we are not practiced in the words to use. For example, what do you explicitly reply when asked such questions as:

1. How do you improve people's lives through your design?
2. How do you change the way people work and improve their performance?
3. How do you enhance a child's learning in school?

It seems we can identify examples of supporting and hindering well-being; the challenge is to document it, even anecdotally. This is something all interior designers do and end up contributing to the existing body of knowledge. Can you document how you have accomplished this or other outcomes? Use Box 3.3 as a guide and complete the activities for two or three of your projects. Use the terms from Box 3.2 as part of your design goals; then, write what design component you used to accomplish this outcome of well-being.

We must document design solutions that support well-being so we have evidence of the interior design practitioner's ability to prevent harm. By documenting the outcomes of several projects, you will be building a small database. Share it with others and use it to support a research project that will inform your next design project. Returning to the wayfinding example, measuring the outcomes of many wayfinding design solutions will provide data from which we may be able to predict a more successful solution. This method also supports evidence-based design and is one way to begin to expand our body of knowledge.

Understanding the definition and components of welfare or well-being is the first step; it is part of your current process, you might simply not articulate it yet. Next, document how these well-being outcomes improve your clients' lives. Finally, share this knowledge with others—your clients, your colleagues, your consultants—to demonstrate how interior designers use their specialized knowledge to transform people's lives. And, incidentally, you are adding to the body of knowledge.

BOX 3.3

DOCUMENTING WELFARE/WELL-BEING

Write one example of a design solution in which you used your interior design knowledge (gained through education and/or experience) to protect people's welfare.

Building type: _____
                (bank, hospital, retail store, residence, lobby, residence hall, classroom, etc.)

User type: _____
          (employees, students, teachers, patients, children, etc.)

When: _____
               (year)

Client/project name: _____
               (if not confidential)

Briefly describe design problem/goals:

Briefly describe design solution/client outcome:

REFERENCES

Health. (n.d.) In *Merriam-Webster's online dictionary* (11th ed.). Retrieved April 23, 2009, from www.m-w.com/dictionary/health

Health and Human Services. (2000, November). *Health.* Retrieved April 3, 2008, from http://www.healthypeople.gov/Document/pdf/uih/2010uih.pdf

Hoist, B. (2004). The safety-sustainability connection. *Interiors & Sources, 13*(8), 58–59.

Robers, G., & Guenther, R. (2006). Environmentally responsible hospitals. In Sara O. Marberry (Ed.), *Improving healthcare with better building design.* Chicago, IL: Health Administration Press, pp. 81–107.

Safety. (n.d.) In *Merriam-Webster's online dictionary* (11th ed.). Retrieved April 23, 2009, from www.m-w.com/dictionary/safety

U.S. Department of Health and Human Services. (2000, November). *Healthy people 2010: Understanding and improving health* (2nd ed.). Washington, DC: U.S. Government Printing Office.

World Health Organization. (2006). *Health and safety.* Retrieved April 1, 2008, from http://whqlibdoc.who.int/publications/2006/GPW_eng.pdf

Welfare. (n.d.) In *Merriam-Webster's online dictionary* (11th ed.). Retrieved April 23, 2009, from www.m-w.com/dictionary/welfare

AUTHORS' NOTE

More information about human welfare can be found in Kopec, D. (2006). *Environmental psychology for design.* New York: Fairchild Books.

> EBD provides an adaptable framework within which to further enhance the value of design in providing innovative solutions that align individual needs and organizational intent.
>
> —Janice Barnes

EVIDENCE-BASED DESIGN

OVERVIEW As pointed out by this chapter's authors in their discussion of evidence-based design (EBD), interior design practitioners need to reevaluate their reliance on normative design—design based on available information or what has been done. We should consider EBD as an integral approach to best practice. An ability to create and substantiate excellent design solutions and build the body of knowledge (discussed in Chapter 4) are but two of the benefits of considering an EBD approach.

D. Kirk Hamilton urges the adoption of a practice model that includes "design based on evidence for key decisions" and provides a process by which to achieve this end. Janice Barnes also makes a case for the use of EBD in interior design practice and asks why we aren't moving along at a better pace. She applauds the work of healthcare designers in EBD and lays out some incentives for the rest of the profession.

The next three authors focus on the challenges of EBD and the possible ramifications of not engaging in EBD. Terri Zborowsky describes how we can embed research into interior design practice, the obstacles that await those who do it, and the fate that awaits those who do not. Jay Brand provides an overview of open office solutions over time and directs interior designers to take another look at the evidence before designing the next office environment. Finally, Caren Martin addresses the role EBD plays in the classroom and the role new graduates play in bringing EBD into the firm. These authors are collectively offering the interior design profession a wake-up call of sorts—to accept the EBD challenge.

> Best practices versus best environment
> practice (design process versus building/type
> specific design decision protocol);
> what is the difference? Are they both
> important to the EBD practitioner?

D. KIRK HAMILTON

EVIDENCE-BASED DESIGN: THE HIGHEST FORM OF PROFESSIONALISM

Interior designers are members of the larger body of design professions. As such, they, like architects and engineers, will often find themselves obligated to refer to the best-available, relevant evidence in the course of making important design decisions together with their client. I have been a proponent of addressing key design issues on the basis of evidence from relevant research findings. I feel strongly that design practitioners who are unable to use these techniques and are unable to measure important results from their own projects lack a fundamental set of professional skills (Hamilton, 2004b). I contend that an evidence-based practice model may be the highest form of professionalism.

PROFESSIONS PROTECT THE PUBLIC

A profession has a higher requirement to protect the public health, safety, and welfare than a trade or vocation. Most code requirements and best practices for health and safety are founded

D. KIRK HAMILTON, FAIA, FACHA, is an associate professor of architecture and associate director of the Center for Health Systems & Design at Texas A&M University. His professional degree in architecture is from the University of Texas and his master's degree in organization development is from Pepperdine University. The focus of his academic research is the relationship of evidence-based health facility design to measurable organizational performance. Hamilton is a board certified healthcare architect with 30 years of active practice and is a founding principal emeritus of WHR Architects. He serves on the board of The Center for Health Design and is co-editor of the peer-reviewed, interdisciplinary *Health Environments Research & Design Journal* (*HERD*). Hamilton is a past president of the American College of Healthcare Architects and the AIA Academy of Architecture for Health. He is the coauthor of *Evidence-Based Design for Multiple Building Types.*

in some form of research, such as flame spread ratings or filtration calculations for recirculated air. The prevailing method of determining whether an interior design practitioner is prepared to protect the public is the National Council for Interior Design Qualification (NCIDQ) examination. To sit for the exam, the candidate must have some combination of education and experience (www.ncidq.org).

Some states have adopted title acts in which the title of interior designer is regulated, and a few states have adopted practice acts that prohibit anyone not registered as an interior designer from practicing. The logic for licensure of interior designers, especially in states with a practice act, is to protect the public's health, safety, and welfare. The American Institute of Architects (AIA) has fought practice acts out of fear that architects might lose work, and because it is nearly impossible to tell where architecture stops and interior design begins. As stated in *The Angle*,

> The AIA's position is that interior designers do not have the education or training necessary to protect the health, safety, and welfare of the public, and giving unqualified individuals the responsibility to do so could have severe consequences. Architects are the only professionals who have a broad enough knowledge base to understand the complexities of the whole building, its parts, and how each are interrelated. (Wesolowski, 2008)

I do not agree with the AIA's position and recognize that both architects and interior designers can be found who do not have all the education or experience to fully protect the public on their own. I am a believer in a collaborative model where practitioners with complementary skill sets work together on behalf of the client, and that true professionals will always recognize when they need help from someone with different skills. I, for example, am licensed as if I have all the structural knowledge to protect the public, yet as an architect I would never attempt designing a client's structure without collaborating with a structural engineer.

SPECIALIZATION WITHIN A PROFESSION

Specialized experience can be a clear benefit for the client on complex projects. I believe the client who needs finish selections for a hospital, criminal justice facility, or classroom will be better served if the practitioner performing the work has prior experience with the specific project type. Just as we expect specialization in medicine (I don't need a neurosurgeon for the flu, and neither my family practice physician nor my cardiologist will ever operate on my brain), there is every reason to expect some future in which architects and interior designers will be able to achieve board certification within specialty practices.

In my own case, I am board certified by the American College of Healthcare Architects (ACHA), which requires candidates to have five years of practice after licensure, and the majority of three years' practice specializing in healthcare before their portfolio is examined to qualify them for admission to the ACHA exam (www.healtharchitects.org). Interior designers have moved in a similar manner. The American Academy of Healthcare Interior Designers (AAHID) offers specialty certification based on five years' experience, an interior design or similar degree, passage of the NCIDQ examination, and a portfolio review to be permitted to take the AAHID exam (www.aahid.org). There is a growing interest in evidence-based design (EBD) within the healthcare specialty (Harris et al., 2008). I predict that other specialties will evolve in the same way, but that there will always be roles for generalist designers, as specialization is not required for every project type.

SOME DESIGN REQUIRES NO EVIDENCE

Aesthetic decisions without important consequence might be described as *decor*, the root word of *decoration* and *decorator*. This, I think, defines the difference between the extraordinary work of skilled decorators and the best practice of a professional interior designer. Much exceptional work is done by decorators and artists who in their respective occupations make important contributions to the quality of the built environment, yet the artful does not necessarily rise to the standard of a profession. If the best of design must be both an art and a science, the decorator model would seem to be all art and no science.

DESIGN WITH EVIDENCE

I have contended that there is a distinction between interior decorators and professional interior designers. I further contend that an evidence-based practice is the highest level of professional practice. So, what exactly is evidence-based interior design? The simplest definition might be the intentional use of the best available knowledge to improve interior design decisions. It would be ridiculous to suggest that designers shouldn't use the best available information. Here is a more formal definition from *Evidence-Based Design for Multiple Building Types* (Hamilton & Watkins, 2009):

> Evidence-based design is a process for the conscientious, explicit and judicious use of current best evidence from research and practice in making critical decisions, together with an informed client, about the design of each individual and unique project. (p. 9)

According to this definition, the key elements of EBD include the commitment to a *process* of making design decisions, informed by the *best available evidence* from science, influenced by the *art of judgment* gained through practice, in *collaboration* with an educated client, *for each* unique and individual project. As I see it, these elements together make up a formula for a successful design practice based on solid work and happy clients.

I have previously written about four escalating levels of rigor that differentiate the ways in which design professionals work with evidence in their practice (Hamilton, 2004a). Each successive level obliges the practitioner to continue to do everything required by the previous level. These levels and the knowledge and actions required for each are shown in Table 4.1.

Level One: follow the literature; link design to research. These designers attempt to stay current with the relevant literature and try to incorporate concepts based on this information in projects. They study completed projects for lessons. Success stories are shared, especially with prospective clients. A real weakness is the self-assessment of completed projects, which can lead to bias.

Level Two: commit to hypothesis and measurement. There is an additional commitment to predict the intended outcomes that are expected to result from proposed design concepts, and the need to confirm whether or not the outcomes were achieved. A chain of logic can be developed from the research on which a specific design concept is based to a prediction of an outcome, or a documented design hypothesis.

Frankly, level two is now my personal minimum requirement for evidence-based practice.

Level Three: share the lessons learned. The next level brings a commitment to share what is learned, and to do so without bias or holding back negative results. These designers will speak about their experience and the results of their studies at conferences or publish their stories. They will openly share their results, good and bad. Post-occupancy evaluations are best performed by independent third parties to avoid self-assessment bias.

Level Four: submit to the review of peers. At the highest level, the design practitioner becomes a researcher, independently, or in collaboration with academic researchers. They regularly subject their work to the scrutiny of peer review, which is the best known way to insure objectivity and to increase the credibility of the findings.

It would be unethical, I feel, for a designer to claim an evidence-based process if they do not understand how to conduct diligent searches, use critical interpretation, hypothesize outcomes, and carefully measure results. Unsupported claims in the face of a lack of skills could diminish the reputation of the interior design profession.

TABLE 4.1

FOUR-LEVEL MODEL OF EVIDENCE-BASED DESIGN

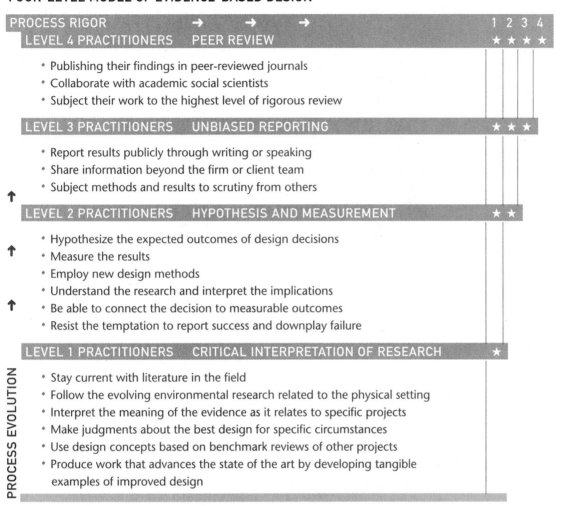

PROCESS RIGOR → → →	1 2 3 4
LEVEL 4 PRACTITIONERS PEER REVIEW	★ ★ ★ ★

- Publishing their findings in peer-reviewed journals
- Collaborate with academic social scientists
- Subject their work to the highest level of rigorous review

LEVEL 3 PRACTITIONERS UNBIASED REPORTING	★ ★ ★

- Report results publicly through writing or speaking
- Share information beyond the firm or client team
- Subject methods and results to scrutiny from others

↑

LEVEL 2 PRACTITIONERS HYPOTHESIS AND MEASUREMENT	★ ★

↑
- Hypothesize the expected outcomes of design decisions
- Measure the results
- Employ new design methods
- Understand the research and interpret the implications

↑
- Be able to connect the decision to measurable outcomes
- Resist the temptation to report success and downplay failure

LEVEL 1 PRACTITIONERS CRITICAL INTERPRETATION OF RESEARCH	★

- Stay current with literature in the field
- Follow the evolving environmental research related to the physical setting
- Interpret the meaning of the evidence as it relates to specific projects
- Make judgments about the best design for specific circumstances
- Use design concepts based on benchmark reviews of other projects
- Produce work that advances the state of the art by developing tangible examples of improved design

PROCESS EVOLUTION

Credit: Kirk Hamilton and WHR Architects Inc. Source courtesy of Wiley & Sons.

EBD is a process of seeking answers to design problems, not a product that supplies ready-made answers or standard solutions pulled out of the practitioner's files. Because the evidence changes daily, and because every project is unique, the implications of research on one project may not be suited to another. The nine-step EBD process illustrated in Table 4.2 is only slightly different than a traditional design process (Hamilton & Watkins, 2009).

Step 1. Establish the client's project goals. Understanding what the client expects or intends is critical to a successful project and every designer will know how to discover the client's goals and objectives.

Step 2. List the practitioner's project goals. The designer must also meet his or her own goals for the project. The firm may need to emphasize profitability, or the project might be an opportunity to showcase a skill for an especially important client.

Step 3. Identify the top 1–3 key design issues. All designers will have been taught to identify issues crucial to the design problem and will be accustomed to focus on these key issues as they initiate the design process. It is impossible to give equal attention to every issue. Current best practice and abbreviated searches should suffice for most, whereas a formal search process can be limited to a manageable number of topics.

Step 4. Convert key design issues into research questions. This step begins to require new skills of a designer. The description of a key design issue is not always in a form that lends itself to research. Each statement of a key design issue must be converted into one or more research questions.

Step 5. Collect information and gather evidence relevant to the research questions. This may require skills the designer hasn't used since graduation, but it is the heart of an evidence-based process. It builds on the skills used in programming and seeks useful information from sources beyond the traditional architectural and interior design domains, often directly related to the client's field. There are nearly infinite possibilities for data that could be relevant to a project. If the designer is tempted to believe the answer is known, an open and inquiring mind is required; if little is known, by contrast, the skill is to carefully narrow the search.

Step 6. Critical interpretation of the evidence. The designer must make judgments about what the multiple forms of information mean to this specific project. Critical thinking must be used to evaluate the collected evidence and the designer must be prepared to deal with conflicting findings. The judgment required makes this step a highly creative moment in the process.

Step 7. Explore design concepts to achieve desired outcomes. Every design practitioner has learned how to develop design concepts intended to produce some intended result.

Step 8. Hypothesize outcomes linked to the evidence-based concepts. The designer must identify the expected outcomes associated with the proposed design concepts. Designers intuitively understand the intention of their design decisions; now they must be documented.

Step 9. Select measures to answer questions posed by the hypotheses. One or more measures by which the hypotheses can be confirmed will need to be identified. It is important to avoid the presumption that these measures will "prove" something about the design; the goal is to determine whether the hypothesis was "supported," or not. Design practitioners performing this kind of applied research can produce important findings that should be shared with the field.

TABLE 4.2
EVIDENCE-BASED DESIGN PROCESS

	TASK	ACTIVITY
1	Identify the Client's Goals	Note the most important and facility-related global and project-based goals
2	Identify the Firm's Goals	Understand the firm's strategic, project, and evidence-based design objectives
3	Identify the Top 1–3 Key Design Issues	Narrow the possible choices; work on high impact decisions
4	Convert Design Issues to Research Questions	Reframe statement of design issues to become research topics
5	Gather Information *(Benchmark Examples, Literature Sources, Internal Studies)*	Infinite possibilities must be narrowed; limited perspectives must be expanded
6	Critical Interpretation of the Evidence	No direct answers; requires open-minded creativity, balance, and critical thinking
7	Create Evidence-Based Design Concepts	Based on creative interpretation of the implications of research findings
8	Develop Hypotheses	Predict the expected results of the implementation of your design
9	Select Measures	Determine whether your hypothesis has been supported

Credit: Kirk Hamilton and WHR Architects Inc. Source courtesy of Wiley & Sons.

I am convinced that this model of practice has the potential to produce higher-quality projects with fully documented superior results. It seems to me, therefore, that there is a moral obligation for the interior designer to use the best available information on behalf of the client. It further seems that the profession will benefit if project outcomes are measured and reported. Credibility of the profession will rise, and the use of better information will result in advances for the entire field.

CONCLUSION

It is my strong opinion that interior designers who have obtained an appropriate education, preferably accredited by the Council for Interior Design Accreditation (CIDA, formerly FIDER), and have passed the NCIDQ examination are qualified for the professional title available in more than 20 states. Those who practice in states that lack licensure laws may still confirm their qualifications with the credentials they have earned. Frankly, I believe those who fail to sit for the professional examination are openly declaring their lesser status as practitioners of the interior decorator vocation or trade. Finally, I believe that the next higher level of professional practice is the adoption of a practice model that includes design based on evidence for key decisions.

I do not contend that what I have written in this brief essay is anything more than one man's personal opinion, no matter how strongly I feel.

I am not a practicing interior designer, although I often played a collaborative role in the design of interior environments during my 30 years of architectural practice. I was "grandfathered" as a registered interior designer in Texas until I relinquished my license in 2004 as I made the transition to academia. All of that notwithstanding, I feel that professionalism for interior designers is based in education, experience, ethics, and contributions that return something to the field. Surely interior designers who obtain rigorous design education that includes a basic understanding of research and how to use it, pass the NCIDQ examination, continue to learn from their research-informed practice, act with integrity, and share findings related to their own projects with the field can be described as EBD professionals practicing at the highest level. I fondly hope it becomes the minimum standard for best practice.

REFERENCES

Hamilton, D. (2004a). Four levels of evidence-based practice: Architecture & environmental research. *AIA/J*, Fall. Retrieved January 3, 2008, from http://www.aia.org/nwsltr_aiaj.cfm?pagename=aiaj_a_20041201_fourlevels

Hamilton, D. K. (2004b, January). The new evidence-based designers. *Interiors & Sources*, pp. 58–59.

Hamilton, D., & Watkins, D. (2009). *Evidence-based design for multiple building types*. New York: Wiley & Sons.

Harris, D., Joseph, A., Becker, F., Hamilton, D., Shepley, M., & Zimring, C. (2008). *A practitioner's guide to evidence-based design*. Concord, CA: Center for Health Design.

Wesolowski, H. (2008, January 31). *Interior design lobby seeks licensure in several states*. Message posted to *The Angle*, AIA Archiblog. Retrieved January 31, 2009, from http://blog.aia.org/angle/2008/01/interior_design_lobby_seeks_li.html

> Does EBD support a human behavior approach, i.e., does it support interior design's strength in regards to accommodating human needs and behavior? Justifying "what I know" with EBD; how does or doesn't that occur?

JANICE BARNES

EVIDENCE-BASED DESIGN: AN INTERIOR DESIGNER'S OPPORTUNITY

Private and public sector organizations now seek evidence that supports design decisions related to capital investments due to the inherent tension between an organization's understanding of its work and an interior designer's understanding of the processes for place-making. Invariably these are two worldviews that seek common ground through design processes, but rarely are cultivated externally to those processes. Current marketplace conditions escalate tensions around decision-making and the degree of risks associated with the same.

As a result, traditional design processes offer little in terms of emotional or capital comfort for real estate decision-makers, who are quite exposed within their organizations in their roles as place-makers as their decisions typically indicate significant capital investments in renovation, relocation/renovation, expansion, or new construction. Given the magnitude of most building projects, the individuals who provide final approval on these investments are

JANICE BARNES, PhD, a principal in the multidisciplinary design practice of Perkins+Will, is the national discipline leader for the planning and strategies practice. As a licensed architect, Barnes brings over 19 years of practice experience and a significant research background to the firm. Her design project experience spans a number of organizational types including corporate, civic, education, and science and technology clients where she focuses on work practices in the context of environmental solutions to better serve client needs. She continues to publish and lecture nationally on these relationships. Barnes received her PhD and MS in architecture from the University of Michigan; she has a MArch, and a BArch. She is a member, reviewer, and former board member of EDRA, an ad-hoc reviewer for the *Journal of Interior Design*, and a member of CoreNet, CIDA's Standards Council, and the University of Michigan College of Architecture and Urban Planning Alumni Board.

typically under enormous scrutiny to both justify the need for the investment in the context of the business and to assure that the investment provides appropriate value for the money.

Evidence-based design (EBD) does exactly this. EBD provides an adaptable framework within which to further enhance the value of design in providing innovative solutions that align individual needs and organizational intent. By providing both clarity of question and evidentiary support, EBD offers decision-makers notable resources for their capital investment decisions. And, as EBD creates a partnering dialogue between interior designers and real estate decision-makers, the role of the interior designer is further enhanced while mutually enhancing that of the real estate decision-maker. As research has long shown, mutual growth creates positive effects in relationships (Baker-Miller, 1986). This mutual growth is an unintended outcome of EBD that further grounds relationships and further enhances the body of knowledge within interior design.

AN INTERIOR DESIGNER'S OPPORTUNITY

As interior designers seek opportunities to provide long-standing value to clients, gaining an awareness of this inherent tension and the ways in which EBD may improve process and outcome is an important step in further enriching the body of knowledge within the discipline and the value of that knowledge for a variety of client types. To situate this statement, having this knowledge means that an interior designer is "capable of participating with the requisite competence in the complex web of relationships among people and activities" (Gherardi, Nicolini, & Odella, 1998, p. 274).

The interior designer's opportunity is to deftly position EBD as a resource within the context of an organization and its work or its complex web. The specificity to the business of the organization is critical. General outcomes tend toward the irrelevant in real estate decision-making. Real estate leaders instead seek very specific applications that relate directly to the decision at hand within the context of their business. Examples include:

1. Demand/capacity confirmation to assure that there is a real need for the capital investment and that other options are fully explored
2. Feasibility assessment to assure that potential reuse and low-cost strategies are compared to proposed new construction
3. Financial impact assessments to assure that the value for money is in alignment with the business plan for the organization or its various departments involved with the capital change

HISTORY

There is precedent for this level of specificity between organizational intent and interior design decision-making, as EBD is by no means a new concept. Although the coining of the term *evidence-based design* by The Center for Health Design and their ongoing research in this area certainly brought renewed focus to the use of research in design decision-making, the legacy of organizational research/environmental design dates to work early in the last century by Taylor, Mayo, and others. "Scientific Management" or "Taylorism" formed the crux of organization/environmental studies during the early part of the last century (Taylor, 1910).

Major theorists/theories included Frederick Taylor/Taylorism and Elton Mayo/Hawthorne Studies (Harvard Fatigue Laboratory, 1927-1932). Over the next 75 years, research on the relationships between environments and the intended work of an organization continued to evolve (BOSTI, 1984; Duffy, 1974; Lave & Wenger, 1991; Leffingwell, 1917; Maslow, 1954; McCoy, 2000; Vischer, 2005; Wineman, 1986).

As a result of this history, there is an extraordinary archive of published research available to the interior design community. Unfortunately, it may be argued that the majority of the published research is not fundamentally grounded in the mental models that real estate decision-makers typically follow. Nor is this research typically published in the press associated with real estate. In fact, recent continuing education seminar titles in corporate real estate consisted of the following:

> Advanced Lease Analysis
> Advanced Real Estate Negotiation
> Corporate Real Estate Finance
> Corporate Real Estate Management in Today's Economy
> Managing Effectively in Global Markets
> Performance Management
> Portfolio Disposition Strategies, Portfolio Management
> Real Estate Transactions
> Impact on Corporate Financial Statements and Strategic Sourcing
> Creating the Right Delivery Model

These are not the seminars that explore findings from the *Journal of Interior Design*, the *Journal of Architecture and Planning Research*, the *Journal of Environmental Psychology*, or even the white papers associated with firms within the interior design industry.

Moreover, in the last 10 years, CoreNet, an international association of professionals who work in some facet of corporate real estate, the *Wall Street Journal (WSJ)*, and *Business Week* independently escalated the topic of design integration as a core business principle. The attention therein suggests that design integration is not initiated from within the design industry, but is in fact in the corporate real estate industry wherein real estate leaders identified the inherent value of aligning design decisions with organizational intent. How is that possible, given that interior designers and researchers or design researchers have been publishing peer-reviewed research in this area for over 75 years?

The question does not discount the history of research in design, but it does emphasize a quiet tension between interior design, industry-focused research, an interior designer's innovations in place-making, and a real estate leader's evaluation of the same. If the findings are not contextually situated, and therefore relevant to the audience that must act on those findings, there will be no action until the audience *finds* that contextual relevance. The escalated attention from *WSJ, Business Week*, and CoreNet is an example of such *found relevance*.

BEST PRACTICE: THE CENTER FOR HEALTH DESIGN

As a comparison, The Center for Health Design (CHD) offers an excellent example of how designers and researchers co-create context and value for clients in the healthcare arena. The work at CHD cultivates the development of common ground between healthcare industry executive leadership and designers who provide place-making for that industry. This effort supersedes the specifics of any one project or any single design firm. Instead, it focuses on the growth of a knowledge base, the development and assessment of associated tools, and the dissemination of findings—all in the service of escalating the value of design decision-making in the context of the mental models of healthcare executives.

From their Web site, CHD (2009) notes that "since 1993, The Center for Health Design has been actively engaged in initiating research to promote the use of evidence-based design to create healing environments in hospitals, clinics, physician offices, nursing homes, and other healthcare facilities." They further identify "the Pebble Project® as a partnership with more than 36 providers nationwide whose goal is to provide documented examples of how using evidence-based design has improved the institution's quality of care and financial performance." (For more information on this resource, see www.healthdesign.org.)

Note the context "improved the institution's quality of care and financial performance" (CHD, 2009). This is not a traditional design statement. This is a statement that directly relates to organizational intent and the success of the business of the organization. CHD's use of EBD as a framework for connecting the value of design that aligns individual needs and organizational intent is an example for the industry. Its basis is patient care and financial success. That example is yet to be replicated outside of healthcare, even though the CHD/EBD lead has been in place for over a decade. And, a strong premise of EBD in general has been in place since the early 1970s. Why is this the case?

INCENTIVES

In a paper presented at the Design Research Society Conference, Sailer, Budgen, Lonsdale, and Penn (2008) suggest the need for an EBD model for office architecture. Watkins and Hamilton (2008) suggest EBD across multiple typologies. With these and other authors lamenting the lack of EBD frameworks outside of healthcare, and with real estate industry representatives addressing the need for more evidentiary support for real estate decision-making, the situation appears ripe for further development. But, is there incentive within other industries to make this sort of investment? Within healthcare, there are two contingents that helped EBD escalate to its current status. In looking at both, incentives in healthcare become quite clear.

The first contingent is the existence of an industry-specific parallel theory. In healthcare that is evidence-based medicine (EBM). The history of EBM is lengthy and well-published, but the basic premise is this: before making a medical care decision, physicians consider the evidence of precedents in similar contexts. In fact, some sources, such as the U.S. Preventative Services Task Force, even stratify the evidence in terms of relevance. This history of evidence-based decision-making is native to the healthcare industry, and therefore EBD is situated soundly on the foundation of the same. There is no theoretical leap required to link EBD to EBM.

The second contingent is that of risk. The healthcare industry is fundamentally challenged with both preventative care and remedial actions. The risk of appropriate response to either is the health and overall well-being of the patient. When risk is high in any organization, systems are comparatively complex and evidence as well as redundancy of backup are required (Weick, 1995; Weick & Roberts, 1993). EBD in healthcare focuses on risk aversion through initial inquiry, predictive modeling, and occupancy evaluation. As such, it provides immediate value in decision-making that is contextually focused to the very real and immediate risks in healthcare environments.

When considering EBD in other industries, the first question is perhaps this: are there industry-specific contingents that EBD must address to be both relevant and persuasive? For example, in corporate real estate, is there a parallel theory to EBD that requires evidentiary support for real estate decision-making?

If EBM is the basis for the same in healthcare, what drives EBD in corporate real estate? Is there an associated risk that requires real estate leaders to develop risk aversion modeling and redundancy measures? With both questions, the leap from healthcare to corporate real estate in general is significant. Concerns in healthcare focused on the life of patients have no direct parallel in corporate real estate.

What then is the potential for EBD in real estate decision-making? What questions require or would be better answered with evidentiary support? By understanding the difficult questions facing corporate real estate decision-makers, and providing specific evidentiary support to the same, EBD may offer a new dialogue between interior designers and real estate decision-makers. As an example, timely questions within corporate real estate focus on limiting marketplace exposure (i.e., costs) through compression planning, lease elimination, increased hoteling and/or telecommuting, and densification. The bottom line of all of these efforts is typically the bottom line, or reducing it. The corporate real estate leader is motivated to reduce costs while maintaining the necessary support for employees. In turn, this leader asks an interior design partner to assist in this endeavor through one of the cost reduction tactics noted above. The interior designer is motivated to gain the contract, conduct the work, and to provide a quality design product that answers the questions asked.

In this context, how might an interior designer best support a client if the question is focused on how to reduce costs? What knowledge could an interior designer provide to improve decision-making and to enhance immediate projects and the long-term relationship? Again, having such knowledge means that the interior designer is "capable of participating with the requisite competence in the complex web of relationships among people and activities" (Gherardi et al., 1998, p. 274). Moreover, what do interior designers need to know to work within the web of relationships in corporate real estate? What structures do interior designers need to understand to situate industry-specific knowledge and design decision-making? How might interior designers provide more than a design-based response to limiting marketplace exposure? Might EBD offer a way to explore the relationships among people and activities that drive the organization's business?

In a recent case, a design team explored these questions by asking the following about a specific client organization:

> What do we know about the value stream of the business, and what do we need to better understand?

> What do we see in our practice with this business that might be improved with a more focused approach to design decision-making, and how does that relate to the value stream?

> What evidence do we have that situates this knowledge within the values of the client?

> What are other organizations doing that directly relate to this same set of issues?

By posing these questions and evaluating results from post-occupancy evaluations (POEs), best practices workshops among peer firms, and comparing these to upcoming projects, the team identified a number of opportunities for real estate cost savings that extended beyond the typical space reduction strategies noted previously. In systematically evaluating these as opportunities within the financial metrics of the client organization, the team initiated a new dialogue with the client, demonstrating value that directly related to the real estate team's assessment of risk (e.g., excess costs) and user satisfaction (e.g., turnover costs).

Because this knowledge came unexpectedly (*without* immediate cost and *with* immediate benefit) from the design team, the real estate team engaged the design team in a completely new way. In opening the dialogue for cost savings in areas that are complementary to the core contract, the design team also began building bridges with associated disciplines within the client organization.

Through both providing immediate value (i.e., cost savings) and initiating a unique dialogue (as a support partner), the design team changed the nature of the collaboration and enriched the overall relationship with the real estate team. Moreover, because all supporting materials were evidentiary-based, the real estate team gained immediate comfort with the concepts at hand and their applicability to future real estate decisions.

This effort did not create a new model of EBD for corporate real estate. Nor did it build a complement to CHD/EBD in healthcare. Instead, this effort was the first step of ensuring that the design team expanded their language to focus on that of the client, and by providing a new lens with which to assess the team's contribution to the value stream, changed the nature of the relationship, building a bridge, and providing immediate and long-lasting value in the client relationship. And, that is where EBD in healthcare gained its initial footing: providing immediate and long-term value to the core business of the healthcare industry through the identification of risks associated with design decision-making and the assessment of the costs of those risks to the financial performance of the organization.

CONCLUSION

As Sailer et al. (2008) and Hamilton and Watkins (2008) suggest, the opportunity to advance EBD in multiple industries is clearly present. The task of the interior design profession is to identify the value streams and associated performance indicators of these other industries and to invest in the development of collaborative models of EBD that are industry-specific (i.e., banking versus healthcare); collaborative (i.e., multiple firms, multiple points of view, voice of the client); and focused on the overall improvement of the provisioning of environments for these industries. Interior designers who choose to participate in the development of this model, much like the team at CHD, will find both immediate and long-term value as trusted advisors with their client organizations.

REFERENCES

BOSTI. (1984). *Using office design to increase productivity, Volumes one and two*. Buffalo: Workplace Design and Productivity.

The Center for Health Design. (2009). Home page. Retrieved February 21, 2009, from www .healthdesign.org

Duffy, F. (1974). Office design and organizations: The testing of a hypothetical model. *Environment and Planning, B*(1), 217–235.

Gherardi, S., Nicolini, D., & Odella, F. (1998). Toward a social understanding of how people learn in organizations. *Management Learning, 29*(3), 273–298.

Hamilton, D., & Watkins, D. (2008). *Evidence-based design for multiple building types*. New York: John Wiley and Sons.

Lave, J., & Wenger, E. (1991). *Situated learning*. Cambridge: Cambridge University Press.

Leffingwell, W. (1917). *Scientific office management*. Chicago: A.W. Shaw.

Maslow, A. (1954). *Motivation and personality*. New York: Harper.

Mayo, E. (1933). *The human problems of an industrial organization*. New York: Viking Press.

McCoy, J. (2000). The creative work environment: The relationship of the physical environment and creative teamwork at a state agency: A case study. PhD Dissertation. University of Wisconsin-Milwaukee.

Miller, J. (1986). What do we mean by relationships? *White Paper Series*. Wellesley Massachusetts: Wellesley Center for Women.

Sailer, K., Budgen, A., Lonsdale, N., & Penn, A. (2007, October). *Changing the architectural profession: Evidence-based design, the new role of the user and a process-based approach*. Paper Presented at Ethics and the Professional Culture Conference October 5–6 inCluj-Napoca, Romania.

Taylor, F. (1910). *Principles of scientific management*. New York: Harper.

Vischer, J. (2005). *Space meets status: Designing workplace performance*. UK: Routledge.

Weick, K. (1995). *Sensemaking in organizations*. Thousand Oaks, CA: Sage.

Weick, K., & Roberts, K. (1993). Collective mind in organizations: Heedful interrelating on flight decks. *Administrative Science Quarterly, 38*(3), 357–381.

Wineman, J. (1986). Current issues and future directions. *Behavioral Issues in Office Design*. New York: Van Nostrand-Reinhold.

> What place does EBD have in interior design? What place should it have? Is EBD a trend or a paradigm shift?

TERRI ZBOROWSKY

INTEGRATING RESEARCH INTO A REFLECTIVE PRACTICE OF DESIGN: MOVING INTERIOR DESIGN INTO THE FUTURE

Design as a discipline means design studied on its own terms, within its own rigorous culture, based on a reflective practice of designing.

—Nigel Cross, *Design Research Quarterly* (2006, p. 5)

As both an interior design practitioner and researcher, I believe that we can effectively integrate research into practice. How successful we are depends on how we approach both the problem and the solution. If we see this as an opportunity to challenge our traditional approach both to education and practice, then we can not only integrate research in practice, but we can sustain it by embedding it into our interior design process.

This essay will outline issues that impede the full integration of research into design practice and discuss the challenges that reside in academia and practice that prevent full integration. For each challenge, opportunities will be

TERRI ZBOROWSKY, PhD, received her doctoral degree in interior design from the University of Minnesota and a BID from the University of Manitoba. For seven years she worked as a registered nurse in Canada. Zborowsky has been at Ellerbe Becket for 12 years, where as a medical planner she focuses on inpatient settings with an interest in the design of nursing units and emergency departments. As director of research, she oversees all research and education efforts. Actively involved in both primary and secondary research, Ellerbe Becket was one of the first firms to create this unique position. Zborowsky also teaches a collaborative, interdisciplinary course that joins the University of Minnesota's Center for Spirituality and Healing and College of Design entitled "Creating Optimal Healing Environments." She was recently selected as "1 of 20 making a difference" in healthcare design by *Healthcare Design* magazine.

offered that currently exist, which will move the integration of research forward. Full integration of research into practice will require a paradigm shift, which this shift provides a tremendous opportunity to advance the interior design profession.

HISTORY/BACKGROUND

Prior to moving this thesis forward, some context is needed. A thorough history of the background of research in the design profession is given by Friedman (2000). He explains that for many years design was taught through apprenticeships—designers were mentored in the field. It is only in recent years that design has found its way into the university setting where both architecture and interior design have been formalized as disciplines of study. Many university-based interior design programs have surfaced through home economics departments, now often known as Human Ecology. Other interior design programs can be found in architecture departments, sometimes referred to as Colleges of Design.

Interior design programs located in land-grant universities have added research to the curriculum to advance the interior design body of knowledge. Currently, most research activity in interior design programs occurs at the graduate level. Very few undergraduate programs offer research opportunities at the undergraduate level. This brings me to the first challenge facing the integration of research into practice—the education of interior designers.

EDUCATING FUTURE PRACTITIONERS

THE CHALLENGE

All the practitioners with whom I work would agree that the notion of research is part of their design process. For example, many practitioners would agree that research occurs during dialogue with their clients in the programming phase. Others would suggest that research is an Internet search on the latest medical procedure that their client is considering for a clinic room. They are right; their understanding of research is as a broad term and can be used to describe data-gathering activities that typically occur during programming. Information practitioners gathering data that is used to inform design decisions on a project-by-project basis is one aspect of research. To build our knowledge collectively, as a discipline, we need to formalize our approach to research by conducting systematic research. In the future, designers will still be surveying clients and utilizing the Internet as a data collection technique for individual projects. It is important to not dissuade this type of activity, but, at the same time, if a systematic approach can work and the resulting data can be used to add to the body of knowledge for interior design, then this approach should be encouraged. To accomplish this goal, research must be integrated further into interior design curriculum.

Part of the obstacle to teaching research and research methods has to do with the faculty available to teach in design schools. Becker (2008) noted that architect educators are "disinterested and often disdainful" (p. 2) when it comes to teaching the role of research in studio classes. This statement could be attributed, at least in part, to the lack of research education in the design field, which may include some interior designer educators as well. However, there is a relationship between what is taught in interior design programs and what is done in practice. Studio instructors and design academics should be prepared to teach research in all studio classes—such as how to integrate components of research into each project—and help students to understand the application of research to improve their designs.

Another challenge that has befallen interior design in academia is the lack of cohesive theoretical frameworks used to underpin design solutions. Theories are needed to advance the discipline as well as to serve as a framework to drive theory development. This concern directly impacts the question of how to integrate research into practice. The interior design profession lacks both formalized theory development as well as validated research tools. These are no small challenges to solve, but the solutions greatly influence the ability to integrate research into practice. Theoretical frameworks and validated research tools are needed to provide practitioners with systematic methods to study the impact of design decisions on the users impacted by the design. The interior design profession needs to encourage approaches to teaching research in both the graduate and undergraduate programs, particularly how research fits into studio classes.

THE OPPORTUNITIES

Just as design requires a certain knowledge base, research has its own philosophies, theories, and methods. Research is a systematic, rigorous, and documented process that requires a certain skill set. Much like interior design, the act of research requires practice and mentoring. There are gaps in our knowledge base that should be filled with courses that focus on teaching interior design philosophy, theory, and research. The need to integrate research into our interior design programs seems apparent just as it is being done at the graduate level for research-based degrees. Research is a tool used to improve design, and as such, should be taught in all first-professional interior design programs, regardless of the degree offered.

Undergraduate students need to be made aware of a philosophy of science for the discipline, interior design theory, and research methods. They may not have to complete a research project that is comparable to a graduate thesis; however, they need to understand how research methods can be used to gather data during design, how to set up design hypotheses (see Zeisel, 2006, for a complete discussion), and how to consider testing these hypotheses. In other words, future practitioners need to learn how to integrate research into practice. They need to discover how research fits into design process, much like any other design tool. Research can be used to help us understand how our designs impact the health, safety, and well-being of the public. If we successfully teach research to undergraduates and graduates alike, we can declare that a paradigm shift has occurred. What a great opportunity for all of us to advance our knowledge base.

DEFINING RESEARCH

THE CHALLENGE

The question posed for this essay included whether or not I felt that evidence-based design (EBD) was a trend or paradigm shift. I feel I must address my concerns about the term *evidence-based design* as it relates to my understanding of research. Stankos and Schwarz (2007) offer a valid critique as they outlined the differences between EBD and evidence-based medicine (EBM). EBD and EBM may have similar intentions, but EBM draws on many more studies than we have amassed in design. Furthermore, limited validity and reliability of many published design studies that have been conducted do not allow for predictions to be drawn. This does not discredit an empirical approach to data collection and analysis, but it does suggest that the types of research methods relevant to studying medical outcomes may not be the same research methods needed to study the impact of interior design.

One challenge to the interior design profession is to consider that our notions of quantitative research may not apply in all circumstances to the phenomenon we seek to study in design. At its very core, design is experiential, yet experiences are hard to quantify. As interior designers seek to understand how our designs make a difference, this approach to research, understanding the experience of design space, may be different from prediction. Perhaps the richest research design to study space is one that uses a multiple method approach so the designer can understand the meaning of elements of the designed space as well as have quantifiable data to support the meaning uncovered. The methods of research that the profession of interior design adopts impacts students who will engage in future research as well as practitioners who will carry out studies in practice.

THE OPPORTUNITIES

As a discipline, we need to define what research means to us. I am frustrated when I hear practitioners or educators tell me that research is something done only during programming. Design, philosophy, theory, and research must progress together, not in isolation. This is a much larger discussion than I can do justice to here, but I would encourage readers to review Groat and Wang's (2002) chapter on design in relation to research as well as Friedman's (2000; 2003) discussion of a progressive research program for design knowledge.

A holistic dialogue of design, philosophy, theory, and research in this manner is a task for students, educators, and practitioners in which to engage together. Interior design educators, challenge your students to explore these relationships, to help us all define what research means to design, and what design means to research. By challenging students to think about the role of research in design, we will be creating future practitioners who have examined these relationships and are positioned to help us understand what this means to practice.

We also must agree to disagree. Rigorous discourse is an aid in the progression of knowledge. We must encourage theory testing and the use of alternative research methods. For example, we do not fully understand how the brain works, particularly related to memory recall or spatial thinking. As we develop this understanding further, we may need to adapt our theories and research methods to this changing paradigm. As researchers, we strive to define theory and methods most appropriate to the questions we ask, but we must remember to remain open to our changing world of knowledge.

Practice-based researchers are in a unique position to advance our discipline as we conduct primary and secondary research to explore the most appropriate theoretical models and research methods for our practice-based inquiries. We have a unique ability to advance aspects of research and theory through the direct application of our findings. The activities of practice-based research fall into the category of field research or action-based research. We have an opportunity to impact design decision-making during the design process, to document our findings, and to contribute to our larger body of knowledge.

INTEGRATING RESEARCH INTO PRACTICE

THE CHALLENGE

The practice of design exists in a very competitive market. Many architectural and interior design firms do not want to share their internal information with other firms because their information is proprietary. I predict that companies that do not embrace sharing and integrating new knowledge successfully will have a hard time keeping practitioners who are trained to seek this out. It is time for architectural and interior design firms to focus on ways that they

TABLE 4.3
RESEARCH ACTIVITIES RELATED TO PHASES OF DESIGN

PHASES OF DESIGN	SUGGESTED RESEARCH ACTIVITIES
Pre-Design/ Master Planning	Literature review focused on building type or specific issues identified Historical analysis
Schematic Design	Identify design hypotheses and design interventions Room mock-up evaluation User surveys Person or place-based observation Conduct research on existing spaces (for pre- and post-test designs)
Design Development	Clarify and integrate design interventions Develop research design (framework) for the design hypotheses identified earlier
Construction Documentation	Limited research design activity at this time
Post-Occupancy	Post-occupancy evaluations

can best impact the future of our profession, to consider what role they have in moving forward our profession and how they would value the skills of research in practitioners.

Practice-based funding for research is another challenge. Little money is spent on research and development in architectural and interior design firms. Most firms operate on a profit margin that does not allow for money to be set aside to grow design knowledge. The challenge is how to calculate what percent of the firm's profit should be dedicated to research activities. This is a particular challenge for smaller firms that have limited resources.

THE OPPORTUNITIES

Integrating research into practice can and does take many forms. Not all firms will be able to—or will want to—add research to their list of services. However, if we can teach research as a tool to design students, then all students will come equipped to utilize research more effectively in their process. With research taught effectively in

academia, firms will be engaged through synthesis when these students become practitioners.

Practice-based research exists on a continuum. Some firms conduct secondary research by gathering and synthesizing existing studies to help inform design decisions. Other firms conduct primary research to inform design decision-making. For example, one firm conducted a study on noise levels related to carpeting or resilient flooring in a particular type of hospital unit to help the firm select a flooring finish. In this way, research informed their decision-making. Other researchers conduct studies that are theory-driven. The research team at Ellerbe Becket completed an empirical study on the impact of decentralized nursing stations on nursing work environments based on a work-environment theory. Others have documented ideas relating specific research activities to phases in design (Geboy & Keller, 2007; Groat & Wang, 2002; Ziesel, 2007). A review of research activities related to design phases can be found in Table 4.3.

During pre-design or during a master planning stage, secondary design research can be gathered to help identify design issues, based on existing literature. Historical analysis falls nicely into this phase. Clients may also identify a specific need or question during the initial stages of design. Early design phases are also the best time to identify the design hypotheses and proposed design interventions that will be implemented to overcome the design challenges identified. Schematic design is an appropriate time to build room mock-ups to be tested as well as to prepare for pre- and post-test studies. Other research activities that may be used at this time include conducting user surveys or behavioral observations. Gathering this type of information along with the programming and schematic design exercises ensures that all information will converge to inform design decision-making during the earliest stages possible.

These activities can continue to a lesser degree during the design development phase, but with design refinement occurring now, it is better to limit studies to specific design interventions, such as deciding which type of medical gas delivery system to use in a patient room, rather than test an issue such as the room size. It is important to note that research should be used to inform design, not disrupt its progress.

Research should be conducted following occupancy. Much has been written on post-occupancy evaluations (POE). Although conducting a POE seems a logical and necessary integration of research into practice, it is my experience in healthcare design that POEs are the most difficult form of research to get initiated. After a space is occupied, clients often feel that POEs are disruptive to the occupants of a new space. Introducing the idea of a POE to the client through an early research brainstorming session may help with later dialogue.

Finally, we all need to encourage funding sources for research in practice. Partnering with nonprofits is one way to find funding sources for important studies. Nonprofit clients are very willing to lend their expertise to proposals, which brings diversity to the study as well as builds our knowledge base. Healthcare clients understand the inherent value of research, but this level of commitment can be achieved in other building types as well. Another source of research partnering is in the manufacturing world. There are many industry partners who also want to move forward our knowledge base, largely because many of them are interior designers as well. If your research questions are well grounded and relevant, then you will find others with whom to share your efforts. Professors who work in land-grant universities are a great place to start.

INTEGRATING RESEARCH INTO PRACTICE: THE DEVELOPMENT OF A REFLECTIVE PRACTICE OF DESIGN

Integrating research into practice is a complex problem, one that will require more than practitioners simply becoming aware of research, reading research articles, and stating design hypotheses. The real integration of research into practice will occur when research becomes part of a reflective practice of design. Schon's (1983) concept of reflective practice is the best example. He describes reflective practice as the form of bringing unconscious patterns and tacit understandings to conscious understanding through articulation. I see reflective practice as an iterative process, not unlike Zeisel's (2006) design development spiral. In design, each phase offers a natural time for reflection— a time to reexamine the problem-solving process with others, or alone. Interior designers naturally engage in this activity.

I am advocating for the integration of research into this process. Research should be viewed as a tool to enhance the interior designers' decision making while they reflect on the issues at hand. Research should be integrated into an interior designer's thought process with the tools of research becoming another way to gather information. Designers do not need to know how to conduct primary research studies themselves—larger firms or land-grant universities have trained design researchers to conduct more complicated studies—but the designer should be able to articulate research questions related to their design. They should be able to state design hypotheses and have an idea of how it will be studied either during design or after. The notion of research should be part of the design process of a reflective practitioner.

CONCLUSION

It is hard to know whether research will be sustainable in interior design or architectural practice even if it is the mainstay of many university programs. There are many challenges to overcome both in academia and in practice. Paradigm shifts will be needed. In academia, further curriculum development is needed. In practice, funding and valid resources are needed. In both, more work has to be done to define and develop design, research, philosophy, and theory for interior designers. However, for every obstacle there are at least as many opportunities. The profession of interior design and the challenges that it faces as we move our profession into the 21st century and beyond must be seen as opportunities to enhance and change our process, our educational systems, and the practice of our profession. The integration of research in our reflective practice provides such an opportunity.

REFERENCES

Becker, F. (2008). Closing the research-design gap. *Implications, 5*(10). Retrieved February 14, 2008, from http://www.informedesign.umn.edu/_news/oct_v05r-p.pdf

Cross, N. (2006). Forty years of design research. *Design Research Quarterly, 1*(2), 3–5.

Friedman, K. (2000). Creating design knowledge: From research to practice. *IDATER 2000 Conference.* Loughborough: Loughborough University.

Friedman, K. (2003). Theory construction in design research: Criteria; approaches and methods. *Design Studies, 24*(6), p. 507–522.

Geboy, L., & Keller, A. (2007). Research in practice: The design researcher perspective. *Implications, 4*(11). Retrieved March 15, 2008, from http://www.informedesign.umn.edu/_news/nov_v04r-p.pdf

Groat, L., & Wang, D. (2002). *Architectural research methods.* New York: John Wiley & Sons.

Schon, D. (1983). *The reflective practitioner: How professionals think in action.* London: Temple Smith.

Stankos, M., & Schwartz, B. (2007). Evidence-based design in healthcare: A theoretical dilemma. *Interdisciplinary Design & Research e-journal, 1*(1), 1–15.

Zeisel, J. (2006). *Inquiry by design.* New York: W. W. Norton.

AUTHOR'S NOTE

The thoughts represented here are not just my own, but arrived here after many hours spent in discussions with my peers and colleagues. I am grateful to Lou Bunker Hellmich and Justin Wilwerding for their critique of this essay.

> What does the evidence tell the interior design industry about the effects of the design of the open-plan office?

JAY L. BRAND

CAN WE RESCUE THE OPEN-PLAN OFFICE VIA EVIDENCE?

To provide a concise discussion framework, the evolution of open-plan office design can be reduced to two contrasting goals—investing in organizational effectiveness or a strategic investment in employees, and saving money, mostly through reducing real estate costs. We now turn to brief descriptions of these often conflicting purposes for office design.

ROO VERSUS SVO VISIONS

Both now and in the past, two visions compete for the soul of office design. One vision involves cost savings and embraces office design as a tool to minimize space and thus save money. Using math any schoolchild would understand, this vision has launched a thousand spreadsheets demonstrating that indeed putting more people into less space is cost effective. Because this *reduction of overhead* (ROO) viewpoint links easily to the bottom line, it has always been, and remains, popular with

JAY L. BRAND, PhD, a cognitive psychologist, holds a BA in psychology/English and an MA and PhD in experimental psychology. Before joining Haworth as an organizational behavior specialist, Brand was associate professor of psychology at Loma Linda University. He is an adjunct professor at Andrews University, Hope College, Grand Valley State University, and Davenport University. Brand has given over 350 presentations nationally and internationally and has authored over 70 publications. He conducts pre- and post-occupancy evaluations and adjacency and work process analyses; consults on organizational strategy, workplace strategy, organizational culture, and knowledge worker productivity; and evaluates and implements human factors and ergonomics programs and organizational strategic alignment. A past public director on AIA's national board, and an ASID distinguished speaker, Brand is a member of SIOP, APS, HFES, APA, and Sigma Xi, and serves as Haworth's liaison to the New Ways of Working Network.

business leaders—particularly those charged with cutting costs. From this orientation, office space functions indirectly as a business tool by reducing the amount subtracted in the familiar "income − costs = profit" (admittedly simplified) equation.

In contrast to the ROO viewpoint, the *landscaped office* idea—with its elaborate programming process—as well as Bob Propst's subsequent *action office* concept (and many similar notions since then) represent the *strategic vision for office* (SVO) design. Largely through the lens of the behavioral and social sciences (and employing much of the language of the currently popular green building and social networking movements), proponents of this approach view office design as a strategic investment in people—office occupants. Seen in this way, office space functions as a business tool by making people more effective, thus increasing the beginning amount of the "income − costs = profit" equation just mentioned.

Because the ROO approach embraced any product that subdivided space (for obvious reasons), this perspective soon corrupted Propst's action office idea by increasing occupant densities to reduce costs; with the arrival of pre-wired panels, the cubicle, for better or for worse, was born. Acoustic panels arrived shortly thereafter, and they promised the best of both visions— space reduction (ROO) AND employee effectiveness (SVO)—through increased privacy.

Unfortunately, privacy was (and usually still is) defined as a product characteristic, e.g., the noise reduction coefficient (NRC) or the sound transmission class (STC), rather than a dimension of occupant experience. This led to the design of offices that indeed saved lots of money (compared to drywalled offices), but fell short of their goals for occupant experience because occupancy quality was rarely rigorously defined or measured.

The intent to integrate two fundamentally competing visions for office design—to "have our cake and eat it too"—remains with us today. Additionally, this ambivalent model helps explain the tremendous popularity of the cubicle because it promises to unite the ROO and SVO visions. If we design offices with cubicles, we can presumably save money *and* improve employee effectiveness. However, early concerns about possible disadvantages of open-plan offices (Hedge, 1982) compared to traditional private (cellular) offices (single-occupant workspaces featuring four walls to the ceiling with a closeable door—usually along the perimeter of a building) have been largely replicated and extended by more recent reviews (Brand, 2008; Oomen, Knowles, & Zhao, 2008). The field of interior design has mostly ignored this body of evidence, and this ignorance has unwittingly taken the form of various attempts to "rescue" the open-plan office concept from its frequently observed problems.

ADDRESSING PRIVACY ISSUES

Lack of privacy, especially acoustic privacy, was one of the first (and remains one of the primary) concerns of occupants in open-plan offices. Systems furniture (cubicles) featuring acoustic panels addressed this dilemma, providing visual privacy as a bonus. Following their introduction, such partitions did seem to improve subjective measures of privacy—particularly when coupled with sound masking and absorptive ceilings (see Figure 4.1). Unfortunately, the ROO (cost-savings) focus for office design pressured corporate real estate and facility executives to increase occupant densities and reduce enclosure to levels that effectively end any functional privacy.[1]

FIGURE 4.1. Combining private and open workspaces (Tengborn's "combi-office" idea focused on this) is another way to improve open-plan designs.

SUPPORTING COMMUNICATION

Communication and, by proxy, collaboration represent a second attempt to rescue open-plan offices. Less enclosure allows line-of-sight interaction, improving communication; and nearby conversations—far from being distractions—actually allow employees to learn, serendipitously and vicariously, from each other. Thus, open-plan offices transform collections of previously isolated, individual employees into learning organizations (see Figure 4.2). Unfortunately, the literature does not support this rosy scenario (Monk, 1997).

This second attempt to rescue the open-plan concept also includes the changing nature of work and thus anticipates changing work styles and related trends (e.g., cells, hives, dens, and clubs). Because work is becoming mobile and distributed, future offices will function more like gathering places than locations for individual, private work. Positive results along these lines have not been forthcoming (De Croon, Sluiter, Kuijer, & Frings-Dresen, 2005; Monk, 1997).

FIGURE 4.2. A first step to improving open-plan offices involves using full-height movable walls to define functional areas larger than individual workstations.

ADEQUATE CHANGE MANAGEMENT PROCESSES

A third rescue attempt argues that if accompanied by the right change management process, moving to open-plan from more traditional (private) offices can not only revive communication and collaboration, but reinvent entire organizations! (See Figure 4.3.) Due to most people's ability to adjust to change, initial complaints soon give way to satisfied employees, all working in unity toward a shared horizon. Unfortunately, the few longitudinal studies available to explore this notion suggest less favorable outcomes (Brand & Smith, 2005; Brennan, Chugh, & Kline, 2002).

GENERATIONAL DIFFERENCES

Interior designers' commonly held assumption that younger generations of workers multitask and handle distractions much better than their older counterparts summarizes a fourth rescue attempt. We thus do not need to provide privacy because these up-and-coming prodigies can ignore distractions in more open environments. Therefore, interior designers can freely concentrate on saving space (and money) because the SVO vision now nestles beyond the confines of office design *per se*, remaining safely ensconced in the advanced cognitive abilities of the young (Palfrey & Gasser, 2008; Small & Vorgn, 2008; Tapscott, 2009).

However, careful laboratory experiments have shown this to be largely a myth, in spite of abundant anecdotal evidence. Basically, for all age groups, doing two (or more) things at once negatively impacts primary task performance compared to single-task conditions (Meyer & Kieras, 1997a, 1997b; Pashler, 1994). Certainly task complexity, experience level, strategy differences, and other factors can influence this dual-task performance deficit, but it has proven quite robust—particularly for difficult (e. g., generative) tasks (Glass et al., 2000; Hans Korteling, 1994; Payne et al., 1994; Schumacher et al., 2001).

GREEN BUILDINGS

Sustainable design embodies a recent, and fifth, rescue attempt for the open plan due to such designs offering their occupants exterior views/daylight (and interior views) along with several other desirable occupancy quality features. Unfortunately, potential disadvantages of largely transparent exteriors, such as increased glare, are rarely mentioned much less prevented (Orfield, 2004), and views often conflict with needs for privacy (Strasser, Gruen, & Koch, 1999) (see Figure 4.4).

CORPORATE CULTURE

One of the latest manifestations of this design *non sequitur* (there exist office designs that reduce costs endlessly yet improve employee effectiveness *at the same time*) involves attempts to inform or align open-plan office design with the prevailing organizational culture. Presumably, if the physical design of the workplace reflects the culture, organizational effectiveness can be improved. As of this writing, this remains largely an interesting design hypothesis; hopefully, future investigations can decide the issue (Mars, 2008).

FIGURE 4.3. A large open-plan office of these workstations would create a distracting environment for knowledge or creative workers.

FIGURE 4.4. Low-density, visually interesting spaces vastly improve the monotony of more typical "cubicles"; however, daylighting glare can hinder performance.

SUMMARY AND SUGGESTIONS

It would appear that most if not all attempts to rescue the open-plan concept from its weaknesses have proven inadequate. Perhaps floor-to-ceiling enclosure should get a second look, particularly if glazed and with acoustic properties. At the very least, group and individual work areas should be acoustically separated.

Work does appear to be shifting across generations from primarily individual to more collaborative, interactive tasks, and this shift seems to be enhanced in more open workspaces (Brand, 2008). However, sacrificing support for individual work requiring concentration in favor of facilitating collaboration may not be the panacea often assumed.

Perhaps mobile/distributed work programs will figure prominently in the ideal solution; these allow choice regarding when and where to perform individual work, contributing to a sense of personal control and allowing office design to concentrate on supporting interactive tasks and informal, group activities. But researchers have noted possible hurdles inherent in this approach (Cooper & Kurland, 2002; Golden, Veiga, & Dino, 2008).

Finally, providing a variety of workspaces differing in size, formality, and privacy levels with ubiquitous support for technology may define a "sweet spot" for office design. Should this variety of spaces be defined with floor-to-ceiling, mostly transparent walls rather than cubicles? Floor-to-ceiling walls—even movable ones—would move office design away from open-plan by definition. That might not be a bad thing; recent research suggests possible advantages from eliminating any discrepancies between what employees expect an office to do and how it actually performs (Maher & von Hippel, 2005), and cubicles promise privacy but often don't deliver (at least not acoustically). Nonetheless, a variety of spaces that allows employees to self-select where to work may not offer the consistent support for knowledge work that dedicated workspaces provide.

Is there a solution to the challenges posed by open-plan offices? Frankly, that's a difficult question. Continuing economic pressures will likely balance occupant-centered design with cost-effectiveness. But, because these represent essentially competing definitions of success, design and science must work together to create beautiful, useful workspaces. Design must first create what research then evaluates, and design must use what researchers provide. Working together, research and design may yet rescue the open-plan office.

NOTE

1. Speech privacy can be defined as the inverse of speech intelligibility. Up to 80% redundant, speech (spoken language) is well-learned and processed to the level of semantics (meaning) automatically; thus, neither younger nor older employees can "learn" to ignore speech around them. The physical conditions that provide speech privacy to any arbitrary level within open offices are well-known (Orfield & Brand, 2004), and include absorptive ceilings, sound masking, absorptive floors; absorptive, low-transmitting walls or panels; and low occupant densities. It is meaningless to determine which of these factors contributes "the most" to privacy, because, if they are not jointly present, speech privacy is not achieved due to redundancy levels in the stimulus.

REFERENCES

Brand, J. (2008). Office ergonomics: Pertinent research and recent developments (pp. 245–281). In C.M. Carswell (Ed.), *Reviews of human factors and ergonomics, 4*. Santa Monica, CA: Human Factors and Ergonomics Society.

Brand, J., & Smith, T. (2005). Effects of reducing enclosure on perceptions of occupancy quality, job satisfaction, and job performance in open-plan offices. In *Proceedings of the Human Factors and Ergonomics Society's 49th Annual Meeting* (pp. 818–822). Santa Monica, CA: Human Factors and Ergonomics Society.

Brennan, A., Chugh, J., & Kline, T. (2002). Traditional versus open office design: A longitudinal field study. *Environment and Behavior, 34*, 279–299.

Cooper, C., & Kurland, N. (2002). Telecommuting, professional isolation, and employee development in public and private organizations. *Journal of Organizational Behavior, 23*(4), 511–532.

De Croon, E., Sluiter, J., Kuijer, P., & Frings-Dresen, M. (2005). The effect of office concepts on worker health and performance: A systematic review of the literature. *Ergonomics, 48*, 119–134.

Glass, J., Schumacher, E., Lauber, E., Zurbriggen, E., Gmeindl, L., Kieras, D., & Meyer, D. (2000). Aging and the psychological refractory period: Task-coordination strategies in young and old adults. *Psychology and Aging, 15*(4), 571–595.

Golden, T., Veiga, J., & Dino, R. (2008). The impact of professional isolation on teleworker job performance and turnover intentions: Does time spent teleworking, interacting face-to-face, or having access to communication-enhancing technology matter? *Journal of Applied Psychology, 93*(6), 1412–1421.

Hans Korteling, J. (1994). Effects of aging, skill modification, and demand attention on multiple-task performance. *Human Factors, 36*(1), 27–43.

Hedge, A. (1982). The open-plan office: A systematic investigation of employee reaction to their work environment. *Environment and Behavior, 14*(5), 519–542.

Maher, A., & von Hippel, C. (2005). Individual differences in employee reactions to open-plan offices. *Journal of Environmental Psychology, 25*(5), 219–229.

Mars, G. (2008). Corporate cultures and the use of space: An approach from cultural theory. *Innovation: The European Journal of Social Science Research, 21*(3), 185–204.

Meyer, D., & Kieras, D. (1997a). A computational theory of executive cognitive processes and multiple-task performance: Part 1. Basic mechanisms. *Psychological Review, 104*, 3–65.

Meyer, D., & Kieras, D. (1997b). A computational theory of executive control processes and human multiple-task performance: Part 2. Accounts of Psychological Refractory-Period Phenomena. *Psychological Review, 104*, 749–791.

Monk, R. (1997). The impact of open-plan offices on organizational performance. *International Journal of Management, 14*(3), 345–349.

Oomen, V., Knowles, M., & Zhao, I. (2008). Should health service managers embrace open plan work environments? A review. *Asia Pacific Journal of Health Management, 3*(2), 37–43.

Orfield, S. (2004, June 1). Critique: occupancy quality: Putting forth a new agenda for sustainable design. *Contract Magazine.* Retrieved April 12, 2009, from http://www.contractmagazine .com/contract/search/article_display.jsp?vnu_ content_id=1000534804

Orfield, S. & Brand, J. (2004). *Better sound solutions: Applying occupant and building performance measurement and design to improve office acoustics.* Washington, DC: American Society of Interior Designers.

Palfrey, J., & Gasser, U. (2008). *Born digital: Understanding the first generation of digital natives.* New York: Basic Books.

Pashler, H. (1994). Dual-task interference in simple tasks: Data and theory. *Psychological Bulletin, 116*(2), 220–244.

Payne, D., Peters, L., Birkmire, D., Bonto, M., Anastasi, J., & Wenger, M. (1994). Effects of speech intelligibility level on concurrent visual task performance. *Human Factors, 36*(3), 441–475.

Schumacher, E., Seymour, T., Glass, J., Fencsik, D., Lauber, E., Kieras, D., & Meyer, D. (2001). Virtually perfect timesharing in dual-task performance: Uncorking the central cognitive bottleneck. *Psychological Science, 12*(2), 101–108.

Small, G., & Vorgan, G. (2008). *iBrain: Surviving the technological alteration of the modern mind.* New York: HarperCollins.

Strasser, H., Gruen, K., & Koch, W. (1999). Office acoustics: Analyzing reverberation time and subjective evaluation. *Occupational Ergonomics, 2*, 67–80.

Tapscott, D. (2009). *Grown up digital: How the net generation is changing your world.* New York: McGraw-Hill.

> How can evidence-based design be introduced into the educational curriculum and/or to design practitioners?

CAREN S. MARTIN

EVIDENCE-BASED PRACTICE: FROM THE CLASSROOM INTO THE FIRM

From all indications, evidence-based design (EBD) is here to stay. EBD has caught the attention of the interior design community via trade publications; the work of the Pebble Project® from The Center for Health Design (CHD) (2009); and presentations at conferences and conventions such as Healthcare Design sponsored by the CHD, NeoCon World's Trade Fair held in Chicago, and IIDEX/NeoCon Canada held in Toronto. EBD's foundation in the precepts of evidence-based medicine has been recognized in the current discussion of EBD. Also, EBD's use of key "evidence" by interior designers in the creation of interior environments (Rhoads, 2008) has been presented as parallel in purpose to the International Code Council's (ICC) development of performance-based codes and standards (Brothers, 2009)—keeping people safe. Furthermore, InformeDesign®, an EBD tool that provides evidence-based design criteria, has been available to design practitioners since January 2003, well before the phrase EBD was commonly discussed.

CAREN S. MARTIN, PhD, CID-MN, FASID, IDEC, IES, IIDA, is an assistant professor of interior design at the University of Minnesota. Before earning her master's and PhD, she practiced institutional, corporate, and healthcare interior design and project management for nearly 20 years, which she shares with her undergraduate and graduate students. Martin served two terms on Minnesota's professional licensing board and chaired NCIDQ's Model Language Committee. She serves on ASID's Legislative and Codes Advisory Council and the Steering Committee of Minnesota's legislative coalition. Her scholarship focuses on opportunities and threats facing the interior design profession. Martin authored "Rebuttal of the Report by the Institute for Justice Entitled 'Designing Cartels: How Industry Insiders Cut Out Competition'" (*Journal of Interior Design*, 2008), and the book *Interior Design: From Practice to Profession* (ASID, 2007). With Denise Guerin, she coauthored *The Interior Design Profession's Body of Knowledge, 2005 Edition*. Together, they co-created InformeDesign® and Martin serves as its director.

But, EBD is not part of best practices for the vast majority of interior designers yet. Why? Some mention anticipated negative aspects of engaging in EBD: the degree of effort required in terms of costs to the firm (i.e., billable hours, the learning curve, encouraging participation by designers) or the possibility of compromising creativity.

Based on experience throughout my career as an interior design practitioner, engaging in EBD is a leap. What was wrong with designing based primarily on creativity, intuition, and past practice experience? Like most interior design practitioners educated in the last century, my approach to design was primarily normative: "I think it will work"; "I've always wanted to try it this way"; "I've seen it done before"; or "My colleague told me about it." The good news is that most times this intuitive, informed "guess" or hypothesis worked—at some level. Creativity was the driver leading to solutions where function was also typically satisfied, though we were never totally certain (in a qualitative or quantitative manner) about how well our designs "fit" our clients and/ or the occupants of the space. This uncertainty occurred from never pre-determining our goals (via measured outcomes) for the design solution, nor measuring them using post-occupancy evaluation (POE). Our perceptions were just that,

typically gathered from our personal observations or comments made by the client or end-users.

Today, in the wake of clients' growing demands for an improved "bottom line," how do interior designers begin to "prove" that the design of a new facility can increase productivity in the office, accelerate patient discharge rates from the hospital, increase student learning in the classroom, or improve visitors' wayfinding through a museum?

EBD purports a method by which to identify evidence that a specific design decision will result is a specific, measurable outcome. But, how much evidence is enough, and how does one determine if the evidence available is sound and applicable for a specific project or client (Hamilton, 2009)? In fact, some interior designers and architects engaged in the EBD movement worry that EBD is merely being utilized as a marketing tool by design practitioners (Levin, 2008). Further, researchers fear that study findings will be misused, i.e., that one finding from a single study will be used as the basis to design a space (Hamilton, 2009; Martin, 2009). These concerns can be resolved through learning opportunities for interior designers at all levels—as an undergraduate student, a graduate student, or an experienced practitioner.

EBD IN THE CLASSROOM

Future interior design practitioners are being afforded the opportunity to engage in EBD while in the classroom. This effort is being facilitated by the availability of resources mentioned previously. Also, within the last year alone, numerous textbooks have been published that define, describe, and illustrate an EBD approach for use by interior design and architecture faculty and students, such as *Evidence-Based Design for Multiple Building Types* (Hamilton & Watkins, 2009), *Evidence-Based Healthcare Design* (Cama, 2009), *Informing Design* (Dickinson & Marsden, 2009), *Programming and Research: Skills*

and Techniques for Interior Designers (Botti-Salitsky, 2009), and *Evidence-Based Design for Interior Designers* (Nussbaumer, 2009).

Teaching undergraduate and graduate students about EBD varies in exposure, approach, and activities developed to support curricular objectives, goals, and learning outcomes. These differences regarding EBD will be discussed with examples of course specifics as illustrations of how EBD is being embedded into the curriculum with the goal to prepare entry-level interior designers to take this knowledge and process into the firm.

EBD AND UNDERGRADUATE EDUCATION

Today, undergraduate students are being educated about EBD as part of the design process. They are also learning about how they can contribute to the multidisciplinary design team in a meaningful way using EBD. The goal is for the undergraduate student to be prepared to begin using an EBD approach in practice upon graduation. The driving force for a focus on EBD—not to the exclusion of other philosophies, theories, and approaches, but as a complement to them—has been the EBD movement through cutting-edge interior design practitioners as expressed through the analysis of practice that contributes to the refinement of the accreditation standards for interior design education addressed by the Council for Interior Design Accreditation (CIDA).

As of June 2009, CIDA accredits 169 interior design programs in Canada and the United States (S. Wright, Site Visit and Meeting Coordinator, personal communication, June 23, 2009). EBD is addressed in CIDA's 2009 *Professional Standards* in Standard 4. Design Process as one of the "Student Learning Outcomes." For context, first, the standard itself states,

> Entry-level interior designers need to apply all aspects of the design process to creative problem solving. Design process enables designers to identify and explore complex problems and generate creative solutions that support human behavior within the interior environment. (CIDA, 2008, p. 13)

The "Student Learning Expectations" specify abilities that must be met as an indication that the interior design program is in compliance with Standard 4. One expectation states, "Students are able to . . . b) gather appropriate and necessary information and research findings to solve the problem (evidence-based design)" (CIDA, 2008, p. 13). This expectation specifies knowledge and ability to apply an EBD approach within the design process.

Educators have been addressing the need to, at a minimum, expose undergraduate interior design students to the concept of research, typically by having them engage in the process itself. They integrate a research process that is systematic and scientific and begins with a research question for which data must be collected and analyzed. For example, for the design of a dining hall/cafeteria in a student union, designers need to know "what is the busiest time in the student center food service area?" The research method used to answer this question could be observation, such as by watching student customers to see who goes into the food service area throughout the day to make purchases, or using content analysis by reviewing records from the cash register logs to determine peak times for purchases.

Students also may be required to identify and gather primary and secondary data from research conducted by others and reported in refereed journals, trade publications, proprietary studies, InformeDesign's Research Summaries and *Implications*, the client's corporate business documents, and manufacturers' Web sites. For example, in an office design studio, interior design students may need information about factors that influence workplace design for their client. Research findings could be identified, analyzed, and developed into evidence-based design criteria for their program. Documentation of both research finding and the design criteria would be required. A model of this type of activity is shown in Table 4.4, which also shows the purpose of engagement with workplace research, some of the topics to be examined, and instructions for presentation of findings.

Assignments such as the one shown in Table 4.4, offer undergraduate students insights that enable them to identify and solve a design problem based on evidence they have gathered. An EBD approach does not exclude creativity, but rather the relationship between evidence and creativity are synergistic—just as a well-developed programming document fuels the basis of an excellent design.

TABLE 4.4

UNDERGRADUATE WORKPLACE RESEARCH ASSIGNMENT

PURPOSE

- Develop research, summary, and synthesis skills
- Investigate four types of sources (e.g., InformeDesign®, industry reports, association publications, or trade publications) for findings that relate to:
  - Workplace factors that might influence the occupants
  - Human behaviors that might influence the design of the workplace
- Identify how findings might inform design criteria; applicability to design solution

TOPICS (*PARTIAL LIST*)

- Audio/visual, telecommunications
- HVAC/indoor air quality (IAQ)
- Influence of personal culture/ethnicity
- Lighting/daylighting
- Physiological needs and factors/ergonomics
- Psychological needs and factors
- Safety/security
- Sensory responses/multiple chemical sensitivity (MCS)

PROCESS

1. Write up a summary/abstract for each of the sources (100-150 words); relay key information from the source, with the citation (i.e., an "annotated bibliography").
2. Write an analysis of your findings. Relate information about how they address the workplace as an environment and/or the behavior of workers within it.
3. Develop a table that includes findings you have gleaned from your research and pair them with evidence-based-design criteria that you have ascertained relates to the finding (note the example in the table).

FINDING	EVIDENCE-BASED DESIGN CRITERIA
Diversity in worker height and weight	Flexibility in furniture fit; adjustable seating

It is essential for undergraduate students to be exposed to a basic level of information that defines the meaning and purpose of "research" versus "information" and gives them a basic foundation in research vocabulary and research methods. Without these tools their quest for knowledge will be little more than a fishing trip. One source for basic research information is the research tutorial (*Research 101*) on InformeDesign, offered free of charge in three segments that present research vocabulary, research methods, and the rationale for use of research-based findings in design solutions (InformeDesign, 2002).

Quality levels of research are also introduced to undergraduate students so that they can begin to determine the difference among the robustness of findings from a blog, Wikipedia™, a newspaper, a trade magazine, a book, or a refereed-journal article; each has its purpose, but *not all findings are created equal* in terms of validity and reliability.

Graduate design students learn about EBD for a different purpose and focus. Graduate students with future goals to teach or to engage in design research in their firms will find themselves learning how to engage in EBD, but moreover to engage in understanding the philosophical underpinnings of EBD. Both aspects have substantial benefits for those with graduate degrees headed back into interior design practice, a growing trend among medium- and large-sized firms practicing primarily in nonresidential design, especially healthcare at this time.

It is essential that graduate students have knowledge in design and human behavior theories and understand the purpose this knowledge serves. For example, common theories can offer perspective to an EBD approach by identifying the connection between humans and their environment (Human Ecosystem Theory), preference for types of environments as they relate to human welfare (Environmental Preference Theory), and the relationship of human behavior to spatial layout characteristics (Space Syntax Theory).

Graduate students typically must be able to ground their application of an EBD-approach to their understanding of practice and research methods (both qualitative and quantitative methods), which are typically a curricular requirement. Theoretical knowledge underpins inquiry and enables graduate students to develop research questions applicable to a specific project or project type and hypothesize design/human behavior outcomes.

Typically, the graduate EBD-focused course will begin by defining EBD, its origins, use across disciplines, and likely benefits and possible challenges of use. Table 4.5 suggests curricular learning objectives to be considered for such a course. It is important to achieve a balance between their individual design experiences and readings via texts and current research and practice readings identified and shared by students during discussion.

Additionally, such a course encourages critical thinking skills through application of the EBD process to a "real" or possible/future project identified by the graduate students, specific to their area of practice or research topic. It is crucial that students identify a research question(s) and develop a hypothesis to identify what they believe applying EBD criteria will bring as an outcome to their design solution. This approach can also be used well by students in the class who will approach the EBD method as a future client. For example, students could come from design-related professions such as facilities management or user

TABLE 4.5
SUGGESTED EBD GRADUATE COURSE LEARNING OBJECTIVES

COURSE OBJECTIVES:

1. Understand the meaning and origins of EBD.
2. Study the development of EBD using innovation theory as the framework for exploration.
3. Identify the "early adopters" of EBD and obstacles to adoption.
4. Explore the advantages and disadvantages of EBD as a process as compared to the current "best practices" design process approach; consider incorporation of evidence-based design criteria in contrast to design decisions consistent with a normative design approach.
5. Identify and analyze EBD tools available to practitioners across design disciplines (e.g., architecture, interior design, landscape architecture) and apply them to a specific design project.

groups such as healthcare administration. An administrator of low-income housing who wishes to ascertain the appropriateness of a proposed housing policy focused on the relationship of square footage allowance and children's success rates in the elementary school years could benefit by knowing how to use and assess evidence that can support design policies or modifications.

All graduate students benefit from design research findings that build the body of knowledge and inform future design solutions—when the findings are disseminated, e.g., as a case study or POE. This knowledge and experience with theory, research methods, experience in working with and/or creating research findings, and disseminating findings via refereed publications and applying research findings—evidence—enables interior designers with advanced degrees to be what Hamilton refers to as "Level 4" practitioners (Hamilton, 2005).

EBD INTO THE FIRM

Hiring entry-level interior designers with undergraduate degrees that had experiences integrating an EBD approach to design can benefit interior design practitioners who have been out of school for more than 5 or 10 years and want to begin to engage in EBD. These new practitioners bring knowledge of this advanced practice approach into the design firm. They have learned to identify evidence-based design criteria and to weave research findings into their programming. This knowledge serves as the foundation for EBD design concepts and subsequent design solutions. Bringing this knowledge to the firm enables practitioners to move beyond normative design in creation of design solutions for savvy, sophisticated clients who demand positive improvements to their "bottom line." And, it must be noted, these clients are often business professionals who are accustomed to having evidence guide their business decisions. They ask no less of interior designers.

Firms are also hiring interior designers with advanced research degrees (master's or doctoral) to engage in building-type or project-specific research or to head up the firm's research department. Additionally, they guide the firm's project teams to sources of evidence-based design criteria and orchestrate the appropriate integration of such evidence into the programming data.

CONCLUSION

EBD has an important place at the table with the aesthetic, creative, and intuitive aspects of interior design, as all components contribute to the final design solution and what is termed best practice (Hamilton, 2009). Interior design practitioners have an ethical obligation to educate themselves about the true spirit of EBD and proper use of this design method/ approach—one of many. Interior design students, whether they come into the firm with undergraduate degrees and knowledge as good consumers of research or with graduate degrees and experience as conductors of research from their own course of inquiry, all can contribute to an improvement of the interior environment beyond what we are capable of providing today.

Martin)⋈(Evidence-Based Practice)⋈(155

REFERENCES

Botti-Salitsky, R. (2009). *Programming and research: Skills and techniques for interior designers.* New York: Fairchild Books.

Brothers, J. (2009, March). Changing a culture of mine to a culture of ours. *Interiors & Sources, 16*(2), pp. 58–59.

Cama, R. (2009). *Evidence-based healthcare design.* New York: Wiley & Sons.

The Center for Health Design. *The Pebble Project®.* Retrieved June 23, 2009, from http://www .healthdesign.org/research/pebble/

Council for Interior Design Accreditation. (2008). *2009 Professional Standards.* Retrieved June 22, 2009, from http://www.accredit-id.org/June%20 2008%20Standards_changes09.pdf

Dickinson, J., & Marsden, J. (Eds.) (2009). *Informing design.* New York: Fairchild Books.

Hamilton, D. (2005, July). *Four levels of evidence-based practice.* AIA Journal of Architecture. Retrieved September 9, 2005, from http://aia.org/nwsltr_aiaj .cfm?pagename=aia_a_20041201_fourlevels

Hamilton, D. (2009). Evidence, decisions, guidelines, and standards. *Health Environments and Research Design Journal, 2*(3), 51–55.

Hamilton, D., & Watkins, D. (2009). *Evidence-based design for multiple building types.* New York: Wiley & Sons.

InformeDesign®. (2002). *Research 101.* Retrieved June 23, 2009, from http://www.informedesign .umn.edu/Page.aspx?cId=182

Levin, D. (2008, September). Defensive driving. *Healthcare Design, 8*(9), p. 8.

Martin, C. (2009). The challenge of integrating evidence-based design. *Health Environments and Research Design Journal, 2*(3), 29–50.

Nussbaumer, L. (2009). *Evidence-based design for interior designers.* New York: Fairchild Books.

Rhoads, E. (2008, January/February). Prescribed design: Employing evidence-based design ensures public welfare while building the body of knowledge. *Interiors & Sources, 15*(1), pp. 57–58.

Today, our process is changing from a linear process to an iterative and concurrent process . . . moving forward in a dance that circles back on itself, leaps forward, skips some steps all together . . . adds new process components, and does so with an increasingly more complex team of experts and potential outcomes.

—Eileen E. Jones

FACTORS INFLUENCING PRACTICE

OVERVIEW Many factors affect the state of practice of interior design. However, two stand out—interior designers' characteristics as practitioners and their focus on human-centered design, and the omnipresence of technology and its perceived conflict with creativity. Interior design practitioners' engagement in the design process is first discussed by Eileen Jones. She proposes an interdisciplinary design process model that allows us to be the expert specialist within a team—or the generalist when appropriate. Anita Barnett continues with recognition of the characteristics of excellence in interior designers she supervises from multiple generations. Rita Carson Guest suggests the knowledge and skills needed for entry-level interior design in context of the firm's role to educate. Interior designers' ability to focus on human-centered design is explored by Louise Jones as she clarifies the differences among universal design, designing for disability, and accessible design.

She gives us a good look at the progress toward designing for all. In contrast, ergonomist Alan Hedge provides us with an "outsider's" view and implores interior designers to take an increased level of responsibility for the physical health and safety of occupants.

In the second part of the chapter, technology's influence on practice is explored first by Mark Nelson, who raises provocative questions about the relationship between creativity and technology. Janice Stevenor Dale speaks to the benefits of embracing technology to enhance your creativity and efficiency. This view is further elaborated by Charisse Johnston in her exploration of technology in context of the design process. Rochelle Maresh presents a discussion of BIM and how it is changing the way interior designers are thinking and working within the design team. Few factors have as much power over interior designers' futures as the influence of the human and technological aspects of practice.

> Are interior designers generalists in a collaborative world or specialists within a design team?

EILEEN E. JONES

A CASE FOR INTERDISCIPLINARY DESIGN

CLIENT-CENTRIC DESIGN APPROACH

If you look at a design problem through the lens of a client, chances are you will see a different opportunity than when viewed through the lens of an interior designer. You are likely to discover that outcomes are not always defined by a product, but rather by a bigger problem definition. With a traditional filter and teaming model, an architect might ask, "What kind of building do you want?" and an interior designer might ask, "What kind of space do you want?" whereas a client-centric view might stimulate a different question: "What is the problem you're trying to solve?" This is the typical "need" versus "want" perspective. The need might uncover that a building or a space is not the starting point of the conversation, but rather only one outcome in a bigger problem definition. The client may want a new building, but what they really need is a redefinition of organizational culture or work styles, a new

EILEEN E. JONES, CID, LEED® AP, AIGA, is a principal and national discipline leader for Perkins+Will | *Eva Maddox Branded Environments*. She uses a research-based design approach that identifies and integrates a client's unique vision, mission, values, and culture into tangible brand expressions, experiences, and environments. Jones has been instrumental in the development and practice of *Branded Environments'* approach. She has led strategic research, community cultural interpretation, brand master planning and positioning, identity, product, and design development. Jones is frequently recognized for design excellence, garnering multiple awards with her project teams, and speaks regularly at many educational and professional venues, advancing the ideas of *Branded Environments*. She is an advocate of interdisciplinary design and is working within Perkins+Will to advance work process change in support of this model.

product strategy, or an approach to marketplace that positions them with clear competitive advantage. When viewed in this light, you begin to realize that the opportunity for problem solving expands beyond traditional design roles and suggests that the team at the table is much more diverse. With an interdisciplinary project team, new outcomes are almost always possible, and everyone's expertise is brought to bear to ensure that the correct problem is first identified and then solved.

Interdisciplinary design teams are quickly becoming the norm rather than the exception in the delivery of design services when solving complex needs. The interdisciplinary design process assumes a collaborative approach to answering the client's questions where multiple service lines are required to meet the needs of the design challenge.

For Janice Barnes of Perkins+Will, interdisciplinary design "refers to the collaborative process that brings appropriate and diverse expertise" together to solve a client's problems, and "retains those voices of experience" throughout the project process. In addition, Barnes observes that as marketplace complexities increase in diversity, and "as numerous stakeholders seek a broader understanding of the role that design plays in supporting organizational requirements, there is a required complement of interdisciplinary perspectives" that enhances the solution to a client problem. Finally, Barnes states that if diverse expertise is not present, then the decision-making is not as strong (personal communication, December 9, 2008). In short, the interdisciplinary design team will deliver the most cohesive and comprehensive design and market knowledge to answer the client's questions.

DESIGN TEAM MEMBERS AND CLIENT ALIGNMENT

Let's say that the client has multiple challenges facing them:

> Issues around recruitment and retention (human resources)
> Desire to redefine corporate culture (C-Suite)
> An evolving brand message in response to marketplace needs (marketing and brand management)
> Obsolete space standards and a desire to move toward a more collaborative work method (facilities, directors, and managers)
> Outdated information technology infrastructure (IT)
> Staff growth and building expansion needs (facilities, C-Suite, directors, and managers)

In parentheses after each challenge is the assumed client stakeholder from the client team. Although each of these topics requires a design response, each also requires an aligned design team member to speak the client's language,

bring best-practice examples and benchmark solutions to the table, speak from a place of knowledge, and demonstrate the ability to work with multiple discipline representatives. The design team, therefore, might be composed of a diverse array of experts such as:

> A cultural anthropologist
> A change management or change communications expert
> A workplace planner and strategist
> An interior designer
> An architect
> A landscape designer
> A brand strategist
> A graphic designer
> An IT specialist and program analyzer

Aligning design team members with client team members builds client confidence. The client brings not only their localized experience but the experience from within their industry of peers. The design team member brings market segment expertise around the clients' challenge and a problem-solving methodology that results in effective and well-informed design solutions.

Alignment of design team members with client team members ensures that design solutions are viewed from the perspective of multiple stakeholders and the needs of all client groups within an organization. This further ensures that the voice of the client is heard by a design team member who understands each specific part of the client question and is able to respond from a corresponding position of knowledge.

COMPOSITION OF TEAM MEMBERSHIP

It can be difficult to work as an interdisciplinary team member. Individual, interdisciplinary team members need to possess two key attributes: a deep, specialized ability, and a broad set of interests and crossover knowledge. Additionally, they must be able to translate their knowledge across a broad platform of diverse problems and sectors. This enables them to collaborate with other team members at a higher rate of success.

Tom Kelley notes that an IDEO team member with this profile might be called a "T-shaped individual," which represents a "breadth of knowledge in many fields," while also having "depth in at least one area of expertise" (2005, p. 75). Jean Egmon of 3rd Angle describes this model as "broad translational knowledge and deep technical knowledge" (personal communication, February 8, 2008). For example, a friend of mine has a bachelor's degree in interior design, a minor in fine arts, a master's degree in marketing communication, and a strong personal interest in material science. Although her expertise is in interior design, she brings a diversity of broader knowledge to the client question and is able to answer those questions from various viewpoints and collaborate with other experts engaged in the design problem. In other words, she is a strong interdisciplinary design team member. She can solve clients' questions around interior design and workplace from a position of expertise; she can connect with them at a business and marketing communications level, understanding how to identify solutions that may impact the built environment and integrate them with other experts; and she can respond to sustainable issues around material appropriateness and innovative material solutions.

Achieving success as a "T-shaped individual" (Kelley, 2005, p. 75) within an interdisciplinary design team requires collaboration. According to Tim Brown (2008), "The increasing complexity of products, services, and experiences has replaced the myth of the lone creative genius with the reality of the enthusiastic interdisciplinary collaborator" (p. 87). This suggests that today's interior designers are both generalists in a collaborative world *and* specialists within a design team. Through collaborative integration of diverse capabilities and expertise, the collaborative interdisciplinary work model and the individuals engaged in delivering services in this manner increase client satisfaction and service, foster partnerships with other collaborators, and deliver client value.

A diverse team of equals at the table expands the thinking, enriches the web of potential solutions, and eliminates silos. Silos happen around closely held areas of knowledge, establishing distinct boundaries. Silos may also contain similar staff profiles, where skill sets complement each other and the specific body of knowledge. A more complex model that embraces collaboration and multi- or interdisciplinary team members expands the possibilities of knowledge, leveraging diverse sets of information, and broadening the perspective and possible outcomes. It allows for the transfer of knowledge and skills and focuses the team on a one-customer solution.

The interdisciplinary design process requires a new way of working and delivering work product. This probably comes as no surprise. For as long as we've been delivering design services, we've been reinventing the delivery process. Or have we? In 2002, *Interior Design* magazine with McGraw-Hill published a book entitled the *Handbook of Professional Practice* (Coleman, 2002). The book posed these questions:

> What kinds of knowledge do interior designers need to do their work?

> What knowledge does the interior design profession require to remain viable now and not merely relevant in the future, but a powerful force for social change?

> How can this body of knowledge put designers on a level playing field with other professions, sustain the profession over the long term, and give designers opportunities to influence new thinking in the industry, the academy, and society? (inside cover)

In all, six categories of information were organized around responses from design voices in the field. Of particular interest to me is the section entitled "Part 4: Process." It consists of 14 chapters from 14 different voices, each describing or charting the various phases of the design process. In the opening comments of chapter 22, the editor concludes that although "approaches vary due to the size of a project, project type and the design firm's philosophy and resources, the basic scope of services is generally consistent from project to project and firm to firm" (Coleman, 2002, p. 483). A Scope of Service chart follows these comments, identifying areas of work and the process steps required around each service component. The process steps included everything from project initiation to project close-out (Maddox, 2002, pp. 484–485). Other contributors go on to identify in detail each individual phase of work and the process engaged.

Whereas many of these process steps are relevant today, the method by which we go about achieving results in an interdisciplinary team may be rapidly changing. It is fair to say that as recently as 10 years ago, the design process was one that would generally be described as linear in nature, moving carefully from one phase to the next with client sign-offs and approvals prior to moving to the next phase of work. This is primarily because we saw design as a process that built on itself, requiring decisions in sequence to move forward in the design process. Therefore, project initiation led to programming, which led to schematic design, which led to design development, and so on. You rarely stepped out of bounds into the next phase without careful sign-off on the currently completed phase.

Today, our process is changing from a linear process to an iterative and concurrent process, all the while moving forward in a dance that circles back on itself, leaps forward, skips some steps altogether, moves backward to reassess, adds new process components, and does so with an increasingly more complex team of experts and potential outcomes. Most significantly impacting our process are issues such as:

> Speed to market
> Communications and technology
> Complexity of business issues including global networks and methods of delivery
> Sustainability
> Market share, voice, brand
> Experience for our customer's customers
> Design awareness of the general public
> Product and service differentiation

With these issues, it is more likely that a team of multidisciplinary experts must be gathered to solve the problems. It is equally likely that the process takes on a new shape and form.

THE INTERDISCIPLINARY PROCESS MODEL

The basic process for delivering a project with an interdisciplinary design team can be reduced to five steps. Although the number of steps may not be too different from previous models, the definition of these steps shows significant change.

Step 1. Engage + Research: Conduct a multifaceted series of exercises aimed at:
- Mobilizing the team and all its players
- Engaging in data collection
- Conducting interdisciplinary design workshops for goal setting
- Reviewing and analyzing all data

Step 2. Prototype: Test opportunities through various exercises including:
- Brainstorming exercises
- Conducting design workshops
- Completing concept testing

Step 3. Develop: Develop preferred model based on outcomes of Step 2, including:
- Rapid prototyping
- Design workshops
- Integrated design strategies
- Concept refinement

Step 4. Implement: Take all necessary steps to see project through to completion, including:
- Assumptions workshop
- Document all decisions
- Bid
- Build
- Move-in

Step 5. Assess + Broadcast: Assess success and challenges of the project, including:
- Document the outcomes
- Share key learning with project and client team members
- Share key learning with the academy and practice at large
- Invite the client's business peers to engage in the learning

The iterative component in this five-step process is the design workshop. A design workshop is structured to speed the design process along in a more informed manner, with all relevant parties at the table, sharing expertise and bringing the best minds together to solve the client's problems. It may cause us to reevaluate assumptions made in earlier process steps. It will help align different experts who may be moving through the process steps at different rates. It will force design decisions and in-depth design thinking. It will create a more robust outcome by engaging all parties, including the client, in simultaneous activity. It will increase our knowledge and leverage our expertise around a certain set of problems. It will deliver a better, more informed solution.

WHAT DO INTERDISCIPLINARY TEAMS MEAN FOR INTERIOR DESIGNERS?

Interdisciplinary teams give interior designers a new way to think about the contribution they make to a project team. In a way, it's the "good news" we've been looking for in the profession. It gives us a way to lead the process where we add the most value, contribute to the process when others lead, and to be the expert with expert knowledge in our discipline throughout the design cycle. It means that one should:

> Take ownership of your knowledge
> Learn to collaborate (look it up: collaborate means "to work together, especially in a joint intellectual effort") (*American Heritage Dictionary*, 2000)
> Develop listening, translation, and analytical skills
> Think inside and outside of the box
> Never stop learning

> Expand your worldview
> Develop areas of diverse interest
> Challenge yourself
> Get to know your clients
> Do it quickly

At the risk of being redundant: today's interior designers are both generalists in a collaborative world *and* specialists within a design team. They must be the carrier of expert knowledge in the field of interior design and contribute this knowledge to the client and project team. They must bring a broader *generalist* perspective to the table, know how to translate information, and understand how others' expertise impacts their work. In the very near future, if you're not practicing in an interdisciplinary, integrated, collaborative manner, chances are you won't be at the table.

REFERENCES

Brown, T. (2008, June). Design thinking. *Harvard Business Review*, pp. 85–92.

Coleman, C. (Ed.) (2002). *Handbook of professional practice.* New York: McGraw-Hill.

Collaborate. (2000). In *American Heritage dictionary* online (4th ed.). Retrieved March 20, 2009, from http://www.bartleby.com/61/

Kelley, T., & Littman, J. (2001). *The ten faces of innovation.* New York: Doubleday.

Maddox, E. (2002). Scope of service chart. In C. Coleman (Ed.), *Handbook of professional practice*, (pp. 483–511). New York: McGraw-Hill.

> What is the upside of a downturn in the economy for the interior design practitioner or firm? How to get the Generation Y staff on board with the challenges and increase their professional potential in the eyes of their supervisor/principal.

ANITA L. BARNETT

ADVICE TO GEN Y: BECOME THE GENERATION OF EXCELLENCE

Carpe diem, or seize the day, is the best advice for anyone in this current economic situation. I recently had lunch with my mentor, and as he walked out of the restaurant the last thing that he said was, "Remember, Anita, the harder you work, the luckier you get." When the going gets tough, the tough start businesses, innovate, and often follow the opposite of conventional wisdom (Count, 2008). This can be an excellent time to provide your "voice" to help your design firm stay viable and powerful with their existing and new clients.

The current economic situation in our country, which is linked to the global economy, has made this a critical time for everyone in the building industry to bring real value to our clients. This value translates into jobs in our industry. People who are truly excellent will be the ones who will be retained by their firms and build the foundation for continued excellence for their companies. But, how do you recognize or become one of these excellent interior designers?

ANITA L. BARNETT, FIIDA, is a principal with Perkins+Will and the corporate, commercial, civic market sector leader in Minneapolis. Having earned recognition for her project leadership and strategic business development expertise, she has maintained a critical focus on the strategic business development of her clients' facilities and corporate headquarters. Committed to building team-oriented cultures and environments, Barnett's blend of innovation and collaboration has allowed her to build and sustain highly successful client relationships. The quality of her community and professional organizational leadership has also positioned her as a major contributor to the advancement of the interior design profession. Acknowledged with prestigious design recognitions for her work on multiple projects throughout her career, Barnett was recently a finalist for the *Business Week* Design Awards, as well as having her work featured in the *Wall Street Journal* for delivering strategic business results.

Throughout my career, there are individuals I have met in our industry as they start their careers. They have intrigued me by their thirst for knowledge and their comprehension of the larger world of which the interior design profession is but a small piece. These are the new members of our profession who I want to watch as they develop their careers and also to help along their career path. These individuals are contributing at an accelerated level on their projects within their firms and also establishing their voice in the community at professional leadership levels and perhaps as teachers. They are innovating and creating new ways of looking at problem solving and becoming the leaders of tomorrow. Life is never linear; therefore, it is important to develop a strong vision and flexible approach to use as a framework for our careers. These excellent interior designers start with a vision of their tomorrow and maintain flexibility in their careers so they can take advantage of unexpected opportunities. As I watch these excellent people, I note that they belong to Gen Y.

ADVICE FOR GENERATION Y: THE GENERATION OF EXCELLENCE

Generation Y (1977–1990 birth years) interior designers have the ability to become designers of excellence by increasing their potential in this very interesting economic time. Following are several suggestions for them to build their vision and framework.

DO A GREAT JOB

This is the time for us to do our best to deliver an outstanding job for each client and project we work on. Be passionate about learning, collaborating, and contributing on every endeavor. Your attitude is very important, and we always want to work with people who have a can-do attitude that inspires all of us to make significant contributions.

INNOVATE

Understand the client's needs and desires so you can create ideas that better meet their requirements. You can contribute by innovating processes, information technology (IT) interactions, communication techniques, and, most importantly, possible new solutions for the client. This moves what you do from a tactical view with limited value creation to a strategic view that leads to dramatic new forms of value. This thinking can make a decisive difference and is linked to a key value of problem solving to which interior designers contribute—"a design thinker's personality" (Brown, 2008).

CONSIDER LIFELONG LEARNING

Always look to continue specialty learning. For example, complete the Leadership in Energy and Environmental Design (LEED®) training to increase your sustainability knowledge; continue along the path to your top level of professionalism with certification exams; participate in professional associations like the International Interior Design Association (IIDA), the American Society of Interior Designers (ASID), or the American Institute of Architects (AIA) and their education programs, to continue to learn about your profession.

CONTRIBUTE TO INTERNAL COMMUNICATION

Projects go through inspiration, ideation, and implementation phases. Create your viewpoint and "voice" on design and contribute your voice to your projects, design charettes, and business discussions. Your firm and team members will then recognize and respect *your* view.

FACILITATE EXTERNAL COMMUNICATION

Remember that when in public you are always a firm's representative. The person sitting next to you on the bus or your neighbor could be aware of an upcoming project or work and are interested in what you do as an interior designer. Connect that information back to your principals in your firm that are in charge of marketing. Extend your *network* in the community and develop friends in other areas of business to bring design thinking to them. Develop relationships early in your career with friends and associates who will someday be top leaders of their companies.

Recently, we were discussing a new public project for which a request for proposal (RFP) had been issued for design services. A student intern was sitting next to us, and he turned to our group and started to tell us some key facts about the project because he had attended a public design charette a few months earlier on this same project.

A recent article in the *Harvard Business Review* focused on the key attributes of very successful people and suggests that they are tied to how people spend their spare time. Research demonstrated that a great "new employee" interview question is "How do you spend a typical day?" (Gregran, 2009, p. 4). Understanding their intrinsic obsessions presents a link to their sources of motivation. Typically, very successful people use their spare time in the day to continue to learn and be associated with issues related to their profession. An example was the "miracle on the Hudson" airplane landing and the gliding experience of the pilot that he could so excellently put to use that day. The intern in our office demonstrated the same successful instincts to learn all he can about our industry in his spare time.

PAY ATTENTION TO LIFE LESSONS

The Adventures of Johnny Bunko is a great book by Daniel Pink (2008) that presents a comic book–style superhero who learns six fabulous life lessons applicable for today. Those lessons are very applicable to all professions; I've included them here and related them to the design profession.

1. *There is no plan.* It is true that "if you want to get ahead in life you have to have a plan." But, you can't map out your life as the world changes, and you also change. A well-known person in the industry told me early in my life, "Always write your goals in pencil, as they will change." Realize that you can't plan all aspects of your life, but that you can focus on work that is interesting to you, and you can have a vision of your future. The key, it seems from Pink, is to maintain a level of flexibility.

2. *Think strengths, not weaknesses.* No matter what you are working on at your job, do the best that you can possibly do even if the tasks are not your passion. Capitalize on your strengths in life and things that bring you "energy." We are very lucky to work in our profession, as it is a combination of art, science, and business, and what we do can make a tremendous impact on our clients' businesses. Have you ever worked so hard on a project that you are "in the zone" where everything is going well, and you can't believe the quick passage of time? That is when you are working to your strengths and concentrating on your passion.

3. *It's not about you.* Always remember that your focus should be on your project, or firm, or clients with whom you are working. You are here to provide service and to improve the lives of others. I have learned working with clients that my job is to make them successful at their work and, if they succeed, so does everyone on our team.

4. *Persistence trumps talent.* Your attitude at work is so important. Top performers "show up" and remember to excel at any part of their craft. We must practice, practice, and then practice some more. Study people who are successful in their careers, and you will come to realize that they do so well because they are working to their "intrinsic" motivation or passion. Persist and you are likely to succeed.

5. *Make excellent mistakes.* Too many people avoid making mistakes in their lives, but spend all of their time planning on what they are going to do, and they never really accomplish anything. Most successful people make spectacular mistakes and then get better and move a little closer to excellence.

6. *Leave an imprint.* As you are starting your career, think about looking back and ask questions: Am I making a difference? Does my being here matter? Think about your purpose in life; realize that your life isn't infinite; and your limited time here should matter. Think big and develop your own voice in the profession.

CONCLUSION

Know that change is happening even as you read this essay. In the world today, exponential change is part of our lives (Sony, 2008). Did you know that the top 10 jobs in 2010 didn't even exist in 2004? Did you know that if "MySpace" was a country that it would be the fifth-largest country in size in the world?

Weathering the current economic situation is an opportunity to learn and study how to contribute to excellence. Focus on your passion and building your "voice" in what you do. You are developing your life and your career, and when it is built on a foundation of excellence, innovation, and contribution to others you will find it to be a life-fulfilling career, leaving your company, clients, and communities a little better because of you. Carpe diem!

REFERENCES

Brown, T. (2008, June). *Design thinking.* Retrieved June 25, 2009, from http://web.me.com/deatkins/CIC/Seminar_Schedule_files/HBR-Timbrown.pdf

Court, D. (2008, December). *The downturn's new rules for marketers: The old recession playbook won't work this time around.* Retrieved June 25, 2009, from http://www.mckinseyquarterly.com/the_downturn_new_rules_for_marketers_2262

Gregran, P. (2009, January 27). *What do you do in your spare time?* Retrieved January 27, 2009, from http://harvardbusiness.org/

Pink, D. (2008). *The adventures of Johnny Bunko: The last career guide you will ever need.* New York: Riverhead Books.

Sony. (2008, June). Education and the future of technology. *BMG Executive Presentation.* Retrieved February 6, 2009, from http://www.flixy.com/education-and-technology-2008

RITA CARSON GUEST

EXPECTATIONS OF NEW GRADUATES: A VIEW FROM PRACTICE

The role of an interior designer is continually evolving within a changing political, social, and economic culture. As in other fields, continual learning is required throughout a career as society, materials, and technology evolve and change. New problems require new approaches for creative solutions. A graduating interior design student will never learn in school all they need to learn to practice effectively in the business world. A first-professional degree curriculum is developed to create world-class problem solvers; much time is spent on theory, design elements and principles, ethics, knowledge of codes, acoustics, lighting, human interaction within the built environment, and space planning, to name a few of the critical knowledge areas. However, students also must learn basic technical skills to become productive employees immediately upon starting their first interior design position.

Today's technical skills are immediately valuable to their employer. In today's fast-paced

RITA CARSON GUEST, RID-AL/DC/FL/GA, FASID, is president and director of design at Carson Guest, Inc., a firm specializing in law office design. She was Georgia's first registered interior designer and first interior designer appointee to the Georgia State Board of Architects and Interior Designers, where she served for 10 years. Guest is also registered in Florida, Alabama, and Washington, DC. She serves on the technical committee for Means of Egress for the National Fire Protection Association, contributing to the last two publication cycles of NFPA 101 and NFPA 5000. Guest was ASID national president (2008-2009). She served on the board of directors for the Museum of Design–Atlanta for eight years, and currently she serves on the advisory board of Bauder College. Guest often writes articles for interior design and business publications and is a popular speaker throughout the United States.

society, companies cannot afford to employ graduates who must spend two years in training before becoming productive. For example, in our company the most productive interior designers we have employed right out of college have technical drawing skills in CAD or Revit, in addition to their knowledge base in interior design, as described above.

When I graduated from college with a four-year degree in interior design and minor in art history, I thought I knew it all! And, I thought my employer was lucky to hire me. It didn't take more than a week to learn that I knew very little about the professional practice of interior design. I had so much to learn! Yet I knew how to draft (no CAD in those days); I knew how to sketch and render; and I had a good sense of scale and proportion and a good color sense. My first assignment was a rendering on my first day of work. After that, my drafting skills were put to work; I was so fast at drafting, I would run out of work, so I was given design problems to solve that would normally fall to a more senior designer. Luckily, I was a quick learner and was handling my own projects as a project manager within a year in the architectural department of the firm. I succeeded with much help and direction from experienced interior designers and architects. I always had someone to go to, to ask questions of, and to help solve the problem at hand. I didn't even realize how much responsibility I had, or that I was doing what a project manager does today. I was very fortunate to grow up quickly in interior design.

Today, it is impossible to teach all the skills needed to practice interior design independently in a two-year or four-year, first-professional degree program, so I believe we need to promote advanced degrees in interior design that include a practicum where experience in the real world is gained. Educators have to choose what is most important to teach their students, given the broad range of critical knowledge and skills to be learned—and it is not an easy decision, I'm sure. So, in this essay I am defining the knowledge and skills needed and not needed to start work in our firm.

MY WISH LIST

After 36 years in the interior design business, I've seen many different practice types. Interior design is a broad field with many opportunities for different types of work. A wish list for knowledge and skills an interior design graduate would possess, for our interior design firm, will look different from those required for other interior design firms.

Our interior design practice is a full-service, commercial design practice. We design the entire space for our clients, including the wall layout, the dimensional volume of the space, the lighting and fixture specifications, the placement of power/data, the millwork, the details of intersections of materials, the hardware, as well as the finishes and furnishings along with accessories and artwork. We also provide a purchasing service for products used in the space when needed by our client, and we hire consulting engineers as needed, based on the scope of work for the project. Knowledge and skills required, then, for a firm that specializes in furnishings, fixtures, and equipment (FF&E) rather than full-service interior design will be different. Knowledge and skills of an interior designer who is employed by Carson Guest are also different depending on the position in the firm. Basic knowledge we would like everyone to have include:

> Good written and verbal communication abilities and knowledge to carry out Internet research
> Entry-level understanding and willingness to contribute to a team preparing a set of interior design construction drawings

- An ability to engage in code research and understand of the basics and importance of complying with building and life safety codes
- A basic understanding of the importance of ergonomics
- A basic understanding of how to use materials and sources properly
- Ability to work within a team
- Sustainable design knowledge is a plus, but willingness to learn how to specify products and materials that are healthy for our environment is critical
- A basic understanding of professional ethics
- Willingness to continue learning

Basic skills we would like everyone to have include:

- Proficiency in Word, Excel, Outlook
- Good computer technical skills including Photoshop, Revit, and AutoCAD

Graduates who are competent in BIM technology or Revit will not have trouble finding a job. Today, there is a void in the market for interior designers who are trained on Revit or BIM technology. BIM drawings are the future for design and implementation. We believe that Revit/BIM technology will replace CAD within the next 10 years. At that time, CAD will be less important than Revit or BIM.

If interior design graduates have a good understanding of the entire body of knowledge (BOK) (see Martin & Guerin, 2006, available at www.careersininteriordesign.com) then they would have knowledge in the areas defined as follows:

1. *Human Environment Needs* knowledge basics including programming, research, analysis of needs, accessibility issues, cultural factors, strategic planning, survey of site, human factors (i.e., ergonomics, anthropometrics), sustainability, indoor air quality, human behavior, psychology of color, social factors, conflict resolution, etc.

2. *Interior Construction, Codes, and Regulations* including building codes, laws and regulations, life safety standards, lighting, building systems, working drawings for non-load-bearing interior construction, permitting, specifications, power/data specifications, fire and life safety principles, acoustics, security, etc.

3. *Design Knowledge* areas including design and detailing of custom furniture, cabinetry, millwork, selection of textiles, an understanding of the design process, aesthetics, etc.

4. *Products and Materials* ranging from various finishes that comprise walls, floors, ceilings, furnishings, etc. A subset of this category is understanding sustainability and the materials needed as well as what materials are needed to meet health and life safety codes.

5. *Professional Practice* including a basic understanding of business types and processes and legal responsibilities to professional ethics.

6. *Communication* is the single ingredient that separates the successful interior designer from others. If you are a good communicator, you can better understand your client's needs. Education will teach you visual communication methods such as sketching, drawing, and rendering.

The BOK knowledge areas are critical for those who want to own an interior design practice; however, the knowledge and associated skills needed will vary depending on the graduates' practice area. For example, some knowledge areas and skills are less important for our firm because we already have leadership in place in those areas. It is very important to have exposure to and awareness of the knowledge areas in the following list, but in-depth understanding or expertise are not expected of entry-level interior designers who are employed by Carson Guest. They include:

- Professional practice knowledge of how to set up a business and legal responsibilities; although, basic business knowledge and ethics are important. Human environment needs knowledge basics (programming, research, analysis of needs, cultural factors, strategic planning, survey of site, indoor air quality, social factors, etc.). Although a basic understanding is important, we will train our designers on programming, needs analysis, how to survey a site properly, and what is needed to provide for the needs of our clients.
- Design knowledge areas including expertise with the design process. We train all of our designers about our interior design process, which will vary depending on the project and scope of work.
- Products and materials are large topics. Finishes and products make up walls, floors, ceilings, furnishings, etc. Although a basic understanding of what is available is good, we have a librarian and librarian assistant keep up-to-date on the latest products in the market and set up weekly updates to keep our designers informed. Our leadership will also help our designers with any sources needed. How to use different materials and sources is more important than the actual source.
- Our designers do not need to be competent to set up business processes. We have standard forms, templates, and materials for everything they will do, and we will train designers to use them. Templates include drawing sheet set up by category, standard notes by category, transmittal forms, budget templates, programming templates, stacking templates, etc.

In 10 years, the basic knowledge needed will be similar, yet technology and the requisite skills will continue to evolve. Graduating interior designers must be prepared to continually learn. There will always be a gap between interior design education and the practice of interior design due to the ongoing evolution of the interior design profession, vast differences in design firm culture and practice between firms, and changes in technology. Mary Knackstedt, in her book *The Challenge of Interior Design*, writes,

> It used to take 50 years for information to become obsolete. Now it happens in less than a few months. University professors are required to spend a minimum of one day a week researching their fields. We are in the same situation. Interior designers cannot afford to spend less than one solid day a week keeping up with design issues. (2008, p. 137)

Today, interior design has become such a complicated business, graduating interior designers need to determine if they want to try to learn it all and own their own business or if they want to specialize in one area of design. If they become an expert in one area and learn all they can, they will be invaluable to a future employer. Interior designers who specialize have a leg up on their competition. Our firm's specialty is law office design; we study the business of the practice of law so we can better meet our client's needs. Clients are impressed when they know you understand their business and their needs.

Whichever route new graduates consider their preferred career path, I believe graduates are always best served by working with an established interior designer or firm before starting their own business. They will learn quickly by doing and learning the way the business operates—if they are perceptive. They will also quickly learn what they enjoy versus what they do not enjoy. Interior design practice should be fun. New graduates should be passionate about what they do and love coming to work every day. If you are passionate about your practice, you will excel!

MY VIEW OF THE FUTURE

I believe we need to make sure interior design students understand that a major goal of interior design is to make the world a better place to live, work, heal, and play. Interior designers are problem solvers who need to be outcome driven with a love of people and a concern for how the power of design can change people's lives. Interior designers solve problems for individuals, their businesses, their employees, their stores, and their schools to enhance those environments in support and preparation for a better future.

Interior designers often create an outcome that their clients can't imagine, but know it is just what they want when they see the outcome. To be a good interior designer, you need a passionate love of people, to support quality of life, and hence you will be fulfilled by knowing you made life better for one or many. Like magic, interior designers turn abstract conceptual thoughts from their imaginations to paper and then apply them as practical solutions in support of better lives.

REFERENCES

Knackstedt, M. (2008). *The challenge of interior design: Professional value and opportunities.* New York: Allworth Press.

Martin, C., & Guerin, D. (2006). *The interior design profession's body of knowledge, 2005 edition.* Retrieved February 16, 2009, from www.careersininteriordesign.com

Universal design, barrier-free, ADA: which horse has crossed the finish line? What do these labels mean to interior designers and the public?

LOUISE JONES

ACCESSIBLE, UNIVERSAL, INCLUSIVE DESIGN: HAVE THE HORSES REACHED THE FINISH LINE?

WHAT IS UNIVERSAL DESIGN?

Confusion continues as to what constitutes universal design (UD). It is often associated with barrier-free design codes, the Americans with Disabilities Act (ADA), life span design, and the U.S. Fair Housing Act. But UD is not a euphemism for accessible design—it is much more than that. UD is a design philosophy that values and celebrates human diversity by considering the needs of all users of a space regardless of their age, ability, or physical stature.

Barrier-free guidelines from the 1950s and accessible design standards from the 1970s were incorporated into building codes to initiate the process of removing barriers in the built environment for people with disabilities. In the 1980s, life span design and transgenerational design extended the concept of accessibility to compel consideration of age when planning residential environments. The U.S. Congress passed civil rights legislation, including the Fair

LOUISE JONES, Arch.D, LEED® AP, IDEC, is a professor emeritus of Eastern Michigan University (EMU) with bachelor's and master's degrees in interior design and a doctorate in architecture. Jones, who has practiced and taught design for over 30 years, was a professor at EMU from 1988–2008 and director of the undergraduate and graduate interior design programs. Her research interests include universal design, interior design education, and green/sustainable design. She served as interim associate dean at EMU to design an environmentally responsible interior for a new campus building, utilizing universal design precepts. Jones served on the IDEC executive board and the *Journal of Interior Design* editorial board, and was deputy editor for the *Journal of Housing for the Elderly.* In addition to presentations and workshops at conferences in North and South America, Asia, Europe, and the Middle East, she has over 50 publications, including a textbook, *Environmentally Responsible Interior Design.*

Housing Act (FHA) and the ADA, that made it illegal to discriminate against people with disabilities. In 1990, the ADA Accessibility Guidelines (ADAAG) became the minimal standard of accessibility; however, the primary focus was to create barrier-free environments for people who used wheelchairs.

Instead of exemplifying good design, compliance with ADAAG often represented the worst possible design that could be legally executed. For example, minimal clearance for a doorway was set at 32 inches wide—even though people who used wheelchairs often scraped the doorway with their knuckles or had to partially disassemble their chairs to gain passage. UD emerged as (1) a more creative response to accessibility needs, (2) in recognition of the "graying of America," and (3) as a consequence of increased attention to equity and social justice.

Vitruvius, a Roman architect who lived 2000 years ago, identified three criteria for good design: *firmitas* (solidity of construction), *voluptas* (positive aesthetics), and *commoditas* (usability). He recommended a design so astute that nothing would impede its usefulness (Vitruvius, 1965 translation). UD considers human needs to be the starting point for design decisions regarding interior environments—but UD is not design for "special needs."

Planning a 60-inch-diameter turning circle to accommodate people who use wheelchairs is "barrier-free design"—it meets the needs of people who have a specific need, but this is not universal design. Planning a bedroom door opening that is at least 32 inches wide accommodates people who use wheelchairs or walkers or crutches, but it also makes it easier to move furniture or suitcases or a baby stroller through the door and provides easier access for people who are obese—this is UD. Selecting an interior paint that does not off-gas volatile organic compounds (VOCs) accommodates the needs of people with multiple chemical sensitivities (MCS) or with chronic obstructive pulmonary disease (COPD), but it also protects indoor air quality (IAQ) for anyone with asthma or allergies or for anyone who wants to avoid exposure to potentially carcinogenic chemicals—this is UD. Specifying a lever door handle that can be manipulated with the side of a hand or with an elbow accommodates people who have difficulty twisting a doorknob due to arthritis, a splint, or missing fingers, or for anyone who has their hands full of groceries, or laundry, or a baby—this is UD.

Leon Pastalon, professor emeritus at the University of Michigan, College of Architecture, advocates focusing on the context of the human condition rather than the characteristics of vulnerable population groups (Mace, 1988). Creating interior spaces for elders, children, and people with disabilities is not design for the special needs of specific groups within the population; instead, it is designing for the full scope of human-environment interactions (Welch, 1995). Ron Mace (1985), who is credited with coining the term, described UD as meeting the needs of most of the people, most of the time.

TABLE 5.1
DISABILITY PREVALENCE IN THE UNITED STATES IN 2006

GROUP	DEMOGRAPHIC CHARACTERISTICS
All Americans* Aged 5 and Older	• 15.7% (1 in 6) have one or more disabilities† • 9.9% (1 in 10) have a physical disability (i.e., limited in one or more basic physical activities such as walking, climbing stairs, reaching, lifting, or carrying)‡ • 3.5% have a self-care disability (i.e., dressing, bathing, or getting around inside the home)‡ • 4.6% have a sensory disability (i.e., blindness, deafness, and severe vision or hearing impairment)‡ • 6.3% have a mental disability (i.e., learning, remembering, or concentrating)‡
Age Specific Subgroups of the American Population	• 7.2% (aged 16–64) have an employment disability (i.e., working at a job or business)‡ • 6.1% (aged 16 and older) have a go-outside-the-home disability (i.e., mobility problem)‡ • 43.4% (aged 65 and older) have one or more disabilities†

Source: U.S. Census Bureau. (2006). American factfinder. Retrieved March 18, 2009, from http://www.census.gov/hhes/www/disability/disability.html

*2006 American Community Survey was the first U.S. Census survey to include civilian, noninstitutionalized individuals; people living in institutional group quarters; and those in the armed forces. See http://www.census.gov/hhes/www/disability/GQdisability.pdf

†The Census Bureau (2006) defines disability as "a long-lasting sensory, physical, mental, or emotional condition or conditions that make it difficult for a person to do functional or participatory activities such as seeing, hearing, walking, climbing stairs, learning, remembering, concentrating, dressing, bathing, going outside the home, or working at a job."

‡2006 American Community Survey Subject Definitions available at http://www.census.gov/acs/www/Downloads/2006/usedata/Subject_Definitions.pdf

THE NEED FOR UNIVERSAL DESIGN

Statistics are often cited to demonstrate the urgent need for UD. Life expectancy was only 44 years old in 1900—there were few physical limitations associated with old age. People who are disabled and/or elderly, most of whom want to maintain independent lifestyles, make up increasingly larger segments of the population. Table 5.1 reveals disability prevalence in the United States: one in six people report having one or more disabilities (U.S. Census Bureau, 2006).

In 1900, there were three million Americans aged 65 or older (1 in 25); by 2000, the numbers had grown to 31 million (1 in 8); by 2030, it is predicted that 67 million people (1 in 5) will be 65 or older (U.S. Census Bureau, 2002). Of the population aged 65 and older, 44% have a disability (U.S. Census, 2006). Longer life span means developing coping strategies for more disabling conditions. UD precepts can address functional problems to maintain elders' independence, autonomy, and dignity without introducing the stigma associated with negative stereotypes of aging. As the median age increases, more elders will require the services and supportive environments that are currently earmarked for people with disabilities.

However, age-related impairments differ from those stemming from genetic or traumatic causes. Multiple, progressive, chronic conditions can seriously affect the quality of life without necessarily being recognized as a disability. Michel Philibert, a French philosopher and gerontologist, believes new understanding has emerged wherein aging is defined as a pattern of change throughout the entire life span (Byerts, 1977). As the population ages, age-related changes in vision, hearing, posture, and mobility affect workplace design (Mueller, 2001). Implementation of UD can allow older adults to continue to be productive members of the workforce.

GLOBAL PERCEPTIONS OF UNIVERSAL DESIGN

The International Classification of Functioning, Disability, and Health (ICF) is the World Health Organization's (WHO, 2001) framework for measuring health and disability at both the individual and the population levels. The ICF is an international standard that addresses health and disability with a new perspective. It acknowledges that every human being can experience a decrement in health and thereby experience some degree of disability. Disability is not something that only happens to a minority of people. The ICF thus "mainstreams" the experience of disability and recognizes it as a universal human experience.

> By shifting the focus from cause to impact, it places all health conditions on an equal footing, allowing them to be compared using a common metric—a ruler of health and disability. Furthermore, ICF takes into account the social aspects of disability and does not see disability only as medical or biological dysfunction. By citing contextual factors, including environmental factors, ICF allows the impact of the physical environment on the person's functioning to be recorded. (World Health Organization, 2009)

With this underpinning, UD precepts can be utilized to respond to a range of human conditions, exceeding far beyond what is possible by using barrier-free codes to create accessible spaces for people with disabilities.

UD is not a truly international concept—it is contextual (Parker, 2001). Cultural, political, legal, and economic circumstances all play a role in how needs, wants, and aspirations are addressed. Although fundamental human needs remain constant, there are vast differences in the understanding and practice of UD in the East and West, in developed and developing countries.

In economically developing countries (where the majority of the global population lives), there are few, if any, public safety nets (e.g., health insurance, social security, pension plans). The strength and coherence of family units are critical in providing care for elders and for people with disabilities (who seldom venture away from home). Multigenerational families are still prevalent, and family bonds are strong. Large, extended families provide the support network for aging parents and for those unable to care for themselves (including orphans and those who are disabled). There is often a divide between rich and poor. Servants provide care and assistance to those who can afford to pay for services; for people without family support (common in war-torn countries), life on the streets often leads to illness and early death.

The prevalence of oppressing realities such as poverty, population pressures, illiteracy, and lack of infrastructures calls for universal design solutions vastly different from those elsewhere . . . the kind that suit the people's needs . . . their physical, social, cultural, and psychological needs. (Balaram, 2001, p. 5.3)

Asia has the world's fastest-growing elderly population. Although UD is largely unacknowledged in most of Asia, in the more rapidly developing countries, some basic UD precepts are beginning to emerge—focusing on design of environments for the increasing number of elders. "Design of suitable habitats for older people must be considered as a natural subset of universal design, supporting the maintenance of personal independence and dignity as people age" (Harrison, 2001, p. 40.1). Developing "elder-friendly" environments is critical; with time this may evolve into "people-friendly" environments that are inclusive of all users, in the true spirit of universal design (Parker, 2001).

In Japan, by the year 2015, more than 25% of the population will be 65 or older—an experience unprecedented in human history. Japan is the first Asian country to persuade the general public to accept UD precepts for dwellings and may be the only country to use economic incentives at the national level to address the implications of a rapidly aging society on the built environment (Kose, 2001). They have emerged as leaders in the development of innovative products and design strategies that exemplify UD precepts.

In 2000, the Commission of the European Communities of the European Union (EU) issued *Towards a Barrier Free Europe for People with Disabilities* to strengthen the concept of inclusiveness for people with disabilities. However, notwithstanding EU legislation that mandates buildings be accessible, a lack of political will by national and local authorities has led to countless barriers to accessibility in the built environment (Walsh, 2001). "Person-centered design" evolved from an understanding that accessibility of the built environment is approached and effectively solved in human scale. In Europe, the concept of person-centered design has evolved to

place real people at the centre of creative endeavors and gives due consideration to their health, safety, and welfare in the built environment. It includes specific performance criteria such as a sensory rich and accessible environment (regarding mobility, usability, communications, and information). (European Charter on Sustainable Design and Construction, 1995, Appendix III)

In the United States, environmentally responsible design and UD are typically taught and practiced as two facets of good design. However, in Europe, they are much more tightly aligned in a broader definition of inclusive design, which also encompasses equity and social justice. Nearly 20 years ago, the United Nations (1992) stated, "Human beings are at the centre of concerns for sustainable development" (p. 2). A sustainable building will be person-centered and socially inclusive, flexible and adaptable, in harmony and balance with the natural environment (Walsh, 2001).

A comprehensive understanding of inclusion was reflected at the United Nations' Earth Summits with the Rio (1992) and Kyoto (1998) Protocols. This definition of sustainable development includes responsible and equitable human, social, cultural, and economic development. Roger Coleman (2001), of the Royal College of Art in London, succinctly expresses the European perspective: "Place the user on center stage and create sustainable environments that are environmentally responsible, age-friendly, barrier-free, and inclusive" (p. 4.22).

In the United States, most nonresidential interior environments are accessible to people who use wheelchairs, though the needs of all of the users are seldom addressed. Although there has been a grass-roots movement to utilize UD to create residential environments that allow their occupants to age-in-place, little headway has been made in creating residential environments that respond to the needs of a succession of residents, their extended families, friends, and guests. A few municipalities have broken new ground by passing *visitability* legislation that mandates new homes provide accessibility for visitors who use a wheelchair (minimum door width, a clear path, and access to a toilet). "Smart House" technology can be used to anticipate the needs of residents and respond accordingly, but the cost is still prohibitive in most instances.

Globally, the outlook is even gloomier. In developing countries, food, shelter, and safety have priority over good design. Although the European construct of inclusive design is broader than the American interpretation of UD, inclusive design is primarily an academic concept rather than a reality in designed environments. Much of Europe still struggles with basic accessibility. The aging of the population may be the stimulus that leads to broader implementation of UD precepts. Asia is aging even more rapidly than the United States, and Japan is leading the way in the universal design of residential environments—this horse may be in sight of the finish line.

Balaram, S. (2001). Universal design and the majority world. In W. Preiser & E. Ostroff (Eds.), *Universal design handbook*. New York: McGraw-Hill.

Byerts, T. (1977). Prologue. *Journal of Architectural Education, 31*(1), v.

Coleman, R. (2001). Designing for our future selves. In W. Preiser & E. Ostroff (Eds.), *Universal design handbook*. New York: McGraw-Hill.

Harrison, J. (2001). Housing for older persons in Southeast Asia: Evolving policy and design. In W. Preiser & E. Ostroff (Eds.), *Universal design handbook*. New York: McGraw-Hill.

Kose, S. (2001). The impact of aging on Japanese accessibility standards. In W. Preiser & E. Ostroff (Eds.), *Universal design handbook*. New York: McGraw-Hill.

Mace, R. (1985). *Universal design, barrier free environments for everyone*. Los Angeles: Designers West.

Mace, R. (1988). *Universal design: Housing for the lifespan of all people*. Washington, DC: U.S. Department of Housing & Urban Development.

Mueller, J. (2001). Office and workplace design. In W. Preiser & E. Ostroff (Eds.), *Universal design handbook*. New York: McGraw-Hill.

Parker, K. (2001). Developing economies: A reality check. In W. Preiser & E. Ostroff (Eds.), *Universal design handbook*. New York: McGraw-Hill.

United Nations. (1992). Declaration on environment and development. *United Nations Framework Convention on Climate Change*. Retrieved March 1, 2009, from http://www.un.org/geninfo/bp/enviro.html

U.S. Census Bureau. (2002). *2000 census of the population and housing summary social, economic and housing characteristics of the United States*. Washington, DC: U.S. Government Printing Office.

U.S. Census Bureau. (2006). American factfinder. Retrieved March 18, 2009, from http://www.census.gov/hhes/www/disability/disability.html

Vitruvius. (1965 translation). *Les dix livres d'architecture*. Paris, France: Les Libraires Associes.

Walsh, C. (2001) Sustainable human and social development: An examination of contextual factors. In W. Preiser & E. Ostroff (Eds.), *Universal design handbook*. New York: McGraw-Hill.

World Health Organization. (2001). *International classification of functioning, disability and health*. Retrieved January 10, 2009, from http://www.who.int/classifications/icfbrowser/

World Health Organization. (2009). *ICF*. Retrieved January 10, 2009, from http://www.who.int/classifications/icf/en/

> How can interior space
> leverage human capital?

ALAN HEDGE

INTERIOR DESIGN:
SATAN OR SAVIOR?

THE PROBLEM

According to the National Council for Interior Design Qualification (NCIDQ),

> Interior design is a multi-faceted profession in which creative and technical solutions are applied within a structure to achieve a built interior environment. These solutions are functional, enhance the quality of life and culture of the occupants, and are aesthetically attractive. (2004)

Not surprisingly, interior design magazines are replete with stunning photographs of beautiful interiors. Anyone looking at such information immediately knows that interior designers are educated to create spaces that are aesthetically pleasing, possibly cost effective, and supposedly functional for their client. Interior designers are rewarded for their innovative solutions, but mostly the praise of colleagues

ALAN HEDGE, PhD, CPE, is a professor in the department of design and environmental analysis at Cornell University. He is a fellow of the Human Factors and Ergonomics Society (HFES), the Ergonomics Society (UK), and the International Ergonomics Association, and is a certified professional ergonomist. Hedge received the 2003 Alexander J. Williams Jr. Design Award from HFES. His research and teaching activities focus on issues of design and workplace ergonomics as they affect the health, comfort, and productivity of workers. Hedge researches workstation design and ergonomic risk factors, alternative keyboard and input systems, the health and comfort impacts of indoor air quality, and the effects of office lighting on computer workers. He co-edited the *Handbook of Human Factors and Ergonomics Methods* and coauthored *Keeping Buildings Healthy: How to Monitor and Prevent Indoor Environmental Problems*. Hedge has published 30 chapters and over 180 articles in ergonomics-related journals.

focuses on the visual impact of the design its colors, forms, and materials used to shape the interior space.

As a professor of human factors and ergonomics in a design department, seeing the imagery presented in interior design and architectural publications is troubling to me. Why, you may ask? The answer is simple; the answer is "people," or rather the lack of them. The imagery that so often characterizes innovative interior design solutions invariably is devoid of any human content. Rooms, office floors, and other spaces are shown in all of their empty glory, untouched by the hands of messy occupants. Only when occupants get to touch and interact with a design solution can one know its level of success.

Unfortunately, many people in my profession of ergonomics spend their days dealing with occupants who have been injured or who are at risk of injury because of poor design decisions, and much of our time is spent correcting the design mistakes made in the creation of aesthetically pleasing but ergonomically suboptimal spaces. Like the stunning Lion fish, many designs are wondrously beautiful, but they also can pack a deadly punch when touched! Instead of leveraging human capital by creating optimal workspace, the design of many modern workplaces does just the opposite. This, then, is the theme of my essay. My focus is the modern office environment because this represents the workspace for many millions of people, and it is where I have done much of my own research over the last 30 years.

In any commercial office building, the major cost to an organization is not the building, its contents, or the energy that it uses, but rather the people. People costs typically can be 90% of all costs paid by an organization to occupy a building (Center for the Built Environment, 2000). The skills, knowledge, and labor activities of the building occupants are the *human capital* that generates economic value and that

is the lifeblood of any organization (Sullivan & Sheffrin, 2003). The square-foot space cost of any office is a tiny fraction of the labor cost of the employees. For example, office space rent is around $20 per square foot, the energy costs around $2.50 per square foot, and the salaries and benefits of the average employee are around $320 per square foot. Anything that improves the productivity of employees by just 1% (which is a mere extra 45 seconds of work per hour) results in a benefit of almost $4 a square foot, which is much greater than any energy savings that could be achieved. Even though so much attention now is rightly focused on sustainable designs that reduce energy consumption, energy costs typically are only 1% to 2% of labor costs! To date, almost no effort has been expended to considering ways that interior spaces can be leveraged to protect workers from injuries and maximize their productivity.

Almost two decades ago Danko, Eshelman, and Hedge (1990) showed that many interior design decisions are not benign, but they can either beneficially or detrimentally affect human health and productivity. Today, the interior design profession is coming to grips with the view that a goal of interior design is to produce interior environments that are comfortable, safe, and healthy places for the occupants. The American Society of Interior Designers (ASID) says that "an interior design professional contributes at every phase of your project to ensure that the final result exceeds your expectations and ensures the health, safety, and welfare of all who may use or occupy the space" (2009). In other words, well-designed interior spaces must leverage human capital.

Unfortunately, not all workplaces have benefited from the involvement of professional interior designers. In pursuing their practice, some interior designers or other design professionals unwittingly have created many of the workplace problems that ergonomists then have to solve.

ERGONOMIC ISSUES

Poor head/neck posture
Poor hand/arm posture
Poor back/torso posture

www.asid.org

ERGONOMIC ISSUES

Poor head/neck posture
Poor back/torso posture
Forward leaning on a hard surface

www.asid.org/about

ERGONOMIC ISSUES

Laptop user—poor hand/arm posture
Window light will veil/reflect in laptop screen
Colleague—poor back/torso posture

www.asid.org/bcdevelopment/running/
Surviving+in+the+Economic+Downturn.htm

FIGURE 5.1. Images from the ASID Web site that actually illustrate how one should not work.

Misguided workplace design is responsible for hundreds of thousands of workplace injuries each year and billions of dollars in lost productivity!

So what needs to change? Although ASID recognizes that interior designers need to have some familiarity with ergonomics, this remains a poorly addressed topic in many interior design education programs. Interior designers need to receive systematic educational exposure to the fundamental principles of ergonomic design so that they can cut through the manufacturers' marketing hype and misleading materials that permeate the marketplace. I am not suggesting that interior designers become ergonomists, or vice versa; merely that interior designers will benefit from taking an appropriately developed ergonomics class. Perhaps even more important, they also should seek impartial advice from ergonomists or reliable sources of ergonomics

information when they are developing their design solutions. Unfortunately, a cursory surfing of the ASID Web site as of May 2009 shows images of people working in postures that fill ergonomists with dismay because they illustrate the wrong ways of working with a laptop computer rather than a proper way (see Figure 5.1). If these are the images being shown by the professional society, how can we really expect interior designers, who are visual thinkers, to create workplaces devoid of ergonomic pitfalls?

Interior designers need to be familiar with various ways of allowing people to work in neutral postures that will not facilitate injuries and also ways of delivering the work tools to users rather than forcing them to adopt contorted postures to access their work tools. The principles of neutral posture working for computer users are readily available from professional sources (see http://ergo.human.cornell.edu/ergoguide.html).

Unfortunately, the word *ergonomic* has been used in a cavalier, liberal manner by many manufacturers, and wary interior designers may believe that they are specifying ergonomic products in their solutions when, in fact, this is not the case. As an example, most if not all office chairs carry a "label" that they are an ergonomic design, yet there is enormous variability among different manufacturers and models, so how can this be? Some manufacturers promote so-called "ergonomic designs" that provide no lower back support, an essential element in any ergonomic chair. Some chairs provide inadequate ranges of adjustments for the target occupants. Some designs are so complex that their occupants never figure out how to properly adjust them. A chair may look "cool," it may be called "ergonomic" but, more often than not, nothing could be more misleading! If this were not the case, when we ergonomists look at modern offices we should never see any design problems, and we should never have to deal with occupants getting injured at work. Just the opposite is true. At Cornell University, we have created checklists that can help ergonomists and interior designers alike to evaluate the quality of the ergonomic design of a chair (see http://ergo.human.cornell.edu/ahSEATING.htm) as well as other office products (see http://ergo.human.cornell.edu/cutools.html).

We can also question who should shoulder responsibility for sub-optimal ergonomic design. Is it the fault of product manufacturers—many of whom never consult with ergonomists during their own design process? Is it the fault of interior designers because they select products from furniture companies that make their lives easy through provision of CAD templates, or that are told that all of a company's products are "ergonomic," or they are misled into believing that all their products are equally effective? Or, is it the clients' fault for not demanding that all designs be vetted by a certified professional ergonomist?

WHO IS RESPONSIBLE?

I contend that, at the moment, the responsibility lies with the interior design profession. Why do I say this? Imagine that the behavior of the typical interior designer was that of a physician, and that the design problem was a patient trying to get well and lead a healthy lifestyle. What if the physician simply listened to their patient, their client, who told them that they wanted to "get better," but they never systematically examined the patient to determine the cause of their complaint? What would we say if we found that the physician chose medications because they were pretty colors or pills because they were nice shapes or had interesting names that were appealing to the patient? What if that physician told the patient that all drugs produced by a company must be equally effective because the company has a good reputation? What if the physician afforded patients (clients) the discretion to choose whatever medications they liked based on their "look"? What if the physician always chose the cheapest medication for a cost-conscious patient, or for a high-net-wealth patient, the most expensive medication irrespective of its efficacy? What if the physician prescribed a treatment regimen with no evidence of its effectiveness? Such situations would be untenable in medicine. Pharmaceutical drugs have to undergo extensive human trials and evidence has to be independently evaluated by the Federal Drug Administration. Physicians have to undergo extensive education in diagnosing illness, in evaluating research evidence, and in prescribing effective treatments. So why should an interior designer, whose decisions can impact the lives of many, be held to a lesser standard?

Of course, interior designers are educated to listen to their clients, but seldom are they given the tools and education to really critically investigate their client's real issues and/or goals. Interior designers are educated to select items based on shape, color, texture, and cost, but seldom based on their efficacy as low-risk-injury work tools for their users. So, when an office worker develops a serious injury, such as carpal tunnel syndrome caused by inappropriate keyboard and mouse use because these work items were incorrectly positioned in a workstation; and the office chair was unsuitable for its user which resulted in awkward, contorted work postures; who is responsible?

We ergonomists typically are called in as "firefighters" to change how the person works, and usually we do this by changing what they are sitting on and how their keyboard, mouse, and screen are positioned. And, we are extremely successful at doing this, but also we are seen as an additional cost over and above the original design, and our post-hoc design interventions are seen as aesthetically undesirable (by the way, I completely agree that many so-called ergonomic products are ugly, and there is no reason that this needs to be the case).

So, who was responsible for the injury? Was it the employee who couldn't work in an appropriate way because of decisions made by the interior designer? Was it the furniture manufacturer who assured the interior designer that their products were "ergonomic"? Or, was it the interior designer who failed to critically evaluate the design solution based on evidence of the efficacy of the products and/or concepts employed? Who simply provided what the client asked for rather than challenging the client to invest in what they really needed? Who focused more on finishes, forms, and color than on functional effectiveness and real ergonomic design? Who never evaluated the impact of the design beyond receiving accolades from colleagues for images of an empty space? Who never followed through to ensure that their design decisions were successful and did not ultimately produce misery for many people?

I contend that making an *informed* design decision is the responsibility of interior designers and that their professional judgment should be based on the best available scientific evidence about the efficacy of design elements.

An additional incentive for interior designers to pay more attention to ergonomic design and to collaborate with ergonomists has recently emerged. Designs that promote good ergonomics can now earn a point in the Leadership in Energy and Environmental Design for Commercial Interiors (LEED-CI®) rating system for commercial interiors in the "Innovation in Design and Innovation in Operations Credit" (Hedge, 2008). The requirement for this point involves the development and implementation of "a comprehensive ergonomics strategy that will have a positive impact on human health and comfort when performing daily activity for at least 75% of Full Time Equivalent building users." The U.S. Green Building Council (2008) gives detailed guidance on a four-step process to attain this point:

> **Step 1:** Identifying activities and building functions for which ergonomic enhancement (I.e., ergonomic strategies that exceed standard industry practice) is both possible and desirable through education and equipment, and wherever possible building users should be consulted on their preferences.
>
> **Step 2:** Define a set of performance goals and expectations for the ergonomics strategy that address productivity, comfort, and health. Develop a plan and design process to meet them. Provide procedures to track and report the results of the ergonomics strategy, ensure that the performance goals have been met, and identify areas of potential improvement.
>
> **Step 3:** Provide machines, equipment, tools, work-aids (METWAs), furnishings, and accessories that reduce the risk of work-related musculoskeletal disorders and are acceptable to a wide range of building users.

Step 4: Provide ergonomics education to building users. Provide at least two opportunities for building users to understand and take advantage of ergonomic features in their environment. At least one of these opportunities must be interactive, and at least one must include an explanation of the provided METWAs and furnishings, preferably by the manufacturer. Post-education evaluations must be conducted. (Hedge, 2008)

CONCLUSION

Are interior designers artistic saviors battling against banal and boring workspaces, or are they sometimes, unwittingly, the stealthy and satanic purveyors of designs that inadvertently perpetrate human misery? It is my contention that the interior design profession has a responsibility to create pleasing interior spaces that also minimize or, better still, eliminate the risks of design-related injuries for occupants. If interior designers do not feel equipped with the necessary knowledge and skills to do this, then it is their responsibility to seek out this expertise for their design team. Yet, from the thousands and thousands of workplace injuries stemming from poor workspace design, it is all too obvious that some professional interior designers often have failed to achieve ergonomic goals.

Interior design is poised at an important juncture in which interior designers are being asked to shoulder more responsibility for the human impact of their designs. For the interior design profession, this is an opportunity to broaden its role beyond the creation of aesthetically pleasing spaces to also ensure that by applying good ergonomics, designs will foster healthy conditions and productive working environments and deliver interior spaces that truly will leverage human capital.

REFERENCES

American Society of Interior Designers. (2009). *Commercial design.* Retrieved May 28, 2009, from http://www.asid.org/designservices/whyhire/commercial/commercialdesign.htm

Center for the Built Environment. (2000). *Task/ambient conditioning systems.* Retrieved April 13, 2009, from http://www.cbe.berkeley.edu/underfloorair/tacguidelines.htm

Danko, S., Eshelman, P., & Hedge, A. (1990) A taxonomy of health, safety, and welfare implications of interior design decisions. *Journal of Interior Design Education Research, 16*(2), 19–30.

Hedge, A. (2008) The sprouting of "green" ergonomics. *HFES Bulletin, 51*(12), 1–3.

National Council for Interior Design Qualification. (2004). *NCIDQ definition of interior design.* Retrieved April 13, 2009, from http://www.ncidq.org/who/definition.htm

Sullivan, A., & Sheffrin, S. (2003). *Economics: Principles in action.* Upper Saddle River, NJ: Pearson Prentice Hall.

U.S. Green Building Council. (2008). *The ergonomics strategy: Innovation and design credits.* LEED Project Certification Credit Interpretation Rulings - LEED-EB 2.0. Retrieved May 29, 2009, from http://www.usgbc.org/Docs/LEEDdocs/IDcredit_guidance_final.pdf

> Has technology influenced creativity?
> Is technology an impediment to creativity?
> Is technology an aid to creativity?

MARK S. C. NELSON

CREATIVITY IN A SEASON OF TECHNOLOGICAL CHANGE

Technology and creativity have historically circled around each other, with first one leading and then the other, while dancing in step together across the centuries as fresh technologies cut in and tired technologies limp out. Over the last 20 years, however, some observers note that technology has not only led the dance with creativity, they feel that technology has continually bruised the toes of its partner. Others might even say that technology will someday dance on its own without needing a creative partner. Does technology hinder creativity or enhance creativity? How is technology changing the nature of creativity in the practice of interior design? These are the core issues examined here.

IMPORT

Interior design is a professional business activity, where creativity and originality have traditionally played a central role in the public's image of interior designers as well as in interior

MARK S. C. NELSON is an associate professor at the University of Wisconsin-Madison. He ushered in his professional career in 1985 with a position as a pen-and-ink architectural illustrator, reasoning that after 600 years of tradition, becoming an expert at Renaissance perspective was a stable career move. Of course, four years later, the PC had rendered those skills obsolete, leading Nelson to spend the last 20 years immersed in digital visualization. Over much of the same time span, he also had ample opportunities to observe creativity first hand while working on award-winning interiors projects headed by talented designers that included three *Interior Design* Hall of Fame inductees. Since becoming a full-time academic in 1999, Nelson has published numerous papers and articles addressing digital technology as well as creativity. Having learned about obsolescence the hard way, he is revisiting his watercolor skills in anticipation of a glut of digital designers.

designers' own self-image (Portillo, 2002). Creativity is an intangible that represents an essential part of the services for which interior designers charge fees. If interior designers' creativity is diminished as a result of new technology, then technology is a threat to interior designers' livelihoods and identities.

Likewise, if technology promises to alter the nature of creativity's relationship with interior designers, then interior designers may find that some traditional skills and services are no longer marketable. If interior designers and interior design educators do not begin to identify ways that the nature of creativity will change as a result of new technology, then creative activities may be taken over by people (or machines) outside of the interior design profession (Celento, 2007), and students will have difficulty entering the workforce.

SETTING

As the winds of spring first blow in and bring a new season, each branch of an apple tree may be in a quite different state from other branches on the same tree. Some twigs sport buds that have barely begun to open; some support unfurling petals; and others are awash with the full, aromatic blossoms that eventually cover every branch. Without warning, the blossoms quickly fall away as green leaves unfurl, but soon firm, new fruit slowly grows around the seeds of future life, bearing no resemblance to the fragile flowers that preceded them. Nature is not always this idyllic, however, and sometimes spring winds blow in a late frost that brings everything to a halt, leading to a fruitless season.

Today, digital technology is a spring wind blowing in a new season, and interior designers are the branches of an apple tree. Some interior designers are still waiting for the buds of creativity to open, other designers are already seeing creativity start to unfurl, and other designers are awash in a burst of creativity. As with the apple tree, what may come next is that, without warning, these fragile blossoms of creativity fall away, leading to new fruits and new seeds of creativity that become the next stage in the life of interior design practice. On the other hand, technology may be a frost that brings creativity to a halt. The discussion that follows leaves metaphor behind and examines the issues more concretely.

DISCUSSION OVERVIEW

Moving beyond apple blossoms to a more detailed discussion of digital technology's impact on creativity in interior design will proceed by first describing how these terms are used. Next, a look back at the typewriter's impact on creativity will suggest a parallel historical example of the dance between creativity and technology. A discussion of interior designers' perceptions of technology as both hindrance to and enhancer of creativity follows. A concluding discussion contemplates possible ways that creativity, its roles, and its processes will be redefined by digital technology.

CREATIVITY, TECHNOLOGY, AND DESIGN IN THE CONTEXT OF THIS DISCUSSION

Creativity can be discussed in many contexts. Some of the more popular contexts include discussions of genius or visionary design. For the purposes of this discussion, however, the intent is not to focus on something that applies to an elite few; creativity refers to the insights that occur during the daily activities of a typical interior designer, leading to new relationships, ideas, or concepts.

For the purposes of this discussion, technology is envisioned in its broadest sense as a tool, system, or method. Technologies may be as concrete as the wheel or as esoteric as the alphabet. Current technologies of most relevance in this discussion of creativity and interior design are digital computing and its related applications, including drawing, visualization, artificial intelligence, prototyping, and manufacturing.

The public commonly associates designing with creating drawings or plans. Interior designers tend to think of designing as problem solving in general, and more concretely as a sequence of steps that begins with programming and ends with design development. Ways that technology influences these perceptions and technology's relationship to creativity will be discussed as follows.

HISTORICAL CASE STUDY: THE TYPEWRITER AND CREATIVITY

If someone had never watched an apple tree change with the seasons, it would be difficult for him or her to envision that fruit would emerge because spring blossoms bear little resemblance to fall apples. A person experienced with flowers of all types would be especially disadvantaged because roses and most other flowers never give way to juicy fruit. On the other hand, watching a time-lapse film of last year's pear tree might make it easier to envision this year's apple tree. In that spirit, a look at the typewriter (one of yesteryear's recently vanished technologies) and its relationship with creativity should help us envision the still blossoming history of digital technology.

The emergence of the typewriter as a creatively focused technology, with an early version first patented sometime near the beginning of the 18th century, may have been the most radical technological development affecting the act of creativity in writing since the invention of the Greek alphabet (written using a stylus, about 400 BC), which in Plato's time radically altered the nature of creativity and discourse (McCluhan & Fiore, 2001). The typewriter's predecessor, the quill pen, was a new technology in 700 AD and was the dominant technology of creative writing for about 1000 years. The typewriter combined the reproductive functions of the printing press with the creative writing functions of the quill. Its development may have had more to do with a search for increased productivity than with a desire to enhance creativity. The first commercially marketed typewriter is credited in 1870. Mark Twain's novel *Tom Sawyer*, published in 1876, is often credited as the first major literary work to be wholly created with the typewriter.

However, the typewriter does not seem to have been an idyllic enhancer of creativity—the paper was facedown so that the typist could not see what was being typed until after removing the paper; that challenge was not removed until after 1895. Over the next 100 years, the typewriter continued to be refined, eventually saturating all creative endeavors that used text to such an extent that typing became a defining activity among serious literary writers. During that same period, whole occupations related to typing became universal. Then, about 20 years ago, typewriters and the many occupations that depended upon the typewriter vanished overnight as they were replaced by personal computers (IBM Office Products Division, 2007).

The typewriter's relationship with text and creativity is similar to digital technology's relationship with visuality and creativity, suggesting a pattern that can be used to predict the future. First, a new technology is developed for business purposes as a way to enhance efficiency and speed. Creative people initially avoid the new technology because creativity is overshadowed by inertia as well as the amount of time investment needed to deal with technical issues. Eventually, however, technology becomes user-friendly enough that creative people who show determination can use it. In the long run, the new technology begins to balance the needs of efficiency, speed, and creativity, becoming ubiquitous and universal. For the typewriter, this pattern took almost 300 years; it looks like it will be much more time compressed for digital technology.

TWO SIDES OF THE SAME COIN?

Many studies and discussions of the relationship between digital technology and creativity often seem a bit like walking into a room with an apple twig in a vase and then using observations of that twig to draw conclusions about the life cycle of an apple tree. The observations may be factual and objective, but at the same time, it is difficult to use these observations to draw inferences about more than the twig itself. In this vein, both practitioners and researchers assert in some cases that digital technology hinders creativity and in other cases that it enhances creativity (Brandon & McLain-Kark, 2001; McLain-Kark & Tang, 1986). Although it is convenient to dismiss all of these perceptions by pointing to the history of the typewriter and asserting that digital technology will inevitably become an indispensable marker for creativity, interior designers have projects that need to be completed now, and they cannot wait for some elusive future creative paradise. Concrete factors that contribute to perceptions of technology as both hindrance and enhancement to creativity can be classified as cultural, technical, conceptual, and pedagogical. A discussion of both hindrance and enhancement examines both sides of the issue in relation to each of these classifications.

PERCEPTIONS OF TECHNOLOGY AS HINDRANCE

Perceptions that digital technology is a hindrance to creativity have strong cultural support, typified by an interior design textbook's emotional characterization of CAD as "potentially dangerous" (Gibbs, 2005), whereas digital renderings and virtual reality have been called distractions (Helmick, 1993). Technical hindrances are well documented and include factors such as a long learning curve, software that was designed by people who do not have extensive experience as interior designers, and physical limitations on computing speed and storage. Conceptual hindrances include the need to pay more attention to computation as well as learning to use what are essentially new languages with a variety of unfamiliar syntaxes. Pedagogical hindrances include traditions that sever skills teaching from conceptual thinking (Marx, 2000). Lastly, it seems natural that interior designers might find it hard to be creative amid constant change and uncertainty.

PERCEPTIONS OF TECHNOLOGY AS ENHANCER

Perceptions that digital technology is an enhancer of creativity seem to be moving more to the mainstream of design culture, as interior design practitioners begin to take technology for granted and in turn make informed choices about when to use it (Pable, 2009). Digital technology has also begun to address multiple physical senses (Nelson, 2005). Technical reasons for enhancements to creativity include ever more computing power at less cost, software that begins to reflect the needs and thinking patterns of designers, and the ability to visualize entire environments and quickly explore alternatives. Conceptual reasons for technology as enhancement of creativity especially revolve around new ways of thinking about traditional design activities within the context of digital technology (Sakr & Johnson, 1991), about when to let the computer do the thinking (Nelson, 1998), and about how knowledge is understood and created (Matthews, 2003). Pedagogical reasons for enhancements to creativity include a new breed of academics who feel comfortable teaching digital media and design at the same time (Seidler, 2008), the introduction of hybrid digital/traditional techniques (Menelly, 2007), and the teaching of technology choices as part of what designers do during the creative process (Taute, 2005). Lastly, to recontextualize a quote commonly attributed to T. S. Eliot, perhaps technical anxiety is the handmaiden of creativity; many creative people thrive amid constant change and uncertainty.

TECHNOLOGY AND NEW VARIETIES OF CREATIVITY

As noted, it seems difficult to envision what type of fruit will eventually grow on a tree simply by looking at its blossoms. Nevertheless, that is the position that interior designers find themselves in right now; what will creativity in interior design look like once the spring petals fall to the ground? Unlike apple trees, where the same type of fruit will return year after year, new technologies can engender new types of blossoms and fruit from the same tree. Which traditional applications for creativity will adapt and thrive, which will stop bearing fruit, and what completely new varieties will ripen?

Discussing three potential areas out of the many possible new aspects of creativity brought about by new technology should serve as examples as well as a starting point for others to theorize along similar lines. These potential areas are a change in the workflow of interior design practice, a change in the boundaries of interior design practice, and a redefinition of what it is that interior designers create.

CREATIVITY AND CHANGE IN DESIGN PRACTICE WORKFLOW

The workflow of traditional interior design practice begins with creative decisions and proceeds in a more or less linear fashion through a series of refinements, followed by an equally long time spent documenting the creative decisions. This often leads to two or more types of specialized interior design practitioners: one with a focus on creativity applied to a design and another with a focus on creativity in visual documentation. This works because concise paper drawings take time, and creativity (in the form of changes) during the documentation phase can be time consuming and wasteful.

With digital technology, however, there is no reason that the documentation cannot start right at the beginning of a project and that the creative decisions cannot continue at least until the bidding phase. This workflow is most efficient when all of the people on a design team are adept at both creative decisions and documentation. To address this, many current practitioners may need to be retrained to be more creative, and students will need to be taught creativity and technical skills side by side.

CHANGING BOUNDARIES OF CREATIVITY

The boundaries of creativity found in traditional interior design practice may be impacted by new advances in software and artificial intelligence (Artificial Intelligence, 2009) that take over routine design processes such as kitchen design and office space planning. Likewise, the Internet allows documents and other items traditionally produced for a fee by local interior designers to be outsourced to markets with lower wages. Whereas these developments may be seen as an assault on interior designers' livelihoods, another way to look at it is that the capacity for creativity will become the primary valuation of each interior designer. Interior designers will no longer perform repetitive or predictable tasks, and will be called in for complex projects or other situations where creativity is a necessity. This will require current practitioners and students to especially focus on processes, creative thinking, and decision-making in lieu of technical skills. Furthermore, digital technology supports routine creativity in areas such as perceptual lighting that have traditionally been addressed by specialists rather than typical interior designers (Han & Nelson, 2006).

REDEFINITION OF CREATIVITY

The proliferation of digital prototyping and manufacturing, virtual reality, affordable immersive reality in the home, and, perhaps someday, nanotechnology (Nelson, 2004) stand to dramatically redefine the meaning of creativity within interior design. The public's conception of what interior designers do is tied to creating drawings that others use to fabricate a design, and interior designers adhere to traditions about how interior design's body of knowledge overlaps with other disciplines (Marshall-Baker, 2005).

These technologies mean that interior designers will directly create a design, no longer making drawings. Modes of creativity for interior designers may begin to look more like those of artists, industrial designers, apparel designers, and filmmakers. For example, interior designers may need to focus more on divergent thinking (i.e., looking for a series of multiple solutions or alternatives) as opposed to convergent thinking (i.e., looking a single best solution) because these technologies allow people to change a design like they change clothes. Digital manufacturing may routinely focus creativity on personally tailored custom items, whereas immersive reality may focus creativity on mass-marketed designs of entire environments that are sold on disks in a bin next to music and games; interior designers may become both artisans and rock stars.

CONCLUSION

In the final analysis, it would seem that creativity in interior design is presently alive and well, both in spite of technology and because of it. It seems that the relationship between technology and creativity is difficult to pin down in the present because no one is quite sure how the new fruit of creativity will eventually taste. However, history has shown a pattern of other new technologies gradually becoming first an enhancer and eventually an integral partner with creativity. There seems to be no reason to doubt that this pattern will continue.

Based on past experience, it should not be a surprise when both creativity and technology head in directions never intended. For example, although the personal computer doomed the typewriter, the typewriter did not doom the pen. Someday soon, the computer keyboard may be replaced by a "digital quill" or even, in a move that would support Socrates' critique of writing (McCluhan & Fiore, 2001), by the human voice that was supplanted by the alphabet. As creativity is redefined, interior designers should be ready to rethink their place in the world of creativity, venturing into new territories and regrouping in old territories, but hopefully bringing apple blossoms wherever they go.

REFERENCES

Artificial Intelligence. (2009). *Encyclopedia Britannica.* Retrieved January 26, 2009, from http://www .britannica.com/EBchecked/topic/37146/ artificial-intelligence

Brandon, L., & McLain-Kark, J. (2001). Effects of hand drawing and CAD techniques on design development: A comparison of design merit ratings. *Journal of Interior Design, 27*(2), 1–13.

Celento, D. (2007, Spring/Summer). Innovate or perish: New technologies and architecture's future. *Harvard Design Magazine, 26,* 70–82.

Gibbs, J. (2005). *Interior design: A practical guide.* London: Laurence King Publishing.

Han, L., & Nelson, M. (2006). Light and pattern: Can digital rendering expand how we think about design? *Representation 2005–06, The Journal of the Design Communication Association,* 32–38.

Helmick, R. (1993). Virtual reality: A design simulation technique that overpowers design content. *Journal of Interior Design, 19*(1), 19–24.

IBM Office Products Division. (2007). *The typewriter: An informal history.* Retrieved June 1, 2009, from http://www-03.ibm.com/ibm/history/ exhibits/modelb/modelb_informal.html

Marshall-Baker, A. (2005). Knowledge in interior design. *Journal of Interior Design, 31*(1), xiii–xxi.

Marx, J. (2000). A proposal for alternative methods for teaching digital design. *Automation in Construction, 9,* 19–35.

Matthews, D. (2003). The problem of knowing: Digital technology, design, and cyberspace. *Journal of Interior Design, 29*(1&2), v–vii.

McCluhan, M., & Fiore, Q. (2001). *The medium is the message: An inventory of effects.* Madera, CA: Gingko Press.

McLain-Kark, J., & Tang, R. (1986). Computer usage and attitudes toward computer usage in the interior design field. *Journal of Interior Design Education and Research, 12*(2), 25–32.

Menelly, J. (2007). Motive, mind, and media: Digital sketching in the creative culture of design. *Journal of Interior Design, 32*(3), 69–90.

Nelson, M. (1998, Summer). Techniques and trends: Visual vs. computational rendering, *Convergence,* 6.

Nelson, M. (2004, January). design FUTURE ing. *Interiors Korea,* p. 221.

Nelson, M. (2005). Hygienic architecture and the defeat of the sensual: Is digital visualization the ultimate tool of conquest or an agent for liberation? *Proceedings of the 2005 Design Communication Association Conference,* Montana State University, Bozeman, MT, pp. 144–147.

Pable, J. (2009). *Quick sketches in interior design practice: A descriptive analysis of practitioners' perceptions, use, and competencies.* Retrieved January 26, 2009, from http://mailer.fsu.edu/ ~jpable/

Portillo, M. (2002). Creativity defined: Implicit theories in the professions of interior design, architecture, landscape architecture, and engineering. *Journal of Interior Design, 28*(1), 10–26.

Sakr, Y., & Johnson, R. (1991). Computer aided architectural design strategies: One size does not fit all. In G. Goldman, & M. Zdepski (Eds.), *Reality and Virtual Reality.* Newark: Association for Computer Aided Design in Architecture.

Seidler, D. (2008). Who's teaching technology? Methods and strategies to develop effective digital design curricula. *IDEC Proceedings, 2008 Annual Conference.* Montreal, Canada, pp. 942–953.

Taute, M. (2005, Winter). Compass vs. computer: Is technology hindering creativity in interior design or fostering it. *Perspective,* pp. 22–25.

Waxman, L., & Zhang, H. (1995). Computer aided design training methods in interior design professional practice. *Journal of Interior Design, 27*(1), 28–36.

Has technology influenced
the "practice" of interior design?

JANICE STEVENOR DALE

MOMENT BEGUINE

New thinking begins with the realization that a technological transformation is replicant, as if fused to an imaginary mind constructed from organic and computerized components. In design, a distinctly three-dimensional form more expressive than ever before has arisen, afforded by the art of digital technology.

If design is defined as the balance of science and art, science fiction is proving out to be truth—not fiction, revealing pure art. Art in design lives somewhere between reality and imagination. It is in that cerebral moment that our imagination is assisted by technology. Whereas science emphasizes logical, objective thinking, art counters with sensitivity and intuition.

It is a time of accelerating change. The speed and fluidity with which one form is ideated and morphed into another and the saturation of digital effects deliver us to another visual environment. The exploration of visual form is giving design new meaning and life. It is aligning its place in history within the

JANICE STEVENOR DALE, CID, FIIDA, is president of J S D A Inc. in Los Angeles, with satellite offices in Chicago and Boise, Idaho. Designing more than 7 million square feet of workplaces for clients including The Boeing Company, State Farm Insurance, Keynetics, and Remax International Real Estate, J S D A Inc. has received multiple awards for design leadership, design excellence in graphics, corporate office design, and historic preservation. Stevenor Dale's master's degree in educational technology centered on the development of a global online interior design program (www.designu.us). She founded IIDA's Southern California Calibre Awards and has contributed significantly to professional licensing efforts and development of the International Building Code. She serves on IIDA's Government and Regulatory Affairs Committee, has chaired CIDA accreditation teams, authored sustainable design guidelines, and developed NCIDQ practice exam sections. Stevenor Dale is a national interior design expert witness on code issues and frequent speaker and author on the future of design.

195

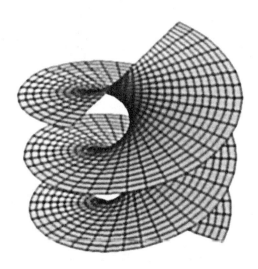

FIGURE 5.2. A helicoid.

vocabulary of art. Greater self-expression in design is possible with less risk than before (Portillo, 2002). No longer are there coordinated planes, but a shifting composition of planes, connectivity, and creative freedom of form. It is technology combined with our imaginations that provides us this capacity, and it is the very same imagination that is required to embrace technology and its impact on the future of design.

CENTERING TECHNOLOGY

The core of design communication—drawing, drafting, and sketching—remains viable visual communication methods transferred into technology-enabled techniques. AutoCAD and ArchiCAD are as central as the parallel rule, accessorized by Creative Suite, the new triangle, and reliant on Microsoft Office, the new scale. Three-dimensional model building is accomplished through Google SketchUp, Autodesk 3D StudioMax, Rhino, Revit, Solidworks, and Apple iMovie. The creation of client communication videos, Web sites, file management sites, and file translation protocols are accomplished with programs such as Flash, HTML, XML, PHP, and Javascript. Digital scripting language offers customizable tools to communicate design ideas (Khemani, 2005). In interior design practice, we are accepting and integrating these tools, which have modified our practice and our process—no less our thinking—and have increased our capabilities.

The effects of digital design are epic and monumental. Posit the computerized application of the design of a helicoid curvilinear stair (see Figure 5.2) floating as it ascends through a conceptual upper-story atrium among five highrise floors. The design experience visualized in minutes is mind-opening; equally rapid can be its implementation into physical reality.

Design must be visualized to be understood. Verbalizing or even sketching may not be enough. A convincing inspiration must be translated into the computer to test the hypothesis. This techno ability stands proudly on the shoulders

FIGURE 5.3. Disney Concert Hall, Los Angeles 2003, by architect Frank Gehry.
(Photo courtesy of Scott L. Dale)

of science. "Designers are exploring forms that until recently could only exist in imagination—sinuous curves, sharp angles, syncopated juxtapositions—extremely complex forms" (Cramer & Simpson, 2002, pp. 5–6) (see Figure 5.3).

Design imagination and creativity are rapidly approaching the fourth dimension through the intelligence of computing technologies as visual thinking connects multiple brain centers, speeding the creative process. Movement from the information age into the "conceptual age" (Pink, 2005), has created a paradigm shift for design. The electronic transfer of information continues to maximize design productivity, to produce three-dimensional (3-D) solutions (as easily as seen at home improvement stores), and to find ways to transform design into profitability.

Virtual reality (VR) content remains key to end users' attention. Quality VR of design solutions provides assistance in selling the idea internally (to executives) or externally (to funding sources), or creating further understanding.

End users are goal-driven and impatient, so VR must provide fast answers and exhibit a fluid delivery. Clients may require plug-ins to manage project data like e-Plan Check software. As designers, VR process modifies our perception critical to design judgment (Blossom, 2002). For example, VR was created and applied by J S D A Inc. for ARCO Plaza by cutting between documented video and proposed CAD-generated design solutions, overlaid with hand-renderings (see http://edtech2.boisestate.edu/stevenordalej/multimedia/arco.mov).

TRANSFORMING DESIGN

When interior designers first glance at a building footprint or elevation, we imagine the shape of the interior cavity, but only through a 3-D view or the analysis of the structural documents do we really begin to see it. We eagerly anticipate receipt of the electronic files from the base building architect so that we can either extract the 3-D information, or create it from the two-dimensional (2-D) documents. Our 3-D drawings accurately

FIGURES 5.4a and 5.4b. *(above and opposite)* Fluid lines contrasted with angular walls create the consciousness of an alternate environment for Remax International Real Estate (Courtesy of J S D A Inc.)

and fully illustrate the spatial cavity, revealing more information than we can quickly assemble in the human mind. Often, nuances of the structural design provide visual cues toward a design solution that may or may not yet be mentally available at that time. Testing and manipulating the program components to align with building parameters or details and the client's goals can be explored and enhanced through full immersion in 3-D.

New 3-D technologies and their constant improvement continue to morph designs toward a new organic statement of spatial experience as digital media liberates design from physical space into new virtual concepts (Liu, 2001). Unifying new sustainable materials provides the seamless integration of spatial form where there is no delineation between surfaces (see Figures 5.4a and 5.4b). Organic shape has emerged from the more malleable interiors to exteriors. In the Remax space, the functional core is an undulating avionic satellite in space, providing for concentric off-jet assistant pods that are circular and rotational in design. Transparent planes envelop ceilings flowing to large daylight pores as one living organism. Rather than distinction between forms, connections are softened radii of organic materials, warm to the touch, and contributing an acoustical quiet.

Sustainable solutions seek to follow nature, its pattern, processes, and solutions. Inspired by biomimicry (Benyus, 1997), we study nature for more cues. Our time-honored, educational foundation shifts from Euclidean to non-Euclidean geometry, the latter responsible for organic fractals in nature. Form is the essence of design; therefore, technologies that support the exploration of form will continue to expand our imagination and embed new organic fluidity and transparency into the design of physical space.

Minimizing chaos is building information modeling (BIM), which manages 3-D information captured within construction documents. BIM increases productivity in building design and construction for both the designer and the general contractor. It renders and measures quantities and interactions of materials to more accurately define the scope of work; meanwhile, it is changing the firm's design process. BIM storming, ideated by Kimon

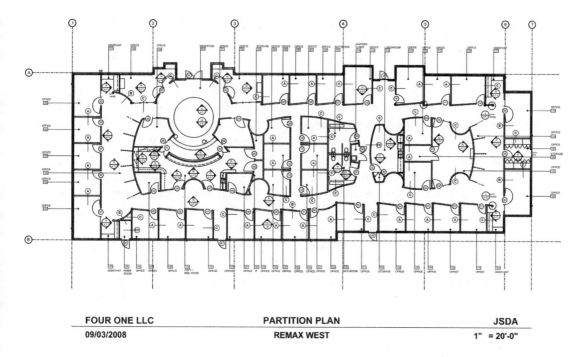

FOUR ONE LLC	PARTITION PLAN	JSDA
09/03/2008	REMAX WEST	1" = 20'-0"

Onuma, FAIA and based on the premise of open source, organizes virtual minds from around the globe to participate in intense brainstorming sessions to proposing intelligent design solutions (http://www.onuma.com/services/BimStorm.php).

PACING DELIVERY

When explored, the pace of design accelerates as long as that goal is mutual among the team members, consultants, and general contractor, no matter how small their role. As a downside, the speed of execution can outpace the client's ability to maintain good standing with payment, creating basic contract changes. Any flaw in the team system can have a great impact on others, their efficiency and their ability to deliver as promised, i.e., *speed to market.*

Accommodating this interior design paradigm shift is virtual asynchronous design communication, driven by efficiency and productivity across multiple time zones. High-speed information transmission and access to evidence-based design rooted in scientific research assists design in achieving connections and collaboration with global team members and clients as the project advances. Expedited communication and accelerated project design progress on digital documents without time loss in real time demand new means to manage high volumes of information.

A robust descriptive, verbal command of the English language is an absolute requirement: " . . . in the southwest quadrant of the 36th floor, the east wall near column B2 where the glass wall intersects the continuous ceiling soffit. . . ." This intricate communication technique is a significant challenge to those working in offices without a full command of the primary language.

GLOBALIZING TECHNOLOGY

Power exists in technique, not in place. Digital design has transformed design, making place relative at best. Changing world demographics underscore the market transfer toward globalization; location is becoming less relevant, and travel is only required for face-to-face meetings. Only the most conservative clients require a hands-on location. Higher design fees are possible, but so is a lack of understanding of the possibilities of online communication tools. On-call meetings can be facilitated with travel. For sustainably minded forms, brick and mortar has become more of a status symbol than a necessity. Work occurs where there is technology and high-speed access.

Online social networking, access to information, product and subcontractor recommendations and research, and people-to-people connections are being redefined by availability of FeedBlitz, Twitter, blogs, podcasts, wikis, YouTube, webinars, client Web pages, and avatars. These technologies tempt designers to design out of state or out of country, where they are not familiar with codes or construction techniques. Potentially, they may not be technically competent to design in that locale, necessitating that design firms team with a local firm. "Practicing within your area of expertise" is a wise admonition to those venturing out toward national or international contracts.

PROVOKING THOUGHT

While the advantages mount, some of the beauty and humanity of the practice may be lost.

> Can a Photoshop-generated materials board viewed online ever replace the artfully arranged materials on a conference table, allowing the client to experience the tactile qualities of their project?
> Does the digitally produced drawing with its crisp lines and accuracy convey the sheer creativity and fluidity inherent in it at a conceptual phase?
> Does a PDF sketch e-mailed to a client at midnight properly replace the presentation of the sketch that a designer might have prepared, carefully constructing the reasons behind the design and at the appropriate moment revealing the design?
> How do we learn from the client by reading their facial expression upon presentation?
> Working virtually, are we freer or less influenced by the water cooler effect of spontaneous creativity?

These perceived challenges simply offer opportunities yet to be solved with new applications. Exploring technology is an integral component of interior design practice. Facilitating this change in design and design practice are the new abilities to share:

> 3-D online redlines, for review anywhere from plane to office
> 3-D models with graphically identified issues replacing lists
> Real context design solutions imported into Google Earth imaging
> Transport of 3-D details to fabricators for mockup construction
> Real-time animation describing the path of travel through a space to demonstrate design (see http://edtech2.boisestate.edu/stevenordalej/multimedia/staples.mov)
> Daylighting analysis to render and compare different curtain wall eyebrow design elements
> A solar environmental modeling program to test alternative light fixtures and solutions (see Figure 5.5)

- Common software (PDF) affords a movement toward FedEx
- Office support rather than specialized "blueprinting" firms
- Preparation of virtual boards online, enhanced with animation and Web design FTP sites that allow for the loading and unloading of massive files and consideration of security risk, and construction management sites posting plans, images and communication files
- Online libraries replacing physical libraries
- Mindjet creative software designed to assist in ideation, leaving paper and markers far behind (see Figure 5.6)
- Real-time project teaming with WebEx and Adobe AcrobatConnect (formerly Macromedia Breeze) for online meetings and video conferencing
- Mobile, handheld telephonic technology connects to the Internet 24/7 with voice-over-Internet-protocols (VOIP)

The technology-enabled design practice shares communication methods with the client and general contractor, creating momentum and affecting the caliber of the entire project team. Often, the use of leading-edge technology itself becomes a marketing advantage to the design firm.

FIGURE 5.5. Internal eyebrow at the corporate headquarters of Keynetics, design by J S D A Inc.

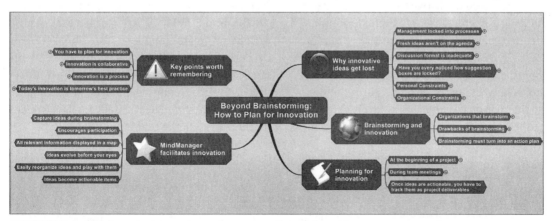

FIGURE 5.6. Mindjet mind-mapping software, an illustration of brainstorming and innovation.

Graphisoft, a leader in computer-aided architecture and design, reported in 2006 that after speaking with many designers, much confusion exists about the benefits of moving to a 3-D virtual building environment. Whereas a few firms grasp the basic concept, developers continue to build collaborative, concurrent, enterprise-scale solutions. It is essentially a technological paradigm shift that all interior designers may not be eager to adopt. Although some have embraced the advent of technology, it is more often feared and resisted, resulting in a design populous of illiteracy, paralleling the proportion of females in this profession. Similarly, design education has yet to be an adopter. So, greater advancement may lie in wait with future generations.

Pushing the technology envelope are the medium-sized firms accustomed to participation in national competitions, large presentation formats, and larger building footprints. Additionally, the more complex the architectural base building drawings, the more assistive the computer-aided 3-D capabilities. As an example, the new organic spiral shapes of Calatrava's Chicago skyscraper (Kamin, 2007) have ventured far from the regular rectangular footprint so common 20 years ago (see Figure 5.7). Structural steel banding and innovative cross-bracing led to unique building shapes; limits are now expanded with twisted steel forming the building structural frame. The exterior skin is clearly separated from the interior volumes in Gehry's Disney Concert Hall (refer to Figure 5.3); there is honesty and a newborn professional respect in that separation.

International engineering firm Ove Arup pushes the limit on creative, performance-based, fire solutions with water-filled cylindrical steel beams that release the water at the proper melt point. Design is long-distanced from the confinement of rectilinear form. The merging of disciplines blurs the lines of practice into newfound collaborative solutions. Collectively, these are the legendary *butterfly effects* that the architecture and design profession commonly release. The waves of these subtle new ideas result in a profound effect on the overall cultural dynamic of our defined environment.

What effects lie beyond our imagination? Could "thought identification," research of the functional MRI (fMRI) at Carnegie Mellon, yet further shape our design consciousness? The newly researched capacity to read our intentions (USNSF, 2008), our reactions to design, aesthetic imagery, and brain patterning could launch a revolution in spatial branding far beyond the graphic advertisorial motifs applied to spaces today. Internal and external neuro-marketing for the workplace or retail space supplant branding, as exhibited visually in the film *Minority Report*.

The space age is advancing in equilibrium with the reapplication of gadgets and gizmos in a 3-R (reduce, reuse, recycle) survivor world and mapping activation of voxels (3-D volume elements identifying a computational model) in the brain. What if we learned that design involves a greater number of functional areas of the brain, beyond the "what do we do" with an apple, or the sensory-motor functions to those that influence feelings, behaviors, new thought? Does design stimulate virtually explosive electrical activity in the brain?

Markedly affected by technology, interior design is clearly entering a new dimension of practice, a new moment to begin. The new thinking of large and small interior design firms has to support the emergence of the professional reputation of the interior designer. With more than 26 states enforcing practice or title acts for interior designers, professional recognition is ours. We prepare computerized construction documentation that directly affects the health, safety, and welfare of the public. Contrasting this advancement, we remain at odds with those who either refuse that responsibility (interior decorators) or those who wish to mistakenly associate our profession under another (interior architects). Yet, significant media resources such as the *Wall Street Journal*, the *New York Times*, the *New Yorker*, and other non-industry media utilize the misnomer "interior decoration" to describe 3-D work.

Embracing technology is now an essential part of interior design. It involves computerization of not only construction documents and 3-D imaging, but an arsenal of software that enables greater efficiencies in the process of design and new freedoms for the practice of design. Unfortunate are the contradictions spawned by intense competition or ego. The evolution of our collective clay molded from both extremes has yet to evidence intent and interest toward a meeting in the middle, where the acceptance of standardized practices and technology could bind.

The vision of digital design is global, with people working together in real time. It embraces cross-platform technology as leading-edge software expands our design imagination and our ability to communicate with one another and with our clients. Integrated communications and access to information through collaborative portals provides a higher quality and faster work process that surpasses client demands.

FIGURE 5.7. Santiago Calatrava's Chicago Spire (construction began in 2007).

Humanity is searching now to cooperate in so many areas, and technology avails this integration. Design is central to humanity's self-expression. Past NeoCon speaker Jean Houston (2007) deems this time as a matter of *kairos*, an ancient Greek term referring to the "moment when the shuttle passes between the warp and woof threads," vibrating as fabric takes form. Woven into the fabric of design are these virtual technologies as principal communication methods availing new design. New visualization processes, incorporating organic informational design provide interactive, changeable, visually refined environments. The dynamics of systematic change vividly influence our practice and design education. Encircled with this pristine opportunity, both interior design practice and educational pedagogy can thrive. Digital design is transformative.

REFERENCES

Benyus, J. (1997). *Biomimicry: Innovation inspired by nature*. New York: Quill.

Blossom, N. (2002, Spring). Linking interior design education and practice. *Perspective*, pp. 24–29.

Cramer, J., & Simpson, G. (2002). How firms succeed: A field guide to design management. *Osteberg Library of Design Management.*

Fowley, D. (2006). *Digital workstyle: The new world of work*. Presented at the Microsoft on-line conference. Retrieved January 11, 2007, from http://www.microsoft.com/southafrica/office/new_world.mspx#E5B

Houston, J. (2007). *2012 predictions, prophecies & possibilities*. Boulder, CO: Sounds True.

Kamin, B. (2007, January 21). New twists for lakefront skyscraper. *Chicago Tribune*. Retrieved January 22, 2007, from http://www.chicagotribune.com/news/local/chi-0701210430jan21,1,6381991.story?track=rss

Khemani, L. (2005, February 28). Prefabrication of timber buildings based on digital models: A perspective from Norway. *AECbytes Features*. Retrieved July 7, 2005, from http://www.aecbytes.com/feature/Norway_prefab.htm

Liu, Y. (2001). Evolving concept of space. In *Defining digital architecture, 2001 FEIDAD award*. Boston: Birkhauser.

O'Brien, J. (2009, January 19). Saving Easter Island. *Fortune, 159*(1), 94.

Pink, D. (2005). *A whole new mind*. New York: Riverhead Books.

Portillo, M. (2002). Creativity defined: Implicit theories in the professions of interior design, architecture, landscape architecture and engineering. *Journal of Interior Design, 28*(1), 10–26.

Stebbins, J. (2009, January 20). *Emerging trends in BIM*. Retrieved January 20, 2009, from http://www.digitalvis.com/bim/?gclid=CLbGqbHwnZgCFRwpawodQ0eY3A

U.S. National Science Foundation. (2008, May 30) *A computer that can 'read' your mind*. Retrieved January 21, 2009, from http://www.nsf.gov/news/news_summ.jsp?cntn_id=111641

CHARRISSE JOHNSTON

TECHNOLOGY'S ROLE IN THE DESIGN PROCESS

Animated "fly-throughs" of virtual 3-D models (computerized space-planning programs that calculate circulation ratios at the touch of a button), custom wall covering and carpeting patterns, all designed and scaled on a desktop PC—these are just a few of the whiz bang tools available to interior designers today, not only those working for large A&D firms with substantial capital budgets, but also to single practitioners in home offices. Software manufacturers imply that armed with the proper technology, we can all turn out dazzling images that recall the graphic impact of Florence Knoll's paste-ups and the exquisite detail of Mark Hampton's meticulous watercolors.

Today, thanks to computer wizardry, a napkin sketch can morph into a fully formed design in a matter of days, let alone weeks or months, appearing to skip blithely over the carefully prescribed steps of the design process. The sequence and definition of these steps—programming, schematic design, design development,

CHARRISSE JOHNSTON, LEED AP®, ASID, Associate AIA, is an associate at Gensler's Workplace Studio, Los Angeles office, where she designs corporate offices for clients in the entertainment, financial, and professional services industries. A graduate of Johns Hopkins University and Columbia Business School, with a BA in behavioral sciences and an MBA in management and marketing, Johnston was a strategic planning executive on Wall Street and founded a corporate event planning firm before earning her degree from UCLA Extension's professional interior design program. She served on ASID's National Student Advisory Council from 2006–2008 and is now a director-at-large on ASID's National Board of Directors. Johnston is involved with design education and professional development efforts within Gensler and through ASID, and often speaks to interior design and architecture students about integrated design teams and the profession of interior design.

construction documents, and contract administration—are so universally accepted that they form the basis for standard architecture and interior design contract documents. Like the scientific method, the design process uses logic and rigor to funnel macro issues down to a specific outcome. But, has technology changed the rules of the game so drastically that it's now time to reexamine and perhaps redesign the design process itself?

This has certainly occurred in other industries. The introduction of computerized airline reservation systems in the 1970s followed two decades later by online fare comparison sites, for example, has all but eliminated the role of independent travel agents in the trip-planning process. AOL's Moviefone obviously changed the way moviegoers select and purchase their movie tickets; less well known is how its upcoming movie search and advance purchase data have upended multiplex operators' traditional scheduling methods. More recently, the last two presidential elections have witnessed a sea change in the dynamics of political fund-raising due to the advent of Internet-based, social networking sites.

The design process, though, is independent of application; it is a systematic approach to a problem. Technology is merely another arrow in a 21st-century interior designer's quiver, to be selectively employed as appropriate. New gadgetry does not replace the traditional phases of the process, nor is it meant to take the place of traditional means of expression. Now, as in the past, design intent should predicate the means used to express that intent; technology follows design trends rather than dictates them.

Technology plays three roles in the interior design process:

1. Automating manual tasks while improving precision
2. Enabling and enhancing ideation
3. Improving communication

AUTOMATING TASKS

Just as the cotton gin revolutionized the cotton industry at the turn of the 19th century, accomplishing in an hour what had previously taken men days to do by hand, so have technological developments—especially computer-aided design, or CAD—helped improve efficiency in all phases of the design process. Here are some examples.

PROGRAMMING

Bubble diagrams and adjacency matrices will always have a place in an interior designer's repertoire. But, now, dedicated software programs have automated the data collection and analysis aspects of programming. Earnest SRP (http://www.earnestdevelopment.com/desk_srp.asp), for one, is a database solution that gathers program and project requirements and runs projections and other scenarios based on industry and custom space standards.

SCHEMATIC DESIGN

Sun-path studies used to involve diagrams, calculations, and viewing physical models under various light conditions. Now, we simply enter the date, latitude, and longitude into SketchUp and other popular 3-D modeling programs, and the resulting images show us precisely how light and shadows will fall in a virtual space.

DESIGN DEVELOPMENT

Rendering modular carpet patterns often entails digitally pasting scanned or downloaded images of individual carpet tiles into desired configurations. In 2008, Mohawk Industries began offering scaled, high-resolution images of some of its modular carpets in various installation formats (e.g., monolithic, vertical ashlar, etc.) that can be easily dragged and dropped into 3ds Max (formerly 3D Studio Max), SketchUp, and other 3-D rendering programs. Called "Drag and Fly," this software is available free of charge on Mohawk's Web site and won the 2008 *Environmental Design + Construction* magazine's Reader's Choice award for best software.

CONSTRUCTION DOCUMENTS

The introduction of CAD and large-format laser printers led to the virtual extinction of drafting departments and blueprint companies. Not only has the work of producing CDs shifted from specialists (e.g., draftsmen, CAD operators, and print shops) to designers, but the process has also become faster, more accurate, and universally accessible.

CONTRACT ADMINISTRATION

Reviewing shop drawings and answering Requests for Information (RFIs) are straightforward but tedious parts of CA. Thanks to scanners, digital photographs, e-mail, and Adobe Acrobat, many of these tasks have become easier.

Rather than redlining multiple copies of shop drawings, we can now mark up one copy, scan it, and return an electronic copy to the contractor. Instead of going out to the site every time a construction question arises, we can now view digital photos taken in the field on our computers or Blackberries and respond by e-mail.

There is little controversy over the use of technology to automate rote processes, for it unshackles interior designers from the drudgery of production. But the popularity of these new tools does not mean that hand-sketching and drafting have become completely outmoded. On the contrary, to use CAD and rendering and modeling software effectively, there's no substitute to learning the traditional methods first. Ironically, now that anyone with a PC can turn out photorealistic renderings, the imperfect, hand-drawn look is often still the most prized. In fact, SketchUp and Autodesk Revit users trade tips online on how to give their immaculate digital drawings a hand-drawn appearance.

IDEATION

Automating existing processes is usually the first stage of information systems' assimilation into a business. The secondary, more evolved stage is when those same systems help create a strategic advantage for the business. The corollary for interior designers is that technology can not only free up more of our time to come up with creative ideas, but it can also actually help us develop better, more innovative ideas, especially during schematic design.

The simplest way in which technology can help ideation is by becoming transparent and eliminating obstacles, allowing the interior designer's mind to work without distraction. As Amazon's Jeff Bezos (2008) said about the key design goals for the Kindle reading device:

> The [physical] book's most important feature is that it disappears. When you're reading, you don't notice the paper and the ink and the glue and the stitching. All of that dissolves and what remains is the author's world, and you go into this flow state. That ability for a book to disappear is something that became our top design objective for Kindle. . . . Books get out of the way and leave you in that state of mental flow.

Similarly, Saffet Bekiroglu (Proceedings from Design Process Symposium, 2008) of Zaha Hadid Architects describes his computer-based design process as follows:

> I repeatedly model, print, sketch, and model again. I believe there's a link between the artistic eye and your hand, and it doesn't go through your head. Suddenly, during this very intense design process—it's like being in a trance—suddenly your intuition kicks in, you think you find the right design solution and then you just go with it. You learn as you're doing.

Casey Reas (Proceedings from Design Process Symposium, 2008), who writes software to create abstract forms, says,

> Just as [you found it] difficult to learn to write but now you're probably very fluid with it, the same happens with programming. [Programming] ceases to be a technical activity and just becomes a way of thinking and expressing and communicating.

This ability of a powerful interface to disappear and allow the mind to work freely is exactly what SketchUp promised new users in 2000. Billing itself as an intuitive, easy-to-learn, 3-D tool to be used "during the conceptual phases of design," SketchUp successfully positioned itself as a creative visualization tool, differentiating it from AutoCAD 2000, which had a steeper learning curve and was used primarily as a graphic documentation tool. One of the keys to SketchUp's meteoric success was that it conformed with and complemented AutoCAD, and it wasn't meant to supplant it.

Another way technology improves ideation is by capitalizing upon computers' massive processing powers to generate incremental iterations and prototypes. The ability to produce infinite variations quickly, thoroughly, and systematically is often beyond human capabilities—but it's a simple task for a computer. Running prescribed design algorithms can result in serendipitous, random beauty. Reas (Proceedings from Design Process Symposium, 2008) calls these aspects of computer graphics parameterization and emergence, respectively.

> The power of using software in parameterization is seeing hundreds or hundreds of thousands of variations in a very short time span. You can make very slight changes to the software and get very macroscopic results. . . . Emergent form is generated by parts acting in concert. The phrase the sum is more than the whole of its parts comes to mind. It's just a few rules you follow that cause dynamic form to emerge out of their individual behaviors.

DOON (http://www.studiodoon.com), for example, is a graphic design firm that creates custom patterns for architects and interior designers. Intricate patterns are generated digitally; their scale, color, and repeats can all be infinitely tweaked to fit the application. This sort of design work could not be undertaken manually; technology is what gives DOON its competitive advantage. Rather than manually producing variations, DOON designers spend the bulk of their time refining and honing images and let the computer do the heavy lifting.

The jagged fractals and swooping curves that characterize many of today's interiors and furnishings are all hallmarks of the electronic age. They could hardly be designed, let alone constructed, without the computer's ability to synthesize design, structure, and fabricate. Zaha Hadid Architects (2006) state that the concept behind their "Seamless" collection of polyester resin furniture was "ultimately driven by the new possibilities created by significant technological advancements in 3-D design software, as well as our inherent desire to test and engage with the very latest manufacturing capabilities."

Plasma Studio's jagged stainless steel corridors in Madrid's Hotel Puerta were also designed and fabricated using computer technology. A computer model mathematically crumpled the walls and ceiling in a nonrepetitive rhythm, and then lit the space asymmetrically with LED lights programmed on a color gradient.

SHORTCOMINGS OF TECHNOLOGY USES

One of the dangers of using the computer during ideation is that because the output appears so finished looking, one may accept a design solution prematurely rather than push forward with more revisions. The same could be said of composing on a word processor versus by hand. "Handwriting encourages students to focus on the writing process . . . keyboarding encourages students to focus on the end product" (Wilson, 2006), spending more time tweaking the appearance of the printed assignment rather than the content.

Michael Bierut (2009), a partner in the graphic design firm Pentagram, expresses similar concerns:

> The technology we have at our disposal is dazzling, and our efficiency is such that clients expect fast solutions and instantaneous updates. We are proud to deliver them. Still, I wonder if we haven't lost something in the process: the deliberation that comes with a slower pace, the attention to detail required when mistakes can't be undone with the click of a mouse.

COMMUNICATION

Improving communication among the design disciplines, between interior designer and client, and between interior designer and the greater community, is a major benefit of technology. Commercial interior projects these days are extremely complex, requiring large, interdisciplinary teams to work closely together for long periods of time. Even straightforward tenant improvement projects involve a slew of stakeholders: client, building owner, contractor, interior designer, allied professionals, consultants, and trades. Making sure all parties are up-to-date is of paramount importance to the success of a project, and, thanks to FTP sites, e-mail, online meeting Web sites, and smartphones, it is easier than ever to keep in touch.

With sustainability on everyone's minds these days, it is more important than ever to form integrated design teams from the very outset of a project. Shared software platforms serve as a common language among a myriad of disciplines. Revit, for example, can reveal potential design conflicts early on in the process (e.g., between mechanical ductwork and lighting layouts) when these issues are easier to address.

Designer-client communication can also be enhanced using technology. Design concepts can be conveyed using a huge range of methods, from quick hand-sketches and foam core models to photorealistic renderings and digital models. The difficulty lies in choosing the right method to fit the project, client, design phase, and type of feedback desired. For example, the artistic, open-ended feeling of a hand-sketch is great for eliciting general "look and feel" reactions. It allows a client to "walk through and look around" a virtual 3-D model and even change finish palettes in real time. It can vividly convey key spatial relations, scale, and other experiential aspects of the design. Additionally, 3-D photorealistic animated fly-throughs might be shown to employees or tenants to generate excitement about their soon-to-be-built new space.

Visualization methods have become so sophisticated that neuroscientists can even observe users' brain responses to simulated architectural environments rather than relying on their verbal feedback. University of California–San Diego researchers have developed a device that immerses users in a 360-degree, full-scale, virtual reality environment called "CAVE" and measures their brain waves. "Unlike an MRI, where you have to lie still, we've synchronized the technology in the CAVE so that we can record a person's brain waves at the same time they're moving about in a simulated architectural environment," says Eve Edelstein, PhD (cited in Oberlin, 2008, para 5):

So with this technology, we can test out architectural designs without having to build them. We can test which features work and which features don't work by measuring the influence of architectural features on mental function and stress levels as people try to navigate their way through simulated buildings using different architectural cues.

Technology can even be exploited after project completion and move-in: post-occupancy surveys can be administered online. Respondents often are more likely to open up online rather than in face-to-face interviews, and the pre- and post-occupancy results can be quantified to demonstrate the value of design.

CONCLUSION

In this digital age, it is hard to resist the novelty of the latest electronic innovations. After all, who doesn't love experimenting with new toys? And, clients can be impressed by the latest bells and whistles. But, it's important to stay focused on the fact that when the project is complete, it's only the built space that matters to the end user; whether or not technology was used to design that space is the concern of only the interior designer. In the end, the best technology is the one that makes the most sense for the project, whether it's a humble Prismacolor pencil or a state-of-the-art animation.

REFERENCES

Bezos, J. (2007, November 19). Interviewed by Charlie Rose. Retrieved and transcribed February 7, 2009, from http://www.charlierose.com/view/interview/8784

Bezos, J. (2008, May 22). Interviewed by *Portfolio* magazine editor Kevin Maney at New York University's Stern School of Business. Retrieved February 7, 2009, from http://www.wired.com/techbiz/people/news/2008/05/portfolio_0522

Bierut, M. (2009, February 8). Drawing board to the desktop: A designer's path. *The New York Times*, p. B2.

Oberlin, J. (2008, October 6). *HMC architects using neuroscience to inform architecture*. Retrieved February 7, 2009, from http://www.healthcaredesign magazine.com/ME2/Segments/NewsHeadlines/Print.asp?Module=News&id=56AB4499E44246D490623351E5B625CA

Proceedings from Design Process Innovation Symposium at A+D Museum, Los Angeles. (2008, December 6). Retrieved February 8, 2009, from http://www.vimeo.com

Wilson, S. (2006, January 30). The surprising process of writing. *Inside Higher Ed*. Retrieved February 8, 2009, from http://insidehighered.com/views/2006/01/30/wilson

Zaha Hadid Architects. (2006, October 24). *The seamless collection*. [Press release.] Retrieved February 17, 2009, from http://www.dezeen.com/2007/03/28/seamless-collection-by-zaha-hadid

> Is BIM appropriate for
interior design practice?
Is it an aid or an impediment?
What advantages does it afford?

ROCHELLE A. MARESH

BIM: IS IT FOR INTERIOR DESIGNERS, TOO?

There is much discussion that building information modeling (BIM) is a great tool for the design of the exterior of the building. We have read about its benefits for architectural design, energy modeling, and construction management. But, what about the interior? BIM is appropriate for interior designers; it is an aid to the profession and offers many advantages.

The three key advantages to utilizing BIM will be discussed. They are not limited to a specific group or specialty within interior design (e.g., healthcare, corporate, education, retail); these are key advantages for any interior designer:

> BIM blurs the lines between interior design and architecture by allowing further collaboration between the two professions.
> BIM challenges interior designers to think through design ideas, solutions, and their final design decisions by modeling spaces three-dimensionally.
> BIM enables interior designers to create better design solutions.

ROCHELLE A. MARESH, CID-MN, LEED® AP, IIDA, is an interior designer with BWBR Architects Inc., St. Paul, Minnesota. Maresh received her BS in interior design with an emphasis in architecture from the University of Minnesota. Maresh typically works concurrently on multiple project teams with other interior designers and architects within BWBR's staff of 100 architects and interior designers. She has helped envision and bring the interior environments of offices, churches, colleges, and medical facilities to life for clients and occupants of these spaces for over 13 years. She has been with BWBR since early 2003. Maresh served as IIDA's Northland Chapter president (2002–2003). In 2004, she traveled to South America to participate in a Rotary Group program that brings design professionals from different cultures together for a collaborative learning experience and professional exchange.

BIM software system addresses the geometry, spatial relationships, geographic information, and quantities and properties of building and interior components (e.g., furniture symbols or manufacturers' details). By doing this, BIM is able to model every part and piece of the exterior and interior of the building, right down to the furniture—hence, creating the geometry of the walls, ceilings, floors, casework, and details. You are able to then extract geographical information on where these items are located, including the quantities, materials, and properties of these items. This is all located within the "model," similar to the term for "drawing" in AutoCAD. BIM can be used to demonstrate the entire building's life cycle including the processes of construction and facility operation. Scope or segments of work can be easily isolated and defined. Systems, assemblies, and sequences are able to be shown in a relative scale with the entire facility or group of facilities (Goldberg, 2004). For example, through proper documentation it would be easy to extract which rooms have carpet versus resilient flooring including the information on the different types of flooring. This can be used for material takeoffs as well as material schedules in specifications.

ADVANTAGES FOR THE FIRM

What does this really mean for me and for my firm? BIM is a process that goes far beyond switching to a new software system. It requires changes to the definition of traditional design phases and entails more data sharing than engaged in by most interior designers, architects, and engineers. BIM improves modeling representations of the actual parts and pieces being used to build a building (Goldberg, 2004). This is a substantial shift from the traditional computer-aided drafting (CAD) method of drawing that has been utilized for the past two decades.

The production of construction documents and specifications includes the drawings, details, site conditions, submittal process, and other specifications for the building's quality. Utilizing BIM, there is less information loss for the design team (architecture and interior design), consultants, and owners by allowing each group to add to and reference all of the information within the set of drawings by seeing it in the model. For example, if there is a question on casework shop drawings, such as a reception desk detail, you are able to see how the reception desk was intended to be built, in a BIM three-dimensional (3-D) model. This allows for easier understanding of how the casework was designed and clearly answers questions regarding design intent so that the casework can be built correctly.

For the firm's design team, BIM allows various team members to work within one drawing at the same time, working in multiple views. This means whenever someone changes something within a view, it changes it within every view for every team member. For example, if you delete a wall, the wall is deleted from everyone's view. In addition, because BIM has links to other objects (e.g., the sconce, header, doors, and windows) that are "sitting" on the wall, they are all deleted from the model as well. Simultaneously, all of the schedules and material take-offs are updated. This allows designers to have a reliable, coordinated, and consistent set of working drawings. At all points in time, this is the primary reason many firms are changing to BIM software systems.

BLURRING THE LINES

When designing spaces using BIM, as offered by Revit Architecture, ArchiCAD, or Vectorworks, the interior designer and architect work closely together when designing and modeling space. Coordination via this collaboration is necessary for a successful design solution as represented via the model and subsequent documentation set. As discussed previously, whenever one person changes a piece or segment of the design, it changes it in every view. So, if the interior designer is going to make any changes to a space, they need to be aware of what is also "located" in that space that they may not be "seeing" (e.g., doors, sconces, ceilings, etc.). This allows the interior designer and the architect to discuss changes prior to making these changes to the drawing. In AutoCAD, objects would be left over and hang out in space from this wall change. With BIM, the object information, no longer part of the design solution, is removed because all the information is "linked" together. As the team works together, making changes in real time, the team can work in a cohesive manner, blurring the lines between interior design and architecture, that is, between the interior components and the building components.

THINKING AND WORKING DIFFERENTLY

Utilizing the BIM system for 3-D modeling allows interior designers to easily see spaces in 3-D. Because everything is built/drawn as a 3-D model, the space already has all the floors, walls, and ceilings; your 3-D model and view are ready to go. Through simply placing a "camera," you are able to create multiple views. These views can easily be named and are automatically saved. Changing the camera view or the width or height of the view box occurs by dragging the camera view or utilizing grips along the side of the view box.

By creating these views, BIM allows design practitioners to produce visualizations continuously as a natural part of the design process. This ability to easily visualize designs in 3-D without using specialized tools and the effortless model/image coordination is the driving force behind BIM's adoption by interior designers (Rundell, 2005). When designing projects, we are constantly creating views to determine how to design a space. For example, when we were designing an atrium space we had curved balconies that move in and out of the space, each with its own wave or ribbon and columns on the exterior and interior (see Figure 5.8). When designing these elements, we created multiple views to determine the best and most appropriate way to complete each component.

Creating these views and modeling the space was critical and allowed us to investigate all areas of the building throughout the design process.

BIM challenges interior designers to *really* think through design ideas, solutions, and final decisions by modeling the spaces in 3-D and then fine-tuning them via their ongoing investigation.

FIGURE 5.8. Avera McKennan Cancer Institute East Atrium.
(Courtesy of Avera McKennan Cancer Institute, Sioux Falls, South Dakota)

BETTER DESIGN SOLUTIONS

When designing spaces, interior designers need quick, easy, and efficient ways of determining if something works in the space or not. BIM helps facilitate this investigation. Utilizing BIM, interior designers are able to have the floor plan, reflected ceiling plan, elevations, and a 3-D view of a space all up on the monitor simultaneously. Making a change to any of these drawings automatically updates and changes the design solution on all other drawings and within the 3-D view. This real-time viewing allows the interior designer to make quick, studied design decisions.

Often, when designing a space, one wonders if the ceiling is too high or too low; is the signage visible at critical junctures down the corridor; is the rhythm or pattern of the partitioning of the space the right proportion? How does the light come into the space at different times of the day? We have all asked these questions and many more. BIM is a tool that expresses these

FIGURE 5.9. Avera McKennan Cancer Institute East Atrium with shadow.
(Courtesy of Avera McKennan Cancer Institute, Sioux Falls, South Dakota)

ideas to team members during in-house critiques. By utilizing the 3-D modeling capabilities of BIM, the interior designer is able to view the space, make critical decisions as a result of testing out various solutions in a timely manner, and present solid design solutions. As shown in Figure 5.9, it was necessary to view this atrium space at different times of the day, allowing the design team to determine floor finish and pattern based on how the light would fall within the space.

BIM facilitates better design solutions beyond pure CAD software systems, such as AutoCAD. BIM's 3-D models allow interior designers to understand the entire project, yielding more examined, thoughtful design solutions. As stated by Rundell,

A purpose-built BIM solution provides the interior designer with a unified environment for conceptual design, design development, visualization, rendering and documentation without any duplication of effort or replication of model information. For interior designers, as for architects and other building professionals, BIM is a power tool for thinking and communicating about design. (2005, p. 4)

Because of the power of BIM, the line between interior design and architecture is blurred, allowing further collaboration between the two professions—3-D allowing the individual with the design ability to shape the design, regardless of title. The end result benefits the design team, the firm, and ultimately the client.

REFERENCES

Goldberg, H. (2004). AEC from the ground up: The Building information model. *Cadalyst.* Retrieved November 1, 2004, from http://aec.cadalyst .com/aec/BIM/AEC-From-the-Ground-Up-The-Building-Information-Mo/ArticleStandard/Article/ detail/133495?contextCategoryId=8578

Rundell, R. (2005). 1-2-3 Revit: BIM for interior design; Interior designers have their own ways of using BIM. *Cadalyst.* Retrieved December 15, 2005, from http://aec.cadalyst.com/aec/article/ articleDetail.jsp?id=258241

As the emphasis of interior design moves beyond an aesthetically applied, product-based, business model . . . to a more knowledge- and service-based profession, visionary ethics facilitates our professional relevance.

—Judith Fosshage

ETHICS AND LEGALITY

OVERVIEW The foundation of the interior design profession—any profession—is its ethics. A code of ethics is an internal force that informs decisions about how interior designers conduct themselves, run their businesses, relate to their clients, provide for users of the built environment, and support and protect society as a whole. The profession is also affected by and even driven by the legal and legislative arenas—external forces.

Authors included in this chapter raise concerns about ethical and legal issues as they discuss these issues in context of the profession today. They also shed light on how ethical behavior can elevate the profession as it moves forward. Judith Fosshage provides an overview of ethical development and moral values grounded in the works of ethical visionaries, whereas Allan Guinan explains how interior designers must define and defend the ownership of our work to the public and specifically to clients—and be compensated appropriately. Looking from both ethical and legal viewpoints, Cindy Coleman defines and discusses interior designers' intellectual property in terms of infringement of ideas, design, and processes, while Susan Farley tests interior designers' knowledge of knockoffs both as imitations of a single product to a complete project. And finally, Don Baltimore explains the ethical and legal implications of being regulated as a profession in the context of professional liability and explores the boundaries of malpractice as it relates to the standard of care. Like no other influences, ethics and legality could guide our profession's evolution or leave interior designers wondering what happened.

> How ethical are we?
How do interior designers view
client desires versus protecting the
environment, people, business?

JUDITH FOSSHAGE

THE ETHICAL IMPERATIVE: RELEVANCY OF THE INTERIOR DESIGN PROFESSION

The word *ethic* comes from Latin *ethikos*, which means "character" or is defined as "a theory or system of moral values" (The Compact Edition, 1997). Ethics implies empathy, fairness, loyalty, honesty, and respect (Haidt in Pinker, 2008, p. 8). It is the Golden Rule: "Do to others as you would have them do to you" or Hippocrates' admonition to "do no harm." Ethics goes much deeper, and we need to understand the various definitions and implications of ethics and moral values as they relate to our client populations as well as our practice.

"The stirrings of morality emerge early in childhood. Toddlers spontaneously offer toys and help others and try to comfort people they see in distress" (Pinker, 2008, p. 7). Animal research verifies that other species share similar impulses, e.g., rhesus monkeys choosing to starve themselves for days to prevent other monkeys from receiving a shock (Gilbert, 2008). "Although no one has identified genes for morality, there is circumstantial evidence they exist. The character

JUDITH FOSSHAGE, CID-NY/NJ, FASID, CSI, IIDA, heads her own firm, Judith Fosshage Interiors, Inc., which specializes in healthcare, educational, and affordable housing projects. She has worked as a consultant to several architectural firms including Roberta Washington Architects in New York. Fosshage is a graduate of Hans Krieks Masterclass and holds certificates from Harvard Graduate School of Design and New York University. She is an active member of ASID serving both locally as New Jersey Chapter president (2000–2001) and nationally on several ASID councils; she became a fellow of ASID in 2009. Actively involved in legislation, she served as president of the New Jersey Coalition for Interior Design Legislation (2003–2007). Fosshage was an instructor for NYU's Healthcare Design Certificate program and currently serves on the advisory board for the Interior Design Program at Berkeley College, and on the InformeDesign® technical review board.

traits conscientiousness and agreeableness are far more correlated in identical twins separated at birth than adoptive siblings raised together" (Pinker, 2008, p. 7). Keltner (2004) in *The Compassionate Instinct* notes:

> when young children and adults feel compassion for others . . . their heart rate goes down from baseline level, which prepares them not to fight or flee but to approach and soothe. . . . Being compassionate causes a chemical reaction in the body that motivates us to be even more compassionate. (p. 24)

Haidt (2007, p. 999) identifies five moral values that seem to be universal and have evolutionary roots. How cultures prioritized these values differs, posing similar characteristic ethical dilemmas common to most established codes. Pinker (2008) summarizes the moral dialogue by quoting Singer's theory of the "Expanding Circle" where

> the optimistic proposal that our moral sense, though shaped by evolution to overvalue self, kin and clan, can propel us on a path of moral progress, as our reasoning forces us to generalize it to larger and larger circles of sentient beings. (Singer as cited in Pinker, 2008, p. 14)

Empathy catalyzes an ethical response demonstrated in altruistic rescuers of Jews during the Holocaust:

What is of final importance is that receptivity to such diverse catalysts did not suddenly emerge in the context of the traumas of the Holocaust. Rather, preparation began long before in the emotions and cognitions through which rescuers normally and routinely related to others and made their decisions. Thus their responses were less explicit conscious choices than characteristic ways of attending to routine events. (Oliner & Oliner, 1988, pp. 221–222)

Fisher (2005) examines three types of ethics:

- ➤ Virtue ethics, with its focus on character traits . . . demand that we look to the well-being of others and that we live modestly and with humility;
- ➤ Deontological ethics, with its concern for doing what is right regardless of consequences, reinforces our responsibility toward other species and future generations; and
- ➤ Utilitarianism, with its goal of maximizing the happiness of as many as possible, demands that we include all other beings . . . with attention to the process and consequences of all that we do. (pp. 4–5)

There are many examples of ethics and morality that impact the world around interior design. Further, we have our own ethical models.

DEVELOPMENT OF ETHICS FOR INTERIOR DESIGN

A business model of ethics concerns fundamental issues of practical decision-making, including activities of ultimate value and standards that determine acceptable behavior. For interior design and other organizations, a code of ethics is established to clarify members' activities in regard to one another, to their clients, their employer/employee, and to their business. These codes are established with their mission statement and goals to provide professional foundation to the organization.

Piotrowski (2008) discusses both the American Society of Interior Designers (ASID) and the International Interior Design Association's (IIDA) codes of ethics; she gives hypothetical examples of common dilemmas interior designers encounter. Along with a consensus-derived definition of interior design published by NCIDQ (2004), these core ethical standards propel the guidelines for establishing a profession and determine the framework of subsequent regulation.

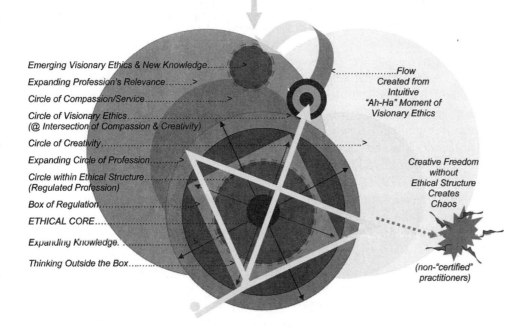

ROLE OF ETHICS

Expanding
INTERIOR DESIGN PROFESSION
Beyond [Regulation]
[Thinking outside the Box]
With
KNOWLEDGE
Making
PROFESSION RELEVANT & DISTINCT
Propelled By

Emerging Visionary Ethics & New Knowledge...........>

Expanding Profession's Relevance.........>

Circle of Compassion/Service.............................>

Circle of Visionary Ethics...................................>
(@ Intersection of Compassion & Creativity)

Circle of Creativity...>

Expanding Circle of Profession...........>

Circle within Ethical Structure.........................
(Regulated Profession)

Box of Regulation.........................>

ETHICAL CORE.....

Expanding Knowledge......>

Thinking Outside the Box...........>

<..................*Flow*
Created from
Intuitive
"Ah-Ha" Moment of
Visionary Ethics

Creative Freedom
without
Ethical Structure
Creates
Chaos

(non-"certified"
practitioners)

"When knowledge is applied and shared, it is advanced to new
levels of understanding. It 'flows' from one person to another, from
past experience to future application, and in that flow it becomes
richer in meaning and usefulness." Bruce Blackmer (2005)

FIGURE 6.1. Role of ethics expanding the interior design profession beyond regulation.

REGULATION OF PRACTICE AND ETHICS

As the emphasis of interior design moves beyond an aesthetically applied, product-based, business model through legislation protecting public health, safety, and welfare to a more knowledge- and service-based profession, visionary ethics facilitate our professional relevance. Figure 6.1 has been included to illustrate the complexity of actions and their contributions and interaction with the role of ethics for the interior design profession, now and in the future, which will be discussed throughout this essay.

Unlike regulation of practice and the profession, dialogue about ethics is an ongoing, fluid process that creates, defines, and determines the direction of a profession. Ethics both precedes regulation to define it and continues beyond its confines, responding to an ever-changing world. Ethics is at the epicenter of the required education, experience, and examination that precludes certification/licensure of interior design.

Although regulation standards are confining to some creative practitioners who have not pursued higher education or who do not test well, they express an external, minimum-level qualification for entrance into the interior design profession and mirror similar professions' requirements. Regulation, by definition, is restrictive, but it is the only means in our current culture to demonstrate levels of competence. The problem is that it is minimal, only qualifying certain knowledge and skills and has limited means to quantify and verify ethical behavior, level of knowledge, or creative talent. The other problem is that because regulation is primarily static, it is often viewed as the end rather than beginning step to establish a profession.

However, ethics, like knowledge, is an internal, ongoing process that depends upon the ability to integrate one's experience, perception, and response within one's intrinsic moral framework. By recognizing that both ethics and knowledge evolve by responding to complex changing experiences, the definition of the profession is further explored and expanded (Blackner, 2005).

When a creative interior designer comprehends a need within the culture, begins to envision a solution within the context of the need, and then implements it, a paradigm shift occurs. This moment is the pivotal point and impetus to a new vision of ethics where the "circle of compassion" intersects the "circle of creativity." It is an *ah-ha* epiphany, a *thinking-out-of-the-box* moment.

However, "thinking outside of the box" has often become a cliché where a strategic facilitator breaks apart the puzzle expecting members of a management team to put it back together without the conceptual and ethical framework supporting the box. Mission statements and creative thinking should be based in realistic evaluations of where we are now and where we need to go, not just where we want to go.

For example, a few years ago medical researchers discovered that a normal heart rhythm mirrored baroque music and introduced the music in the intensive care unit hoping to stabilize heart patients. However, introduction of the music often created additional stress, until they realized it was necessary to mirror the patient's present irregular heart rhythm and then gradually adjust the music to mirror the normal heartbeat. This demonstrates how it is essential to understand the context of the *box* and its limitations, and recognize the unrealized need to think outside of it. After the insight is realized, it is impossible to return to a prior approach, beginning the "optimal experience where time no longer has meaning" and when there is flow, defined by "a self-contained activity, one that is done not with the expectation of some future benefit, but simply because the doing itself is the reward" (Csikszentmihalyi, 1990, p. 67).

ETHICS AND INTERIOR DESIGN'S SOCIAL OBLIGATIONS

In an effort to define interior design as a profession, Anderson, Honey, and Dudek (2007) differentiate interior design's unique role in society from other professions, in particular, architecture. Although, as in all other professions, interior design is mandated to protect public health, safety, and welfare, Anderson, Honey, and Dudek (2007) assert interior designers' expertise is more weighted in welfare issues. They state, the basis for a social compact for the interior design profession is designing physiologically and psychologically supportive interior environments that enhance quality of life (p. vi). Our hope is that when interior designers focus on the unique value of their work in society, they will find greater meaning and purpose in that work. (p. vii)

Interior design needs to define itself in terms of its social obligation and focus more on quality of life issues (Anderson, 2005, p. xi). However, interior design does not *own* this concept. Although our education and particular talents lie in our ability to listen to the undercurrent needs of the often unrepresented client (i.e., patient in hospital setting, student in educational facility, etc.), only a limited number of interior designers have embraced a more humanitarian commitment. Our organizations, design publications, and ultimately public perceptions of our work are distorted by the commoditization of our profession. Too much emphasis is placed on product, branding, marketing, and individual celebrity interior

designers. Rarely are the designs of spaces demonstrating a social consciousness published, thus distorting the breadth and depth of services interior designers are prepared to and do provide (Farson, 2008).

At this critical juncture, the interior design profession is in the regulatory process, while being threatened by allied professionals and unregulated practitioners (both groups perceiving threats to their bottom line). Simultaneously, the interior design profession is moving toward a more service-oriented ethical model. The question remains: where are we going? Farson (2008) and Hamilton and Watkins (2009) question the wisdom of regulation, feeling it isolates a profession (architecture) from being fully open to progressive ideas, stagnates its higher purpose, and promotes ego building and commoditization. However, I believe our profession will be professional when we expend our energies to collaborate rather than compete, and when we suspend judgment, opening ourselves to the diversity of ideas percolating, awaiting recognition.

ETHICS BY EXAMPLE

Ethical visionaries remain centered in their intrinsic, inner, ethical core (similar to the rescuers of the Jews). They are described by Farson (2008) as "metadesigners" who lead with wisdom, utilizing design as the organizing discipline of the future. Or envisioned as Re: Visionaries who "take a look at the world around them, then look deep inside themselves to ask What If and find ways to make it What Is" (Urban Revision, 2008). Or as subversive leaders:

If architecture (design) is going to inspire community, or stimulate the status quo in making responsible environmental and social structural changes now and in the future, it

will take what I call the "subversive leadership" of academicians and practitioners to remind the student . . . that theory and practice are not only interwoven with one's culture but with the responsibility of shaping the environment, of breaking up social complacency, and challenging the power of the status quo. (Mockbee, 1998, p. 1)

These ethical visionaries have certain identifiable characteristics (e.g., compassion, commitment, creativity, cooperation, and sense of community) that take them beyond the ordinary, implementing ideas with rippling consequences (McDonough & Braungart, 2003). For example, ethical vision can be borne out by a single person, as in the case of Tony Torrice. As one of the first designers to design from a child's perspective, he designed spaces focusing on their needs through the child's eyes to create a magical world not based upon cartoon characters or other adult-imposed perspectives but captured dreams within their personal space. "In building rooms for people with special needs, I consider three 'C's': Choice, Color and Convertibility. It is very important that choice comes first" (Torrice, 1989, p. 37).

Ethical vision can also embrace a philosophy as in humanitarian design. This approach did not begin with the development of Auburn University's "Rural Studio" by Samuel Mockbee, but it was elevated by his foresight to include bringing beauty and design to impoverished areas, giving respect and understanding to neglected populations as well as giving students an opportunity to design and build both relationships and buildings:

> what is necessary is a willingness to seek solutions to poverty in its own context, not outside it. What is required is the replacement of abstract opinions with knowledge based on real human contact and personal realization applied to the work and place. (Mockbee, 1998, p. 1)

CONCLUSION

Usually ethical responses are triggered by an event (e.g., Hurricane Katrina, 2005), an individual (e.g., Victor Papanek's view of universal design, 1972), an idea/invention (e.g., Steve Jobs's personal computer), or a previously unseen or not fully understood need (e.g., diversity). As ethical insights begin to be accepted within the larger cultural context, revised conceptual guidelines are required to support the ethical core. When the concept of patient-focused care began to take hold, much of the healthcare industry did not comprehend the ethical concept and utilized the term for marketing purposes without implementing the intrinsic philosophy. When implementing a humanitarian project, there is a dangerous possibility of creating an overly designed aesthetic without understanding the community's needs (i.e., Coke bottle in the movie *The Gods Must be Crazy*).

Expanding the interior design profession beyond regulation to a more comprehensive ethical vision based on integrating a deeper and broader body of knowledge further evolves professional standards. Now is the opportunity to foster an emerging model that ensures integrity and accountability through performance by defining levels of competency. Hamilton and Watkins (2009) delineate incremental levels of expertise for individual practitioners in evidence-based design. Similarly LEED® (Leadership in Energy and Environmental Design) identifies and certifies incremental levels of a building project and its continuing sustainability (U.S. Green Building Council, 2009). Although LEED encourages their own (i.e., LEED AP) certification through testing, it does not restrict who participates in the design team. This approach encourages interior designers' participation to challenge creative new methodology in leadership and recognizes the ongoing process of learning on all levels of competency (Green Building Certification Institute, 2009).

To ensure that the interior design profession has a viable future, *evolving ethics* are an essential ingredient. Hopefully, new emerging ethical visionaries will arrive to both redesign our thinking and revitalize our profession with meaning, "to enlarge our sense of what matters . . . to embrace the fact that there is far more that unites us than divides us" (Wechkins, Masserman, & Travis, 1964 as cited in Gilbert, 2008).

REFERENCES

Anderson, B., Honey, P., & Dudek, M. (2007). Perspective: Interior design's social compact: Key to the quest for professional status. *Journal of Interior Design, 33*(2), v–xiii.

Blackner, B. (2005). Knowledge on knowledge. *Journal of Interior Design, 31*(1), p. 8.

The Compact Edition of Oxford English Dictionary. (1987). Oxford: The Clarendon Press.

Csikszentmihalyi, M. (1990). *Flow: The psychology of optimal experience.* New York: Harper Collins.

Farson, R. (2008). *The power of design: A force for transforming everything.* Norcross, GA: Ostberg Library, Greenway Communications.

Fisher, T. (2005). The ethics of housing the poor. *Implications, 4*(1), Retrieved March, 2006, from http://www.informedesign.umn.edu/_news/jan_v04r-p.pdf

Haidt, J. (2007, May 18). The new synthesis in moral psychology. *Science, 316*(5827), p. 999.

Hamilton, D., & Watkins, D. (2009). *Evidence-based design for multiple building types.* Hoboken, NJ: Wiley & Sons.

Green Building Certification Institute. (2009) *Professional credentials.* Retrieved May 30, 2009, from http://www.gbci.org/DisplayPage.aspx?CMSPageID=28

Keltner, D. (2004). *The compassionate instinct.* Retrieved February 4, 2009, from http://greatergood.berkeley.edu/greatergood/archive/2004springsummer/keltner_spring04.pdf

McDonough, W., & Braungart, M. (2003). *The Hannover principles: Design for sustainability.* New York: McDonough Braungart Design Chemistry.

Mockbee, S. (1998, November 15). *The rural studio. Architectural design everyday and architecture.* Retrieved January 17 2009, from http://speakingoffaith.publicradio.org/programs/ruralstudio/mockbee_ruralstudio.shtml

National Council for Interior Design Qualification. (2004). *NCIDQ definition of interior design.* Retrieved March 11, 2005, from http://ncidq.org/who/definition.htm

Oliner, S., & Oliner, P. (1988). *The altruistic personality: Rescuers of Jews in Nazi Europe.* New York: The Free Press.

Papanek, V. (1972). *Design for the real world.* New York: Pantheon.

Pinker, S. (2008, January 13). The moral instinct. *The New York Times*, p. 1.

Piotrowski, C. (2008). *Professional practice for interior designers.* Hoboken, NJ: John Wiley & Sons.

Torrice, A. (1989). Color for healing. *Journal of Health Care Interior Design, 37.*

Urban Revision. (2008). *Urban revision.* Retrieved January 8, 2009, from http://www.urbanrevision.com/biography/revisionaries

U.S. Green Building Council. (1988). *Project certification.* Retrieved March 15, 2009, from http://www.usgbc.org/DisplayPage.aspx?CMSPageID=64http

Wechkins, S., Masserman, J., & Terris, W. (2008). Cited in M. Gilbert (Ed.), *The 2008 shift report: Changing the story of our future.* Petaluma, CA: Institute of Noetic Sciences.

> How is the commoditization of interior design affecting the future value of the profession?

ALLAN GUINAN

COMMODITIZATION OF INTERIOR DESIGN

The question I was asked to consider was, how is the commoditization of interior design affecting the future value of the profession? A better question may be: historically, how has the continued commoditization of interior design consistently undervalued the profession? In practical experience over the course of 25 years, I have witnessed a sea change in the tools and methods utilized by interior designers in the practice of interior design. Although the quintessential design process is not fundamentally different, the scope of projects has changed exponentially, often involving highly strategic initiatives with client business leaders as they look to interior designers to develop real estate solutions tailored to support business needs.

Throughout this period of rapid change and exciting challenges for our profession, the industry has become predominantly commoditized as fee schedules decline. The perception of clients that interior design services are limited to quick aesthetic solutions and most

ALLAN GUINAN, ARIDO, IDC, is a founding partner of Figure3, Toronto, Canada, and has been in practice for over 25 years. He is an NCIDQ certificate holder and has a BID from the University of Manitoba. Guinan's clients include diverse global brands where he has led teams on workplace, retail, and hospitality projects in North America, Asia, and the Middle East. Projects from Figure3 consistently have been published and received considerable recognition for design innovation. Guinan has served on the board of ARIDO for seven years and was its president in 2001. He has juried for NCIDQ and serves as a CIDA site visitor in North America. Guinan has spoken at numerous conferences in Canada and Asia and often participates as a guest critic, lecturer, and thought leader on the future of the interior design profession.

often awarded based upon little more than price does little to increase our value.

Commoditization is the process by which goods or services that have economic value and are distinguishable in terms of unique attributes end up becoming simple commodities in the eyes of the market or consumers. How do we protect against commoditization from continuing to happen in interior design? I believe that our profession must engage in three distinct actions to address the challenges facing our industry:

1. Educate interior designers and inform business leaders to the true value of design thinking.
2. Resist the speed-trap of faster implementation versus deeper engagement with clients.
3. Protect our industry through intellectual property laws .

This essay will explore how lack of movement on these actions has restricted interior design fees in the past, and how the profession can create real financial value for practitioners and our clients in the future.

Consulting in today's business world requires interior design practitioners to react quickly to the demands of the market and often to produce solutions at an accelerated pace. Project solutions are required to meet the quantitative needs of clients and expected to do so with creativity and innovation. Working faster can mean we are not necessarily working smarter nor realizing the full potential of client opportunities. Speed, as a client priority, causes shortcuts of the design process by minimizing design thinking. The time for thoughtful client interaction to produce an intelligent, informed solution is rarely allocated to interior designers in a commodity-driven fees market.

In an effort to meet the demands of the marketplace, new technologies in the design field intended to minimize mundane, repetitive tasks have inadvertently jeopardized our ability to undertake a thorough design process. This design process involves disciplined research, benchmarking, and a deeper discovery process related to greater human interaction and understanding of the user needs within the context of an organization's strategic business objectives. Rather than providing opportunities to spend quality time in discovery processes, technology is instead viewed as a tool for speed to expedite a constrained schedule.

Clients see little value in front-end investment in research and analysis and often demand fast solutions to drive down costs to solve an immediate business need. If a business case were presented by interior design practitioners to justify the added investment, perhaps this perception would be much different. Unfortunately, developing clear rationale and a financial return on investment (ROI) is not a trained expertise of the majority of interior design practitioners. When interior designers can provide no evidence of how the tangible results of an interactive design process provide financial benefits to a business via the design of their space, they go unmined, and the commodity cycle is reinforced.

Even when an informed client does recognize those benefits and separates the strategic services from the implementation stage, an all-too-common practice is that interior designers provide this research and analysis as a loss leader to win the more lucrative future implementation stages of a major project, again devaluing the intelligence of those strategic services. This trend undermines the profession's inability to own an in-depth and meaningful design process and to charge accordingly for these valuable services.

Ownership of the intelligence piece of strategic project work is further undermined by current intellectual property laws in North America, which cannot protect a practitioner's ability to copyright the intangible thing the building industry calls a design concept or even ultimately the contract documents that comprise significant liabilities for our practitioners. Until we resolve the legal battles over property rights or ownership of ideas, we will continue to see our services devalued and commoditized by our clients.

Next, this essay will explore the root causes of commoditization and shifts in thinking around the value of interior design services that the profession must provide to survive and thrive as a viable business consultancy in the future.

DESIGN THINKING (AND ITS TRUE VALUE TO BUSINESS)

If interior design is being threatened by commoditization, why then is the advent of design thinking supported by business schools such as Rotman School of Management in Toronto so compelling to business leaders? Rotman, led by Dean Roger Martin, was among the first business schools to begin teaching design as a strategic advantage. This education occurs through product development and prototyping classes that pair designers at Toronto's Ontario College of Art with Rotman's MBA students. They work through Designworks Research Center and internships that give students hands-on experience in research and development. There are now over 22 so-named *D-Schools* worldwide (D-Schools, 2009).

Advocates of design thinking include authors such as Daniel Pink (2005) and industrial design firms such as IDEO, led by CEO Tim Brown (2008). They advocate design thinking as the new Holy Grail for business in the race to early identification of new market opportunities, innovative product ideas, integration of technological advances, and ultimately smarter business solutions. Pink and Brown argue that "integrative thinking" can bridge the divide by helping business leaders think like designers and designers to think like business leaders through a collaborative process. So, why have industrial designers gained the respect of business leaders (and enjoy the rewards of fees and royalties from their design work) while interior designers continue to lose valuable market share? Perhaps some of the answers can be found in the people initially attracted to the profession and the interior design educational system.

Most individuals who pursue an education and career in interior design have strong creative and problem-solving capabilities. The classically educated interior designer instinctively relies on intuitive cognitive thinking to work through a series of optional solutions concurrently until the best solution is reached. In his book *The Opposable Mind*, Martin (2007) identifies this unique thinking style as integrative thinking, an innate ability widely accepted as the norm in the design world, but underutilized in the business world. Martin believes that the integrative thinkers (designers) and analytic thinkers (business leaders) need to understand and respect the critical role both play in successful problem solving. For interior designers, the missing link has historically been the ability to back up a creative solution with analytic research and to successfully articulate how a proposed design solution supports the goals established by the business as important.

Although use of evidence-based design (EBD) within undergraduate interior design programs is becoming more common, most programs place little or no emphasis on research, analytical thinking, prototyping, or the establishment of metrics to determine if the final solution meets the objectives initially established. Within a four-year program, technical skills and aesthetic-based abilities seem to continue to take precedence as the major factor in grading an interior design student.

The result is interior designers who have not been educated to gather research, disseminate information, develop strategic options, and use relevant metrics to critically evaluate those options. Most certainly, interior designers are not educated to develop financial business models to support proposed design solution recommendations. What is also evident is that people initially drawn to the profession and who are not taught to value this process are unlikely to put value on it within their professional lives.

TECHNOLOGY (AND HOW IT ENABLES AND LIMITS PERCEIVED VALUE)

If the market perceives that the primary value of interior design services is predominantly the documentation of design ideas, and if the speed of documentation is most influenced by the acceleration afforded by new technologies of integrated computer-aided design (CAD) software, then does this explain why our profession is caught in the treadmill of faster production for work of reduced value?

Through the use of CAD in the design process, the time required to complete manual work has been dramatically reduced and resulted in practitioners' ability to compress the implementation portion of a project schedule. Other technologies have also fueled the pressure on project timelines. With the advent of the fax machine, Internet, and PDF imaging formats to communicate an idea, clients have learned to expect faster turnaround times through instant communication tools. Thus, interior designers have lost the ability to charge for valuable strategic thinking because emphasis has been placed on implementation and immediate response time.

The time to complete a design process is, in fact, no less time-consuming, and the expertise and software technologies are no less complex to master, but clients continue to undervalue the knowledge driving the process and focus on implementation instead. They begin to devalue a process where there is less engagement with them and they are unable to value something that appears too easy and fast to produce.

In North America 15 years ago, a typical design process for 20,000 square feet of office required three to six months of design time from the beginning of the assignment to commencement of construction. Fees per square foot for this work would range from $2.50 to $3.50 per square foot (Loebelson, 1990). In 2009, that same process has been accelerated to occur in as little as four weeks, with similar fees. During the same period, salaries and business costs have continued to rise. With the added expense for firms to purchase and maintain software and technology, the result is reduced profitability for the industry.

So where does this trend toward increased speed and reduced client engagement lead us? We have only to look at markets outside of North America where the value of the design process has been commoditized to an extreme. During the boom in Shanghai over the last five years, the market demands interior design firms to provide design/build services for the commercial office sector. In this market, the client representative is the real estate broker who issues a request for a proposal (RFP) to interior design firms. They must submit a fully evolved design concept and a total flat cost to construct and furnish the project; this is the ultimate in one-stop-shopping.

In Asia, and elsewhere, this contractual approach is not unusual. However, the more disturbing element is that a design firm is typically given only one week, from receipt of an RFP outlining the client's program requirement, to produce a design and price the solution. Interior designers have little or no client contact and are required to provide a solution completely within a vacuum of relevant knowledge about the business.

In this emerging model, there is no value placed on research and understanding the needs of the corporation or employees, and no perceived need to articulate the objectives and goals or to establish metrics for success for the client. Success is defined solely by aesthetics and price alone. If this is the value of interior design in this market, and within an increasing global marketplace, can North America be far behind?

It is a disturbing trend that destroys the value of analytical research and what design thinking can do in achieving a strong solution. If we continue to produce faster, do the solutions become routine and unoriginal? Do we begin to shortcut the investigation of a client's individual needs and produce space as a commodity product without defining success for that particular client?

There is no question that a creative process requires time to produce a solution to meet the individual needs of clients. Clearly, the trend of extreme commoditization of the global interior design profession is a very dangerous one and a trend that must be monitored very closely.

INTELLECTUAL PROPERTY (AND HOW IT HAS FAILED TO PROTECT THE INTELLIGENCE OF OUR PROFESSION)

Historically, the legal profession has focused its attention not on protecting our intellectual property rights, but on protecting design firms from liabilities resulting from errors and omissions. But ownership of our intellectual property (i.e., copyright) lies at the core of the business of any interior design firm. Coke doesn't sell the formula for its drink; Toyota doesn't sell the patents for the components in its cars; recording artists don't sell the unrestricted right to replay their music; and industrial designers do not design products for manufacturers without advance royalty agreements. Yet, interior designers sell the products of their expertise and creative intelligence for a relatively low percentage of the total, one-time project cost.

Why does the customer of an interior designer fail to value a similar creative expertise that results in spaces experienced every day by the client's employees or customers? Clearly the laws of supply and demand apply to our industry like any other creative work product, but I also believe that a fundamental reason for our inability to protect our work legally is the difficulty we face in demonstrating financial return on the often significant investment required to design an environment to meet specific business objectives.

Royalties and the legal protection of copyright laws are only possible when buyers understand the potential financial reward of their initial investment. In the interior design industry, the usual protocol is to retain the intellectual property rights of the design, but provide the client with a right to use the design, only in connection with the project at hand. Clients usually retain copies of the design for their own use in connection with what a design firm has been contracted to design and have built. Copyright law, however, does not protect interior designers from clients who reuse a concept to build subsequent versions of the original design. Currently, in practice, if the original work product has been paid in full, the client owns the copyright of that design and is free to replicate that design in any other project.

I believe that our profession must earn legal ownership of our own creative intelligence by demonstrating to business leaders the quantitative and qualitative benefits of investment in design. In other words, only when we prove our worth will we finally be able to charge for our value and retain ownership of our work.

SUMMARY

How does our industry change the trend of continued commoditization of our professional services? There are no easy solutions, but certainly I believe that education—of our own profession and our clients, will be critical in the coming years to reverse the trend toward commoditization. I suggest the following steps:

1. Educate the next generation of interior designers to understand design thinking processes and concepts and to integrate *D-thinking* into disciplined discovery processes.
2. Work with business leaders in a deeper discovery process in determining success factors for a business that can be measured and demonstrate the value of design.
3. Educate interior designers to become versed in developing evidence-based, business case models to support investment in interior design services.
4. Educate the legal profession to protect our intellectual property as effectively as our liabilities.

Our profession must continue to reinvent itself through the education of our practitioners and our customers. Certainly, it will take time for interior design educators, graduates, and practitioners to gain the knowledge and confidence to successfully articulate the value that these influences have on business leaders. Our reward? A much more challenging professional experience for practitioners, more evidence-based and intelligent design solutions for our clients, and financial compensation that recognizes the unique expertise we offer to well-satisfied clients.

REFERENCES

Brown, T. (2008, June). Design thinking. *Harvard Business Review, 86*(6), pp. 85–92.

D-Schools. (2009). D-schools: The global list, *Newsweek*. Retrieved February 2, 2009, from http://bwnt.businessweek.com/interactive_reports/talenthunt/index.asp

Loebelson, A. (1990). 100 interior design giants of 1990. *Interior Design*. Retrieved February 2, 2009, from http://www.highbeam.com/doc/1G1-9254597.html

Martin, R. (2007). *The opposable mind: How successful leaders win through integrative thinking.* Boston: Harvard Business School Press.

Pink, D. (2005). *A whole new mind: Moving from the information age to the conceptual age.* New York: Riverhead Books.

> How would you define *design ownership*? When is an idea "mine," i.e., intellectual property?

CINDY COLEMAN

IDEALS + IDEAS + INFRINGEMENTS

The stature of an individual or a profession doesn't happen simply from legacy, a code of ethics, or a statement of beliefs; it comes from how the legacy is manifested and experienced. Interior design's legacy is revealed through notions of use: how places and spaces are both utilized and inhabited. To get there, interior designers practice a combination of theory, knowledge, humanity, and artistry. What distinguishes one interior designer's practice from another is how this combination is applied and how it informs the basis for a designer's unique ideas. Ideas—the power, value, and responsibility they yield—are the mark of great design.

Ideas are the legacy of both great interior design and great interior design practice. Interior designers by nature are prolific in the creation of new thinking and ideas. The ownership of these ideas—to whom the idea belongs and how to protect it—falls under the category of law called intellectual property. Understanding the ethical and legal implications of intellectual property is the subject of this essay.

CINDY COLEMAN is a graduate of The School of the Art Institute of Chicago in interior architecture with over 20 years in the design industry. She has had diverse experiences in interior architecture, product development, and journalism. In 1998, Coleman and Neil Frankel established Frankel + Coleman, focusing on architecture, design, and journalism. She is the author of *Interior Design Handbook of Professional Practice* (2001). Currently, Coleman is a contributing editor of *Interior Design* magazine and *Chicago Architect*. She is an assistant professor at The School of the Art Institute of Chicago in the Department of Architecture, Interior Architecture and Designed Objects, and is the professional advisor for the Marcus Prize, a $100,000 biannual architectural prize administered through the University of Wisconsin–Milwaukee School of Architecture and Urban Planning and the Marcus Corporation Foundation.

> We do not act rightly because we have virtue or excellence, but we rather have those because we have acted rightly.
>
> —Aristotle

Since the time of Aristotle, the practice of design has been portrayed as a truly noble profession. A few centuries later, in the *Ten Books on Architecture*, Vitruvius advocated a profession that was diverse in building skill, scholarship, practice, and theory. When it came to the subject of ethics and philosophy, Vitruvius' treatise described scholarship as what makes a designer "high-minded and not self-assuming, but rather renders him courteous, just, and honest without avariciousness" (Vitruvius, 2005, p. 7).

Fast-forward a couple millennia. Ask a group of contemporary interior designers why they chose design as a profession and more times than not the answer still centers on Vitruvius' noble ideals about scholarship, practice, and theory. Today, this triad drives the foundation of design ideas and ideals—intellectual property. Intellectual property forms the foundation of a practice ethic.

According to the World Intellectual Property Organization's (WIPO) *Guide to Intellectual Property Worldwide* (2009), intellectual property refers to the creations of the mind and includes inventions, literary and design works, symbols, images, and more. Intellectual property falls into two categories: (1) industrial property, which includes invention patents and trademarks, and (2) copyright, which includes literary and artistic works like drawings, paintings, photographs, and designs.

Ethics and law, while different, are often linked together in the context of intellectual property because they are based on similar principles of rules of behavior. Ethics and one's ethic are the moral principles that guide behavior and the knowledge that informs the sense of obligations people have to themselves and to society (*Merriam-Webster's Online*). The law is rules of behavior established by a governing authority and enforced by a penalty system (*Merriam-Webster's Online*).

A further distinction is that the law is written and applied in the public realm to protect order and regulate the actions of the public. Conversely, ethics are conceived as private acts, sometimes in the context of an individual, a family, a community, a religion, or an organization. Although some may believe it's unethical to lie to a friend, it isn't illegal. And, though it is illegal to steal a loaf of bread, for some it may not be unethical if it will save someone from starvation. The ethics behind intellectual property suggest acting responsibly with one's own work or invention and respecting the ownership of the work or invention of others. Like law, the study of ethics is complex and looks to uncover the origins of our principles. It is understood that a person's moral reasoning develops in different ways for different reasons; sometimes it is cultural, environmental, or spiritual or through education, knowledge, and reflection.

Lawrence Kohlberg, a leading expert in the subject of ethical reasoning at the University of Chicago, theorized that people learn to reason morally and ethically in a sequence of stages. Kohlberg's (1969) research, as cited in Trevino (1992), describes six primary stages of moral reasoning:

- First stage is based on notions of obedience and doing the right thing to avoid negative consequences.
- Second stage understands the difference between right and wrong, but the moral reasoning centers on concerns over one's own self-interests.
- Third stage of reasoning is about doing good for praise and approval.
- Fourth stage reasons that law and order and being a good, dutiful citizen are important to society's well-being.

> Fifth stage centers on the social contract and how, when one person falters, social conventions risk degradation.

> Sixth stage is considered the most evolved and reflective stage of ethical reasoning that opts for good based on a more global perspective regarding the respect for the rights and dignity of all people.

Protecting ideas and the taking of other's ideas falls into the purview of both law and ethics and converge when someone breaches or infringes on another's intellectual property. To avoid potential conflicts among design practitioners, many professional associations set in place a standard of "professional ethics" to clearly define a criterion of conduct on a broad range of issues including intellectual property.

A profession's code of ethics establishes a baseline standard of conduct and behavior for professional members. Failure to comply with a code of professional ethics may result in censure from the profession or the professional association or some other sanctions.

Generally, for the interior design profession, a professional code of ethics attempts to inspire and encourage respect toward fellow professionals, the industry, and the public. Codes of ethics (International Interior Design Associa-

tion, 2001) mandate a standard of behavior that centers on issues of responsibility including:

> Responsibility to the public in the professional's careful and knowledgeable execution of the work

> Responsibility to the client by being qualified to do the scope of work contracted and executing the work in a highly professional manner

> Responsibility to other professionals through one's honesty and integrity

> Responsibility to the profession by contributing to the body of knowledge, advocating contribution, and continuing the professional's own education

A proponent of professional codes of ethics will place value in having clear codes that help professionals understand the principles behind the expectations and creation of an ethical framework that is applied openly and fairly. An opponent will question the validity of relying on codes of ethics to promulgate good professional conduct because it sets a minimum standard rather than a high standard. Opponents also take issue with creating a fixed document with a pre-established set of ethics (and sanctions when violated) because it can be perceived as self-serving.

IDEAS

Thinking is easy, acting is difficult, and to put one's thoughts into action is the most difficult thing in the world.

—Johann Wolfgang von Goethe

For the most part, with or without a code of ethics, a true professional understands the ethical and legal implications of infringing on someone's intellectual property and goes to extremes to avoid conflicts. However, the boundaries are not as clear when it becomes the owner's (i.e., client's) rights versus the interior designer's

right to the intellectual property, specifically as it relates to the interior designer's instruments of service. An instrument of service is generally defined as any tangible work product prepared by the interior designer on behalf of a client and where, once again, ethics and law intersect. Here, ethics perform the preface to the application of intellectual property law.

Depending on how an interior designer's work contract or proposal is worded, the owner may have full rights or limited-use rights to use and distribute these instruments of service (e.g., design sketches and construction documents) for the sole purpose of executing the construction of the project. According to Barry B. LePatner, Esq., a leading authority on corporate, real estate, and design law, this is an often-confused area of intellectual property from both sides of the negotiating table.

An interior designer's instruments of service fall into the category of intellectual property known as copyright law. The following briefing is a summary of a discussion with LePatner (personal communication, January 2009) on the rights, risks, and liabilities associated with copyright and copyright infringement related to an interior designer's instruments of service.

COPYRIGHT

The basic premise of copyright law states that anyone who sketches an original graphic symbol, i.e., makes a drawing, essentially has an automatic copyright the minute this person takes pen to paper. Although copyright exists when the original works appear in a tangible medium like a drawing (whether or not it is registered), good practice dictates that the author of the drawing(s) registers it with the U.S. Copyright Office (2009).

In general, registration occurs at the completion of the work, specifically if the work is going to be published, or if there's something unique about the work. For example, if an interior designer or firm plans to submit the work for a design competition and the project is likely to receive notoriety, it's important to register the work.

When an interior designer or firm transmits in-progress design documents to a client that have yet to be registered with the U.S. Copyright Office (2009) (in progress prints, schematics, design proposals, etc.), it is still good practice to place the copyright notice on each document (© year, name of firm or person). It's also good practice to insert "not for construction" on all in-progress drawings. A copyright created after 1978 is protected for the life span of the author plus an additional 70 years after

death or, in the case of multiple authors, 70 years after the death of the last living author. In the case of a work made for hire, the author is the hiring party. The duration of copyright for works made for hire is 95 years from the first publication, or 120 years from creation, whichever expires first (U.S. Copyright Office, 2009).

When or if someone has access to an interior designer's or firm's copyright and copies it to use without compensating the original designer/firm at an agreed value, that person has infringed on a copyright. The interior designer or firm whose copyright is infringed can take legal action against the other party. The first step is to seek counsel. It's usual to send a letter to the offending party putting them on notice that it is the interior designer's or firm's belief that the offending party has access to the works without permission. The letter will outline the remedies the interior designer or firm seeks.

In collaborative engagements, generally, each collaborator retains the intellectual property of his or her interest. For example, if a structural engineer adds design elements to a drawing, the engineer retains the copyright of the structure and the same is true for the other collaborators. When the boundaries are unclear, specifically when multiple designers or firms take on shared roles or engage in joint venture partnerships, it's advisable to establish the parameters of copyright ownership at the start of the engagement.

When, or if, a client seeks ownership of the documents beyond a limited-use as instruments of service, language stating this transfer of ownership must appear in the agreement between the client and interior designer or firm. In this case, the interior designer or firm may want to seek counsel to avoid negative implications and liabilities from the transfer.

When or if a client has multiple project locations and intends to utilize planning concepts designed by one firm and later executed by another, the interior designer or firm can arrange to have a two-part agreement: one for the prototype that includes the design concept and branding, etc., and another for the site-specific adaptations. The copyright for the intellectual property belongs to the first interior designer or firm, no matter if the project moves forward or stalls. When it comes to the site-specific work, the contracts vary; sometimes the interior designer or firm is involved for each location, or involved minimally, and their compensation and intellectual property rights are negotiated accordingly.

Specific care about intellectual property and indemnification should be taken when or if the interior designer or firm's contract is terminated. The interior designer or design firm has the right to be paid in full for the services and expenses rendered to date. If the project is under construction, the interior designer or firm should apprise the governing agencies of the project's status.

Next is the issue of credit for authorship. If the project was substantially designed under the first designer's/firm's contract, that interior designer/firm will want to pre-arrange with the second interior designer/firm how the credit will be documented. Finally, the first interior designer/firm will want to be indemnified from responsibility for the project since he/she is no longer in a position to review the project's development. The second interior designer/firm taking over the project from another firm is required to obtain consent from the original interior designer/firm and have it in place before the second designer/firm can ethically begin work on the project. (Note: end of LePatner's scope of contribution.)

INFRINGEMENTS

A lotta cats copy the Mona Lisa,
but people still line up to see the original.

—Louis Armstrong

Beyond the context of instruments of service, intellectual property rights for works of design are more difficult to protect from infringement. Appropriators don't necessarily require an original drawing to copy the design—the information is readily available in catalogs and Web sites and by examining or simply engaging with the physical, designed object, building, or space. In addition, making slight alterations to an original design is a simple defense some copyists use if an infringement case goes to court.

In the realm of product or object design, "original" status comes from designers and/or manufacturers who maintain the exclusive right to manufacture and/or distribute the works. When a manufacturer hires a designer to design a specific work or works, it is likely that that manufacturer retains and owns the works. An independent designer of an original work may also sell the exclusive right of production to a manufacturer. In this case, the manufacturer who owns the exclusive right is considered to produce the original works (Berry, 2008). An example of this is the Mies van de Rohe Barcelona collection, which he designed in 1929. In 1948, Mies sold the exclusive rights to Knoll to manufacture the collection (Schiffer, 2006). There are many entities that sell the Barcelona collection, but it is the Knoll-manufactured version that is considered the original.

The pervasiveness of infringements from copyists is not an indication that it is either ethically or legally more tolerable than other breaches; rather, it is because the burden of proof is the responsibility of the designer or manufacturer of the original work. Engaging in legal action against an intellectual property infringement is both costly and time-consuming and is the greatest deterrent in stopping knockoff proliferation.

CONCLUSION

Real wealth is ideas plus energy.

—Buckminster Fuller

Ethics are often considered one's private philosophy, so they are rarely discussed in context of defining a professional legacy. Interior designers understand their obligation on behalf of the client in economic, schedule, budget, and environmental concerns; the mission is less clear when it comes to acting responsibly toward the protection of ideas, knowledge, and intellectual property—specifically how each is shared, protected, and preserved. Law and ethics converge on this subject. Codes, laws, and rules of conduct set standards and mitigate misappropriation. Ethics, values, and high ideals, however, transcend notions of authenticity and are critical in the promotion of a profession's new thinking and invention.

It is as true today as it was in Vitruvius' era: interior design's legacy is the reflection of the profession's ideals and values. The power and influence interior design wields—whether in its usability; its economical or environmental impact; or as new and original invention, thought, and wisdom—must be exerted in balance with great ethics, morals, and a sense of responsibility. Interior design's legacy depends on it.

REFERENCES

Berry, J. (2008, December 12). Knock-offs: Flattery or fraud? *Contract*. Retrieved March 12, 2009, from http://www.contractmagazine .com/contract/content_display/design/essay/ e3i4c4c27b6bb76d9d1f17fa95db552ff3c

Ethic. (n.d.). In *Merriam-Webster's online dictionary*. (11th ed.). Retrieved April 30, 2009, from http://www.m-w.com/dictionary/ethic

International Interior Design Association. (2008). Policy & procedures, D.8., *Code of ethics for professional and associate member conduct*. Chicago: Author.

Law. (n.d.). In *Merriam-Webster's online dictionary*. (11th ed.). Retrieved April 30, 2009, from http://www.m-w.com/dictionary/law

Margolin, V., & Buchanan, R. (1995). *The idea of design*. Cambridge, MA: The MIT Press.

Schiffer, N. (2006). *Knoll home & office furniture*. Atglen, PA: Schiffer Publishing.

Trevino, L. (1992). Moral reasoning and business ethics: Implications for research, education and management. *Journal of Business Ethics, 11*(5–6), 445–459.

Tuan, Y. (1989). *Morality and imagination, paradoxes of progress*. Madison, WI: University of Wisconsin Press.

U.S. Copyright Office. (2009). Frequently asked questions about copyright. Retrieved March 15, 2009, from http://www.copyright.gov/help/faq/

Vitruvius, P. (2005). *Ten books on architecture*. (M. H. Morgan, Translation, 1914) Stilwell, KS: A Digireads.com Book.

World Intellectual Property Organization. (2009). *Understanding copyright and related rights*. Geneva: WIPO.

AUTHOR'S NOTE

C. Coleman would like to thank Barry B. LePatner, Esq., Hon. AIA, founder of the New York–based law firm LePatner & Associates LLP.

SUSAN E. FARLEY

WHEN IS AN IMITATION AN ILLEGAL KNOCKOFF?

When an imitative product or design[1] triggers a mental connection to the product it imitates, it is often called a *knockoff*. The critical question is whether the knockoff is illegal. Volumes of legal treatises recite the legal standards used to answer this question. The relevant volume depends largely on the type of product imitated and the protection sought: namely, whether the original product is protected by a design patent, a trademark and its subsidiary law governing trade dress, or a copyright. Any one product may be subject to one or more areas of intellectual property law. Consequently, it can be a challenge for the non-lawyer to predict whether an imitation is illegal.

Having seen thousands of knockoffs and examining the facts surrounding their creation and marketing, certain trends predict the answer to whether a knockoff is illegal. These trends are not universal truths because there are exceptions to every rule. But, for the non-lawyer who cannot examine in detail the legal standards for three or more relevant areas of law, the following list of universal trends points to an illegal knockoff.

SUSAN E. FARLEY, Esq., is a registered patent attorney whose practice is heavily focused on patent, trademark, and copyright legal issues involving design commercialization, and she frequently lectures on these topics. As a partner in the intellectual property law firm of Heslin & Rothenberg Farley & Mesiti, P.C., Farley represents a wide range of businesses whose products are in demand largely because of their design aesthetics. As lead trial counsel in a number of landmark trade dress and patent cases, Farley has also been instrumental in several precedent-setting Federal Appeals Court decisions. She coauthored an Amicus Brief on behalf of a group of design-oriented businesses at the United States Supreme Court. Farley is a consulting legal advisor to the Foundation for Design Integrity, a nonprofit organization of design industry professionals whose principle goal is to educate the industry on the importance of protecting, rewarding, and encouraging the creation of designs.

THE ORIGINAL IS THE TEMPLATE FOR THE IMITATION

Although there are exceptions, if the imitation is created using the original as a template, there is an obvious question as to its legality. Two questions should be asked and answered by a lawyer: (1) why was the original needed? and (2) why wasn't the product created as an original work using the imitator's own creativity? The answer to these questions may reveal some of the additional trends identified in the following sections.

THERE IS NO SUCH THING AS THE 10% RULE

There is a popular urban legend that if an original design is changed by 10%, then it is not an infringement. This is a fantasy. There is no such rule, and in practice, a 10% change in a distinctive or unique product or design may be inconsequential. This assumes for a moment that changes can be so quantified and tallied into percentages. This is another fantasy. Even if a 10% design change could be quantified, in some instances it may be more than enough to avoid illegality. This would occur if, for example, the field of the prior art was very crowded or the change affected the one distinguishing feature of the original over the prior art. On the other hand, one can imagine a scenario where a hefty percentage is changed, and the imitation still looks very much like the original. Rather than a percentage test, the law provides that if an imitator attempts to design around the original, it must follow these legal standards to avoid liability:

1. If patent infringement is to be avoided, the imitation must not be substantially similar to the eye of the ordinary observer, giving such attention to detail as an ordinary observer would give. In making this determi-

nation, the prior art must be kept in mind. Employing this standard, the ordinary observer is not the professional interior designer who notices subtle differences. Instead, it is the typical end-purchaser. One way to look at this is if the imitation looks closer to the patented piece than it does to any of the prior art, it is probably an infringement.

2. If copyright infringement is to be avoided, the imitation must not be copied. If copying is denied, it is presumed to have occurred despite the denial if the imitation is substantially similar to the original and the imitator had access to the original. Access is presumed if the original is subject to a filed copyright application.

3. If trade dress infringement is to be avoided, the imitation must not be confusingly similar to the original, and the original must either be distinctive (if it is something other than a product), or it must be very famous such that relevant consumers recognize the product from its appearance as coming from a single source, even if they are not sure of the name of the source. In other words, it must be an icon.

THE PRODUCT IS MARKED

Frequently patented products are marked with a patent number or a patent pending warning. Similarly, copyrighted works are often marked with a notice. If the imitator sees either marking, and nonetheless proceeds to use the product or work as inspiration without advice of counsel, then the imitation is highly suspect. Sometimes, emboldened imitators actually remove the notice or otherwise obliterate it to obtain the assistance of unwitting third parties, who are also liable, despite their lack of knowledge. One cannot rely on a lack of marking. In most, if not all trade dress infringement cases, there is no marking. Also, liability exists in both copyright law and patent law in the absence of marking. Only the size of the monetary award is affected by a lack of marking.

THE SAVVY IMITATOR TURNS A BLIND EYE

Incredibly, all too often, an illegal knockoff is marketed by an entity that has its own design protection portfolio, and sometimes has taken measures to enforce it, including conducting lawsuits against others. These imitators are highly sophisticated in the area of design protection, so it seems incomprehensible that they would blatantly imitate that which is not theirs and not know it is a problem. This behavior can be only explained as willfully turning the blind eye. If the imitator fails to ask for an opinion of counsel prior to the product launch, if the imitator is aware of the original and yet does not question its proximity to it, if the imitation is marketed in the same channels trade because of the known desire for the product, the prediction is the eye has been blinded intentionally. The most plausible explanation is that the imitator believes the knockoff is illegal. Turning a blind eye is strong evidence of the imitator's state of mind. Consequently, if the imitator suspects that the imitation may be illegal yet chooses not to find out, then it is most likely illegal. After the willful blind eye is established, if the knockoff is illegal, the damages can be increased exponentially.

THE IMITATOR HOPES TO REAP WHERE IT HAS NOT SOWN

If the imitator was motivated to create an imitation to take advantage of the status, goodwill, and/or reputation of the original, then the imitation may be illegal. Further predictors of illegality can be found if the imitation was created in an unreasonably short period of time with minimal or less than reasonable amount of expense, trial, and error. Additional predictors exist if, after the imitation hits the market, it succeeds sooner than is reasonably expected without the same level of marketing and advertising as the original. A plausible explanation of this overnight success is that the imitation unfairly benefited from the original. Because our legal system is based in equity and fairness, judges and juries typically do not like it when an imitator unfairly reaps from the labor and investment of others. They typically find this good fortune to be illegal.

CONFUSION HAPPENS

If anyone along the chain of purchase or anyone after the purchase mistakes the imitation as being an original, or is induced to purchase it believing it is an original, or sponsored or affiliated by the maker of the original, then the imitation is almost certainly a knockoff. Two situations come to mind. The first is where the imitation is labeled with its own brand,[2] but looks virtually identical to the original. Courts have routinely held that labeling is not enough to overcome the confusion created by the virtual imitation. Perhaps the confusion was only used initially to attract one to the imitation. Such initial interest confusion is enough to establish illegality. Another situation is where the purchaser knows the imitation is a knockoff, but observers after the point of sale may be or are confused. Courts again have held this type of post-sale confusion is sufficient to establish illegality.

BAIT AND SWITCH

Where a specifier or end user's agent requests an original product, and the imitator fills the order with its own look-alike product or "reinterpreted design," this is strong evidence of an illegal knockoff. This fact pattern occurs where the agent attaches to its purchase order a specification (i.e., spec) sheet for a product not made by the "custom manufacturer." Seldom, if ever, is there a follow-up inquiry to determine if the agent or purchaser wanted the original product as attached to the purchase order or if they really wanted a knockoff. Most of the time, it is understood. The agent wants the knockoff. It is impossible to know what the end user was told or wants. In some cases, the end user is willing to sign an affidavit that the agent (typically the purchasing agent, or site contractor for a commercial project or in limited situations in which the interior designer is specifying and selling the product directly to the end user) told or misled them to think they were buying the original. Sometimes the agent showed pictures of the original and made the sale based on that image, and sometimes they even charged the end user for the original and kept the difference. Even if the savings is passed on to the end user or the end user knows this is a "custom" imitation of an original, it is highly unethical. Sometimes a case of fraud can be made against the interior designer if they have acted as the agent. At a minimum, a case for copyright infringement of the specification sheets is actionable along with a case for patent and/or trade dress infringement if the protection exists. More than one manufacturer and agent have had their cases collapse after this evidence is uncovered. It should be a huge red flag.

Similarly, where an original work is specified in a bid package, identifying by name a design or product and/or its equal, this is not a license to knock it off. "Or equal" means the specification can be legally satisfied by another product of equivalent quality and a satisfactory albeit different design aesthetic. If the substitute is an illegal knockoff, not only is the manufacturer of the knockoff liable, but so is the party who approved it as an equal and anyone else in the chain of sale. If the product is patented or copyrighted, the end user is also independently liable. Interior designers have suffered significant embarrassment and liability when contacted after a project is completed by an end user charged with a claim of infringement under this scenario.

THE IMITATION IS A KNOCK-DOWN, IT MAY BE A KNOCKOFF

The converse of this is an even more accurate predictor, namely if the imitation is a "knockup" such that its quality or its design is an improvement over the original, it is highly unlikely that it is an illegal knockoff. The purpose of an illegal knockoff is to take sales away from original, using the benefit of the original's market presence. This usually requires a comparatively smaller price, which often occurs when corners are cut and quality is less. If the imitation is higher in quality, it usually is not cheaper. In this instance, the imitation will stand on its own merit and will not unfairly or illegally gain from the original's goodwill, investment, and/or the talent of its designer. A big exception to this predictor is in the area of patent law, where an improved imitation may still infringe a patent if it contains all the elements of the patented invention, or its equivalent or, in the case of the design patent, where the imitation is substantially similar to the design as illustrated in the patent and less similar to what is already known in the prior art.

IMITATOR ACTS ABOVE THE LAW IN OTHER MATTERS

After dealing with thousands of imitators over the past 25 years, it is my opinion that certain common characteristics have emerged. Frequently, the imitator exhibits a "rules don't apply to me" mentality, which can be identified in their personalities and in other areas of their business dealings. Although the relationship between those other areas and the motivation to sell illegal knockoffs may be unproven, its coexistence is undeniable. Therefore, it appears to be a predictor. Areas of concern include poor or nonexistent record keeping; noncompliance with discovery demands and other legal deadlines; chronic misrepresentations and blatant lying, in some cases amounting to perjury; avoidance or noncompliance with employment laws; tax evasion; bullying others, including the owner of the original for which protection is legally sought; a complete lack of empathy or recognition of the harm the illegal knockoff is causing; extreme arrogance; aggression; and denial.

THE COMMON SENSE "DUCK" RULE

After looking at the original and the imitation, if there is no reason, other than those mentioned previously, for the two designs or products to be so undeniably similar *and* if the imitator provides none, while simultaneously denying any copying or imitation, then trust your instincts. Citing the old "duck" rule, if it looks like an illegal knockoff, sells like an illegal knockoff, and acts like an illegal knockoff, then probably it is an illegal knockoff.

NOTES

1. For the purpose of this essay, a "product or design" includes any tangible design, such as two-dimensional works including fabrics, wallpaper, floor plans, and three-dimensional works such as furnishings, accessories and adornments, jewelry, silverware, toys, lighting, space designs, architectural works and details, and color schemes.

2. These situations are not to be confused with counterfeiting, which is where the virtually identical imitation carries the original's trademark label or brand without permission. Counterfeiting is illegal in all situations, whether or not confusion is established. Counterfeits are the most serious class of illegal knockoffs. Criminal sanctions are available against counterfeiters, but are not available against knockoff artists.

H. LADON (DON) BALTIMORE

WHAT IS THE EFFECT OF REGULATION ON LIABILITY?

With several states regulating interior design and many others considering regulation, important questions arise for the interior design profession:

- ❯ What is the effect of regulation of interior designers on their liability?
- ❯ Why should interior design professionals care about liability?
- ❯ If you are a professional and careful, does the potential of liability affect you?
- ❯ Are lawyers waiting for regulation to hold interior designers to higher standards, or are lawyers already circling the profession?

These questions also provide an opportunity to review the liability of interior designers without regulation:

- ❯ What liability does an interior designer have?
- ❯ What acts or failure to act can incur liability?

H. LADON (DON) BALTIMORE has been a licensed attorney for 34 years. His practice emphasizes government relations and administrative law. He has represented individual interior designers, as well as the Tennessee Interior Design Coalition, the Tennessee Chapter of ASID, and the Tennessee Chapter of IIDA. Baltimore has represented interior designers individually in court and during administrative hearings, as well as the interior design profession in the legislature and before the Tennessee Board of Architectural and Engineering Examiners. Baltimore also has represented businesses and associations in courts, administrative agencies, and legislative bodies. Baltimore is a member of the American, Tennessee, and Nashville Bar Associations. He is past chairman of the Tennessee Bar Association Governmental Affairs Committee and of the Nashville Bar Association Legislative and Governmental Relations Committee. He was a consultant for the National Council for Interior Design Qualification's By-Laws and Policies and Procedures Committee.

- What standards are imposed on interior designers even without regulation?
- Are the standards under regulation different from the standards without regulation?
- Other trades and professions, without regulation, have been held to a high standard of care, which has resulted in liability. Does this mean the same for the interior design profession?

The profession has been busy designing homes and commercial spaces; educating interior design students; informing the public of the profession's impact on safe environments, ergonomic workspaces, proper egress, and accessibility for the handicapped; and designing for an aging population and others with special needs. During these efforts, our society has been improving standards of care for professionals and specialists to hold them accountable for ignorance or disregard of those standards. Interior designers' liability has come to the forefront of the profession's concerns because of lawsuits against interior designers and other design professionals, the adoption of practice acts (i.e., regulation that controls the practice of interior design), and consideration of proposed practice acts in several states. Liability lawsuits against interior designers in states without practice acts have been pursued to the natural concern of the profession. A combination of these events has interior designers wondering what the actual and potential exposure for liability is in their profession, with or without regulation. An interior designer can legitimately ask,

- Is my liability higher in a jurisdiction with a practice act?
- Will my liability increase if the state or province adopts a practice act?
- What liability exposure do I face in the absence of a practice act?
- Should the profession maintain high standards and practices even without regulation to avoid or, at the very least, minimize exposure to liability claims?

LIABILITY: YES, NO, OR MAYBE?

For an issue that has caused concern for interior designers, there is *no concrete evidence* of regulation increasing interior designers' liability in their practice. A definitive answer is difficult because there are few reported cases of liability to date in states with or without regulation. In states with interior design regulation, there has been no evidence that regulation has caused an increase in interior designers' liability. Though even without a number of decisive court cases and academic treatises, a discussion of the issue is beneficial to interior design practitioners so they can make an informed and intelligent assessment of the effect of regulation on liability, an issue of importance to individual interior designers and to all segments of the interior design profession.

The vast majority of court cases involving interior designers are concerned not with liability but with clients not wanting to pay ("I am not paying for this!"). Usually, these cases involve interior designers suing to be paid when a client refuses and the client, in turn, pleading defenses of incompetence on the part of the interior designer, not delivering the services and products as promised, breach of contract, or the client not being pleased with the result. A disgruntled client often counters that the interior designer is in actuality, under state law, an unlicensed general contractor, an unlicensed home improvement contractor, or other unlicensed regulated trade or profession and, therefore, cannot recover for services rendered. This can occur because many state laws prohibit unlicensed practitioners from recovering all or part of their fee.

Other legal matters involving interior designers are administrative actions in practice or title acts (regulation of the use of the title, but not of the practice of interior design) alleging the interior designer is holding himself or herself out as a licensed or registered professional when, in reality, they are not a licensed or registered professional. Even in states without interior design practice or title acts, administrative actions involve interior designers (and others) practicing in other licensed professions when not qualified, for example, as an architect, engineer, or contractor. Such legal action is not restricted to interior designers; architects, engineers, and contractors are often taken to task for invading the territories of other professions.

The lack of reported cases of interior designers being sued for liability as a result of professional malpractice makes it difficult to assess the potential of increased liability under regulation. However, there is no evidence that regulation has increased liability for interior designers. The same legal standards of care to hold an interior designer liable for professional malpractice can be applied in jurisdictions with or without regulation.

What is liability? What liabilities for interior designers are we talking about? And, more specifically, what liability might be affected by regulation? Liability is defined as the state of being liable (American Heritage College Dictionary, 1997). Not much help there, but the dictionary goes on to further define *liability* as an obligation, a responsibility (*American Heritage College Dictionary*, 1997). With that further refinement of the definition, we are getting closer to what liability means for interior designers in their profession. An even more enlightened explanation of liability can be found in synonyms for *liability—accountability, exposedness, being made accountable* (*Webster's New World*, 1999). In other words, interior designers can be exposed to liability and made accountable for their actions or failure to act as a professional. A review of some liability exposure for interior designers can show what, if any, effect regulation will have on liability.

Some liability will not be affected by regulation. For example, liability for practicing architecture, engineering, general contracting, or other licensed profession without a license is now, and will continue to be, a violation of law, with or without regulation. Ancillary to such liability is holding oneself out as an interior designer or using the title "interior designer," "certified interior designer," "licensed interior designer," or "registered interior designer" as defined in a practice act state or title act state. Such liability is also obvious and not under question in this essay. Other obvious forms of liability that will not be affected by regulation are breach of contract, adherence to employer/employee laws, and compliance with tax laws. Interior designers are liable for their actions or non-actions (especially nonpayment of taxes) concerning these laws, regulation or no regulation of interior design practice.

The liability we are concerned with is professional malpractice under a practice act. *Malpractice* is defined as any professional misconduct, unreasonable lack of skill or fidelity in professional duties (*Black's Law Dictionary*, 1968). In other words, professional liability (as in professional liability insurance) is our topic of concern.

Detractors of the interior design profession have stated, "while bad taste might be offensive, there is no evidence that anyone has been killed by a bad color scheme" (Report from the, 2000). Not only does this statement denigrate the interior design profession, it misses what the profession does and the serious issue of professional liability. Decisions regarding means of egress and specification of furniture, fabrics, and finishes to meet fire codes are just two examples of how interior designers affect the public health, safety, and welfare. Such decisions also potentially expose interior designers to liability.

Negligence for an interior designer, or anyone else for that matter, is the absence of care that is necessary under the circumstances. It is the violation of a "standard of care" for the profession and the specific project. If a designer violates that standard of care, he/she is negligent and incurs liability. If a designer does not violate a standard of care, the designer is *not* negligent and does *not* incur liability.

What is a standard of care? There is no one perfect standard of care. The standard of care is determined by analyzing if the interior designer has the requisite minimum knowledge, ability, and experience to perform the particular project and if the interior designer exercised reasonable care; in other words, performed as would other similarly situated interior designers.

As a practical matter, if an interior designer is sued for negligence or professional malpractice in a court of law, experts would be called to testify as to the standard of care and if the interior designer met that standard of care. Specifically, an interior designer would want an expert witness to testify along the lines that "I have an interior design education; I passed the National Council for Interior Design Qualification exam; I have 20 years experience in interior design. I have reviewed the plans, specifications, and the project itself; and, in my expert opinion, there are no errors or omissions. The standard of care has been met." Of course, it goes without saying (but I will say it), the litigant on the other side wants an expert with the same or similar credentials to conclude that "I have reviewed the plans, specifications, and the project itself and, in my expert opinion, the standard of care for the community in a project of this nature has not been met." This scenario would be played out in jurisdictions with or without regulation.

One consideration of regulation is that regulation could be cited to set the minimum standards of education and experience. The next step would be to determine if the interior designer exercised reasonable care as any other such interior designer in the same circumstances would have exercised. In other words, how would a similar interior designer perform in the same circumstances? The answers to the second step and last question are likely to be determined by the same analyses regardless of regulation.

Lack of regulation does not make a profession or trade immune from liability. Interior designers, as are other professionals, are required to not only exercise reasonable care in what they do, but to also possess a minimum standard of special knowledge and ability. Even skilled trades that do not require regulation are held to a standard of care and incur liability if that standard of care is violated. Courts have imposed liability on unregulated professions and trades such as thresher operators, restaurant owners and managers, and oil well shooters (increase oil well production with explosives), just to name a few.

Using fire safety as a specific example for potential liability, interior materials play a major part in flame spread and toxic gas production. In the event of a devastating fire occurring within a space in which an interior designer was involved, does anyone doubt the interior designer would be sued only in a jurisdiction with regulation and not sued in a jurisdiction without regulation? Any lawyer worth his/her salt is going to sue all those who participated in the design, selection, and construction of the project—the interior designer, architect, engineer, contractor, and manufacturer. The interior designer is not going to be immune by the status of regulation or no regulation in the jurisdiction. If a thresher operator can be sued for violating a standard of minimum special knowledge and ability, so can an interior designer— whether or not regulation is involved.

Though a discussion of means and methods to protect an interior designer from liability is beyond the scope of this essay, some guidance on liability avoidance can be offered. To protect interior designers from and, at the very least, minimize exposure to liability, interior designers should only practice in their area of competence, participate in continuing education, consult an attorney to ascertain if liability can be limited by contract, and maintain professional liability insurance. Of course, this is a list of minimum recommendations and not exhaustive.

CONCLUSION

Though there is no definitive answer, it appears regulation will not significantly, if at all, increase liability of interior designers. There is no evidence of an increase in liability in practice act states. Liability, also known as professional negligence or professional malpractice, can be alleged and incurred in jurisdictions with or without regulation. Professionals such as interior designers are held to a standard of care, and if that standard of care is violated, liability can be incurred. As discussed previously, disgruntled clients or end users of interior design projects can, and will, pursue liability actions against interior designers regardless of regulation or no regulation of the interior design profession. As a result, interior designers should take steps to protect themselves from or, at a minimum, reduce exposure to liability. In our litigious society, it is safe to say that an interior designer is a target of liability actions with or without regulation. An interior designer should always maintain high professional standards of care whether or not practicing in a jurisdiction with regulation. Professional liability has not raised its head only in regulated environments. Professionalism, in and of itself, imposes a higher standard of care.

REFERENCES

Giattina, J. (2000, May). Direct connection. *A report from the president*. Retrieved May 8, 2009, from http://www.ncarb.org/NewsClips/may00.htm

Liability. (1997). In *American heritage college dictionary*. Boston. Houghton Mifflin.

Liability. (1999). In *Webster's new world Roget's A-Z thesaurus*. New York: Macmillan.

Malpractice. (1968). In *Black's law dictionary*. St. Paul: West Publishers.

It is not enough that the spaces are aesthetically pleasing and can be maintained successfully, but they must meet both physical and psychological needs of occupants and owners of the space for the life of the space. . . . Simply, regulation protects the health, safety, and welfare of the public.

—Janice Roberts Young

REGULATION OF PRACTICE

OVERVIEW The interior design profession has advocated for regulation of practice for over 35 years, and yet attainment of regulation—especially regulation of practice—is proceeding at a snail's pace, at best. The authors of this chapter explore the disconnect among qualifications and responsibilities of interior designers; the needs of the public as considered by legislators as gatekeepers of regulation; and the mounting, though not always quickly apparent, evidence that the public is at risk—or is it?

In the face of the fuel load interior content contributes to fires, Katherine Setser recounts the tragedies that can occur without interior designers' specialized knowledge used to create fire-safe environments. Janice Roberts Young focuses on the need for regulation of interior design practice through an examination of how practice is regulated and legislators' obligations to keep the public safe. A systematic delineation of minimum requirements to practice regulated interior design is recounted by Diane Goté, and then she asks us to consider if these are sufficient. Wondering why professional interior designers are typically not identified as "professionals," David Stone proposes a "hybrid" regulation act that will provide the best of all worlds—both title and practice. Meanwhile, Phyllis Moore reveals the controversy that surrounds those who oppose interior design regulation and their motives—some from our own profession. And, continuing on that path, Caren Martin examines the battle of wits and words ensuing between the interior design profession and external forces as well as from within facets of the interior design profession and explores the systemic challenge of misinformation. This chapter begs the question: what/who is the most serious threat to the profession's right to practice and the ability of the profession to protect the public?

> Is regulation of practice the best way to prevent harm? Does regulation of interior design truly protect the health, safety, and welfare of the public?

KATHERINE S. SETSER

THROUGH THE CRACKS: FAILURES IN THE IMPLEMENTATION OF FIRE AND LIFE SAFETY STANDARDS IN THE SELECTION, SPECIFICATION, AND INSTALLATION OF INTERIOR CONTENT[1]

My morning started badly. I took a break and read the newspaper. I read about the uphill battles of people involved in humanitarian efforts to end hunger and malaria or finding a cure for cancer. What was I doing? Designing spaces so that my clients would feel better about themselves? No, that wasn't all I was doing. I was potentially saving countless lives. And with luck, no one will ever realize it.

The first priority of interior designers must be the protection of the health, safety, and welfare of the public (American Society of Interior Designers, 2006, § 2.3; International Interior Design Association, 2009, ¶ 3).[2] This responsibility is paramount. Proper selection of interior content,[3] the very issue with which interior designers—knowingly or unknowingly—grapple daily and for which many are specifically trained, is a primary determinant of whether accidents become tragedies (National Fire Protection Association, 1997).[4] Uninformed choices can have devastating results. Yet, the value interior designers offer

KATHERINE S. SETSER, IIDA, earned a BS in interior design at Miami University (Ohio). Her award-winning career spans more than two decades and includes design of specialized facilities for the elderly, psychiatric patients, prisoners, and juvenile offenders. In 1999, Setser cofounded enterprise resource group, LLC in Nashville, focusing on project planning services—programming, user-needs analysis, research, implementation and occupancy strategies, as well as forensic performance evaluation and litigation support consulting. Much of her work relates to the function of design and interior content in project performance and failure. Since 2003, Setser has been instrumental in developing interior design legislation, fostering her role as consultant to coalitions, and as an extensive lecturer. She serves on both state and international boards of numerous professional and civic organizations; chairs the NCIDQ Multiple Choice Examination Development Committee; and has held faculty appointments at Western Kentucky University, the University of Tennessee–Knoxville, and Watkins Institute.

for protection of life and property within the built environment is woefully underappreciated and largely unrecognized by the public, code officials, and allied professions—even by some within the field of interior design. Not only is the interior designers' role often minimized during the design/construction process, but also their participation in the development and implementation of life safety codes is seldom sought.

SCOPE OF THE PROBLEM

This devaluation of the expertise and contribution of interior designers is surprising because there is overwhelming evidence that the fire and death rates in North America are among the deadliest in the industrialized world[5] (International Association for the Study of Insurance Economics, 2008, pp. 4–6). A specially commissioned task force on fire and the built environment[6] determined that two of the most significant reasons for the high fire mortality rate in the United States fell precisely within the interior designer's domain—interior content. These reasons were:

1. A failure of standards to control building content presents serious dangers, particularly when incremental occupancy or use changes occur; and

2. Most interior content modifications in existing buildings are governed by superseded codes until significant alterations trigger implementation of current standards (Federal Emergency Management Agency and U.S. Fire Administration, 1987).

Both issues underscore weaknesses in comprehensive life safety code enforcement over a building's life. Regulation of a building's interior content often slips through the cracks and, as a result, compromises the public's safety.

IMPEDIMENTS TO PRODUCTIVE COLLABORATION

The general public assumes that current legal, regulatory, and oversight systems adequately safeguard its health, safety, and welfare. Similar misconceptions are common among allied professionals (e.g., architects, engineers, interior decorators), often driven by lack of knowledge, perspective, institutionalized beliefs, and protectionist motives.

The interior design practitioners' ability to collaborate meaningfully is impeded by numerous factors. In particular, interior designers face a number of hurdles founded upon erroneous perceptions from outside and, interestingly, within their own profession.

Misconception #1: The practice of interior design does not impact public health, safety, and welfare because interior design services only pertain to aesthetics.

The rhetoric is familiar and all too common. A spokesperson for a coalition against interior design regulation stated, "Not a shred of evidence has ever been presented to support a conclusion that the unregulated practice of interior design places the public in any form of jeopardy whatsoever" (Morrow, 2008, p. 21). And, a national voice for architects railed against licensure of interior designers by stating, "… while bad taste might be offensive, there is no evidence that anyone has been killed by a bad color scheme" (Giattina, 2002, ¶ 8). Such statements are easily refuted. But, if not addressed, the myth becomes the reality. These statements imply interior designers have no impact on public health, safety, and welfare. And yet, according to the National Fire Protection Association (NFPA) (Assembly Occupancies, 2009), interior finishes and

SIGNIFICANT FIRE INCIDENT	DATE OF INCIDENT	CIVILIAN DEATHS	CIVILIAN INJURIES
The Station, West Warwick, RI	February 2003	100	200
Fraternity House Fire, Chapel Hill, NC	May 1996	5	3
Board and Care Fire, Mississauga, ON	March 1995	8	12
Stadium Fire, Atlanta, GA	July 1993	0	0
Stadium Fire, Atlanta, GA	October 1993	0	0
Private Club Fire, Indianapolis, IN	February 1992	1	4
Board and Care Fire, Colorado Springs, CO	March 1991	25	8
Hotel Fire, Miami Beach, FL	April 1990	9	21
Fraternity House Fire, Berkeley, CA	September 1990	3	2
Fatal Board and Care Fire, Bessemer, AL	September 1990	4	—
Fatal Office Building Fire, Atlanta, GA	June 1989	5	20
High Rise Apartment Fire, Manhattan, NY	January 1988	4	9
First Interstate Bank Building, Los Angeles, CA	May 1988	1	—
Rooming House Fire, Massapequa, NY	August 1986	5	—
DuPont Plaza Hotel Fire, San Juan, PR	December 1986	97	140
Haunted Castle Amusement Fire, Jackson Township, NJ	May 1984	8	—
Boarding House Fire, Beverly, MA	July 1984	15	9
Hotel Fire, Peterson, NJ	October 1984	13	70
Central Community Home Fire, Worcester, MA	April 1983	7	—
Annandale Village Fire, Gwinnett County, GA	August 1983	8	—
Hotel Fire, Dayton, OH	November 1983	1	20
Hotel Fire, Las Vegas, NV	February 1981	8	350
Hotel Fire, Las Vegas, NV	November 1980	85	700
Hotel Fire, Cambridge, OH	July 1979	10	—
Hotel Fire, Greece, NY	November 1978	10	—
Beverly Hills Supper Club, Southgate, KY	May 1977	165	70
Night Club Fire, New Orleans, LA	June 1973	32	12
Totals		**629**	**1632**

FIGURE 7.1. Design tragedies: proof of interior content as contributor to fire loss. NFPA fire investigations indicate interior finish and content are consistent, direct contributors to loss of life and property in these and other fires.

furnishings in public assembly spaces[7] have more impact on the protection of life and property than any other issue except the actual fire ignition source itself.

Since the early 1940s, the fire investigations division of the NFPA has investigated and analyzed fires of technical or educational significance in the interest of loss prevention.[8] Even a cursory examination of these reports provides compelling evidence that interior content is a significant contributor to loss of life and property. Twenty-seven fires in public and other high-risk occupancies[9] specifically point to one or more aspects of interior finishes, furnishings, and arrangement of furniture as significant contributing factors in the loss of 629 lives (see Figure 7.1). Furthermore, the use of highly combustible interior finishes, content, and/or overwhelming interior fuel loads, especially in access or exit corridors, exacerbates loss through rapid flame spread and smoke development (NFPA, Fire Investigations, pp. various).[10]

A more detailed look at fire data for specific occupancy types reveals causal relationships between interior content and fire loss (Ahrens, 2006). Interior content in public and high-risk occupancies is responsible for more than 1,400 fires, 100 civilian injuries, and 16 civilian deaths every month (see Figure 7.2). The percentage of fires in which interior content is a first ignition source is 12% of all fires; the percentage of deaths (32%) and injuries (20%) where interior content is a first ignition source is much greater. To the point, if interior content is a first ignition source, risk of injury and death dramatically increases, particularly in occupancy types that present the greatest challenges in code compliance and enforcement over the useful life of the building.

A more comprehensive measure of loss from substandard interior content is provided by an examination of the extent of damage. The ability to contain fire (to object, room, floor of origin, or beyond) is an indicator of the speed at which fire and smoke spreads. The rates of flame spread and smoke development are determined in large part by the interior fuel load (consisting of wall, ceiling, and floor finishes; window treatments; movable partitions; furniture, decoration, accessories; and other content). Abnormal and improper fuel loads impede the ability of occupants to exit safely and can be devastating in the loss of life and property (Fitzgerald, 1997, pp. I–26–27). For example, in Figure 7.2 the two occupancy types Rooming/Boarding/Lodging and Hotels/Motels have a significantly high proportion of deaths, 46% and 38%, respectively, that occur in spaces well beyond the fire origin even though the number of fires first ignited by interior content in these occupancies is low, 20% and 24%, respectively.

Simply stated, proper design, selection, installation, and maintenance of interior content are critical to the health, safety, and welfare of the public (Hall & Coté, 1997, pp. 1–12). This is knowledge in which trained interior designers excel, regardless of the color scheme.

Misconception #2: Interior content may pose a hazard to the health, safety, and welfare of the public in high-risk occupancies; however, the risk of harm is mitigated by participation of licensed professionals and code officials within the existing regulatory environment.

The position of the American Institute of Architects (AIA) is symptomatic of this attitude. Its public policy states:

> that it is in the public interest for architects to design all structures primarily intended for human habitation or use. There are considerable differences between architecture and other licensed professions that significantly affect public health, safety, and welfare. The architect's comprehensive education and training encompass the impact of design and technology on the health and well-being of the public and on the built and natural environments. Each jurisdiction has a responsibility to its citizens to ensure that structures used or occupied by the public are designed by licensed architects. (2007, p. 6)

The built environment is not quite this simple nor the architects' scope of services and knowledge often this comprehensive.

There is a typical regulatory path for new construction and substantial building renovation: contract documents, signed and sealed by a licensed architect or engineer, are reviewed by code enforcement officials, and projects are visited periodically during construction to check regulatory compliance. However, the public (and many oversight participants) is largely unaware of the magnitude and

OCCUPANCY TYPE	TOTAL ANNUAL FIRES (AVG)	FIRES INVOLVING FIRST IGNITION OF INTERIOR CONTENT (ANNUAL AVERAGE)				EXTENT OF DAMAGE (LOSS OUTSIDE FLOOR OF ORIGIN)
		ANNUAL FIRES	CIVILIAN DEATHS	CIVILIAN INJURIES	DIRECT PROPERTY DAMAGE	
Rooming, Boarding/ Lodging	1,830	370 (20%)	8 (62%)	44 (44%)	$5.6 mil (32%)	46% deaths 27% injuries
Hotels/ Motels	4,550	1,110 (24%)	4 (25%)	61 (31%)	$18.9 mil (22%)	38% deaths 20% injuries
Dormitories, Fraternities/ Sororities, Barracks	2,340	310 (13%)	3 (100%)	29 (36%)	$16.9 mil (53%)	33% deaths 9% injuries
Religious and Funeral Properties	1,760	260 (15%)	1 (100%)	5 (25%)	$25.3 mil (26%)	100% deaths 20% injuries
Public Assembly Occupancies	3,890	490 (13%)	2 (100%)	14 (33%)	$22.9 mil (28%)	50% deaths 23% injuries
Eating and Drinking Establishments	9,910	600 (6%)	0 (0%)	4 (3%)	$14 mil (12%)	100% deaths 19% injuries
Educational Properties	7,070	640 (9%)	—	15 (13%)	$10 mil (9%)	3% injuries
Care for Aged Facilities	3,680	560 (15%)	3 (27%)	70 (41%)	$3.4 mil (27%)	0% deaths 5% injuries
Health Care Facilities	3,150	350 (11%)	0 (0%)	36 (41%)	$2 mil (9%)	0% deaths 6% injuries
Store/ Mercantile	17,200	2,000 (12%)	1 (11%)	27 (9%)	$245 mil (38%)	67% deaths 27% injuries
Office Properties	4,900	460 (9%)	1 (25%)	3 (6%)	$13 mil (9%)	50% deaths 8% injuries
Multi-Family Properties	91,300	9,800 (11%)	160 (3%)	890 (19%)	$198 mil (18%)	31% deaths 23% injuries
Totals	**151,580**	**16,950 (12%)**	**183 (32%)**	**1,198 (20%)**	**$575 mil (21%)**	

FIGURE 7.2. Causal relationship: interior content and fire loss; annual averages for high-risk occupancies (1999–2002). Fires in which interior content is a first ignition source are a small percentage of total fires, but a high percentage of those that cause damage, injury, and death.

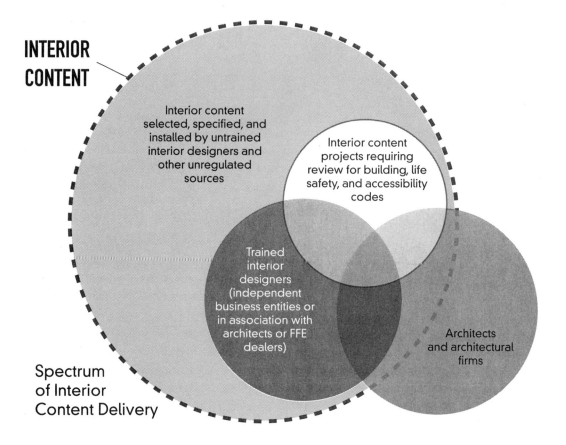

INTERIOR CONTENT

Interior content selected, specified, and installed by untrained interior designers and other unregulated sources

Interior content projects requiring review for building, life safety, and accessibility codes

Trained interior designers (independent business entities or in association with architects or FFE dealers)

Architects and architectural firms

Spectrum of Interior Content Delivery

FIGURE 7.3. A view of the regulatory cracks: spectrum of interior content delivery. Many interior content decisions, without the assistance of trained design professionals or regulatory oversight, are made by property owners; managers; end-users; finish and furnishings, fixtures, and equipment (FF&E) manufacturers; vendors; and a host of others—retailers, remanufacturers, installers/reconfiguration specialists, and untrained design practitioners.

frequency of change in interior content after initial occupancy that occurs without a review for building and life safety code compliance and/or without the involvement of licensed design professionals. Interior content, the very element that NFPA has stated is critical for life safety concerns, is often selected, specified, installed, and reconfigured outside of and/or after the project's review and permitting process (see Figure 7.3).

Over the life of a building, incremental change to interior content can profoundly affect life safety performance. This incremental modification may be driven by changes in ownership, tenancy, occupancy, and capacity or motivated by aesthetics, deterioration, obsolescence, and flexibility (reconfiguration of partitions, furniture, fixtures, and equipment). These unregulated modifications, because of their frequency and incremental nature, far outnumber new construction or significant renovation projects; new office construction completed in U.S. markets during the second quarter of 2008 made up less than 1% of available office square footage (Cushman & Wakefield, 2008, p. 1–2).[12]

Small, incremental modifications implemented by untrained participants can have severe repercussions. One small drip of the faucet does not cause damage; it's the cumulative body of water that overflows the sink.

Emblematic of this problem was the 1988 fire at the First Interstate Bank in Los Angeles, California (construction completed in 1973). The fire investigation proved to be "of great technical significance" with respect to interior content (Klem, 1988, p. i). The close, geometric configuration of the workstations, which provided a greater than average fuel load, in concert with the large open space, accelerated the fire (Klem, 1988, p. 29).[14] The fire resulted in one fatality, nearly 40 injuries, and total loss of the use of the 62-story structure for more than six months. The actual monetary loss has been estimated to be in the hundreds of millions of dollars.[15]

One might ask why anyone, trained or not, can specify, reconfigure, or install workstations, regardless of content or layout, in any high-rise building without the oversight of a licensed professional. Successful fire protection is based on a balanced, redundant system that allows for failure of any one of the multiple approaches (Hall & Coté, pp. I–11–12). In the United States, emphasis is often placed on fire suppression and response rather than on comprehensive preventative measures, perhaps in part because of such gaps in the delivery of interior content. A trend toward lessening more passive fire safety restrictions in buildings with sprinklers may point to a dangerous overreliance on automatic fire suppression systems. The problem inherent in this approach is epitomized by a 2001 recall of 35 million potentially faulty sprinkler heads (Mayer, 2001, p. H–01).

To return to the AIA's public policy, the members of the AIA are not (nor would one imagine they really want to be) the sole purveyors of life safety protection for interior content. As the life safety cracks in the regulatory framework expand in number and scope, interior designers should embrace, fill, and work to correct these voids. Otherwise, the codes are at best a tool to help find fault after a disaster has already occurred.

Misconception #3: The interior design field and its collective participants are prepared to share the mantle of public health, safety, and welfare responsibility.

The first two misconceptions recount distorted impressions of interior design harbored by allied professions. The interior design community rallies in near unanimity to counter these attitudes that facts discredit. But, an objective, introspective reflection of interior design practice proves much harder to solicit complete agreement. Are the collective participants truly ready to "share the mantle of responsibility?" If one gauges the readiness by its pursuit of regulatory accountability, then the practice is indeed equipped and ready to transition to the new archetype: interior designers as recognized, licensed professionals in the design industry.

A tremendous effort over decades has developed a thoroughly documented body of knowledge (Martin & Guerin, 2006), advanced academic curricular standards (see Council for Interior Design Accreditation at www.accredit-id.org), and a comprehensive competency examination (see National Council for Interior Design Qualification at www.ncidq.org). However, within the interior design field is a large group of practitioners who call themselves "interior designers"[16] but who have disparate definitions of the nomenclature than those developed for the professional licensure track. With an absence of regulation, and acting independently, they have few practice norms and no discernable standard of care. More importantly, their commitment to an evolving, regulated profession varies from apathy to downright hostility. These attitudes accentuate the public's confusion about what is an interior designer, a confusion made worse by the excessive exposure in the media of interior design as mere entertainment (HGTV among others). Such superficial perceptions return the argument full circle to misconception number one, interior designer as color picker.

One might say there is a widening gulf within the interior design field, pitting those in favor of professional accountability against those in favor of an absence of regulation. It becomes a matter of differentiation of services—those interior designers who prepare for and want to apply their knowledge in these challenging life safety conditions and those who choose other paths of participation in the interiors industry. The issue is not a casual disagreement. As building and life safety requirements become more stringent, all parties must realize that licensure of the profession—or some portion of it—will be necessary to improve protection in public and high-risk occupancies. The issue becomes one of survival in an area of practice: interior content in public and high-risk occupancies, for which interior designers are well qualified.

SEALING THE CRACKS

For a long time, many interior designers have sought to convincingly prove that they can play a vital role in protecting public health, safety, and welfare. A segment of the available proof has been provided here. The interior design profession, by its unique position in the delivery of interior content, provides essential knowledge and expertise that can protect property and lives, especially within the unregulated fissures in the implementation and enforcement of fire and life safety codes. And, practitioners who choose to seek licensure supported by their education, training, examination, and experience should participate as equal partners with other professions designing and maintaining health, safety, and welfare within the built environment. But, the interior design profession must effectively communicate this necessity, and it must marshal the fortitude to address difficult questions.

> Is the collective interior design establishment equipped and committed to provide the cohesive leadership and resources necessary to make a forceful argument for licensure? Is it dedicated to the accountability and full participation in the larger design community once licensure is attained?

> Is the establishment willing to acknowledge and accommodate distinct, complementary, professional paths within the field? Should licensure establish qualifications not only for the practice of interior design but also, not unlike the paralegal or the nurse practitioner, for those distinct complementary participants whose work contributes to the broad spectrum of interior design?

> Is the profession prepared to fully contribute as respected participants in a regulated environment? Can those practitioners assume their responsibility to the public and work to *seal the cracks*?

The answers to these and other questions likely will change the face of the interior design profession. One thing is certain: the future for all interior design professionals will be different than the current status quo. To have a seat at the table and to continue to participate in the design of an ever more complex built environment, the interior design profession must collectively take a more proactive role in its own destiny.

1. Although fire and life safety compliance are essential in all occupancy types, this article focuses on compliance with respect to public and other high-risk occupancies.

2. Similar ethical requirements are included in most jurisdictional legislation where the title or the practice of interior design is regulated.

3. For the purposes of this article, interior content includes the selection, specification, arrangement, and/or installation of interior finish materials and interior space content such as furniture, fixtures, and equipment provided as part of a scope of interior design services as defined by National Council for Interior Design Qualification (NCIDQ, 2004, pp. 1–2), accepted in current title and practice legislation and included in model legislative language (NCIDQ, Core Provisions, p. 1).

4. Section 6-5 Interior Finish cites the following few examples of the "deadliest U.S. fires" in which interior finish has been a significant factor in rapid flame spread: 2003 The Station Nightclub, Warwick, RI; 1989 Office Building, Atlanta, GA; 1986 DuPont Plaza Hotel, San Juan, PR; 1981 Hilton Fire, Las Vegas, NV; 1979 Holiday Inn, Cambridge, OH; 1978 Holiday Inn, Greece, NY; 1972 Nursing Home Fire, Springfield, IL, 1970; Pioneer International Hotel, Tucson, AR (pp. 319–322).

5. The United States has the 5th highest number of fire deaths per 100,000 persons out of 26 industrialized nations despite the fact it outspends all but one nation for fire protection (an estimated 12% of the total national cost of building and construction for private nonresidential structures). U.S. fire death rates continue to fall slowly—at a rate of less than 1% a year from 2003 to 2005, largely due to advances in building and fire safety codes as well as improvements in fire analysis (Intl. Assn. for the Study of Insurance Economics, 2008, pp. 4–8).

6. One of seven task forces assembled for a 1987 conference conducted by United States Fire Administration (USFA) / Federal Emergency Management Agency (FEMA), which included individuals from business and governmental organizations with an interest in fire protection. The purpose of the workshop was to achieve a consensus on the nature of the U.S. fire problem, review progress since the 1974 America Burning report (published by the 1971 National Commission on Fire Prevention and Control) and to develop recommendations to reduce further the loss of life and property due to fire. A follow-up commission formed in 1999, America at Risk: America Burning Recommissioned, echoed many of the same concerns expressed over the preceding decades (Federal Emergency Management Agency, 2002).

7. The NFPA defines an *assembly occupancy* as "an occupancy (1) used for a gathering of 50 or more persons for deliberation, worship, entertainment, eating, drinking, amusement, awaiting transportation, or similar uses; or (2) used as a special amusement building, regardless of occupant load. Assembly occupancies might include the following: armories, assembly halls, auditoriums, club rooms, dance halls, drinking establishments and exhibition halls among others" (National Fire Protection Association, 1997, Assembly Occupancies, ¶ 1).

8. NFPA fire investigation documentation includes "details of fire ignition, growth, and development; contributions of building construction, interior finish and furnishings; fire detection and suppression scenarios; performance of structures exposed to the fire; smoke movement and control; human reaction (response) and evacuation; fire fighting and rescue; fire propagation as a function of human reaction time; and the extent of life loss, injury and property damage" (National Fire Protection Association, 2009a, Fire Investigations, ¶ 2).

9. For the purposes of this examination, public and high-risk occupancies are defined as occupancies to which the public has access as passive users—they have had no input in space design decisions—and/or spaces that carry special risk to the occupants during an emergency, and, therefore, are subject to stricter code requirement and enforcement standards. Examples include high-rise buildings because of the complications of rescue in structures where heights exceed that of typical fire department ladder units or the length of time it takes to evacuate non-ambulatory patients in a healthcare setting. Specific occupancies in this compilation include: assembly, residential board and care, business, healthcare, high-rise, hotels/motels/dormitories, lodging/rooming house, mercantile, and multifamily housing including apartments and condominiums.

10. Data review was limited to online NFPA publications of fire investigations in public and high-risk occupancies (National Fire Protection Association, 2009a, Fire Investigations, various). The fire investigation reports for the fires listed above or enumerated in instruction about impact of interior finish in the Life Safety Code Handbook (National Fire Protection Association, 1997, pp. 319–322) clearly identify interior finish materials and/or content as directly contributing to the loss of life or property. Other fire investigations report impact of substandard interior content but do not expressly identify it as a direct contributor to loss. For relevance, only fires since 1973 are listed.

11. Annual averages are national estimates of fires reported to U.S. municipal fire departments during the four-year period of 1999–2002. Data exclude events of September 11, 2001. Fires reported only to federal or state agencies or industrial fire brigades are excluded. Fires are rounded to the nearest ten and direct property damage is rounded to the nearest hundred thousand dollars. Property damage has not been adjusted for inflation (Ahrens, 2006, p.3).

12. Even allowing for a sharp cutback on new commercial office construction starts because of recent economic conditions, a 51% drop over the previous year period, placing new office construction at approximately 1% of the available office space (Cushman & Wakefield, 2008, pp. 1–2).

13. Figure 3 is intended to be illustrative of relationships only.

14. NFPA's fire analysis listed one of the major factors contributing to the loss of life and the severity of the First Interstate Bank Building Fire was the "[r]apid initial growth, development, and spread of the fire due to the combustible nature and geometric arrangement of the office furnishings in a large, open floor plan" (Klem, First Interstate Bank Bldg., p. iii).

15. The NFPA fire investigation report states that "the intensity of the fire was so severe at the First Interstate Bank that the incident commander feared that structural collapse of the [62-story] building might occur. It also took 64 companies and 383 firefighters 3½ hours to eventually get ahead of the floor-to-floor fire spread and knock the fire down . . . " (Klem, 1988, p. 37).

16. In jurisdictions that do not regulate the practice of interior design, anyone may use the title regardless of qualifications. A "[r]uling in the late 1990s by the 11th Federal Circuit [Court] on a lawsuit filed by a Tennessee unlicensed person resulted in the ruling that "Interior Designer" could not be regulated and restricted to only licensed persons since it had been used without restriction and without regulation for a long period of time. At that time, Tennessee's Board [of Architectural and Engineering] Examiners succeeded in gaining their legislature's cooperation in changing their title to "registered interior designer," which could be restricted, regulated, and upheld in court" (NCIDQ, Core Provisions, §. forward). Similar cases continue to be filed in states where interior design regulations use the broad term *interior designer.*

REFERENCES

Ahrens, M. (2006). *U.S. fires in selected occupancies.* Quincy, MA: National Fire Protection Association.

American Institute of Architects. (2007). *Directory of public policy and position statements: As amended by the board of directors December 2007.* Retrieved May 9, 2009, from http://aia.org/aiaucmp/groups/aia/documents/pdf/aias078449.pdf

American Society of Interior Designers. (2006). *ASID code of ethics and professional conduct.* Retrieved May 8, 2009, from http://www.asid.org/about/ethics

Cushman & Wakefield, Inc. (2008). United States office report. *Marketbeat.* Retrieved February 27, 2009, from http://www.cushwake.com/cwglobal/docviewer/US_OFF_2Q08.pdf?id=c21400023p&repositoryKey=CoreRepository&itemDesc=document&cid=c16500002p&crep=Core&cdesc=binaryPubContent&Country=GLOBAL&Language=EN&Country=US&Language=EN

Federal Emergency Management Agency. (2002, June). *America at risk: America burning recommissioned, FA-223.* Washington, DC: U.S. Government Printing Office.

Federal Emergency Management Agency, & U.S Fire Administration. (1987). *America burning revisited: National workshop, Tyson's Corner, Virginia, November 30–December 2, 1987.* Washington, DC: U.S. Government Printing Office.

Fitzgerald, R. (1997). Fundamentals of fire safe building design. In A. Coté (Ed.), *Fire Protection Handbook* (18th ed.). Quincy, MA: National Fire Protection Association.

Giattina, J. (2000). A report from the president. *Direct Connection, 3*(1). National Council of Architectural Registration Boards. Retrieved January 14, 2009, from http://www.ncarb.org/NewsClips/may00.htm

Hall, J., & Coté, A. (1997). America's fire problem and fire protection. In A. Coté (Ed.), *Fire Protection Handbook* (18th ed.). Quincy, MA: National Fire Protection Association, pp. 1–12.

International Interior Design Association. (2009). *IIDA code of ethics.* Retrieved May 15, 2009, from http://www.iida.org/i4a/pages/index.cfm?pageid=304

International Association for the Study of Insurance Economics. (2008). World fire statistics: Information bulletin of the world fire statistics. T. Parish (Ed.), *Geneva Association Information Newsletter.* Geneva, Switzerland: The Geneva Association.

Mayer, C. (2001, July 29). Sprinkler recall sounds alarm: Some safety officials fear buildings depend too heavily on systems. *Washington Post,* p. H–01.

Martin, C., & Guerin, D. (2006). *The interior design profession's body of knowledge, 2005 edition.* Grand Rapids, MI: Council for Interior Design Accreditation, American Society of Interior Designer, Interior Designers of Canada, International Interior Design Association, and the National Council for Interior Design Qualification.

Morrow, P. (2008, November). Anti-licensing: Insurgence of the independents. *Window Fashions Vision.* Retrieved May 7, 2009, from http://idpcinfo.org/Patti_Morrow__Insurgence_of_the_Independents.pdf

National Commission on Fire Prevention and Control. (1974). *America burning: The report of the national commission on fire prevention and control.* Washington, DC: U.S. Government Printing Office.

National Council for Interior Design Qualification. (2004). *NCIDQ definition of interior design.* Washington, DC: Author.

National Council for Interior Design Qualification. (2008). *Core provisions of interior design registration: Model legislation.* Washington, DC: Author.

National Fire Protection Association. (1997). In R. Coté (Ed.), *Life safety code handbook* (7th ed.). Quincy, MA: Author, pp. 319–322.

National Fire Protection Association. (2009). *Fire investigations.* Retrieved January 10, 2009, from http://www.nfpa.org/categoryList.asp?categoryID=241&URL=Research/Fire%20investigations

The following reports and investigations were used for background information:

Best, R., & Demers, D. (1982). *Investigation report on the MGM Grand Hotel Fire: Las Vegas, NV, November 21, 1980 (Rev Jan. 15, 1982)*. Quincy, MA: National Fire Protection Association. Retrieved May 12, 2009, from http://nfpa.org/

Best, R. (1983). *Summary investigation report: Central community home fire: Worchester, MA, April 19, 1983*. Quincy, MA: National Fire Protection Association. Retrieved May 11, 2009, from http://nfpa.org/

Best, R. (1978, January). Tragedy in Kentucky. *Fire Journal*. Quincy, MA: National Fire Protection Association. Retrieved May 16, 2009, from http://nfpa.org/

Bouchard, J. (1984). *Investigation report: Haunted castle amusement facility fire: Jackson Township, NJ, May 11, 1984*. Quincy, MA: National Fire Protection Association. Retrieved May 16, 2009, from http://nfpa.org/

Comeau, E. (1995). *Fire investigation report: Board and care fire: Mississauga, ON, March 21, 1995*. Quincy, MA: National Fire Protection Association. Retrieved May 16, 2009, from http://nfpa.org/

Coté, R., & Timoney, T. (1984). *Investigation report: Elliot Chambers boarding house fire, Beverly, MA, July 4, 1984 (Rev. Oct. 15, 1984)*. Quincy, MA: National Fire Protection Association. Retrieved May 12, 2009, from http://nfpa.org/

Demers, D. (1981). *Fire investigation report: Hotel fire: Las Vegas, NV, Eight fatalities, February 10, 1981 (Rev. Nov. 20, 1981)*. Quincy, MA: National Fire Protection Association. Retrieved May 12, 2009, from http://nfpa.org/

Duvall, R. (2006). *NFPA case study: Night club fires*. Quincy, MA: National Fire Protection Association. Retrieved May 9, 2009, from http://nfpa.org/

Isner, M. (1988). *Investigation report: Apartment high-rise fire: Manhattan, NY, January 11, 1988*. Quincy, MA: National Fire Protection Association. Retrieved May 16, 2009, from http://nfpa.org/

Isner, M. (1989). *Fire investigation report: Fatal office building fire: Atlanta, GA, June 30, 1989*. Quincy, MA: National Fire Protection Association. Retrieved May 11, 2009, from http://nfpa.org/

Isner, M. (1990). *Fire investigation report: Fraternity house: Berkeley, CA, September 8, 1990*. Quincy, MA: National Fire Protection Association. Retrieved May 15, 2009, from http://nfpa.org/

Isner, M. (1991). *Fire investigation report: Board and care facility fire: Colorado Springs, CO, March 4, 1991*. Quincy, MA: National Fire Protection Association. Retrieved May 11, 2009, from http://nfpa.org/

Isner, M. (1992). *Fire investigation Report: Private club fire: Indianapolis, IN, February 5, 1992*. Quincy, MA: National Fire Protection Association. Retrieved May 11, 2009, from http://nfpa.org/

Isner, M. (1993). *Summary fire investigation report: Two stadium fires: Atlanta, GA, July 20, 1993 & Irving, TX, October 13, 1993*. Quincy, MA: National Fire Protection Association. Retrieved May 10, 2009, from http://nfpa.org/

Isner, M. (1996). *Fire investigation summary: Fraternity house fire: Chapel Hill, NC, May 12, 1996*. Quincy, MA: National Fire Protection Association. Retrieved May 11, 2009, from http://nfpa.org/

Klem, T. (1983). *Investigative report: Travel Master Inn motel fire: Dayton, OH, November 23, 1983*. Quincy, MA: National Fire Protection Association. Retrieved May 11, 2009, from http://nfpa.org/

Klem, T. (1986). *Investigation report on the DuPont Plaza Hotel fire: December 31, 1986, San Juan, Puerto Rico*. Quincy, MA: National Fire Protection Association. Retrieved May 11, 2009, from http://nfpa.org/

Klem, T. (1988). *Fire investigation report: First Interstate Bank building fire, Los Angeles, CA, May 4,
1988.* Quincy, MA: National Fire Protection Association. Retrieved May 11, 2009, from http://
nfpa.org/

Klem, T. (1990). *Summary fire investigation report:
Fatal board and care fire: September 19, 1990.*
Quincy, MA: National Fire Protection Association.
Retrieved May 11, 2009, from http://nfpa.org/

Kyte, G. (1986). *Fire investigation report: Rooming
house fire: Massapequa, NY, August 23, 1986.*
Quincy, MA: National Fire Protection Association. Retrieved May 12, 2009, from http://nfpa
.org/

National Fire Protection Association (2009). *Fire
safety in assembly occupancies.* Quincy, MA:
National Fire Protection Association. Retrieved
January 9, 2009, from http://nfpa.org/

Peterson, C. (1984). *Investigation report: Alexander
Hamilton Hotel fire: Patterson, NJ, October 18,
1984.* Quincy, MA: National Fire Protection Association. Retrieved May 11, 2009, from http://
nfpa.org/

Robertson, J. (1990). *Fire investigation report: Hotel
fire: Miami Beach, FL, April 6, 1990.* Quincy, MA:
National Fire Protection Association. Retrieved
May 11, 2009, from http://nfpa.org/

Swartz, J. (1979). Human behavior in the Beverly
Hills fire. *Fire Journal* May 1979. Quincy, MA:
National Fire Protection Association. Retrieved
May 15, 2009, from http://nfpa.org/

Timoney, T. (1983). *Summary investigation report:
Annandale Village fire, Gwinnett County, GA,
August 31, 1983.* Quincy, MA: National Fire
Protection Association. Retrieved May 16, 2009,
from http://nfpa.org/

Willey, A. E. (1974, January). The upstairs lounge
fire. *Fire Journal.* Quincy, MA: National Fire
Protection Association. Retrieved May 17, 2009,
from http://nfpa.org/

➤ Is regulation of practice the best
way to enforce the right to practice?

JANICE ROBERTS YOUNG

THE NEED FOR REGULATION OF THE INTERIOR DESIGN PROFESSION

SCOPE OF INTERIOR DESIGN PRACTICE

Interior design practice is one of the last professions relating to the built environment to become a regulated profession, joining allied professions of architecture, engineering, landscape architecture, and construction, in a natural and logical evolution. As all these professions incorporate knowledge of many content areas, so does interior design. Interior design knowledge areas include interior construction (e.g., nonstructural versus structural elements), psychology, cultural anthropology, ergonomics, materials, acoustics, lighting, maintenance, furnishings, and decorative arts. And, certainly, and always, aesthetics.

In the public's view, interior designers select colors and materials (Sawasy, 2009), long having been perceived as the experts in that endeavor. However, well-designed spaces do not happen by accident, nor do they magically appear because someone can blend color and materials (Sawasy,

JANICE ROBERTS YOUNG, FIIDA, ASID, is an interior design practitioner in Jacksonville, Florida. She received a bachelor of interior design from Auburn University and has practiced for over 30 years in the design of airports, banks, offices, institutions, resorts, restaurants, and residences. Young was invited to serve on the Interior Design Associations Foundation, Inc. (IDAF), the Florida coalition for interior design, later becoming its vice president and acting president, and as president through 2010. She was appointed by Governor Chiles to serve on the Board of Architecture and Interior Design (BOAID) from 1991–1996 and was the first interior designer to serve on the Probable Cause Panel. Young served as IIDA's director of Government and Regulatory Affairs (1996-1998), was Florida's delegate to NCIDQ (1996-2002), and served as an NCIDQ board member and then president in 2005. She has served for many years on NCIDQ's IDEP and Model Language committees.

2009). Although there are certainly individuals who have innate abilities and talents (sometimes referred to as *taste*) to succeed in various vocations to produce a beautiful environment, those skills and talents are not enough to satisfy the challenges for today's interior design practice, nor to satisfy the public's expectations for their completed interior design projects.

With growing awareness of sick building syndrome (SBS) and building-related illness (BRI), interior designers who are experts in materials and finishes, must be conscientious and accurate at selecting materials and specifying the installation techniques for the initial installation and long-term effect of materials in place during the lifetime of the space. Issues of geography, climate, moisture, and volatile organic compounds (VOCs) of the materials must be considered in developing a healthy environment.

Since the passage of the Americans with Disabilities Act (ADA) in 1990, interior designers must also incorporate the guidelines for accessibility and barrier-free spaces in projects. Incorporation of these guidelines determines the success or failure of the functionality of the space, apparent to users immediately and thereafter every day, whether the project is a residence, an office, a hotel room, or hospital lobby. It is not enough that the spaces are aesthetically pleasing and can be maintained successfully, but they must meet both physical and psychological needs of occupants and owners of the space for the life of the space. Beyond these concerns and overall design considerations, interior designers must also work with a variety of state and local codes as interpreted by local building code officials and fire marshals for specific project parameters. As a result, the practice of interior design has grown more complex and challenging and requires those who practice it to be regulated.

INTERIOR DESIGN PRACTICE AND REGULATION

Throughout history, professional membership organizations have typically initiated the profession's movement toward regulation as a natural evolution of the development of the profession's specialized and abstract knowledge (Martin, 2008). In addition to formal education, followed by experience in the field, and formalized and standardized examination, the profession identifies and builds its body of knowledge (Martin, 2007). Though the practice of interior design did not achieve the first jurisdictional regulation until 1973 (Puerto Rico), 76 years after architecture was first regulated (Illinois in 1897), the profession of interior design has evolved in the same manner as architecture and other professions (Martin, 2007).

Interior design practice regulation came about for several reasons. The first and foremost issue is protecting the public even when they do not have the knowledge to understand some of the consequences of their needs not being met. Occupants' needs can only be assured through identification of practitioners' abilities to meet the standards needed to provide such services, and that practitioners accept responsibility for their work, including essential, ongoing training and continuing education as knowledge grows.

In the past, the terms *designer*, *decorator*, *interior designer*, and *interior decorator* have been used without restriction, and this has led to confusion by the public. They questioned, "Is this person who I am considering working with for my new office/new home knowledgeable so I can expect that the environment created will be healthy, safe, aesthetically pleasing, and work well for me?" The public needs substantiation that the persons they consider for the design of their projects do have the ability to protect their health, safety, and welfare even when they did not know what specific decisions would be required to achieve this end and their specific goals.

For example, consumers benefit from the licensing of physicians because it is costly for consumers to judge the quality of medical care, and the receipt of medical services from unqualified personnel can have dire consequences (Sass, 1993). Likewise, without clarification of the parameters of essential knowledge through regulation, there is confusion over the simple matter of who has the qualifications to create a safe interior environment.

With interior design title and/or practice regulation, titles that have otherwise been used commonly by the public can only be restricted when they appear with a "qualification" (i.e., a qualifier) in the title. For example, "professional engineer" is the regulated title for qualified, licensed engineers that interior designers and architects collaborate with in the design of the built environment because the term *engineer* had been in the public realm and used by many individuals to describe several distinct job titles (e.g., train engineer, traffic engineer, network engineer). Likewise, the term *interior designer* cannot routinely be restricted because the public has used it and applied various definitions or skill sets to those persons before any regulations ever existed. This means that titles such as "registered interior designer," "licensed interior designer," or "certified interior designer" can be valid and regulated titles. The preferred title is based upon jurisdictional precedence and preference.

Two specific opinions, one relating to a Florida case in 1992 (*Abramson v. Gonzalez*) and another relating directly to interior design title restriction in Tennessee, pertain directly to titles and restriction. Ultimately, titles cannot restrict if they have been used in common public application unless the practice is also restricted, and even then the restriction must not violate the First Amendment (i.e., freedom of religion, the press, and expression) and the Fourteenth Amendment (i.e., rights of citizenship) of the Constitution of the United States. The measure of title restriction, other than restriction of practice, lies with the protection of commercial speech from unwarranted government regulation: if the use of the term in the context of commercial speech is designed to solicit a commercial transaction, or if it is likely to deceive, or where records show that a particular form or method of advertising has in fact been deceptive (Tennessee A.G., 1995).

DOCUMENTING THE NEED FOR INTERIOR DESIGN REGULATION

There has been an assumption that fire marshals and safety inspectors assume the ultimate responsibility for these significant issues in interior environments such as health and safety outcomes. In reality, it is up to interior designers to incorporate design solutions that promote safe and healthy environments (Danko, Eshelman, & Hedge, 1990). Are there alternatives to regulations that would allow the public to be assured they are getting what they need and want and a safe environment? Yes, by devoting more resources to require all plans for any type of project be submitted to building code officials for review. This would be costly because it would require all plans to be submitted for review, even those not currently required to be submitted (Sass, 1993).

As Carl Sapers, legal counsel to the National Council of Architectural Review Boards (NCARB), said, "The public is only protected if the people who design the built environment for human habitation have been educated, trained, and examined so they are competent to do the work" (Sapers, 2000, p. 6). Protecting the public can only be accomplished when all decisions are made by educated, knowledgeable, experienced persons from the first vision of the project through to its realized tangible form, and interior designers have these competencies.

It is not necessary to have documented deaths, fires, permanent injuries, or sickness caused by unqualified persons practicing interior design before interior design regulation can be considered. Instead, it is routinely the responsibility of lawmakers to be proactive to protect the public (Martin, 2008). Lawmakers should act *before* there are deaths, fires, injuries, or illness—to foresee what may contribute to these. Research has shown that the creation of spaces for working, healing, playing, learning, or resting is not just about the building, but because every decision and the specification of every component within each space affects those within the space, today and for many tomorrows (Martin, 2008).

The regulation of interior design practice is important because through regulation of professions, lawmakers benefit the consumers by identifying who is qualified to perform a specific service so the public can avoid unfortunate outcomes. This is of paramount importance regarding decisions that may not be understood or appreciated during project development, but would be difficult and costly to correct after the fact, especially relevant to code adherence, accessibility concerns, and material selections.

The regulation of interior design practice defines interior design and qualifications held by persons using the term *interior designer* (National Council for Interior Design Qualification, 2008). It relieves the public of having to evaluate relative performance of professional interior designers versus other persons providing design services. The work of built-environment professionals, whether interior designers, architects, or engineers, commonly presents scenarios where there is an overlap in scope of some portion of the work; regulation also permits consumers choices for the same work (within the acknowledged scope of practice for the specific profession), and some of those choices can be cost saving (Sass, 1993).

QUALIFICATIONS FOR INTERIOR DESIGN REGULATION

Whether one is working directly with the client or in a team, professional regulation identifies there is a level of competency that can be expected in the work, and that it is qualified by a standardized method of evaluation (Sawasy, 2009). Those standards include education as the first of five essential components.

EDUCATION

After lengthy research and identification of the unique body of knowledge needed to practice interior design to meet the public's needs and expectations, the Council for Interior Design Accreditation (CIDA) announced that as of January 1, 2010, only those interior design programs that culminate in a bachelor's degree, or higher, would be considered for CIDA accreditation (Council for Interior Design Accreditation, 2009). This important decision by CIDA demonstrated that a broader education was necessary than had been previously considered as a "minimum" for interior designers to meet the challenges in today's complex building environment. This change in a qualification standard exemplifies one of the steps taken by the interior design profession to ensure that the public's health, safety, and welfare needs are safeguarded through initial, formalized education.

EXPERIENCE

The second component describes a specific duration of diversified interior design work experience following the formal education, whereby theory learned is expanded and enhanced by application. This work experience includes working with clients in analyzing their needs and creating a program for planning; researching and preparing schematic or preliminary plans, followed by design development including plans and specifications of ceilings and lighting, floor plans, detailing, specifications of furnishings, equipment, and finishes; and preparing construction documents that provide the details for the execution of the project and all tasks needed to complete the project and its functional requirements. Work experience would also include a review of a finished project to verify that the project has been executed properly and completely as planned. All of this work would be performed with and under the direct supervision of a qualified person (e.g., a professional interior designer).

EXAMINATION

The third component is an examination created to test the knowledge and applied skills necessary to protect the health, safety, and welfare of the public. That examination, produced by the National Council for Interior Design Qualification (NCIDQ), evaluates knowledge regarding the scope of interior design practice elements that relate to and address the health, safety, and welfare of the public (Steinmetz, 2009).

CODE OF CONDUCT/CODE OF ETHICS

The fourth component critical to the practice of interior design is adherence to a code of conduct or code of ethics. Professional conduct and appropriate actions for regulated practice are defined in the jurisdiction's regulatory code (i.e., statutes, rules), as well as parameters for varying levels of censure or penalties for failure to adhere to these requirements, based upon the specific code or action violated. The penalties vary from letters of reprimand to monetary fines, suspension, or even revocation of the license/certification/registration.

CONTINUING EDUCATION

The fifth component, continuing education, is required for renewal of a certificate or license, as well as for maintenance of professional membership in interior design organizations. Continuing education is becoming increasingly important as practitioners must remain current with constantly evolving knowledge related to changing codes, sustainable design developments, accessibility guidelines, and other elements that require greater and greater depths of understanding.

HOW INTERIOR DESIGN IS REGULATED

With the regulation of practice, the practice and scope of practice are defined, i.e., what may and may not be done in the practice (NCIDQ, 2008). Furthermore, the exemptions that are traditionally included in practice regulation also serve to identify and define those occupations and tasks that are not part of regulation. Exempt persons or entities such as those who may only be providing assistance or help for the purpose of a retail sale of any products or allied practitioners (e.g., architects) are protected from having to uphold the same requirements or responsibilities of regulated persons.

When a new regulation is passed by the legislature, there is a period of time for individuals who may not otherwise meet all qualifications required of the practice regulation, but who are currently involved in interior design practice to apply to become a regulated person, known as a *grandparenting* (aka *grandfathering*). Although this period of time is typically a one- or two-year period, it can be extended with the intent that all who want to become licensed for practice will have ample notice and opportunity to do so. In Florida, when the practice legislation was passed in 1994, the grandparenting period was extended twice for an unusual total of six years (Florida Dept. of Business and Professional Regulations, 1994–1999).

Typically, practice regulations include the issuance of a seal that can be used by the licensee for signing and sealing documents required as dictated by local jurisdictions, including construction permits for work within the scope of interior design practice. The International Model Code developed by the International Code Council (ICC) did not identify by profession, per se, documents that required submission or professionals doing the work. Instead, the ICC identified responsible persons as "registered design professionals" and left identification of specific professionals to the local code official to determine based on the appropriate approach for their respective jurisdiction. Only regulated professionals are typically considered for determination as a registered design professional.

CONCLUSION

Interior design practice regulations require that a specific standard of qualifications be met by those ultimately licensed. These standards allow the public the right to choose interior designers or others to perform work when practice scopes overlap with allied professions, thereby granting a broader choice of regulated persons. Consumers can be confident that expectations for their projects will be met when they engage licensed professionals for the design of their built environment—professionals who are held to consistent, high standards and associated prescribed responsibilities over those who are not licensed. Simply, regulation protects the health, safety, and welfare of the public.

REFERENCES

Abramson v. Gonzalez, 949 F. 2d 1567 (11th Cir.1992)

Council for Interior Design Accreditation. (2009). *History.* Retrieved February 9, 2009, from http://www.accredit-id.org/history.php

Danko, S., Eshelman, P., & Hedge, A. (1990). A taxonomy of health, safety, and welfare implication of interior design decisions. *Journal of Interior Design Education and Research, 16*(2), 19–30.

Florida Department of Business & Professional Regulations. *Laws and Rules for the Board of Architecture and Interior Design, Chapter 481, Part 1, Florida Statutes; Rules 61G1, Florida Administrative Code,* State of Florida (October 1994–1999).

Martin, C. (2007). *Interior design: From practice to profession.* Washington, DC: American Society of Interior Designers.

Martin, C. (2008). Rebuttal to the Institute for Justice report entitled "Designing cartels, how industry insiders cut out competition." Journal of Interior Design, 33(3), 1–49.

National Council for Interior Design Qualification. (2008, November). *Core provisions in interior design registration: Model legislation.* Retrieved February 1, 2009, from http://www.ncidq.org/publications/modellanguagedocs.htm

Sapers, C. (2000). *An address on interior design legislation by Joseph P. Giattina, with related remarks by Carl M. Sapers.* Published remarks from the NCARB Annual Meeting, June 14, 2000. Washington, DC: National Council of Architectural Registration Boards.

Sass, T. (1993). *Economic impact statement for Board of Architecture and Interior Design Proposed Rule 21B–11.0017 "Scope of Interior Design Services,"* in association with Thaell & Associates. Tallahassee: State of Florida.

Sawasy, M. (2009, January/February). IIDA notes: Why does the interior design profession need to be legislated? An architect's view. *Interiors & Sources, 16*(1), 58.

Steinmetz, D. (2009, January/February). Filling the HSW vessel: A look at how NCIDQ assesses interior design competencies. *Interiors & Sources, 16*(1), pp. 59–60.

Tennessee, State of. Office of the Attorney General. Opinion No. 95–004, January 19, 1995.

DIANE GOTÉ

REGULATIONS AND MINIMUM PROFESSIONAL COMPETENCY

This essay[1] will briefly discuss the regulation of interior designers and present an overview of the minimum competencies required for the practice of interior design. For the profession of interior design to maintain its boundary of practice, minimum competencies (e.g., academic credentials, professional testing, etc.) must be updated on an ongoing basis. Some of the anticipated gaps in credentialing criteria and core knowledge will be discussed and identified for action. This essay will also describe the general responsibilities of the regulatory boards and their focus.

Finally, I will show that the future expectations for professionals in the built environment are for more intense accountability, higher educational standards, collaboration with an increasing number of allied professionals, and greater public scrutiny. We, as both professionals and members of society, would want it no other way. The speed of technology and the social transformation that

DIANE GOTÉ, CID-NJ, FASID, studied environmental design at Pratt Institute. Her firm, Design Works, Inc., in Summit, New Jersey, manages residential and selected commercial projects. Goté served two terms as president of the New Jersey chapter of ASID, during which the chapter received the "Thousand Points of Light" Citation (G. W. Bush) for the New Jersey Battered Women's Shelter. Goté served on the ASID board of directors (three terms) and has been a member of several national committees. She initiated the New Jersey Coalition for Interior Design Legislation (1986), which led to the Interior Designer Certification Act (2002). Currently, she serves as the New Jersey delegate to NCIDQ and is vice president of the New Jersey State Board of Architects. Goté has appeared on ABC's *Good Morning America* and was a regular contributor on *WOR Radio* in New York City.

are occurring have set both society and the interior design profession on a path of change with quickened footsteps. We are wasting time, and the public needs the protections that knowledgeable interior design practitioners offer.

BACKGROUND

In some sectors of society, regulatory safeguards that are prudent, beneficial, and geared to enhancing public health, safety, and welfare are not being adequately established and effectively enforced. This may have resulted in part from both the speed of change as well as the inability of society to appropriately monitor and regulate the changes when needed. Obvious in what has just occurred in the financial and real estate arenas and the food and drug industries, social responsibility and commitment to the general good in the long run cannot be ignored because the ramifications of not honoring these elements impact society as a whole. Appropriate, effective regulations avoid the potential chaos that accompanies lack of regulations while minimizing the burden and constraints of overregulation.

Over the past 35 years the interior design profession has established standards of practice (Martin, 2007) and partnered with state legislatures for adoption of regulation; these efforts have met with a modest degree of success. Unfortunately, some lobbying and trade groups have recently taken to attacking these standards. These misguided efforts can further undermine the public's confidence in the interior design profession and negatively impact the creation and execution of interior design projects that address environmental and human needs holistically.

For those who want little or no regulation, the idea is "let the public decide" who is a qualified, professional interior designer. Their rationale assumes that the public can protect itself from firms and individuals who stoop to unscrupulous, nontransparent, and unethical business and professional practices. The public complains about fees and costs, but not usually about the less obvious incompetence of a practitioner whose ineptitude is often hidden in jargon and other nontransparent activities. In an effort to save dollars and time on both the client's and builder's part, shortcuts and omissions threaten the proper completion of even the most common building projects. There are health, safety, and welfare issues on every interior design project that may impact the client in the future. It requires an insightful, diligent, consistent, ongoing effort on the part of interior design practitioners to ensure these aspects are appropriately addressed and that the health, safety, and welfare of the client are and will be maintained.

When the correct material choices are made, construction documents prepared, and intentions are good, there is an integration of work by those who participate in a construction or renovation project to ensure that the project is completed as designed. Unless qualified interior designers and architects are engaged throughout the project, the health, safety, and welfare of the client may be jeopardized, and the quality of the project may be affected and compromised.

As in many other complex activities, the clients are unaware of the possible negative consequences of inappropriate selection and installation of design and construction elements. Very often, the architect and the engineer are long gone from a new construction project, or especially from a renovation (many renovations do not include the professional services of architects but are accomplished by the building owner with or without the professional services of a qualified interior designer), but the client's life is affected for many years by the recommendations and knowledge, or lack thereof, of the interior designer on a building project. The properly informed allied professionals and certified interior designers are responsible for protecting the public's interest. The interior designer is often on the project for a greater length of time, post-construction. The interior designer is the one most likely doing the post-occupancy evaluation (POE) study.

There are specific credentials required of regulated professionals by all jurisdictions that regulate (i.e., certify, register, or license) any profession. Of these credentials, the three E's stand out as primary: education, experience, and examination. The first E, education, is the mainstay of any profession (Piotrowski, 2007). The well-prepared professional concentrates a focused period of time studying in an intense, structured, educational program that can be accredited by the Council for Interior Design Accreditation (CIDA), the accrediting body for interior design programs in North America. Most jurisdictions require a CIDA-accredited degree or its equivalent.

There is much debate on issues concerning *substantial equivalency* as related to educational programs. Substantial equivalency does not mean the education is equal. As education is also one of the eligibility requirements to sit for the professional exam developed by the National Council for Interior Design Qualification (NCIDQ), this issue of substantial equivalency has been studied as relevant to regulation. More study by NCIDQ is being done. Review of the substantially equivalent education for candidates as a qualification for testing is a high priority. At their annual conference in 2008, NCIDQ presented for discussion the Broadly Educated Interior Designer concept for consideration, a performance-based knowledge evaluation process (National Council for Interior Design Qualification, 2008). It is parallel in concept to the National Council of Architectural Registration Boards (NCARB) Broadly Experienced Architect program (National Council for Architectural Registration Boards, 2008);

both allow substantial experience as a substitute for otherwise prescribed formal education requirements.

The second E is gained by applying the body of knowledge learned in education. Newly degreed interior designers on their career paths need to count on gaining their qualified, diverse experience under a certified, licensed, or registered interior designer; an NCIDQ certificate holder; or a registered architect. NCIDQ has developed the Interior Design Experience Program (IDEP) to provide entry-level interior designers with a structured and monitored way to obtain diverse experience. The regulatory boards and provincial associations require proof of high quality, diversified interior design experience. What better way to protect the public than to ask those professionals who have made themselves accountable to provide guidance and preparation as mentors and supervisors? Serving in this capacity is essential to the practice for the properly credentialed interior designer.

The examination, or third E, is a two-day practice exam that was developed by NCIDQ in consultation with a professional testing and examination organization. It is evaluated for currency on a regular basis; tested for validity by an independent organization using national psychometric standards (Standards for Educational and Psychological Testing, 1999); and revised approximately every five years. Practice analysis surveys are completed by practitioners from all areas of practice, and the exam is revised to reflect current interior design practice as determined via the practice analysis. As the third step, and culmination of several years of design study for the new interior designer, this test provides regulatory boards with a criterion that is nationally recognized, respected, and valid. With the pace of technology and the growing list of environmental and sustainability concerns, this test will continue to become more comprehensive as time goes on.

Regulatory boards of the individual states and territories of the United States and the provinces of Canada (i.e., jurisdictions) are members of NCIDQ. The requirements for sitting for the NCIDQ examination and becoming an NCIDQ Certificate Holder are noted on NCIDQ's Web site (see www.ncidq.org).

REGULATORY BOARD REQUIREMENTS

Regulations are intended to protect the unwitting public who at times forget the common-sense rule that "if it sounds too good to be true, it usually is." Regulations are intended to focus on the public interest and are intended to guide and proactively protect the general public. Subsets of the general public, e.g., the "consumer" and the "registered professional," are considered special interest groups to regulators (Martin, 2008). Regarding regulators, their focus is on the health, safety, and welfare of the citizens of the state or jurisdiction, the administration of the specific laws and regulations under their purview, and the adherence to those laws by the individuals licensed, certified, or registered by that body.

Whether the title used is "registered" or "certified" or "licensed," there are specific criteria that must be met to practice in a jurisdiction. In the preparation of legislation, legislators want the opportunity to grandparent (also known as "grandfather") candidates that for one reason or another will need to be transitioned into the new law. Grandparenting criteria are not always easy to meet, and the proof of qualification needs to be done on a case-by-case basis. Regulatory boards must be unbiased, consistent, and exercise due diligence in their assessments of grandfathering applicants for credentials. Most boards have dealt with this process and appreciate its importance. But, the health, safety, and welfare of the public receiving interior design services is the foremost consideration in the review of all candidates by the regulatory board members.

Also, as part of state regulation, there is a code of ethics or code of conduct requirement. This is a critical minimum requirement of professional practice. The public expects the credentialed professional to adhere to a code of ethics/conduct. Many of these codes focus more to business practices than health, safety, and welfare issues, also essential to the welfare of the consumer and the occupants of the space. Infractions of the code are cause for action against the regulated professional.

Continuing education (CE) requirements are increasing in many jurisdictions. Not only is the quantity of CE requirements increasing, but also the kind of CE that is specified is changing. Each jurisdiction varies in the number of CE units in terms of what is required in the health, safety, and welfare categories. As the complexity of the built environment increases, the number of CE credits required will continue to become more specific in each of the health, safety, and welfare areas.

Most jurisdictions require the NCIDQ certificate indicating passage of the examination as one of the criteria in the regulatory credentialing process. Other criteria typically include residency requirements, personal legal history, and signature on the code of ethics or code of conduct. The minimum competence (National Council for Interior Design Qualification, 2004) required does vary by jurisdiction and as regulations change over time. This is a good thing. Unfortunately, there is a lag time for the regulations to be updated following revisions of

NCIDQ standards for professionals, advances of technology, and the needs of society receiving the services of interior designers. Also, as time goes on, interior design professionals need to continue to support the jurisdictional regulations and renew their certificates/registrations/licenses. Unless the regulatory credential is respected and valued, the number of participants will decrease and the benefit to the public will diminish.

CONCLUSIONS, IMPLICATIONS, AND CHALLENGES

What follows are issues that continue to evolve and grow as a result of the complex needs of society; the health, safety, and welfare of the public; and the maturation of the interior design profession. These are the next issues to contemplate, address, and resolve.

COMPETENCY CONFUSION

There is tension between established standards and the ongoing improvement of standards. The process is not uniform between the United States and Canada, or even from state to state within a geographical region in the United States. Yet, in the future, the practitioner and public should expect a fair and equitable set of minimum requirements for the profession across jurisdictional boundaries. Standardized, jurisdictional requirements are to be expected to change due to the ongoing need to continually raise the bar of minimum competency. Although NCIDQ tests minimum competency (Steinmetz, 2009), some incorrectly consider it the maximum competency standard. Therefore, it is easy to see how confusion can occur.

OTHER EXAMINATIONS

As NCIDQ sets out the requirements to sit for the examination, it must be noted that there are subsets of examinations in specialty areas collaboratively or outside the current domain of NCIDQ, e.g., the American Association of Healthcare Interior Designers (AAHID) exam, the National Council for Lighting Qualifications for Lighting Professionals exam, the Leadership in Energy and Environmental Design Accredited Professional (LEED® AP) exam, the National Kitchen and Bath Association's (NKBA) kitchen and bath exams, etc. It may be in the near future that NCIDQ will be expected to prepare the testing for subsets of professional practice, as it has done for AAHID. Thus, it would be appropriate for interior designers who have passed the NCIDQ, the minimum competency test, and acquired a regulatory credential, to move on to more specialized areas and advanced, specialized qualification examinations. Where would these subset proficiencies fit in the credentialing process?

FOCUS ON THE "WELFARE" PART OF HEALTH, SAFETY, AND WELFARE

What the interior designer knows and what result that knowledge has impacts the new building or renovation project. As practitioners, we know that our work involves analyzing and integrating many aspects of the project at once like weaving a cloth with many kinds of threads. This process continues until the design is achieved and the solution reached—with the needs of the client being foremost. As practitioners, we spend many hours in meetings with the client, more so than probably any other allied professionals. Greater detail with a greater number of elements involves greater time. This ongoing, face-to-face relationship may account for another difference between the profession of interior design and the other allied professionals; thereby, the interior designer can dramatically affect the welfare of the client.

Correctly addressing their welfare presupposes the knowledge of human environmental needs (Martin & Guerin, 2006), and acquiring that knowledge requires the applied focus by educated, credentialed interior design practitioners and researchers.

QUESTIONS ABOUT INTERPROFESSIONAL WORK

Collaboration of various kinds of design professionals in everyday practice is commonplace. This will increase in the future as our built environment (Bowles, 2007) becomes more complex. Do the minimum competencies we have today as interior designers address the overlap of professional responsibility? Also, how are the emerging integrated technology systems to be addressed in the cross-professional communication (Toy, 2009) and documentation on a project? The professional interior designer needs to be aware that new skills are required and need to be learned at a fast pace.

LAG TIME

How do we address the lag time between effective regulation and current and future evolution and demands of professional practice? The minimum requirements will be impacted at a faster rate of change (e.g., the lack of regulations on newly created financial investments' subsequent impact on society).

COORDINATION OF SERVICE TO THE PUBLIC

Let us remember that we first serve the public. The public needs the services of credentialed professionals who have a working relationship with, understand the same vocabulary, and acknowledge the responsibilities of allied practices. This is the major challenge as we go forward in the area of competency requirements (Sawasy, 2009). With society changing at an unparalleled rate, *no one profession will have all the answers.* It takes all of the built-environment professionals working and partnering together to protect the public.

NOTE

1. This essay is the personal viewpoint of the author and does not reflect the opinion of any board or organization.

REFERENCES

Bowles, M. (2007, Spring). Untapped knowledge, *Perspective*, IIDA Quarterly Magazine. Retrieved January 31, 3009, from www.aia.org/k_a_200706_ftr

Martin, C. (2007). *Interior design: From practice to profession*. Washington, DC: American Society of Interior Designers.

Martin, C. (2008). Rebuttal to the Institute for Justice report entitled "Designing cartels, how industry insiders cut out competition." *Journal of Interior Design, 33*(3), 1–49.

Martin, C., & Guerin, D. (2006). *The interior design profession's body of knowledge, 2005 edition*. Grand Rapids: Council for Interior Design Accreditation, American Society of Interior Designers, Interior Designers of Canada, International Interior Design Association, and the National Council for Interior Design Qualification.

National Council for Architectural Accrediting Boards. (2008). Broadly experienced architect (BEA) program. *Handbook for Interns and Architects*. Washington, DC: Author.

National Council for Interior Design Qualification. (2004). *NCIDQ definition of interior design*. Retrieved January 31, 2009, from http://ncidq.org/who/definition.htm

National Council for Interior Design Qualification. (2008). Annual Council of Delegates, meeting report. Washington, DC: Author.

Piotrowski, C. (2007). *Professional practice for interior designers*. Hoboken, NJ: John Wiley & Sons.

Sawasy, M. (2009). Why does the interior design profession need to be legislated? *Interiors & Sources, 16*(1), p. 58.

Standards for Educational and Psychological Testing. (1999). American Educational Research Association and National Council on Measurement in Education. Washington DC: American Psychological Association.

Steinmetz, D. (2009). Filling the HSW vessel, a look at how NCIDQ assesses interior design competencies. *Interiors & Sources, 16*(1), pp. 59–60.

Toy, J. (2009). IDC Bulletin: The next most obvious thing. *Interiors & Sources, 16*(1), p. 61.

> Is a title act sufficient protection for the public? Is the effort required to pass legislation worth it?

DAVID D. STONE

TITLE OR PRACTICE: WHAT MAKES SENSE? A PERSONAL VIEW FROM AN "UNREGULATED" INTERIOR DESIGNER

My name is David Stone, LEED® AP, IIDA, and NCIDQ certificate holder #8043. I'm a professional interior designer with almost 30 years experience in interior design, having graduated with a bachelor of science in design with a major in interior architecture from Arizona State University. I am a past International Interior Design Association (IIDA) local chapter officer and president as well as international committee member; a past member of the National Council for Interior Design Qualification's (NCIDQ) board of directors and numerous committees; and a member of the Green Building Certification Institute's (GBCI) Credentialing Steering Committee. I have been involved with interior design legislative challenges with the Massachusetts Interior Design Coalition (MIDC) and currently serve as the president of Interior Design Coalition of Arizona (IDCA). Yet, with *all* these credentials, I still struggle to be recognized as the *professional* that I am.

DAVID D. STONE, LEED® AP, IIDA, is an active NCIDQ certificate holder with a BS in design with a major in interior architecture from Arizona State University. Stone is the 2008–2009 president of the Interior Design Coalition of Arizona (IDCA) and a past president of IIDA's New England chapter as well as a former member of NCIDQ's board of directors. Currently, he is a committee member with both IIDA (at the international level) and the Green Building Certification Institute. A native of Endicott, New York, Stone's almost-30-year career in interior design, primarily in Boston, has focused on corporate and commercial projects with commissions completed for Nokia Telecommunications, Raytheon Missile Systems, Nortel Networks, and EMC Corporation. His work has also included projects for a Filipino supermarket/ department store, a Native American casino/hotel in the American Southwest, a bus/train transportation center in the American Northeast, and a Phoenix-area pediatric cardiothoracic intensive care unit.

This struggle for recognition throughout my career has been chronic, starting in college. My college mates and I constantly labored to obtain parity and recognition with our architecture degree peers, an effort that continues today. My education prepared me for the responsibilities of a professional interior designer, one that researches not only trends in materials, but psychological and physiological aspects of how we humans perceive and deal with interior space. I have continued my education regarding issues of life safety and fire code, aging in place, and environmental sustainability and resource management. Interior design is recognized for having its own distinct body of knowledge by numerous state and provincial regulatory agencies through legal recognition (see http://www.iida.org/custom/legislation/statelg.cfm or http://www.asid.org/legislation/state/). It is even recognized by the U.S. government as a distinct profession (see the U.S. Office of Personnel Management Flysheet for Professions, Series GS-1008; the 2007 NAICS #541410 definitions; or see http://www.bls.gov/oco/ocos293.htm#empty). However, I still must explain and defend my profession to non-interior design professionals. Why is this? Can licensure help with better recognition of the profession? I believe it can, and that's why I continue to advocate strongly for legislation that regulates interior design

PRACTICE ACT OR TITLE ACT

Now the big question: What type of legislation makes sense? My personal feeling is that nothing beats a practice act. But in reality, the most practical type of legislation is a title act with lots and lots of substance in it, what I call a "hybrid title act." (For more information on differences between a practice and a title act, refer to NCIDQ's Model Language Draft: http://www.ncidq.org/pdf/model_lang_docs/2008/ModellegislationFINAL08.pdf.) Personal experiences in developing language for both legislation types in Massachusetts and Arizona, where a practice and title act, respectively, are being pursued, along with participating with NCIDQ's Model Language Committee, have greatly influenced this viewpoint.

Although a practice act leaves nothing to chance, it is perceived by many that it excludes some designers and leaves other practitioners of our profession out of the game. It is continually seen by a vocal, minority opposition as an exclusionary approach to protectionism by an elitist segment of interior design. Me, an elitist? All I want is to have recognition for my hard-earned knowledge and capabilities.

I grant that a practice act may prevent some who do not meet the required qualifications from calling themselves an interior designer and from providing anything within the defined "practice" of interior design, but isn't that a good thing? Would you want your nurse practitioner to operate on you to remove a cancerous growth? Or your dental assistant to remove that abscessed tooth? Nor should you want your "decorator" to provide services related to life safety issues pertaining to the layout and placement of walls and furnishings in your office, hospital, casino, or retail establishment. You want a truly competent, qualified, educated, trained, informed, *and* regulated interior design professional making these decisions.

Fortunately, some legal jurisdictions have seen this argument clearly and have embraced the idea of strong standards for licensure by enacting practice acts, requiring specific education, experience, and examination criteria as justifications for licensure. I applaud efforts in Alabama, Florida, Louisiana, Nova Scotia, Nevada, Puerto Rico, and Washington, DC, and hope the rest of North America follows in their footsteps.

However, there have been arguments that the title "interior designer" has been around too long to prevent some lesser-qualified individuals from using it, and so the argument goes that a title act is more appropriate. These are a current string of "wins" by groups opposing interior design legislation that largely hinges on existing title laws regulating the title "interior design," not on the purpose or content of regulating language. But without substance, this type of legislation is nothing better than a paper-mill-type certification, lacking meaning and leaving the consumer without a clear idea of who is capable to offer interior design services and who is not.

Additionally, some political parties (i.e., Republican, Libertarian, etc.) typically make practice acts harder to pass because they are seen as barriers to the right to work or as only one option to protect the public. Massachusetts had hard-line architects who were adamant that only the truly competent should be allowed to practice interior design and, therefore, pushed the community to develop a tight, succinct practice act to keep unqualified interior designers from offering interior design services. And, the legislative bodies' were inclined to agree. (The stance of the architects in Massachusetts has since changed, but the approach of the interior design community toward seeking a practice act has not.) Arizona, on the other hand, is a staunch right-to-work state and frowns upon practice act legislation for any profession, making a title act with specific minimum criteria more appealing. That doesn't mean Arizona legislators are less concerned about public protection; they simply prefer an alternative approach.

HYBRID TITLE ACT

I have been personally involved with numerous conversations, negotiations, discussions, and arguments about interior design regulation in Massachusetts, Arizona, and beyond and have learned much about success and defeat in the process. These "opposite end" experiences have led me to be practical about the type of legislation I want to see achieved, leading me to be a strong proponent of the "hybrid" act. Maryland, as an example, has developed interior design title act legislation that is a great example of a hybrid act (see http://www.dllr.state.md.us/ license/law/cidlaw.htm). By establishing a clear title for qualified interior designers (i.e., registered interior designer) and identifying clear educational and experiential requirements along with a diversified, non-area-specific minimum competency examination, we can protect the rights of interior decorators, non-registered interior designers, and registered interior design professionals. At the same time, we will facilitate the current practice of collaboration between interior designers, architects, and engineers, each within their respective but still overlapping roles. This is similar to the legal competency qualifications for attorneys, paralegals, and legal administrators. It is consistent with the main consideration of any legislation: protection of the public's well-being and safety.

Opponents of legislation—any legislation, that is—say that regulation is not necessary. They suggest that interior designers' services don't protect the public, so there's no need for either a practice or title act. That argument is outmoded, designed to protect their limited knowledge of what has become a technically demanding profession.

Supporters of legislation—any legislation—use examples of public harm (the Rhode Island nightclub and Las Vegas and Puerto Rico hotel fires) as examples of the most drastic types of disasters that can occur when both qualified and unqualified designers misapply their professional knowledge. They also show how these situations can be mitigated by legislation of what has become a distinct profession, i.e., interior design.

Opponents spread fear among those less qualified or untrained that their ability to continue to make a living will be taken from them.

Proponents offer the knowledge that legislation will open the doors for more clarity and distinction between occupations, and allow all design professionals to benefit from better collaboration and understanding of our work's worth.

Opponents suggest that supporters are only looking out for themselves and the here and now. Nothing could be further from the truth in the minds of those proposing legislation. Proponents are looking out for the future, for those entering the profession, and for the consumer and professional yet to come. Some who are advocating for legislation may not be able to achieve licensure under their own proposals, but they have the greater good—both for the public and the profession—in their minds when doing so.

And, that's where the hybrid title act can truly appeal to all. When crafted correctly, a title act can preserve the rights of decorators and tradespeople to continue to advise their clients on accessorizing and decorating interiors while protecting the public's right to seek out appropriately qualified interior design practitioners educated in areas of egress, flammability, and other life-affecting issues when such expertise is needed. It creates consumer choice, not restriction. It provides expansion of business abilities, not restraint of trade. It presents a better, safer living experience for all of us affected by the built environment.

Interior designers have achieved so much in understanding the myriad groups of peoples affected by this progression toward regulation and recognition of our profession; and we still have much to share with each other on our journey. Hopefully, one day soon I will no longer need to explain what I do and what I don't do as an interior designer, that the day will come when television portrays interior design as something a qualified, licensed interior designer does; that the time will arrive when my design profession colleagues treat me with the respect and honor due the true *professional* that I am. I know that day will happen before the sun sets on my career. I just hope it happens early enough that I get to enjoy the sunset with my fellow interior designers: past, present, and yet to be.

> What challenges face interior design legislative coalitions? What opportunities are created via legislative coalitions?

PHYLLIS D. MOORE

REGULATION OPPOSITION: CONTRADICTIONS REVEALED

The right of educated and tested interior designers to legally define their profession is drawing controversy from many directions with some of the strongest opposition coming from within our own industry and design community. We study hard and prepare for a successful career, but as we begin that journey we often come face-to-face with the reality that we must seek permission from others to fully utilize our education and capabilities, or surrender control of our future to individuals who do not understand or are afraid of what skills we bring to the marketplace.

Why would individuals from within our own industry oppose legal recognition? Isn't raising the bar of professionalism by wanting to take responsibility for work done, requiring education and testing, and protecting the public what all professionals should want? Based on the opposition to interior design licensing, apparently this is not so. Is the real issue public protection, or has the desire to protect market

PHYLLIS D. MOORE, FASID, received a BS in interior design from the University of Alabama. She is an NCIDQ certificate holder and is president of Interior Design Source, LLC, in Decatur, Alabama. As a charter member of the Alabama Interior Design Coalition, Moore has served actively for over 14 years. She has been president and has served on the board of the ASID Alabama chapter and has received several awards for her work. Nationally, Moore has served on ASID's board of directors, chaired the Legislative Advisory Council and Student Advisory Council, and served as a member of several committees. In 2002, she became a fellow of ASID and received a national Presidential Citation in 2005. Moore is also a recipient of the Jack Davis Outstanding Alumni Award from the University of Alabama. She serves as an ASID STEP instructor and has served on NCIDQ's IDEP committee.

share eclipsed the desire to provide safe environments where people live and work? Many questions arise, among them:

> If other disciplines within the built environment provide benefit and protection for consumers, then why is there opposition to interior design, and how can we minimize or overcome this controversy?
> Does the public understand the truth about our profession, and do they really care?
> Why do some within the industry seem so threatened and determined in their strong opposition?

If interior designers are going to make a difference on this issue, they must be dedicated to the profession and believe this issue does matter to the public. We all must find a way to control the message, as the future of the interior design profession is at stake.

Interior designers, through their education and experience, contribute to the design of the built environment and should be part of the design team along with architects, engineers, and landscape architects. It takes the expertise of all disciplines working together to ensure the best design solution for a client. However, without legal recognition for interior designers, it is often hard for them to be recognized as design professionals and be granted professional courtesies or permitting privileges from building departments. Some interior designers find themselves limited in their scope of work not by their body of knowledge or skills but rather by the limitations placed on them by allied disciplines. Becoming a partner in a firm as an interior designer is not allowed by law in some states. Simple business issues such as workman's compensation insurance, business licenses, professional liability, and omissions and errors insurance are adversely affected by not having legal recognition of interior design as a profession.

For over a century, architects and engineers have protected their professions (and the public) with professional license qualifications that set standards and define those professions. If the work interior designers contribute to the built environment truly matters, we must parallel the architects and engineers with our own professional qualifications and standards to prevent harm to the public. The fact is, only in the last 30 years have we actively sought legal recognition of interior design.

It is important to understand that our roots have grown from an aesthetic beginning; until recently, we did not have the metrics to support professional licensing. Not until the Foundation for Interior Design Education Research (FIDER), now the Council for Interior Design Accreditation (CIDA), was founded in 1970, and the National Council for Interior Design Qualification (NCIDQ) in 1974 did we have a means to measure our interior design education or test of that body of knowledge, respectively, in a practical application of those abilities. Federal laws such as the Occupational Safety and Health Administration (OSHA) and the Americans with Disabilities Act (ADA) also provided life safety and handicap accessibility requirements, which became part of interior design education and provided an avenue to be part of public safety issues through the building codes. With the inclusion of building code, life safety, and accessibility knowledge into interior design education there became a strong foundation to justify that interior designers impact public health, safety, and welfare (HSW).

Since passage of the first title act for interior design in 1973 (Puerto Rico), efforts to pass license laws in all states, territories, and provinces (Canada) have drawn increasing opposition. Whereas groups such as engineers, home builders, retailers, and others have opposed interior design laws, the primary opposition has come from the architectural community, mainly the American Institute of Architects (AIA). Their main argument is that interior designers are not adequately educated or tested and do not protect the public. A close look at the education requirements by CIDA, the body of knowledge tested by NCIDQ, and the scope of services interior designers offer by definition of the profession in legislative language does not support the AIA position.

Interior designers are not asking to provide any services for which they are not qualified. The National Council of Architectural Registration Boards (NCARB) (n.d.) in its paper "The Five Standards of Professional Regulation: An Examination of the Merits of Interior Design Regulation" compares interior design testing and education to that of architecture, which is not a valid comparison and irrelevant to the practice of interior design. We are not architects and do not offer architectural services, nor do we desire to.

AIA (2007) claims that only tested architects and engineers are qualified to maintain responsibility for the health, safety, and welfare of the public in the built environment because interior designers do not have the educational or training requirements necessary to protect the public. AIA (American Institute of Architects, 2008) and NCARB (n.d.) remain opposed to any form of interior design legislation and insist that interior design services remain under the direct supervision of architects and engineers. Code officials do not universally agree with this position and are beginning to accept the role of the interior designer as a *registered design professional.*

Architecture began its professional path without education or testing requirements and has had the advantage of over 100 years to raise the bar. So too should interior design—a younger profession—have the time to establish its path and unique defined parameters. What interior design legislation seeks is the capability to remove the current barriers that prevent us from using our education and minimize our abilities in the marketplace.

Most recently, opposition has come from the Interior Design Protection Council (IDPC), which operates as a nonprofit business league consisting of smaller individual state groups

as well as larger collaborating organizations such as AIA, NCARB, National Kitchen and Bath Association (NKBA), the Institute for Justice (IJ), the Interior Design Society (IDS), and others (Interior Design Protection Council, 2008a). Being part of this larger organization has allowed AIA and NCARB to be less visible in their opposition by allowing IDPC to be the stronger front voice for them all. The IDPC coalition has mobilized to oppose the passage of any interior design legislation claiming it is anti-competitive, unnecessary, and prohibits their constituents' ability to freely practice their livelihood. The Institute for Justice (IJ), a nonprofit libertarian, public interest law firm, was funded in 1991 by the Koch Family Foundation and offers pro bono legal representation to pursue its free-market agenda (Institute for Justice, 2008). Collaborating with IDPC, they have filed lawsuits in several states to prevent or challenge interior design legislation. IDPC (Interior Design Protection Council, 2009) claims they want to have individuals freely practice their livelihoods without government interference, regulations, or consideration of possible consequences to the environment in which we live and work. Nowhere do they address the concerns of the consumer.

The real intention of interior design legislation is to provide safe environments for everyone to work and live in. If any well-intentioned individual wants to accept responsibility for providing this safe environment, interior design practice laws provide a clear avenue for them to do so. Interior design legislation defines the qualifications required to practice interior design that apply to all equally and fairly, yet opposition would have you believe it exists only to establish a small, elitist group that gives an advantage to a select few. The opposition fears they will be at a disadvantage because they will appear less qualified.

One of IDPC's (Interior Design Protection Council, 2008b) tactics is to send attack-style letters filled with misinformation to state legislators, encouraging them to oppose interior design legislation. They also monitor legislative efforts in all states and publish their viewpoints on the IDPC Web site. They then attack ASID for serving its own members by monitoring and providing information and support to members seeking help with legislation that is written and introduced into state legislatures by coalitions—not ASID.

For those supporting legislation, herein lies the dilemma. AIA opposes interior design legislation because they claim the interior design standards of testing and education do not compare to that of the architects, and they want the bar raised higher. IDPC and the IJ oppose regulation of any kind and want no requirements or qualifications to practice interior design. AIA and NCARB support that position as well. In the spirit of compromise, efforts to try and resolve issues and provide certain protection for those not licensed are considered elitist by IDPC yet far too low for AIA. Coalitions must ask themselves what issues could possibly be common and acceptable ground to both opposition groups, especially when AIA supports both positions?

WORK OF THE COALITIONS

Coalitions must find a way to carve out language to protect those not wanting or qualifying for licensing, yet set the standards high enough to protect the public. Voting consumers can help coalitions win this argument as their voices are important when heard in the statehouses.

Despite these efforts to prevent interior design legislation from passing, it is important to note that 26 states and jurisdictions currently have some form of law or legal recognition of interior design, as shown in Figure 7.4.

Although we solicit help from our clients and consumers, there is much opportunity in the marketplace for our coalitions. For example, as more interior designers become LEED® accredited, and the public demand for energy-efficient solutions increases, we have a great tool to use in promoting a proactive campaign supporting interior design legislation. Energy efficiency, cost-effective solutions, universally designed spaces that allow individuals to live longer in their homes, and more productive workspaces that attract and retain employees are all benefits of good interior design and are supported through ASID research and papers. We should be celebrating these achievements and making sure our legislators and the public are aware of these important issues we address. Examples include:

- Interior designers are a vital part of the Center for Health Design; we know the effect design has on human behavior and design spaces that improve healthcare and healing.
- Interior designers were sought out after 9/11 to help rebuild the Pentagon.
- ASID was sought as a partner to the Government Services Administration.
- Interior designers are a vital part of the U.S. Green Building Council, finding sustainable solutions and design practices that protect and conserve our resources and environment.
- Interior designers specify much of the products and content calculated in a building's fuel load, critical to people's safe exiting during a fire.

It's time we promote the real story to our legislators and demonstrate the truth of what interior designers accomplish and provide.

However, the public is not certain who is qualified to protect them from harm. In June 2007, ASID nationally surveyed 1,000 consumers about their use of design services. The findings indicated that more than half of the consumers surveyed felt not knowing how to distinguish between a licensed and unlicensed interior designer was harmful to their hiring decision, and nearly 7 out of 10 consumers believe

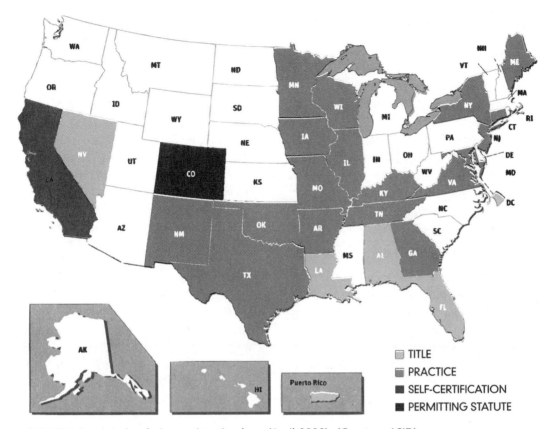

FIGURE 7.4. Interior design registration laws (April 2009). (Courtesy ASID)

Legend:
- TITLE
- PRACTICE
- SELF-CERTIFICATION
- PERMITTING STATUTE

identifying a qualified designer by title is helpful to them (Globus, 2007). There is room for all in the marketplace, but we must allow public need to drive and determine the services hired. This means providing a way for the public to understand and choose between the various services and professions. Clearly, the public is beginning to perceive the value of the interior designer, and we must solicit them to join our voices in the statehouses. The more the public understands the profession and demands professional services, the stronger our voices will become in overcoming the misinformation the opposition is promoting. Educators should continue promoting strong professionalism with students so they complete a monitored experience program and the NCIDQ exam as the next steps in their career path. These efforts and voices are important to the work of the coalitions.

Moving forward to define the profession in all states increases independent control of the scope of services we offer and makes our profession more parallel to the related disciplines in our industry, i.e., classifying roles for the public. Simply put, it's the right thing to do for the public and the profession.

As we prepare to move forward, one thing remains clear. There is a struggle between architecture and interior design that should not exist. If we believe all disciplines bring added value to a project, and each profession has specialized knowledge and skills to benefit the outcome of projects for our clients, we must find common ground and mutual respect. If not now, perhaps a new generation will be able to look beyond the past and embrace the future with an understanding and respected acceptance of the knowledge and skills all professionals have to offer.

REFERENCES

American Institute of Architects. (2007, December). *AIA directory of public policies and position statements as amended by the Board of Directors, p. 6.8. Architectural Practice and Title Regulations.* Washington, DC: Author.

American Institute of Architects. (2008, January 31). Interior design lobby seeks licensure in several states. *The ANGLE.*

Giattina, J.P. Jr. (2000, June 14). *An address on interior design legislation by Joseph P. Giattina, Jr., FAIA, President of the National Council of Architectural Registration Boards (NCARB), with related remarks by Carl M. Sapers, NCARB Legal Council.* Retrieved February 1, 2009, from http://www.ncarb.org/NewsClips/pressaddress.html

Globus, S. (2007, September). *ASID update: Another party heard from.* Retrieved February 1, 2009, from http://www.interiorsandsources.com/ArticleDetails/tabid/3339/ArticleID/5174/Default.aspx

Institute for Justice. (2008, December). *Institute profile: Who we are.* Retrieved February 1, 2009, from http://www.ij.org

Interior Design Protection Council. (2008a). *Collaborating organizations.* Retrieved February 1, 2009, from http://www.idpcinfo.org.about.html

Interior Design Protection Council. (2008b). *Think the biggest threat to interior designers is the slowing economy or the downturn in the housing market? THINK AGAIN!* Retrieved February 1, 2009, from http://www.idcinfo.org-publications

Interior Design Protection Council (2009). *Welcome: Our mission, our vision.* Retrieved February 1, 2009, from http://www.idpcinfo.org/legislation.html

National Council of Architectural Registration Boards. (n.d.). *The five standards of professional regulation: An examination of the merits of the interior design regulation.* Retrieved February 1, 2009, from www.idpcinfo.org/NCARB-5Standards.doc

> There are many opponents against regulation of interior design practice. Who/what is the most serious threat to the profession's ability to protect the public?

CAREN S. MARTIN

DON'T BOTHER ME WITH THE FACTS!

Often, I am questioned about opponents of interior design practice regulation as the development of interior design as a profession has been an area of my scholarship since 1995. Over the last several years, I have been called upon numerous times by state regulatory agencies, interior design coalitions, and professional organizations for consultation regarding right to practice issues. Their specific stories will not be the core of this essay; however, my research and work with them have given me a unique, broad insight into the current state of interior design practice regulation and the groups who oppose it.

The opposition's actions threaten the interior design profession's ability to protect the public and its right to practice. The Institute for Justice (IJ), the National Kitchen and Bath Association (NKBA), and the Interior Design Protection Council (IDPC) have emerged in the past several years. Other groups have been in opposition for some time, such as the American Institute of Architects (AIA) and the National

CAREN S. MARTIN, PhD, CID-MN, FASID, IDEC, IES, IIDA, is an assistant professor of interior design at the University of Minnesota. Before earning her master's and PhD, she practiced institutional, corporate, and healthcare interior design and project management for nearly 20 years, which she shares with her undergraduate and graduate students. Martin served two terms on Minnesota's professional licensing board and chaired NCIDQ's Model Language Committee. She serves on ASID's Legislative and Codes Advisory Council and the Steering Committee of Minnesota's legislative coalition. Her scholarship focuses on opportunities and threats facing the interior design profession. Martin authored "Rebuttal of the Report by the Institute for Justice Entitled Designing Cartels: How Industry Insiders Cut Out Competition" (*Journal of Interior Design*, 2008), and the book *Interior Design: From Practice to Profession* (ASID, 2007). With Denise Guerin, she coauthored *The Interior Design Profession's Body of Knowledge, 2005 Edition*. Together, they co-created InformeDesign®, and Martin serves as its director.

Council of Architectural Registration Boards (NCARB). New entities seem to spring up overnight as offshoots of some of those named above, such as the Interior Design Freedom Coalition. The opposition landscape is shifting at a rapidly increasing rate.

However, when considering this oppositional maelstrom in an objective manner, there are three overarching forces of opposition facing the interior design profession:

1. Architectural organizations that claim interior design is contained within the practice of architecture;
2. Interior decoration and residential interior design entities that claim by regulating interior design, interior designers will be stripped of their livelihood; and
3. The IJ, which claims that no profession should be licensed, i.e., let the free market prevail, public beware.

HOW DID WE GET HERE?

Throughout history, every profession from medicine to engineering has struggled to make a place in society and become a recognized, established profession—interior design is no exception (Abbott, 1988; Martin, 2007; 2008). Therefore, why is the interior design profession surprised that an increasing number of opponents to regulation have emerged? Until the past three or four years, I would have said we were right on schedule in our quest for regulation because it took architecture from 1897 to 1951 to become licensed in all 50 states (Draper, 1977). Further, landscape architecture is not yet fully regulated nationwide.

But, there has been a shift in the tactics opposition groups have taken in their fight against regulation. There is, perhaps, another force at play that focuses on communication of misinformation, instead of facts, via an escalation in dramatic tactics and language used to communicate their stand. Before a discussion of misinformation, first we need to briefly examine the three primary opposition camps: architectural organizations, forces from what might be considered "within" the profession, and the IJ.

OPPOSITION FROM ARCHITECTURAL ORGANIZATIONS

Opposition from architecture, the most closely allied profession, has been ongoing since the interior design profession began its quest for legal regulation of practice. Whited (2009) recounted her unsavory experience while president of the National Council for Interior Design Qualification (NCIDQ) as an attendee at a NCARB meeting (a parallel organization to NCIDQ) in 2000. "NCARB had proposed a resolution that stated that interior design was harmful to the public" (Whited, 2009, p. 19). That specific resolution did not pass.

Most vocal and relentless in opposition to regulation of interior design has been the AIA. It has denounced interior design professionals for practicing architecture without a license. In fact, AIA's national policy requires that components (i.e., chapters) oppose regulation of interior design:

In the public interest, the AIA holds that only architects and engineers licensed through examination possess the necessary education, training, and experience to protect the health, safety, and welfare of the public in the built environment. Other individuals may possess useful skills in designing within the built environment, but fragmentation of responsibility for the building design process endangers and misleads the public as to respective areas of competence and expertise. The AIA opposes practice or title regulation of individuals or groups other than architects and engineers. (AIA, 2008a, p. 6)

Moreover, the AIA has asserted that the profession's work has no influence on the health, safety, and welfare of the public. In *The Angle*, the AIA reported on the IJ's lawsuit opposing the use of the title "Interior Designer" in Oklahoma and noted,

> The AIA opposes the Oklahoma law, as well as all regulation to interior design, because interior designers do not have sufficient education or experience necessary to protect the public, and consequently, according to AIA state relations manager Billie Kaumaya, it should not be a field regulated by the government. "Governments don't typically regulate occupations because it inhibits competition, but when there is a genuine effect on the health, safety, and welfare of the public, they make an exception," says Kaumaya. "Doctors, lawyers, engineers, and architects protect the public, but interior designers do not." (AIA, 2008b)

This official, national policy means they will and have opposed even landscape architecture regulation, which has contributed to the fact that to date only 45 states have practice regulation (American Society of Landscape Architecture, 2009).

However, it must be noted that on an individual level, many, many architects support regulation of interior design, and some have the fortitude to write letters to legislators and testify their support. For their actions, they risk being ostracized by their colleagues and marginalized by their AIA peers. Conversations between an architect and interior designer typically sound like, "Yes, I support your profession's efforts, and interior design work is very important—I depend on the knowledge and expertise of my interior design colleagues—but, if I testify, I can kiss any future AIA design awards or leadership positions away." Furthermore, some interior designers working in firms who support AIA's policy regarding interior design regulation,

even firms that focus primarily on the design of interior spaces (and employ many interior designers), experience the same pressure to remain quiet about supporting their profession. Regardless of the longevity of its opposition, architectural organizations have been quiet in comparison with the din raised by the next two forces. Perhaps the AIA feels it can afford to relax its attack on the interior design profession a bit with other forces taking over the most aggressive stances, and in fact the AIA (2009) reports the anti-legislative efforts of the IJ in their newsletter, *The Angle*.

OPPOSITION FROM WITHIN(?) THE INTERIOR DESIGN PROFESSION

The second opposition group comes from what appears to be *within* the interior design profession, but that depends on how one defines who is and is not an "interior designer" (see the National Council for Interior Design Qualification's *Definition of Interior Design*, 2004). Primary players in this opposition group are the NKBA and the IDPC. As the profession has taken steps to raise the bar and formalize and increase requirements to practice interior design, natural stratification of expertise and knowledge has occurred.

This evolution of the maturing interior design profession has served to further separate interior design from interior decoration (Martin, 2008). Membership organizations such as the NKBA, which strive to be inclusive and do not require the "three E's" (formal education; monitored experience; and a national examination that focuses on health, safety, and welfare of the public) for membership, claim that their members are professional interior designers, too.

However, the scope of work of the design of a residential bathroom or kitchen is not regulated by jurisdictions (considered "exempt" spaces), and therefore, these designers are not required to meet education, experience, and examination qualifications to practice in those spaces, as *anyone* can legally design them. Their work does not affect the health, safety, and welfare (HSW) of the public, i.e., commercial interiors. Their work, though complex and impressive, requires a different body of knowledge than is required by interior designers who design schools, hospitals, or offices (considered "non-exempt" spaces). These interior designers practice in public spaces whose design is regulated by state or provincial laws because they protect the public's HSW.

Another piece of the maturing of the profession is related to required education. The decision by the Council for Interior Design Accreditation (CIDA) to accredit only interior design programs of higher education that culminate in a bachelor's degree (CIDA, n.d.) has also served to separate graduates of associate of arts degree programs. These graduates might provide interior design services or interior decoration services in unregulated (i.e., exempt) spaces, but have not been educated to fully protect the public's HSW (in non-exempt spaces). As has been stated by educational scholars, some represented in Chapter 10 of this book, it is simply not possible to teach the profession's body of knowledge in less than a bachelor's degree—and some believe that is not enough and advocate for a graduate degree (Guerin & Thompson, 2004).

A second "within the profession" opposition group, the IDPC, has a Web site that contains an expansive list of "services" that focus on legislative activities, the core of their mission. Statements such as, "IDPC is committed to helping in any and every way possible to assure that interior designers, ancillary businesses, and students are not now, nor will they be in the future, negatively affected by regulation" and their pledge to "assist the Institute for Justice in defending the constitutional rights of interior designers" (IDPC, n.d.a) speak of "interior designers," confusing what many of

their constituents do as interior design. Showing their concern of who will be affected by this legislation shows their confusion of the facts. Their Web site (www.idpc.org) includes a list of occupations that will be affected by regulation of interior design practice (see Box 7.1) (IDPC, n.d.). The list includes occupations that are not within the scope of regulated interior design, such as "interior decorators," "paper hangers," and "upholsters."

OPPOSITION FROM THE IJ

The IJ, a libertarian organization that focuses its efforts on "protection of First Amendment rights" (IJ, 2009), finds the profession of interior design to be "low-hanging fruit" and has successfully leveraged the fearful practitioner members from within the other interior design organizations noted previously. Their ongoing crusade to stop additional interior design regulation and/or strike existing regulation of interior design in the United States is well known.

Their well-funded litigious activities have emboldened others such as "Live Free and Design!" and "Liberty for PA Designers" to jump in on the attack. Many of these groups are passionate and seem unimpeded in disseminating information that is not always accurate—but dramatic and, unfortunately, believable.

The first scathing IJ publication, *Designing Cartels: How Industry Insiders Cut Out Competition*, was published in September 2006 (Carpenter, 2006). I wrote a carefully researched rebuttal to that report that relayed the activities of the IJ, the three E's, rights of consumers, and protection of the public, as well as delineating between interior design and interior decoration, which was published in the *Journal of Interior Design* in May 2008 (posted in a preliminary format on an accessible Web site in fall 2007). Since that time, the IJ has published three additional, inflammatory reports, plus an update (very minimally) of their original 2006 report (Carpenter, September 2008):

BOX 7.1
OCCUPATIONS CLAIMED BY THE IDPC TO BE AFFECTED BY INTERIOR DESIGN REGULATION

Antiques dealers

Architects

Art dealers

Cabinetmakers

Carpet and flooring suppliers

Decorative hardware showrooms
  and suppliers

Decorative painters

Draftsmen/women

Electricians

Fabric manufacturers

Finish carpenters

Furniture finishers

Furniture showrooms and retailers

Glass suppliers

Home stagers

Home theater personnel

Interior decorators

Interior designers

Kitchen and bath designers

Lighting store personnel

Lumber yard personnel

Manufacturers' representatives

Office furniture dealers

Painters

Paper hangers

Plumbers

Plumbing (fittings and fixture) suppliers

Restaurant equipment suppliers

Tile installers

Tile showroom personnel

Trim manufacturers

Upholsterers

Wallpaper suppliers and manufacturers

Window and door manufacturers

Window hardware suppliers

Window treatment installers

Window treatment workroom personnel

➤ *Misinformation & Interior Design Regulation: How the Interior Design Cartel's Attack on the IJ's* Designing Cartels *Misses the Mark* (Carpenter, July 2008)

➤ *Designed to Mislead: How Industry Insiders Mislead the Public About the Need for Interior Design Regulation* (Carpenter, September 2008)

➤ *Designed to Exclude: How Interior Design Insiders Use Government Power to Exclude Minorities & Burden Consumers* (Harrington & Treber, February 2009)

The July 2008 report was a rebuttal to my rebuttal. In their 11-page report, my name was noted 30 times—none of them complimentary. The alarming issue, though, was that even friends and family (ready to defend my honor)

who read their rebuttal said to me, "Well, they make some good points." This response, unfortunately, is typical of how carefully crafted language can go a long way to make a case, *even if unfounded*. Furthermore, readers are drawn to a powerful visual image.

The first three IJ reports used covers composed of somewhat benign images. However, the February 2009 report (Harrington & Treber) has the image of an evil-looking Mr. Clean (a smiling, Procter & Gamble cleaning product icon as shown in Figure 7.5) in a bouncer-type, arms-crossed pose, heavily shadowed. What is most prominent in this scary image (see Figure 7.6) is the badge Mr. Clean wears on his chest, which says "ASID," appropriate, as ASID is characterized by the IJ as the leader of *the interior design "cartel"* (Carpenter,

FIGURE 7.5. The Mr. Clean icon has been known by television audiences for over 50 years. (Proctor & Gamble)

FIGURE 7.6. IJ's cover for their February 2009 report, *Designed to Exclude: How Interior Design Insiders Use Government Power to Exclude Minorities & Burden Consumers.* (Harrington & Treber, February 2009)

2006). But, the fact is, there is no cartel (Martin, 2008), and ASID is not the only professional interior design organization supporting practice regulation.

To summarize, these three opposition groups continue to attack the interior design profession's efforts to protect the public via the regulation of practice; following are their points.

1. The AIA opposes regulation of all built environment professions except architecture and engineering, and they believe interior design is part of architecture. Is this simply a protectionist attitude? Further, they claim that interior design does not protect the public's HSW; but we can document the myriad ways it does in non-exempt spaces. What do they have left to fight interior design practice regulation with? Misinformation.

2. Organizations such as the NKBA and IDPC oppose regulation of interior design practice because they say their members, or interior designers in general, will not be able to continue their practice. We can document that kitchen and bath designers, interior decorators, and residential interior designers can continue their work/practice in exempt spaces. What do they have left to fight interior design practice regulation with? Misinformation.

3. The IJ opposes all regulation of any profession based on libertarian philosophy, and they do not think interior design practice protects the public. We can document that it does. What do they have left to fight interior design practice regulation with? Misinformation.

The greatest threat to the interior design profession by any and all of these opposition groups is the misinformation they spread. It impedes the public's ability to correctly identify an interior designer who will design interior environments that protect their health and safety and preserve their welfare. Without this ability, there could be severe consequences.

Are the behaviors evidenced in current American culture illustrative of a systemic problem that has made the quest for regulation of the profession more difficult to obtain? In Niccolo Machiavelli's *The Prince*, one learns that the ends justify the means; to gain and hold power is the end goal, regardless of the steps that must be taken in its achievement. It is appropriate to use this infamous treatise as a reference when considering the biased communication by the opposition to all who will listen. With the goal in sight, evidently how one gets there is hardly as relevant as being successful.

Many cite the crisis of ethics we are experiencing today as a society in areas of business (Heineman, 2007; Podolny, 2009), medicine (Gligorov et al., 2009), and education (Bruhn, Zajac, Al-Kazemi, & Prescott, 2002), and *how* we communicate and *what* we say are an important part of the issue. I contend that because opponents of interior design practice regulation do not have documented, factual findings upon which to base their verbal, written, and visual attacks, they are resorting to discrediting the interior design profession through propaganda and repetition of misinformation.

PROPAGANDA

The historic and current use of propaganda in our culture, as well as when used against the interior design profession, is a crucial challenge, interrelated with ethical and moral behavior. Merriam-Webster defines *propaganda* as:

> the spreading of ideas, information, or rumor for the purpose of helping or injuring an institution, a cause, or a person . . . ideas, facts, or allegations spread deliberately to further one's cause or to damage an opposing cause; also, a public action having such an effect. (2009)

Propaganda, a distortion of the facts, enhanced through repetition, serves as a valuable tool for those inclined to undermine those communicating factually and with minimal bias—in this case, the interior design profession. The media and others have used the IJ's attack on the profession as an opportunity to falsely stereotype the knowledge, expertise, qualifications, purpose, and practice of professional interior designers to the degree that most would label it libelous (Neily, 2008; Will, 2007). Somehow, responding in a measured, factual tone is not as interesting and gets far less media coverage.

Outside mainstream media, audience-specific communication delivered in the trade press, inperson, or via e-mail are also impactful. An example of the use of propaganda was witnessed when Ed Nagorsky, Esq., general counsel and director of legislative affairs for NKBA, spoke at a meeting of NKBA's Minnesota chapter two days before a hearing of the licensed interior design bill by a Senate committee. NKBA members were told in reference to the NCIDQ examination, "No way you'll pass." And, regarding the work experience requirements in Minnesota to be a certified interior designer (or licensed interior designer, per pending legislation), "you need to intern from two to five years without being paid!" He repeatedly used the word *internship*—commonly referred to the experience gained while in school—and misapplied it to postgraduation experience, which is paid. Other phrases he used that evening to instill fear in the attendees about the upcoming legislative package included "second-class citizens," "you could take that exam seven times before you pass it," and "this bill will hurt your ability to compete . . . stay in business . . . stay in Minnesota" (January 15, 2009).

REPETITION

The second issue has to do with repetition. Repetition makes it true—or does it? We have learned that beyond the message itself, the delivery method is also important. Consider the familiar phrase "weapons of mass destruction"—now commonly known as WMDs—who is yet unfamiliar with that term? A Google search on July 8, 2009, of "WMD" yielded 4.35 million hits (i.e., results). WMDs were the basis of the United States' entry into the Iraq war (Arsenault & Castells, 2006). The Bush administration used the phrase often to incite fear in Americans about their safety and security. It still has tremendous impact, even though it has been verified by former Vice President Cheney (Johnson, 2006) and others (CNN, 2004; Economist's View, 2006) that WMDs did not exist in Iraq at the time the United States invaded.

Arsenault and Castells refer to this process as the "social production of misinformation" produced by the "interplay between the political and communication establishments" (2006, p. 301). The effects are long term; evidence indicates that the public retains the threat long after its origin and basis have been discredited.

EFFECTS OF MISINFORMATION ON THE INTERIOR DESIGN PROFESSION

The significant effects of use of misinformation on the interior design profession's purpose, need, and role in securing practice regulation are that (1) opinions and facts are not differentiated from one another, and (2) there is little need to substantiate the false statements, as there is no time to do so. Furthermore, when the interior design profession is described by the opposition, *opinions* about the profession are stated and then *are substantiated with unsubstantiated information*, often from spurious sources.

This phenomenon is being referred to in the popular press and the scholarly literature (Jarjour & Chahine, 2007) as a crisis of "objective reality." A lesson we all learned as children to always tell the truth is seemingly going by the wayside, a bit. It boils down to the diminishment of straightforward communication of the facts to statements influenced—to greater or lesser degrees—from a *personal perspective* (Lowry, 2008). This movement away from objective reality has important consequences. As noted by Ryan, "When ideas of diverse political, social, economic, and cultural groups are not objectively reported, good decisions are unlikely" (2001, p. 5).

The following issues of misinformation resulting from compromises to objective reality and propaganda, facilitated via repetition, are examples of how these behaviors have been used by the opposition to impede interior design's quest to protect the public and our right to practice our profession. Purposely, quantitative issues have been selected as they are easily verifiable. Also, as noted, they are from firsthand experiences in Minnesota:

1. Issue: number of persons (certified interior designers) who would be impacted in Minnesota if the proposed licensed interior design bill (SF 376, 2009) did pass: Misinformation stated: 740 CIDs; 80% also registered architects; "only 150 CIDs would be impacted" (testimony of A. Voda on behalf of the MN AIA, February 17, 2009). Facts: 755 CIDs in Minnesota; 51% were also registered architects, 366 CIDs were regulated by the board solely as certified interior designers (A. Barker, MN AELSLAGID board staff, personal communication, February 9, 2009).

2. Issue: passage rate of the NCIDQ examination: Misinformation stated: "[the exam] is extremely costly, restrictive, and has an extremely low rate of passage (approximately 45%)" (NKBA, email to Minnesota chapter members, February 14, 2008). Fact: Spring 2009 pass rates for the exam are Section I: 73%; Section II: 71%; Section III: 84% (*NCIDQ Letter*, e-mail, July 2009). Scores for the previous four years (2004–2008) are within those same ranges (J. Kenney, Executive Director, NCIDQ, personal communication, February 12, 2009).

Another example of these tactics at work can be found in an e-mail that was sent to NKBA members in Minnesota just nine days before the Minnesota Senate Commerce and Consumer Protection Committee was to hear SF 376 regarding the "licensed interior design" practice act (Minnesota has had a title act since 1992). The subject read: "Minnesota Interior Design Practice Act Hearing Scheduled; Act Now to Protect Your Right to Practice!" In the body of the e-mail, these kitchen and bath designers were informed,

> The Minnesota State Legislature has recently introduced an Interior Design Practice Act which, if adopted, will be one of the most restrictive interior design laws in the country. If passed, it will absolutely impact your ability to practice your profession, whether as a kitchen or bath designer, retail showroom or consultant. (E. Nagorsky, personal communication, February 8, 2009)

The fact is, in Minnesota as well as almost all other states and Canadian provinces, single-family homes and duplexes are exempt spaces; therefore, anyone can design the interiors of those spaces; furthermore, in Minnesota, retail sales and consultation in the furtherance of a sale were specifically exempted. In other words, NKBA members were being rallied to oppose a bill that did not apply to them as most NKBA members design kitchens and baths in residences and/or participate in retail sales. After NKBA members are informed of the facts, they often, individually, support regulation of practice as they understand the need to protect the public. In Minnesota there are NKBA members who are also certified interior designers as they practice beyond residential kitchen and bath design and are qualified to use that title.

Many other examples of misinformation propagated by the AIA, the IJ, and the NKBA (all of whom participated fully in Minnesota's legislative situation) can be viewed by reviewing a video of the Minnesota Senate Commerce and Public Protection Committee's hearing (SF 376) on February 17, 2009 (available at https://netfiles.umn.edu/users/cmartin/MN%20Senate%20Commerce%20Comm%20Hearing%202009/CommitteeHearing%20%28D%29/cmte_comm_021709.wmv).

IMPLICATIONS FOR THE FUTURE OF THE PROFESSION

The activities described constitute an abuse of the public's trust, both as they relate to general issues and specifically to the characterization of interior design and interior designers by the opposition. The level of orchestration also speaks to intent—that the manner in which the profession has been attacked is intentional, measured, and planned. So, where do we go from here? Moreover, considering the concept of "social production of misinformation" (Arsenault & Castells, 2006, p. 301), how can the interior design profession get the world to *bother with the facts*?

Surely, education on all fronts will move interior designers toward their regulatory goals—or will it? If we want to fulfill the requirements of being "professional" we must continue to educate the public, legislators, and all factions within our profession in a truthful manner. We must illuminate for these stakeholders how they can separate fact from misinformation.

One option might be to use the type of "truth" tool that gained notoriety during the 2008 presidential campaign via the work of the Annenberg Public Policy Center of the University of Pennsylvania: FactCheck (see www.factcheck.org). They describe their purpose as "a nonpartisan, nonprofit 'consumer advocate' for voters that aims to reduce the level of deception and confusion in U.S. politics" (FactCheck, 2009). They have been around since 1994, but the increase in the level of "spin" created by the last political race gained top notoriety for this organization. This could be a useful approach and/or tool for our profession if we can rely on an objective party to vet the facts.

In our quest for regulation and the right to practice, factual education is especially important when talking with legislators. They are pressed for time; they continually are meeting with individuals and organizational representatives with opposing viewpoints; and they are making complex decisions. Additionally, the most convincing arguments may challenge objective reality, i.e., not be factual, but may resonate with their constituents. How can we be successful with our message in the face of these challenges? We must remind all that everyone is entitled to an opinion—but that the facts do not necessarily support opinion. Everyone enjoys a great piece of theater or an engaging movie, but presenting the facts should not be about the drama.

REFERENCES

Abbott, A. (1988). *The system of professions: An essay on the division of expert labor.* Chicago: University of Chicago Press.

AIA. (2008a, December). Architectural practice and title regulations. *Directory of public policies and position statements.* Retrieved July 13, 2009, from http://www.aia.org/aiaucmp/groups/aia/documents/pdf/aias078764.pdf

AIA. (2008b, October 16). *State and local update: Interior design law causes lawsuit in Oklahoma.* Retrieved October 23, 2008, from http://www.aia.org/gov/angle/angle_nwsltr_current

AIA. (2009, May 28) *Opposition to interior design regulation grows.* Retrieved July 13, 2009, from http://info.aia.org/nwsltr_angle.cfm?pagename=angle_nwsltr_20090528&archive=1&

American Society of Landscape Architects. (2009). *Advocacy & licensure.* Retrieved July 13, 2009, from http://asla.org/StateGovtAffairsLicensure.aspx

Arsenault, A., & Castells, M. (2006, June). Conquering the minds, conquering Iraq: The social production of misinformation in the United States—a case study. *Information, Communication & Society, 9*(3), 284–307.

Bruhn, J., Zajac, G., Al-Kazemi, A., & Prescott, L. (2002, July/August). Moral positions and academic conduct: Parameters of tolerance for ethics failure. *The Journal of Higher Education, 73*(4), 461–493.

Carpenter, D. (2006, September). *Designing cartels: How industry insiders cut out competition.* Arlington, VA: Institute for Justice.

Carpenter, D. (2008, July). *Misinformation & interior design regulation: How the interior design cartel's attack on the IJ's designing cartels misses the mark.* Arlington, VA: Institute for Justice.

Carpenter, D. (2008, September). *Designed to mislead: How industry insiders mislead the public about the need for interior design regulation.* Arlington, VA: Institute for Justice.

CIDA. (n.d.). *Accredited programs.* Retrieved July 8, 2009, from http://www.accredit-id.org/accreditedprograms.php

CNN.com. (2004, October 7). Report: No WMD stockpile in Iraq. Retrieved July 9, 2009, from http://www.cnn.com/2004/WORLD/meast/10/06/iraq.wmd.report/index.html

Draper, J. (1977). The ecole des beaux-arts and the architectural profession in the United States: The case of John Galen Howard. In S. Kostof (Ed.), *The architect: Chapters in the history of the profession* (pp. 209–237). New York: Oxford University Press.

Economist's View. (2006, April 23). 60 minutes: Bush, Cheney, Rice told Iraq had no WMD program before war. Retrieved July 10, 2009, from http://economistsview.typepad.com/economistsview/2006/04/60_minutes_bush.html

FactCheck. (2009). *Our mission.* Retrieved July 9, 2009, from http://www.factcheck.org/about/

Gligorov, N., Newell, P., Altilio, J., Collins, M., Favia, A., Rosenberg, L., & Rhode, R. (2009, June). Dilemmas in surgery: Medical ethics education in surgery rotation. *Mount Sinai Journal of Medicine, 76*(3), 297–302.

Guerin, D., & Thompson, J. (2004). Interior design education in the 21st century: An educational transformation. *Journal of Interior Design, 30*(1), 1–12.

Harrington, D., & Treber, J. (2009, February). *Designed to exclude: How interior design insiders use government power to exclude minorities & burden consumers.* Arlington, VA: Institute for Justice.

Heineman, B. (2007, April). Avoiding integrity land mines. *Harvard Business Review, 85*(4), 100–108.

IDPC. (n.d.a). *Services.* Retrieved July 10, 2009, from http://idpcinfo.org/services.html

IDPC. (n.d.b). *FAQs.* Retrieved July 10, 2009, from http://idpcinfo.org/FAQ.html#anchor_56

Institute for Justice. (2009). *Institute profile: Who we are.* Retrieved July 9, 2009, from http://ij.org/index.php?option=com_content&task=view&id=566&Itemid=192

Jarjour, R., & Chahine, J. (2007, May). Media image of the Middle East. *Media Development, 54*(2), 3–6.

Johnson, A. (2006, September 10). *Cheney: Iraq was right, WMD or not.* Meet the press. Retrieved July 9, 2009, from http://www.msnbc.msn.com/id/14767199/

Lowry, D. (2008, September). Network TV news framing of good vs bad economic news under democrat and republican presidents: A lexical analysis of political bias. *Journalism & Mass Communication Quarterly, 85*(3), 483–498.

Machiavelli, N. (1505). *The prince.* Translated by W. K. Marriott (1908). Retrieved July 9, 2009, from http://www.constitution.org/mac/prince00.htm

Martin, C. (2007). *Interior design: From practice to profession.* Washington, DC: American Society of Interior Designers.

Martin, C. (2008). Rebuttal to the Institute for Justice report entitled "Designing cartels, how industry insiders cut out competition." *Journal of Interior Design, 33*(3), 1–49.

Neily, C. (2008, April 1) Watch out for that pillow. *The Wall Street Journal Online.* Retrieved July 13, 2009, from http://online.wsj.com/public/article_print/SB120701341410579079.html

NCIDQ. (2004). *NCIDQ definition of interior design.* Retrieved July 9, 2009, from http://ncidq.org/who/definition.htm

Podolny, J. (2009, June). The buck stops (and starts) at business school. *Harvard Business Review, 87*(6), 62–67.

Propaganda. (2009). In *Merriam-Webster's online dictionary.* Retrieved July 1, 2009, from http://www.m-w.com/dictionary/propaganda

Ryan, M. (2001, March). Journalistic ethics, objectivity, existential journalism, standpoint epistemology, and public journalism. *Journal of Mass Media Ethics, 16*(1), 3–22.

Whited, L. (2009, March). Occupation? Planet giver. *Interiors & Sources, 16*(2), pp. 18–20.

Will, G. (2007, March 22). Wallpapering with red tape. *Washington Post,* p. A21.

AUTHOR'S NOTE

The author wants to acknowledge Jeffrey Martin's encouragement and insights relative to examining this specific issue facing the interior design profession in the broader context of current societal challenges.

You must take a close look at yourself and your personality and gauge to what extent you are open to people different than you.

—Vincent G. Carter

DIVERSITY

OVERVIEW Diversity presents considerable challenges to interior designers as we strive to meet the needs of people who will inhabit the spaces we design. Diversity is discussed by the authors of this chapter in terms of race, ethnicity, culture, gender, economics and power, and ability level. Vincent Carter truly begins at a foundation level when he says that it's vital to understand what the terms *respect* and *diversity* mean, especially those terms used to describe overt or covert feelings and actions. He gives us several actions to live by that underpin our ability to gain respect. Sherry Bilenduke and Victoria Horobin explore the issues faced by women in this female-dominated practice but male-dominated business world. From their perspective as business owners, they take a look at gender inequity and the double standard for expectation and performance standards. Debora Emert continues this discussion with examples from her global practice. She gives her perception of the acceptance of women's expertise in a male-dominated management system as well as by clients and contractors.

Jack Travis discusses the need to express his black identity via design contributions. His experience has led him to develop 10 Principles of Black Cultural Design. Furthermore, he challenges the interior design profession to bring more black individuals into the profession to begin to embrace diversity. John Turpin finishes this chapter by focusing on the "human-ness" of interiors. He describes the various client or user "types" for whom interior designers problem-solve and provides a checklist to help interior designers become inclusive designers.

The significant and growing impact of diversity is changing the design industry. There are challenges ahead to both design spaces that support and celebrate difference as well as to become, as a profession, a mirror of the diverse culture within our own ranks. Only then will we be able to truly create the type of world we seek to provide.

> How do we get minorities (gender, age, race/ethnicity, culture, socioeconomic standing) into interior design practice, into interior design education?

VINCENT G. CARTER

R-E-S-P-E-C-T

It is possible to achieve respect in a diverse environment as a minority in a majority profession like interior design. To understand what this means, ask what the word *respect* means to you. Does it bring to mind Aretha Franklin? Or, does it take you back to the last time you were disrespected? In this essay, I will begin by offering my definition of respect.

Respect means acknowledgment, honoring an individual or institution, looking up to someone, admiring his or her accomplishments, anticipating good outcomes, listening to opinions other than your own, allowing someone to express himself or herself on a topic, reserving judgment, and being willing to accept an outcome that wasn't planned or initiated by you.

You should always make sure you understand a given term, know in what context it is being used, and, perhaps more importantly, how it is being used. After acknowledging the

VINCENT G. CARTER, CID-MD, LID-DC, FASID, is a native of Milwaukee, Wisconsin. He received a MS degree from the University of Wisconsin–Madison and a BS from the University of Wisconsin–Milwaukee. Carter commutes from Baltimore to Washington, DC, where he is a senior program manager with the Department of Homeland Security. He is active with the Washington Metro Chapter of ASID and has held several national positions for ASID including chair of the National Ethics Committee. Carter also serves on the CIDA Accreditation Commission. He held several positions with NCIDQ, including president. As an initial member of the Washington, DC, Board of Interior Designers, Carter served as vice chair and chair. He also represented the Washington, DC, board on the NCIDQ Council of Delegates and on the National Legislative Coalition for Interior Design (NLCID).

definition, consider if you would like to have it used to describe you or your actions.

Diversity means having choices, good or bad, that involve race; perceptions; opportunities; the leveling of the playing field; consideration for qualifications first, past experiences second, and personality third; and finally, respect for individuals and what they bring to the table.

To put the issues or definitions of respect and diversity into perspective, consider your perception of the following terms: *African American, black designer, interior designer, minority, Section 8, set aside, best qualified, diverse background,* and *diverse experience.* Most people have negative perceptions of these terms—why?

ACTIONS THAT GAIN RESPECT

As a successful African American interior design practitioner, I am often asked, "What must an African American interior designer—regardless of his or her area of specialty—do to gain respect in a diverse environment?" Several actions come to mind immediately.

- Believe in yourself. If you do not believe in yourself and your abilities, you cannot expect anyone else to do so. Know what you are talking about. Conduct research and study to ensure you understand both the question and the topic. Remain current in your field and area of expertise.
- Make yourself visible, yet avoid drawing too much attention to yourself. When seats are not assigned, sit in the front half of the room or near the head of the conference table, even if you are sitting along the wall.
- Dress properly for the occasion, meeting, or gathering. Your goal should be to make your knowledge and intelligence known—at the appropriate time. Think of those who will follow in your footsteps. Make a good first impression and earn their respect.
- Speak up. Enunciate and make sure you are heard. Of course you should watch for cues and understand the modus operandi for the meeting or event, e.g., is there an agenda, is there a procedure for asking questions, has the previous question been answered, are you following Robert's *Rules of Order.* Ask appropriate questions; do not ask simply for the sake of asking.

- Realize trying to stand out may work against you and accept that it isn't always appropriate.
- Admit to yourself that you do not know everything. You will be surprised how much respect you will gain by this admission.
- Always make sure that you find the answer as soon as possible and, if feasible, become an expert on the subject. Follow your gut instinct or intuition; if you have a question, chances are several others in the audience have the same question and will be relieved that you spoke up for them.
- Share ideas. Don't worry about always receiving credit or even acknowledgment. Can you think of a more functional layout for the space you are in right now? If so, what will you do with the idea? Will you merely mention it to the person sitting next to you while in the room and forget it before you leave? Or will you pull one of the sponsors to the side and mention your ideas to him or her? Does it matter that you may not receive credit? What should matter is that when you return to this space you see that your ideas were implemented and perhaps further surprised by being acknowledged for the idea. Keep in mind there are appropriate times we should receive credit and times when it will follow. There will be times when you will not receive credit, and even worse, you know at times someone else will claim your idea. It's OK; your time will come.

- Be observant. Know who is in the audience. Be aware of your surroundings. For example, map out an egress route in the event of an emergency. The leader in you will take charge during an emergency.
- Be sincere. Avoid pretending to be interested; you might be recruited to volunteer for something that doesn't interest you at all. Be honest with yourself and the audience.
- Get involved. There are opportunities for involvement at both local and national levels in organizations that represent your profession and your interests. Make sure you are getting something out of your investment; it should be a wise business decision with appropriate returns. Be careful; it can be costly to belong to multiple professional organizations. Choose one or two and get involved, run for office, or chair a committee. This is the best way to learn the organization and get to know your fellow volunteers.
- Be a role model. Understand that you will be considered a role model by someone. When you become aware that you are a role model, embrace the respect, don't abuse the implied power, and do what you

can to share your experiences with them, preferably in a one-on-one or small group setting. View yourself as a mentor. Share positive and negative experiences with your mentees to help them avoid making the same mistakes.
- Don't give in to stereotypes associated with minorities. We are all minorities in certain situations, e.g., race, age, education, gender, class, etc. Learn to listen and respect others for their words and actions; do not be close-minded by their classification.
- Arrive early. It's the professional thing to do, and it also shows you respect the person who made the appointment, scheduled the room, or booked the entertainment.
- Avoid leaving early. There will be times when you cannot stay until the end, just make sure that before the event or meeting begins you tell someone, anyone (ideally the chair of the committee, the actual speaker, or the person that signed you in) that you have to leave early. This will prevent the chair, speaker, or sponsor from making an incorrect assumption that you were bored or not interested.

ACTIONS THAT PREVENT RESPECT

It is important to understand why we are respected; it is also important to understand why we fail to gain or receive respect. Almost all of the following actions tend to be based on our fear of not receiving credit or acknowledgment for something we've done or suggested.

- Not cooperating with others. We sometimes act solo, want to act alone, and not allow others to help or give help.
- Not sharing ideas or information. We often hold the information too close to our chest for fear that it may get into the wrong hands, or we may not receive credit for it. Think of when you were a student; were you very secretive with your

design solutions? Or did you freely share your ideas?
- Always seeking recognition. Do not think you are the only one worthy of respect or receiving credit. Do not be too concerned with receiving the respect that you have not yet earned.
- Not respecting fellow professionals. We often feel we are the only one who can complete a given task, job, or project. Let others earn your respect.
- Not respecting our customers. Think about it: when was the last time you said the client really doesn't know what's best for him/her? They knew enough to hire you! Now it's your turn to give something back, hopefully for a fee.

My approach to life may be different than yours; perhaps it is similar. Some of you may think of me as a successful black or African American male in the field of interior design. If I thought about it I would probably agree, but on my terms, not yours, which is part of the key. I am often asked how I overcame a given barrier or obstacle. I prefer to think of them as challenges that must be overcome in a specific time frame, not unlike a project with a deadline.

I learned a long time ago that I was going to be a lonely pioneer in many aspects of my life. As a child I actually enjoyed going to school, looked forward to receiving recognition for perfect attendance, and couldn't wait to get home or go to the library to complete a homework assignment. Imagine that—wanting to go to school! I will let you in on a secret—I couldn't wait to get to college, so I attended night classes at a community college while a senior in high school.

I was often the only black person in my classes at the University of Wisconsin, the only black in my former position at the World Bank, the first black president of the Washington Metro Chapter of the American Society of Interior Designers (ASID), the first black international president of the National Council for Interior Design Qualification (NCIDQ), and the first black on the Washington, DC, Board of Interior Designers, as well as the first to serve as chair. In all of these roles, I tried to follow the actions I suggested in this essay.

A few years ago, while I was president-elect of the Washington Metro chapter of ASID, some fellow board members wanted to address the lack of minorities (which commonly means few blacks or African Americans) in the chapter and involved in the field of interior design. They invited Shauna Stallworth of the Organization of Black Designers (OBD) to give a presentation to the board. Shauna did an excellent job explaining why minorities were absent and made suggestions to the board on how to increase minority members and their involvement and active participation.

Although I was glad they thought enough to invite Shauna, it made me question how my own board viewed me. One of my board colleagues commented quietly to me that they could simply have asked me. I could only laugh inside, and, again, wonder how they viewed me. Upon asking this question, I was told, "You are different."

This brings up an interesting dilemma for which I would like to solicit your help. Being the only black or African American at the table can be both an honor and a disappointment. In many ways, the more time I spend representing "US" at these tables, the more I'm seen as alienating myself from "US" by some of "US." Why is that? You can help by joining me at the table.

I am often asked to represent "US" at national events. I receive respect simply by being myself, expressing my opinions, and not biting my tongue. I am often described as quiet, introspective, and always thinking. I agree. The real issue is who is thinking that and why.

CONCLUSION

It is important that we understand the importance of why we are in the profession we have chosen. I am here because I believe in the profession of interior design, am dedicated to it, and feel that I have found my areas of expertise—namely, design of educational facilities and facilities management. I enjoy problem-solving, diagnosing root problems, and proposing solutions to overcome them.

Do you know why you are here? How do you earn respect; give respect; and get to know yourself? You must take a close look at yourself and your personality and gauge to what extent you are open to people different than you. Are you willing to listen before speaking? Would you seek advice or counsel from someone who has a diverse or different background? Are you willing to mentor someone? How would your coworkers describe you? How would a fellow meeting attendee you do not know describe you? Listen and take notes.

Respect yourself. It is the first step in gaining the respect of others.

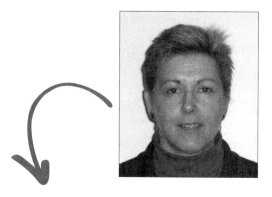

SHERRY BILENDUKE, ARIDO, IDC, holds a bachelor of interior design from the University of Manitoba. In practice since 1982, she has extensive experience in all aspects of the design process with particular expertise in corporate offices and financial institutions. As principal and director of design at KBH Interior Design, Inc., in Toronto, Bilenduke holds the ultimate responsibility for the quality and integrity of all design work produced by the firm. She establishes realistic programs and budgets, develops effective project organization, and has a thorough understanding of the clients' business objectives. Bilenduke has worked with architectural, engineering, and construction firms across Canada. She is an active member of ARIDO and IDC and a CIDA site visitor. She received NCIDQ's highest honor for her contributions to the profession, the Louis Tregre Award in 2005.

VICTORIA HOROBIN, ARIDO, IDC, holds a bachelor of applied arts from the School of Interior Design at Ryerson University in Toronto. In professional practice since 1987, she has many years of experience in both interior design and interior construction management with a concentration in corporate office and retail projects. Horobin is a principal and director of marketing for KBH Interior Design Inc., in Toronto. In addition to her interiors experience, she has worked extensively with architectural firms, focusing on the client's image and business philosophy through the development of their interior environments, while responding to the critical needs of function, budget, and schedule. Horobin is a past president of ARIDO and has been actively involved in leading legislative pursuits related to the regulation of the practice of interior design in Ontario. She also participates in a variety of committees for NCIDQ and received the Louis Tregre Award in 2000 for her contributions.

SHERRY BILENDUKE &
VICTORIA HOROBIN

YOU'RE A WOMAN, AN INTERIOR DESIGNER, AND YOU WANT TO BE IN BUSINESS?

The first and most obvious thought when dealing with the question of "what are the challenges facing a female interior design business owner?" is the balance of work and family. The practice of interior design is deadline-driven and often deals with substantial project budgets. This can mean long hours of work that take time away from family and personal life. Additionally, we are a people-oriented business; throughout the day the design business owner is dealing with clients, consultants, and staff—pursuing new business opportunities, pitching design ideas, attending meetings, talking on the phone, answering e-mails, and dealing with staff questions. There is little "gas left in the tank" at the end of the day to spend energy on family needs. However, is our profession really any different from other professions when it comes to this aspect of work? Likely, this is not the case.

The next thought that comes to mind is that the public at large, whether they are residential or commercial clients, lack understanding of what it is we do as interior design professionals. Although we establish long-term relationships with many clients, we also deal with many first-time clients, those who have never been through the process of working with an interior designer. There exists an inherent lack of knowledge about the depth and breadth of our scope of work and knowledge base. This lack of understanding extends past client relationships to the working relationships we have with others on the interior design project team and to business at large. Engineering consultants, contractors, lawyers, accountants, and bankers—all of these professionals are often unaware of the complexities of the interior design profession.

Additionally, there is still a pervasive assumption by those for and with whom we work that, "because you are young and female, you probably don't know what you are talking about." This is a factor that young, female interior designers commonly face, whether they are presenting design concepts and solutions to clients, or working out construction details with consultants and contractors in the office or on a construction site. Gender inequality is clearly present in the profession of interior design, and is perhaps the most pervasive bias because it affects half the population.

As women progress through their careers, the questions and challenges posed by the stakeholders of any project may change, but the bias remains. Negotiating fees with clients, presenting design solutions, and negotiating costs with contractors are all common tasks we perform. Yet there exists a double standard and lack of confidence that we are really competent to deal with such large decisions and such large sums of money. Does our business really have value and thus merit a fee for service? In business, "professionalism" seems to have a different set of standards for women than it does for men.

Finally, women in business historically have not received as "good a deal" from financial institutions and lenders, despite the fact that female-owned businesses are generally a better risk. Until very recently, the perception of a woman-owned business was "they are small, probably home-based, part-time (i.e., mothers), and probably don't make very much money." Though, as more women have developed successful businesses, the attitudes of lenders have begun to change.

HISTORY AND EDUCATION

Let's start at the beginning—why are there so many more women in the profession of interior design than there are men? The simple answer to this question is that there is gender inequality and sexism in the public education system. In high school, boys showing an interest in design are more often directed to a career in architecture, whereas it is acceptable for girls to opt for a career in interior design. But again, this bias is due to educators in the public education system (and the public at large) not having an accurate understanding of interior design. In terms of post-secondary education, interior design education has its roots in decorating programs, which were typically housed in the fine arts or home economics departments of colleges and universities. Girls were encouraged to pursue support (i.e., "helper") and domestic careers, rather than those based in science or business.

Obviously, this has changed over time. The university education system has become much more equal; there are many more women pursuing careers in architecture and engineering. Interior design programs are valuable to their institutions, ever more commonly accredited and more frequently housed within building science departments. The quality of education provided to both male and female students is equal; yet the vast majority of the student population in these programs is still female. This appears to be a North American phenomenon, where the majority of the interior design industry seems to be made up of women. In Europe and Asia, it appears the industry is more evenly split between the genders.

Thus, the gender inequity would seem to go back to the routing of students into university programs at the public school level. There is still the perception that men are better at math and science than they are at arts and fine arts, that they are more logical and, therefore, better suited to run a business. Career guidance provided to students tends to direct them toward a career that reinforces gender inequality as they enter programs of study in higher education.

After graduation, the challenges faced by young interior designers begin to appear. Why do some people not show respect to a young female interior designer in a business situation? There seem to be two main reasons for this: lack of understanding of the depth of education and the interior design scope of work, and the existence of a male-dominated culture in many of the related professions and industries with which these young interior designers work.

Interior design is a relatively new profession as it exists today. In earlier years, the focus was more on decoration, but as opportunities grew, the scope of work carried out by interior designers expanded to include complete design, documentation, and administration of interior construction projects. Types of projects also changed from what was once purely residential design, which by its nature deals with domestic issues, to design that encompassed all forms of business and institutional space.

Members of the public, both men and women, are not generally aware that interior design education provides a strong foundation in building systems, building codes, and structural systems as well as business and professional practice. These knowledge areas have traditionally been viewed as the domain of architecture. Although this may have been true in the early days of the profession, it is no longer so, yet this outdated notion persists.

Interior design is a profession dominated by women, yet most of the people interior designers interact with on a daily basis are men. These include clients, consultant team members, contractors, and building officials. Paternalistic attitudes are not uncommon toward young female interior designers. The perception is that interior designers are capable of handling the decorative aspects of a project, but that they don't understand how things "go together."

Finally, many still believe that women, and particularly young women, are not serious about their careers and are not fully focused on the business at hand. This idea persists, no matter the experience level or career path of the interior designer.

GENDER BIAS BETWEEN MALE AND FEMALE BUSINESS OWNERS

As interior designers gain experience and progress in their careers, it is common for them to want to own their own businesses. By our nature, we want to be in charge and lead the interior design team and process. Yet, as these young women are continually questioned and challenged regarding their knowledge and ability, they may get frustrated and choose to leave the profession rather than face the challenges of running a business. This seems to carry over into other design professions as well.

In the field of architecture, 170 women surveyed revealed that a gradual erosion of confidence from their relationships with clients, supervisors, and peers led to their reduced self-esteem and poor job satisfaction (de Graft-Johnson, Manley, & Read, 2007). The research concluded that women's decisions to leave the profession were not linked to academic or practical ability or to poor career choice. This would suggest that gender bias also exists in the related professions.

Generally speaking, men and women have different approaches to business and value different things. When it comes to owning and operating a business, standard stereotypes apply:

> Men tend to be left-brain thinkers, focusing on facts, hierarchy, and structure. Women tend to be right-brain focused, which involves values, intuition, and relationship-building. Women business owners tend to be both. They're focused on values, relationships, and

intuition, but at the same time, they want the facts, and they want information. That means some women may take longer to make decisions. They are much more likely to want to consult with others. In general, women tend to focus on collaboration and integration, where men tend to focus on policies and procedures. (Gumpel, 2009)

These should be positive attributes for the female business owner, but perhaps they are not acknowledged.

On the other hand, some people view these attributes as weaknesses to be exploited. This can manifest itself in several different ways in the interior design profession including:

- Clients who agree to fees and then refuse to pay or expect an unwarranted discount
- Contractors who submit unsupportable quotations for changes and expect them to be approved
- Consultants and contractors who will not entertain alternative solutions
- Staff members not adhering to company policy

Women in interior design seem to be viewed as less experienced and capable in business situations. This gender discrimination is not limited to our male clients; female clients tend to have the same perceptions and biases.

ACCESS TO CREDIT AND FINANCING

When it comes to running an interior design business, access to credit is imperative. Without a steady cash flow, businesses cannot grow and thrive. And with knowledge-based consulting practices, investors are uncommon. Is the profession of interior design any different than other professions in terms of our access to financial assistance? Does a gender bias exist in terms of accessing financing?

The image of the woman-owned business used to be that it was small business and not a major contributor to employment or the economy. At question is whether these perceptions are still held in the financial community, given the success rates of women-owned businesses, and the high level of professionalism and sophistication that women take in approaching lending institutions for financing.

Traditionally, cultural and historic situations here pushed women toward service professions more than to the industries. The banking system is not fully aware of how to manage the access to credit for service industries due to the intangible nature of this sector. In the past, banks often felt that this sector was too volatile and

would not risk investment to promote growth (Troiani, 2003).

According to the National Foundation for Women Business Owners (Center for Women's Business Research, 1996), women business owners' sources of capital have changed significantly between 1992 and the present. Nearly three-quarters of women entrepreneurs are using business earnings to finance their firms, double the number from 15 years ago. At the same time, the percent using credit cards as a source of capital has been cut in half, down to 23%, a level very similar to male entrepreneurs.

Although there is growing similarity between women and men business owners' sources of capital, women tend to use their credit for different purposes. Women use credit primarily for growth and expansion, whereas men are more likely to use it to smooth out cash flow and consolidate debt. This should be a reassuring statistic in terms of lending practices (Center for Women's Business Research, 1996).

Relationships with banks, reported by many women entrepreneurs as a problem in the past, are improving. According to surveys conducted by Wells Fargo Bank and AT&T Credit

Corporation (Center for Women's Business Research, 1996), the percent reporting one or more problems in working with their banks has dropped overall and now is at about the same level as men. Today, women business owners are just as likely as men business owners to have bank credit and are just as likely to report being satisfied with the amount of credit available to them. Further, the range of sources that women- and men-owned businesses turn to for capital is very similar (Center for Women's Business Research, 1996).

These statistics show a decreasing gap in the availability of financing for women-owned businesses, as well as in women presenting applications for financing to grow their businesses. So it would seem that although gender disparity still exists in the financial aspects of business, this is not a significant factor or a deterrent for women opening a business.

CONCLUSION

How do we continue to make progress in women's success in this profession at the same rate as men? Is the answer really as simple as enhancing public education about the reality of the profession of interior design and what it is that we do? Should the interior design profession be involved at the public school level to ensure everyone understands their options?

This is a process that will take time. The practices of architecture and engineering have been around for centuries, and likely the members of these professions would also state that their work is misunderstood by the public. But, they are respected professions with perceived value. Interior design, in its current state, has only been around for a few decades. Over time, and with persistence, it will be more commonplace for its value to be understood.

Perhaps it all comes down to the fact that people don't know what we do. It is, thankfully, very common that at the end of a project, those with whom we work have a newfound respect for the interior design profession. They are impressed by the amount of time, work, attention to detail, and energy involved in the process—and they are most often delighted by the outcome. They are surprised by the impact of a professionally designed interior space—whether it is a home, an office, a retail store, a hospitality space, an educational space, or a healthcare environment. The comments and reactions they receive from clients, staff, and colleagues delight them. They are the interior design profession's best advocates.

REFERENCES

Center for Women's Business Research. (1996, October 17). *Women business owners make progress in access to capital.* Retrieved 01/25/09, from http://www.nfwbo.org

de Graft-Johnson, A., Manley, S., & Read, C. (2007, May). *Why do women leave architecture?* Retrieved January 25, 2009, from www.architecture.com

Gumpel, E. (2009). *20 years of advocacy & education: Sharon Hadary looks back on 2 decades as executive director of the Center for Women's Business Research.* Retrieved January 25, 2009, from http://www.womenentrepreneur.com

Stats Canada. (2005). *Women in Canada: A gender based statistical report (5th Ed.).* Government of Canada. Retrieved January 25, 2009, from www.statscan.ca.

Troiani, L. (2003, October 3). *Women in business: A contribution to socio-economic growth in developing countries.* Retrieved January 25, 2009, from www.euromedtds.org

> What challenges face a female practitioner (e.g., female interior designer working with male architects and engineers) in a large firm?

DEBORA EMERT

WHERE ARE THE WOMEN? STATUS OF WOMEN AS DESIGN FIRM MANAGERS

Would you be surprised to hear that only 33% of the executive management positions in major design firms today are held by women? I am one of them. With over 30 years experience as a practicing interior designer, I have had the opportunity to see our profession grow and mature in countless ways.

For example, technology has changed our service delivery; what once was hand drawn is now computer generated, and what once was mailed or hand delivered is now electronically transmitted (and let's not forget the interim Quip technology followed by the now-almost-antiquated facsimile). These technological advancements have resulted in an increased expectation for the speed at which work is generated; many clients literally think that design is but a "click away."

Next, materials technology and design research advancements have resulted in a more thoughtful development of solutions for our clients. Design is a commodity—just look at

DEBORA EMERT, CID-MN, LEED® AP, is the director of the interior design line of business for NELSON and the Design Consortium. A graduate of Northern Arizona University with a BA in applied science/interior design, she has practiced commercial interior design for 32 years. Emert worked for a number of global organizations prior to cofounding E Design (1988) in Minneapolis. In 2004, E Design merged with NELSON, and she was appointed managing director of the Minneapolis office, then director of the interior design line of business and director of design in 2007. Emert's scope of experience covers all aspects of a project and has extended from large corporate headquarters projects in India to radio broadcast facilities, professional practices, healthcare, and hospitality. She has made presentations at EDRA, the Symposium on Healthcare Design, and Minnesota Real Estate Journal–Extreme Office Makeover Conference. Emert has served as a part-time instructor of interior design at the University of Minnesota.

the products on the shelves at your local discount store; no longer is a toaster just a square metal box. Design excellence is an out-of-the-box expectation of our clients now. But, there is one thing that hasn't changed much in the past 30 years: interior design, from the commercial/contract venue especially, is still a male-dominated profession.

THE SITUATION

What I find interesting about this is that although the interior design management is male dominated, the majority of interior designers graduating from Council of Interior Design Accreditation (CIDA) accredited interior design programs are female. I venture a guess that the majority of employees in interior design firms are also female. But, this is not true in the upper ranks of firms' management, which have been male dominated since interior design organized as a profession over 50 years ago.

When you look at the majority of top design firms over the past 30 years, most were founded by men, and most are still managed by men. These include firms where I worked, such as Saphier Lerner Shindler Environetics (SLS); Richmond, Manhoff, and Marsh (RMM); and Griswold, Heckel, and Kelly (GHK); all were founded by men. And, even firms that have stood the test of time like Gensler, Perkins+Will, HOK, and NELSON, for whom I currently work, are still male dominated.

In an effort to verify my opinion on this situation, I conducted an Internet search of the Web sites of the current top 10 "Interior Design Giants" as published by *Interior Design* magazine (Davidsen, Leung, & Grimscheid, 2009) to review the gender-related management statistics. Sadly, it was even worse than I expected! From the information available on the 10 firms' Web sites, the highest percentage of women in senior leadership was 33%; there were a couple other firms in the 20–25% range, several in the 11–14% range, and, amazingly, several were below 10%. In one of the largest and oldest firms, only 5% of the management were women!

It is 2009, and it has been over 170 years since Susan B. Anthony asked for equal pay for women. It has also been 89 years since the U.S. government gave women the right to vote. Is this all the farther female interior design professionals have made it in terms of a management presence in the largest, leading firms of the design industry?

WHY NO WOMEN?

What is the reason for this male dominance? When you look at the commercial interiors segment of the industry, the global business environment is still primarily male dominated. There is an underlying belief that information and recommendations *from men to men* are considered more seriously. Somehow having a man explain construction and building codes to a top executive is more believable, and certainly less humiliating, than from a woman because, as we all know, *construction is man's work*. If we were simply saying what walls to paint certain colors, then it would be OK for the information to come from a woman. But, we aren't; we are truly affecting the built environment with significant impact on the occupants, not to mention the corporate purse strings.

Having been raised as an independent individual, believing that there were no limitations to my abilities other than those self-imposed, it never occurred to me that I, as a female professional, might be treated differently than a male professional. My first eye-opening experience that changed my viewpoint on this issue occurred during my third year out of college. (Actually, that isn't entirely true, as sexual harassment was a real issue during my internship—but that is another subject.)

I had been hired as a project manager for the Denver office of RMM, which was ranked in the top ten interior design giants at the time. One of my first projects was the relocation of a "big eight" accounting firm. The project had been in progress for almost two years, and I was to be the third project manager assigned to the account. The other two had been men who, for different reasons, had not met the client's expectations; thus, I was coming into the project under less than ideal circumstances.

As I walked into the first meeting with the client contacts, the managing partner and office manager (both of whom were men in what also has historically been a male-dominated profession) looked at me, then looked at my male architect boss, looked at each other, and looked back at my boss, and both said, "She's a woman!" Quite observant on their part, I thought. This first encounter set the tone for the project: a continual process of proving my abilities and knowledge.

The project went on for over a year and was completed very successfully and was ultimately published. I will add that they were less than cordial to me through most of the project. One of the only things that kept me going, besides the drive to succeed and prove that I was as capable as a man, was the mental image of the first visit to the construction site by the office manager. He had not adjusted the basket size in his hard hat and, as a result, it dropped down on his head, making him look like a Playskool toy.

For the most part, my experience has been that after a client recognizes the value you bring to the project as a professional interior designer, the acceptance of gender becomes a non-issue. To get to that point, however, as a woman I have had to outwardly show my knowledge to a higher degree than my male counterparts, especially when it comes to the very technical side of our practice, and that leads into gender bias by the construction trade.

IN THE FIELD

Interacting with contractors in the field as a woman is another situation. I cannot tell you how many times male contractors have tried to ignore my input. There is an automatic assumption that, as a woman, I apparently do not have the capabilities to understand the complexities of construction. There have been many times that I have been at a construction site with significantly younger male teammates, and the contractors will speak directly to them as if I am not even present. Because of this, I have made it a point to become knowledgeable about construction and have done construction work myself to expand my academic knowledge to a practical, working-level knowledge. It required extra effort for me to learn construction means and methods, along with building codes, schedules, costing, etc. Although the Council for Interior Design Accreditation (CIDA) accredited programs require these knowledge areas to be included in interior design curriculum today, there is still the need for self-motivated education and research to excel in the professional practice of interior design. One of the best things that I did my first year out of school was to read the current building code, cover to cover.

Regardless of your gender, as a professional interior designer, it is critical that you fully understand what you are designing, whether or not it can be built as designed, and whether the contractor's construction methods and quality are at the highest level possible from your observation. It is easy for a contractor to look at you and say that they cannot get that wall surface any smoother, or that it is impossible to complete a detail the way it is drawn. But, if you can explain to them what technique or what material they should use to achieve the desired solution, it is difficult for them not to comply. There is a different level of respect with the contractor, and a partnership is established that results in superior solutions.

GLOBAL MANAGEMENT GENDER EXPERIENCE

Having worked for a number of multi-office national and international design firms, I have had the opportunity to work on a wide variety of project types, sizes, and locations. Most recently, I have been working on a series of projects for our India offices and spent most of the past year and a half in India. That alone has been an amazing experience, but interfacing with major corporations in a foreign country as a Caucasian female has been very interesting.

Surprisingly, I don't feel that I have necessarily had to prove myself as a woman. I was brought in as an international expert, and my gender didn't matter; there has been an appreciation for the experience, knowledge, and global perspective that was sought to advance these organizations to a global platform. In many ways, it was necessary for me to change my preconceived notions of the relationship between gender and positions at work. In the United States, the majority of administrative assistants and receptionists are women. In India, they are predominantly men because these positions are not considered to be menial but very important to the success of the executives.

Construction in a developing world is fascinating; the resourcefulness displayed is amazing. What was also amazing was to see the number of women on the construction sites of major buildings who, in their saris made of silk and fine cotton, were climbing up and down ladders and bamboo scaffolding, barefoot, carrying baskets of dirt, brick, and concrete on their heads. They would look at me as I walked through the job site in western clothing, a professional woman. They were amazed that I had been able to achieve this kind of status; it was heartening to them.

WHERE DID ALL THESE MEN COME FROM?

The ratio of men to women in management far outstrips the ratio of men to women in practice in interior design; where have all of the men in our interior design profession come from? There might be a few explanations, but one I think is important is this: a very large percentage of the men practicing interior design are actually architects or architects by training who have chosen to practice interior design. Just as the interior design education programs are dominated by women, historically architectural programs have been dominated by men.

Studies have shown that men are encouraged to pursue intellectually challenging studies; that men are "naturally" better at math; and thus, more men are encouraged to pursue or believe that they are capable of completing architectural programs. Thankfully, this is changing as research shows that women are equally capable of understanding math, and that the issue has been a matter of perceived ability and a lack of encouragement. I have to admit that I always had a desire to go back to school and obtain a degree in architecture, but the thought of completing the required math and physics classes kept me from ever following through.

This raises the question of why do these men, educated in architecture, choose to practice interior design? I am not sure that I know the answer, but I would surmise that it is because they prefer the intimacy of designing interior spaces. From my perspective, even in the commercial markets, designing interior space requires you to interact with your client on a more personal level; it requires fully understanding what drives them, how they work, why they work. Our male-dominated society still believes it is more appropriate for men to be educated in architecture rather than interior design, but perhaps men do desire to be engaged in projects in a more intimate way.

LOOKING TO THE FUTURE

The position and importance of women in our society has changed dramatically in the past 30 years; in the history of civilization, this is only a flash. Given the fact that the interior design profession is only about 50 years old, it really isn't that surprising that women haven't played a more dominant role in its leadership. I would guess that even if we went back five years and looked at the same statistics of women in management positions in leading firms, it would be closer to zero, so the current average of roughly 15% is a significant improvement in a much shorter amount of time compared to our overall civilization. If we look at the mid-level management positions in these top 10 interior design giants, the average percentage of women is likely closer to 50%; I know that is the case with NELSON. If you read what thought leaders such as Daniel Pink, Tom Peters, Lance Secretan, or Seth Godin have to say about where business and management are headed, you know that design, innovation, intuition, and insight are going to drive organizational success. All of these speak to the strength of women as being impactful contributors to our design industry in the immediate future. As the slogan says, "You've come a long way, baby," but I think we can realistically add, "Watch where we can go!"

REFERENCES

Davidsen, J., Leung, W., & Girmscheid, L. (2009, January 1). *Up to the challenge: 2009 top 100 giants.* Retrieved July 8, 2009, from http://www.interiordesign.net/article/CA6631078.html

> How do we get minorities
(gender, age, race/ethnicity,
culture, socioeconomic standing)
into interior design practice,
into interior design education?

JACK TRAVIS

BLACK CULTURE IN INTERIOR DESIGN— HIDDEN IN PLAIN VIEW: TEN PRINCIPLES OF BLACK SPACE DESIGN FOR CREATING INTERIORS

Over a decade ago, I posed the question, what makes great buildings, spaces, and places? I contend that it is when a building, buildings, set of buildings, or spaces/places reflect and serve the people of the community for which they are intended. Their design lifts the spirit and provides shelter and functional use that fosters positive aesthetic and tactile relationships between the buildings and/or spaces and the people they are intended to serve (see example in Figure 8.1).

Culture and its impact in the environmental design disciplines are at the front line of debate in my work. For the past 12 years, I have been particularly interested in black culture as an important theme in the creation of space and form. Interest in this subject grew out of an awareness of the lack of an architectural expression that identifies a sensual environmental design interpretation that speaks to African or black sensibilities in ways that other art forms have evolved. Concepts or

JACK TRAVIS, FAIA, NOMAC, RA, established Studio JTA in June 1985. To date, the firm has completed several residential interiors projects for such notable clients as Spike Lee, Wesley Snipes, and John Saunders of *ABC Sports*. Travis is currently an adjunct professor of interior design at Pratt Institute and at the Fashion Institute of Technology. In 1992, he edited *African American Architects: In Current Practice,* the first publication to profile the work of black architects in the United States. In 1977, Travis received a BArch from Arizona State University and a MArch from the University of Illinois, Champaign-Urbana, in 1978. In 2004, he became a fellow of the AIA, and in 2006, Travis was inducted into the Council of Elders of NOMA.

FIGURE 8.1. Buildings in a cultural, educational, and urban context.

themes of blackness reveal themselves in art, music, sculpture, writing, poetry, dance, religion, and in so many other aspects of the African or black experience. These concepts and themes of blackness are neither co-opted nor can they be denied. Architecture, as well as all other environmental design disciplines, has failed to reveal an Africanness or blackness at any time, or on any level. Neither pedagogical arguments nor theories of methodology, discussions of technique, and/or criteria for determining materiality in space/form design from academia or professional practice have ventured to do so.

Currently I am aware of two non-black and one black architect whose bodies of work are solely dedicated to the evolution of an African aesthetic in architectural practice. Patrick Dujarric is a former Aga Khan Award-winning French expatriate and architect living in Dakar, Senegal. Peter Rich is South Africa–based and

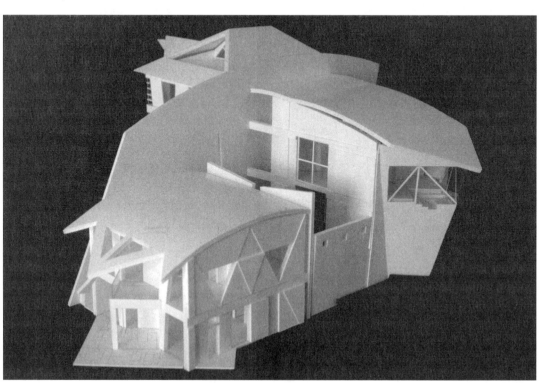

FIGURE 8.2. Single-family resident in a suburban context.

FIGURE 8.3. Single-family resident in an urban context.

has dedicated his practice to emerging connectivity between those who do the work and those for whom the work is done. Pierre Goudiaby is of Wolof tribal descent and is an international figure from his country of Senegal. His work has long been geared toward revealing an aesthetic that is African at its core, and one that connects to the African first and foremost. Figures 8.2 and 8.3 show models of residences with cultural design components with suburban and urban contexts.

There remain no interior design professionals of note who have dedicated their work toward creating a black aesthetic. Recently, an ever-increasing number of non-black and black designers have presented projects that embody a strong black cultural identity. Most notable among the group are Courtney Sloane, Cecil Hayes, and Clodagh. Recently several style books have been published with black cultural themes. Among them are *African Style, Harlem Style, South African Style*, and *At Home with African Americans in Harlem*. One periodical, *Homes of Color*, has emerged in recent years showcasing *Afrocentric* furnishings such as the wall coverings of Sheila Bridges, who has also hosted a home decorating show on cable television called *Sheila Bridges*.

FIGURE 8.4. A child's space in a suburban context.

FIGURE 8.5. A spiritual space in a suburban context.

DESIGNER LIVING

In the wake of all of this progress one must not forget how devastated the initial situation was—and remains, in many circumstances. African Americans are approximately 13.5% of the nation's population. Add to this number the populations of Caribbean and African people now in the United States, and the number increases to more than 17%. The number of black registered architects who are members of the American Institute of Architects (AIA) currently is barely 1%. This means that there should be 13 to 17 times as many black registered architects in that organization than reflected by current membership.

Unfortunately, it must be noted here that the interior design profession has not done nearly as well as the architectural profession. There currently are no records that track membership according to race and ethnicity, which is a comprehensive telling of the inequity of the enrollment of black designers in the professional organizations (or in academia), and there is little or no effort to actively engage, recruit, or encourage blacks to enter the interior design profession. Neither the American Society of Interior Designers (ASID) nor the International Interior Design Association (IIDA) seem poised to tackle the subject with any real fervor in the near future.

Despite the lack of support from the interior design profession and the interior design organizations that support them, several black interior designers have emerged and have sustained practices over a significant amount of time. Some have found black clientele open to exploration of African/African American or black cultural themes, particularly in the residential marketplace. But largely, it must be said that it has been the client and not the designer who has generated the interest in this selective exploration.

WHY A BLACK AESTHETIC INVESTIGATION?

In answering the question "Why a black aesthetic investigation?" the following three reasons are posited.

1. Identity, image, and contribution are vital keys to the success in any community. Children need to see faces that look like their own in the creation, management, maintenance, and design of the communities in which they live and grow. Figure 8.4 (*opposite*) shows the interior of a space designed for a child.

2. What if Africans came to the Americas as immigrants and not as slaves? What then would be the aesthetic manifestations of our communities?

3. Black space/form design does exist under so many layers of resistance that it remains hidden in plain view. Figure 8.5 demonstrates use of form to create a spiritual space.

The formulation of a set of principles of "Black Cultural Design" began to evolve in my work in the last five or so years. The themes that comprise this set of 10 principles grew out of my investigation of the processes and procedures for planning, designing, and constructing medium- to large-scale projects that one might term as essential to the vitality of a community. The projects I worked on that helped me identify these principles include housing, commercial and retail ventures, health and welfare typologies, and educational and civic environments (see Figure 8.6). These 10 principles seem to embody Black Cultural Design at all scales from urban to buildings to interiors.

While still a work in progress, the 10 principles are presented here for discussion, debate, and inquiry purposes as opposed to a dogmatic set of criteria. The first four principles—Economy, Simplicity, Ease of Construction, and Ease of Maintenance—have to do with basic infrastructure of resources and services so necessary and yet so often missing in our communities:

1. Economy. Economy is arguably the most significant of the principles when designing and building in communities of color where resources and expertise are scarce. Economy assures a condition of ease of construction technique. Simpler techniques can be taught informally and in a timely way as well as in need for rapid rebuilding in disaster relief and recovery situations. Economy assures that a larger segment of the community can be involved in the design, construction, and making of the environments where we live, work, and raise our children.

2. Simplicity. Simplicity provides for clarity and understanding in the process of design and construction, thus assuring that a larger portion of the community will be able to understand, learn, and ultimately participate in the design, making, and shaping of the building, spaces, and places of and for the black community.

3. Ease of Construction. Opportunity for training unskilled labor for trade, technical, and professional careers in urban planning, environmental design, management, and construction can act to provide a strong advocacy approach in building and rebuilding efforts during relatively normal courses of events, but especially during emergency and disaster assistance.

Economy, Simplicity, and Ease of Construction act to form the core ingredients for emergence of a Black Cultural Design evolution. Combined, they form the foundation for creative endeavor to serve as a springboard. This infrastructure is necessary but consistently lacking in almost every large-scale endeavor proposed for black communities, nationwide, and is often supplied by other non-black supporters. The fourth principle is one of sustainability—if a design cannot be maintained, it will be replaced.

4. Ease of Maintenance. Promoting the use of materials and methods of construction and detailing that would require a minimum of upkeep, replacement, and/or repair over time within communities where a lack of resources is often at issue is vital to maintaining positive aesthetic value and perception. Too often, funds for upkeep and repair are scarce, nonexistent, or simply not considered due to other immediate concerns of operation in low-income neighborhoods. Concepts and techniques that promote Ease of Maintenance would assist in encouraging longer-lasting upkeep and reverence of properties over extended periods of time.

FIGURE 8.6. Multiresidential urban context.

The next three principles—Spirituality, Heritage, and Duality or Irony of the Condition—address basic "specifics" that, in their manifestations, tend to identify and thus can act to celebrate black culture in ways that differentiate from other cultures, particularly Eurocentric or Western culture.

5. Spirituality. Fundamental and at the core of much of our being and tradition as original Africans and descendants of original Africans in the diaspora is a strong sense of what lies beyond this life. Spirituality, whether group organized or nontraditional and of the individual, has its place and can manifest in every aspect of living, working, learning, resting, and worship. The concept of soul embedded in the roots of the cultural paradigm in virtually every aspect is but one example.

6. Heritage. Information, symbolism, and physical memory of past legacy and achievement of peoples, events, places, and dates act as reminders of what has gone before and is therefore critical to making place in the black community. Perceived evidence of efforts to suppress black heritage makes an inclusive attempt to celebrate legacy in a meaningful way. Educating those severed from such and reaffirming the importance of knowing from whence you came is an important endeavor. Heritage integrated within the design process further fuels other catalysts in unifying and creating healthy growth of our communities.

7. Duality or Irony of the Condition. Past and current situations of the African diaspora cultural enclave manifest attempts to coexist within a dominant culture; however, the former, by nature, being in direct conflict with the latter is an ongoing theme in our lives and in the make-up of our communities. The dual identity one exhibits and the irony of cultural nonacceptance, while the collective is often deemed unacceptable, is real for us and must be revealed for what it is as long as it exists. Artists have found ways to deal with this condition in positive and meaningful ways. The larger art form of environmental design is challenged to seek ways to reveal this condition and its manifestations.

The last set of three principles—Earth Centered/Earth Nurturing; Strong Indoor/Outdoor Relationship; and Intense Use of Color, Pattern, and Texture—relates themes that have direct correlation to environmental design principles as well as green and sustainable principles for making space/form relationships, basic infrastructure of resources, and services so necessary and yet so often missing in our communities.

8. Earth Centered/Earth Nurturing. This principle expresses the need for designers to relate that which is made to that which is found. The African sense is to build with the found in respect and repose, existing with + within as opposed to on or over. Also implied is the respect for the ground or horizontal plane in an informal rather than a formal relationship where functions of movement and rest are incorporated within.

9. Strong Indoor/Outdoor Relationship. This relationship promotes the basic sense that Sub-Saharan tribal groups practice in creating all typologies of shelter. The cultural concept historically affirms the notion that indoor and outdoor spaces are inseparable and crucial to existence due to climatic and other environmental factors. Activities are hybrid in use, and, therefore, both kinds of spaces are often used for the same activity at different times of the day and of the season. Outdoor spaces seen as integral with indoor spaces act as extended reception, gathering, and ceremonial enclaves, fully entrenched in lifestyle beyond climatic challenges.

FIGURE 8.7. Institutional and healthcare in an urban context.

10. Intense Use of Color, Pattern, and Texture. Essential in expression of spatial/formal content elevating the aesthetic qualities of our lives, it is the intensity of the use of these three components, presently and historically, that differentiates the Western and the non Western approaches. Africans and peoples of African descent incorporate color, pattern, and texture in intensities that rival, if not surpass, all other cultures.

CONCLUSION

These 10 principles represent the corner for cultural design constructs at present in my practice. It is my hope that fellow interior designers and architects, both black and other, will consider these concepts for inquiry, debate, polymics, and practice. Until there is a framework of principles and ideals for reference, the evolution of a clear definition of black cultural identity in environmental design will not come to fruition.

Notions of black space/form expression also seek to promote the debate between the appropriateness of *literal* versus *conceptual* expression in the design canon. Black space/form design advances the importance of history and heritage in modern Western canon and will surely evolve a new set of priorities within the American architectural palette when encouraged and thus celebrated within the canon (see Figure 8.7).

Culture will become an increasing theme in our work as architects. Most people of color will not find reference on this theme by restudying architecture. Rather, we must study anthropology, religion, or archeology. Even then we will find ourselves rediscovered, researched, interpreted, and redefined overwhelmingly by members of the dominant culture. Black culture has heavily influenced art, music, fashion, style, and film in modern times. However, within the environmental design disciplines, it remains hidden in plain view.

> Can design for the "majority" meet the needs of the "minority" and vice versa? What crucial issues must be addressed regarding diversity of cultural/ethnicity, gender, age, socioeconomic standing, and ability level?

JOHN C. TURPIN

DESIGNING FOR DIVERSE USERS: A CULTURAL IMPERATIVE

When interior designers speak about "what they do," one thing is perfectly clear: people are their central concern. In the popular press, student textbooks, and academic journals, authors continue to reinforce their fundamental concern for the human condition, and rightfully so; interior designers create spaces for "real people in the real world" (Knackstedt, 2002, p. 1). However, over the last century, the client has become an ever more complex problem. For example, in the early 1900s our predecessors, the interior decorators, focused their efforts mainly on private residences. The client profile was relatively finite—white, Anglo-Saxon, upper class, and female. Though others may have lived or worked in the home, the matriarch made most of the decorating decisions on behalf of the household. Today's interior designer could only hope for such an easy task. The private home can now consist of extended families, foster or adopted children, single parents, two fathers, multiple generations, a slew of pets, and even

JOHN C. TURPIN, PhD, IDEC, is an associate professor and chair of the Department of Interior Design at Washington State University–Spokane. He has an MS in architecture from the University of Cincinnati and a PhD in environmental design and planning (history, theory, criticism) from Arizona State University. Turpin's research has been published in the *Journal of Interior Design,* the *Journal of Cultural Research in Art Education,* and *InForm: the Journal of Architecture, Design & Material Culture.* His last three research presentations have garnered awards for excellence, all of which have focused on the exploration of the early female decorators and interior designers and their role in the development of the history of the profession. Turpin was the 2008–2009 president of IDEC and sits on the board of reviewers for the *Journal of Interior Design.*

a home office; nonresidential interiors offer an even greater challenge due to an increasing diversity of "users."

Numerous factors contribute to the diversity of users, many of which seem to have occurred in the last few decades. Universal design "recognized that the range of human ability is ordinary, not special" (Preiser & Ostroff, 2001, p. 1.3). Issues of age, physical ability, and culture have become common design issues, not unique considerations. This paradigm shift is timely because people are living longer. According to the U.S. Census Bureau (2005), between 2000 and 2050 the population as a whole will increase by 49%; the population of Americans over 65, however, will increase by 147%. This figure represents over 86 million people, and interiors must accommodate their desires to continue to live, work, and/or play. This creates a challenge for the interior designer. They must not only consider the human dimensions of the users, such as their varying body proportions (e.g., height and weight), but also their range of physical and mental capabilities. For example, do they have full control over their legs, or are they required to use a wheelchair? Do their hands function fully, or has arthritis set in, thus limiting their ability to grasp objects in their offices or homes? What is their current mental capacity? Do they have the ability to understand subtle wayfinding cues, or is more direct signage a necessity? All of these factors affect the design solution.

At the end of the 20th century, the concept of social justice gained crucial momentum and changed the manner in which many disciplines viewed their role in society. Generally speaking, social justice "requires the consideration of and sensitivity to all voices and all concerns" (Capeheart & Milovanovic, 2007, p. 2). Interior designers heard the call and began participating in projects for the underprivileged, impoverished, abused, and forgotten. These groups required significant study, as they had been previously ignored by the design disciplines because such projects lacked high-profile status. Important research is occurring in the academy as scholars turn their attention to these groups and their effect on the design process (Awwad-Rafferty, 2008; Jani & Singh, 2008).

Perhaps even more challenging is the ethnic and cultural diversity of the client in this ever-shrinking world. In the 21st century, nations are neighbors and continents are communities. Human migration cultivates cultural engagement to varying degrees. Some people embrace assimilation, whereas others enjoy the celebration of their native values. The importance of cultural awareness is as simple as realizing that a "grasshopper is considered a pest in the United States, a pet in China, and an appetizer in Northern Thailand" (Earley & Mosakowski, 2004, p. 3). If three cultures can perceive an insect so differently, imagine how this might translate to the interior environment with all of its components and rituals.

Needless to say, the interior designer faces an expansive range of variables from human dimensions to daily rituals caused by differences in age, gender, socioeconomic level, ability, and culture. The significance of each of these categories is implied in Havenhand's (2004) poetic description of the purpose of the interior designer who focuses on the "intimate movements, needs, and emotional concerns of the users" (p. 40). The term *intimate* is appropriately employed as it speaks to an individual's deepest nature, which is determined as a result of personal context and individual conditions. With such a variety of considerations, is it possible for interior designers to create spaces for multiple users with extremely diverse needs and profiles?

Before answering this question, criteria for what is "good design" is in order. Ideally, an interior environment should support both an individual's body and mind. This requires interior designers to consider how the function, stimulation, and perception of space affect users. Function has been the primary consideration for the built environment from the moment humans gathered around a fire for light, warmth, and food. Function addresses primarily physical interface between the human body and the environment through objects such as walls, furnishings, and accessories. Stimulation engages the mind through the body. For example, a visual stimulus, such as color, or a tactile stimulus, such as texture, could excite or relax one's mind and thus body. Perception is a process in which the mind filters all of the information in the interior through an individual's values and belief system. The most challenging of the three considerations, perception, requires interior designers to understand an individual's deepest nature.

If interior designers accept that (1) function, stimulation, and perception[1] are the three critical components of an "ideal" design, and that (2) diversity of users must be recognized and addressed, then one could suggest that all interior designers should employ an instrument or process that allows them to evaluate users of spaces using the tool shown in Table 8.1. Interior designers should be asking themselves how gender affects function, how age affects stimulation, or how ability affects perception. For a single user, interior designers can truly create spaces tailored specifically to that individual. However, as additional individuals are added to the program, the interior designer's ability to meet the needs of each user becomes increasingly more difficult, if not improbable.

During the research phase of any given project, interior designers can utilize this simple chart to identify the range of users for intended projects. They can then identify and analyze the manner in which various categories of the client profile would impact the three overarching design goals. Unlikely to satisfy all, interior designers must then prioritize information to reach the final design solution.

Of the three categories, function has the most potential for meeting needs of diverse users because we all share one trait—we have a body. Although the condition of that body makes each of us unique, simple design options exist that make a space usable by most people, if not all. Consider a door handle. Many of us grew up with "doorknobs"—a mechanism based on the dimensions and capability of a healthy human hand. Individuals who have lost some or all of the flexibility of their hands due to arthritis have great difficulty opening doors with these "knobs." Levers, on the other hand, allow people to use more of their body weight to push down on the mechanism as opposed to grasping the object and then using their wrist to turn the knob. Whether young or old, male or female, rich or poor, African or Asian, the door lever is indeed a fairly universal design solution. The ultimate solution may be doors that require no human contact, but only human presence. Automatic doors acknowledge that all people do not have working limbs. This same discussion can be applied to circulation paths that are wide enough for wheelchair access. No one is hindered, whether pushing a stroller, in a wheelchair, or walking on temporary crutches, when they move through a five-foot-wide corridor.

Furnishings become slightly more challenging because of the increased need for varied human dimensions. A chair requires the measurement of heel to knee, knee to back, back to neck, width of shoulders, and so on. The challenge of merging anthropometrics and ergonomics has been achieved in the design of office chairs. Their flexibility allows the furniture to literally adapt to the user, which is particularly important because so many workers spend eight hours a day at a desk with a computer in front of them. However, how many people actually understand how to adjust their work chairs to support varying tasks and functions? For furniture in less task-oriented spaces, interior designers can select seating with firm cushions and appropriate seat heights and arms that allow the elderly to more easily sit down and stand up (Leibrock & Terry, 1999). Such pieces are rarely flexible enough, however, to accommodate

TABLE 8.1.
TOOL FOR ADDRESSING USER DIVERSITY DURING THE DESIGN PROCESS

DESIGN GOALS	CLIENT PROFILE				
	Age	Gender	Socioeconomic Level	Ability	Culture/ Ethnicity
Function					
Stimulation					
Perception					

people of all heights. It is at this point that interior designers (and the users) must compromise by selecting furniture that will suit the "majority" of people. This is not an arbitrary task. Interior designers embark on a prioritization system of users and of needs versus desires.

Stimulation is most closely tied to aesthetics. Interior designers decide what people see and touch. In regards to visual stimuli, studies in retail lighting design by Park and Farr (2007) indicate that lighting affects human behavior. Interior designers can utilize lighting that actually encourages customers to approach a product. However, the majority of studies acknowledge that preference, an indicator of perception, must be considered. Park and Farr also discovered that preferences for lighting differed between two cultures. Warm light enticed Americans, but cool light enticed Koreans. Park and Guerin (2002) further support this finding of cultural preference, but in a color study that demonstrated that Western (United States and United Kingdom) preferences and meaning of color generally differed from Eastern (Japan and Korea) preferences. Research demonstrates that interior designers can employ methods of

stimulation, but they are often generalized for a specific audience.

People's individual perception makes interior designers' tasks the most challenging. Users' perceptions of a space rely rather heavily on "what they know" or have experienced in life, which is very much determined by age, gender, socioeconomic level, physical ability, and, above all, culture. As a result, most studies target specific groups (and many of those acknowledge subgroups). For example, Bradley, Corwyn, McAdoo, and Coll (2001) assessed home environment indicators to determine longitudinal effects of poverty and ethnicity on child development. Some of their concluding recommendations addressed use of light or bright colors to decrease perception of dark and monotonous interiors that are often associated with impoverished homes. This recommendation goes beyond client preference by attempting to combat socially constructed characteristics of poverty-stricken dwellings. For both inhabitants and guests, the unexpected cue of light and color generally challenges people's perception of the socioeconomic level of the family because of the suggestion of cleanliness and upkeep. Other studies examine displaced Somali women's perception of the home (Hadjiyanni, 2007), the elderly's perception of the work environment (Kupritz, 2003), and special-needs children's perception of a library (Banks, 2004). Needs based on perception often conflict between users, but many of them can also be unnoticeable to groups the effect is not targeting.

Considering the number of variables discussed in this essay, the ability to create a truly "universal" interior is unlikely. However, one thing is certain: designing for the "majority" is no longer an option, at least not as that term has been previously understood. The majority does not simply represent groups with the greatest number. In the United States, five-foot, four-inch-tall, middle-class females should be the standard. (Did we ever design for that majority?) Instead, interior designers must design spaces that the majority of people can use.

Of the three considerations, function has the greatest potential to address the needs of the largest range of people, especially with new technologies that continue to allow objects and environments to adapt to people. In addition, function should be the primary consideration; if a space does not "work," then what use is it? Interior designers can employ stimulus to evoke certain responses based on scientific studies; however, preference often plays a role as to how individuals will process that stimulation as a result of perception. These two considerations often need to target specific groups, likely to be primary users.

Interior designers have a moral and ethical responsibility to design spaces that are as inclusive as possible. Research continues to offer new information and products that allow them to achieve this goal. High-style design lacking social conscience is a paradigm of the past. The values of cultural pluralism and social justice have begun to displace values of materialism and exclusion. This shift has (and should) guide the design disciplines as they expand their services and apply their expertise to serve the whole of humankind.

NOTE

1. In this framework, the author considers aesthetics as a crucial component of all three concepts. Aesthetics becomes a tool that can enhance function, drive stimulation, and manipulate perception.

REFERENCES

Awwad-Rafferty, R. (2008). From poverty to prosperity: Making a difference with participatory design. *Interior Design Educators Council Annual Proceedings*, 111–120. Retrieved January 30, 2009, from http://www.idec.org/pdf/idec Proceedings.pdf

Banks, C. (2004). All kinds of flowers grow here: The child's place for children with special needs at the Brooklyn Public Library. *Journal of the Association for Library Service to Children, 2*(1), 5–10.

Bradley, R., Corwyn, R., McAdoo, H., & Coll, C. (2001). The home environments of children in the United States, part I: Variations by age, ethnicity, and poverty status. *Child Development, 72*(6), 1844–1867.

Capeheart, L., & Milvanovic, M. (2007). *Social justice: Theories, issues, and movements.* New Brunswick, NJ: Rutgers University Press.

Earley, P., & Mosakowski, E. (2004, October). Cultural intelligence. *Harvard Business Review*, 1–8.

Hadjiyanni, T. (2007). Bounded choices: Somali women constructing difference in Minnesota housing. *Journal of Interior Design, 32*(2), 13–27.

Havenhand, L. (2004). A view from the margin: Interior design. *Design Issues, 20*(4), 32–42.

Jani, V., & Singh, K. (2008). Bringing hope to a devastated community in New Orleans: An interdisciplinary community service project. *Interior Design Educators Council Annual Proceedings*, 591–607. Retrieved January 30, 2009, from http://www.idec.org/pdf/idecProceedings.pdf

Knackstedt, M. (2002). *The interior design business handbook.* New York: John Wiley & Sons.

Kupritz, V. (2003). The effects of physical design on routine work activities. *Journal of Architectural and Planning Research, 20*(2), 110–121.

Leibrock, C., & Terry, J. (1999). *Beautiful universal design.* New York: John Wiley & Sons.

Park, M., & Farr, C. (2007). The effect of lighting on consumers' emotions and behavioral intentions in a retail environment: A cross-cultural comparison. *Journal of Interior Design, 33*(1), 17–32.

Park, Y., & Guerin, D. (2002). Meaning and preference of interior color palettes among four cultures. *Journal of Interior Design, 28*(1), 27–39.

Preiser, W., & Ostroff, E. (2001). *Universal design handbook.* New York: McGraw Hill.

U.S. Census Bureau. (2005, April 25). *Facts for features.* Retrieved January 30, 2009, from http://www.census.gov/Press-Release/www/releases/archives/facts_for_features_special_editions/004210.html

It appears that after a couple of decades of moving toward globalization, the anticipated growth of economic wealth has been moderately achieved—but at the price of cultural identity and human experience.

—Joseph Pettipas

GLOBALIZATION

OVERVIEW Interior design is a global profession. North American interior designers' experiences beyond their own shores are expanding at an ever increasing rate, offering opportunities to create spaces for clients in other lands from cultures and viewpoints different than their own. Likewise, due to immigration to North America, interior designers shape environments for a broadening range of cultural groups. Many issues have been raised regarding westernization of the world—and the creation of the interior environment is part of that conversation. How do North American interior designers practice in various countries and cultures and, moreover, are their approaches respectful of cultural identity, appropriate, and supportive?

As a Canadian interior designer, Joe Pettipas questions where globalism has taken us—a stifling uniqueness that brands spaces as the same. Americans with extensive international experience, Ken and Faye LeDoux identify the complexities of international design practice from the challenges of vocabulary to the demands of nationalism. In-house interior designers Jeanette Dettling and Kristian Broin describe creating comfortable, functional corporate interiors worldwide that respect culture. Residential environments for immigrant and minority populations are discussed by Tasoulla Hadjiyanni, who suggests that the responsibility of interior designers is to create environments that support cultural identity. Considering globalization most broadly, Valerie Fletcher gives an updated look into the world's view of universal design, focusing on interior designers' roles and responsibilities as they practice globally. It is crucial that as interior designers we consider these prospects of globalization and their inevitable influence on our practice, firm mission, education, and personal worldview.

> Do we export/impose Western interior design/architecture precedents globally? What are the short- and long-term impacts? What are the ethical considerations of engaging in this activity?

JOSEPH PETTIPAS

GLOBALISM IN DESIGN: ARE WE RESPONSIBLE?

"GLOBALIZED" DESIGN TODAY

In the early 1970s, globalism, as a shaper of civilization, was heralded as the key driver in economic leadership. Synonymous with internationalism, globalism suggested that all civilization would be driven by commerce and that politics, social policy, and culture would, therefore, be perceived through the veil of economics.

Ultimately, the goal was to promote the growth of wealth and, subsequently, an elevated lifestyle and well-being. Technology, economics, business, and commerce would dissolve the barriers of time and space that once separated people. Globalization also promised to reduce the cost impacts of transport and communication through the international integration of production and consumption.

With dissolving barriers, North American and European corporations eagerly entered new markets, bringing with them, as they migrated

JOSEPH PETTIPAS, LEED® AP, ASID, IDC, IIDA, RDI, is senior vice president and the regional practice leader of Western Canada for HOK. With nearly 30 years of experience, he has practiced in the corporate, hospitality, retail, and healthcare environments and is responsible for ensuring that all projects exhibit a high standard of design excellence, while supporting clients' business objectives. Pettipas has completed benchmark, large-scale projects in the United Arab Emirates, Doha, Saudi Arabia, Jordan, China, Indonesia, Mexico, Canada, and the United States. Project types include indoor entertainment complexes, large shopping environments, the groundwork for a new city of 150,000 inhabitants, and a recent five-hotel addition to an existing shopping mall. Pettipas has received numerous design and effectiveness awards and has taught at Ryerson University in Toronto. A former president of ARIDO, Pettipas is on the board of both the Design Exchange and CIDA (also served as chair), and is a board member of IFI.

eastward, their concepts of leadership and corporate culture with the related ideas, aesthetics, and beliefs. The net result of which was that globalism was fundamentally based upon the culture and ethos of the West. The design industry was no different.

As these Western ideas, aesthetics, approaches, and beliefs became synonymous with wealth, they quickly turned into must-have status symbols. Purchasing, owning, and consuming products became not only desirable but necessary. The result of this new fashion was that Western design firms provided the Western aesthetic; Western retailers provided the Western brands; and Western hotels provided the Western lifestyle.

Throughout the 1980s and 1990s, economic pressure as the core of globalist theories became a catalyst to produce these same Western products quicker and cheaper in new and emerging marketplaces. This resulted in a chain reaction imbalance where, all of a sudden, the very desirability (uniqueness) of these products has been watered down both in quality and availability. Also, these production and accessibility pressures have caused many, especially those who are involved in shaping the physical environment, to question the appropriateness, suitability, and morality of the imposition of Western ideals, products, and environments upon developing nations. For example, in retail environments, it is now possible to go anywhere, in any country, to places and spaces that look just like the last place or space in the last country.

The quest for Western uniqueness has erased this very uniqueness and created a sameness, or blandness, that is now, unfortunately, global. It appears that after a couple of decades of moving toward globalization, the anticipated growth of economic wealth has been moderately achieved—but at the price of cultural identity and human experience.

As the global marketplace continues to become, necessarily and functionally, smaller, we, as the progenitors of interior design within the built environment, must assume the responsibility of ensuring that the places we create are responsible to the natural environment, the public, the social structures, and the economic climates where we practice. It is as much our job to educate and inform our clients about issues surrounding globalized design as it is to synthesize brand and rationalize our design decisions based upon how what we do impacts the environments in which we do it. The imposition of the Western design solution may not always be wrong; it will, however, always be wrong if we do not approach the question of suitable solution first, with appropriate outcome the direct result.

In the retail and hospitality sectors, the end-user groups now expect that environments provide a place of memory—a place that is unique and memorable to the user. It is far less about consistency and much, much more about the unpredictable, the new, and the unique environment. Although this can be achieved through the stylization or development of a fantasy construct, it is far more impactful when it is based upon tangible and real spaces and places; when it is designed to embrace the social and cultural environment within which it is located. Although one might immediately assume that this approach would result in a slavish reproduction of the local historical vernacular, it need not be so. Inclusion of echoes of a culture, references to local building types, incorporation of local artisan works, and the use of indigenous materials can all contribute to the development of memory for users.

The development of the Eco Tourist tours in Costa Rica, resorts within Bali and Java, the unique qualities of Caribbean resorts, and the increasing popularity of nonthemed destinations seem to support this quest for the *real* and valid. And, whereas a trip to the magical world of Disney can be memorable, would it be as magical if it were found in every city or country? Would the mystery and the magic still be there?

Several large recognized brand retailers and hoteliers are recognizing this opportunity. For example, a hotel giant, whose portfolio contains a chain that is represented by one letter, is one of the front runners in developing unique and wholly different environments in each of its properties. Often keyed to the city or region where they are located, they have managed to connect to the vibe of the place. They are as intrinsic to the city as they are to the neighborhood. A case in point is their property on the lakeshore in Chicago. Through the use of metallic finishes and materials, and lobby lounge bar speaks to the upscale tourists and fashionistas attracted by Oak Street, the Museum of Art, and the Magnificent Mile, whereas their Chicago Loop location, housed in a period structure, appropriately reaches out to the high-powered corporate players in town to make a deal.

Currently most, if not all, hoteliers are embracing the development of environments that respond to their customers' expectations for spaces and places that are distinct. These clients want variety within their brand guidelines and standards that enable the development of memory. These spaces must allow the guest to respond to the "where am I today?" question that so many business travelers face when opting for the service, comfort, and quality guarantee that these larger chains have so ably provided in the past.

There is also change happening among several retail chains where environments are responding to geography and social expectations. These retailers are even stocking their shelves with local-market-specific products because they have recognized the need to target their products to a more discerning marketplace. The use of environments that are unique to each location, that are often in rehabilitated building stock, and that engage their customers in imagining they are somehow transported to another time are all new tools in the arsenal of retail operators and interior designers—and they are proving to be extremely effective.

A Vancouver-based spa and treatment corporation, just completing its fifth location, has embraced the concept of local. Each of their existing locations and all future planning have been developed to *speak* about the local environment. They use local, indigenous materials, and color palettes in harmony with the local environment. They have developed enhanced

FIGURE 9.1. Poolside at the Intercontinental Hotel in Aqaba, Jordan.

services and processes derived from local, historical culture combined with ancient therapy philosophies of India. This relative newcomer to the business has created a strong business and developed a loyal following that make a point of visiting each location when they are nearby.

Another striking example of uniting a global brand with a local flavor is the Intercontinental Hotel in Aqaba, Jordan. This hotel, owned by the government of Jordan and managed by the Intercontinental Hotel Group, has been designed to provide guests with all of the latest in technology, services, comforts, and luxury. Yet, the exterior and interior architecture and interior design have been developed to echo the landscape and climate of this Middle Eastern country that is so steeped in history. This hotel is sited on the shores of the Red Sea with a visual vantage of Israel, Egypt, and Saudi Arabia (see Figure 9.1). Through the use of local stone, color, texture, art, and atmosphere, the hotel design speaks deliberately and clearly about its representation and connection to the countryside, environment, and lifestyle of both historic and modern Jordan (see Figure 9.2).

FIGURE 9.2. Local stone, patterning, and geometry.

In summation, within today's global marketplace, the multinational face of business coupled with an understanding that good design is good business has provided many with the opportunity and the challenge of using our interior design skills within cultures and regions that many of us know little about. These regions are often littered with prospective clients whose primary expectation is buying a little piece of the North American dream. As professional interior designers, we must be economically, socially, culturally, and environmentally responsible, even when it is perhaps at odds with the expectations of our clients. It is the balancing of these factors with those of our clients' perceived needs that are the hallmarks of a successful, responsible, and capable interior designer.

Aiding our clients to embrace a new solution—one where best practices and modern technologies are recognized and incorporated in tandem with environments that are evocative of the locale, society, and geography in which they reside—will ultimately result in financial success. Ignoring these changing expectations of our clients and their target audiences will not.

KENNETH A. LEDOUX, CID-MN, FASID, AIA, IIDA, is a registered architect and an interior design director for AECOM Ellerbe Becket, Inc., an international, full-service design firm. In his 40-year career, LeDoux's national and international design projects have been widely published and have earned over 50 regional, national, and international design awards. His designs for international healing environments are praised for their sensitivity to local nature, history, and culture while incorporating modern details and expressions. K. LeDoux has spoken at numerous design conferences, including Design & Health's 6th World Congress and Exhibition in Singapore, June 2009, on the topic *Integrated Healthcare City Model: A Case Study in Dubai, UAE.*

FAYE LEDOUX, CID-MN, is a principal and senior project manager for AECOM Ellerbe Becket, Inc., an international architecture, interiors, engineering, and construction firm based in Minneapolis, Minnesota. Her career has been devoted to the planning, design, and management of projects located regionally, nationally, and internationally including projects in Canada, Central America, Russia, Egypt, and South Korea. F. LeDoux has focused her interest on the study of the benefits of well-planned and designed environments on their users, as well as their impact on the facility's bottom line. She has spoken at a number of healthcare conferences in the United States, Canada, China, Korea, and Sweden, and has written numerous articles for healthcare journals.

KENNETH A. LEDOUX &
FAYE LEDOUX

ENTERING THE GLOBAL DESIGN MARKET

There is no doubt that we live in a global society with access to information, products, and opportunities we could not have dreamed of 10 years ago—before the Internet explosion. As a result of this technology, much of the world has adopted our Western ideals and now seeks a more Western lifestyle. From fashion to music to interior design, the world looks to the West for inspiration, opening doors to Western interior designers who are interested in pursuing foreign opportunities. But, any interior designer who is tempted by the lure of international design must be aware of the complexities of profitably performing work and producing expected deliverables in unfamiliar cultures.

For interior designers who are considering practicing their profession globally but have little or no exposure to the foreign design experience, we will identify some of the most common issues they might encounter. Examples are presented and recommendations made to help overcome common obstacles. We will also discuss several design trends that are prevalent or are gaining prominence throughout the world. These trends are having a profound effect on interior design practice as it evolves globally.

GLOBALISM ISSUES

Interior design publications tend to depict the world as a singular design forum, a concept that enhances an interior designer's perception of an overall global culture. As a result, interior designers may think of themselves as members of a global community or culture that "speaks the same (design) language," and that easily extends beyond the ordinary limits of national borders and cultural identities. This illusion is further reinforced by the seeming ease with which we electronically communicate with clients, foreign associates, and coworkers anywhere on the planet.

But, the reality is that the demands of nationalism still exist. The organization of the construction industry, as well as that of the interior design industry, varies significantly from region to region. In many countries, there are protectionist barriers to discourage competition from non-national providers of services and products. It is unwise to attempt to do business in foreign locales without seeking legal assistance regarding local policies dictating the provision of services by foreign providers, contractual intricacies, transfer of currencies, and a multitude of other business-related activities.

It is also important to understand a country's customs and local business etiquette to avoid embarrassing social faux pas. Many books are written on the topic, or one can do a Google search by typing in "business etiquette in (name of country or region)" to find helpful information on a specific location. Learning a few local customs—bowing, exchange of business cards, etc.—and using some simple phrases—hello, good-bye, thank you, please—in the local language can endear interior designers to their clients.

COMMUNICATION

The first, and most obvious, obstacle to international work is language differences. English has become the most widely accepted business language. In Asia, especially, parents place a high value on their children becoming proficient English speakers and send them to local English schools, or even to the United States to study English at very young ages. However, one must be careful not to assume a foreign English speaker's proficiency means comprehension. Our use of imprecise English—slang, design speak, or esoteric terminology—with our foreign counterparts may cause a misunderstanding. The English language also contains many words that sound alike but have different meanings, which can cause confusion. For example, we once used the technical term *shear wall* on a teleconference with a Korean architectural firm. The intended use of the term was to describe a structural wall built to resist lateral forces. Our Korean counterpart did not understand the term, nor did they know the proper spelling. So, when they checked their English language dictionary their misinterpretation was "sheer" wall—one that is very thin or transparent!

Often, especially for presentations, Western interior designers may need a translator to ensure that their audience correctly understands what is being said. When working with a translator, interior designers must make points using concise language delivered in bite-sized phrases and pause for the translator to translate before going on to the next point. Avoid using idioms and esoteric descriptors—airy, edgy, crisp, cutting edge—whose meanings may be difficult to translate as intended.

Thankfully, a picture is still worth a thousand words. Graphic communication via photographs, sketches, or computer-aided imagery proves most valuable in delivering a design message. Be aware that others, particularly Asians, excel in producing very lifelike 3-D images and have expectations for high-quality imagery that may be difficult for Western interior designers to meet.

USE OF MATERIALS

The use of materials in foreign settings may differ significantly from our value system. Differences in material values may be based on history, culture, or availability. For instance, Western interior designers may place a high value on the use of stone to denote quality, whereas, in Korea, granite is so plentiful, it is used for sidewalks, curbs, and gutters, and in some areas of Italy marble is used for sidewalks. These value differences can be confounding, but, when understood, offer interior designers opportunities to use plentiful local materials that may be prohibitively expensive in a U.S. application.

The same can be said for construction techniques. In parts of Asia, where steel production and fabrication are commonplace but hardwood lumber is rare, casework may be manufactured with an internal frame of one-inch-square tubular steel clad with veneered top and side panels. When assembled, it is totally indistinguishable from its American hardwood-framed counterpart. Similarly, in Korea, complex articulated ceiling details (coves, stepped ceiling edges, etc.) are often factory formed from metal, screwed into place, and finished. The result is lightweight and perfectly detailed.

COLOR

The application of color can be especially difficult because it can convey meaning in two different ways—natural associations and psychological symbolism. Natural associations, such as the color green as it appears in nature, are global and convey the same meaning to most cultures. Psychological symbolism arises from cultural or contemporary contexts such as flags, political colors, or cultural contexts including tradition, religion, celebrations, and even currency. Without the assistance of a local associate, Western interior designers may misinterpret the symbolism of certain colors. For example, the red for the Asian bride's wedding dress denotes happiness and prosperity, but a white dress depicts death. The use of black can also be quite tricky, so it is best to have a local interior design associate to consult for acceptable color usage.

INTELLECTUAL PROPERTY RIGHTS

Protecting intellectual property rights is an issue with which interior designers must proceed with caution. In some countries, the practice of design knockoffs and ownership of design documents may be problematic. The knockoff of furniture design has become so prevalent, especially in the hospitality industry, that interior designers should take care that they do not unwittingly violate intellectual property rights by allowing a trademarked design to be duplicated. Protection of design documents must be clearly addressed in the contract to prevent reuse of intellectual property without compensation.

There are several design trends occurring on a global level that profoundly shape and influence the interior design profession. For example, universal design and diversity, environmental and social sustainability, globalization of design value and talent, and sensory-emotional research are viewed differently around the world. These trends and influences need to be considered when pursuing and performing design internationally.

UNIVERSAL DESIGN AND DIVERSITY

One cannot discuss the topic of diversity without including universal design in the dialogue. The global population has become more diverse in age and ability, and future projections are sobering. Interior designers are struggling to meet the needs of the more diverse population. Helping shape a world that works for all inhabitants is a formidable goal for interior designers.

Universal design is not a new concept. Employing an inclusive design approach has been a constant theme since the mid-1970s. Practicing universal design with its message of respect for diversity is mandatory as we move into a more globalized society. To produce relevant design solutions, interior designers must understand and be sensitive to cultures and populations outside their own.

In response to a need for universal design and in preparation for the millennium, the government of Korea formed the Presidential Commission for the New Millennium in Korea and, in turn, Yonsei University in Seoul, Korea, created the Institute of Millennium Environmental Design and Research to globally address environmental design issues. Biannually, practitioners from around the world gather to present their research and application of such topics as emerging lifestyle, new technology, innovative materials, and new concepts for the use of space, all with heavy universal design overtones. Participating as American interior designers, it is humbling to note how far we have fallen behind in championing inclusive design principles.

Looking at changing demographics, universal design makes economic sense. Facing a quickly aging global population and a severe economic downturn, the longer people can live independently, the less emotional and financial burdens are placed on families, agencies, and governments. Designing universal environments that promote easy mobility and are pre-wired for future technologies such as motion sensors, video communication, and health and well-being monitors should continue to be our focus.

ENVIRONMENTAL SUSTAINABILITY

As our planet's environment is threatened and grows more fragile, the greater our responsibility as interior designers to create durable, sustainable design solutions. As Americans, we have jumped on the sustainable bandwagon with great zeal, but our European counterparts have made green living a part of their lives for decades. Selecting green materials is a good beginning, but as interior designers we must walk the sustainability walk in our daily lives to really understand its impact on the world. We must continually remind ourselves that the Earth is not ours to keep; we are only caretakers of it for future generations. This credo will help inform our best sustainable design decisions.

SOCIAL SUSTAINABILITY

A partner to environmental sustainability is social sustainability. Attitudes about diversity are changing as communication and media open our eyes to the rest of the world. We need to develop respect for all cultures, not just our own. As environmental sustainability strives to leave a better world through wiser consumption of assets, social sustainability strives to take future generations into consideration by employing a more cultural and people-oriented approach to life and design. We need to recognize how our actions have an impact on the global society. By applying the concept that "no person is an island," we promote a less self-centered view of the world. When contemplating design solutions, we must address issues including the impact of family, parenting, marriage, divorce, community, culture, nationality, and globalization on our society.

GLOBALIZATION OF DESIGN VALUE AND TALENT

In the past, the United States, Scandinavia, and Italy were the recognized global design leaders. Today, there is an explosion of design talent worldwide. Locations such as Australia, New Zealand, the Netherlands, China, Japan, and Brazil, to name just a few, have notable design communities producing significant work around the globe. This explosion is due in part to an increased appreciation of the value of design on an international basis. Many governments and corporations worldwide use design as a means of branding and differentiating their image.

The Target Corporation is a prime example of a company that uses design in its branding effort. From employing international designers to designing clothing and products exclusive to the Target brand, to clever advertising, the message is that by buying good design (at Target), one can create a modern, hip lifestyle.

SENSORY-EMOTIONAL RESEARCH

As markets for products and experiences expand and diversify, interior designers and manufacturers are using sensory-emotional research to gain public approval of their work and increase their bottom lines. This research helps to identify patterns that lead to purchase and is utilized to create a stimulus that interests the viewer enough to elicit a response, i.e., the sale.

Hospitality design, for example, is highly focused on creating environments and products that elicit user emotion. Hotel and restaurant chains and manufacturers faced with the challenge of providing the same experience or product in multiple global markets are using sensory-emotional research to make adjustments to a single product to enhance sales worldwide.

CONCLUSION

Globalization has created opportunities for interior designers to expand their practice into foreign markets that seek their talent and expertise. To capitalize on this market segment, interior designers must be aware of the intricacies of doing work internationally, the trends that drive it, and the issues that may arise for their successful practice. Before bidding or accepting a project, interior designers must carefully research, at a minimum, the client's credentials, the project's funding, and the business laws of the project's location. When into a project, interior designers should involve experienced local partners, research the culture, take copious notes, keep impeccable records, and above all—have fun!

JEANETTE F. DETTLING, CID-MN, IIDA, is manager of interiors and global standards for Medtronic. She has a BS in interior design from the University of Minnesota as well as other study in business. Dettling has over 30 years working as an interior designer and project manager on a wide range of project types including corporate, medical, institutional, and residential in the United States, Europe, and Asia. She is responsible for hiring and managing architectural consultants for all corporate projects at Medtronic, where they follow LEED® principles. She manages the design staff responsible for global interior projects including U.S. sales offices and global offices.

KRISTIAN BROIN, CID-MN, LEED® AP, IIDA, is the principal project manager for interiors and global standards at Medtronic. She has a BFA in design and has over a dozen years' experience in design practice as an interior designer and project manager. Her work includes projects in the corporate environment, residential design, and dealerships. Current responsibilities include full-scope construction and design for sales office projects across the United States as well as international assignments around the world. Broin is an Art Buddies mentor and volunteers as an art leader in local elementary schools that have lost art education positions.

> Why are culturally relevant interiors important to the employees of a global corporation? What does it communicate to employees in different cultures and geographies when we integrate their culture?

JEANETTE F. DETTLING &
KRISTIAN BROIN

CULTURALLY RELEVANT INTERIORS

We are interior designers for a U.S.-based global corporation that invents, manufactures, and distributes precision equipment. We have an employee population in 120 countries, so cultural diversity, globalization, and meeting employee needs are issues that we work with daily. Our goal is to connect our employees through our environmental brand and not through U.S.-dictated design or strict corporate standards. This goal communicates to our employees that we respect their culture, value our differences, and promote a one-company image universally. As our corporation matures, we integrate acquisitions worldwide and by incorporating our visual brand, we link our facilities together. This goal ensures that design integrity and consistency are established without submerging the cultural differences. Implementing this goal within diverse physical environments is a challenge for the interior designers on our staff.

Globally, our environments articulate a sense of innovation, passion, creativity, and forward thinking. However, there are three design strategies that we have found to be internationally preferred, and we incorporate them in varying degrees in all employee environments: precision in the designed environment, access to daylight, and employee amenities. We also integrate these goals with two underlying components of the corporate philosophy: ensure company identity and integrate sustainability.

347

FIGURE 9.3. Corporate entry showing clean lines and rectilinear forms.

FIGURE 9.4. Fireplace area designed for informal gatherings.

PRECISION IN THE DESIGNED ENVIRONMENT

Precision detailing reflects our ability to use precision to invent and distribute complex, lifesaving products. This design strategy is manifest in buildings and interiors through use of architectural forms that use clean lines, simple forms, and lack of ornamentation. Precision detailing can be seen in Figure 9.3, which shows a corporate entry using the precise lines and forms that reflect the foundation of our inventions.

ACCESS TO DAYLIGHT

Interior spaces optimize views and include access to daylight for all employees, plus incorporate a connection to nature. We design interior environments with the offices in the core and workstations on the glass for light-filled spaces for all employees. Our cafeterias are open and multipurpose rooms that serve as employee gatherings for town hall meetings.

FIGURE 9.5. Interior branding through mission statement as art.

FIGURE 9.6. Product display to remind employees of their contributions.

EMPLOYEE AMENITIES

Amenities are incorporated to ensure a work/life balance for all employees. Patios are incorporated off the cafeterias, skyways connect buildings, and window treatments can be controlled by the employees. We have wellness and fitness centers, healthy food choices in cafeterias, company stores, on-site dry cleaning, banks, signature coffee spaces, ability to purchase event and movie tickets at discounted rates, on-site child care facilities, and in house health clinics. Bike racks with on-site showers are provided. Many of our common spaces include fireplaces with soft seating incorporated (see Figure 9.4) and wireless access that provides employees with the ability to work and collaborate anywhere.

COMPANY IDENTITY

Our company has a strong commitment to our corporate identity and our history. We have pride in our beginnings, development, and innovative products. We use this identity to establish our environmental brand and display our mission statement (see Figure 9.5), products (see Figure 9.6), historical images, core behaviors, company logo, and exterior signage as part of our design scheme. These items are applied consistently in our offices worldwide and remind employees that they are contributing members to our organization and society. Displaying our identity this way is a powerful tool used to communicate our brand to our employees as well as our customers.

To educate our design and real estate partners, we send or personally present a photographic guideline document as an inspirational document to introduce our design tenets and help our partners understand who we are as a company. These images include exteriors, public spaces, workspaces, signage examples, exterior and interior landscaping, and lobbies. This shows the complexity of our company, but that we project friendly, collaborative, and inviting environments that support our employees and their work, as well as show a global connection. In this way, we use graphic design to extend our brand by focusing on the company identity and mission.

SUSTAINABLE DESIGN

We follow LEED® principles in design solutions because we are an environmentally responsible company. For example, we institute global contracts to leverage our budgets, but look to incorporate locally produced products. We hire local architects, interior designers, and feng shui consultants to help us achieve culturally relevant environments through the use of color, finishes, and open office workspace layouts. We require that finishes and furniture be locally produced whenever possible because it is the right thing to do from a sustainability standpoint.

We have also established a landscape tenet by creating a strong relationship between the interior and exterior of our campus buildings. We consciously extend the interiors into the landscape, and vice versa, and use primarily native plants with a contemporary approach. This approach reinforces our mission as maintaining good citizenship.

INTERNATIONAL VERSUS REGIONAL DIFFERENCES

We have international goals, yet we have learned to identify and honor regional differences. For example, in color, we have learned anecdotally that employees from different cultures universally like warm versus cool colors. Additionally, the use of wood is viewed as a warm element universally. However, as interior designers we must be aware that visible color is based on the amount of light in a region. For example, our Latin American interiors incorporate strong saturated colors; Finland employees prefer blues; Copenhagen staff members prefer bold reds; and China employees prefer reds, oranges, yellows, and citrus greens.

We also embrace the spiritual nature of a culture when appropriate. In greater China, Hong Kong, and Japan, we hire local feng shui experts to review all space plans, and we incorporate their suggestions. Additionally, the workforce is hierarchal and less democratic than the West; there is a greater distinction between management and staff so management is sited away from the office workers. Yet, we strive to have designs take on an international look rather than an historic or culturally traditional reference. Other interesting design outcomes we have found:

1. United States, Canada, and Australia
   - We use more traditional design.
   - We include more private office spaces for management to reflect the more hierarchical work style.
   - We specify panel-based workstations that are typically in the 65-inch range.

2. Latin American countries
   - We use vibrant color and lean toward international design.
   - We design with workstations that are desking systems with more open office space and less hard walls.
   - We have found a collaborative work style, which means more open plan layouts.

3. European countries
   - We have found a more socialistic work environment, so there are fewer private, enclosed offices and more open work-spaces.
   - We pay attention to employee concerns that U.S. corporate aesthetics and standards will be forced on them.
   - We listen hard to their concerns and issues because they assume that an architect or interior designer from a country different than theirs could not possibly understand their needs.

4. Middle East countries
   - We design private offices to house several staff members per office versus an open office due to the social and expressive nature of employees.

5. Eastern Europe (Russia and the Baltic region)
   - We use open office spaces with only eight employees per area to reflect employees' desires to be more enclosed.

CONCLUSIONS

When meeting with employees around the world, interior designers must listen more and talk less. We must do our homework before traveling to have at least a minimal understanding of others' culture, art, and language. We try to learn a few social phrases and make an effort to communicate general greetings in their language. We let all with whom we meet know that we are there to develop a shared interest, mutual respect, and a long-term relationship based on trust. These strategies and interpersonal practices provide us a better relationship with our global colleagues, allow us to create interior environments that carry our brand and support all employees, and provide a better economic bottom line for our company through satisfied employees.

How can the built environment create/reflect cultural identity without becoming stereotypical?

TASOULLA HADJIYANNI

GLOBALIZING INTERIOR DESIGN: REFLECTIONS ON DIFFERENCE AND TRANSCULTURALISM

Inherent in globalization is the movement of people, products, and ideas. Long seen as immigrants who left their home countries in search of opportunities, today's "global souls" (Iyer, 2000) are positioned as diasporas, defined as people who have "exemplary multiple belonging" (Tölö-lyan, 1996, p.8), tight connections to their motherland, and overidentification with their cultural identity (Mehta & Berg, 1991). This discourse runs parallel to the many studies that situated the built environment as a cultural medium, as both impacting and being impacted by culture and identity (Duncan, 1981; Low & Chambers, 1989; Low & Laurence-Zúñiga, 2003).

For nearly two decades, multiple voices in architectural education have called for more research and education around cultural differences from a design perspective (Dutton, 1991). However, according to Fisher, "architects talk a lot about the benefits of good design for people's lives, but we do very little to quantify those benefits or to document their effects" (1996,

TASOULLA HADJIYANNI, PhD, is an assistant professor in the interior design program at the University of Minnesota. She holds a BArch and a MS in urban development and management from Carnegie Mellon University as well as a doctoral degree in housing studies from the University of Minnesota. Her doctoral work led to her book *The Making of a Refugee: Children Adopting Refugee Identity in Cyprus* (Praeger, 2002), which established her scholarly focus on the interrelationship among design, culture, and identity under conditions of displacement. Hadjiyanni is now investigating the role of residential environments in cultural identity construction among five of Minnesota's new immigrant and minority groups: Hmong, Somali, Mexicans, African Americans, and Ojibwe Indians. An advocate for culturally sensitive designs and an internationalized curriculum, she disseminates her teaching pedagogies, theoretical and practical research findings, and outreach activities in leading interdisciplinary academic journals, conferences, and exhibits.

p. 42). Thirteen years later, this statement still resonates with culturally minded educators. Exploring how interior spaces and the field of interior design relate to the *similarity* and *difference* that defines the cultural identities of the diaspora (Hall, 2000) has an added sense of urgency; research shows that mental, emotional, and physical health problems abound among displaced people who lose their cultural connections (Adler, 1995; Bammer, 1994; Papadopoulos, Lees, Lay, & Gebrehiwot, 2004).

Experiencing *difference* does not imply embarking on an international trip. These last few decades, the American cultural landscape has dramatically changed, and we are now surrounded by signs we cannot read; ethnic markets to shop; and people who dress, eat, pray, and live differently. In the United States, 11.1% of the population is foreign-born and 17.9% speak a language at home other than English (approximately 53,592,328 people) (USA Census Quickfacts, 2000).

Belonging to what Anderson (1983) calls "an imagined community," members of the diaspora have identities that are "constantly producing and reproducing themselves anew, through transformation and difference" (Hall, 2000, p. 31). The questions, then, facing any interior designer working with the notion of culture under the globalization umbrella are many.

> How different are we from each other?
> How long will these differences last?
> What is cultural, and what is due to other factors?
> Which practices are we to support through the design of interior spaces and which are not to be supported?
> How do we avoid stereotyping the people we are trying to serve?
> How do we make sure that what we design will survive the test of time and market changes?
> How do we even begin to answer these questions?
> What role can interior design play in the debates around difference?

This essay reflects on trajectories by which interior design can navigate the complex intertwining of cultural interactions and highlights the challenges and opportunities this endeavor entails. Drawing from interdisciplinary knowledge, I posit that the built environment can respond to cultural identity both conceptually and practically. By engaging in dialogues and debates around globalization, I argue interior design education can better prepare students to be competent practitioners, critical thinkers, and responsible designers. A student's work will be used as an example.

UNDERSTANDING AND RESPONDING TO DIFFERENCE

Although meaningless borders, fragmented cultures, and weakened nationalism are often perceived as synonymous with globalization, the challenge to designing for culture in this global era is that we are "living in an increasingly diversified world which only has the trappings of homogeneity" (Long, 2000, p. 185). Focusing on identifying what makes us different from one another is thereby the first step to creating culturally sensitive designs; that is, designs that support various ways of living (Hadjiyanni, 2005). The question is: How does something achieve the status of a *transcultural value*? Answering this question, Gates (1996) argues: "You make it transcultural. You 'teach the world' to sing . . . Coca-Cola jingles" (p. 60). It is this duality, then—*difference* and *transculturalism*—that defines practicing under the globalization umbrella. For interior designers to be globalized, they must be able to negotiate between these two, and often disparate, forces.

Cognizant that some form of change is bound to ensue when displaced people find themselves in new circumstances (Camino &

FIGURE 9.7. Responding to culture with motifs.

Krulfeld, 1994; Shryock & Abraham, 2000), interior designers can turn *difference* into an opportunity. Difference can be deciphered through theoretical paradigms such as Fischer's cultural logic (1999), exposing the glue that holds a culture together and keeps it from dissipating under Western influences. Anthropological discourses on cultural change have long identified its selective and appropriative nature—members of cultural groups actively choose which elements of their culture to change and how to change them (Pilkington, Omel'chenko, Flynn, Bliudina, & Starkova, 2002). Cultural expressions such as language, food, and music have been found to be more likely appropriated and adapted to a group's own ideals than cultural values such as religion (Karam, 2000). Variability and a dynamic character are also integral to these processes of change. There are many ways through which an individual or a collective can

identify with a culture, both at one point in time and across time—in a few words, there are many ways to belong (Hadjiyanni, 2002).

The multiplicity in modes of belonging can make responding to difference in the global era irresistible for interior designers. As responses can be both conceptual and programmatic, I will delve deeper into each in an effort to shed light on how to address the challenges brought forward due to our increasingly complex world.

CONCEPTUAL RESPONSES

Typical design responses to cultural identity are often limited to the exterior of buildings and the replication of architectural elements, such as roofs, columns, and decorative features from that group's past or place of origin, i.e., the Ojibwe Indian motif used on the exterior of the Mille Lacs Indian Museum in Onamia, Minnesota (see Figure 9.7). These approaches fail to account for the complex, multidimensional, and dynamic facets of identity definition, perpetuating stereotypes of what belonging to a specific group implies (Mazumdar, Mazumdar, Docoyanan, & McLaughlin, 2000).

At the same time, limiting design responses to ornamental treatments does not engage one of architecture's biggest assets, that of form. In his book *Philosophy of the Arts: An Introduction to Aesthetics*, Graham (1997) positions aesthetics as a "source of understanding" (p. 64). He goes on to say that buildings can be "vehicles for the exploration and elaboration of certain human ideals" (p. 154). Taking this idea further, buildings can act as a medium for starting a dialogue around what makes us different from each other, becoming storytellers that recite what it means to be a member of a marginalized group or celebrate the excitement that can come out of diversity. Such a conceptual approach can incite transformational learning, implying a change in consciousness that will have lasting effects on the students' self-definition (Clark, 1993). I therefore call these concepts *transformative concepts.*

For transformative concepts to be efficacious, they must be grounded in thorough research of the issues surrounding the cultural group at hand. Furthermore, their development and communication must be undertaken through both written and visual elaborations: a title, a statement, and a visual. The title captures the essence of the concept; the statement builds on what the title alluded to; and the visual helps interior designers organize and synthesize their thoughts in something with fewer prerequisites than a building. A sketch, for example, does not have to meet codes or programmatic guidelines. With multiple ways to tell the concept's story, it becomes easier to convey the idea to others, to illustrate its relevance to the project and the proposed solution and also to evaluate one's level of understanding of what it means to be different and how cultures interact.

Strong concepts have to be complex; must account for variability, the many ways one can belong to a culture; and they must be dynamic, not static, revealing the changes that accompany cultural interactions—the potential growth but also the limitations or suppressions that can be a result of a power imbalance. What is fascinating here are the opportunities that arise when these concepts are translated in the built environment (Hadjiyanni, 2008).

PROGRAMMATIC RESPONSES

Given the diversity of the American cultural landscape and the mobility of the American population, culturally sensitive designs must retain resale value; that is, they cannot be culturally specific. Instead, they must accommodate the needs of various cultural groups. Adopting a transcultural perspective, the practical implications of this essay relate to the development of transcultural programmatic guidelines that support varying cultural practices. Let's take, for example, residential environments. With a home's spatiality hosting many cultural practices and impacting social change (Pader, 1993), interior designers who are sensitive to how the built environment relates to culture and identity can begin to ponder:

1. How are living rooms, dining rooms, kitchens, bedrooms, and bathrooms used by different cultural groups?
2. Which uses are similar among diverse groups and which are different?
3. What kinds of spaces support basic practices like cooking, eating, sleeping, grooming, and storing possessions?
4. How do activities, such as decorating for a preferred aesthetic, dressing according to one's cultural norms, and practicing a religion, manifest themselves spatially?

By determining the various functions and users of spaces, design parameters can be developed, such as room size, shape, adjacencies, wall and window placement, colors, furniture, lighting, materials, equipment, and storage requirements.

Coming to the United States to escape a devastating war in their homeland, Somalis face a host of challenges. Some of these challenges stem from their Muslim religion and the fact that Somali women often choose to wear the *hijab* to cover their hair in the presence of unrelated males (Hadjiyanni, 2007). On the conceptual level, the interior design student team of Lisa Antenucci, Daniel De Lambert, and Lynn Skowronski used a fence to capture the multiplicity of identities and interactions that form a diverse community (see Figure 9.8).

In her individual translation for her design, Antenucci conceived the house's first floor as a series of distinct boards, held together by a central corridor that speaks of a community's shared values (see Figure 9.9). Variability is shown by the grid being interrupted through a dynamic diagonal on the second level (see Figure 9.10).

Antenucci went a step further and incorporated a coffee shop on the master plan of the proposed site of this housing development in South Minneapolis where her residence for Somalis is located. Its presence engenders neighbor interaction, strengthening community relationships. Inside the home, on the main level, Antenucci created separate social areas for men and women to gather so that women can cook and attend to children unveiled. A semi-enclosed porch on the upper level further caters to women's needs because it allows women to get fresh air without being veiled (see Figure 9.11).

Through understanding of the clients' cultural norms, a residence can be designed to fit their cultural needs, yet not be designed as a culturally specific residence.

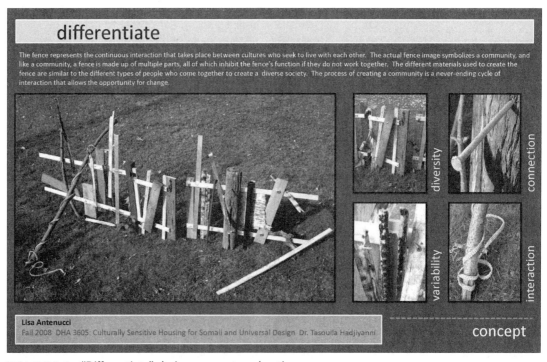

FIGURE 9.8. "Differentiate" design concept exploration.

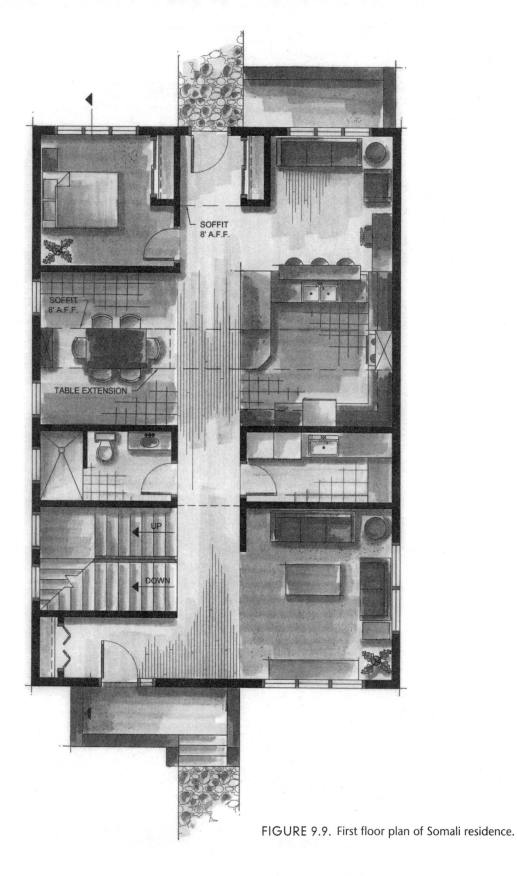

SOFFIT
8' A.F.F.

SOFFIT
8' A.F.F.

TABLE EXTENSION

UP

DOWN

FIGURE 9.9. First floor plan of Somali residence.

FIGURE 9.10. Second floor plan of Somali residence.

Within the figure:
SOFFIT
0' A.F.F.

DOWN

FIGURE 9.11. A semi-enclosed porch of Somali residence for privacy.

CONCLUSION AND IMPLICATIONS

By adopting an interdisciplinary perspective, interior design can actively respond to *difference* in ways that start a dialogue and inform current debates. Key to interior designers' ability to overcome stereotypical accounts of what it means to be a member of a culture is being mindful of the many questions that complicate the interrelationship among design, culture, and identity at a time when "everywhere is so made up of everywhere else" (Iyer, 2000, p. 11). Is it politically correct to design spaces that support gender separation, such as the previous example? Making this inquiry all the more intriguing is the awareness that there is not one answer to the problem of responding to difference. Instead, the many ways to belong and the selective, dynamic, and appropriative nature of cultural change allude to the need for flexible

and adaptable interior spaces that support various ways of living.

Forming synergies with others involved in the thinking, making, and operating of buildings as well as collaborating with academics and practitioners from other fields are instrumental means through which interior design can raise awareness about difference among the general public and policy makers. With social justice and cultural sustainability at the top of its 21st-century agenda, interior design can lead the way for cultural sensitivity to be embedded in buildings ranging from residences to schools, hospitals, airports, offices, and retail venues. Although the establishment of a cultural-code check is an ambitious vision, interior design can become the catalyst that makes a difference.

Adler, S. (1995). Refugee stress and folk belief: Hmong sudden deaths. *Social Science & Medicine, 40*(12), 1623–1629.

Anderson, B. (1983). *Imagined communities: Reflections on the origin and spread of nationalism.* London: Verso.

Bammer, A. (Ed.). (1994). *Displacements: Cultural identities in question.* Indianapolis, IN: Indiana University Press.

Camino, L., & Krulfeld, R. (Eds.). (1994). *Reconstructing lives, recapturing meaning: Refugee identity, gender, and culture change.* Switzerland: Gordon and Breach Publishers.

Clark, C. (1993). Transformational learning. *New Directions for Adult and Continuing Education, 57,* 47–56.

Duncan, J. (Ed.). (1981). *Housing and identity: A cross-cultural perspective.* London: Croom Helm.

Dutton, T. (Ed.). (1991). *Voices in architectural education: Cultural politics and pedagogy.* New York: Bergin & Garvey.

Fischer, E. (1999). Cultural logic and Maya identity: Rethinking constructivism and essentialism. *Current Anthropology, 40*(4), 473–488.

Fisher, T. (1996). Three models for the future of practice. In W. S. Saunders (Ed.) *Reflections on architectural practices in the nineties.* New York: Princeton Architectural Press.

Gates, H., Jr. (1996). Planet rap: Notes on the globalization of culture. In M. Garber, P. B. Franklin, & R. L. Walkowitz (Eds.) *Field work: Sites in literary and cultural studies.* London: Routledge, 55–66.

Graham, G. (1997). *Philosophy of the arts: An introduction to aesthetics.* New York: Routledge.

Hadjiyanni, T. (2002). *The making of a refugee: Children adopting refugee identity in Cyprus.* Westport, CT: Praeger Publishers.

Hadjiyanni, T. (2005). Culturally sensitive housing: Considering difference. *Implications, 3*(1), 1–6. Retrieved April 26, 2009, from http://www.informedesign.umn.edu/_news/jan_v03-p.pdf

Hadjiyanni, T. (2007). Bounded choices: Somali women constructing difference in Minnesota housing. *Journal of Interior Design, 32*(2), 17–27.

Hadjiyanni, T. (2008). Beyond concepts: A studio pedagogy for preparing tomorrow's designers. *International Journal of Architectural Research, 2*(2), 41–56.

Hall, S. (2000). Cultural identity and diaspora. In N. Mirzoeff (Ed.), *Diaspora and visual culture: Representing Africans and Jews.* London: Routledge, 21–33.

Iyer, P. (2002). *The global soul: Jet lag, shopping malls, and the search for home.* New York: Alfred A Knopf.

Karam, A. (2000). Islamisms and the decivilising processes of globalisation. In A. Arce & N. Long (Eds.), *Anthropology, development and modernities: Exploring discourses, counter-tendencies, and violence.* London: Routledge, 64–73.

Long, N. (2000). Exploring local/global transformations: A view from anthropology. In A. Arce & N. Long (Eds.), *Anthropology, development and modernities: Exploring discourses, counter-tendencies, and violence.* London: Routledge, 184–211.

Low, S., & Chambers, E. (1989). *Housing, culture, and design: A comparative perspective.* Philadelphia, PA: University of Pennsylvania Press.

Low, S., & Lawrence-Zúñiga, D. (Eds.). (2003). *The anthropology of space and place: Locating culture.* Malden, MA: Blackwell Publishers.

Mazumdar, S., Mazumdar, S., Docoyanan, F., & McLaughlin, C. (2000). Creating a sense of place: The Vietnamese-Americans and Little Saigon. *Journal of Environmental Psychology, 20,* 319–333.

Mehta, R., & Belk, R. (1991). Artifacts, identity, and transition: Favorite possessions of Indians and Indian immigrants to the United States. *The Journal of Consumer Research, 17*(4), 398–411.

Minnesota Quickfacts (2000). Retrieved February 3, 2009, from http://quickfacts.census.gov/qfd/states/27000.html

Pader, E. (1993). Spatiality and social change: Domestic space use in Mexico and the United States. *American Ethnologist, 20*(1), 114–137.

Papadopoulos, I., Lees, S., Lay, M., & Gebrehiwot, A. (2004). Ethiopian refugees in the UK: Migration, adaptation, and settlement experiences and their relevance to health. *Ethnicity and Health, 9*(1), 55–73.

Pilkington, H., Omel'chenko, E., Flynn, M., Bliudina, U., & Starkova, E. (2002). *Looking west? Cultural globalization and Russian youth culture.* University Park, PA: Penn State University Press.

Shryock, A., & Abraham, N. (2000). On margins and mainstreams. In N. Abraham and A. Shryock (Eds.). *Arab Detroit: From margin to mainstream.* Detroit, MI: Wayne State University Press, 15–35.

Tölölyan, K. (1996). Rethinking diaspora(s): Stateless power in the transnational moment. *Diaspora, 5*(1), 3–36.

U.S.A. Census Quickfacts. (2000). Retrieved February 3, 2009, from http://quickfacts.census.gov/qfd/states/00000.html

> ➤ What does *universal design* mean
> in today's globalized practice?

VALERIE FLETCHER

A GLOBAL PERSPECTIVE: UNIVERSAL DESIGN AS SOCIALLY SUSTAINABLE DESIGN

DEFINING CONCEPTS

Universal design—is it a big idea that delivers vision and substance or just accessible design dressed up to look more interesting? Is there evidence of global impact? Is there potential for igniting the kind of zeal that we witness daily for environmental sustainability? It depends on how you define it and where you look but the concept of universal design has gained slow but steady traction, globally.

What is universal design? Inclusive design? Design for all? The nomenclature is settling down after some years of mostly geographically based camps defending an interpretation peculiar to one of the terms. There is a broad acceptance today that a variety of terms share the same meaning. Choice is determined by local habit and tailoring words to resonate with different audiences.

Universal design (UD) is a way of thinking about design, a framework for the design

VALERIE FLETCHER is executive director of the Institute for Human Centered Design, an educational nonprofit organization founded in 1978 and based in Boston, Massachusetts. The Institute's mission is to advance the role of design in expanding opportunity and enhancing experience for people of all ages and abilities. Fletcher writes and lectures internationally. She currently oversees design projects ranging from the development of a global, Web-based collection of case studies of universal design in nine categories of the built environment; renovation of an historic public building for a school of architecture; and research on universal design in classrooms, workplaces, and homes. Fletcher is a special advisor to TOTO Ltd., and to the U.N. Department of Economic and Social Affairs. She has a master's degree in ethics and public policy from Harvard University. The Boston Society of Architects awarded Fletcher the Women in Design award in 2005. She's a trustee of the Boston Architectural College.

362

Variation on the Principles of Universal Design

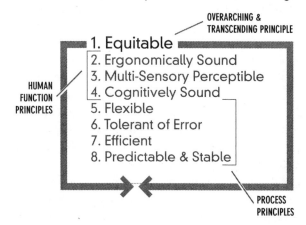

FIGURE 9.12. Principles of Universal Design with equitable use around human function principles and process principles.

of places, things, information, communication, and policy that focuses on the user, on the widest range of people operating in the widest range of situations without special or separate design. This statement builds from a simpler definition offered by Ron Mace, widely considered the father of universal design in the United States (Preiser & Ostroff, 2000).

Our organization, founded in 1978 as Adaptive Environments, chose to change its name in celebration of our 30th anniversary in 2008 and became the Institute for Human Centered Design. We chose to use plain descriptive language as a definition: universal design is human-centered design (of everything) with everyone in mind.

The original set of universal design principles was developed by a group of U.S. designers and design educators from five organizations, including ours, in 1997. The principles are copyrighted to the Center for Universal Design, School of Design, State University of North Carolina at Raleigh. The principles are used internationally, though with variations in number and specifics (see http://www.design.ncsu.edu/cud/about_ud/udprinciples.htm).

USEFUL VARIATION OF BOTH UD PRINCIPLES AND ORGANIZATION

Today, universal design—or human-centered design—includes the overarching principle of Equitable Use wrapping around the dual categories of Human Function Principles and Process Principles. This model is derived from the work of Erlandson (2008). He focuses on engineering and products, and his ideas have relevance for the interior environment. Figure 9.12 shows this relationship and further identifies the factors of each principle. The three broad factors of functional limitation are:

> Ergonomic (i.e., mobility, dexterity, strength limitations)
> Perceptible (i.e., sensory including sight, hearing, speech, touch)
> Cognitively sound (i.e., brain-based learning differences, intellectual limitations, psychiatric conditions, brain injury, and issues from simple memory loss to dementia related to aging)

In this variation of principles of universal design, the process principles, similar to the original principles of universal design, guide the iterations of the design process and name a characteristic outcome of a successful universal design. Is the design flexible enough to accommodate different needs and preferences? Has the designer anticipated a diversity of users and circumstances without jeopardizing safety? Can someone use the design without burdensome complication or excess effort? Is the design as a whole intuitive, and do the details of the design align with familiar patterns of use (e.g., location and type of controls, orientation of hot and cold). The overarching principle of *equitable* is the ultimate measure of design.

Erlandson's organization of principles addresses a central pair of vulnerabilities in universal design. First, there is an assumption that *universal design* is a synonym for *accessible design* with a little more attention to aesthetics, but still focused on addressing the dominant concerns of accessibility, i.e., people with mobility limitations, especially wheelchair users and people who are blind. The second weakness in universal design is the challenge of designing across the full spectrum of functional issues. If it's too open-ended, it becomes

meaningless—more aspiration than design strategy. The Erlandson scheme of adopting three broad categories of human function captures the majority of conditions, makes it possible for a client to appreciate the conceptual difference with accessibility, and makes it more likely that practitioners and clients appreciate the need for research and innovation to expand a repertoire of design solutions.

In addition to principles, universal design is defined by the engagement of "user/experts" (Ostroff, 1997), people who have garnered expertise from personal experience in solving problems with the environment. They may be the parents of toddlers, people with disabilities, or older people who are experiencing the functional changes in each physical system related to aging. Many interior designers, especially young interior designers, have little direct knowledge of functional limitation and the ways in which design can either impede or enhance daily life and choice. We see the same concept in the United Kingdom in the use of the term *critical users;* similar to user/experts, critical users are people with functional limitations of ability or constraints of circumstance (e.g., caregivers) who build critical awareness of design that fails (Dong, Simeon Keates, Clarkson, & Cassim, 2003).

ETIOLOGY OF THE GLOBAL MOVEMENT

A pairing of insights from experience and demographic facts gave birth to universal design globally. The experience of accessible/barrier-free policy in developed nations such as the United States, Canada, Western Europe, Australia, and New Zealand generated insight that design could do more than reduce barriers. It could enhance everyone's experience. Although an important impetus to interest in the United States and some other developed nations, there's little doubt that the most potent catalyst to attention to universal design is the aging of the world's population.

Life expectancy has been extended by an average of 30 years since 1900 in developed nations. Though far less dramatic in emerging nations, the demographic phenomenon of aging impacts the entire planet. Globally, the percentage of people aged 60 or more will triple by 2050. Even though the percentage of total population over 60 is more dramatic in wealthier developed countries, the absolute number of people over 60 years of age is larger in the developing nations because of the enormous populations of nations in the developing world (see Figure 9.13). In 2005, it was 64% of all people 60

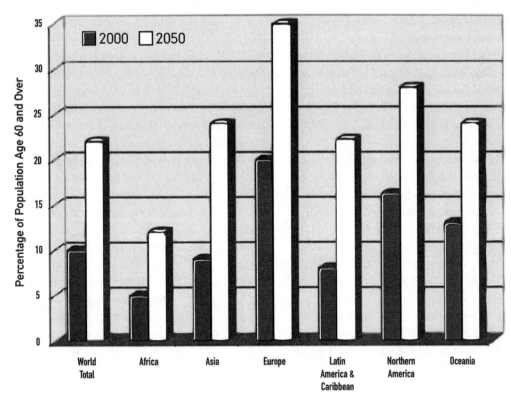

FIGURE 9.13. Percentage increase in age 60+ by region, 2000–2050 (World Population Prospects, 2006).

or older in the world and is expected to be 80% by 2050 (Executive summary, 2007). The demographic markers for development are lower fertility rates and longer lives. To appreciate the magnitude of the issue, consider that China projects over 400 million people over 60 years of age by 2050 (see http://english.peopledaily.com.cn/200605/13/eng20060513_265381.html).

INTERNATIONAL POLICY ON UNIVERSAL DESIGN

Not surprisingly, global insights and demographics have generated a set of international policies on the role of design in human experience and social participation. The World Health Organization's (WHO) new definition of disability, the International Classification of Function, Disability, and Health (WHO/ICF), issued in 2001, delivers an unparalleled call to action for interior designers. Disability was once assumed as a way to characterize a particular subset of people with largely stable limitations.

The WHO/ICF mainstreams the experience of functional limitation as intrinsic to human experience and defines disability as a contextual variable, dynamic over time, and in relation to circumstances. One is more or less disabled based on the interaction between the person and the physical, communication, information, social, and policy environments with which one interacts. The WHO/ICF called for the identification of "facilitators" that go beyond barrier removal to enhance the experience of all people and specifically referenced universal design as the most promising framework (*Towards a common language*, 2002).

The United Nations' Second World Assembly on Aging: Madrid Political Declaration and International Plan of Action 2002 addressed the potent role of design in its Priority Direction III: ensuring, enabling, and supporting environments. The Priority incorporates as assumption that we've moved beyond barrier removal and accessibility to the language of *enabling and supporting*. At that event, then U.N. Secretary General Kofi Annan embraced the vision of inclusion in his opening remarks at the Madrid event: our fundamental objective is building a society fit for all people of all ages (see http://www.unis.unvienna.org/unis/pressrels/2002/soc4603.html).

Another international policy support for universal design is the 2008 Treaty on the Human Rights of Persons with Disabilities, the 3rd Supplement to the International Human Rights Treaty that adds people with disabilities to the earlier supplements for women and children. The new treaty begins with the framework of the WHO/ICF and codifies design as a human right. Delegates from the developing world drove an agenda during the five-year-long process of drafting the treaty for a commitment to universal design as the framework that would ensure integration of inclusive design features at the point of development. Given scarce resources, they had little hope that there would ever be resources specific for meeting their needs. But, if universal design was integrated into every investment made in development, people with disabilities would benefit from a wide array of opportunities for equitable participation. As of June 17, 2009, the treaty has been signed by 139 of 192 United Nations' members, though not the United States. As a presidential candidate, Obama stated his intention to sign the treaty (Obama & Biden, n.d.) and has restated that intent as president (Calabro, 2009).

REGIONAL PRECEDENT: EUROPE, JAPAN, AUSTRALIA, DEVELOPING NATIONS

The founding of European Institute for Design and Disability (EIDD) in 1993 in Dublin, now renamed as Design for All Europe, established a uniquely design-driven vision. Though the pattern of commitment from nation to nation varies substantially across the European Union (EU), the leadership of the design community distinguishes the European position.

Laws and design guidance regarding accessibility occur at the national level throughout the EU, but the overarching vision to enhancing the quality of life through *design for all* occurs at the EU. By means of policies that have evolved in the last five years, the European Commission (2007) has established requirements for design-for-all as a condition of public purchasing. The EU funds for local planning have also mandated that a participatory planning process include people with disabilities and older people.

Throughout the EU, one can find numerous examples of the integration of design-for-all and environmentally sustainable design. Although the integration is not mandated at the EU level, there are expanding examples in single and multifamily housing, hospitality, schools, urban design, and transport in Italy, Sweden, Spain, Portugal, Germany, and throughout the United Kingdom.

The Commission on Architecture and the Built Environment in the United Kingdom (www.cabe.org.uk) offers an example of leadership on both inclusive design and environmental sustainability. Originally created by Prime Minister Tony Blair to improve the quality of design in public architecture, it has become a powerful vehicle for sharing precedent, driving policy, and spurring innovation.

Today, Japan has the world's oldest population. The population is presumed to have peaked in

2007 at 127 million for the world's second largest economy and, with steady patterns of low birth rates and long life span, expects to have a population of only 100 million by 2050, 40% of it over 60 years old. Given deep cultural values of respect for elders, accommodating an aging population is an indisputable national priority. However, the traditional assumption of family support evaporates when there are too few caretakers in relation to the size of the older population.

Japan has made an unrivaled commitment to universal design and, since 2002, leads the world in both public awareness and depth of commitment. Unlike any other nation, the Japanese business community leads the movement. Following the international universal design conference in Yokohama in 2002, Japanese business executives, government officials, scientists, and designers created the International Association for Universal Design (IAUD), which has an average of 150 dues-paying corporate members including leading Japanese-based multinational corporations. As a testament to their success, the July 2007 Nikkei Design Japanese reported that 67.5% of the Japanese population is familiar with universal design (personal communication, Yas Harai, Professor, User-Centered Design Institute, Kyushu University, Fukuoka, 2008).

Similar to the European Union, one can find frequent examples of products and built environment projects in Japan that integrate universal design and environmental sustainability. Sekisui House, the largest residential developer in Japan with over four million units sold, offers a wide variety of housing designs with a menu of environmentally sustainable and universally designed features. Sekisui runs a large public laboratory and showroom just outside of Osaka that allow visitors not only to see but also to experience design solutions. Panasonic, though not a housing developer, develops residential appliances and products that integrate green and universal design. They opened a model "Eco-UD" home in late 2005, which is open to the public and is steadily refreshed with new products and features.

Evidence builds annually of universal design as an appealing concept in the developing nations where most growth will occur in the 21st century. In the fall of 2008, Latvia and Cuba, poor nations with educated populations, hosted conferences on universal design. Throughout Latin America, and most especially in Brazil, municipal policy promoting universal design for all new construction projects aligns with a political vision of social equity. Pockets of leadership in India are establishing universal design portfolios of projects that include both new construction and renovation. The U.N. has adopted universal design as policy for post-conflict reconstruction. The new U.N. Treaty on the Human Rights of People with Disabilities creates a diverse and widespread demand for practical information about universal design that poses a dissemination challenge that will permit building on good precedents rather than reinventing the wheel.

UNIVERSAL DESIGN INTEGRATED INTO SOCIAL SUSTAINABILITY

Over the last 15 years, universal design has achieved a slow but steady increase in awareness; however, outside of Japan, it remains largely a niche concept still conflated with accessible design. Over a little longer period and most especially in the last five years, we have witnessed an extraordinary embrace of sustainability as central to good design. In much of the world, sustainability is understood to be the triple bottom line of environmental, social, and economic sustainability. Even the American Institute of Architects' (AIA) Committee on the Environment (COTE) envisions a multifaceted understanding: Sustainability envisions the enduring prosperity of all living things. Sustainable design seeks to create communities,

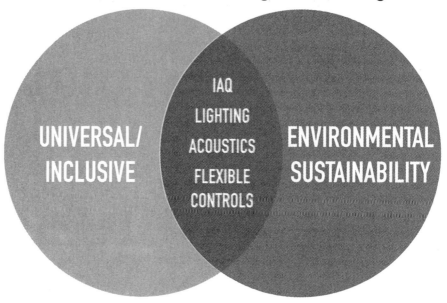

With Increasing Attention to Improving
Human Health and Well-Being in Green Design

UNIVERSAL/
INCLUSIVE

IAQ
LIGHTING
ACOUSTICS
FLEXIBLE
CONTROLS

ENVIRONMENTAL
SUSTAINABILITY

Significant and Growing Overlap

FIGURE 9.14. Integration of universal and sustainable design.

buildings, and products that contribute to this vision (see http://www.aia.org/practicing/groups/kc/AIAS074684). The United States tends toward a narrower view equating "green" and sustainability.

It is time to consider the strategic value and practical opportunity of bringing universal design under the tent of sustainability (see Figure 9.14). Socially sustainable design, where it is not endorsed as a summons to equitable design, tends to be the "mother and apple pie" element of the sustainability tripod—full of vague good feeling, but lacking substance. Universal design

is real and meaty and is responsive to the truth that no design in the 21st century can be sustainable without attention to the facts of human diversity in age and ability.

In a current project to create a universal design global collection of case studies in the built environment, we find that the best examples seamlessly combine a commitment to environmental sustainability and universal design. We intend and expect that the inspiration of those good stories will drive fresh thinking and a new excitement about the power of design as a transformative power in people's lives.

REFERENCES

Calabro, T. (2009). *Pittsburgh stands in world disability rights spotlight: Breaking down barriers.* Retrieved June 17, 2009, from http://www.post-gazette.com/pg/09168/977756-114.stm

Durocher, J. (2009, March). Presentation at the Convention on the Rights of Persons with Disabilities/Legal Ramifications and Trends. Indiana University. Indianapolis, IN.

Dong, H., Simeon Keates, P., Clarkson, J., & Cassim, J. (Eds.). (2002). Implementing inclusive design: The discrepancy between theory and practice. *Universal Access Theoretical Perspectives, Practice, and Experience.* ERCIM International Workshop on User Interfaces for All. Berlin: Springer, 106–117.

Erlandson, R. (2008). *Universal and accessible design for products, services, and processes.* Boca Raton: CRC Press, Taylor & Francis Group.

European Commission. (2007, December). Policy M/420 EN Brussels, standardisation mandate to CEN, CENELEC, and ETSI in support of European accessibility requirements for public procurement in the built environment.

Executive Summary. (2007, December). *The official world population estimates and projections (2006 revision).* New York: The Population Division of the Department of Economic and Social Affairs of the United Nations Secretariat.

Obama, B., & Biden, J. (n.d.). *Barack Obama and Joe Biden's plan to empower Americans with disabilities.* Retrieved June 17, 2009, from http://www.barackobama.com/pdf/DisabilityPlanFactSheet.pdf

Ostroff, E. (1997). Mining our natural resources: The user as expert. INNOVATION. *The Quarterly Journal of the Industrial Designers Society of America, 16*(1), 27–30.

Preiser, W., & Ostroff, E. (2001). Dedication. *Universal design handbook.* New York: McGraw Hill.

Towards a common language for functioning, disability and health ICF. (2002). Geneva: World Health Organization.

World Population Prospects. (2006). *Volume II: Sex and age.* The Population Division, Department of Economic and Social Affairs. New York: United Nations Secretariat.

> With such strong outside forces influencing the way the interior design profession is evolving, shouldn't we be more critically examining what knowledge . . . and type of educational model will best prepare entry-level interior designers to address the future needs of the profession?
>
> —Allison Carll White & Ann Whiteside Dickson

CONFRONTING EDUCATIONAL CHALLENGES

OVERVIEW Interior design education is confronting several issues that will shape the future of the profession. Two of these issues are the focus of this chapter: the shortage of educators and new models for educating practitioners and educators. Authors of this chapter bring to light these issues and propose some clarifications, solutions, and challenges for us to discuss.

The shortage of qualified interior design educators is documented by Georgy Olivieri, who represents an engaged practitioner viewpoint. She recognizes that the shortage will impact the entire profession, not just educators. Denise Guerin offers a process for educators to use with administrators that supports a different definition of "qualified" and supports practitioners as educators. Jane Kucko focuses on the role educators play in shaping people as well as practitioners; the role of graduate education in shaping interior design educators; and the role of master's degrees in shaping the livelihood of the profession.

Responding to the issue of new knowledge in practice, Tiiu Poldma suggests a new educational model that prepares entry-level interior designers for a critical thinking approach to practice. Allison Carll White and Ann Whiteside Dickson present an education model that increases the amount of education required to attain the first-professional degree based on the increased knowledge required for practice.

John Weigand and Buie Harwood clarify the differences among the many types of master's degrees in interior design and introduce a model for a master of interior design as the first-professional degree. Margaret Portillo offers the hybrid MID degree, which embraces students with bachelor's degrees in majors that are not related to design.

The last two essays focus on the administration of educational programs and support interdisciplinary and collaborative approaches to all design education. Henry Hildebrandt discusses an integrative and entrepreneurial approach to education and scholarship. Jo Ann Asher Thompson suggests that now is the time for academic institutions to boldly embrace interdisciplinary design education. This chapter has new roles and ideas for practitioners and new educational models for educators and students. Let's prepare future interior designers for the practice world that they will enter!

GEORGY OLIVIERI

WHO IS PREPARING NEW PRACTITIONERS?

Can you imagine the dilemma of design firms as we run out of qualified interior design educators? Practitioners in firms are already working harder, spending more of their valuable time to integrate interior design graduates into their practices. Because of the shortage of interior design educators, any new entrants to the interior design profession have been educated in overcrowded classes and programs. Currently, there are studio classes, within highly regarded interior design programs, reported to have a 36:1 student to teacher ratio. The situation is quickly deteriorating, moving from bad to worse. Several industry supporters have answered the initial question with a resounding, "No!" (See Figure 10.1.)

GEORGY OLIVIERI, MBA, LEED® AP, is the founder of GO Initiatives. She has a BA in interior design and has served in leadership roles within the built environment industry and the interior design profession. She is a tenured advocate for the value of design and interior design education. She is the initiator of the Kimball Office Work Group on Sustaining Interior Design Education. Olivieri has coauthored the book *Design Does Matter* and authored numerous articles that were published in IIDA's *Perspective, Interiors & Sources, Contract, PR News,* and *Going Green: Case Studies in Outstanding Green Business Practices*. She also is a frequent contributor to the design industry periodical *officeinsight*.

SHORTAGE OF QUALIFIED INTERIOR DESIGN EDUCATORS

The interior design profession needs to wake up and smell the coffee. *We are running out of qualified interior design educators.* It is a fact

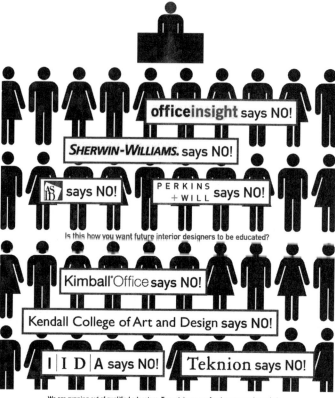

FIGURE 10.1. Firms, industry, and organizations who have said "no" to educator shortage.

documented by survey data collected and analyzed by the Interior Design Educators Council (IDEC) (2007) and the Council for Interior Design Accreditation (CIDA). Reasons for this shortage include the aging and retirement of baby-boomer educators, increased number of students, institutional growth within interior design programs, and newly developed institutions and specialty programs.

Currently, 50% of all interior design programs have open positions (121 at the time of survey Fall, 2007); 88% will have openings within three to five years (167+ positions will be open); 50% of respondents have conducted searches for more than one year; and typical size of pools of viable applicants range from one to six for 85% of respondents with 48% having only one to three

persons in their pools (Interior Design Educators Council, 2007). The interior design profession has reached an educational crisis brought on by the shortage of qualified educators. Most practitioners and leaders in the profession are unaware of this shortage and its impact on the future of the interior design profession.

Members of the interior design academy are all too familiar with this situation, having dealt with its challenges for years. Students and interior design graduates have known the problem. They personally experienced overcrowded classrooms and frustrations being taught by teachers with master's degrees or PhD's in disciplines *other* than interior design. Many institutions require a minimum of a master's or PhD to teach in any discipline on a full-time basis, including interior design. How many interior design practitioners do you know with an advanced degree? There aren't many.

Almost two years ago, during a design association board meeting including representatives from interior design education, practice, and industry, an update was shared about the declining pool of qualified interior design educators. It was accepted as matter of fact by educators and interior design program chairs in the room. But, it startled other board members from practice and the built-environment industry. Bringing them to their feet with alarm, it sounded a wake-up call for our profession.

As one of those surprised by the news, I could not believe that this problem, a threat to the success and future of the interior design profession, was not communicated with other stakeholders in the industry. Quite frankly, I was outraged. How could educators not have told practitioners that we are running out of qualified educators? How could practitioners not have asked, keeping a pulse on education, the very source of their business enterprise? How could the two groups not have communicated? Unfortunately, the answer was simple. They have stayed in their separate silos, worlds apart from each other.

To sustain the profession of interior design, we must tear down these silos. The relationship between interior design education and interior design practice is mutually dependent. We need to think of it as a closed-loop process. Educators cannot affect the resolution of the declining pool of qualified interior design educators alone. They have worked to build awareness within the academy; by generating significant white papers, defining the problem through research, providing recommendations for advanced degrees in interior design, petitioning institutions to accept less than the master's degree requirement for part-time educators, and recruiting practitioners as potential new educators. The result of their efforts established an excellent foundation for potential resolution. But, acting alone, they have not effectively stemmed the tide. And, the situation continues to worsen.

I challenge practitioners and interior design firms to recognize their responsibility to "feed" the educational process. How dare they complain about the current skill set of interior design graduates entering the profession if they have not assumed an active role in providing students with the valued benefit of practitioners' experience? If interior design firms do not recognize, reward, and encourage their talented practitioners to secure advanced degrees and teach interior design in both full-time and part-time capacities, how can our profession survive? Do we need to remind them of the existing threat posed by others ready to assume our role?

Interior design firms sometimes subsidize master of business administration (MBA) degrees for their top performers. However, I have yet to witness any interior design firm provide support for an employee's endeavor to earn an advanced degree that will further employees' professional development and prepare them to teach interior design. I know of one instance where a leading firm denied a request for funding of an advanced degree for this purpose. They provided only a wish of good luck.

THE BEGINNING OF A SOLUTION

The solution lies within a three-legged stool approach, integrating the shared actions of interior design educators, practitioners, and industry associates working together against this threat to the interior design profession. In the fall of 2008, a working group of representatives from all three groups was sponsored by Kimball Office with a charge of making recommendations to affect a solution. The initiative, shepherded by IDEC, brought together a group of five people selected from a large pool of qualified candidates. The group assumed responsibility for defining the problem and developing proposals designed for maximum impact. They were named the Kimball Office Work Group (KOWG), and their full report is available at http://www.goinitiatives.com.

The result was the creation of an overall strategy for resolution with a five-year implementation plan entitled "Sustaining Interior Design Education." The emphasis shifted reporting on the declining pool of qualified interior design educators to development of a road map for sustaining interior design education.

The KOWG (2008) created a vision statement, as follows: "Our preferred vision is that interior design stakeholders mutually invest resources of time and money to ensure the future of the Interior Design profession by providing an appropriate number of qualified educators via the foundation of robust education" (p. 1).

CHALLENGES

The group then identified the main challenges in reaching this vision:

1. There is insufficient knowledge and communication exchange between stakeholders including:
   - Little knowledge among practitioners about the shortage of qualified educators
   - Lack of data dissemination
   - Lack of knowledge of financial impact of interior design educator shortage on all stakeholders
   - Continued development of silos among associations, school curricula, interior design schools, profession, etc.

2. There is insufficient knowledge and communication about interior design education as a career including:
   - Practitioner-educator career path often not discussed in first-professional degree programs
   - Graduate education frequently not discussed as a stage in the practitioners' career path
   - Few interior design practitioners with advanced degrees
   - Practitioners lack clarity on what is graduate education
   - Graduate interior design not valued by design firms via increased compensation, position, or even development support
   - Practitioners lack knowledge of how to access graduate programs
   - Practitioners unaware of how to become an educator
   - Practitioners generally lack awareness and understanding of nuances in teaching positions

3. Institutional (colleges and universities) roadblocks exist that are both perceived and real including:
   - Lack of institutional valuing or acceptance of a diverse educational team
   - Inequity of facilities and other resources compared to other programs
   - Too many students for the number of faculty (full-time and part-time)
   - Addition of many part-time faculty who only teach and do not contribute to scholarship, do not contribute to program administration and engagement, and who must be supervised by full-time faculty to maintain consistency
   - Perception that recruiting students is unnecessary due to current demand
   - Inequality for interior design educators within academia in terms of pay and workload, grant money available, etc.
   - Emphasis on object over design thinking

4. There are perceptions and myths about interior design including:
   - Public and related design community lack a common understanding of what interior design is
   - False perceptions of interior design have been created by media, such as HGTV
   - Belief that educators' base pay/salary is significantly inferior to practitioners
   - Belief by the public and some practitioners that one teaches because one cannot practice
   - Belief among educators that practitioners don't want to leave design practice
   - Lack of knowledge of available sources for graduate degree funding
   - Lack of demographic diversity within interior design practice and education

STRATEGIC GOALS

The KOWG members reached two overarching goals after analyzing the situation and challenges:

STRATEGIC GOAL 1

Promote interior design education by developing ways for practitioners to reach students via classroom teaching and other learning opportunities.

   - Identify diverse credentials of educators that fit institutional needs to bring practitioners into the classroom at a consistent level,
   - Develop and disseminate information about methods by which interior design practitioners can contribute to the body of knowledge,
   - Develop and disseminate information about graduate programs that prepare practitioners to teach, and
   - Create relationships that foster understanding of students', educators', and practitioners' needs.

STRATEGIC GOAL 2

Develop a communication plan for practitioners and all stakeholders to learn about the lack of qualified interior design educators, careers in higher education, and graduate education opportunities.

   - Create connections for educators and practitioners, providing personalized coaching assistance on how to move into education.

The KOWG report continues with a full listing of recommendations and tactics to support these strategic goals. This report has been shared with the Issues Forum—an informal association of the American Society of Interior Designers (ASID), CIDA, the Interior Designers of Canada (IDC), IDEC, the International Interior Design Association (IIDA), and the National Council for Interior Design Qualification (NCIDQ). This group is essential to continued focus on sustaining the pool of qualified interior design educators.

I was one of the people who stood up at the initial design association board meeting, shocked by the news of the declining pool of qualified interior design educators. For almost two years, I have served as a volunteer organizer, spokesperson, fund-raiser, and marketer, authoring eight articles regarding this important cause. Having witnessed the response from all groups, I have two very different reactions. I continue to be amazed by the behaviors of educators, practitioners, and associations maintaining separate silos. How can they feel their interests and mutual survival are different? In the business world, this is a supply chain relationship: education feeds practice and practice feeds education with experience.

Many members of the built environment industry have called to express their thoughts. A good number of architects have initiated contact. They are more than happy to help educate interior design students, even though they admit to not having an interior design education or practice experience. I found it bothersome when one architect said it is much easier to teach interior design to architects. Many architects have advanced degrees (e.g., MArch) and, therefore, meet the academy's qualifications of a master's degree and therefore can teach interior design students. Should we relinquish the future of our profession to architects?

I have been encouraged by positive responses from people determined to make a difference. One day after publishing an article in *officeinsight*, over 170 postings on Facebook were made by young interior designers and students supporting the cause. Individual practitioners have reached out for help in moving into education. Interior design firms have requested help for their members seeking to become educators. Industry partners have made tremendous monetary contributions to help support this initiative. IDEC's KOWG has worked to aggressively move forward with strategies for resolution.

Hopefully, this wake-up call will serve to bring together all three legs of the stool: educators, practitioners, and professional design associations to sustain interior design education. IDEC leadership has willingly assumed this role, now it is our responsibility to support them. IDEC has assumed "Sustaining Interior Design Education" as a key mantra for their organization. Their leadership has my hope and full support. We have a lot to lose and more to gain.

REFERENCES

Dohr, J. H. (2007). Continuing the dialogue: Interior design graduate education inquiry and scholarly cultures. *Journal of Interior Design, 33*(1), v–xvi.

Guerin, D., & Thompson, J. (2004). Interior design education in the 21st century: An educational transformation. *Journal of Interior Design, 30*(1), 1–12.

Interior Design Educators Council. (2007). *Quantitative data supporting need for new strategies.* Retrieved February 5, 2009, from http://www.idec.org

Kimball Office Work Group. (2008). *The Kimball Office Work Group report: Sustaining interior design education.* Retrieved February 5, 2009, from http://www.goinitiatives.com

Olivieri, G. (2007, May). *Call to action: Dialogue about sustaining the future of interior design education.* Retrieved February 8, 2009, from http://officesight.com

Olivieri, G. (2008, April). *What ever happened? From declining pool of interior design educators to enhancing the pool of educators.* Retrieved February 5, 2009, from http://officesight.com

Olivieri, G. (2008, November). *Ah-ha moment on Facebook.* Retrieved February 9, 2009, from http://officesight.com

> Are there ways in which the shortage
> of interior design educators can be addressed
> in the short term? The long term?

DENISE A. GUERIN

REDEFINING "QUALIFIED"

Interior design education is facing a severe shortage of qualified interior design educators. For the last 8 to 10 years, there have been over 100 interior design faculty positions (generally full-time), open annually, across North America; most of these positions go unfilled (Interior Design Educators Council, 2007). Reasons for this shortage include the increasing number of students who are interested in interior design as a career and the subsequent increasing enrollment in existing programs, causing an increase in the number of faculty required to teach. The increased numbers of students have also encouraged more higher education institutions to offer a degree in interior design, again, reflecting an increasing need for more faculty to teach in these new programs. Next, a significant number of current faculty are baby boomers and are, or will be, retiring. Finally, because the first-professional degree (the one generally required to practice) for interior design is the bachelor's degree, we have few practitioners who have a master's degree,

DENISE A. GUERIN, PhD, FASID, FIDEC, IIDA, is a Morse-Alumni distinguished professor and director of interior design, University of Minnesota. She earned bachelor's, master's, and a PhD in interior design. She teaches undergraduate studios, ethics and professional practice, and interior design research methods and advises both master's and PhD students. Guerin's research focuses on post-occupancy evaluation in sustainable buildings and implementation of evidence-based design in practice. She has served as president and vice president of the IDEC Foundation, on several task forces for NCIDQ, and as editor of the *Journal of Interior Design*. Currently, she serves as a CIDA site visitor, actively participates in Minnesota's interior design practice legislation efforts, and is president-elect of IDEC. She is coauthor of *The Interior Design Profession's Body of Knowledge: Its Definition and Documentation,* 2001 and 2005, and is coordinator of InformeDesign®. Guerin is a recipient of IIDA's Michael Tatum Excellence in Education Award, NCIDQ's Louis Tregue Award, and ASID's Distinguished Educator for 2007.

379

unlike related fields such as architecture and landscape architecture where the first-profession degree is typically at the master's level. The significance of this is that institutions generally require faculty to have a master's degree to teach, even part-time. This lack in supply of interior design educators with master's degrees is being filled by architects who have master of architecture (MArch) degrees. This credential might be appropriate if they have extensive interior design experience.

The point is, no matter how we got here, and no matter who is filling the gap, we have a problem and we need to solve it fast—but in a way that is logical and accepted by administrators in colleges and universities. One part of that solution is to redefine the idea of a master's degree as the minimum education requirement for teaching, especially for part-time faculty, in lieu of extensive interior design practice experience. Let's take a look at why that is a requirement so we can understand how to make a change.

WHY IS THE MASTER'S DEGREE AN INSTITUTIONAL REQUIREMENT TO TEACH?

The reasons behind the requirement of a master's degree as a teaching credential by most institutions rest with institutional accreditation. Higher education institutions, whether public or private, are generally accredited by regional accreditation agencies such as the North Central Association Commission on Accreditation and School Improvement (NCACASI) or the Southern Association of Colleges and Schools Council on Accreditation and School Improvement (SACSCASI). One of the accreditation standards is related to credentials of "qualified faculty." Indicators of this standard require that, at a minimum, faculty education is a master's degree. Therefore, most administrators and faculty include the master's degree as a minimum education requirement when developing a position description and searching for new faculty. Some schools employ this restriction when searching for any position, including part-time, temporary, full-time, or tenure-track ones.

In academia, the graduate degree, even for part-time faculty, brings greater prestige to the faculty position, program, and college; assures administrators that scholarship can be addressed by the faculty; and outside agencies see a credible, valid program. Earning a master's degree in your field suggests you have adequate content knowledge of your discipline, and you have moved beyond entry-level and gained a level of expertise in some aspect of your discipline. Most institutions assume the additional expertise is in the area of scholarship, thereby beginning to prepare you to do research or creative production. It also provides you with a credential that is helpful when applying for grant funding, which brings money into the institution and the program. The PhD assures administrators that you have content knowledge, research expertise, a research agenda, and a greater potential to secure grant funding for research projects.

A SHORT-TERM SOLUTION

I contend that a closer reading of the accrediting bodies' standards, e.g., NCACASI and SACSCASI, will show that the master's degree is suggested or required for the *majority* of positions, not necessarily *all* positions, and that there can be *extenuating* or documented *special*

circumstances. Interior design faculty must make a case to their administrators that having experienced interior design practitioners in the classroom, without a master's degree, especially for part-time teaching positions, is important to program excellence. Extensive interior design practice experience (to be defined by the interior design program) can and does, in some cases, meet the extenuating/special circumstances indicator. We know we need faculty in the classroom who have interior design practice experience to support a first-professional degree program. We need to redefine how this experience is valued by administrators so that it can serve as a component of the education and experience credential that underpins qualifications. We must redefine "qualified."

In 2007, five interior design practitioners and educators were appointed to a working group, which was funded by Kimball Office and called the Kimball Office Work Group (KOWG). They developed five recommendations, strategies for implementation, and budgets. (You can read more about this group and all recommendations in Olivieri's essay that precedes this one. The name of this initiative is now Sustaining Interior Design Education, or SIDE.) All recommendations from this report and progress made can be viewed at http://www.idec.org/careercenter/becomeide.php.

In this essay, I am offering a short-term solution to SIDE's Recommendation 1: *identify credentials for several types of ID education positions*—in a way that reflects the need to have experienced interior design practitioners in the classroom (whether or not they have master's degrees). Administrators are looking for ways to creatively solve their shortage of interior design educators, so let's give them a logical method by which to act. In other words, let's help academic institutions develop a way to document the level of qualifications required for each type of faculty position that they are trying to fill, i.e., part-time, temporary, full-time, tenure track, etc.

I developed the Interior Design Educator Credential Matrix (see Table 10.1, following page) to be used to define the qualifications are for each type of open position a program has. This idea was first discussed and published in 2007 (see Guerin, 2007), and is being

reintroduced here with expanded dialogue. This Matrix can be used immediately by interior design educators and administrators as they develop their strategic plans for faculty positions. Working together, they can develop the mix of credentials that is a good fit for their institution and program.

The Matrix includes Institution Type, which defines types of degrees offered. This generally determines the Role of the Educator including the teaching requirements such as history, healthcare studio, or lighting. Next, the Matrix includes Scholarship Expectations, which may include basic and applied research and/or creative work. For the purpose of this framework, scholarship is defined to include faculty contribution to interior design's body of knowledge as determined by the institution's governance. Scholarship expectations may be defined by the program in a way that allows practitioners to bring their "lessons learned" in practice into the classroom and disseminate them in a way that adds to the body of knowledge. This will take mentoring by existing program faculty, who will also learn from practitioners and vice versa.

Teaching and scholarship roles then should determine the Degree Required; the extent of Experience Required is then identified to reflect the specifics of the educator's role. Also, please note that *all* positions require the successful completion of the National Council for Interior Design Qualification exam.

All institution types and mixes may not be reflected here. The examples shown in the Matrix are limited by my experience at two institution types, a teaching university and a research university. This Matrix can be a starting point for faculty at any institution type; I invite you to continue further development of this matrix for your institution and position type to redefine "qualified." It can offer academic institutions a logical method for addressing the shortage of interior design educators

TABLE 10.1
INTERIOR DESIGN EDUCATOR CREDENTIAL MATRIX

INSTITUTION TYPE	ROLE OF EDUCATOR	SCHOLARSHIP EXPECTATIONS	DEGREE REQUIRED	EXPERIENCE REQUIRED
Research and Teaching • First- and post-professional degree in ID offered; PhD offered	• Teach in first-professional degree program • Teach in post-professional degree program (MA, MS, PhD) • Scholarship • Outreach • Service	• Research grants • Refereed publications • Creative scholarship • Refereed presentations • Other as determined by institutional needs	• PhD or post-professional master's	• NCIDQ certificate holder (requires minimum of two years' practice experience)
Teaching • First- and post-professional degree in ID offered	• Teach in first-professional degree program • Research or creative scholarship/practice • Service	• Creative scholarship • Refereed presentations • Other as determined by institutional needs	• First-professional degree in interior design and post-professional degree	• NCIDQ certificate holder • Contributions to the profession via practice or service • Excellence in design practice (to be determined by institution)
Teaching • First-professional degree in ID offered	• Teach in first-professional degree program • Creative scholarship/practice • Service	• Continued practice • Other as determined by institutional needs	• First-professional degree in interior design	• NCIDQ certificate holder • Contributions to the profession via practice or service • Excellence in design practice (to be determined by institution)
Teaching • Associate's degree or certificate offered in ID	• Teach in pre-professional degree program • Creative scholarship/practice • Service	• Continued practice • Other as determined by institutional needs	• First-professional degree in interior design	• NCIDQ certificate holder • Excellence in design practice (to be determined by institution)

due to the lack of interior design practitioners who hold a master's degree. By defining the mix of education and experience with the role and expectations of the institution, an alternative way to determine an educator's credentials can be determined.

A BRIEF CASE STUDY

At the University of Minnesota, we have made the case for extensive interior design practice experience in lieu of a master's degree for part-time faculty. We also have architects with MArch degrees and full-time faculty with doctoral degrees, e.g., PhD and EdD. This is the mix that is the right fit for our program. The journey to develop our balance is what led to the development of this Matrix, although it wasn't around when we began this effort. I hope it can help other programs to move along a bit faster than we did!

Because of the need for practice-experienced faculty in the classroom (an extenuating circumstance) and the shortage of interior design educators (a special circumstance), we sought a way to not be limited by administration's requirements to hire interior design faculty with a minimum of a master's degree; we made a case for experience. We searched out the data upon which administrators made their decisions. We reviewed applicable accreditation standards; searched for documentation that allowed interpretation of those data, i.e., *most* faculty needed a minimum of a master's degree; and developed the position description(s) to meet the experiential nature of a first-professional degree in interior design.

We have also defined our full-time, tenure-track interior design faculty position to require the minimum of a master's degree, extensive interior design practice experience, and the ability to contribute to scholarship, either research or creative production. This is a far different position and type of faculty than is generally accepted at Tier One Research Institutions. Gaining approval for these credentials for part-time and full-time positions took our efforts over time, with our department head's support, to convince our college- and university-level administrators that these credentials were imperative to success in the interior design classroom, especially the studio. The point is, we defined our needs via the position and expectations, then defined the credentials that would support such a position, which is done whenever there is an open faculty position. What is different is the use of the Matrix to make the case for redefining qualifications.

It is a logical path, and we found our administration receptive. As a result, we have about half of our part-time faculty with bachelor's degrees in interior design complemented by extensive practice experience. And, when we have need of additional part-time faculty, we are able to hire those without master's degrees but with extensive experience. We also have a full-time, tenure-track position available that has as its minimum requirements: a master's degree, extensive interior design practice experience, and an ability to contribute to creative scholarship or research. Both of these strategies have opened up the pool of "qualified" educators, and because more part-time faculty are interior design practitioners, we have increased interaction among practitioners, students, and faculty.

SUMMARY AND CONCLUSION

It is the mix of degree and practice experience defined by the role of the educator (i.e., studio responsibility, graduate advising) within a specific institution type that reflects the goodness of fit of any educator at any given point in time. And, in a single program, there must be a balance of different degree types and disciplinary backgrounds so that all purposes of the institution and curriculum are served. Using this Matrix is an alternative way to redefine "qualified" credentials of interior design educators. At first examination, do not be dissuaded by your institution's practices, investigate further, and start a dialogue. Make the case based on goodness of fit and program excellence.

The additional benefit of broadening faculty qualifications is that more practitioners will be in the classroom increasing interaction among faculty, students, and practitioners. Also, practitioners may find out just how much they like teaching. In the long term, this may be a solution to the declining pool of qualified educators.

REFERENCES

Guerin, D. (2007). Continuing the dialogue by defining "qualified." *Journal of Interior Design, 33*(2), 11–14.

Interior Design Educators Council. (2007). *Quantitative data supporting need for new strategies.* Retrieved April 16, 2009, from http://www.idec.org

> How does the world (clients, the public) benefit from a person with a master's degree in interior design? With a bachelor's degree in interior design? What is the downside?

JANE K. KUCKO

BECOMING AN INTERIOR DESIGN EDUCATOR: THE ROLE OF THE MASTER'S DEGREE

The week had been challenging with the intensity of students completing their final design projects; the inherent "when it rains it pours" cliché, which we all understand; and the onset of the U.S. holiday season. As final exam week approached, a non-traditional student (an individual returning to university after years of another career) came to my office asking for advice. The conversation evolved from providing encouragement into one of those meaningful conversations that occurs only on rare occasions.

In the midst of the pressure of school, this individual was also attempting to balance a job and a personal life. After a somewhat lengthy conversation, the student looked me in the eye and asked, "What is it like being in the position to shape, mold, and educate young, beautiful minds?" I was spellbound as I pondered the question. I loved teaching—it has been my career. I answered the question by explaining that indeed it is an incredible opportunity

JANE K. KUCKO, PhD, FIDEC, currently serves as faculty for the interior design program at Texas Christian University and director for the Center for International Studies: TCU Abroad, where she oversees the development of international opportunities for students and faculty. She is also an NCIDQ certificate holder. A long-standing member of IDEC, Kucko has served the profession through various leadership roles in IDEC, including the role of president in 2007–2008. She previously served on CIDA's Accreditation Commission. Kucko's leadership for CIDA, IDEC, and various other leadership roles led her to becoming an IDEC fellow in 2002. Her emphasis on international education led to a collaborative effort between five North American institutions to develop a model for international distance learning. Other areas of scholarship include the work of E. Fay Jones and narrative research on North Texas quiltmakers. Kucko is also a quilter and has won various awards at North Texas quilt shows.

to be in the academy that fosters creativity, exploration, and discovery. As educators, we are fortunate to be in an environment of teaching young minds and developing our future interior designers. And yet, teaching is a lofty responsibility. Of course interior design educators' goal is to prepare future designers according to Council for Interior Design Accreditation (CIDA) *Professional Standards*, to become a National Council for Interior Design Qualification (NCIDQ) certificate holder, and fulfill qualifications to meet state regulatory requirements. However, beyond these professional requirements, one's education is an optimal time to explore, question, and create without parameters that will otherwise exist from the moment one is professionally employed.

The question posed by my student has remained with me for several years and, honestly, there isn't a week that goes by that I don't think about the incredible role interior design educators play in developing the interior design profession. Interior design education is an extraordinary profession that fosters the morphing of education with practice.

As recently revealed by Olivieri (2008) and the Kimball Office Working Group (IDEC, 2008), there is a serious need for qualified interior design educators. This recent attention to interior design educators has brought to light the question: what does "qualified" mean? In the midst of a variety of different institutional models (Guerin, 2008), ultimately educators need to define long-term goals and frame their credentials accordingly. An equally important point is that interior design education must be composed of a team of educators representing varied experience in education, practice, and research in order to engage and prepare students for an interdisciplinary world. The purpose of this essay is to shed light on the rationale for requiring interior design educators to hold a minimum of a master's degree to teach interior design.

WHAT IS A QUALIFIED INTERIOR DESIGN EDUCATOR?

The Interior Design Educators Council (IDEC) tenure and promotion document (IDEC, 1993) describes several issues related to teaching in higher education including the minimum requirement of a master's degree *and* a minimum of two years of professional experience to be tenurable. Furthermore, IDEC's tenure and promotion document states that interior design education should be composed of educators who represent an array of professional design experience (IDEC, 1993). For more than 20 years, institutions of higher learning have recognized that educators with master's degrees frequently bring practical experience into the classroom—a critical component of students' education. In addition to IDEC's tenure and promotion document, accrediting agencies such as the Southern Association on Commission on Colleges (http://www.sacscoc.org/about.asp) maintain master's degree accreditation requirements for faculty teaching in accredited colleges and universities. You may ask, however, what about those of us who have bachelor's degrees in interior design and years of practical experience? Why does the academy generally refuse to accept these professional credentials as equivalent to a master's degree? To answer the question, the role of the master's degree will be presented, followed by five reasons that explain the importance of the master's degree:

1. Building a bridge between teaching and practice
2. Learning evidence-based design
3. Development of an area of expertise
4. The technology revolution
5. Today's student culture

These five points will be discussed to answer the question: Why is a master's degree required to teach interior design?

TABLE 10.2
BECOMING AN INTERIOR DESIGN EDUCATOR

Qualifications	Minimum of two years' practice experience plus a master's degree

PURPOSE OF POST-PROFESSIONAL MASTER'S DEGREE	
To prepare the practitioner for teaching in higher education.	Master's degree teaches how to: • Bridge practice with education • Learn evidence based design • Develop an area of expertise • Address the technology revolution • Teach today's college student

THE ROLE OF THE MASTER'S DEGREE

The academic environment is appealing because teaching provides an opportunity to create, design, and share expertise in collaboration with students. For many educators, teaching brings back the reason why we entered design in the first place—to create enriching interior environments. The design studio fosters creativity, exploration, and dialogue. The creative synergy that evolves in the classroom is stimulating and today's college student is capable of creating innovative and effective design solutions to challenging and global problems.

A post-professional master's degree in interior design prepares the practitioner for teaching in higher education. Institutions of higher learning embrace individuals entering education from practice. The practical knowledge gained from the real world is critical to students' education. However, the master's degree is equally important for the individual to authentically develop an area of scholarly expertise; discover the culture of the academy, which is quite different than practice; and learn to teach in a transformed educational environment.

Although positions such as instructor and "professional in residence" (rather than tenure track) have begun to emerge in higher education, the master's degree remains the predominant minimum requirement to teach in a full-time, tenure-track capacity in higher education (see Table 10.2). Beyond the reality of this requirement, holding a master's degree is a necessary credential and incredible journey in order to be an effective interior design educator.

BRIDGING TEACHING AND PRACTICE

Effective teaching requires substance, instructing students to become consumers of knowledge, and bridging the gap between theory and practice (Leblanc, 1998). Pursuing a graduate degree prepares the future interior design educator for the responsibility of teaching beyond a practical approach. Graduate education provides the venue for interior design educators to go beyond practical application and be visionary consumers of design theory that guide us through process and interdisciplinary relationships impacting design (Leblanc, 1998). Effective teaching must also act as a liaison between the academy and the design community. Professional practice experience provides the connection with design practice while the master's degree is important to advance one's education beyond practical application, understand the academy, and learn to teach.

The art of teaching requires the educator to be able to utilize models of teaching that inspire students while building the bridge between practice and education. One example, the refraction model (Pagano & Roselle, 2007), requires students to understand the differences between reflection (subject matter, e.g., interior design), critical thinking (practice), and refraction (context). The master's degree allows future educators to build upon their practical knowledge by exploring design theory as it relates to practice and, most importantly, how to create pedagogical strategies to teach interior design.

LEARNING EVIDENCE-BASED DESIGN

The definition of interior design in part states that interior designers create design solutions that enhance the quality of life and culture of the occupants (NCIDQ, 2004). According to the definition, interior designers must create interior environments that respond to the social context of the project and are based upon research and analysis. Furthermore, "Standard 4. Design Process" of CIDA's *2009 Professional Standards* states that students must be able to "gather appropriate and necessary information and research findings to solve the problem (evidence-based design)" (p. 13). Harwood and Weigand (2007) called for graduate programs specializing in evidence-based design that bridge the gap between design education and practice. Evidence-based design (which is also prevalent in other professions such as nursing and engineering) requires the interior design educator to teach students the application of research to the design solution. Obtaining a master's degree provides the necessary research skills to develop a grounded approach to evidence-based design, which is then integrated into undergraduate education.

DEVELOPMENT OF AN AREA OF EXPERTISE

Graduate education often requires exploration of a particular area of expertise by providing a mechanism to study your curiosities and more fully develop research skills. Seeking a master's degree is an exciting opportunity; you can immerse yourself into a particular area of emphasis to fully explore its application to interior design. Examples of areas of expertise include practice (e.g., healthcare and gerontology), social justice, sustainable design, social/psychology of interiors, color theory, pedagogy related to interior design, technology, and interdisciplinary design, to name a few. The master's degree extends beyond an advanced education by offering research and teaching assistantships allowing the graduate student time to learn research skills and glean practical experience in teaching. Today's college student constitutes a very different culture from years past. What has become known as the narcissistic generation (Twenge, 2006), college students require innovative teaching and styles of engagement to learn. A master's degree provides the opportunity for innovation, research that contributes to evidence-based design, and an understanding of the revolutionary pace of information that dominates our students and classroom.

Interior design education and the academy require educators to keep abreast of the profession through scholarship, whether creative activity or research. Scholarship provides exciting opportunities for educators to "practice what they preach" by focusing upon a particular area of study, learning both teaching and research skills, and fostering innovative approaches to creative activity.

TECHNOLOGY REVOLUTION

During the past 20 years, higher education has been transformed into a highly interactive and technologically advanced environment (eSchoolNews, 2006). Today's classroom and students are quite different than even five years ago. Beyond the software packages that we utilize in practice and education, engaging students in learning, communication, and the design process has been revolutionized through technology. One simple example is the penetration of Facebook, MySpace, and other interactive technology into the student culture. Whereas e-mail used to be an effective mode of communication with students, e-mail is now considered old-fashioned—meaning educators over age 30 are utilizing a means of communication with students that is now considered out of date (eNews, 2006). This is just one example of how the college teaching environment has drastically changed over the years. Teaching strategies that address rapid technology shifts are continually evolving in the academy. Institutions of higher learning have been transformed through technology, globalism, shifts in student culture, and pedagogy. Obtaining a master's degree not only allows an individual to develop expertise, it provides emersion in the culture of the academy—a critical step to being an effective educator.

TODAY'S STUDENT CULTURE

Perhaps one of the most important reasons for earning a master's degree to teach interior design is to learn the culture and mind-set of today's college student and the academy. As a long-standing design educator, I could not image returning to practice without an intensive practical internship any more than I could recommend that a practitioner enter the realm of education without preparing for the culture of today's student, including how to teach so that today's students learn. Popular magazines such as *Time*, *Newsweek*, and *The Economist* have published numerous articles on Generation Y. The most recent research comes from Twenge and Campbell (2009) in their work entitled *Narcissism Epidemic: Living in the Age of Entitlement*. They describe today's college students as entitled, assertive, and confident. Seasoned educators can no longer place their values and learning styles upon this generation of students (eNews, 2006). To the contrary, teaching methods must continue to be developed that communicate and engage college students without demeaning educational standards and simultaneously preparing students for reality. The master's degree prepares the educator for teaching within the culture of today's colleges and universities.

CONCLUSION

Being an interior design educator in higher education is an extremely rewarding career. The environment is challenging and synergistic between students, the community, and the world. Institutions of higher learning require a master's degree to prepare the individual for a career in collegiate teaching, which requires expertise in a specific area and development of a scholarship agenda. Beyond institutional and accreditation requirements, earning a master's degree is an incredible journey that allows focus on *you*—your education, your area of expertise, and your desire to pursue new directions, and to prepare you to become an interior design educator.

REFERENCES

Council for Interior Design Accreditation. (2009). *Standard 4. Design process*. Retrieved January 30, 2009, from http://www.accreditid.org/June%20 2008%20Standards_changes09.pdf

ESchool News. (2006). *For students, email already outdated*. Retrieved February 11, 2009, from eschoolnews.com/news/topnews/index .cfm?&&i=36982D

Guerin, D. (2008). Defining graduate education in interior design. *Journal of Interior Design, 33*(2), 11–14.

Harwood, B. (2006). The 1995 hypothesis + the 2015 hypothesis, *Journal of Interior Design, 31*(2), xi–xxii.

IDEC. (1993). *Appointment, tenure and promotion*. Retrieved February 17, 2009, from http://www .idec.org/members/index.php?direct=05ffg788jk0

IDEC. (2008). *Declining pool of interior design educators: Professionals engage in roundtable at NeoCon 2007*. Retrieved February 9, 2009, from http:// www.idec.org/pdf/Declining Pool/pdf

Leblanc, R. (1998). *Good teaching: The top 10 requirements*. Retrieved January 30, 2009, from http://honolulu.hawaii.edu/intranet/committees/ FacDevCom/guidebk/teachtip/topten.htm

National Council for Interior Design Qualification. (2004). *The definition of an interior designer*. Retrieved January 11, 2009, from http://www .ncidq.org/who/definition.htm

Olivieri, G. (2008, April 21). What ever happened?: From declining pool of interior design educators to enhancing pool of educators, *officeinsight*, article 619. Retrieved from http://www.officein-sight.com/query?body=Kimball+Office+working+ group&limit=15

Pagona, M., & Roselle, L. (In press). Knowledge development cycle: Refraction theory. *Frontiers: The Interdisciplinary Journal of Study Abroad*.

Twenge, J. (2006). *Generation me: Why today's young Americans are more confident, assertive, entitled and more miserable than ever before*. New York: Simon & Schuster.

Twenge, J., & Campbell, K. (2009). *Narcissism epidemic: Living in the age of entitlement*. New York: Simon & Schuster.

Weigand, J., & Harwood, B. (2007). Defining graduate education in interior design. *Journal of Interior Design, 33*(2), 3–10.

JOHN WEIGAND, MArch, IDEC, is professor and chair in the Department of Architecture and Interior Design at Miami University (Ohio). He earned architectural degrees at Miami and the University of Illinois (MArch) and worked professionally in Chicago for 11 years. Weigand developed and directed Miami's BFA in interior design (1995–2006). He serves on the CIDA board of directors; he has served as a reviewer for the *Journal of Interior Design* and member of IIDA's Strategic Planning Committee; and co-chaired the 2003 Body of Knowledge Conference. Weigand chaired the IDEC White Paper Committee on Graduate Education, the outcome of which was published in the *Journal of Interior Design* (2007). He authored *The Nature of Design* and is a contributor to *Schools that Learn* (Senge, 2000). In 2001, he was awarded the NCARB Prize for creative integration of practice and education in the academy. Weigand is also the 1999 winner of Miami's Crossan Hayes Curry Effective Educator Award.

BUIE HARWOOD, MFA, CID-VA, FIDEC, Honorary FASID, received her MFA and BFA degrees in interior design from Louisiana Tech University. She practices both residential and commercial interior design and consults with interior design programs on curriculum and accreditation. Harwood is a professor emeritus from Virginia Commonwealth University, where she served as department chair (for programs in Virginia and Qatar) and coordinator of the MFA program. Her numerous awards and honors include ASID Educator of Distinction, ASID Honorary Fellow, and IDEC Merit awards. Harwood serves the profession via leadership positions with IDEC, NCIDQ, IDCEC, ASID, and CIDA. She participated in the initial development of the Interior Design Experience Program (IDEP). She coauthored publications including *Architecture and Interior Design, From the 19th Century: An Integrated History* and *Architecture and Interior Design Through the 18th Century: An Integrated History*. Harwood publishes articles in research journals and professional association publications.

❯ What are the terminal degrees in interior design? What challenges and benefits do each offer?

JOHN WEIGAND &
BUIE HARWOOD

CLARIFYING GRADUATE DEGREES IN INTERIOR DESIGN AND PRESENTING THE MID

As it exists today, interior design graduate education is defined by various degrees with different missions, professional content, research content, degree nomenclature, accreditation status, credit-hour requirements, and curricular focus. These multiple degree offerings create a lack of clarity for interior design practitioners who may want to pursue a graduate degree and for institutions of higher education that must define minimum academic requirements for their faculty hires. Although undergraduate, first-professional degrees in interior design are acceptable for practice in the field, they generally do not qualify as adequate preparation for college-level teaching. Academia recognizes both the PhD and master's degrees as "terminal teaching degrees" (terminal herein defined as qualifying the degree-holder for college-level teaching). But the degree offerings are varied and distinct.

In spite of this lack of clarity surrounding degree offerings, there is an increased emphasis on interior design graduate education due to several factors. The interior design knowledge base is arguably more complicated and continues to increase in complexity, as evidenced by rapid change in sustainable design practices and digital technologies. These and other examples of increased quantity and complexity of knowledge raise the question of the need for additional or graduate-level education as a requirement for practice. Increased disciplinary collaboration also requires that today's graduates understand design in a broader sense, that they receive appropriate liberal arts education, and that they are able to work in multidisciplinary team settings. This increasingly pushes disciplinary expertise beyond the baccalaureate level. An increased emphasis on evidence-based design (grounding design decision-making in design research) places a priority on interior designers' knowledge of the types of research activities common to graduate education. Further, as interior designers work in this collaborative environment, it is important to create parity in the degree tracks among design professions. For example, architecture requires a minimum of five years (BArch) or six years (MArch) of professional education as the first-professional degree, which is a prerequisite for licensure. Interior design, by contrast, requires a minimum of a four-year (BA/BS/BFA/BID) first-professional degree as a requirement for practice. All of these factors have moved graduate education front and center in discussions about academic requirements for practice as well as teaching.

This increased emphasis on graduate study is underscored by interior design educators: "The 21st century will require individuals to hold master's and doctorates in a given perspective of interior design while at the same time understanding, collaborating, and sharing across perspectives" (Dohr, 2007, p. viii). In this essay, we will clarify the purposes of current graduate degrees and propose that the profession adopt a single master of interior design (MID) degree in parity with the MArch degree and as a complement to the PhD degree. We will identify it as the first-professional, accredited degree in interior design.

CURRENT GRADUATE DEGREES

THE PHD DEGREE

The role of the PhD is clearly understood by most practitioners and academics. Historically, and in most disciplines, the PhD is established as the benchmark degree for college-level teaching, signifying the highest level of academic achievement in the field and defined by the creation of new knowledge through research in a specific area of expertise. Although PhD programs in interior design exist, none are specifically housed in departments of interior design. Instead, PhD programs are associated with disciplines such as human ecology, environmental design, or sociology, so the degrees earned relate to interior design, yet are distinct. They are characterized by a deeper knowledge of design and human behavior research, typically within a more focused content area or surrounding a specific issue. In academic settings, where deeper knowledge is required (teaching at the graduate level or teaching in support areas such as human factors or design history), the PhD is perceived to be of higher value than the master's degree. However, because the PhD is frequently earned in disciplines related to, but distinct from, interior design, there is no guarantee that the PhD candidate demonstrates a more holistic competency in interior design practice. Nor is explicit knowledge of interior design practice the goal of most PhD programs.

THE MASTER'S DEGREE

The types and goals of master's degrees are quite varied. They include a first-professional degree so that one can practice design and teach (e.g., master of architecture/MArch), a terminal post-professional degree (master of fine arts/MFA) so that one can gain depth in an area of interest and teach, and a post-professional, research-oriented degree (master of art/MA or master of science/MS) so that one can prepare to teach or prepare for further study in a PhD program. Even within academia, varied types and goals for each degree, and varied pathways for acquiring a master's degree, exist, creating confusion for academics as well as interior design practitioners. Figure 10.2 shows the existing paths of various bachelor's degrees to master's degrees and ultimately to a PhD. Also shown is the requirement for a leveling transition stage to accommodate the extent, or lack thereof, of design education at the bachelor's level prior to attempting a master's degree.

The master's degree is commonly accepted by the academy as an alternative to the PhD as a teaching qualification in professional programs. The master of fine arts, master of architecture, master of landscape architecture, master of furniture design, and master of historic preservation are well-established examples of professional degrees that are grounded in design practice

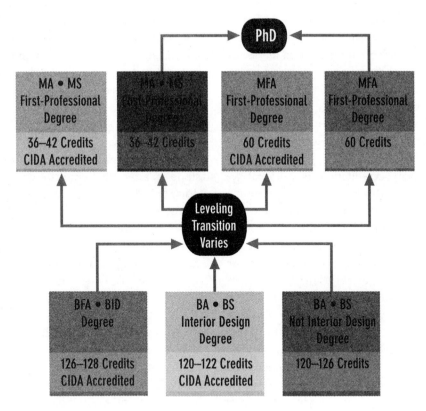

FIGURE 10.2. Existing graduate degree pathways.

and recognized by the academy as qualifying the degree-holder for college-level teaching. Unlike the PhD, these master's degrees promote expertise in design and design process that, by definition, requires broad knowledge across a range of content areas. Design decisions are informed by (and evaluated against) this broad knowledge. It is precisely this broad-based design focus that distinguishes these masters' degrees from the PhD. Typically, these master's programs also provide initial exposure to research experiences as well as classroom teaching through research or teaching assistantships. A thesis experience that promotes the concept of evidence-based design and that integrates research into the design process is common.

Master's degree level programs are equally likely to vary in terms of their curricular content or emphasis. They offer varying degrees of professional education, research education, teaching methods (and teaching experience), and exposure to the liberal arts. By default, they also evidence bias toward the unit in which they're housed (e.g., Human Ecology, Art, Architecture), thus offering varying exposure to the behavioral sciences, to the studio arts, or to architecture. Additionally, the time to degree varies among programs, but is typically between one and three years.

FIRST-PROFESSIONAL MASTER'S DEGREE

A number of master's level programs are first-professional, recognizing the need to provide professional education for students lacking the undergraduate degree in interior design. Typically, the curriculum in these programs is a combination of baccalaureate and advanced-level professional studies and may include some initial exposure to research and teaching. However, because much of the professional content is shared with the baccalaureate level, there is no guarantee that research methods and studio-based design work are integrated. In fact, some first-professional programs provide only professional education and exclude the research component altogether. Although this experience may prepare the graduate for practice, it cannot adequately prepare the graduate for college-level teaching.

Professional accreditation is optional for first-professional master's degree programs. Some of these programs pursue, and are granted, accreditation through the Council for Interior Design Accreditation (CIDA), but this number is small. Further, the minimum requirements for accreditation at this master's level are identical to those for baccalaureate programs because CIDA accredits only first-professional degree programs. There is no expectation for a higher level of achievement or significantly advanced coursework at the graduate level. As a result, students earning the first-professional master's will demonstrate varying degrees of professional knowledge and skill.

In schools of architecture, the MArch degree likewise qualifies the degree holder for college-level teaching, and it is also a first-professional degree (along with the five-year BArch). This "first-professional degree is a stipulated requirement for licensure. Most educational programs offer either a four-year degree leading to a master's program or a five-year baccalaureate degree" (Harwood, 1991, p. 9) with one or two additional years of advanced study (often referred to as 4+2 or 5+1 programs). It should be noted, however, that the National Architecture Accrediting Board (NAAB) has stated that all first-professional accredited architecture programs must be offered at the MArch level by 2011 (National Architecture Accrediting Board, 2009).

In limited cases, the master of interior design (MID) degree is offered, and it may be positioned as the terminal degree. Similar to the MArch, a student might enter this program with a bachelor's degree in a design-related area and completes the MID with two to three years of advanced study. As a new(er) degree, the MID is not well understood in the academy, and its status as a terminal teaching degree is unclear.

POST-PROFESSIONAL MFA DEGREE

Programs housed in art schools most commonly offer the MFA degree. This is understood as a terminal graduate degree in design disciplines for college-level teaching. Typically in interior design, students enter this program with a bachelor's degree in interior design or a closely related area. The MFA requires a concentrated design studio experience along with advanced scholarly research.

POST-PROFESSIONAL MA AND MS DEGREES

Interior design programs housed in human ecology, family studies, or home economics historically offer the MA or MS degrees. These are typically understood as leading to the PhD, but can also be positioned as terminal teaching degrees, *even though* they may not emphasize professional content. Schools can require those who apply for the MA or MS to have an existing bachelor's degree in interior design, which then gives more credibility to the concept of the post-professional degree. But, confusion develops when some schools offer these degree options to students who have bachelor's degrees in other non-design-related fields and, therefore, are not participating in a sequential in-depth building-block experience, which is a criterion for post-professional degrees.

The majority of post-professional programs typically focus on beginning research methods, design research, and possibly teaching methods. "Post-professional graduate degrees build on an existing foundation in the field, provide opportunities for specialization, and focus on the generation or reinterpretation of knowledge and the testing of design theories" (White & Dickson, 1994, p. 28). Generally, the presumption is that students who are accepted to and enter these master's programs have earned a professional interior design baccalaureate degree, but this expectation varies from institution to institution. The prerequisite baccalaureate degree may be either from an accredited or non-accredited interior design program. Or, in fact, it may not be from an interior design program at all. The determination of professional competency as a prerequisite for post-professional study is made on a case-by-case basis by each program.

RELATIONSHIP OF MASTER'S DEGREES TO TEACHING QUALIFICATIONS

This variety in program attributes confirms that interior design graduate education is driven as much by market need as by any consistent set of expectations developed by the profession or enforced through the accreditation process. When the master's degree is defined by some institutions as a terminal degree for teaching, this lack of clarity is problematic because it is not clear what combination of undergraduate and graduate degrees and practice experience this degree represents.

Interior design administrators will often seek master's-qualified candidates who possess strong design ability and an understanding of issues directly related to design practice. Professional practice experience is frequently a priority in search descriptions as a complement to the master's degree. This more comprehensive design ability is valuable to undergraduate teaching and to a professional, design-based curriculum, both of which comprise the majority of teaching positions in interior design. And, it is especially valuable to small teaching faculties (also prevalent in the discipline), where teachers must be able to cover multiple courses and content.

THE PROPOSED TERMINAL MASTER'S DEGREE IN INTERIOR DESIGN

There is no clear definition in the interior design discipline of what constitutes the professional and terminal master's degree and how this is distinguished from master's programs that lead to the PhD. Such a definition has not been adopted, or promoted, by any of the various professional organizations or formalized through the accreditation process. Although the diversity of master's level degrees is arguably healthy, an agreed-to definition of the "professional" master's degree is critical because this is established as an alternative to the PhD and a prerequisite for college teaching. The profusion of graduate degrees makes it unclear which degrees do and do not qualify the degree-holder for college-level teaching. As a result, institutions are able to develop different interpretations for what constitutes the terminal teaching degree and disqualify some master's degrees positioned as terminal. This underscores the need for a clearly identified master's degree track, grounded in evidence-based design practice, and positioned as an alternative to the PhD as a qualification for teaching.

A terminal master's degree in interior design, then, must be grounded *both* in design practice and in research. If it is purely a post-professional, research-oriented degree, then it is not adequately distinguished from the PhD and will not be viewed as comparatively rigorous. Likewise, if it is a practice-based degree only, disconnected from research and evidence-based design (EBD), then it is not appropriately critical and does not prepare the graduate for college-level teaching or EBD practice. By placing the design process at the core of the curriculum and by allowing student-directed research to inform this process, the master's degree is positioned as distinct from the PhD, but as providing qualifications for teaching.

It may not be enough, though, to define the terminal master's in a conceptual sense; it must also have a clear identity. One way to provide this identity is to prescribe a degree name. The MA and MS are not obvious choices here, given that these are historically understood as degrees earned en-route to the PhD. Perhaps the degree that provides the most identity is the MID, given its specific reference to "interior design." Guerin and Thompson (2004) propose,

> The transformation of interior design is dependent upon the master of interior design (MID) becoming accepted as the first professional degree. . . . The MID provides the opportunity to gain breadth of knowledge in emerging content areas such as sustainability, universal design, indoor air quality, and other quality-of-life issues. (p. 1; p. 4)

Similar to the MArch, it offers a very clear identity. It is also a relatively new degree name and thus able to be defined by the profession.

Although a commonly understood degree name will provide identity, perhaps the only way to insure conformance with the intent of the professional master's is to require accreditation of this degree, likely through CIDA. This accreditation would need to recognize the value added above and beyond the baccalaureate, so the guidelines would be more rigorous. These guidelines would clearly communicate the value of this professional master's degree as a "terminal teaching degree," qualifying graduates for entry-level teaching positions, as well as a "terminal practice degree," qualifying graduates for entry-level practice. It is important to point out that more stringent accreditation requirements would not be driven by the accrediting organization, but rather would be created in response to demands by the academy, professional organizations, testing and regulatory agencies, and employers. Accreditation guidelines would also regulate "time to degree." Existing one-year master's degrees (associated with 4+1 programs) might need to increase the number of total required credit hours. And, MA and

MS degrees could initially be grandparented in under an adequate grace period.

Finally, in recognizing that graduate applicants will demonstrate differing levels of professional competency, it is important to carefully define a leveling component for an accredited MID degree. Figure 10.3 shows the proposed MID pathway with students earning a design or non-design-related bachelor's degree, the leveling component, and the MID as the first-professional, accredited degree. The duration of the leveling component will logically vary for each student. Thus, the total time to degree for the MID would need to be flexible.

For now, this new accreditation level need not impact existing accreditation of baccalaureate programs. Over time, however, redefinition of the MID as the sole terminal teaching and practice degree at the master's level would clarify the degree track and create a degree identity in much the same way that the shift to baccalaureate-level accreditation did in 2000.

ARGUMENTS FOR THE FIRST-PROFESSIONAL MASTER'S IN INTERIOR DESIGN

If the MID was to be defined, over time, as the first-professional degree (meaning that accreditation would no longer occur at the baccalaureate level), this would add clarity to the degree track and create degree identity at the graduate level. But, there are other advantages. Such a shift also responds to increasing complexity in the profession and in the interior design knowledge base. Graduate-level study can emphasize a more critical and research-driven design and greater depth of study. Practical experience can be incorporated more fully into the curriculum. Further, by shifting some professional content to the graduate level, a greater exposure to liberal studies and to more general design study is possible at the baccalaureate level.

Another benefit of shifting first-professional accreditation to the master's level is its significant and immediate impact on the pool of qualified, college-level educators. A critical mass of

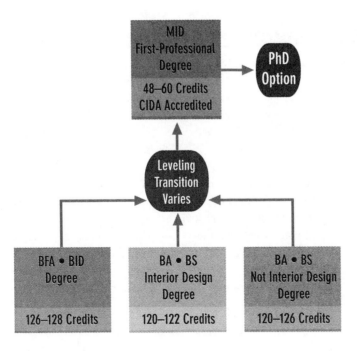

FIGURE 10.3. Proposed MID process.

experienced and qualified practitioners is currently not eligible to pursue full-time teaching
at a later point in their careers because the first-
professional accredited degree is defined at the
baccalaureate level. By mid-career, when these
practicing interior designers might consider a
shift into teaching, they are not degree-qualified
to do so. Returning for post-graduate study is
an option, but is often impractical due to family
obligations or constraints related to location or
finances.

Finally and importantly, a shift to first-professional graduate education would place interior design and architecture education on a
more equal footing by equating their career
tracks. This would counter arguments in the
licensing arena that interior design education is
not adequately extensive and would positively
impact efforts to secure interior design practice acts. If both interior design and architecture supported the first-professional, accredited
master's degree, aligned programs could more

easily pursue shared content knowledge at the
undergraduate level and specialization at the
interior (or architectural) scale at the graduate
level, allowing for greater collaboration between
design disciplines. Alignment of these related
academic tracks ultimately will strengthen—
not weaken—interior design.

This essay notes the confusion that currently exists in interior design education surrounding graduate degrees. The rationale for
moving the terminal degree to the master's
level was given. Introducing the MID as the
future of interior design education and, therefore, practice will respond to the confusion
and, more importantly, the increasing complexity of the profession, increased depth of
knowledge required to practice, and the growing importance of an evidence-based approach
to interior design. The MID serves to respond
to these issues, and colleagues are invited to
add their voices to its definition, role, and
outcomes.

REFERENCES

Dohr, J. (2007). Continuing the dialogue: Interior design graduate education inquiry and scholarly cultures. *Journal of Interior Design, 33*(1), v–xvi.

Guerin, D. (1991). Issues facing interior design education in the twenty-first century. *Journal of Interior Design Education and Research, 17*(2), 9–16.

Guerin, D., & Thompson, J. (2004). Interior design education in the 21st century: An educational transformation. *Journal of Interior Design, 30*(1), 1–12.

Harwood, B. (1991). Comparing the standards in interior design and architecture to assess similarities and differences. *Journal of Interior Design Education and Research, 17*(1), 5–18.

Harwood, B. (2006). The 1995 hypothesis + the 2015 hypothesis. *Journal of Interior Design, 31*(2), xi–xxii.

National Architectural Accrediting Board. (2009). *Accreditation eligibility.* Retrieved May 29, 2009, from http://www.naab.org

Weigand, J. (2004). *Assessing commonality and distinction within the knowledge base in interior design and architecture.* Presentation at the Interior Design Educators Council Annual Conference, Pittsburgh, PA.

Weigand, J., & Harwood, B. (2007). Defining graduate education in interior design. *Journal of Interior Design, 33*(2), 3–9.

White, A., & Dickson, A. (1994). Practitioner's perceptions of interior design graduate education and implications for the future. *Journal of Interior Design, 20*(1), 27–35.

> What issues are at the core of sustaining interior design education? Is it a master's degree? Where does that fit into the future of the profession?

TIIU POLDMA

SUSTAINING EDUCATION: FUTURING INTERIOR DESIGN DIRECTIONS?

As we consider the different issues surrounding the state of the interior design profession, we are compelled to consider the diverse issues that will affect future directions for interior design education. Whether it is the values that underlie what we do and how we do it (Vaikla-Poldma, 2003; Weigand, 2006), a body of knowledge of interior design that is dynamic and changing (Marshall-Baker, 2005; Martin & Guerin, 2006), or the fact that emerging interior design research happens to advance a holistic, sustainable environment (Marshall-Baker, 2004); these are all factors at the heart of sustaining a future education for interior designers within the built design disciplines.

This essay proposes that a sustainable education requires critical thinking and development of an inquiry-based education specific to interior design values and knowledge. Educational contexts for this type of education may include:

TIIU POLDMA, PhD, IDC, IDEC, ARIDNB, AERA, earned a BID, an MA, and a PhD. She is associate professor and vice dean of graduate studies and research at the Faculty of Environmental Design, University of Montreal, Quebec. She teaches interior design studios, theories, practices, and advanced research methods for the built environment disciplines. Current research interests include qualitative and experience-based design research; arts-informed research methods; intelligent, virtual, and physical aspects of designed spaces; light and color; phenomenology; new technologies and emerging interior design practices; and integrating theory with process. As researcher with Artful Analysis and Representation in Research Collective, Poldma explores collage as a scholarly research method. She serves as a site visitor for CIDA, a board member for the DRS Society, a member of the editorial board of *Inderscience,* regional editor of the *Journal of Design Research,* and associate editor of the *Journal of Interior Design. Taking Up Space: Exploring the Design Process* is Poldma's first book (2009).

- Developing appropriate educational/pedagogical approaches that respond to emerging and changing realities in a worldwide context
- Developing specific learning activities to situate interior design and its specificity within inter-disciplinary and multi-dimensional contexts

- Understanding what underlying core values affect and inform interior design practices and processes

Also, we ask ourselves, given these emerging contexts, what, in the end, constitutes a sustainable future education for interior design? This question forms the basis for the following discussion.

UNDERSTANDING THE ROLE OF EDUCATIONAL PRACTICES WITHIN INTERIOR DESIGN EDUCATION

First and foremost, developing educational practices requires what Hernandez (1997) calls "critical pedagogy" that is situated within:

> The need to develop theory by theorizing the practice, what (Henry) Giroux would refer to as theory emerging in concrete settings, although not collapsing in them, in order to analyse them critically and get into action based on informed praxis . . . the use of everyday concepts, such as voice and dialogue . . . to deconstruct and reconstruct the terrain of everyday life. . . . The need to have conception of subject, in the context of the current controversy of this topic, to develop political action and a sense of agency. (p. 14)

For interior design education, this could begin with learning and understanding what the underlying values are that we use to both teach and learn interior design processes, methods, and practices (Poldma, 2008; Vaikla-Poldma, 2003). For this critical learning to happen, we need to help students investigate what interior designers do and how, through the acquisition of both design studio learning and theory acquisition. We can build educational experiences into student learning by using dynamic learning activities (such as the social construction of space through dialogue) or static learning activities (such as planning and designing interior space) (see Figure 10.4). Teachers using both types of thinking become facilitators of student learning, helping them to develop the capacity to ask relevant questions about the design process and the role of the interior designer in society. This moves interior design education away from prescriptive practices and toward inquiry-based learning and reflective thinking.

This type of thinking is not easy, and students may sometimes find themselves in uncomfortable spaces trying to understand how the design decisions they make affect and sustain the planet. However, when students are put into different learning situations or interdisciplinary or multidisciplinary situations, teamwork and problem-solving frame and act as the catalyst to this type of learning *by doing*.

FIGURE 10.4. Students examining concepts, design projects done as creative exercises for examination in theory course on advanced conceptual processes.

THE DILEMMA OF PEDAGOGY AND PRACTICE

It is important to understand the nuance between effective teaching practices that hone student understanding versus instilling pedagogical practices that are prescriptive in nature. Hernandez discusses this dilemma:

> What is pedagogy anyways? Pedagogy is a deliberate attempt to influence how and what knowledge and identities are produced among particular sets of social relations. . . . How knowledge gets produced/communicated and how students participate in the process as either objects or subjects are fundamental political aspects to be taken into account. All these elements speak for a practice that is about much more than teaching strategies

> or concerns of mere practitioners. That is, pedagogy refers to a necessary dynamic of theory and practice with political and ethical concerns leading to a process of reflection and reorganization. (p. 12)

In a sustainable model of interior design education, students become agents of discussion and change and are no longer *objects*, while teachers use design problems and issues as the catalyst for facilitating learning through dialogue. For example, in Figure 10.5, we see how the student applies learning from dialogue about the project (see Figure 10.4) to examine the design decisions being made.

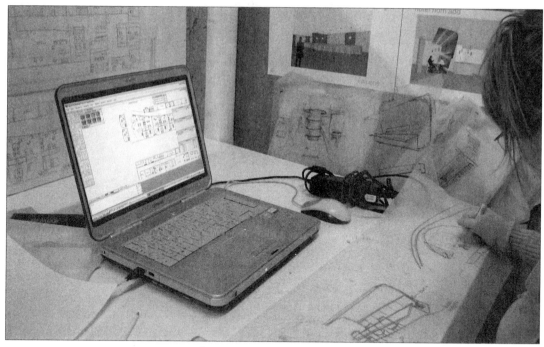

FIGURE 10.5. Student working on her final project in the interior design studio.

A PROPOSED MODEL FOR SUSTAINING INTERIOR DESIGN EDUCATION

When we understand the educational practices that can be encouraged, we can examine the specific knowledge components of interior design processes and practices that can be considered as fundamental. These include:

> Understand that interior design projects are solved using a *complex design process*

> Understand that *empathy and meaning* play a role in studio learning

> Develop *critical thinking skills* through the exploration of situated contexts that provide a place for theoretical and critical reflection

> Explore the *whole design experience* through the development of design sensibility using specific interior design project processes

> Understand how *ethics, empathy, and service* (Nelson & Stolterman, 2003) are core interior design values

When this specific knowledge is addressed, we can then make suggestions about how to create a model for sustaining interior design education. This model may include the following six characteristics.

1. *Situating learning experiences in real-time experiences of designers as users.* Interior design students need learning experiences where they can grasp how users will actually live within the spaces that they design. Exercises promoting how interior designers are the experimental users of the place that they will design are necessary. This means advocating that students gain an understanding of the actual lived experiences of their clients, within the design studio milieu, alongside aesthetic and functional learning exercises.

FIGURE 10.6. Collage of students' examination of issues during the research phase of the project.

2. *Bringing theory and practice into the design studio as components of critical thinking.* Practice must be brought directly into theoretical learning. This begins with students doing research collected with an evidence-based approach, which in turn supports the design proposals made, and then link these experiences to the theoretical and epistemological aspects of the design. Concepts are examined as these occur in interior design project research and development, considered through critical reflection, and then new ideas and solutions are proposed in an iterative and formalizing process. For example, in Figure 10.6 we see how students take research and information gathered in interior design studios and work in groups in early brainstorming design stages by expressing their ideas in a series of collaged images and text.

3. *Understanding interior design learning as part of a multidisciplinary approach.* Learning from different disciplines should be integrated into the core interior design curricula. Disciplines such as semiotics, cultural theory, phenomenology, pragmatic philosophy, and social psychology have much to offer in the evolution of design discourse in the design studio milieu.

4. *Develop curricula based on a critical values-oriented perspective that is culturally diverse.* A culturally diverse approach considers the experiences of users through the lens of a critical and dialectical nature of the local and cultural perspective. For example, in the project shown in Figure 10.7, cultural, social, and urban issues frame the contexts within which students create projects for a multifamily residential space. Students learn to develop empathy for a diverse range of users in diverse cultural and social situations.

5. *Developing a "broad view" of the design process and practices in interior design.* Characteristics expressed through items 1 through 4 build toward the idea of a broad, values-oriented education (Friedman, 1997; Nelson & Stolterman, 2003). Friedman (1997) argues for a broad view of design education as a means to move from a craft-based education toward a design, science-based education situated in inquiry, when he states:

> *every intelligent design professional in the knowledge era—graphic designer, information designer, design manager, industrial designer—must increasingly be a hybrid professional trained with a broad view. These professionals must draw on a number of disciplines to understand the nature of their task in solving specific problems: design leadership, philosophy, psychology, physiology, sociology of knowledge, research methodology, information, strategic*
>
> *design, combining these with an integrate perspective of critical studies and history of ideas. Is this too broad a range of studies for a single profession? Not in terms of education. It is a matter of practical simplicity in curriculum development. (p. 22)*

6. *Putting the interior design process into context.* Putting the design process into context is vital. Multiple contexts in learning are a necessary means to give students the experience of constraints and limits that will be imposed in the profession (Poldma & Joannidis, 2008). Too often, it is the context in the real world that determines problem parameters, and too often the design problem within contexts and constraints is not adequately explored nor critically examined. Design education must provide opportunities for students to experience these constraints, but also question and test them.

MAKING A SUSTAINABLE EDUCATION INQUIRY BASED

Friedman (1997), in his seminal paper "Design Science and Design Education," makes the argument for design education maturing when it moves from the crafts-based education of its history toward an inquiry-based education. How do we make this happen? Inquiry begins with the integration of critical thinking and theory-based thinking in theory courses in senior-level baccalaureate and master's programs, alongside the technical knowledge acquired and currently privileged as a preparation for both practice and master's level professional programs. This is easily done with the integration of seminar-format discussions that promote group dialogue as a vital mimicry both of how designers work with clients in the profession and as needed learning tools of scientific inquiry, or to discuss the larger ethical, global, and contemporary issues that affect how designers think and work (see Figure 10.8).

Not only must we learn how to design, but also we must learn how to create designs that work in the context of the realities within which the design finds itself. As Friedman notes:

> The search for artistic effect as a primary value in design has given us far too many disasters: teapots that don't pour . . . chairs that tip over. . . . Every design professor can add examples to this list. The challenge is not to recognize obvious disasters in design after they're made. That is easy. The challenge is to shape an effective process of design that yields effective outcomes. This must be an inquiry-based process, a problem-solving process linked to effective methods of design development. This, in turn, requires the use of systematic thinking, a scientific approach. (1997, p. 4)

By scientific, Friedman (1997) refers not to a positivist approach but rather a systematic approach that requires research as its core value. This scientific approach requires "the tradition

FIGURE 10.7. Examining issues in a social and cultural context. Exploring three generations in the urban milieu.

FIGURE 10.8. Final interior design project model (M-C. Tremblay).

of research, writing and professional dialogue" (p. 4). Friedman (1997) suggests that this is, for the most part, absent in design school learning. Inquiry requires the integration of theorizing with the practices of doing, of writing, and contemplating as much as creating and designing. As he continues:

The design process begins, above all, with inquiry. . . . A good design process must embrace the aesthetic as well as the scientific. The central difference is that one does not start with the look and feel, but rather with the parameters of the problem. (p. 5)

The interior design process considers the parameters of the problem first and foremost. This includes putting the interior design project into context while developing good and effective problem-solving skills. This type of design process embraces a broad view and becomes a holistic education where values of critical thinking and service are honed (Nelson & Stolterman, 2003).

CONCLUSION

Many interior design educators already integrate characteristics of this model into their programs. However, to make education sustainable, we need to imagine the future including the issues raised herein. Business management professor Mintzberg (2009) has suggested that the business leaders of tomorrow will be effective if they integrate "conceptual ideas" into their thinking. In interior design, we have these skills at our fingertips, and we develop effective solutions through inquiry, critical thinking, problem solving, and an understanding that innovation happens when we bring people and interior environments together through the vehicle of interior design processes. It is this model for interior design education that we need to promote in the future.

REFERENCES

Friedman, K. (1997). Design science and design education. In *The Challenge of Complexity*. Peter McGrory (Ed.), Helsinki: UIAH, 54–72.

Hernandez, A. (1997). *Pedagogy, democracy and education: Rethinking the public sphere*. New York: State University of New York Press.

Marshall-Baker, A. (2004). A new paradigm. In *Forum IDEC*. Retrieved March 1, 2009, from ISdesigNET/ Magazine/Back Issues/October 2004/IDEC

Marshall-Baker, A. (2005). Knowledge in interior design. *Journal of Interior Design, 31*(1), xiii–xxi.

Martin, C., & Guerin, D. (2006). *The interior design profession's body of knowledge, 2005 edition.* Grand Rapids, MI: Council for Interior Design Accreditation, American Society of Interior Designers, Interior Designers of Canada, International Interior Design Association, and National Council for Interior Design Qualification.

Mintzberg, H. (2009, March 14). *Scully* (Television broadcast). Burlington, VT: Public Broadcasting Service.

Nelson, H., & Stolterman, E. (2003). *The design way: Intentional change in an unpredictable world.* Englewood Cliffs, NJ: Technology Publications.

Poldma, T. (2007). The proposal for a pluralistic discourse in interior design education, research and practice: Issues, values, and foundations for the future. In S. Caan, & B. Powell (Eds.), *IFI Roundtable Conference Thinking into the Future* (pp. 149–172). Singapore: International Federation of Interior Architects/Designers.

Poldma, T. (2008). Interior design at a crossroads: Embracing specificity through process, research and knowledge. *Journal of Interior Design, 33*(3), vi–xvi.

Poldma, T. (2009). *Taking up space: Exploring the design process.* New York: Fairchild Books.

Poldma, T., & Joannidis, M. (2008). *Understanding today's interior design project: Putting the design process into context.* Paper presented at the IDEC East Regional Conference, Toronto, Ontario.

Vaikla-Poldma, T. (2003). *An investigation of learning and teaching processes in an interior design class: An interpretive and contextual inquiry.* Unpublished doctoral dissertation. Montreal: McGill University.

Weigand, J. (2006, Winter). Defining ourselves. *Perspective*, 26–34.

ALLISON CARLL WHITE, PhD, CID-KY, FIDEC, FIIDA, is a professor in the School of Interior Design in the College of Design at the University of Kentucky. She also holds a joint appointment in the graduate program in the Department of Historic Preservation. White has published extensively on various aspects of the design profession, with a special focus on the need to promote the value of interior design to the human experience. She became an IDEC fellow in 1999 and currently serves as the chair of IDEC's College of Fellows. White also has served as a reviewer and a publication board member for the *Journal of Interior Design*. In 2000, she was made a fellow of IIDA after serving as the director of the Education and Research Forum and president of the IIDA Foundation.

ANN WHITESIDE DICKSON, CID-KY, FIDEC, IIDA, is an associate professor and the director of the School of Interior Design in the College of Design at the University of Kentucky. She served on the executive board of IDEC for nine years and became a fellow in 2000. Dickson has been the school's director since 2001, and her work with the Provost was instrumental in creating the College of Design, bringing together interior design, architecture, and historic preservation. Dickson has written extensively about the relationship between the value of a profession, its body of knowledge, and graduate education. She and Allison Carll White organized and hosted the Polsky Forum, a think tank composed of the profession's leaders, to discuss the status of research and graduate education. Dickson has served as a CIDA site visitor since 1988 and as a reviewer for the *Journal of Interior Design*.

> With all there is to teach,
> what is "falling off the table"?
> How can interior design programs handle
> the explosion of knowledge?

ALLISON CARLL WHITE &
ANN WHITESIDE DICKSON

"ON THE TABLE": THE NEW FIRST-PROFESSIONAL DEGREE

It is certainly not news that there is an information explosion in the design professions that will continue to expand at an increasingly more rapid pace. This phenomenon is made even more complex by overlapping boundaries of practice with allied professions, diminishing natural resources, endangered environmental quality, globalization, and fluctuating economies. Whereas some may ask what is "falling off the table," maybe the question should be posed differently. With such strong outside forces influencing the way the interior design profession is evolving, shouldn't we be more critically examining what knowledge must remain "on the table" and what type of model is needed to best prepare entry-level students to address the future needs of the profession?

The accepted model for the academy to prepare students to enter the world of work continues to be a four-year bachelor's degree. The domino effect of the imploding forces influencing interior design practice is dictating that the bar be raised in education, the impact of which is becoming overwhelming within the constraints of the academy. Council for Interior Design Accreditation (CIDA) guidelines and standards have been the yardstick for professional education since 1973, and the most current version has been dramatically revised to focus on core values and knowledge that reflects where the profession is at this time. To quote CIDA's philosophy (2009), "The best preparation for the future is an education that will enable graduates to adapt to a changing world" (p. 2).

The first CIDA accreditation standards were established after an extensive study of the state of interior design education as well as the state of professional practice based on prototypes drawn from allied and non-aligned professional accrediting bodies and in consultation with the U.S. Department of Education (R. Rankin, personal communication, May 28, 2009). These standards have evolved and been revised numerous times based on changes in professional practice and projected future trends. Do the accreditation standards, which ensure minimum competencies in education, provide a platform that enables programs to educate students for entry into the profession?

We believe that the recently revised 2009 CIDA accreditation standards allow for greater flexibility within the academy for a program to capitalize on the goals of the institution, program objectives, unique opportunities afforded by the program's context, and available resources. This is a much-needed step in the right direction. We expect that as a result of the implementation of the 2009 standards, there will be much greater diversity found within accredited interior design programs across the country, and this diversity will benefit the profession to some degree.

However, this solution is inadequate to address the needs of our rapidly changing profession. Given the velocity of change in both the world and professional practice, is the current four-year educational model relevant? Although posed in the context of educational training for another discipline, the quote by French philosopher Bruno Latour (2004) seems appropriate to ask with regards to the current model for interior design programs:

> It does not seem to me that we have been as quick, in academe, to prepare ourselves for new threats, new dangers, new tasks, new targets. Are we not like those mechanical toys that endlessly continue to do the same gesture when everything else has changed around them? (p. 1)

Is this statement true for the educational model found in most universities and institutions of higher learning where interior design is located? If so, what change is possible to best prepare our students to be members of a global community, to demonstrate a greater social consciousness, and to promote the value of interior design?

The recently revised CIDA standards ensure a basic core of knowledge and begin to address values that are important to the profession as a whole. What the current standards cannot do is help define the value of interior design and convey to others how interior design supports and enhances the human experience. But, why is this important to the educational process and the profession? Over 10 years ago, Boyer and Mitgang (1996) discussed the importance of engagement in the university experience, which they suggest must clarify the public benefits of design, promote the creation of new knowledge, and stress the importance of ethical, professional behavior. We believe that with an educational structure that facilitates a higher level of engagement than currently possible in undergraduate programs, individuals graduating with first-professional interior design degrees will have a much-enhanced sense of how their work affects others, what value it brings, and how it addresses societal needs. Greater engagement will become self-sustaining to the profession.

We agree with Guerin and Thompson (2004), who have identified "three challenges [that] provide the critical underpinnings required for the continuing evolution of any profession and academic discipline" (p. 1). These three underpinnings are a "breadth and depth of knowledge required to solve complex interdisciplinary problems of human behavior and design" (p. 1), evidence-based design criteria, and the value of research. We further agree that a master of interior design (MID) must be considered the first-professional degree. However, Guerin and Thompson's 4+1 (4-year bachelor's degree plus a one-year master's degree) model is not sufficiently forward-looking to meet the future demands of the profession. What is required is a radically different model that addresses what needs to be on the table.

We propose the new table to be a 3+2 model for the first-professional degree in interior design. This new model will increase the value of the profession by providing both breadth and depth of knowledge for graduates, allowing for the exploration of evidence-based design thinking, cultivating specialization, and expanding the knowledge base of the profession. A three-year undergraduate degree, patterned after prestigious institutions such as Oxford and Cambridge, has been proposed by both academic and legislative bodies as an alternative to the traditional four-year degree. It is now under serious consideration by some American institutions in the wake of current economic conditions (Jaschik, 2009; Lewin, 2009; Strauss, 2009). Former education secretary and university president Lamar Alexander calls three-year degrees the "higher ed equivalent of a fuel efficient car, compared to the traditional gas guzzling four-year course" (Jaschik, 2009, p. 1). Tightening up the average number of credit hours taken per semester, students can accomplish 120 credit hours in three years. Such a model would save time and, therefore, money in acquiring a bachelor's degree prior to entering a specialized area of study within the profession that leads to a master's degree. A student completing the BA or an interior design studies degree would have two options: finalizing their education without becoming a professional interior designer or completing two additional years of professional degree requirements by entering into a graduate program after completing a certified work experience in the profession.

In three years, all aspects of CIDA's core knowledge cannot be addressed. As with allied professions, the core knowledge by which accreditation standards evaluate a program will be spread throughout the entire first-professional degree program. The new model should not be viewed as simply an undergraduate degree followed by a master's degree, but rather as a totally integrative experience that will better prepare students to meet the needs of the profession. Graduates need both a core interior design knowledge base that is broad as well as a depth of knowledge in a specialized area. In addition, in today's globalized world, a strong liberal arts background is more important than ever and would be completed with the BA degree.

The proposed 3+2 model will require new ways of thinking and doing with regards to adopting new instructional formats that foster integration of subject matter with application, while not forsaking problem solving, critical thinking, and design innovation. A change in mind-set needs to occur to allow students to explore knowledge within a broader context, not simply as a series of separate courses within a semester. While maintaining a strong academic core of knowledge integral to the profession, technical knowledge and other skill-based information could be moved to a course-within-a-course, workshops, and intensives to allow students to progress more rapidly. This will facilitate an understanding of the connectivity of subject matter to encourage "the integration, application, and discovery of knowledge inside and outside the profession" (Boyer & Mitgang, 1996, p. 27).

Further, the interior design profession as a whole needs to step up to the plate and work collaboratively with educators to develop standards for a required certified work experience that initiates engagement with the real world. A portion of this requirement would need to be met prior to embarking on the final two years of study. Facilitating the tracking of an internship to meet professional education and registration requirements could be handled by the National Council for Interior Design Qualification (NCIDQ) (Harwood, 1995; 1996), just as it is by

National Council of Architectural Registration Boards (NCARB) (2009). After completing this initial experience, students will be much more knowledgeable about how their work fits into the context of the global community and brings value to society as a whole.

The final two years, culminating in an MID, would provide students with a depth of knowledge in an area of specialization, demonstrate evidence-based design solutions in a focused area, and help them gain a true understanding of the value that research adds to practice and contributes to the body of knowledge of the profession. Drawing on the strengths of their university and their faculty, programs could develop unique areas of specialization that would feed into the differing needs of the profession. Students could elect to complete their first professional degree in the same program as their undergraduate degree or transfer to another university with a specialization supporting their particular interest. This will allow for cross-pollination of programs by providing students the opportunity to draw from the strengths of more than one program in obtaining a first-professional degree.

We believe that the Guerin and Thompson 4+1 model (2004) provides a solid stop-gap measure to address the immediate needs of the interior design profession, particularly for facilitating enhanced engagement between the profession and the academy. However, the 3+2 MID first-professional degree provides the foundation required for the long-term health and future of the profession. We believe that to fully develop an area of specialization and gain a true understanding of research processes that support evidence-based design, a program of study of no less than two years is required. The current CIDA standards lead to a generic degree in interior design and do not prepare graduates for specializations now needed for practice, engagement in interior design education, and the cultivation of our body of knowledge. The current CIDA standards could be modified to define the guidelines necessary for the development of a specialized area as part of the requirements for the first-professional degree.

We believe that the adoption of the 3+2 model as the first-professional degree in interior design is critical to sustain the future of the profession. Graduates with an area of specialization rather than a generic interior design degree will be able to engage more quickly with the challenges facing the profession and the global issues impacting society. What remains on the table is a strong liberal arts foundation, a base core of interior design knowledge, and the development of an area of specialization with an understanding of research practices that bring value to a profession.

All professions have moved toward specialization, which has influenced their educational process. Interior design must move in a like direction. With the rapidly changing world and the accompanying explosion of knowledge, the interior design generalist is no longer relevant. The first-professional degree must begin to address a broader scope of values achieved through the rigor of specialization. Latour (2004) has reminded us that the academy has been slow to prepare for change, and our professional history reflects a similar trend. As we are reminded by Williams (2005), "The willingness and speed at which [the profession] agree[s] to change [is] a challenge that historically has proven to be one of the biggest hurdles of all" (p. 40). Now is the time for the profession to adopt the 3+2 model for the first-professional degree in interior design. We cannot afford to move at a snail's pace given the outside forces influencing our profession.

REFERENCES

Boyer, E., & Mitgang, L. (1996). *Building community: A new future for architecture education and practice.* Princeton: The Carnegie Foundation for the Advancement of Teaching.

Council for Interior Design Accreditation. (2009). *Professional standards 2009.* Retrieved May 30, 2009, from http://www.accredit-id.org/profstandards.php

Guerin, D., & Thompson, J. (2004). Interior design education in the 21st century: An educational transformation. *Journal of Interior Design, 30*(1), 1–12.

Harwood, B. (1995). An interior design experience program, part I: Defining the need. *Journal of Interior Design, 21*(2), 39–51.

Harwood, B. (1996). An interior design experience program, part II: Developing the experiences. *Journal of Interior Design, 22*(1), 15–31.

Jaschik, S. (2009, February 17). The buzz and spin on 3-year degrees. *Inside Higher Ed.* Retrieved on May 29, 2009, from http://www.insidehighered.com/news/2009/02/17/three

Latour, B. (2004). Why has critique run out of steam? From matters of fact to matters of concern. *Critical Inquiry, 30*(2). Retrieved on May 8, 2009, from http://criticalinquiry.uchicago.edu/issues/v30/30n2.Latour.html

Lewin, T. (2009, February 24). An option to save $40,000: Squeeze college into 3 years. *The New York Times.* Retrieved May 29, 2009, from www.nytimes.com/2009/02/25education/25hartwick.html

National Council of Architectural Registration Boards. (2009). Internship development program. Retrieved June 3, 2009, from http://www.ncarb.org/idp/index.html

Strauss, V. (2009, May 23). Colleges consider 3-year degrees to save undergrads time, money. *The Washington Post.* Retrieved May 29, 2009, from www.washingtonpost.com/wpdyn/content/article/2009/05/22/AR2009052203681.html

Williams, S. (2005, Winter). Measure of success. *Perspective,* 36–40.

⟶ How does the world (clients, the public) benefit from a person with a master's degree in interior design? With a bachelor's degree in another field? What are the obstacles?

MARGARET PORTILLO

COMPLETING THE CIRCLE: THE PLACE OF THE MID IN INTERIOR DESIGN

From his cultural vantage point as a Tuscarora Indian, Ken Rhyne sees his design practice as a circle: a shape without beginning, without end. A circle composed of practitioners, affiliated industry professionals, educators, researchers, and students increases in scale and dimension with each component part. Each member has a place in the circle. A special opportunity to reshape and expand the circle is presented by those who are educated in what I will call the hybrid master's of interior design. These hybrid master of interior design (MID) graduate programs have a track that enable graduates with a bachelor's degree from another field to become competent in entry-level interior design skills while gaining a specialization through thesis research or creative scholarship. This segment of the circle should be celebrated as enlarging the discipline's reach and connectivity to other fields.

At the core of this essay, narratives describe the educational experiences and professional

MARGARET PORTILLO, PhD, IDEC, is professor and chair of the Department of Interior Design, College of Design, Construction & Planning at the University of Florida. During her academic tenure, she has studied environmental color, creative design thinking, and topics in design pedagogy and narrative inquiry. Portillo is the author of *Color Planning in Interior Design: An Integrated Approach to Color* (Wiley, 2009). The book presents a criteria-based framework for color planning featuring original design process narratives by interior designers and clients. Portillo also held national leadership positions, serving on the CIDA Standards Committee, leading the *Journal of Interior Design* publications board, and as chair of the Research Council for FIDER. Portillo also served as guest editor for a special issue of the *Journal of Interior Design* on narrative inquiry and currently serves as the journal's editor in chief.

aspirations of MID students with such diverse educational backgrounds. Some argue that this population yields inherently weak designers and second-tier educators. I argue the opposite view: you will not only find strong interior designers and first-rate educators from the hybrid master's track pool but that these individuals may be best able to leverage their diverse interdisciplinary knowledge into creating remarkably well-designed spaces for clients and the public, and that these individuals also are well positioned to advance research and creative scholarship in the academy. Investing in this segment of the graduate population will lead to a healthy repositioning of evidence-based design practice and scholarship. That being said, I do recognize that it is critical for the hybrid MID to achieve core competencies in interior design and demonstrate a mastery of the discipline. I strongly believe that the role of the hybrid MID does not diminish the role of more traditionally educated interior designers. Further, I also want to acknowledge the obstacles that sometimes face these programs and their students. Critically reexamining the role of graduate education offers insights into ways of reshaping the field and best positioning the discipline to address future challenges and opportunities.

CROSSING INTERDISCIPLINARY BOUNDARIES IN GRADUATE EDUCATION

The Carnegie Foundation for the Advancement of Teaching commissioned a five-year project, *The Carnegie Initiative on the Doctorate,* to critique the status of doctoral education in the United States and make recommendations for its future (Golde & Walker, 2006). One of the foremost suggestions for change focused on interdisciplinarity as a means to ensure innovation and vibrancy in growing the knowledge base across disciplines. Again and again, leading scholars, charged with envisioning the future of graduate education in mathematics, chemistry, neuroscience, education, history, and English, saw the refusal to accept disciplinary boundaries as essential to reinvigorating doctoral education and expanding the pool of knowledge. In his analysis of the ideas put forth, Prewitt (2006), Columbia University, underscored the importance of crossing boundaries:

[Disciplinary] boundaries . . . are there to be crossed, blurred, merged, reconfigured, and even ignored. There is no neuroscience without cognitive science, no history without demography, no chemistry without biology, no education without sociology, no mathematics without computational sciences, no humanities without the arts, and on and on. (p. 29)

Cutting-edge programs in doctoral education promote "new intellectual groupings" and recognize that great opportunity for innovation lies exactly on the intersection point between fields: an assertion fully supported in the creativity literature (Csikszentmihalyi, 1999).

Likewise, hybrid MID programs have the potential to strategically form new intellectual groupings. We see interdisciplinarity not only as a driver in research and graduate education but in practice. For example, innovative global design consultancies, such as IDEO, leverage content knowledge and processes from across disciplines into award-winning design breakthroughs (Hargadon, 2003).

To explore the place of the hybrid MID in the disciplinary circle, student narratives are presented in Boxes 10.1–10.3. These narratives express the potential and complexities faced by three students who came to the study of interior design with undergraduate degrees in anthropology, architecture, business, and hospitality management. Lessons from their individual stories translate into larger ideas that can be explored by those delivering hybrid master's programs, those enrolling in such programs, and those hiring their graduates.

Clients, the public, educators, and practitioners, all can benefit from an investment in this segment of the circle. Finally, some of the obstacles will be presented that must be resolved if this connectivity with other fields is to be reached.

BOX 10.1
JIMMY'S STORY[1]

NARRATIVE OF AN ANTHROPOLOGY UNDERGRADUATE STUDENT EXPERIENCING THE HYBRID MID

I first was exposed to interior design in 2001 when I came to the university as a freshman. I had previous experience in drafting in high school, but that was more about technical execution than idea creation. At the university, I continued in architectural design studios for three semesters and after that left the program because I was frustrated with the purely theoretical approach to design. Architectural studios in this particular program focused more on form-making and less about a buildable design. I missed the technical and practical aspect of drafting from my high school. I felt there needed to be some place between theory and practice. For the remainder of my undergraduate education, I bounced between majors including, in order, history, building construction, back to architecture, and eventually to anthropology. I loved anthropology as an academic discipline, but had difficulty seeing how I could directly translate my anthropology education to a career in anthropology. . . .

I began exploring the possibility of applying my anthropology education to a graduate course of study that would result in a profession . . . I wanted to do something creative. I decided to revisit the reasons why I left the field of architecture as an undergraduate. I also considered both graduate school in architecture and interior design, but in the end I felt that interior design had the component that I was still searching for—which was to bridge the creative process of the designer to real-world design applications.

I started the master's program in the fall of 2006, and found that I had made the right decision. The program contained the practical aspects that I felt were missing from my undergraduate experience with the highly theoretical components of architectural design, and also included a research component that provided purpose for a design. . . .

I have found that anthropology definitely has helped in my MID program because in anthropology you are forced to see what is not there, and you are forced to discover things that people do not tell you. . . . Sometimes it requires a fresh pair of eyes to see all that can be.

BOX 10.2
ALEXIA'S STORY[2]

NARRATIVE OF A HOSPITALITY UNDERGRADUATE STUDENT EXPERIENCING THE HYBRID MID

My bachelor of science degree was a business degree in hospitality management, and I specialized in business operations. The work required for the degree was writing and research, but I really hadn't had any arts training since high school. Getting into the MID program and taking design studios for the first time . . . was a challenging transition. I was prepared for theory and methods but not the basic foundation design classes for the program. [As time went on] I felt that I had fully adapted to the program, and now I am able to apply the studio design foundation to research in design hospitality.

BOX 10.3

TIFFANY'S STORY[3]

Business was the field that I was most drawn to given the limited options on the Caribbean island where I grew up. In high school, I was on a business track, and college was a continuation of what I had done in high school. I guess I liked learning the business skills that were part of the curriculum—this was a combination of what I liked and what was available.

I have a long-standing appreciation of arts and crafts, and I realized that there was a field of interior design, yet I did not have the opportunity in my college to pursue interior design, given the limited offerings. When I finished my business degree, and I was working in my field for a time, I began thinking about pursuing a master's degree. Interior design was one of the options I thought about. My initial interest in interior design had never really waned, but I never had the opportunity to pursue it.

The transition from the curricular structure of business to a design-orientated field was not easy. The curriculum is structured very differently. Design is much more visual whereas business involves creativity in higher-level courses (such as creating a business plan), but the visual is not the primary focus. There is, especially in advanced [business] coursework, the opportunity to use creativity in a different way, in a different product. There is more writing in a business curriculum, although in the interior design graduate program there is writing as well. Papers require creativity but in the design studio the project is the visual product unless you are in some design graduate seminars [requiring writing]—this was easier. Ideally I could see myself teaching and practicing.

THE PLACE OF THE HYBRID MID

These three stories illustrate examples of new intellectual groupings that connect interior design and other disciplines. The narratives show that students who have committed to pursuing a master's degree in interior design often retain an affinity with their undergraduate fields of study and would like to inform their theses with this knowledge base. This type of student has acquired discipline-specific knowledge (such as history), and understands its key theories, central figures, discipline-specific language, research methods or processes of creative scholarship, as well as the field's evolution. Framing interiors-based research from another disciplinary perspective, these relative newcomers to the field are well positioned to create new, creative insights into interior design.

OBSTACLES

When first introduced to the studio culture, novice graduate students may feel intimidated and frustrated, like foreigners in a hostile land. To mitigate such experiences, hybrid MID programs should communicate performance expectations to potential program applicants who lack design experience. Further easing the transition into studio learning, faculty in such programs also can consider offering peer mentoring, skill development workshops, and incorporate select vertical studio experiences where more experienced students partner with less experienced ones. When possible, interior projects can be tailored to reinforce specialization areas such as hospitality design or historic preservation in the studio curriculum.

FIGURE 10.9. Main circulation through leisure area of airport features an abstracted Chinese ribbon element defining spatial zones and programmatic areas.

With the mastery of design thinking and skill sets, hybrid MID students seem satisfied with their ability to design and growing fluency in a new visual language. At this stage, MIDs are better able to integrate acquired disciplinary knowledge into their thesis work. For example, Jimmy applied his knowledge on culture and participant observation methods learned in anthropology to his thesis study of place making. In studio, he led his team in developing cultural references for a proposed airport project in Beijing (see Figures 10.9–10.12). Team members included James Wall, Katie Chapman, Danielle King, Jenna Lychako, and Ashley Moore.

Alexia's degree in hospitality management and related work experience alerted her to shortcomings in the design of hotel reception areas. Armed with interdisciplinary education and experience in hospitality and design, she is well prepared to study this problem in the field and develop recommendations. In Tiffany's thesis, she examined Caribbean influences on a significant historic building reflecting her life experience. These students have essentially become true hybrids and, while their design knowledge and skills and career aspirations vary, they can compete with the best traditionally educated students.

How can we recruit more MID students like Jimmy, Alexia, and Tiffany into the field? These students come to the interior design with another degree commitment, and life experience to draw upon in their work. Sometimes it takes time to discover interior design and maturity to venture into a less-traveled path compared to studies in traditional liberal arts and sciences or well-established professional schools.

Just as law and medical students now come to these professional programs from disciplines other than political science or pre-med tracks, so too can the master's of interior design student. Whether aligned toward practice, teaching, or research, the hybrid MID is ideally positioned to advance the practice and scholarship of evidence-based design. One such student entering a master's of interior design from another discipline lamented that she felt she had to "fight for your place when you come from another field." Is this necessary? Shouldn't we be focused on developing untapped potential?

FIGURE 10.10. Leisure area with stage for performances contains LED panels that offer a dynamic backdrop for performances as well as serve as a wayfinding device during non-performance times.

OPPORTUNITY TO CLOSE THE CIRCLE

Across the United States and Canada, hybrid MID programs, with a track for students from non–interior design degrees housed in research-intensive university settings, may want to consider forming a consortium. Programs in the Association of American Universities (AAU) and Carnegie I status schools are well positioned to support interdisciplinary, evidence-based graduate education. United, these programs could more powerfully engage interiors faculty, students, practitioners, allied contributors, and collaborators in strategic partnerships. Separately, interior graduate programs in general are fairly insular but together can have greater effectiveness in locating opportunities for funding, conducting, and disseminating interdisciplinary work (e.g., pre-design research, post-occupancy evaluations, or narrative case studies).

Working in tandem with other like-minded programs, interdisciplinary research can cumulatively expand the knowledge base. Interior design faculty members who oversee the thesis process should strive to create productive alliances across campus with faculty from other departments who contribute to a MID student's thesis. Further, interior design leaders from practice and industry should seriously consider the benefits of allowing students to investigate their processes and products using an interdisciplinary approach. One thing is for certain: we have to move beyond Balkanizing to better leverage scholarly work that crosses disciplinary boundaries. Together, each component of the circle from students to practitioners is called upon to imagine and act on the possibilities of crossing disciplines to raise our collective level of impact and innovation. Remembering the Carnegie Initiative . . . the time could not be more compelling to rethink the possibilities and potential of the hybrid MID. Who will participate in the process?

FIGURE 10.11. Atrium arrival area at night features large-scale LED panels with a "you are here" map designed to be seen from across the open atrium.

CONCLUSION

A discipline is only as strong as its knowledge base (Golde & Walker, 2006), and the knowledge base in interior design can be greatly developed by graduate research and education. Hybrid MID programs, existing and new, can and should be given the opportunity to demonstrate that their graduates meet CIDA-accreditation standards and offer specialized, interdisciplinary knowledge to the field vis-à-vis evidence-based practice, creative scholarship, and research. MID programs aligned with research-intensive institutions may be best able to meet this charge.

Changes are needed in attitude and action. Programs willing to recruit master's students from non-design backgrounds need to attract and retain the right caliber of graduate students. These students must be able to gain the necessary interior design foundation and bring their previous educational and life experiences to bear on their thesis research. Graduate coordinators and faculty members in such MID programs are encouraged to make strategic alliances across campus and encourage interdisciplinary connections in both graduate coursework and research. For example, I have chaired graduate committees that involve faculty members from departments including business, education, history, and urban and regional planning; unequivocally, outside faculty members make significant contributions to the framing of the research problem as well as its methodology and interpretation. To grow and develop the hybrid MID, we need to consciously cultivate interdisciplinary connections. As MID programs continue to mature and grow in legitimacy, we must explicitly capitalize on the multidisciplinary roots of the graduate students who are particularly well suited to engage in interdisciplinary research and creative scholarship that underscores the real-world relevancy of interior design. Are we ready to complete the circle?

FIGURE 10.12. Information desk in arrival area contains abstracted Chinese lattice work to define the space as well as provide opportunities for displaying arrival and departure information.

NOTES

1. James Wall, born and raised in Rockledge, Florida, spent most of his time as a boy drawing, coloring, and imagining far-away places. He completed a bachelor's degree in anthropology and is enrolled in the MID program at the University of Florida.
2. Alexia Cazort Thomas, born on the West Coast and raised in Atlanta, completed her undergraduate degree in the Hotel School at Cornell University. Her master's thesis, being completed in the MID program at the University of Florida, focuses on hospitality environments.
3. Tiffany Lang, born on St. Croix, U.S. Virgin Islands, completed a bachelor's degree in business. Her MID thesis investigated Caribbean influences on the Hamilton Grange property in New York. She is now enrolled in the University of Florida interdisciplinary doctoral program, concentrating in interior design.

REFERENCES

Csikszentmihalyi, M. (1999). Society, culture, and person: A systems view of creativity. In R. J. Sternberg (Ed.), *The nature of creativity* (pp. 325–330). New York: Cambridge University Press.

Golde, C. M., & Walker, G. E. (Eds.). (2006). *Envisioning the future of doctoral education: Preparing stewards of the discipline.* San Francisco, CA: Jossy-Bass.

Hargadon, A. (2003). *How breakthroughs happen: The surprising truth about how companies innovate.* Cambridge, MA: Harvard Business Press.

Prewitt, K. (2006). *Who should do what*: Implications of institutional and national leaders. In C. M. Golde & G. E. Walker (Eds.), *Envisioning the future of doctoral education: Preparing stewards of the discipline* (pp. 23–33). San Francisco, CA: Jossy-Bass.

> What are the challenges and opportunities when the design disciplines share an administrative home?

HENRY P. HILDEBRANDT

SUSTAINING DESIGN PEDAGOGY: STRUCTURE AND CONTENT OF INTERIOR DESIGN PROGRAMS AND AN EMERGING ACADEMIC CONTEXT

AT ISSUE

Professional design education is losing ground with the design profession it serves. Professionally generated research and design expertise are far ahead of schools and programs. Innovations in software and digital technology, sustainability knowledge, and management practices are being advanced within the profession that is now serving a more diverse client base and is working harder to maintain competitiveness (Gutman, 2007). Architecture and interior design programs are lagging behind professional firms as academic, administrative structures remain unchanged and unresponsive to new opportunities and challenges.

Interior design programs, together with other professional environmental design disciplines, organize curricula based on a number of principle factors. They include a model of professional traditions that has been embedded into the discipline's educational belief of professionalism; a context within the (university's) institutional

HENRY P. HILDEBRANDT is a registered architect with a BArch from the University of Nebraska, and a MArch from Kent State University. At the University of Cincinnati, he has been the coordinator of the Interior Design Program and associate director of Undergraduate Programs. Under Hildebrandt, the Interior Design Program achieved top national ranking by *Design Intelligence*. Hildebrandt was the Hyde chair, visiting professor, University of Nebraska, and has received several College of Design, Architecture, Art and Planning teaching honors, and UC's Faculty Achievement Award. He has been featured as one of five "A+ Teachers" in *Perspective*, received *Cincinnati Magazine's* Interior Design Professor of the Year, and IIDA's Michael Tatum Excellence in Education Award. Hildebrandt has been active in the AIA Interior Architecture Knowledge Community, has served as president of IDEC, and is a CIDA site visitor and team chair.

expectation of knowledge advancement; and the greater societal goal of protecting the health, safety, and well-being of its citizens.

Currently, American universities and higher educational institutions have expanded the idea of their roles from an educational focus to research and knowledge-generators and income-generating service centers. Responding to financial pressures and accelerated costs, traditional pedagogical principles have been questioned and as a result have begun to direct a new focus toward funded research. Professional design programs do less in developing connections to industry and research-granting sources than other professional disciplines such as medicine and engineering.

One of the problems in architectural education, according to Gutman (2007), is that the focus in the last several decades has been on curricula development and faculty output in design, criticism, and theory content. This has left building technologies and construction, the nuts and bolts of how to build, with less invested curricular energies, leaving graduates technically deficient. As Gutman (2007) points out, this reversed a pattern dominant until the mid-20th century where schools were connected to a background in the building trades. This trend has diminished the potential for academically funded research where the primary occupation of its professional activity is the design and building of buildings. This dialogue of academic and professional mission applies to interior design as well. Still, these disciplines and their programs have, as a whole, maintained a fairly solid status within the university and continue to enjoy high prestige with the public.

A major condition in the discussion of interior design's capability to contribute to a sustained dialogue of the new roles within the university and demanded by the profession is the specific governing, administrative structure of each program. This has been historically, and is currently, a major distinguishing factor in program output alignment within the institution.

Interior design programs and their curricula have been, with few exceptions, housed in quite different administrative locations within the university than architecture programs. Having different curriculum and enrollment projections, architecture schools often evolved into their own administrative units as schools or college. It has allowed each architecture program to maintain the traditional, monolithic, and time-honored design-studio-centered teaching vehicles and has structured a curricula heavily invested in studio pedagogy.

Interior design programs, on the other hand, have been grounded in human behavioral interests and centered in a more pure, academic research, output model—less invested in studio teaching. This left technical areas—issues of core and shell construction and the tasks of building—underrepresented or minimized in core curricula. Much of this is because interior design programs have had their roots deep in home economics and husbandry-type colleges dating from the 19th and early 20th centuries (Nutter, 2001). They have often maintained a non-studio and behavioral science discipline orientation and have been slow to adapt administrative restructuring and realignment toward a professional curricula structure. Only the last two decades have seen shifts in administrative alignments.

One of the most important potential components in aligning new educational strategies for universities—and interior design programs—is the shared administrative umbrella. This alignment provides both challenge and opportunity.

The next section of this essay discusses the emergence of interior design education and reconsiders its educational parameters regarding both the professional and academic world as opportunities for new platforms of learning pedagogy and effective theoretical and research studies. The goal is to frame a position for pedagogical content and to set agendas for potential curricula innovation to sustain a dialogue and process of action for problem solving and problem setting that structures discipline integration and collaboration.

Currently, much attention has been given to a more effective and collaborative professional practice in the design and building processes. Interior design and architectural firms; construction industry partners; and the architecture, engineering, and construction (AEC) industry have embraced new and emerging practice formats for collaboration and different types of networking teams in the delivery of design and building services.

A highly competitive global and regional market for design services has reset professional agendas. New modes of practice steer firms to engage in more cultural, ecological, and technical cross-disciplinary design teams. According to publisher James Cramer (2006), firms are increasingly engaging in an integrated practice where projects are designed, developed, and executed by interactive teams composed of several disciplines. These teams openly share information and ideas within streamlined delivery protocols fueled by a single technology platform.

This technology platform is known as integrated practice (IP) and realized through building information modeling (BIM). Digital platforms of drawing sharing and data integrated delivery type programs make it easier for more architectural firms and the AEC industry to switch to timesaving IP formats and BIM programs to improve design quality and effectiveness in service and product delivery. And, owners themselves are demanding more streamlined services that integrate design and construction services and are faster in delivery while focused on outcomes. Firms need to be more competitive, brand conscious, and develop responsiveness to clients' programs (Cramer, 2006). This involves firms increasingly using 3-D and 4-D technologies to study and deliver multiple design options in a shorter amount of time.

This emergence of IP in the AEC industry involves improving efficiency in the design/build process and is organized around collaborative sharing of information. However, the focus has largely been limited to only a localized collaboration—architects, interior designers, builders, and owner—with knowledge sharing and collaborative arrangements kept within this small circle and held within the scope of a single project. Firms are transitioning themselves into knowledge providers and resource generators with collaborative IP programs. As expanding market pressures drive firms to a more dynamic knowledge base of professional services delivery, IP and BIM will continue to become more common (Cramer, 2006).

CURRICULA STRUCTURE AND SUSTAINING THE CURRICULUM

The critical issue for current discussion is recognizing the potential for professional programs of interior design and architecture as potential partners for developing mutual collaborative service agendas—both within the institution and out. As Gutman (2007) notes, industry and the design profession have now taken the lead in knowledge generation and new paths of technology utilization for practice. The competitive professional world has demonstrated an agile ability to adapt and make innovative changes for healthier modes of operation and is accomplishing this evolution rather quickly.

The educational environment within the traditional university has not. There has grown a troublesome disconnect between education and practice, as noted by Burns (1997), which she terms "increasing emphasis on the production of scholars, rather than the production of professionals" (p. 36).

Universities customarily operate on set patterns that schedule and codify disciplines in complete, neat packages, wrapped for quick degree delivery. They are organized in a hierarchical pyramid structure of colleges, schools, and departments—and structured in top-down management fashion. They are often insular within individual departments and colleges and layered with tenure career-path professors, all of which contribute to an environment of isolation from competitive pressures and removed from the world of business effectiveness. This has established a context that discourages new trajectories of exploration in educational cross-disciplinary collaborations and off-campus partnerships.

Colleges in the U.S. typically administer several similar disciplines within their budgetary umbrella and are often housed within the same building or complex. In environmental design, architecture, and design college units, combinations of several disciplines may exist. Programs such as architecture; landscape architecture; design—industrial, graphic, fashion, interior; fine arts—painting, sculpture, art history; planning—urban and community; and building or construction science may be represented in various combinations under one administrative unit. College or school administrative groupings tend to have a kind of organizational logic that follows along professional service relationships such as the combination of architecture and interior design. However, as is often the case with many interior design programs, they are housed according to a distant historical relationship particular to the institution such as interior design and textile programs within a Human Ecology college.

In the university's centralized and autocratic administrative structure, funds and resources are distributed in a trickle-down process where resources filter down to the lowest administrative strata of department and then program. This often is an unhealthy arrangement for smaller programs, which is often characteristic of interior design programs. Within a limited resource environment, this establishes a guarded, turf mentality mind-set that discourages exchange

and interactive curricula development involving interdisciplinary and cross-disciplinary programs. Sharing of teaching means sharing resources; resources that are needed to support core curriculum teaching; resources needed for degree-granting classes; and resources needed for faculty support, supplies, and lecture series.

Academic research also suffers. The enterprise of knowledge production is kept inside the academic unit or within the discipline's own scholarship circle; research is viewed for short-term internal ends of promotion or tenure. And unlike industry, where high-risk and proprietary practice is one of the costs of knowledge generation, institutional production of scholarship is supported by sabbaticals, grants, release time, and graduate assistants. Just as new opportunities and new models for collaboration have developed in the profession, design education has opportunities to develop innovative and dynamic scenarios for reexamining the educational matrix and its pedagogical methodologies. Interior design, architecture, and other environmental design programs share many advantages of being housed together. Just as the profession uses integrated disciplines to deliver comprehensive services as in IP, this model's relevance is applicable to the academy. Shared formats of curriculum and crossover courses present opportunities for new platforms of learning, research, and effective administration.

Colleges and schools possess an army of talented and well-educated faculty directing equally talented and energetic students. These are resources to be utilized. If one of the goals of higher education is to harness collective energies to solve urgent problems, then the opportunity to assemble faculty and students to act on a wide range of critical issues should be a high priority. Positioned as research and analytical think tanks, and armed with new and powerful virtual tools, design studios and seminar classes can and have become significant, collaborative partners for new knowledge generation and the development of new priorities.

The need in the profession for hard research and analysis-formulated information is greater than before (Gutman, 2007). Although the goal of the university is to provide an education free from everyday demands of a commercial landscape, research and scholarship that involve community partnerships of interdisciplinary teams—professional and academic—can help sustain program curricula and activate critical dialogue to stimulate innovation and leadership (Burns, 1997; Friedman, 2007).

For example, research in behavioral and evidence-based design (EBD) processes could provide market value and utilize an intelligent, technologically savvy student/faculty labor force for such analytical services as post-occupancy evaluation (POE) (Hamilton & Watkins, 2009). All this is available as a rich research resource within design schools and interior design programs. Programs that partner with outside industry and professional firms as collaborative research-driven clinical laboratories can engage in complex, real-world projects that offer opportunities to weave together data-gathering and problem-setting strategies to solve community problems and sustain curricula teaching objectives.

Interior design, design (such as graphic design, product design, and fashion design), and architecture programs in comprehensive environmental design or architecture administrative units are just beginning to recognize this potential. Although the university system is still tied to an academic process of singular scholarship and individual, autonomously driven products such as a written research thesis, design curricula allows for flexible formats of the design studio employed as case method pedagogy (Friedman, 2007).

In large, multidiscipline design colleges, cross-disciplinary faculty and students can be assembled as research teams or in knowledge communities composed of a diverse pool of collaborative experts. At the University of Cincinnati, College of Design, Architecture, Art, and Planning (DAAP), a college with four schools, 11 sub-discipline units, and 2,300 undergraduate and graduate students, this has become one of the six guiding principles in the college's strategic plan.

One example of this is Professor Brian Davies of DAAP and Program of Interior Design. Professor Davies offered an interdisciplinary, experimental design studio on design for extreme environments. This involved faculty and students from medicine, geology, psychology, interiors, architecture, and industrial design to define and develop building for extreme conditions (Davies, 2008).

Although a history of interior design and design education has been largely ignored and must be explored in greater depth, individual program backgrounds and their changes within the last 50 or 60 years are equally void. Interior design programs and other design disciplines in the universities' structure are diverse, having many affiliations and relationships to other academic units. This has been consistent with interior design's historical development as a discipline and its current professional setting.

Harnessing intellectual energy and the skills of an analytical, research labor force are largely untapped within interior design programs and within the university structure. Although a few graduate programs have developed a framework for entrepreneurial models, more research program integration with the design industry has not yet developed a sustained tradition of partnership history such as in engineering or medical schools.

Most environmental design colleges and schools have not established many long-term collaboration goals with outside partners, nor have they set guidelines and assessment platforms for successful measurements. Without any long-term, ends-means testing beyond annual budgetary benchmarks, planning strategies remain unmeasured and success elusive.

To sustain curricula, grow programs, and contribute to the dialogue of new and needed knowledge for practice and curricula content to maintain authority over the inside of the building shell, and to advance the ethical commitment to resource usage, an integrated and entrepreneurial educational culture must be engaged. This provides challenges and offers opportunities for new platforms of learning pedagogy and new theoretical and research avenues.

REFERENCES

Burns, C. (1997). An approach to alignment: Professional education and professional practice in architecture. *Practices, 5/6*, 33–39.

Cramer J. (2006, June). *Scenarios shaping the next architect's success. Design Intelligence* [Bulletin]. Number 199. Greenway Communications LLC, pp. 3–9.

Davies, B. (2008, December). *Partner and prosper: The new academic paradigm.* Design Intelligence [Bulletin]. Number 219. Greenway Communications LLC, pp. 83–87.

Friedman, D. (2007). Architecture education on the verge. In J. Nasar, W. Preiser, & T. Fisher (Eds.), *Design for designer: Lessons learned from schools of architecture*, pp. 19–26 New York: Fairchild Books.

Gutman, R. (2007). Redesigning architectural education. In J. Nasar, W. Preiser, & T. Fisher (Eds.), *Design for designer: Lessons learned from schools of architecture.* pp. 11–18. New York: Fairchild Books.

Hamilton, D., & Watkins, D. (2009). *Evidence-based design.* Hoboken, NJ: Wiley & Sons.

Moe, K. (2007). Integrated curricula. In proceedings from the American Institute of Architects and Association of Collegiate Schools of Architecture Cranbrook 2007 Conference, *Integrated practice and the twenty-first century curriculum.* Cranbrook Academy of Art, Bloomfield Hills, MI.

Nutter, K. (2001). *Tracing the paths of interior design education.* Unpublished master's thesis, School of Architecture and Interior Design, College of Design, Architecture, Art, and Planning, University of Cincinnati.

Sanoff, H. (2007). Historical development of architecture schools. In J. Nasar, W. Preiser, & T. Fisher (Eds.), *Design for designer: Lessons learned from schools of architecture*, pp. 27–33. New York: Fairchild Books.

> What are the challenges and opportunities when the design disciplines share an administrative home?

JO ANN ASHER THOMPSON

INTERDISCIPLINARY ACADEMIES: CHALLENGES, RISKS, AND OPPORTUNITIES

In an unstable and unpredictable world, universities are being asked to produce graduates who will help solve complex societal and environmental problems—with fewer and fewer resources. In this challenging situation, traditional academic organizational and administrative models are being called into question. As a result, formerly accepted administrative units within universities (e.g., departments, institutes, schools, and colleges) are being merged, reconfigured, and—in some cases—eliminated.

Many scholars argue that transformational change within the academy can only occur when there is a focus on multidisciplinary and interdisciplinary collaboration (Ewel, 2001; National Academy of Sciences et al., 2005). Given this assertion, it should be expected that the design disciplines—often touted as the foci of innovation and creativity within universities—will take the lead in transforming from discipline-specific to interdisciplinary, shared administrative units

JO ANN ASHER THOMPSON, PhD, FIDEC, FIIDA, serves as professor of interior design at the Interdisciplinary Design Institute at Washington State University Spokane, where she served as vice chancellor (2003–2008). She is an NCIDQ certificate holder and practiced professionally for 15 years. A longtime site visitor and team chair for CIDA, Thompson has held national and international leadership roles including serving as IDEC's president and as the editor-in-chief of the *Journal of Interior* from 2004–2009. IIDA awarded her the Tatum Educator of the Year Award (2002). Thompson's research interests include the development of an interdisciplinary theoretical framework for interior design; interdisciplinary research and scholarship curriculum models; conceptual models that link interior design research to the process of design problem solving; critical linkages between the design educator's and design practitioner's roles; and graduate education and research opportunities for interior designers. She is the author of numerous journal articles and book chapters.

where collaborations in teaching and research could more naturally occur and with the added benefit of lower administrative overhead costs. Unfortunately, however, design faculty often resist efforts to change, entrenching themselves in the security of old mores and traditions rather than open-mindedly examining possible opportunities offered by an interdisciplinary home.

A BRIEF LOOK BACK

In most American universities, the idea of disciplinary isolation from other disciplines began in the late 19th century with the creation of the concept of an academic major. The development of majors soon began to underpin both the curriculum offered and the organization of American universities, with specializations (majors) widely adopted for undergraduate, graduate, and professional studies.

The most prominent organizational component to emerge from the concept of academic majors was departments. Within American universities, a department is usually understood to be the academic and administrative home of a discipline. According to the literature,

> A discipline is literally what the term implies. When one studies a discipline, one subjugates the ways one learns about phenomena to a set of rules, rituals, and routines established by the field of study. A student learns to study according to these rules, classifying phenomena according to commonly adopted terms, definitions, and concepts of the major field. Relationships among phenomena are revealed through the frames provided by the discipline, and the researcher or student arrives at conclusions based on criteria for truth or validity derived from the major field. (Radcliff, 2008)

Within the context of this history, university cultures soon began to emerge that further promoted discipline specificity, resulting in the development of departmental silos.

CHALLENGES TO SHARING AN ADMINISTRATIVE/ACADEMIC HOME

When conversations about possible reorganization begin, the historical evolution of departments as the organizational representative of a discipline reinforces the tendency of design faculty to "hunker down" and "protect their turf." This mind-set becomes ingrained; often limiting opportunities to create new, interdisciplinary administrative/academic models that can be more nimble and responsive to real-world issues that require more than one area of expertise.

Interestingly, this entrenchment stance runs counter to the philosophy of many professional design firms. For example, the widely respected design firm of Sasaki Associates declares on their Web site,

> Because we represent a wide variety of professional perspectives and experiences, and because we routinely consult with one another we can handle complex challenges more readily than other firms . . . Sasaki Interiors draws on the interdisciplinary philosophy on which our firm was founded. Our design is a process—not just an outcome. This process is collaborative and client focused. (Sasaki Associates, n.d.)

Although departmental silos are a primary barrier, there are many other individual, disciplinary, and programmatic barriers to interdisciplinary collaborations in American universities. These barriers include turfism, ego, extended time requirements, differences in methodologies and disciplinary norms, and the lack of funding for interdisciplinary efforts (Morse et al., 2007).

Disciplinary isolation and lack of funding for interdisciplinary approaches have been recognized not only by academicians, but also by leading design practitioners such as Eva Maddox, founder of Eva Maddox Branded Environments and Design Principal at Perkins+Will in Chicago. In 1999, Maddox lamented,

> Why do most design schools keep people from different disciplines isolated from one another? There are too many tensions between departments. . . . Those few institutions that even have engineers and architects and materials scientists all on the same campus tend to pit those groups against one another. The goal seems to be to get people to compete for funding. So why would those groups want to collaborate? (Lieber, 1999)

Several other organizational barriers and traditions extending beyond those already mentioned inhibit the creation of interdisciplinary, shared units. Traditional academic systems for hiring, tenure, promotion, and other rewards at most academic institutions are controlled by departments, and faculty often receive credit only for the teaching and research actually performed in their departments. Faculty who teach in interdisciplinary teams or classes outside the department may receive little or no departmental credit (Project Kaleidoscope, 2006).

Although the department continues to stand as the most universally accepted administrative unit in universities, and serves to define the discipline as it is owned by the faculty, further university traditions exacerbate resistance to interdisciplinary models. Things such as the names of degrees conferred, the reward structures that control the dissemination of knowledge, the assessment of mastery, and even the assignment of space and facilities significantly impacts transformation from a discipline-specific departmental model to an interdisciplinary model (Simpson et al., 2008).

Lastly, some of the greatest obstacles to shared, interdisciplinary units are disciplinary bigotry and lack of collegiality and respect that permeates many university cultures. Regardless of the specialization—be it in arts, sciences, humanities, business, engineering, agriculture, or design—there are those who will always view one discipline as beneath another. This assignment of second-class citizenry to design specializations and disciplines is embedded in many university cultures—and, unfortunately, it is often reinforced by university administrators.

In far too many cases, these biases reach into the ranks of design faculty, creating conflict—rather than collegiality—among faculty in the design disciplines. This lack of respect between disciplines is often evident among interior design and architecture faculty, thereby limiting the opportunities for meaningful collaboration. Upon graduation, students from such programs continue to view the world from a biased point of view, many times poisoning the potential for interdisciplinary collaboration in the professional design community at large. According to Eva Maddox, "It's one thing to dissolve the barriers that exist between the academic world and real life. It's another thing altogether to tackle the barriers that exist among designers on both sides of the divide" (Lieber, 1999). This concern is seconded by Stanley Tigerman, an architect and close associate of Maddox, who bluntly proclaims, "Architects have always treated designers badly" (Lieber, 1999).

Why then, with all these traditions and biases in place, should interior design programs fight the status quo? Are the benefits of interdisciplinary, shared experiences, and academic homes worth the risk to challenge these barriers? To answer these questions, it is important to first contextualize the status of American universities in today's world.

It is becoming widely acknowledged by educational and governmental leaders that transformational change is necessary if American universities are to continue to occupy a leadership role in higher education worldwide—and that key components of this change are interdisciplinary programs and research models. Major funding agencies such as the National Science Foundation (NSF) and others are increasingly demanding that interdisciplinary teams be the focus of grant applications, and leaders in reform of higher education are pinpointing interdisciplinary collaboration as essential.

For example, the Council of Graduate Schools clearly articulates the need for universities to incorporate interdisciplinary approaches in its 2007 Report by stating, "The United States must increase the number of graduate education programs that reflect the interdisciplinary dynamism characteristic of most innovative research centers" (McAllister & Redd, 2007).

Others point to a greater sense of urgency than ever before. This is due in large part to increasing competition in design and innovation around the globe. This competition has generated a desire for much broader design skills in the workplace, requiring academic institutions to respond. As globalization moves disciplines such as engineering, business, and design closer together, many argue that interdisciplinary undergraduate and graduate design programs are necessary for the United States to maintain its leadership in the future.

Recently there is evidence that the tide is beginning to turn and challenges are being overcome that have previously prohibited meaningful interdisciplinary discourse and the creation of shared, interdisciplinary homes (Simpson et al., 2008). Given the environment in higher education in the United States, opportunities for interdisciplinary exchange and collaboration have never been greater for the design disciplines. Funding opportunities for interdisciplinary teams are becoming more available; universities are beginning to embrace interdisciplinary programs and research by restructuring their reward systems to encourage interdisciplinary scholarship; the global community is quickly recognizing that the complexity of today's issues requires cross-disciplinary and interdisciplinary exchange to address them; and graduates from design programs are facing the need to perform in collaborative, interdisciplinary teams in the real world of practice.

A particularly inspirational example from the world of professional practice—where interdisciplinary dialogue and exchange underpins every decision—is IDEO. Founded by David Kelley in Palo Alto, California, "design thinking" is IDEO's primary praxis.

> We refer to our overall approach as "design thinking": a means of problem solving that uses design methodologies to tap into a deep reservoir of opportunity. . . . An inherently shared approach, design thinking brings together people from different disciplines to effectively explore new ideas—ideas that are more human-centered, that are better able to be executed, and that generate valuable new outcomes. (IDEO, 2009)

Just as at IDEO, when the design disciplines share an administrative/academic home,

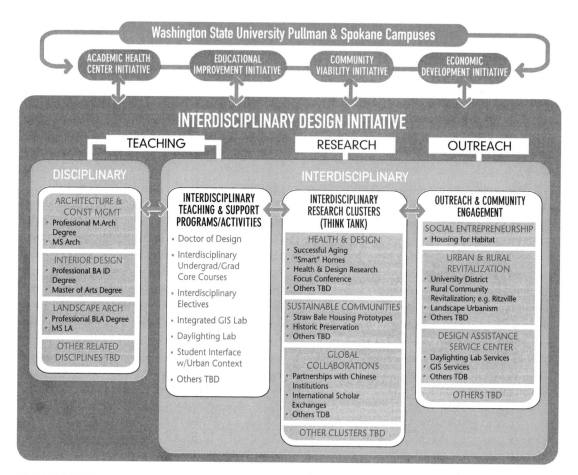

FIGURE 10.13. Proposed interdisciplinary model for a multi-campus system at Washington State University (Thompson & Blossom, 2008).

"it enables us to collectively tackle problems and ideas that are more complex than the lone designer can imagine" (IDEO, 2009). In such an interdisciplinary setting, students have the benefit of being grounded in their own discipline, while at the same time gaining insights into others. In an interdisciplinary and shared environment, faculty have more opportunity to exchange dialogue, identify issues, and collaborate with colleagues from different points of view. When a culture of mutual respect can be modeled by faculty, students soon follow—and both benefit.

Interdisciplinary, shared administrative/academic models within institutions of higher education provide a provocative and collaborative setting that allows faculty and students the opportunity to go beyond and between traditional boundaries. In such an academic environment, each design discipline reinforces individual disciplinary knowledge and skills, while developing additional interdisciplinary depth of understanding. This model advances both the art and science of design within the philosophical and pedagogical framework of interdisciplinary inquiry, critical synthesis, and problem solving (Guerin & Thompson, 2004). To those who assert that the risks of creating shared administrative/academic homes for the design disciplines are too great, or that the challenges are impossible to overcome, it is important to point out that there are interdisciplinary models being adopted at universities across the country.

Figure 10.13 (opposite) shows an interdisciplinary academic model for a design education initiative. The structured yet complex model reflects the complexity of interdisciplinarity at academic institutions. No model is perfect, and many universities are still dealing with the numerous challenges previously discussed. However, the time could not be better to boldly move forward, recognizing that at the root of every university's mission is the goal to provide students with an education that prepares them to succeed in a diverse, complex, and global community. Academic and administrative models, such as that shown in Figure 10.13, that combine disciplines and emphasize interdisciplinarity offer the design disciplines a tremendous opportunity to fulfill this vision in new and innovative ways.

REFERENCES

Brewer, G. D. (1999). The challenges of interdisciplinarity. *Policy Sciences, 32,* 327–337.

Ewel, K. C. (2001). Natural resource management: The need for interdisciplinary collaboration. *Ecosystems, 4,* 716–722.

Guerin, D., & Thompson, J. A. (2004). Interior design education in the 21st-century: An educational transformation. *Journal of Interior Design, 30*(1), 1–12.

IDEO. (2009). Design thinking. Retrieved January 23, 2009, from IDEO Web site: http://www.ideo.com/thinking/approach/

Klein, J. (2004). Interdisciplinarity and complexity: An evolving relationship. *E:CO, 6*(1/2), 2–10.

Lieber, R. (1999). Design: Eva Maddox. *Fast Company,* (30). Retrieved January 19, 2009, from http://www.fastcompany.com/magazine/30/maddox.html

McAllister, P., & Redd, K. (2007). International graduate applications and admissions in science and technology: The role of graduate education in supporting innovation. *Research Report.* Retrieved January 19, 2009, from http://www.cgsnet.org/portals/0/pdf/GaTech_ConfPaper_CGS.pdf

Morse, W., Nielsen-Pincus, M., Force, J., & Wulfhorst, J. (2007). Bridges and barriers to developing and conducting interdisciplinary graduate-student team research. *Ecology and Society, 12*(2), 8. Retrieved January 21, 2009, from http://www.ecologyandsociety.org/vol12/iss2/art8/

National Academy of Sciences, National Academy of Engineering, and Institute of Medicine. (2005). *Facilitating interdisciplinary research.* Washington, DC: National Academy Press.

Project Kaleidoscope. (2006). What works—an essay from the community: How academic institutions can facilitate interdisciplinary research. Retrieved January 23, 2009, from http://www.pkal.org/documents/InstitutionsAndInterdisciplinaryResearch.cfm

Radcliff, J. A. (n.d.). The academic major—The rise of the disciplines and majors, structure, interdisciplinary majors, academic majors, students and disciplinary knowledge, Retrieved January 23, 2009, from http://www.education.stateuniversity.com/pages/1726/Academic-Major.html

Sasaki Interior Design Services. (n.d.) Retrieved January 20, 2009, from http://www.sasaki.com/how/services.cgi?m=4

Simpson, T., Barton, R., & Celento, D. (2008, September). Interdisciplinary by design (A discussion). *Mechanical Engineering: The Magazine of ASME.* Retrieved, January 20, 2009, from http://memagazine.asme.org/Articles/2008/September/interdisciplinary_by_design.cfm

Thompson, J., & Blossom, N. (2008). Washington State University Spokane program prioritization report. Unpublished report. Spokane, WA: Washington State University.

11

PERCEIVED
IDENTITY

OVERVIEW What's in a name? This question has been asked about people, objects, locations, and, yes, even professions. Has the perceived identity of the interior design profession not allowed us to gain recognition for all we can do? We prevent people from being harmed in the interior environments in which they live, work, and play, but we are not exactly known for determining safe solutions. The underlying perception of the interior design profession varies widely—by the public, by related design professions, and even within our own profession.

This is the issue addressed by this chapter's authors—and they have divergent viewpoints! Shashi Caan suggests that it is important to create an identity for interior design that reflects the deep and palpable effect interior environments have on human experiences. Further, Crystal Weaver says, we must continue to define our work different from architecture—are we a separate profession or not? Janice Linster feels there is significant ambiguity in the name, whereas Lisa Whited and Mary Anne Beecher both call for us to determine if it's the name or the profession that needs changing. Eric Wiedegreen suggests more than one name is appropriate—is that a problem?

The last two essays examine what influences how the public perceives the identity of interior design. Lisa Waxman and Stephanie Clemons report on the influence of television media on our perceived identity. Theodore Drab concludes the chapter by declaring that we must help ourselves by using a better-informed design vocabulary when we talk about our design decisions, especially to those who publish our solutions. So, the question to you is this: should we change our name, or have we developed a good, solid brand that just needs a stronger presence?

SHASHI CAAN

FROM SHELTER TO COMFORT: EXPLORING THE INTERIOR DESIGN IDENTITY

INTERIORS AND THE WIDER DEFINITION OF DESIGN

Design is an essential discipline in the 21st century, one whose horizons seem limitless. Design affects and shapes the entire physical and sensory world we inhabit, and design practice has evolved from its roots in traditional craft, industry, and making toward a more sophisticated and comprehensive notion of design thinking. Business and marketing sectors have generated this groundswell in recognizing design as an ability and tool to organize; its adherents hold that design has evolved beyond the creation of physical objects or environments toward a new identity as a strategic thinking process combining rational analysis with creative thought. The advocates of design thinking argue that its rise has also spelled the demise of specialized sectors of design by focusing on process and giving little or no credence to the benefit of specialized knowledge of typologies, circumstances, or human behavior.

SHASHI CAAN is principal of The Shashi Caan Collective, New York City, and a former design director and associate partner with the New York office of Skidmore Owings and Merrill. She is the current president of IFI. She served as the chair of interior design at Parsons The New School for Design in NYC. Caan was *Contract* magazine's national Designer of Year (2004) and Educator of the Year for Greater NY (2006). She holds master's degrees in architecture and industrial design from Pratt Institute and a BFA in environmental design from the Edinburgh College of Art, in the United Kingdom. Caan is currently involved with New York's Columbia University, where she leads a research effort to establish the parameters and content for a design curriculum. She is a member of the executive board of the IDA (The International Design Alliance) and was recently made a fellow of the Royal Society for the encouragement of arts, manufactures, and commerce.

Even as the business-oriented sides of design advocate the merit of the generalized design process, leading designers and academics, in contrast, hold that design has no single identity, but rather must be seen as a constellation of distinct disciplines. In this view, the need for a depth of expertise in distinct design outcomes—as in product or communication design—has never been more essential. As a result, we can witness conflicting trends in design simultaneously, one moving toward unification and simplification and another to further expansion and depth.

Where do interiors fit in this map? Interiors as an area of interest have reached an unsurpassed global popularity, yet their increased visibility has only compounded the confusion over just what interior design is and what the interior designer does or should do. For interior design to evolve as a more distinct and meaningful discipline within a 21st-century conception of design, we must clearly define and address the

content and substance of what makes interior design unique. With a more comprehensive definition in place, we can then establish a continued relevance for an essential, rigorous, and evolving practice of interior design, even as the wider practice of design continues to encompass an ever larger scope.

But, the need for a comprehensive appraisal of the interior identity is critical for another and even more fundamental reason, one far beyond any struggle over professional turf. The vast majority of our lives is spent inside one space or another, yet we have a limited vocabulary with which we can speak about the very qualities that interiors, and only interiors, can address. By accepting the notion that interiors have a palpable effect on us, we can bring interior design forward as a discipline and practice whose identity and distinct importance to human well-being are clear to all of those in the profession and in the world at large.

DECORATION, DESIGN: TWO POLES OF IDENTITY

The public's current understanding of the term *interior designer* covers a wide range of professionals and trade-related individuals, ranging from the amateur decorator to the sophisticated and highly educated interior planner and problem solver, who deals with complex, large-scale commercial interiors. The gap between these two extremes is so vast that the profession and the general public have difficulty making sense of the merits of retaining a decorator versus an interior designer, and of what education and professional experience one would need to claim either mantle.

The problem is perhaps even more intractable than it seems and is one of a fundamental misperception because the most common popular conception of interiors is, as a profession, more concerned with the surface effects of style and fashion rather than substance. This stereotype is entrenched in the media, and in particular home-makeover shows, which continue to

reinforce the notion that interior design is simply a room-by-room styling exercise that can be implemented by just anyone with taste visiting one of the major retailers—and the residential examples given tremendously discount the knowledge required to design appropriately for the complexity of family life. Yet this stereotype also offers the opportunity to highlight the stark contrast between decoration and the comprehensive practice of interior design. Simply considering the difference in skills and ability that a decorator needs for a single-room, decorative makeover against the skills that an interior designer needs for the design of three million square feet of commercial interior space makes that point.

This bona fide interior designer must have a vast professional expertise in strategy, systems, planning, and environmental issues, which is knowledge that is recognized as important by the business community when offering design thinking as training for creative decision-making. The interior designer also needs a detailed understanding of structure, construction, regulatory requirements, building codes, and, above all, a worldly cultural awareness with a comprehensive education in the formal effects of spatial manipulation that go well beyond decorating and taste-making.

So what is this formal vocabulary? It involves manipulating volume, light, color, sound, smell, proportion, texture, and pattern to optimally support the functional and operational requirements of a space or sequence of spaces. The designer must also be able to plan both flexibly and strategically for the best, long-term potential of real estate, using its technological and practical opportunities to sensitively address a client's changing needs and culture. All of these aspects must be considered volumetrically and be envisioned in a spatially unifying concept that gives a client specific experience and provides users and occupants with a desired emotional impression.

It is the depth of thinking, the rigor of research, and the design process that distinguishes and sets apart the quality of successful interior design. Decoration is not exiled from this vocabulary, but must be integral to the experience and function as a critical, finishing touch. By carefully layering in these decorative elements, spaces can be completed. That completion—the Gestalt moment—represents the great unification of formal means that the serious interior designer must be educated to achieve.

INTERIORS AND BEING

The articulation of this formal visual and physical vocabulary is, however, not enough to establish the distinct role the interior designer must play and the identity the discipline must have. Interiors practice will always remain incomplete and unresolved if the emotive and sensory elements of interiors that directly affect us are not given a weight equal to the other and perhaps more easily taught formal elements. Thus, an interior's identity must evolve from primarily offering physical interventions to the inside of the built environment toward a broader practice that takes into account the effects those interventions have on the well-being of people who inhabit the space.

Fundamental to interiors practice is the human occupation of space. Thus, the interior affects humans at more intimate and individual scale than architecture. Further, the functionality of the interior can be both practical and uplifting, and invigoratingly affect people in not only who they are but also in whom they can become. That need to transform the experience is so poetically stated in the words of Lao-Tzu: "The reality of the building does not consist in roof and walls, but in the space within to be lived in" (see http://www.famousquotesandauthors .com/authors/lao_tzu_quotes.html). Frank Lloyd Wright was so struck by this quotation that he had it written on the wall of the auditorium in Taliesin West, Phoenix, Arizona.

Put more simply, the designer must consider the interior as the response to a question: "Who am I, and who do I become upon entering the designed space?" That question is the essence of what interior design needs to answer for people in the physical world. When the interior designer's intention invokes the user's innate desire, then the space has been successfully designed. When a space is transformed into a useful and appropriate experiential environment that fully supports the people for whom it is designed, it becomes much more than just a sum of its formal visual elements. Yet, these experiential requirements for interiors are least recognized by the general public as integral components of interiors practice; even those practicing interior design professionally are not always conscious of these requirements. Thus, the most significant leap in the definition of interior design that needs to be made is the need to integrate this experiential knowledge into education, profession, practice, public awareness, and ultimately into the identity of interior design. With this integrated knowledge, interior design will stand more clearly on its own and will no longer be seen through the lens of other design disciplines.

THE ANALOGY TO PSYCHOLOGY

The development of other disciplines, particularly of psychology, may offer useful insights in and analogies for the development of interior design as a distinct discipline. Psychology offers two relevant aspects for comparison: first, in its struggle to emerge as a profession separate from the traditional practice of medicine; and second, in the acceptance of the possibilities of offering rigorous, empirical treatment for the inner qualities of the mind. The great advance in experimental psychology was made in arguing that there were direct, externally introduced measures that could affect internal mental processes, which for centuries had been thought unknowable. Psychology was able to identify and describe bona fide emotional states that had been previously thought of in purely physical terms. The interior design discipline must make a similar step forward in understanding better the profound effect it has and relate it to the seemingly intangible qualities of interior experience.

Although architecture and interior design have a symbiotic relationship, they are distinct and individual professions, often with different goals not unlike the doctor and the psychologist. Whereas the medical doctor has an expertise that focuses on a person's physical and bodily health (the external phenomena), the psychologist addresses a person's internal or the emotional, perceptive, and behavioral health. Because the interior similarly deals with these latter qualities, we must offer interior design as a design discipline that addresses human problems that allied design practices are simply ill-suited and ill-prepared to address.

Thus, we must build rigorously a comprehensive base of knowledge on these sensory, perceptive, and behavioral issues *in terms of design.* This new experiential and emotive knowledge will have to flow from empirical research to build a design knowledge that is now barely present.

The development of empirical design research must be a vital center of the interior design process that will allow us to create a usable, wide-ranging knowledge of fundamental human behavior that interior designers can use to better serve people. By folding this new learning into the existing knowledge of designing environments responding to functional and programmatic needs, the built space that results—whether a hospital, a multistory office complex, a school, an airport, a single-room restaurant, or a residence—will sing with a completeness that would otherwise be absent.

REDISCOVERY OF ROOTS

The complexity of inside space has vastly increased in the past century—roughly the life span of modern interior design practice—and today we deal with numerous interior typologies of widely varying scales and functions. From supporting the most essential and basic needs to the most transient pleasures, today the interior comes in a myriad of shapes, sizes, and configurations. However, the apparent complexity of interiors practice belies and obscures the common origins and roots. The recovery of the roots of interiors—the deep-seated needs for shelter and comfort—is essential.

The earliest interior, the cave, predates any notion of building or design. It attempted to fulfill a more fundamental internal quest for psychological equilibrium and delight rather than to serve merely as physical shelter. The earliest forms of habitation did provide a direct barrier from the hostile forces of the external world, but they also satisfied—or attempted to satisfy in a minimal and primal form—the deep human desires for emotive and sensory experiences that the outside world alone could not provide, as so richly evidenced by the early cave painting from our prehistoric ancestors.

The identification and recovery of the fundamentals of this common origin will aid interior designers in their attempt to address human needs in occupied space, a purpose that, as stated earlier, must form the core of the interior design profession. Whatever the typology of the interior, we should be able to fulfill the individual and collective needs of the occupants to better let them live their lives in comfort and security.

INTERIORS PRACTICE INFORMS ALL DESIGN

Interior design elevates, but not in the traditional sense that decoration might be said to elevate, through taste. Instead, good interior design is not based in style or fashion but on realizing the most appropriate and livable environment to support people. In its primary emphasis on human qualities, interior design also offers a better pathway to all design to consider more fully the role of humans in a designed world. Seen this way, and returning to the two different points of view posed at the beginning of this essay, the advocates of design thinking and strategy have merely isolated and magnified what is latently an integral part of all design practice.

What needs to be added to this thinking is the other dimension. Good design is when the human spirit is uplifted and piqued by the unfolding of discovery and delight. But, as with any of the classical arts, good design requires cultivation and learning. Good design is not about trends or fashion, but rather about smart solutions infused with empathy and beauty.

CRYSTAL D. WEAVER

ALLIED PROFESSION OR SUBSET OF ARCHITECTURE: THE DILEMMA

Interior design is, by definition, preparation, and practice, an allied profession of architecture. This relationship, based on the shared common purpose that joins the two professions, is both reciprocal and open to other professions that impact the built environment such as engineering, urban design, and landscape architecture.

DEFINITION

The definition of interior design, as endorsed by the Council for Interior Design Accreditation (CIDA) and published by the National Council for Interior Design Qualification (NCIDQ) in 2004, is clear in delineating the role and responsibilities of the profession:

> Interior design is a multi-faceted profession in which creative and technical solutions are applied within a structure to achieve a built interior environment. These solutions are

CRYSTAL D. WEAVER, PhD, IDEC, associate AIA, has been a professor of interior design at the Savannah College of Art and Design (SCAD) in Savannah, Georgia, since 1992 and served as chair of the interior design department from 1997–2001 and dean of the School of Building Arts (Architecture, Urban Design and Development, Historic Preservation and Interior Design) from 2000 to 2007. She was one of the founding members of the executive committee for the USGBC, Savannah chapter, and has served on the national USGBC LEED® Curriculum & Accreditation Subcommittee. Weaver also coauthored the LEED® CI *Technical Review* for the USGBC. Her work over the past eight years with the AIA and ACSA has resulted in numerous awards. Weaver received her MS and PhD from the University of Tennessee, Knoxville.

functional, enhance the quality of life and culture of the occupants, and are aesthetically attractive. Designs are created in response to and coordinated with the buliding shell, and acknowledge the physical location and social context of the project. Designs must adhere to code and regulatory requirements, and encourage the principles of environmental sustainability. The interior design process follows a systematic and coordinated methodology, including research, analysis and integration of knowledge into the creative process, whereby the needs and resources of the client are satis-fied to produce an interior space that fulfills the project goals. (NCIDQ, 2004)

The definition further, through elaborating on the scope of services performed by an interior designer, establishes the professional as one whose services may include, among other services, "Coordination and collaboration with other allied design professionals who may be retained to provide consulting services, including but not limited to architects; structural, mechanical and electrical engineers; and various specialty consultants" (NCIDQ, 2004).

PREPARATION

The preparation required for the practice of interior design reinforces the allied relationship between interior design and architecture. Although both professions subscribe to the three E's of education, experience, and examination, they do so independently of one another. Each discipline engages in design education that is specific to the respective profession.

Beginning with formal academic prepa ration, which is subject to the rigors of professional accreditation requirements for both interior design and architecture, the educational process for the two disciplines runs on parallel tracks. Both CIDA and the National Architectural Accrediting Board (NAAB) engage in distinctly independent accrediting processes designed to ensure that educational programs meet established standards for the respective professions.

Similar to the educational process, the experience leg of preparation for professional practice for interior design and architecture runs on parallel tracks as well. Whether via the Interior Design Experience Program (IDEP) administered by NCIDQ or the Intern Development Program (IDP) administered by the National Council of Architectural Registration Boards (NCARB), the programs provide a structured transition from the academic experience to the professional world, independently and in isolation of one another.

Examination requirements, as with both education and experience mandates, continue the independent and parallel preparation of the professional interior designer or architect. Requirements of graduation from an appropriately accredited CIDA or NAAB program and completion of the IDEP or IDP experience serve as eligibility precursors for both examinations, the NCIDQ and Architect Registration Examination (ARE), respectively. Sharing a common mission to protect the health, safety, and welfare of the public, the NCIDQ and ARE independently establish minimum competencies for professional practice in interior design and architecture.

PRACTICE

The practice of interior design establishes the allied relationship between interior design and architecture. Since the earliest days of the profession, the practices of interior design and architecture have been intertwined. This historical and reciprocal relationship between interior design and architecture has at times placed each profession in both a dependent and independent alliance with respect to one another. Historically, this relationship between interior design and architecture has adapted to the needs of each of the professions individually and collectively, as well as the economic realities of the day. The adaptation by the two professions continues into the present day.

The definition of interior design was created by a task force of appointed members of interior organizations, including the Association of Registered Interior Designers of Ontario (ARIDO), the American Society of Interior Designers (ASID), CIDA, the Interior Design Educators Council (IDEC), the International Interior Design Association (IIDA), and NCIDQ, that published it in 2004. This definition has been endorsed by all of these organizations. It references the dependent yet independent relationship between interior design and architecture in stating, "Interior design is a multi-faceted profession in which creative solutions are applied within a *structure* to achieve a built environment. . . . Designs are created in response to and coordinated with the *building shell*" (NCIDQ, 2004). Interior design relies only upon architecture to supply the canvas upon which to work, yet is independent of architecture in the work upon the canvas. In the end, the success or failure of the interior lies solely upon the interior design, as does the structure upon the architecture.

Professional organizations play a vital role in the allied relationship of interior design and of architecture. In addition to providing a code of ethics and professional conduct by which all members agree to abide ASID, IIDA, and the American Institute of Architects (AIA) serve a vital role in representing the interests of their membership through advocacy, education, and professional development. Membership categories in ASID, IIDA, and AIA acknowledge the successful completion of the NCIDQ or ARE and provide membership opportunities for allied professionals. Operating as parallel organizations, IDEC and the Association of Collegiate Schools of Architecture (ASCA) have as their core missions the advancement of interior design education and architectural education, respectively.

THE DILEMMA

That the question "Is interior design an allied profession or a subset of architecture?" must be asked is indicative of the current state of the interior design profession. Two major issues are at play in addressing this dilemma, one of definition and identity and another of perspective.

Since the earliest days of the profession, interior designers have struggled to create an identity by which to define themselves and their profession. From the never-ending discussion of "interior designer" or "interior decorator" to the adoption in 2004 of a definition of interior design endorsed by CIDA and approved by NCIDQ, the struggle has been played out individually and collectively by academicians, practitioners, and their respective professional organizations.

Presently, the struggle to create and communicate a common identity and definition continues. Whereas IDEC, CIDA, and NCIDQ all endorse the 2004 definition of interior design, which clearly establishes interior design as an allied profession of architecture, IIDA promotes a variation of the definition on their Web site that has reference to, but is not the same as, the endorsed definition:

> The interior design profession provides services encompassing research, development, and implementation of plans and designs of interior environments to improve the quality of life, increase productivity, and protect the health, safety, and welfare of the public. The interior design process follows a systematic and coordinated methodology. Research, analysis, and integration of information into the creative process result in an appropriate interior environment. (IIDA, n.d.)

As if to compound the struggle of identity and definition, ASID, the oldest, largest, and leading professional organization for interior designers, provides no direct reference to the definition of "interior design" or "interior designer" on its Web site (ASID, n.d.). The endorsed definition is found about three levels down (in "clicks") under "Design Services," then "Interior Design Basics," where, in the third paragraph, the NCIDQ Web site is linked, and one goes directly to the definition (http//www.asid.org.designservices/basics/).

The academic (IDEC), accrediting (CIDA), and examination (NCIDQ) arms of the profession, i.e., the entities responsible for the preparation of professional interior designers, endorse a definition of interior design that varies or is missing from the two major organizations representing the profession. Accredited interior design programs across the United States deliver educational programs based upon standards established by CIDA that lead to eligibility to sit for the NCIDQ exam. Yet the students of these programs enter into a profession that has been defined differently, if at all, by the two primary professional organizations than the definition that served as the underpinning of their formal academic preparation. Lacking a common accepted identity or definition that unifies the educational, examination, and professional practice areas of interior design, the

struggle continues in frustrated attempts to educate the public of the role and responsibility of interior design within the built environment.

The second issue at play in addressing the dilemma of interior design as an allied profession or a subset of architecture is that of perspective. The documented struggle to define interior design has been exacerbated by a skewed perspective of the profession by both its members and the public at large. Historically, the profession of interior design has sought to identify and define itself through the mirror of architecture, placing interior design in a subservient and dependent relationship with architecture. The resulting status and image of the interior design profession has been that of a subordinate subset of architecture.

This subordinate placement of interior design as a subset of architecture is still prevalent today within both academic and professional practice settings. In numerous academic institutions, interior design programs exist under the larger umbrella of architecture. Typically staffed with fewer faculty, lower student numbers, and smaller budgets and faculty salaries, these programs perpetuate the dependency and subset nature of interior design to architecture. Similar relationships exist within professional practice in architecture and design firms as interior design, again viewed through the mirror of architecture, serves as a dependent subset of architecture rather than an independent allied profession.

The placement of interior design as a subset of architecture is a result of several contributing factors, the primary of which is the lack of unity and clear identity coming from the profession. Beginning with the absence of a singular, shared identity and definition of the profession by its invested members and organizations to the unwillingness to be represented by one all-encompassing, professional organization, the segmentation of the interior design profession has undermined the profession's power and allowed others to make the argument that interior design is a subset of architecture.

THE SOLUTION

To unequivocally establish interior design as an allied profession of architecture within the profession and greater public arena, three actions must occur. First, a clear, concise definition of interior design must be adopted and vigorously promoted by all bodies and organizations involved in interior design. From academic preparation through professional practice, a singular definition of interior design will serve to unify the numerous players in the profession and solidly secure the rightful identity of interior design as an allied profession of architecture.

Secondly, with a single, concise definition in place, the academic, practitioner, and professional organization bodies of interior design must collectively and simultaneously address the issue of public perception and identity of the profession. The public must be educated as to the role and responsibilities of interior designers without viewing the profession in the mirror of architecture. The responsibility for this public outreach must be borne by educators, practitioners, and the professional organizations of ASID, CIDA, Interior Designers of Canada (IDC), IDEC, IIDA, and NCIDQ, working together as a single entity representing the profession.

And finally, interior designers at all levels and positions within the profession must conduct themselves as allied professionals of architecture. From educators and students at academic institutions to practitioners and professional organizations, members of the profession must establish and unceasingly reinforce the independent and allied relationship between the professions of interior design and architecture.

CONCLUSION

Is interior design an allied profession or a subset of architecture? Interior design and architecture are allied professions, sharing a parallel yet independent pathway through professional preparation and practice. The current state of the profession, however, creates a dilemma in the lack of acceptance and adoption of a singular, unifying definition and common identity for interior designers. Compounding this lack of a shared definition and identity is the skewed perspective of the profession by its members and the public.

The time has come for interior design to firmly establish itself as an allied profession of architecture for its members and the public through the adoption of a singular definition of the profession, the creation of an accurate public identity, and a shared commitment to the independent, yet shared focus of the profession. The time is now to remove the question of "allied profession or subset of architecture" from discussions of the profession of interior design.

REFERENCES

ASID. (n.d.) *About ASID*. Retrieved January 30, 2009, from http://www.asid.org/about/default.htm

IIDA. (n.d.). *Definition of an interior designer*. Retrieved January 30, 2009, from http://www.iida.org/i4a/pages/index.cfm?pageid=379

NCIDQ. (2004). *Definition of interior design*. Retrieved January 30, 2009, from http://www.ncidq.org/who/definition.htm

> Does the client know your interior design background (education, experience, examination), and does he/she care? Is your interior design background ever a liability? Do you hide your background?

JANICE CARLEEN LINSTER

PERCEIVED IDENTITY

The conversation usually starts with a very simple question, "What do you do for a living?" "I'm a designer. I own an architecture and interior design firm. We design mainly commercial environments such as . . ." "Where did you go to school?" Easy, "the University of Minnesota." "What was your degree in?" Here's where the pause comes in, I look up hoping for a large jet to fly over and muffle the conversation or for a distraction in the crowd that draws attention elsewhere. My mind reels—name, rank, and serial number only—do whatever you can to avoid "it," the degree, the title. Here it comes. "My degree is in interior design." I hear back, "Oh, how fun, so you pick colors!"

The introduction or elevator speech is always short, sweet, and to the point. Unfortunately, the minute you spit out the words *interior designer,* you've lost them. There's no time for the "I actually have a four-year degree; I took a test that covered . . . ; I think three-dimensionally; I deal with codes and . . ." It's too late. They've made up their minds; they have you pegged.

JANICE CARLEEN LINSTER, CID-MN, LEED® AP, ASID, is a graduate of the University of Minnesota. Her 25-year career has focused primarily on the workplace. Linster is a principal and one of the founding partners of the Minneapolis-based architecture and interior design firm Studio Hive, which specializes in the design of corporate, learning, and living environments. Prior to establishing Studio Hive, Linster was a principal and director of interior design for Ellerbe Becket. Linster's industry participation includes serving as president of the University of Minnesota's College of Design student and alumni board. She has also served as a board member of Minnesota's state licensing board, ASID's board of directors, and InformeDesign's technical review board, as well as an NCIDQ delegate. She has also been a juror for local and national design competitions, and a panelist, speaker, and guest critic for interior design programs.

To be very clear, my viewpoint, although shared with many others, represents only a segment of the interior design population. Not a superior segment, but a critical mass practicing primarily commercial interior design and complex residential interior design. For those of us who've accrued education; passed the industry's national examination by the National Council for Interior Design Qualification (NCIDQ); and practice in a firm providing a broad scope of professional, creative, and technical services, the mental picture the general public associates with the interior design profession is often disturbing.

Is interior design fun? Definitely. It is creative, inspiring, and always changing. But there is much more to it. There is a sector within the profession capable of influencing health and wellness, productivity, sales transactions, concentration, communication, inspiration, personal safety, and brand recognition. Under one umbrella, we have a population of highly educated interior designers impacting our lives through the design of some of the most notable environments in our society. Under this same umbrella, at the opposite end of the spectrum, we have another population, gifted in color and decor, who overnight have claimed the title "interior designer." At what point do we call "time out"? Do we continue to wade through the flock, doing our best to claim the piece of the profession that reflects our education, experience, and testing? Or is it time for a title adjustment? And if so, what should it be?

As with most professions, interior design has evolved immensely since its inception. External influencers such as technology, globalization, the economy, sociology, human health, and life safety have progressed the profession; CIDA (Council for Interior Design Accreditation) accredited interior design educational programs and the NCIDQ examination have continued to transform it. Training, internships, and continuing education have also expanded to keep pace with these ongoing changes. At the same time, we celebrate these more stringent benchmarks

for education, experience, and examination, we've seen a plethora of "do-it-yourself" programs, certificates, and advertisements promoting an "easy entrance" job market. Even television shows have sprung up highlighting "interior design makeovers in a week," giving a face to the occupation that clearly does not define the career path many of us pursued.

The profession has matured and branched off into multiple directions; all the while, the title "interior designer" has stretched to cover everything this field was and everything it has grown to be. Herein lies the problem; "interior designer" has become a catch-all title, a label trying to mean everything to everyone.

As interior designers, we all need to take responsibility for our own career destiny. At the same time, however, we are branded by external viewpoints of client perception, public perception, or word-of-mouth delivered by friends. Our label, or professional title, forms an immediate impression and signals a series of stereotypes. For those of us who have attended one of the highly regarded interior design educational programs offered around the country, the degree itself is not the root of the problem. Speaking personally, my education was well rounded, and my own drive positioned me in the role I had expected. The title assigned to me, however, is ambiguous and has initiated a few unexpected challenges throughout the course of my career. The primary battles I see for interior designers seeking to pursue this complex and comprehensive side of practice are proving self-worth to allied professionals engaged in the collaborative design process, meanwhile dispelling the stigma that wraps artificial boundaries around an interior designer's scope of work.

Although uphill battles exist in the effort to gain prominent recognition in the commercial interior design profession, achievement comes from perseverance and making your own mark. It takes a determined individual to not just break the mold but to define the mold, and fortunately the stage has been set by many successful interior designers.

As we enter the field, our first challenge is to establish our personal brand. Those who rise to the top often take on additional efforts, additional coursework, essentially going the extra mile. Determination is, therefore, a key element in shaping one's individual destiny. Life will certainly be easier if you affiliate yourself with a firm whose brand and reputation embody the interior design profession you are pursing. In addition to one's own determination, riding the coattails of a successful, industry-leading firm can lead to recognition by association. There are many design firms all over the country that embrace the full scope of interior design and are recognized by allied professionals and clients for their unique knowledge.

INTERIOR DESIGN AND ARCHITECTURE

Impressing an employer is often more difficult than impressing a client. There are still many design firms that do not understand the wide-ranging role of a professional interior designer. As a result, many interior designers choose to avoid these employers, whereas others pursue a more limited role in these firms, focusing on furnishings and finishes. This, too, is a valued occupation but dramatically different than the more complex, comprehensive side of the profession that encompasses the full use of specialized knowledge. I frequently see interior designers settling into a compacted role in an architecture firm. This reality is as much about interior designers, their understanding of the business, and their aspirations for practicing as it is about preset stereotypes in the design firm. This situation is representative of a multifaceted issue. Interior designers have to want the broader role and prove their self-worth, and the firm has to be accepting of the role.

Architecture and interior design are too connected to ignore the benefits of collaboration. For some professionals in both industries, the road to an amicable relationship may be rough going at first. Creating synergy and partnerships, however, is at the root of success for professionals and clients alike, and those with the perseverance to pursue these alliances will yield the greatest benefits.

INTERIOR DESIGN AND THE PUBLIC

Client perceptions of interior designers are a slightly different animal. Because our clients are "the public" before they are our clients, they form opinions based on preconceived notions. Many clients may not recognize interior designers in architecture and interior design firms as interior designers. Because many architects have chosen to focus their careers on the design of interior environments, clients may easily assume interior designers are architects and architects are interior designers.

When interior designers speak eloquently and intelligently about design, space, experience, codes, or sustainability, the client's or contractor's limited perceptions about the role and value of interior designers will be modified, and this new knowledge about interior designers' reputation and performance will supersede any preconceived stereotypes. Clients will most often recognize the firm and the individuals in the firm for what they do and not give consideration to title, let alone specific education or examinations.

Most firms will hone individual talent in a manner consistent with the values, vision, and philosophies of the firm. Therefore, education and examination are important parts of entry into the profession, and experience is a determining factor in how one's career unfolds and varies from that of another. If interior designers make the right professional moves, showing their worth to a client becomes less of a battle than fighting misperceptions in the public eye or even proving our value to architects.

I have had the title ambiguity discussion with many designers. It's an old conversation for many of us. It's interesting that when established, many commercial interior designers share a common habit of ditching the formal "interior designer" title and opting for the abbreviated title of "designer" simply to avoid stereotypes and misjudgments. The vagueness of this "designer" label is apparently a better bet than risking being slotted in the *wrong* category altogether. Over the years, my colleagues and I have been tagged with a variety of titles resulting from the diversity in our profession. The list includes interior designer, of course, as well as decorator, finish picker, architect, interior architect, and my favorite–WPPO (wallpaper-picker-outer).

If a young brilliant individual came to me expressing interest in pursuing a career designing all aspects of interior environments, I might struggle with the advice on the appropriate career path. Highly regarded interior design programs definitely provide the best education, yet the all-encompassing title carries an unfair burden. Architectural programs may appear to have won the more prestigious title contest, yet the education is too broad for anyone with no intention of designing skyscrapers and too weak in regard to the unique knowledge of interior design. Interior architectural programs may be a solution for providing clarity in the future, but they do not seem to be welcomed by either the interior design or architecture professions as a professional career path. The bottom line is we are long overdue for an assessment of our industry and an evaluation of the definition of the title "interior designer." It is not enough to have a career path with a bachelor's or master's degree and a national examination that tests competency to perform our roles. The pool of individuals falling under the "interior designer" umbrella is simply too broad, too diverse. Even with licensing and registration of the profession, the confusion continues to exist.

Not everyone pursuing a career in interior design is after the same professional role. As the profession matures and only a segment of that profession becomes increasingly responsible for the public's health, safety, and welfare and for influencing the overall human experience, the assignment of distinguishable titles based on specific roles and responsibilities becomes eminently important. Precedence has been set outside of our profession as new titles, job descriptions, and even industries have surfaced and branded themselves in a fraction of the time our profession has been in existence. Interior design is an industry that embraces progression, sets trends, and commends innovation. Let's apply this science, this mind-set, to our own profession. We should be proud of our history and, at the same time, prepare for the future.

> What is the nature of the identity crisis that seems to have hit the interior design profession? Do we differ from other professions in our development? What is the answer?

LISA M. WHITED

THE IDENTITY CRISIS OF INTERIOR DESIGN

"The first step to wisdom is getting things by their right names," wrote Edward O. Wilson (1999), in *Consilience: The Unity of Knowledge.* Interior design continues to struggle with its identity as a profession. Achieving regulation in just 26 jurisdictions has taken more than 30 years and, as of 2009, seems to have hit a wall. Is reconsidering our profession's name one of the first steps to achieving wisdom? Have enough factors adversely affected interior designers' ability to regulate our profession that we need to abandon the name *interior designer* in favor of a new title? Or, has the profession evolved to the point that we should consider combining it with architecture?

PUBLIC PERCEPTION AND TITLE CONFUSION

I have struggled with the identity of my vocation for years. Numerous medical and insurance forms with my name on them have countless titles listed: educator, facility planner, consultant,

LISA M. WHITED, IIDA, has owned a consulting firm, Whited Planning + Design, in Portland, Maine, since 1986. In her ongoing efforts to enhance the credibility and value of professional interior designers, she served as head of the interior design department within an architectural college for three years and an adjunct professor to several New England design schools. She presents seminars, publishes articles, and speaks to groups across the country on the value of interior design. Whited also served on NCIDQ's board of directors for several years and served as its president in 2000. She has a reputation for being an informed, outspoken visionary, and, as one client recently stated, "has an ability to look at things from an angle no one else had considered." A sought-after speaker and accomplished writer, Whited has an MS in management and an AA in interior design.

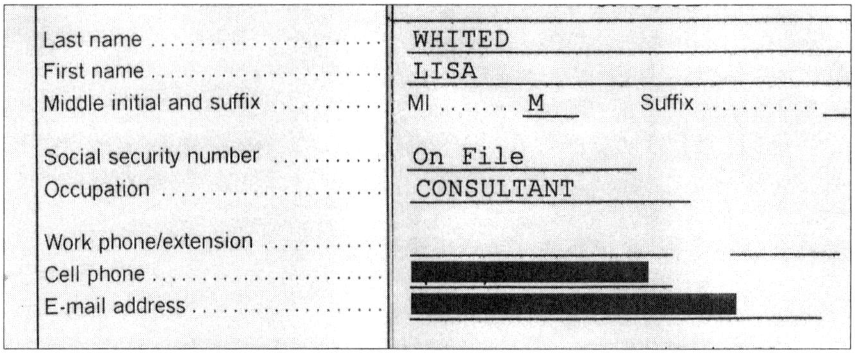

FIGURE 11.1. My identity crisis with a simple medical form.

and, yes, even certified interior designer (see Figure 11.1). When asked at a party, "What do you do?" I do not say, "I am an interior designer." Instead, I *describe* what I do, launching into my 30-second elevator speech: "I consult with organizations that are trying to improve work productivity and enhance employee surroundings. Sometimes that work results in facility change and sometimes not." The title of my profession simply does not convey the breadth of my work. The persona of interior design is too wrapped up in glossy magazines and do-it-yourself television shows. And, perhaps there is nothing wrong with that, but it seems that the perception of my profession is in purgatory, perpetually suspended between a legitimate career and a Sally Struthers correspondence course ("be a designer—or look just like one!"). My experience with the profession's title is not unique to me—many practitioners can share similar stories.

What started as interior decoration in the 19th century evolved into interior design in the 1960s; today the title *interior designer* is used to describe a spectrum of expertise. Under the heading "Interior Design" in the *Yellow Pages* one will find a wallpaper installer with a high school education listed next to an individual with an advanced degree who designs complex healthcare environments. The title has little meaning in the public realm and simply does not convey the depth of knowledge, education, and experience required to design safe, functional interiors that enhance the inhabitants' quality of life.

The media constantly interchanges the words *designer* and *decorator*. The American Society of Interior Designers (ASID) is often cited as the American Society of Interior Decorators in print publications. Clients, who have had professional relationships with their qualified, registered interior designers for years, will still introduce them to acquaintances as "my decorator." Despite attempts to educate, explain, and clarify to the public what we do and what we are called, gaffes persist.

It is no wonder there is so much confusion. The U.S. Standard Occupational Classification system (SOC) and the North American Industry Classification System (NAICS) have two separate definitions of interior design. However, *both* systems use a singular definition for interior decorating and interior design. According to the SOC, "interior designer" and "interior decorator" share the same classification code (27-1025-263). NAICS identifies interior design services with number 541410. Again, the same definition and classification number is used for interior decorating and interior design (Whited, 2007).

GENDER INEQUALITY

There is a long history of interior decoration being dominated by women. "Throughout the early 20th century, interior decoration was one of the few careers considered appropriate for women to be engaged in outside of the home, as salaried work was largely reserved for men" (Martin, 2007, p. 18). Male-dominated architecture and female-dominated interior design have been at odds for years. Perhaps a not-so-subtle form of professional harassment against interior design began in architectural firms in the mid-20th century. Practitioners from that time will tell you of disparaging remarks from their architect peers about interior *desecrators* and *inferior decorators*. Sadly, these terms can still be heard in traditional architectural firms today. These monikers, even offered in a bantering fashion, are of course insulting to a professional and a profession.

Beyond the equivalent of collegial slurs, is there a correlation between the high number of males practicing architecture and the high number of females practicing interior design? If interior design did not exist as a career choice, would more of its practitioners have become architects? This question may seem too hypothetical to consider—perhaps akin to saying if nursing did not exist as a profession, would there have been more female doctors earlier in the history of medicine.

Consider the strides made in other professions toward gender equality based on data from the U.S. Department of Labor (2008). Medicine has increased its number of female, licensed doctors steadily for the past 30 years, growing from just 7.6% of all practitioners in 1970 to 27.8% in 2006 (American Medical Association, 2008). Women have joined the law profession at a similar rate: 30.7% of all attorneys in the United States are female (American Bar Association, 2007). Yet, 80% of all interior design practitioners in the United States are women (American Society of Interior Designers, 2004) and more than 78% of all licensed architects are men (U.S. Department of Labor, 2008).

These statistics have remained relatively static for years. Unlike medicine and law, architecture has not shown a significant increase in the number of female licensed professionals, which hovered at 13% for many years, and is now said to be 20% (Walsh, 2007). At least medicine and law have gained enough female members to be considered "traditional" careers for women. But, for women wanting to study architecture, the profession is still considered a non-traditional career choice, according to the U.S. Department of Labor (2008).[1] Additionally, the number of licensed, female architects remains small because many female architects go into partnership with their husbands, and frequently only the husband will get the license for the firm (Taylor, 2001).

OVERLAP OF KNOWLEDGE

In 2008, a group of academics, led by a former president of the Association of Collegiate Schools of Architecture (ASCA), Ted Landsmark, PhD, convened to study the similarities between architecture and interior design. His goal with this initiative was to have a conversation take place within the professional colleges and universities where both interior design and architecture are taught. Among other findings, the educators discovered "the [architecture and interior design] curricula actually taught have significant areas of overlap and convergence that significantly blur the definitions of each discipline" (Landsmark, 2009, p. 25). Among several concerns cited by the group, the next statement in particular is of interest to me:

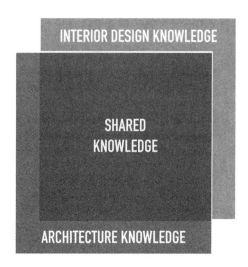

FIGURE 11.2. Area of shared knowledge between architecture and interior design.

"What is and would be a culture of equality across disciplines, programs, and schools, and how might that be affected by other factors such as gender, regional or urban/rural differences, or professional expectations?" (Landsmark, 2009, p. 25). According to Dr. Landsmark,

> John Weigand's (Miami University) analytical paper on curricular overlaps was summarized: interior design is not a subset of architecture, in that it "owns" a distinctive territory and body of knowledge. About 70% of the [architecture and interior design] disciplines' knowledge overlap under current accreditor standards. The study of human behavior and technical requirements diverge at advanced levels of study; and there is a need to offer advanced or specialized knowledge and research in problems related specifically to the uses of interior spaces. (Landsmark, 2009, p. 26)

Figure 11.2 is an image I created to demonstrate this overlap of content visually.

Weigand's study, coupled with Landmark's commentary, and my 20+ years as an interior design practitioner, 10 years as an educator, 7 years service on a joint state regulatory board, and participation in National Council for Architectural Registration Boards (NCARB) and National Council for Interior Design Qualification (NCIDQ) conferences since 1993 led me to the following question: Have enough factors adversely affected interior designers' ability to regulate their profession that we need to abandon the name *interior designer* in favor of a new title? I believe the answer is "Yes."

I believe we need to consider another title for the work that we have claimed is interior design. *Interior design* permeates the public domain of language; it is too difficult to wrest it back from its encompassing meaning of anything to do with an aesthetic impact on an interior environment—from light switches to window treatments to wall covering—and little or nothing to do with an inhabitant's safety, health, and well-being.

For a few years I believed that we, female interior designers, were partly to blame for slow approval of interior design regulation by legislators. I thought sexism and discrimination were behind some of the fights and sparring over the legitimacy of the profession. However, I now prefer the point of view posited by linguist professor Deborah Tannen, author of several best sellers including *You Just Don't Understand: Men and Women in Conversation* and *The Argument Culture*.

Tannen quotes Maureen Dowd, commenting on why there are not more female newspaper columnists: "Men enjoy verbal dueling," said Dowd. "As a woman," she explained, "I wanted to be liked—not attacked" (Tannen, 1998). In her exploration of why "fighting speech" is used to explore ideas in Western culture Tannen continues,

No one bothers to question the underlying notion that there is only one way to do science, to write columns—the way it's always been done, the men's way. This brings us to our political discourse and the assumption that it must be agonistic in method and spirit. If we accept this false premise, then it is not surprising that fewer women than men will be found who are comfortable writing political columns. But looking for women who can write the same kind of columns that men write is a waste—exactly the opposite of what should be the benefits of diversity: introducing new and different ways of doing things. (Tannen, 1998)

As I re-read Tannen's comments, I cannot help but insert "to design buildings," as in: "No one bothers to question the underlying notion that there is only one way to do science, to write columns, *to design buildings*—the way it's always been done, the men's way." And, again, *"But looking for women who can design the same kind of buildings that men can is a waste*—exactly the opposite of what should be the benefits of diversity: introducing new and different ways of doing things."

Consequently, as I further consider the state of the interior design profession, I wonder if we can apply Tannen's approach to a new profession. Female students have written of bias experienced in male-taught architecture studios (Guo, 2006). As an educator in one of the oldest architecture schools in the country, I witnessed a male tradition and "way of doing" that was often considered "right" for a female-dominated interior design program.

If we were to dissect architecture and interior design—not just based on current curricula but also based upon the most recent practice analysis studies of NCARB and NCIDQ—is it possible we would find even more than 70% overlap of required knowledge? And, if we did, what would that discovery mean? What if, in all of its politically incorrect crassness, the following joke was true? "What do you call a female architect? An interior designer."

The method of principled negotiation developed at the Harvard Negotiation Project (Fisher, Ury, & Patton, 1991, p. xii) is to decide issues on their merits rather than through a haggling process focused on what each side says it will and will not do. It suggests that you look for mutual gains whenever possible, and that where your interests conflict, you should insist that the result be based on some fair standards independent of the will of either side. Any method of negotiation may be fairly judged by three criteria:

> It should produce a wise agreement if agreement is possible.
> It should be efficient.
> It should improve or at least not damage the relationship between the parties (Fisher, Ury, & Patton, 1991, p. xviii).

A wise agreement can be defined as one that meets the legitimate interests of each side to the extent possible, resolves conflicting interests fairly, is durable, and takes community interests into account (Fisher, Ury, & Patton, 1991, p. xviii).

Using this principled negotiation method, I would like to see a framework for discussion around a combined body of knowledge of architecture and interior design. Finding truly neutral parties to engage in this discussion may be difficult, but perhaps the previously convened group of academics from schools that teach both interior design and architecture is a place to begin. Conducting similar discussion circles with seasoned and recent practitioners of architecture and interior design should give us enough documentation to seriously consider the merits of either changing the title of the interior design profession or creating a new profession altogether. This analysis may reveal several things:

1. The closely related professions of architecture and interior design should remain separate entities.
2. There is so much overlap between architecture and interior design that we are really talking about one profession.
3. Both professions have evolved to such an extent that purposefully combining accreditation standards and examination mechanisms is a natural next step in the progression of the professions.

Conducting a thorough analysis of accreditation and examination standards (including the most recent practice analyses for interior design and architecture) and then using the tenets of principled negotiation to facilitate a conversation may result in discoveries that do not thrill either side of the debate. On the other hand, I can imagine the richness of the process alone having positive repercussions for all involved.

NOTE

1. A nontraditional occupation for women is one in which women comprise 25% or less of total employment.

REFERENCES

American Bar Association. (2007). *Commission on women in the profession.* Chicago, IL: Author.

American Medical Association. (2008). *Physician characteristics and distribution in the U.S.* Author.

American Society of Interior Designers. (2004). *The interior design profession facts and figures.* Washington, D.C: Author.

Fisher, R., Ury, W., & Patton, B. (1991). *Getting to yes: Negotiating agreement without giving in.* New York: Penguin Books.

Guo, J. (2006, February 28). Women in Arch. voice complaints. *Yale Daily News.* Retrieved February 9, 2009 from http://www.yaledailynews.com/articles/view/16832

Landsmark, T. (2009, Winter). *Inside: Out II, practice.* Boston: Boston Architectural College.

Martin, C. (2007). *Interior design: From practice to profession.* Washington, DC: American Society of Interior Designers.

Tannen, D. (March 15, 2005). The feminine technique. *Los Angeles Times.* Retrieved February 9, 2009, from http://articles.latimes.com/2005/mar/15/opinion/oe-tannen15

Taylor, S. (2001, August 23). Women's numbers in professional schools still low. *Women's E News.* Retrieved February 9, 2009, from http://www.womensenews.org/article.cfm/dyn/aid/628/context/archive

U.S. Department of Labor, Women's Bureau. (April, 2008). *Quick facts on nontraditional occupations for women.* Retrieved February 7, 2009, from http://www.dol.gov/wb/factsheets/nontra2008.htm

Walsh, S. (2007, March/April). Designing new spaces: Women in architecture. *Journal of Undergraduate Research, 8*(4). Retrieved February 8, 2009, fromhttp://www.clas.ufl.edu/jur/200703/papers/paper_walsh.html

Whited, L. (2007). *Causes of harm: How interior design protects the public health, safety and welfare.* Washington, DC: National Council for Interior Design Qualification.

Wilson, E. O. (1999). *Consilience: The unity of knowledge.* New York: Random House.

> Should interior design adopt
"interior architecture" as its new name?

MARY ANNE BEECHER

THE NAME IS NOT THE PROBLEM

Fear of a name increases fear of the thing itself.

—J.K. Rowling, *Harry Potter and
the Sorcerer's Stone,* 1997

J. K. Rowling's point about the danger of allowing a moniker to take on too much significance is well taken. When too much power is ascribed to a name, it is sometimes tempting to confuse its purpose to describe with its ability to signify status. Some labels conjure up images of quality whereas others call to mind ordinariness. Yet, it may be human nature to seek out simple yet memorable tags to summarize even the most complex entities or circumstances. Hence, one can explain the prevalence of acronyms, logos, and slang in today's culture.

Perhaps contemporary culture's preoccupation with labels and its propensity to brand everything explains interior design educators' recent fixation on what might be described as a grand branding debacle: the debate over what term should be used to name their discipline. Despite the fact that *interior design* has been

MARY ANNE BEECHER, PhD, heads the Department of Interior Design at the University of Manitoba in Winnipeg, Manitoba. She is an associate professor and teaches courses on the history of interior spaces and furniture and interior design studio. Beecher holds a doctoral degree in American studies with an emphasis in material culture studies from the University of Iowa and interior design degrees from Iowa State University. Her research explores the evolution of interior space in the 20th century by investigating the reciprocal influence of design and culture, especially as it is evidenced in the design of storage space and storage objects. She is also interested in the evolution of the interior design profession in the period following World War II. Beecher is a member of IDEC and the Vernacular Architecture Forum and serves on the Council of the Professional Interior Designers Institute of Manitoba.

used to describe this profession for nearly 100 years, many consider it uncomfortably ambiguous. The root of this problem may be that in North America, the public has used the phrase *interior design* interchangeably with *interior decoration* since its introduction, and today's dictionaries still list *interior decoration* as its synonym (*Merriam-Webster's online dictionary*). Some dictionaries also conflate the identity of interior design with other design fields, describing it as "a branch of architecture" (dictionary.com). Confusion around what the term *interior design* actually signifies, therefore, may explain why some interior designers seem to fear the use of this name and seek other alternatives.

In response, the latter part of the 20th century saw a flurry of effort on the part of some educators to shift the names of their programs from the commonly used *interior design* to the more obscure term *interior architecture*. Public debates over the appropriateness of this move have been aired at recent meetings of interior design educators, indicating the contentiousness of the proposition.

The debate around the appropriateness of new nomenclature centers, at least partly, on whether having a different name also signifies a redefinition of the profession or the scope of the practice it implies. In some cases where a clear distinction is drawn between interior design and interior architecture, it seems that it does. Students at the Rhode Island School of Design's Interior Architecture program are taught to alter load-bearing or structural aspects of a building's interior, whereas students who want to study interior design as a specialty at Auburn University can enroll in an interior architecture program that mandates dual admission to the architecture program.[1]

Other programs called "interior architecture," such as those at the University of North Carolina–Greensboro and Kansas State University, seem to define their "new" discipline as a kind of hybrid located outside the bounds of either traditional interior design or architecture, instead integrating the study of interior design, architecture, and industrial design.

At least one U.S. design program has used the term *interior architecture* historically. Educators at the University of Oregon called their interior design program "interior architecture" from its inception in 1928. Originators conceptualized this program as a specialty within the discipline of architecture, but it has since emerged as a separate curriculum centered on interior design knowledge. Other programs such as those at the University of Wisconsin–Stevens Point and Ohio University have more recently employed the name interior architecture without clarifying how or if their programs differ from interior design.

Although *interior architecture* may be a term commonly used throughout Europe and Scandinavia to describe professionals who design interior spaces, the individual states and provinces of the United States and Canada place limits on who can use the term *architect* to describe themselves in those countries. This alleged confusion over what to call interior designers' credential is, therefore, rendered moot in North American practice. Whether students study "interior design" or "interior architecture" has no impact on the term with which they are allowed to describe themselves once they enter the profession.

Interior designers often make the seemingly reasonable argument that the term *interior architecture* is a more accurate reflection of the range and type of problem solving that many of them provide, but there is no sign that the architectural profession will be giving up control of the term anytime soon. One might say, then, that the name issue is actually a nonissue. The debate over what interior design should be called is a distraction from the real problem—that after nearly 100 years of existence, interior designers are still trying to communicate to the general public, to their peers in other design disciplines, *and* perhaps even to themselves, that their name and their work make a unique and valuable contribution to the quality of the built environment—especially at its most intimate level.

What else might interior designers do to clarify the identity of their brand to others? Interior designers have excelled at establishing detailed criteria for the educational content that provides accredited credentials in the field (i.e., Council for Interior Design Accreditation's *Professional Standards*). They have succeeded at articulating and expanding the body of knowledge on which educational content relies. They have been, however, tragically ineffective at securing a clear expectation for the type of educational preparation (accredited, or not) a professional interior designer can be expected to have, and their ability to bolster their profession's image through the work of a cohesive professional organization has been likewise compromised.

Persons interested in studying interior design in North America find themselves faced with a diverse range of academic program types from which to choose. Two-, three-, four-, and five-year programs that result in a range of certificates, diplomas, bachelor's degrees, and master's degrees all exist. Students can choose to study interior design at top research universities or small community colleges, art institutes, or private liberal arts colleges. Interior design programs are housed within schools of design or architecture, within the realm of human ecology (or similarly named entities), or alongside the fine arts. Some institutions even have more than one interior design program, usually with strongly different emphases.

This variety creates a confusing challenge to persons trying to navigate the differences among program types and to understand what significance accreditation actually holds. Since its inception in 1970, the Council for Interior Design Accreditation (CIDA, formerly FIDER) has accredited a range of program types and will only cease accrediting programs that do not terminate in a minimum of a bachelor's degree as of January 2010. The variety of programs also contributes to the public's challenge to understand what type of background one might expect a professional interior designer to have. And because there are still professionals in practice from all types of backgrounds, interior designers have been reluctant to introduce restrictions on the types of educational credentials professionals are required to attain.

In addition to the challenge of raising the level of expectation for the educational preparation of professional interior designers, the widespread use of a professional examination is an important step toward securing its identity as a profession. Although there is no standardized nationwide licensure for interior designers in the United States or Canada, an examination—known as the National Council for Interior Design Qualification (NCIDQ) exam—has been used since 1974 to recognize that minimum competency requirements have been met by persons who have successfully completed it.

One might assume that, as in other design disciplines, it is having an accredited degree that determines whether a graduate can eventually access the profession's examination for certification. This is not the case, however. The current structure allows multiple paths to sit for the exam and become an NCIDQ certificate holder and is an unfortunate reflection of the educational diversity still dogging the profession. The nonprofit organization that oversees the writing and administration of NCIDQ's examination currently allows persons with five different combinations of education and practical experience—from having a CIDA-accredited bachelor's or master's degree to having as few as 40 semester hours of interior design coursework culminating in a degree—to sit for the examination.

The number of supervised hours in professional practice required prior to taking the exam varies depending on the type of educational background an individual holds. Persons with a bachelor's or master's degree (in any discipline, accredited or not) must complete 3,520 hours of experience under the supervision of an NCIDQ certificate-holder, or an architect who offers interior design services, whereas persons with the least amount of formal education allowed must attain at least 7,040 hours of supervised hours of experience.[2] With a system such as this in place, the credentials of practicing interior designers vary wildly, and the current exam eligibility structure strongly communicates that persons in practice benefit more from their practical training than in the study of their discipline. Is it really any wonder that others sometimes view interior design more as a trade than a profession?

Often professional organizations serve to present a cohesive image of a profession to the public and communicate its value and merit. Although some consolidation occurred toward the end of the 20th century, interior designers have always found themselves represented by a fractured array of such groups. The largest of them, the American Society of Interior Designers (ASID), was formed in 1975 by bringing together two formerly splintered societies whereas the International Interior Design Association (IIDA) formed in 1994 through the union of three smaller groups.[3] Interior design educators formed their own organization—the Interior Design Educators Council (IDEC)—in 1962, and in Canada, the Interior Designers of Canada (IDC) has served as the national association for its professional designers since the early 1980s, even though the provinces maintain individual associations that do not, as of this writing, have consistent educational requirements for membership from province to province (Birdsong & Lawlor, 2001).

PROFESSIONAL CULTURE

For all of these "technical" inconsistencies in how the interior design profession is understood and defined, its own culture may be the biggest roadblock in determining how it, as a profession, is perceived. The culture of interior design has always been inclusive, resulting in a reluctance to restrict who is "allowed" to practice. Its legitimacy as a profession has been questioned historically from within and without, due, at least in part, to the fact that interior design has always attracted more women to its pursuit than men, which has resulted in the creation of many gender-based and sexual stereotypes used to characterize its practice. These conditions may cause some interior designers' internal discomfort with their own roots. But, rather than capitalizing on how the differences between interior design and the other design disciplines might be used to express the uniqueness of its contributions to the designed built environment, interior designers have relied far too much on stressing the similarity of their perspective on the world to that held by others.

Havenhand (2004) articulates what is lost in this process by proposing that when interior design's supposed association with the feminine is suppressed, interior designers diminish the value of what they do and how they employ their knowledge in comparison to the approaches taken by other designers. Pable (2009) expands on this position by asserting that interior designers' own discomfort with their use of subjective ways of knowing undermines their ability to capitalize on the use of intuition and emotion to enhance their approach to solving interior design problems.

Although internal, cultural turmoil may be at the heart of some designers' lack of professional self-confidence, the occasional destructiveness of the rhetoric produced by factions outside of the profession must also be acknowledged as a source of the misperceptions that exist about the profession. But, just as interior designers do not have a choice about using the term *architecture* in their name, what others say about the profession is also something interior designers cannot control. Now may be the time for interior designers to choose whether or not they want to continue to view themselves through someone else's lens, or to ask themselves how much longer they will tolerate the persistent use of a narrative of oppression in their own telling of their story. Was nothing learned from *The Feminine Mystique*, which proposed nearly 50 years ago that women seek positive ways out of the culturally created cycle of teaching their supposed limitations back to them until they see no option other than to believe them?

CONCLUSION

Until interior designers give up their reluctance to claim ownership over certain areas of knowledge; until they are willing to challenge the legitimacy of contingents who infringe on these areas in their own practices; and until they are prepared to engage in the unpleasant task of restricting the use of the name "interior designer" from persons who do not have professionally robust accredited credentials in the specialized study of interior design (even if they have credentials in another design discipline), interior designers cannot hope to achieve public understanding of the profession's significance and that the practice of interior design is intuitive or akin to the practice of a trade will be sustained by some. If a singular yardstick is to be used to measure the importance of the roles played by the various design professions, then interior designers must be willing to uphold consistent standards that merit the public's respect. Likewise, the embrace of ambiguity about the profession's relationship to "allied" design disciplines by interior designers must be replaced by a claim of a self-generated and unique knowledge base.

NOTES

1. Although the interior architecture program is not CIDA-accredited, Auburn University also offers an accredited Bachelor of Science, Interior Environments degree from its College of Human Sciences that is.

2. This restriction on who is eligible to supervise is only in effect for persons who initiated supervised work on or after January 1, 2008. Prior to that time, unlicensed practitioners could qualify as supervisors of future examination candidates.

3. The ASID formed by combining the National Society of Interior Designers (NSID) and the American Institute of Interior Designers. The IIDA is made up of members formerly belonging to the Council of Federal Interior Designers (CFID), the Institute of Business Designers (IBD), and the International Society of Interior Designers (ISID).

REFERENCES

Birdsong, C., & Lawlor, P. (2001). Perceptions of professionalism: Interior design practitioners working for the top 100 firms. *Journal of Interior Design, 27*(1), 22–34.

Dictionary.com. (n.d.). In *WordNet® 3.0*. Retrieved March 6, 2009, from http://dictionary.reference.com/browse/interior design

Havenhand, L. (2004). A view from the margin: Interior design. *Design Issues, 20*(4), 32–42.

Interior design. (n.d.). In *Merriam-Webster's online dictionary*. Retrieved March 6, 2009, from www.m-w.com/dictionary/interior%20%design

Pable, J. (2009). Interior design identity in the crossfire: A call for renewed balance in subjective and objective ways of knowing. *Journal of Interior Design, 34*(2), v–xx.

> Should interior design adopt
"interior architecture" as its new name?

ERIC A. WIEDEGREEN

WHAT'S IN A NAME? THE ISSUE WITH INTERIOR DESIGN AND INTERIOR ARCHITECTURE

ERIC A. WIEDEGREEN, FIDEC, IIDA, Allied ASID, is a professor and chair of the Department of Interior Design at Florida State University. He holds a BA in history from Stetson University and a BDesign and MArch from the University of Florida. Wiedegreen has practiced architecture and interior design in Florida and Virginia. Previously, he was an associate professor in interior design at Virginia Tech, and program director for interior design at the International Academy of Design and Technology–Chicago. Wiedegreen has won numerous national and regional design awards, has led many student summer abroad programs, and travels extensively. He served as the 2006–2007 IDEC national president, and was a charter member of IIDA and a former member of AIA.

Much debate and angst have occurred among interior designers over the terms *interior design* and *interior architecture*. To some, they are one in the same; to others, distinctly different. One practitioner may fiercely guard one term as the very definition of who they are as a professional, and yet another may graduate under one term and practice seamlessly under another. Although definitions exist for each, the average designer would be hard pressed to come up with substantive differences between what the terms represent.

Today, the interior design profession is at a critical crossroads in regards to self-definition (establishing a "body of knowledge"), public perception (the blurring of *design* and *decoration* on popular television), and attacks from outside forces working to diminish the legal standing of the profession (Institute of Justice, National Kitchen and Bath Association). Added to this "directional challenge" is the shifting relationship interior design holds with the profession of architecture that at times upholds, and at other times fights, our best interests. The dual terminology of interior design and interior architecture seems to further exacerbate these issues.

Without taking on ALL the issues before us, how might we best deal with this (seemingly) competing terminology? Must we support one term over the other, or is there another alternative to better serve the future of the interior design profession?

There is little doubt that if our profession had a single designation, the public would be better informed, there would be more clarity between professional education and licensing, and the profession could (at least potentially) speak with one voice. In 2006, the American Society of Interior Designers (ASID) took a firm stance against the use of the term *interior architecture* and asked fellow members of the Issues Forum elected and executive leadership from ASID, the Council for Interior Design Accreditation (CIDA), the International Interior Design Association (IIDA), Interior Design Educators Council (IDEC), Interior Designers of Canada (IDC) and the National Council for Interior Design Qualification (NCIDQ) to write letters in support of this stance.

This proved more difficult than expected. The board of directors of IDEC felt strongly that it had a responsibility to its members housed within programs of interior architecture (who had little or no ability to change the designation) not to appear to undermine their programs. No support letter for the ASID stance was written. In a letter to Issues Forum members, dated December 14, 2006, the IIDA board of directors stated, "We have not fully ascertained the breadth of information available on this topic, and we are conducting a more extensive evaluation on how the terms are being defined, employed and utilized." The letter ended in semi-support:

> We are in full agreement with the American Society of Interior Designers that the usage of the above-referenced terms [Interior Design/Interior Architecture] is indeed confusing to

the public, students and practitioners, and that consideration of this matter by all stakeholder groups represents a defining moment in the continuing evolution of the profession of Interior Design. (IIDA, 2006)

CIDA simply stated that they accredited design programs, regardless of what the program called itself. Thus, the end of 2006 found the profession without agreement on a stance regarding the two terms.

As IDEC's response showed, design education has not been able to come to any consensus as to how to address the use and, perhaps, the meaning of the two terms. Interior architecture programs are found naturally within some colleges of architecture, but are also found housed outside such obvious entities. No consistent standard exists. As an illustration, a Google search of "interior architecture" found the Program of Interior Architecture, within the Department of Architecture, within the School of Architecture and Allied Arts at the University of Oregon. The program's Web site mixes terminology freely:

> The Interior Architecture program has a national reputation for excellence in interior design education. It is highly regarded by both design educators and leading design firms from across the country and is consistently listed as one of the top interior design programs in the country. . . . Opportunities for graduates include interior design practice within an architectural firm or as an independent interior designer, lighting design, exhibit design, set design, facilities management and furniture design. . . . Students study interior design within a broad architectural context to prepare them for positions of leadership as interior designers in an increasingly complex professional context. (University of Oregon, 2009)

Another confusing element in distinguishing between interior design and interior architecture is the varied use of both terms globally. As many practicing interior designers in Europe are educated within programs of architecture, they thus become "interior architects." On the other hand, South Korea often has programs of interior design and thus graduates "interior designers."

A review of international design organizations confirms this mixed message. The International Federation of Interior Architects/Designers (IFI), while a "global" organization, has predominant membership in Europe. The IFI mission statement is "to expand internationally the contribution of the interior architecture/interior design profession to society through exchange and development of knowledge and experience, in education, practice and fellowship" (International Federation of Interior Architects/Designers, 2009a). Note that both terms are used, with the inference that they are interchangeable. This use of terms becomes even cloudier when a further search of IFI's Web site reveals

> The content of the IFI Yearbook 2009 will be made up essentially of the works of the *Interior Designers* within our member countries and a limited amount of IFI specific information. This is the one way that IFI can showcase the effort put into *the profession* by member associations. (International Federation of Interior Architects/ Designers, 2009b)

The italics in the previous statement is mine, but clearly *interior design* and *the profession* are seen here as the same.

A European-based umbrella organization, The European Council of Interior Architects (ECIA)

> is the representative body for the European professional organizations in Interior Architecture and Design. Founded in 1992, ECIA currently represents 14 members-national organizations, with over 7000 practicing Interior

Architects . . . ECIA is the common voice of Interior Architects on European and International levels, promoting this profession as vital part of society and economy. (The European Council of Interior Architects, 2009)

A review of its member organizations leaves little doubt of the preponderance of the term interior architect in Europe, attested by such terms as *Interieurarchitecten* (Netherlands), *Innen Architekten* (Germany), *innanhussarkitekta* (Iceland), and *Architectes d'Interieur* (Belgium). Yet, the Italian organization *Associazione Italiana Progettisti d'interni* (AIPi) in English refers to "interior designers." Here again, global terminology for the interior design profession, as we know it in North America, coalesces around interior architecture but still references the term *interior design*. Of course, the 800-pound gorilla in the room is "how does the profession of architecture view this issue of dual terminology?" If all practitioners of interior architecture were graduates of architecture programs and licensed within the architecture profession, the designation would be clear; it would belong fully to architecture. Much like the global examples presented, the North American model interchanges the two terms, but to a lesser degree. There is little to no expectation that a graduate of an interior architecture program could practice architecture. In fact, educational publications (such as that coming from the University of Oregon previously cited) state that graduates of interior architecture programs practice within the profession of interior design. In fact, the use of the title interior architect by an interior designer who does not hold a license to practice architecture is violating applicable state statutes governing the practice of architecture. Why, then, has the profession of architecture not come down hard on the use of the term *interior architecture*?

The current American Institute of Architects' (AIA) policy opposes any type of practice regulation with the exception of architects and professional engineers (American Institute of Architects, 2008). AIA policy on practice regulation is based on the supposition that only architects' and professional engineers' education, experience, and examination are stringent enough to provide an adequate level of protection of the public's health, safety, and welfare. In the public interest, the AIA holds that only architects and engineers licensed through examination possess the necessary education, training, and experience to protect the health, safety, and welfare of the public in the built environment. Other individuals may possess useful skills in designing within the built environment, but fragmentation of responsibility for the building design process endangers and misleads the public as to respective areas of competence and expertise. The AIA opposes practice or title regulation of individuals or groups other than architects and engineers (American Institute of Architects, 2008).

After much preparation and review, the board of directors of the Association of Collegiate Schools of Architecture (ACSA) published "Reports from ACSA Topic Groups Preparing for the October 2008 NAAB Accreditation Review Conference." Under *Topic Area: Interiors*, this report listed the following recommendations to the National Architectural Accrediting Board (NAAB): that NAAB should accredit Interior Architecture programs; that ACSA and NAAB should expand their memberships to include Interior Architecture programs; that NAAB should recognize degree titles that include "Interior Architecture"; that a NAAB-accredited Interior Architecture program could be independent, or it could be affiliated with art, architecture, human ecology, or engineering departments; and that NAAB should be the accrediting body that recognizes both Interior Architecture and Architecture as related but distinct domains of education and practice (Association of Collegiate Schools of Architecture, 2008).

Upon receiving these recommendations, ASCA did not choose to support the

recommendations, nor did NAAB choose to act on them. Despite the lack of support for the recommendations, several crucial points had been stated publically (and even published): the recognition that interior architecture may very well exist within the profession of architecture; and most importantly, interior architecture (and certainly by association interior design) exists as a separate and distinct profession from architecture.

So where does that leave the discussion of interior architecture and interior design and what is to be done from here? There appears to be two courses open to the interior design profession:

1. Stick to "principle" and embrace the term *interior design* as the sole way to describe the profession.
2. Embrace the two terms as equal (or at best only marginally different).

There is no global recognition of a distinction between interior architecture and interior design, nor is there a clear perception of difference in North America. Both terms appear to be valid descriptors of a profession that safeguards the health, safety, and welfare of the public within interior environments. Proponents of each term believe in the validity of the term in self-description. Perhaps we have a situation where it would be better to view the two terms with an inclusive viewpoint.

There now appears to be a good chance that architecture could take control of the term *interior architecture*. Were they to do so, it is likely that a case would be made that interior architecture is somehow superior to interior design, which could strengthen the public's perception that interior design and interior decoration are strikingly similar, if not one in the same. This marginalization would weaken interior design's recognition as a profession, endangering the careers of current and future practitioners, design education, and, surely, public welfare.

Now is the time for the profession of interior design to stop being a divisive factor and start being a unifier by embracing BOTH terms as valid and meaningful, nullifying any differences in meaning and status. With several forces conspiring to diminish our profession, we need all within our ranks to work toward common goals. If interior architecture was fully and successfully embraced within the current profession of interior design, there would honestly be the possibility that architecture would fight vigorously to deny the term *interior architecture* for public usage, as infringement on their professional nomenclature. This would, in fact, solve the entire dilemma. What is critical, however, is that *we* (whether we call ourselves interior design or interior architecture) control the development and design of interior environments as a recognized profession distinct from architecture. In terms of survival, what's in a name? Perhaps everything.

REFERENCES

American Institute of Architects. (2008). Architectural practice and title regulations. *Directory of Public Policies and Position Statements as amended by the Board of Directors December 2008*, Position Statement 8.

Association of Collegiate Schools of Architecture. (2008). *ACSA Board of Directors, Delivery of Reports from ACSA Topic Groups Preparing for the October 2008 NAAB Accreditation Review Conference,* December 7, 2007, p. 17. Retrieved April 30, 2009, from https://www.acsa-arch.org/files/about/ACSA-ARCTopic%20Reports--Complete%2010-07.pdf

The European Council of Interior Architects. (2009). *Definition of ECIA.* Retrieved February 5, 2009, from http://www.ecia.net/index.php?page+2

International Federation of Interior Architects/Designers. (2009a). *IFI mission statement.* Retrieved February 5, 2009, from http://www.ifiworld.org

International Federation of Interior Architects/Designers. (2009b). *Content of the IFI yearbook.* Retrieved February 5, 2009, from http://www.ifiworld.org/index.cfm?GPID=67

University of Oregon. (2009). *Description of the program of interior architecture.* Retrieved February 1, 2009, from http://architecture.uoregon.edu/index.cfm?mode = programs&page=intarch

LISA K. WAXMAN, PhD, FIDEC, IIDA, is a professor in the Department of Interior Design at Florida State University, where she has taught for over 20 years. She has received two teaching awards and was the 2006 recipient of the university Graduate Faculty Mentor Award for her work with graduate students. Waxman has been an active member of IDEC, serving in numerous leadership roles at the regional and national level. In 2007 she was elected an IDEC fellow. Waxman has presented and published articles on topics related to the use of technology in design, issues of place and place making, as well as design and popular culture. She regularly wins presentation awards for her outstanding verbal and visual refereed presentations at IDEC conferences. She resides in Tallahassee, Florida, and if not in her office, can be found at the pool, on her bike, or in the garden.

STEPHANIE A. CLEMONS, PhD, FASID, FIDEC, has been teaching interior design for over 20 years at Colorado State University (CSU), where she is a professor in the Department of Design & Merchandising. She has been the recipient of both the Outstanding Teacher and Advisor awards from her college and Best Teacher Award from the Alumni Association. Clemons's research focus is related to infusing interior design content into elementary and secondary education levels (K–12). Clemons has held numerous leadership positions including president of both IDEC and the IDEC Foundation, and currently serves as chair of the *Journal of Interior Design* board. Clemons also serves on the national board of directors for ASID. She has published numerous journal articles and, with colleagues, has received multiple outstanding research paper/presentation awards from IDEC. She was elected a fellow by both IDEC and ASID in recognition of her contributions to each organization and the profession of interior design.

> How is television influencing enrollment in interior design programs and future and current students' professional identity once in practice?

LISA K. WAXMAN &
STEPHANIE A. CLEMONS

THE IMPACT OF TELEVISION ON THE PUBLIC'S PERCEPTION OF INTERIOR DESIGN

After more than 25 years of teaching interior design, we find that we still need to explain the profession of interior design—not only to our students, but also to our clients, friends, and even parents. We've been doing this since we were undergraduate students and assumed then that in relatively short order the public would understand the contribution interior designers make in the design of interior environments. Over the years, great strides have been made in terms of establishing the professionalism of interior design. Many states have recognized the knowledge and skills needed to successfully practice interior design and have passed legislation to regulate interior designers.

Still, it seems that for every step forward, there is a gentle creep backwards in terms of public perception. Some of these negative forces are highly visible, with chronic challenges to jurisdictional (i.e., state, province, territory) regulations coming from a number of organizations. Other forces have been more subtle, but still negatively impact the public perception of interior design. One of these challenges has come in the form of entertainment, specifically design-related, reality television. Currently there are several high-quality, design-related television shows, though the vast majority inaccurately depicts the profession of interior design. Developed primarily for entertainment purposes, the inaccurate portrayal of interior designers on television has created a challenge in terms of depicting interior design professionalism and their responsibilities for the health, safety, and welfare of the public.

In the late 1980s and early 1990s, the popular sitcom *Designing Women* featured four designers and their intertwined personal and working lives. Although the owner of the firm was elegant and articulate, most of the other designers were portrayed as ditzy and self-centered. Although humorous, this show did very little to raise the public opinion of the interior design field. In 1998 another sitcom, *Will and Grace*, featured Grace as an interior designer who managed to run a design office with a funny, but alcoholic, receptionist. Although Grace seemed to be educated and qualified, this show portrayed the life of an interior designer as easy and something that can be done in your spare time with unqualified support staff.

More recently, reality television has grown in popularity. Over 25 new design-related reality shows were developed and aired between 2000 and 2006 (Smith, 2007). Regarding current television trends, Thompson, director of Syracuse University's Center for the Study of Popular Television, notes there has been a shift in the last five years in the focus of home improvement shows from those that instruct to those that entertain (Bien, 2003). A 2003 episode of *Trading Spaces*, "100 Grand," was the highest-rated program ever on The Learning Channel (TLC) with 9.1 million viewers, topping programs on ABC and CBS in prime time among women ages 25–54. Home and Garden Television, (HGTV) added *Design Star* in 2006, a show with 10 aspiring designers who seek to impress viewers and win their own design-related reality show (Reality Competition Genre, 2006). In 2006, HGTV was distributed to more than 89 million U.S. households and was seen in 48 countries with an average of 5.2 million viewers per month (Dream Home Delivers, 2006). In 2007, as the housing market began to collapse, HGTV drew some of its biggest audiences ever as more people became interested in renovating their existing houses (Weber, 2007).

One positive result of these television shows has been an increased interest in interior design and the importance of interior environments. However, research indicates that television audiences have great difficulty distinguishing nonfictional from fictional media presentations (Banks & Banks, 1995), and that audiences learn from and construct knowledge from both types of presentations. Inherent in the phrase "reality show" is the understanding that what audiences see depicted in a particular television show is

real. In the case of interior design, the reality seen on the screen is not an accurate portrayal of the profession.

Several years ago, the American Society of Interior Designers (ASID) conducted a survey of both interior designers and consumers to determine differences between their perceptions of design-related reality shows (American Society of Interior Designers, 2004). Results indicated that there were some similarities and some differences in how these shows were perceived. When ASID asked consumers if the design-related reality shows present a realistic view of the interior design process, 55% of responding consumers felt they did, whereas 23% felt they did not. Eighty percent of consumers responding said they were familiar with interior design before the design television trend, and 25% felt that design television had influenced their thoughts on interior design.

Martin (2004), a practicing professional interior designer turned educator, went further by watching dozens of episodes of design-related reality shows and developing a list of six "myths" about the profession as portrayed on television. These myths include:

1. The goal of the design process is to surprise the client.
2. Quality and speed are synonymous.
3. Anyone can be an interior designer.
4. Good design is trendy and cool.
5. Designing your space will be super expensive.
6. Interior designers are zany, flamboyant airheads.

Martin proceeded to debunk these myths and explained the realities faced by practicing interior designers. Her concern was not only for the misuse of interior finishes (e.g., painting a sofa to match the walls), but in the extremely inaccurate portrayal of the profession itself. She explained that the client should be an integral, ongoing part of the design process. In addition, she emphasized the time it takes to create a design concept that supports a client's needs and to document how it will be constructed, as well as specifying materials, selecting contractors and suppliers, and building the space. The myth regarding who can practice interior design is clarified by Martin as well when she explained that states and jurisdictions that certify or license interior designers require them to be qualified by education, experience, and examination.

It is not too difficult to understand how the public can be confused regarding the qualifications required to be an interior designer. Many times the "designer" on the show has little to no education or training in the field. Instead, they are seemingly selected for their visibility and popularity. For example, in 2009, a popular professional football player, with no design background, was invited to host a reality television series about becoming an interior designer. The television vice president stated, "Sports fans know he has formidable skills on the field, but will be surprised by his talent as a designer" (Harris, 2009, p. 74). One of the first design-related reality shows, *Trading Spaces*, rehired their popular host after she completed her role in a Broadway show. She also has no education in the discipline. Regarding the hidden complexity in a show called *Top Design*, Collins (2008) stated, "Soon it will all return: the mammoth egos, the nasty feuds, the career fates that teeter on choosing just the right fabric swatch" (p. E1). What is the public to make of this? The message seems to be that interior design is not a profession but a fun hobby that requires no education or experience to practice.

Another misperception portrayed through design-related reality shows is the amount of time it takes to complete a design project. One show creates amazing high-end renovations of homes, but the entire renovation from start to finish can be viewed in a one-hour show. Again, this can be misleading to the public. As a response to this situation, a Canadian designer launched her own "reality" video blog online to show the real renovation process stages, including the demolition, the disruption of home life during the renovation, and the delays that often occur with such a project (Laporte, 2007). She wanted clients to understand what the process would look like, the steps involved, the mess that would be created during the process, and how long it would take to finish.

Curious about the impact of these design-related television shows on our interior design students, we decided to assess student perceptions at Florida State University and Colorado State University concerning design-related reality shows (Waxman & Clemons, 2007a; 2007b). Findings indicated that there were some positive perceptions about (1) the creative ideas gleaned from the shows, (2) an appreciation of an increase in the public's appreciation of well-designed environments, and (3) an awareness that interior design enhances the human condition. However, there were negative opinions as well. Students were concerned that the shows portray an inaccurate perception of the profession by oversimplifying the process of creating an interior environment. One student respondent said, "They give the public the wrong impression of design and perpetuate the idea that we are merely crafty decorators." There was also concern that the work shown on many of the design-related television shows was of poor quality. In addition, these projects often have extremely low budgets and short timelines. This concern was reflected in a quote from a student respondent stating, "They [television shows] use the cheapest quality product on a $1,000 budget, and people think they can do the same thing on a $1,000 . . . but they don't see the furniture falling apart as soon as the cameras leave [the scene]."

Other students' concerns focused on the way interior designers were represented. They felt that, on some television shows, the image of interior design was tarnished because of the portrayal of the designers as "flighty." In addition, students discovered that many of the "designers" on these design-related television shows had no degree or credentials in interior design. This was verified when exploring the Web site of one of the interior design–related shows. Only two of the 15 television "designers" had degrees in interior design, and one had a degree in architecture. Although many practicing interior designers spend years in school (education), followed by at least two years of practice (experience) before they take the National Council for Interior Design Qualification (NCIDQ) examination, 80% of these television "designers" lacked that type of preparation. No wonder the public is confused.

The profession of interior design has evolved significantly over the last 30 years. However, students, educators, and practitioners face a public who lacks the knowledge to distinguish between interior design and interior decoration. Although interior design educators and practitioners are calling for implementation of evidence-based design criteria into the design process (Guerin & Thompson, 2004), the "designers" on *Trading Spaces* are degrading the profession by painting the carpet to resemble wood (Peterson, 2004).

Interior designers are aware that many of their clients are watching or have watched these shows. Although some of them are quite realistic and may be worth watching, others present an inaccurate portrayal of the profession. In academia, educators should be prepared to address the perception of the profession during orientation sessions and/or in their introductory courses. Students may arrive on campus without a clear understanding of the demands that will be made on them during their interior design education or when they enter the profession. Students must be aware the curriculum will include technical classes (e.g., lighting), graphic communication courses (e.g., sketching), history, theory, computer-aided design, and complex studio experiences designing residential and commercial interiors. In addition, students must learn and apply life safety codes, the Americans with Disabilities Act, and universal design strategies, among other topics, and will ultimately take the NCIDQ exam to become regulated practitioners and/or to be a professional member of an interior design organization.

There has been some progress in public awareness of the interior design profession since our undergraduate years. Today, there are over 30 states or provinces in North America with regulations established for interior design (International Interior Design Association, 2009). These states, provinces, and territories have recognized the need for educated and experienced interior designers. In addition, many clients and end users have benefited from the work of qualified interior designers and now value the contribution they make to a project. However, more must be done to offset the potentially inaccurate perceptions created by the recent popularity of design-related reality shows. Interior design students, educators, and practitioners must continue to be involved in their communities and their organizations to speak up for the profession and explain the value of their work in the creation of well-designed spaces to the public.

REFERENCES

American Society of Interior Designers (2004, month). Design TV: What's hot and what's not. *ICON*, pp. 30–31.

American Society of Interior Designers (2004–2006). *American Society of Interior Designers Strategic Plan FY, 2004-06.* Retrieved September 13, 2004, from http://www.asid.org/ASID2/resource/resource.asp

Banks, J., & Banks, C. (1995). *Handbook of research on multicultural education.* New York: Macmillian Publishing.

Bien, L. (2003, October 31). Renovating how-to TV shows in a race to duplicate success of "Trading Spaces." *The Post Standard (Syracuse, NY)*, p. E1.

Collins, S. (2008, August 11). Hidden complexity in design. *Los Angeles Times*, p. E1.

Crupi, A. (2006, March 27). TLC puts learning back in its lineup. *Adweek.* Retrieved June 8, 2009, from http://www.adweek.com

Dream Home Delivers Dream Traffic for HGTV (2006, May 2). *Business Wire.* Retrieved September 15, 2006, from http://www. Businesswire.com

Guerin, D., & Thompson, J. (2004). Interior design education in the 21st century: An educational transformation. *Journal of Interior Design, 30*(1), 12.

Harris, B. (2008, November 6). Just give me the damn wallpaper! *Toronto Sun*, p. 74.

International Interior Design Association. (2009). *Interior design laws of North America.* Retrieved May 18, 2009, from http://www.iida.org/custom/legislation/statelg.cfm

Laporte, D. (2007, October 13). Interior designer uses YouTube to show what a job in progress is like. *Toronto Star*, p. CO02.

Martin, C. (2004, August). TV design myths. *Midwest Home & Garden*, pp. 159–163.

Peterson, C. (2004, February 29). Designed for TV. *Chicago Sun Times*, South Edition, Homelife News, p. 1.

Reality Competition Genre Gets Makeover with HGTV Design Star. (2006, April 12). *PR Newswire US*, Retrieved September 15, 2006, from http://www.prnewswire.com

Smith, N. (2007, February 2). Design for delirium. *The Wall Street Journal.* Review: Television, p. W5.

Waxman, L., & Clemons, S. (2007a). Students' perceptions: Debunking television's portrayal of interior design. *Journal of Interior Design, 32*(2), vii–xi.

Waxman, L., & Clemons, S. (2007b). Student perceptions concerning the influence of design-related reality shows. *Housing and Society, 32*(2), 147–160.

Weber, J. (2007). Housing woes? Not at HGTV: The home improvement network is attracting new viewers and mass market advertisers. *Cable Television*, 4050, p. 74.

> When interior designers talk about their practice and/or design solutions, why and how do they sabotage their professional identity?

THEODORE DRAB

THE PROBLEM:
PLAY VERSUS WORK

"Oh, how fun!" This is all too often the reaction when an interior designer tells someone what she/he does for a living. The inappropriateness of this response would be apparent if the career in question was professor, attorney, nurse, physician, dentist, or accountant, but its familiarity to interior designers signals that, in our current society, "fun" is an acceptable descriptor of interior design activities. The official "Definition of Interior Design" (NCIDQ, 2004) presents the "professional design practitioner" as a person "qualified by means of education, experience, and examination to protect and enhance the life, health, safety, and welfare of the public." However, few Americans would list interior design as a profession, and most would be surprised to learn that a 4-year degree, 2-year internship, and passage of a national examination are part of the practitioner's background.

The low number of practice acts in states, provinces, and territories testifies to the public's perception that interior designers select

THEODORE DRAB, ASID, IDEC, IIDA, is an associate professor in the Department of Design, Housing, and Merchandising at Oklahoma State University. His teaching focuses on design history, professional practice, lighting, and large-scale commercial interior design studios. Drab practiced interior design in both New York City and Washington, DC, for Swanke Hayden Connell Architects. His research includes the design of group homes for special populations, the Middle Eastern roots of the Gothic style, and the language used to describe interior design and interior designers in periodicals. His findings have been published in various journals in design and culture. He has been named to the Distinguished Speakers Series (2008, 2010) by ASID for his language research and has served in leadership positions in Oklahoma chapters of both ASID and IIDA. Drab currently serves as president of the IDEC Foundation.

476

colors and furniture rather than protect public health, safety, and welfare. Resistance to the inclusion of interior designers with architects and engineers as "registered design professionals" in the International Building Code (ICC, 2005) revealed a reluctance even among fellow professionals to correct the popular misconception. These allied professionals, frequent collaborators with interior designers, perhaps preferred to be viewed by the public as the only *serious* design practitioners, the only ones capable of protecting and enhancing the life, health, safety, and welfare of the public, hence the only ones worthy of *professional* status. Why have interior designers been unsuccessful in achieving that status with both the public and allied design professionals?

History provides a rich record of interiors designed to accommodate the needs of people through the ages, yet architects and engineers claim a longer tradition of practice (if not education and examination). Treatises from pre-Christian Rome (Vitruvius' *De Architectura*) and Renaissance Italy (Alberti's *De Re Aedificatoria*, Vignola's *Regole delli Cinque Ordini*, and Palladio's *I Quattro Libri dell' Architettura*) are still quoted by architects today, but there are no comparable texts from these eras tracing the long tradition of interior design. Although the design of significant buildings of the past can be attributed to specific individuals, like Michelangelo, it was not until the 19th century that designers such as Percier and Fontaine became known through the publication of their work, and interior designers finally arose from anonymity.

THE BACKGROUND: GIRL TALK

The language introduced by the early authors of interior design texts in the late 19th and early 20th centuries established the first lexicon of interior design, and, for a variety of reasons, initiated the misperceptions that still prevail. The Aesthetic Movement popularized the use of the word *taste*, with Charles Eastlake's *Hints on Household Taste* (1868) followed by Elsie de Wolfe's *The House in Good Taste* (1913). These widely read books (the former has seven editions in the United States alone from 1872 to 1890) were popular because the authors directly addressed the reader, and, in the case of Eastlake, criticized the work of professional decorating firms while urging the reader to exercise his/her own *taste* in making a house a home.

The connection between *taste* and *fashion* in our understanding today makes taste a changeable thing, no match for the lofty changelessness of Vitruvius' *utilitas, firmitas,* and *venustas* (i.e., commodity, firmness, and delight; translated by Henry Wotton, 1624), and understood today as "function, structure, and aesthetics" (Pile, 2005). Similarly lofty were the aims of the Roman and Renaissance texts relative to building scale and variety; the seminal texts dealt with technical complexities involved in numerous building types. The 19th- and 20th-century writers focused on interior design; however, they dealt exclusively with residential interiors. The seriousness of the words employed to establish theory and discuss large, complex design problems differentiates the early architectural texts from their later interior design counterparts. To continue the use of Latin terminology, it's clear that Palladio's *Four Books of Architecture* would not have the same *gravitas* if he had entitled it *Hints on Designing Villas*.

A significant gender distinction has also contributed to public perception of architecture and interior design. The former has been considered a male domain due to its perception as more technical, mathematically oriented, and grounded in science, whereas the latter is seen as more artistic and expressive of emotion, considered by many the natural domain of the female. Just as the first books affected perception, the first academic programs also played a part. The academic programs in both architecture and interior design were inaugurated during the late 19th and early 20th centuries. Massachusetts

Institute of Technology (MIT, founded 1865) accepted only male students at that time, whereas Frank Parsons's interior design program in New York (the first interior design program in the United States, 1904) geared the curriculum primarily to the daughters of upper-class families (Lewis, 2001). Although today there are many women with degrees in architecture and men with degrees in interior design, the gender of early educational program graduates continues to influence public perception.

It is also relevant that the majority of books dealing with architecture are authored by males and those dealing with interior design have female authors. Beginning with Edith Wharton's collaboration with Ogden Codman (*The Decoration of Houses*, 1897), women continued as the voice of residential decoration, with Elsie De Wolfe, Ruby Ross Wood, and Candace Wheeler writing books, with articles in magazines such as *Home Chat* (1865–1968), *Ladies' Home Journal*, and *House Beautiful* providing advice to homemakers.

These authors developed a vocabulary suited to woman-to-woman dialogue about domestic issues. The conversational tone was especially prevalent in the popular technique of answering readers' questions in a regularly published newspaper column or magazine feature. Easy-to-grasp concepts such as De Wolfe's "suitability" and Wood's "common sense" (Pile, 2005) simplified the tenets of design theory for the mass audience. Most important was the underlying assumption that, given a few "tips" and "pointers" and "rules of thumb," any woman could develop her "taste" and "create" a beautiful home for her family. If her ability to do so was somehow hampered, she could "enlist the aid of a decorator" to "help" her make her dream home a reality. The whole subject of interior design became part of the female realm, akin to romance novels in the literary sphere. The discipline's stature was diminished, such as the *chick flick* that has no chance of being nominated for an Academy Award. De Wolfe stated in 1913 that "it is the personality of the mistress that the home expresses. Men are forever guests in our homes, no matter how much happiness they may find there" (Massey, 2001, p. 126). This basically Victorian concept of a woman's role, and of taste as the emblem of social status, has colored our thinking, speaking, and writing ever since. Matthews and Hill (2007) have also shown that language classified by linguistics scholars as specifically female, hence discounted by society, still characterizes interior design discourse.

CONTRIBUTING FACTORS: PROBLEM PERPETUATION IN PERIODICALS

The definition of the word *profession* provided by Abbott (1988) and others stresses the requirement for specialized training and education enabling the professional to perform at a level substantially higher than an individual without such a background. An examination of interior design magazines over the past decade reveals that the conversational tone and simplified vocabulary that typified early 20th-century women's magazines still dominates today. The words one might expect to encounter that would signal specialized training and education are absent, and a lack of seriousness in the language used instead communicates a message damaging to the recognition of interior designers as protectors of the public's health, safety, and welfare. Words such as "knowledge" and "research," prominent in NCIDQ's "Definition of Interior Design" (2004), rarely occur in magazine articles about interior design, diminishing the stature of interior designers as individuals with specialized education. When the words *knowledge* and *research* do appear, they invariably refer to interior designers knowing where to find a specific product or the process of discovering that source. Interior designers are thus portrayed as shoppers, not distinguished from the layperson who also can shop.

Another common quality of interior design journalism is its emphasis on personal

TABLE 11.1

VERBS USED IN INTERIOR DESIGN MAGAZINES TO DESCRIBE INTERIOR DESIGN ACTIVITIES

VERB	VERB COUNT ALL ARTICLES	VERB COUNT "PRO" ARTICLES	FREQUENCY ALL ARTICLES	FREQUENCY "PRO" ARTICLES
Design	1184		2.62	
Create	449	80	.99	1.35
Help/assist	75	1	.17	.02
Select/choose	74	1	.16	.02
Space plan	65	1	.14	.02
Draw/draft	17	1	.04	.02
Listen	13	1	.03	.02
Specify	13	3	.03	.05
Research	12	5	.03	.08
Solve problems	11	0	.02	.00
Organize/manage	8	1	.02	.02
Assess/evaluate	3	0	.01	.00
Educate/teach	2	1	.002	.02
Coordinate	1	0	.002	.00
Sell	1	0	.002	.00
Analyze	1	1	.002	.02

preference. Homeowners "fall in love" with a neighborhood, a house, a chair, or a color. This emotional reaction is seldom explained or its root causes explored. Significantly, professional interior designers, when directly quoted in magazine articles, also provide a statement of personal preference more frequently than a reasoned explanation. Residential interior designers "love," "adore," or "favor" particular period styles, palettes, or patterns whereas commercial designers rarely supply the reason behind what they want to convey in their designs. Professional interior designers are portrayed as similar to the layperson—able to like or dislike something without the need to articulate thoughtful reasons.

A recent study identified the most common word used by professional interior designers to explain their activities, and linked that frequency of use with the word's prevalence in magazine articles. The word is *create*, and this verb and its derivatives are also among the most frequently used words in magazines. Interior designers tend to "create" (verb) by using their "creativity" (noun), "creatively" (adverb), or providing their clients with "creative" (adjective) results. The difficulty of the overuse of these words lies in the lack of clarity surrounding their meaning. Although scholars like Portillo (2002) have provided careful definition, the idea remains only a subjective "beauty is in the eye of the beholder" phenomenon to the average citizen.

Most Americans tend to link "creativity" to "art" rather than with "profession," and would not connect "creativity" with "mathematics," "science," "knowledge" in general, or "research" in particular. Creativity, to most, is indefinable, yet with qualities of innovation, or at least novelty embedded in its meaning. Creative effort produces a "new look," a space that is "different" from the norm, somehow distinctive. To label someone as "creative" is a safely vague compliment, a positive statement that requires no explanation, just as "good taste" was in the past. In many ways, "creative" has become the new "tasteful," with its overuse similarly diluting its meaning and impact.

Table 11.1 compares the use of selected verbs, including "create" and "analyze," as they

TABLE 11. 2
VERBS USED BY PROFESSIONAL INTERIOR DESIGNERS OVER THREE TIME PERIODS TO DESCRIBE WHAT THEY DO

1996–2000 (N=150) VERB USED	%	2000–2005 (N=180) VERB USED	%	SEPTEMBER 2006 (N=97) VERB USED	%
Create	**21**	**Create**	**46**	**Create**	**56**
Organize/manage	**15**	Design	36	Select	16
Design	14	Select	21	Draw/draft	12
Solve problems	12	Solve problems	15	Research	11
Space plan	9	Space plan	14	Design	10
Listen	7	Draw/draft	14	Specify	10
Draw/draft	6	Specify	13	Solve problems	9
Select	5	Coordinate	11	Space plan	9
		Organize/manage	**11**	Coordinate	7
Sell	5	Research	9	Help/assist	7
Research	4	Listen	9	Listen	7
Educate/teach	4	Educate/teach	9	**Organize/manage**	**6**
Coordinate	4	Help/assist	8	Educate/teach	5
Specify	2	Sell	7	**Assess/evaluate**	**2**
Analyze	**2**	**Analyze**	**4**	**Analyze**	**1**
Assess/evaluate	**2**				

appeared in 360 articles in professional magazines ("Pro") and design magazines aimed at the public in 2006. Articles that depicted designed interiors were reviewed for the words used by article authors to describe the design thinking and activities of the interior designers of the spaces. Notice that the frequent use of "create" and the infrequent use of "analyze" in these magazines, even those directed at a professional audience (like *Interior Design, Interiors & Sources,* and *Contract)* are mirrored in Table 11.2.

In Table 11.2, interior designers were asked to respond to the question "What do you do as an interior designer?" Verbs were provided by 427 professional interior designers who were surveyed over a 10-year period

(1996–2006). Note that the verb "create" consistently tops the list of verbs used by professional interior designers during three time frames (1996–2000; 2001–2005; September 2006). Note how the use of the words *manage* and *organize* decline in use over the course of the 10-year study. Finally, note the consistently infrequent incidence of the words *analyze, assess,* and *evaluate.* Yet, it could be argued that interior designers' abilities in the areas of analysis, assessment, and evaluation are those that are most highly valued by clients. These words denote activities that only those with the appropriate education and experience are qualified to perform successfully, whereas *create* can be used to describe activities performed by children.

INTERIOR ARCHITECTURE: DEVELOPMENT OR DETRIMENT?

An increased frequency of the word *architecture* and its derivatives in interior design magazines over the last few years has found its way into interior designers' vocabulary and beyond. Advertisements in the interior design magazines promote "kitchen architecture" (cabinets, counters, and appliances), "bathroom architecture" (plumbing fixtures and shower enclosures), "architectural seating" (auditorium fixed seating), "architectural paneling" (paneling of high quality), and "architectural hardware" (hardware of modernist style). As part of their marketing strategy, manufacturers use "architectural" to distinguish their products from those offered by competitors, although the competitors' products are similar. Magazine articles extol the "architectural" qualities of moldings, flooring materials, and even paint colors, with the word *architectural* used as a positive modifier indicating some sort of distinctive quality. As a result, the word *architecture* and its derivatives are very often used far more frequently in interior design magazines than the term *interior design.*

In crediting published interior design installations, several magazines use the term *interior architecture,* particularly when the interior design was completed by an architecture firm. A growing number of colleges and universities offer "interior architecture" degree programs, with the term strategically used to project the notion that they are separate, distinct, and different from "interior design" degrees. Interestingly, the faculty in these programs are often members of the Interior Design Educators Council (IDEC) and typically pursue national accreditation from the Council for Interior Design Accreditation (CIDA).

CONSEQUENCE OF LANGUAGE

The phenomenon of "interior architecture" is best understood against the backdrop of the interior design vocabulary that developed over the last century. The casual phrases of the early interior decorators lack the seriousness sought for in our value-oriented society. Consumers don't want to pay someone who "plays" with color, planning, or systems layout. Contemporary interest in sustainability, environmental psychology, life-cycle cost, universal design, and healing environments make earlier emphases seem trite in comparison; generating a new "look" or providing an indefinable "feeling" for a space is less desirable (and marketable) in the "information age," when knowledge and expertise and technology trump "taste," "sensitivity," and the "signature style" of the practitioner.

Two conclusions can be drawn from the previous paragraphs, and each presents a viable alternative for the interior design profession. One is to embrace the term *interior architecture* as one that appropriately distinguishes interior designers from architects and interior decorators and effectively communicates a message of rigor and tradition clearly understood by the general public. The other option is to focus on developing a distinctive vocabulary, teaching it to our students, using it in our daily discourse, and promoting its use by magazines publishing our work. Neither direction is free of discomfort, potential controversy, or significant challenge, but it seems clear that maintaining the *status quo* is not a productive option if our aim is solidifying expanding the influence of the interior design profession.

REFERENCES

Abbott, A. (1988). *The system of professions: An essay on the division of expert labor.* Chicago: University of Chicago Press.

Drab, T. (2002). The impact of periodicals on the perception of interior design as a profession. *Proceedings of the Interior Design Educators Council, Santa Fe, 30–31.*

Drab, T. (2008). Defining interior design: Professional language vs professionals' language. *Proceedings of the Interior Design Educators Council, Montreal, 358–367.*

Lewis, A. (2001). *Van Day Truex: The man who defined 20th-century taste and style.* New York: Viking Studio.

Massey, A. (2001). *Interior design of the 20th century.* London: Thames & Hudson.

Matthews, D., & Hill, C. (2007). Sexism, femininity, and the language of interior design. *Proceedings of the Interior Design Educators Council, Austin, 241–248.*

National Council for Interior Design Qualification (NCIDQ). (2004). *NCIDQ definition of interior design.* Washington, DC: Author.

Pile, J. (2005). *A history of interior design.* New York: Wiley & Sons.

Portillo, M. (2002). Creativity defined: Implicit theories in the profession of interior design, architecture, landscape architecture, and engineering. *Journal of Interior Design, (28)*1, 10–26.

CHALLENGES

OVERVIEW The final chapter of this book presents a summary of challenges to interior design practitioners, educators, students, researchers, and friends of the profession. The authors were each asked to identify the most compelling challenge facing the profession or the call to action they would ask us to heed. The overlap among authors indicates, to us, the compelling need to create actions to respond to those challenges. The differences in their challenges, coincidentally, seem to fall right along the lines of the issues each chapter addresses.

Bruce Brigham begins the chapter by basing the value of interior design on the belief that we change people's lives through the creation of spaces and that we must find a way to teach the public about the value of design. The same action is indicated by Rosalyn Cama in her challenge to practitioners to get design goals related to business outcomes—all based on evidence. Her call to action is to dispel four myths about the interior design profession, instilling value and identity, or consider losing the profession. Scott Ageloff challenges our identity as a profession. If we are a profession, then we need to solve our identity crisis, establish collaborative working relationships, and support visionary leaders.

Robert Nieminen and Bradford Powell support the identity and value issues as well. Nieminen says that developing the identity of interior design is of key importance to remaining a vital profession. He calls for unification of the profession and development of a brand. Powell agrees and surmises that without a single professional organization to steer the ship our professional growth will be diluted.

Trevor Kruse focuses on education and regulation as challenges to the profession. He asks if standardizing interior design education is weakening the output of entry-level interior designers and supports a method for identifying alternative yet rigorous paths to become a regulated practitioner. Michael Kroelinger ends the chapter by pulling together the relationships that underpin our profession. He identifies specific, urgent issues and suggests a point of national dialogue must be reached for the interior design profession to grow to its national stature. As you consider these challenges and ponder these actions, the question you must answer is, what can *you* do to sustain and develop the interior design profession? It is *your* future.

> Interior design is at a crossroads.
> What is your "call to action" to sustain
> and grow the profession of interior design?

BRUCE J. BRIGHAM

WHAT MAKES US GREAT? DISCOVERING THE UNIQUE VALUE OF INTERIOR DESIGN

What is so important about interior design? Why should a developer, an hotelier, a retailer, or a homeowner bother to retain us? What do we do that is so special . . . that makes us valuable? What do we do that other members of a design team do not do? Interior designers have been struggling with these questions for years. We all know that we are important to a project . . . we just can't quite say how.

The discussion of buildings and urban environments has been part of our societal chatter for decades. Since the art and science of building first began thousands of years ago, people have been talking about and critiquing these spaces and structures they build, trying to understand their significance, their meaning, and their value.

Let's face it, a whole industry of magazines, writers and critics, formal educational writings, and even television shows has existed for decades to encourage and support this discussion. And, it is an important discussion; it forms

BRUCE J. BRIGHAM, FASID, RDI, IES, is currently a principal of Retail Clarity Consulting, a retail brand development and design company based in San Carlos, Mexico. Prior to forming his own consultancy, Brigham was the founder and managing principal for nine years of Planet Retail Studios, an international branding and retail design company, based in Seattle, Washington. He has designed and supervised more than 400 design projects, mainly in the fields of retail and hospitality, and won awards from ASID, *Chain Store Age,* and the National Association of Store Fixture Manufacturers. Brigham's work has included development of store design projects throughout the United States and in Asia; hospitality and hotel planning and design; mixed-use components planning; regional mall design; and adaptive reuse of historical properties. He has written extensively on the subjects of retail trends, store planning and design, brand differentiation, and branding strategy and has been a featured guest on ABC's *Good Morning America.*

a critical part of our society, our discussion on the nature of art, and our advancement of science—and the quality of our lives in general.

But it seems that, most of the time, the discourse is held in the language of architecture and structure. We tend to think of the entire built environment in terms of its relationship to the precepts and goals of fine architecture. And, we tend to speak about the built environment always in these architectural terms. The architects have framed our environmental conversation. (It's only natural; they have been leading it all of these years.)

We have allowed the discussion of interior design to take place within these architectural parameters, too. As we have searched the scope of our work to find the deeper intrinsic value that we know is hidden in there—if only we can define it and bring voice to it—interior designers have spent time looking at the tangible effects of our work. We have tried to define our value in the same terms architects use.

Lately, the focus of these studies has been to look at the health, safety, and welfare aspects of the interior designs that we do. We have believed that perhaps this truly represents the heart and soul of the value of interior design. We have been determined to prove that interior designers, even more than architects, implement the most critical aspects of health, safety, and welfare for the protection of the public. As a profession, we have spent the last decade trying to prove our case for this with hard data. For a variety of reasons, too diverse to delve into here, we have been unable to do this convincingly—even though we know it to be intrinsically true.

But is this the unique and defining trait of our profession? Can we really define the essence and the value of our entire profession through our implementation of the health, safety, and welfare aspects of design?

This argument, it seems to me, misses the real mark completely: for it is an attempt to define the value of interior design within the framework of this architectural discussion. Health, safety, and welfare (or HSW, as it is typically known) is an architectural idea and a long-standing architectural term, whether we like it or not. And, it is an area of responsibility that the architects seemingly own, again, whether we like that fact or not.

We will never convince the public at large that, somehow, the deepest value of good interior design is the way it *protects* them in the environments in which they live, work, and play. There is nothing compelling about this HSW argument (although it is true). More to the point, there is nothing unique about it, either.

As interior designers, we know that there is something unique about what we do to a space. We start from an empty shell, concrete, and drywall—a blank canvas. Then we use our knowledge and imaginations to "bring this space to life."

I think that the phrase "bring this space to life" may be one of the keys to the value of what we do. It suggests that there is something *intangible* about the result that interior designers achieve . . . that the result of a great interior design is more connected with the concept of "life" (whatever that is), and less to the physical nature of the architecture, or the design tools we have used to achieve our result.

Another clue: one could argue that interior design predates architecture as a social need—and as a profession. As my friend and colleague Shashi Caan, principal of Shashi Caan Collective and past chair of Interior Design at Parsons School for Design, says,

> Just look at where we've come from. Man originally lived in caves, not architectural buildings. The interior was found space as it still is today, and predates engineering or architecture. And what did he do? He decorated the walls of his space with painting and symbols of his life. Since there was human consciousness to do this, then it is feasible that there was other spatial or functional awareness that we do not know about. Surely, this is the beginning of interior design! It also could be

FIGURE 12.1. Chartres Cathedral in Paris is magnificent architecture, but the ultimate purpose of this structure is to create an interior space that lifts your soul. © John Kellerman / Almay.

argued that the beauty of Chartres Cathedral [see Figure 12.1], while although certainly existing in the fantastic engineering of the walls and roofs with their flying buttresses and magnificent spires, rests in the *interior space this structure creates*. It is an interior space and a design so lofty and inspiring that it literally allows your soul to reach up and touch God. Now, that is interior design at its finest! And that act of touching God is the very purpose of that space. It is why it exists. (Personal communication, December 2008)

Where do these clues on design value seem to point? To me, they suggest that the real and fundamental value of interior design rests with this idea: *as interior designers, we literally change people's lives with the spaces we create*. I

think the fundamental value of interior design does not reside in the physical things we do, the clever manipulation of space, light, color, and texture that come together to make a marvelous interior. Architects often talk about their use of these elements to create their magnificent structures. And they are right: these tools we use in our design work cross many professional lines and are not unique to us.

I believe our fundamental value as interior designers lies in the fundamental concept that *we create environments that sociologically and psychologically change people's lives*. Engineers don't do this. Graphic designers don't do this; architects don't do this—at least with the designs of their buildings. It is only when the interior design of a building is completed, and we enter the spaces the architect has created and the interior designer has completed, that we really experience the wonder of a building.

Actually, this is not news to many accomplished interior designers. We have been well aware of the impact our work can have on the lives of our clients. It is one of the fundamental reasons we love to practice our profession. After these days, as the work we do becomes more complex and sophisticated, we are finding ourselves increasingly aware of the way our design work is sociologically and psychologically affecting people's lives. We are beginning to try to quantify the effects our design work has on the people who use it.

I practice retail design. This is a field in which we have measured the effects of our design work in a very immediate fashion for some time. When you get to the bottom line, my clients really want only two things from my interior design work: that it builds their brand and makes them a profit. Great interior design, in the world of retail, has always been equated with financial success, and in that sense it has always been measurable. It usually is something that is quick and easy to measure by looking at sales figures. Perhaps the connection has not been made yet in the most scientific manner, but at least it can be made with one's gut, as most savvy retailers know.

This is another clue to the intrinsic value of successful interior design. It seems it needs to be measured in ways that are *less tangible* than other design professions: the way a resort hotel makes you unwind and feel carefree; the way a well-designed hospital interior can lift you up and make you feel better; the way a perfectly suited home design can allow its owners to effortlessly enjoy their lives in exactly the way they want to live (for many years to come); the way a newly renovated office space can increase work pleasure, creativity, productivity, and reduce sick days, too. These are some of the intangible ways interior design improves multiple aspects of our lives and can instigate meaningful change.

These hard-to-measure effects of interior design on the way we live our lives, on the way we move every day through the interior environments all around us, are, in my opinion, the basis for the intrinsic fundamental value of interior design. Our value does not reside in our skilled choice of wallpaper or the fancy Italian floor tile. It lives in the sum total of all the decisions we make in our design work, turning a space into something alive, which brings about change in the way we live, work, play, and heal. It is a work of art—a work of art that *has an effect on people's lives.*

We can say that this is a very difficult thing to measure. This is true. And, it is one of the reasons the value of our work has been so elusive. If we can't really put our fingers on its effects, on this essential value, is it really real?

Of course. I think the answer to this question is twofold. First, even looking at these values from a purely empirical perspective, I would say that they are still very real—because we can *feel* them, everyone can feel them. Feeling something, having something affect one's inner being, is not an easily measured trait, but that does not mean it is therefore invalid. We see the effects of our design work all around us every day. We may not be able to find scientific proof that we have changed people's lives, but we know we have.

Secondly, I think empirical proof is close at hand. I believe we are on the verge of finding ways to properly measure the effects of our designs on the people who use our environments every day, across the various interior design specialties in which we practice.

As I have said, in retail design we have been measuring the effects of interior design for years. When I say that my clients only want two things, to build their brand and to make money, I am disguising the real work of the talented interior designer. To achieve these goals, we must create an experience for the store guest that is perfectly targeted to a specific set of sensibilities; that makes our target guest feel good about themselves and their personal aspirations;

that is more than a "pretty store" but is an effective selling environment—one that has meaning in some way for the people to which it is targeted. A well-designed retail environment connects with guests, has meaning for them, and ultimately affects their lives. One can debate the importance of this effect, but I believe that it is real.

This is the essence of what is called evidence-based design (EBD). We have been practicing it in the world of retail design for years. What is exciting about the future for interior design in general is that EBD is becoming a part of many other design specialties these days, especially in healthcare. It will prove to be the tool with which we can begin to measure this otherwise intangible nature of the fundamental quality and value of what we do.

Office design is one field of interior design in which EBD measurement is beginning to take hold. Studies are being done to measure staff productivity, number of sick days, and even staff contentment with the new environment. Hospitals are leading the way in trying to measure the effects of good interior design on the healthcare environment: decrease in doctors' and nurses' mistakes; faster recovery times; happier, healthier patients; better work flow and efficiency; and so on. For them, this satisfies the same basic goals as for my retail clients: hospitals need to make money, too. And more than ever today, they are interested in building themselves a meaningful brand.

To move this idea forward, we first have to acknowledge and research this value proposition, and then define it for ourselves and for the general world as our professional manifesto. With a proper definition of what we do and why it is so valuable, many things can follow. The ramifications of this value proposition are huge.

First, we would obtain our long-fought legitimacy in the design/build world. We would have a chance to be properly recognized in the construction community as an important—some would say critical—part of the design and construction team. At the budget table, we would be much less likely to see our work cut out of construction budgets (or in fact minimized). A case could be made that the interior design elements were a cost-effective part of the design, with tangible (as well as intangible, but measurable) long-term ramifications and meaningful results.

Interior design would come into its own as an important design profession, separate from architecture, with a manifesto for its intrinsic value much stronger and more heartfelt than ever before. Interior design would take its place alongside the other design disciplines as a unique and essential part of the design continuum.

Standing in the nave of Chartres Cathedral and gazing up into the seemingly infinite, sunlight dappled space, who hasn't felt the touch of the hand of God? This feeling, this effect, I propose is the essence of our profession and our art. A little piece of that feeling can truly exist in any of the projects that we create—if we are great interior designers.

> Interior design is at a crossroads.
What is your "call to action" to sustain
and grow the profession of interior design?

ROSALYN CAMA

THE EMERGING PROFESSION OF EVIDENCE-BASED INTERIOR DESIGN: FOUR MYTHS ABOUT INTERIOR DESIGN THAT MUST FIRST BE DISPELLED

Evidence-based interior design will be an essential component of interdisciplinary design team makeup (Cama, 2009). Without a link to human, organizational, and economic outcomes, interior design is a discretionary service and therefore expendable. Through application of an evidence-based interior design approach, a body of knowledge (Martin & Guerin, 2006) is growing, and professional leaders from organizations such as the American Society of Interior Designers (ASID), the International Interior Design Association (IIDA) and the Center for Health Design should use it to develop a business case.

HISTORIC DRIVERS THAT DEVELOPED A WEAK FOUNDATION

The profession of interior design has suffered from a weak foundation for a number of reasons, including:

ROSALYN CAMA, FASID, is president and principal interior designer of the evidence-based planning and design firm CAMA, Inc., in New Haven, Connecticut. The firm's mission is to partner with its clients in support of their strategic plan to create interior environments that improve outcomes. Founded in 1983, CAMA, Inc. has completed design work for many clients nationwide in the areas of healthcare and academic settings for higher education. Cama has served as national president of ASID and also currently serves as chair of the board for the Center for Health Design. Cama holds a BS degree with distinction in interior design and textiles from the University of Connecticut. She is a frequent writer and lecturer on the topic of evidence-based healthcare design. Cama authored *Evidence-Based Healthcare Design* (Wiley, 2009).

1. Historically it has been associated with the luxurious, nonessential embellishment of the built environment available only to the carriage trade.
2. It grew out of the art of decorating and the trade of selling furniture.
3. It was predominately practiced by women who at best were educated within a school of home economics at an accredited land grant university (yours truly included).
4. Its value has been grossly misunderstood because of the lack of data that links its merits to a beneficial outcome.

Much has happened in the last century to grow the profession and the perception of its value, but much more has to happen to tip the scale to bring interior design into its own in the new millennium. We must examine and dispel myths about interior design.

CROSSROADS: MYTHS ABOUT HISTORIC DRIVERS MUST BE DISPELLED

Myth #1: Design is only for the wealthy.
Fact: What was once privileged is now common.

Good design does not cost more, but a premium is paid if that design does not improve the human condition. The halls of Versailles were not created for common folk but rather for royalty. To this day, we visit Versailles to observe with awe the formal symmetry of the architecture and interiors, the impressive gardens, the gilded decoration, and the design of a total package that is the result of a masterful union of an integrated, interdisciplinary team of designers and master artisans. Many centuries later, the fruits of the labor of similar professionals and artisans moved beyond royalty's private sanctuaries to an elite class with discretionary income to improve the image of their surroundings.

In the last century, magazines began to publish a view into the homes, offices, and grounds of the rich and famous—at first directed to the trade and then available on egalitarian newsstands. By the late 20th century, it became easy to subscribe to these publications, search electronically, or watch a television broadcast of worldly places embellished with what was once only available to the elite. Today, the worldview of professional interior design has flattened. Friedman (2005) notes in his book *The World Is Flat*, three great eras of globalization:

The first lasted from 1492—when Columbus set sail, opening trade between the Old World and the New World—until 1800 . . . or Globalization 1.0. It shrank the world from a size large to a size medium . . . Globalization 2.0 lasted roughly between 1800 to 2000, interrupted by the Great Depression and World Wars I and II. This era shrank the world from a medium to a size small . . . around the year 2000 we entered a whole new era: Globalization 3.0. Globalization 3.0 is shrinking the world from a size small to a size tiny and flattening the playing field at the same time. (pp. 9–10)

The world of interior design has shrunk as well. The myth that good design is for the wealthy is thankfully no longer true. It is readily available through a range of affordable professionals and accessible sources. Current trends encourage us to take a do-it-yourself approach to replicate similar, quite appropriate images borrowed from the media, using products readily available through less expensive sources. What is missing from this voyeuristic approach to interior design is the acknowledgment that there is a base of knowledge that takes a designed interior from image creation to functional excellence. It is here where the profession has lost ground and must redefine itself to build value.

The value proposition in this first myth is to change the perception that interior design services are about finish and product selection (easily available in a flattened world) and more toward human, organizational, and economic outcomes.

Myth #2: Designers have secret sources.
Fact: "To-the-trade" is now a mouse click away to open sources.

The trade of identifying and selling product, once a secretive privilege, is no longer where the value of interior design services is placed. Much information is readily available to anyone willing to recognize a credible source after a quick Google search. The unusual decorative object, the perfect paint color, the most suitable piece of furniture is no longer privileged information (see Figure 12.2).

Most of the to-the-trade discounting has also disappeared in this tight economy. A 60-minute makeover on a national television network cannot completely educate the unsuspecting public on how to organize and execute a design project any easier than a television show about an extreme personal makeover can teach how to practice plastic surgery. Instant gratification through a good television set crew who has done their homework will not marginalize the efforts it takes to investigate, hypothesize, and execute a well-intentioned interior design solution—but it changes the rules of the game.

I believe that if the general population has access to this information then we, as professionals, must be steps ahead. Using an evidence-based approach, we must create environments that impact human behavior. This means selecting the best color from nature is only part of the equation; we need to know what that color elicits in terms of a mood or behavior and understand how it changes under various light sources, especially if we are interested in controlling circadian rhythm.

The value proposition in this second myth is to let a strategic outcome be the design

Benjamin Moore Launches iPhone App

If you're more of a Benjamin Moore fan than Sherwin-Williams, then today is your lucky day! The Benjamin Moore iPhone app called ben® Color Capture™ launches today. It lets you snap a picture of any color inspiration and instantly match it to one of the more than 3,300 hues that comprise Benjamin Moore's color system. FUN!

Go download it on iTunes or the App store now soon?!

FIGURE 12.2. Benjamin Moore Paints has launched an iPhone application called Color Capture. It allows you to take a picture of any color inspiration and match it instantly to one of more than 3,300 hues that comprise Benjamin Moore's color system. It then allows you to save your favorite colors.

driver—not let a product drive the next best design idea. If interior designers lead with outcomes, then we become the translators of all of the resources that are available. In the words of Gladwell (2000) in his book *The Tipping Point*, "translators take ideas and information from a highly specialized world and translate them into a language the rest of us can understand" (pp. 199–200).

Myth #3: A four-year degree program leads to professionalism.
Fact: Requisite for a professional degree is a graduate degree.

Typically, male-dominated professions such as medicine, law, and architecture have advanced their professional degree requirements from baccalaureate degrees with apprenticeships to post-baccalaureate degrees with internships. Collins (2001) talks about how great leaders "first got the right people on the bus, the wrong people off the bus, and the right people in the right seats—then figured out where to drive it" (p. 13).

I have been in this profession since 1975, and since then we have struggled with who is qualified to be on the bus. First, it was a discussion about level of education, two-year programs versus four-year programs. Then, it was about NCIDQ-based state registration laws qualifying professionals. But, really it is about being afraid to get inadequately educated people off the bus for a more tightly defined profession. We are complacent about being *good*, never allowing our profession to become revered as *great*.

The interior design profession needs perceptions to change by offering services where the most value occurs. It requires an epiphany beyond our professional organizations that have not been able to successfully move the topic forward. It has to come from a client-driven shift in service requirements. In the economic turmoil that is upon us, most projects will emerge with a heightened sense of purpose and outcome-driven goals. I foresee a much more accountable, evidence-based, outcome-driven interior design world in the not too distant future. *Iconoclast* author, Berns (2008) discusses where breakthroughs occur.

> But epiphanies rarely occur in familiar surroundings. The key to seeing like an iconoclast is to look at things that you have never seen before. It seems almost obvious that breakthroughs in perception do not come from simply staring at an object and thinking harder about it. Breakthroughs come from a perceptual system that is confronted with something that it doesn't know how to interpret. (p. 33)

Our current economy, and all that will change as a result of it, can finally be the catalyst to alter the perception of what interior designers bring to the interdisciplinary team's table. That value will grow as our educational programs grow and more research is provided to build a base of knowledge about the interior

design interventions that impact human, organizational, and economic realms of the projects in which we participate.

The value proposition in this third myth is that interior designers have much to offer to improve the human condition. Our body of knowledge is growing, and we have responsibility for many of the design interventions that have proven positive outcomes. We need to begin to move beyond four-year degrees. As we discover the need to incorporate more research into our projects, graduate and post-graduate degrees will become the norm.

Myth #4: "Trust me, I have an amazing portfolio of award-winning work."
Fact: Time-honored traditions need validation. "Show me results."

An evidence-based approach to professional practice justifies decisions made. In our unsettled world as a new economy emerges in the first half of the 21st century, this type of practice method is poised to emerge as a new way of conducting business.

In his classic book *Notes on the Synthesis of Form*, Alexander (1964) states:

> Unselfconscious cultures contain, as a feature of their form producing systems, a certain built-in fixity—patterns of myth, tradition and taboo which resist willful change. Form builders will only introduce change under strong compulsion where there are powerful (and obvious) irritations in the existing forms which demand correction. (p. 48)

As we follow our colleagues in medicine, time-honored approaches to practice will be pushed to the mat, irritated by the need for qualification through quantifying data. As goes evidence-based medicine, so will go evidence-based design (EBD). This final myth will be dispelled by peer review.

The future is clearly laid out. The myths I have outlined need to be dispelled by the following actions:

> Interiors need to be created within an interdisciplinary team using evidence-based, hypothesized, outcome-driven solutions for all who inhabit built environments.
> Interior designers need to be the translators of productive, safe environments for the betterment of humankind.
> Post-graduate programs need to evolve around a finite group of topics that can build a strong foundation for the profession and all whom they serve.

> A shift in practice methodology must lead to EBD.

The call to action is simple. Make a compelling business case for the right design interventions. Show how the investment in good design by a qualified, professional interior designer who is part of a larger interdisciplinary team will align strategically with the goals of a project and will create a return on the project's investment of resources. It is here and only here where the value proposition for the profession of interior design will be made. We need "the strength and presence of mind to seize this opportunity" (Gladwell, 2008, p. 267) to sustain and grow our profession of interior design.

REFERENCES

Alexander, C. (1964). *Notes on the synthesis of form.* Cambridge: Harvard University Press.

Berns, G. (2008). *Iconoclast.* Boston: Harvard Business Press.

Cama, R. (2009). *Evidence-based healthcare design.* Hoboken, NJ: John Wiley & Sons.

Collins, J. (2001). *Good to great.* New York: Collins.

Freidman, T. (2005). *The world is flat.* New York: Farrar, Strauss and Giroux.

Gladwell, M. (2000). *The tipping point.* Boston: Little, Brown and Company.

Martin, C., & Guerin, D. (2006). *The interior design profession's body of knowledge, 2005 edition.* Grand Rapids, MI: Council for Interior Design Accreditation, American Society of Interior Designer, Interior Designers of Canada, International Interior Design Association, and the National Council for Interior Design Qualification.

> What is the greatest challenge facing the interior design profession today?

SCOTT M. AGELOFF

ARE WE THERE YET?

The interior design profession does not exist. If we use commonly accepted measures to determine if interior design is a profession, the result is no. Not yet anyway. Depending on where you are located, confusing as it is, the answer is no, yes, or maybe.

According to Bullock and Trombley (1999), a profession is established when an occupation transforms itself through "the development of formal qualifications based upon education and examinations, the emergence of regulatory bodies with powers to admit and discipline members, and some degree of monopoly rights" (p. 689).

Putting aside for a moment that this is also a global matter, approximately half of the jurisdictions in the United States permit absolutely anyone, regardless of their knowledge or skills, to print a business card, call themselves an interior designer, and sell interior design services. In these places, there is no agreed-upon definition of what interior design is, and no guideline as to who is an interior designer. It is a free-for-all.

SCOTT M. AGELOFF, IDEC, ASID, AIA, is senior vice president for academic affairs and dean of the New York School of Interior Design. He has degrees from Carnegie-Mellon University (BArch) and from Yale University (MArch). He has served as treasurer of ASID (New York Metropolitan Chapter), IDEC board of directors member, treasurer and board member of Interior Designers for Legislation in New York, NCIDQ exam grader, and is a CIDA site visitor. He has practiced as an architect and interior designer with firms in Pittsburgh, Seoul, New Haven, and New York. Ageloff & Associates was established in 1987, specializing in high-end residential interiors. Ageloff is licensed to practice architecture in New York, New Jersey, and Massachusetts, and is a New York State Certified Interior Designer. His work has been published in the *New York Times*, *New York Spaces*, *Industry*, and *Architectural Digest*.

And, even in jurisdictions where interior design is a legally recognized profession, such as in my home state of New York, the public does not know or care. The sad reality is that if you ask 20 people on the street what an interior designer is, you will likely get 20 different answers.

Although I applaud the media's role in raising public awareness of the value of good design, many TV productions have communicated the false notion that anyone, regardless of education and experience, can design an interior. Even worse, the public is led to believe that it can be achieved in a 30-minute time slot. This could not be further from the truth. It is all too easy for the average person to forget that reality TV is commercial entertainment, not real life.

What is real is that the discipline of interior design is not unique in its efforts to reach professional status. Every profession, including law, medicine, engineering, and architecture, just to name a few, had to cross similar thresholds. A common body of knowledge becomes defined, formal education is established, a professional association is founded, a code of ethics is written, a method for testing knowledge and competency is put in place, and regulation in the form of licensing is adopted and enforced. Without any one or a combination of these things, a profession is not fully matured, and its very existence is in question.

Similar to the path that other professions have taken in the past to reach maturity, the road to a future where interior design is universally accepted as a profession is proving to be long. The question is, "Will it happen, and how do we get there?" I believe it is inevitable. But, for those among us who are committed to this goal, beware. It is critical that we not delude ourselves into thinking that it has already happened. Interior design is only midway along the road to maturity as a profession, and forces exist that are determined to derail its further advancement. And, if we are not careful, what already has been achieved can be rapidly undone.

There are those who question if interior design should even be a profession and all that comes with that status. Contrary to what they say, much like law, medicine, architecture, and engineering, the knowledge and skills necessary to successfully design interior environments are substantial and complex. It requires intelligence, talent, rigorous education, experience in the form of a monitored apprentice period, and after that, passage of a test to ensure minimum competency, and renewal through continuing education.

Doubters, take note. Qualified and competent interior designers successfully tackle an amazing array of project types, as the discipline of interior design embraces every kind of building and use. This includes schools, libraries, hospitals, restaurants, laboratories, hotels, homes, community centers, nursing homes, places of worship, airports, and every other building type one can imagine. Along with being beautiful, a properly designed interior is well crafted, functional, sensitive to the environment, economically viable, and above all, safe to occupy, and safe to exit in case of an emergency. Anything less than that is unacceptable; what interior designers do, if done improperly, can kill people in the case of an emergency, like fire. The formation of spaces, and the furnishings and materials they contain, should be visually appealing, but must also be selected and arranged to allow safe passage, discourage the spread of fire, and not produce toxic fumes via off-gassing or when ignited.

Much in the same way that no one thinks to question that doctors should have a formal education, be licensed, or be the only ones able to legally perform surgery, I foresee a time in the future when the public will have the same notion about interior designers. Like architects and engineers, all interior designers will be understood as highly skilled professionals, fully knowledgeable in the art and science of creating interior environments, who are essential in ensuring that the interior of every type of building is designed in a way to accommodate its function; to be beautiful and sustainable; and to protect the life, health, safety, and welfare of the public.

To reach this goal, it is critical that interior designers come together, work to resolve certain matters, and actively drive the process toward maturity or the road to the future may be extended beyond the horizon. It will require visionary leadership and a tremendous amount of work. There can be no spectators, only doers. And if we don't do it, no one will do it for us.

What can we learn from other professions? Thirteen architects convened in 1857 to "promote the scientific and practical perfection of its members" and "elevate the standing of the profession," and founded what became the American Institute of Architects (AIA) (American Institute of Architects, 2005). Until that time, there were no schools of architecture and no licensed architects in the United States. Today, there are more than 300 chapters of the AIA and nearly 100,000 licensed architects in the country. It is illegal to use the title "architect" unless you are one of the license holders, both in the United States and Canada. And no one would think to question their exclusive right to use that title or to suggest that the practice of their profession be unregulated.

The titles "doctor," "lawyer," "engineer," and "architect" are clear. If you design the interiors of buildings, you are known as an interior designer, right? Well, not necessarily. You might identify as an interior architect (though unless you are a licensed architect you may not legally use this term), an environmental designer, a space planner, an interior decorator, a kitchen and bath designer, a facilities manager, a home fashions professional, a stylist, or just a person with an artistic flair. Then again, you might be an interior designer. If interior designers hope to ever find the end of the road and establish a clear and unified profession, they must first agree what to call themselves and their profession. The public cannot be expected to know

who we are and what we do if we cannot decide what to call ourselves—and stick to it.

Along with the challenge of identity is the need to end the turf war that still is being waged in some quarters between interior designers and colleagues in related professions. On one side is the architecture establishment, which often resists the legal recognition of interior design and the goal of empowering interior designers to take full responsibility for their work, while also claiming that only architects are qualified to protect the health, safety, and welfare of the public, as it relates to the interior environment. At the other extreme are groups such as the Interior Design Freedom Coalition, which also argues against legal recognition and licensing, claiming that they cause restraint of trade, and that there are no risks to the public anyway. The banner on their Web site includes a quote from Mark Twain. "No man's life, liberty, or property is safe while the legislature is in session." Supporters of this coalition include the National Kitchen and Bath Association (NKBA), and many others.

For those who contend that the public does not need to be protected, I ask them to remember the 100 people who died at The Station nightclub in Warwick, Rhode Island, on February 21, 2003. Had the interior of that club been designed properly, many or all of those people might still be alive today. As reported by CNN,

The fire was caused when pyrotechnic sparks ignited flammable sound insulation foam in the walls and ceilings around the stage, creating a flash fire that engulfed the club in 5½ minutes, 230 other people were injured and another 132 escaped uninjured. (Cable News Network, 2003)

A survivor is quoted as follows:

There was a table in the way of the door, and I pulled that out just to get it out of the way so people could get out easier. And I never expected it to take off as fast as it did. It just—it was so fast. It had to be two minutes tops before the whole place was black smoke. (Cable News Network, 2003)

As a young idealist, I believed I lived in a forward-thinking, progressive society, but as time has gone by, I have learned that is not the case. It seems we Americans are most comfortable with the status quo. Left to our own devices, we tend to be reactive at best. Following the tragedy in Warwick, the Rhode Island State Senate introduced the Interior Design Practice Act in 2005. That legislation is still pending and has significant opposition.

To move forward, we must solve our identity crisis, establish a truly collegial and collaborative environment, and support the visionary leaders in our discipline. And, we must all embrace the fact that the definition of interior design overlaps the definitions of related fields. This is no different than the situation of architecture, engineering, and landscape architecture. Rather than reinforce clearly defined boundaries, we must celebrate our common ground and take advantage of the abundant opportunities for collaboration. To reach our future, we must work together to raise our entire industry up and leave the squabbling over turf and ownership behind.

The challenge of identity extends to the realm of academia. Though I heartily support the notion of varying philosophical approaches in interior design education, the road to the establishment of interior design as a profession will be made even longer unless all educators embrace a single term that identifies the academic programs that teach the body of knowledge. And, we must use that same nomenclature on the diploma that we give to our graduates— interior design. With all due respect to my North American colleagues who have made eloquent pleas for inclusiveness, diversity, and differing philosophies, it should not be *environmental design*, it should not be *interior architecture*, and it should not be *space planning*. A true

profession can have only one name. So when we educators get together to talk, as educators love to do, let's try to keep our eyes on the future, and do what is best for our discipline and our students. We can and should have differences, but we can only have one name.

It is high time that that same spirit of agreement and cooperation lead to the establishment of a single professional organization in the United States that would bring all interior design practitioners together to work toward common goals. Interior designers must have a unified voice. The roadblocks to the establishment of the profession will not be removed without it. The American Society of Interior Designers (ASID), the International Interior Design Association (IIDA), and others have to put aside self-interest and concentrate on the future.

I am reminded of riding in the back seat of my parents' car in the early 1960s along Ocean Parkway in Brooklyn during one of our frequent trips home from New England to visit family. I could see a mixture of old houses and new apartment buildings as we drove along this main artery. Among this jumble were many small synagogues in what had been private homes, some sitting right next to each other. I asked my parents why there were so many small synagogues. Why not just one larger one? I remember my father's simple explanation: "Two people had a disagreement." We cannot afford to let that be our model for dealing with differences. We must all get under the same roof if we are ever going to become a true profession.

I would sum it up this way. I want my home to contain a creative and well-planned interior with good light, pleasing materials, and comfortable, great-looking furnishings. I want those things, and I want to be sure having them still preserves our planet's resources for future generations. Moreover, in the case of some unexpected accident or illness leading to a disability, I want to be able to continue to live in my home. And, if tragedy strikes and it catches on fire, I don't want my home to kill me. I have similar aspirations for my workplace, the places I go see movies, the restaurants I eat in, the supermarket, the bank, the train station, the resorts I visit, the club I belong to, the department store, the drugstore, the museums—in fact, all the spaces I visit.

Though my passions are design and education, I think I'm a pretty average guy. And because I want those things, then I assume most people do. In my vision of the future, professional interior designers will be at the center of satisfying those wants. They will be rigorously educated; they will belong to one professional organization; they all will be called interior designers; they will be licensed; they will have to adhere to a standard code of ethics; and they will be respected for their many contributions to society. One day the profession of interior design will exist everywhere. We are not there yet. It is up to all of us to make it happen.

REFERENCES

American Institute of Architects. (2005). *History of the American Institute of Architects*. Retrieved May 25th, 2009, from http://www.aia150.org/hst150_default.php

Bullock, A., & Trombley, S. (1999). *The new Fontana dictionary of modern thought*. London: Harper-Collins.

Cable News Network. (2003, February 21). *At least 96 killed in nightclub inferno*. Retrieved May 25, 2009, from http://www.cnn.com/2003/US/Northeast/02/21/deadly.nightclub.fire/

> What is the greatest challenge facing the interior design profession today?

ROBERT NIEMINEN

CRITICAL CHALLENGES FACING THE PROFESSION OF INTERIOR DESIGN: SHORT- AND LONG-TERM VIEWS

What is the greatest challenge facing the interior design profession today? If there was ever a better illustration of a loaded question, I haven't found it. Interior designers face a myriad of challenges every day—from project management to budgets, from branding to programming, from staying current on the latest products, trends, building codes, and sustainable design to . . . the list goes on. But among the trials facing the profession, I believe two of them stand out from the rest as being the most pressing: surviving the current economic recession in the short term; and, in the long term, overcoming what can be likened to an identity crisis.

What I mean is that, as a relatively young profession having only gained recognition in the last half of the last century, the practice of interior design has experienced its share of growing pains and, I believe, is in yet another stage of development. Much like other professional practices serving the public—such as doctors, architects, lawyers, and nurses—interior designers

ROBERT NIEMINEN is the editor of *Interiors & Sources* magazine, a national trade publication focused exclusively on the interior design of commercial spaces. *Interiors & Sources* is dedicated to the advancement of the profession of interior design and promotes the value of design services in the creation of functional, sustainable, and aesthetically pleasing environments. Under Nieminen's direction, *Interiors & Sources* has been the recipient of several industry awards, including a 2007 Maggie Award for Best Overall Magazine (Trade, under 50,000 circulation), and a 2007 Gold Eddie Award from *Folio* magazine for editorial excellence and design. Nieminen has also served on the ASID annual awards committee (2008, 2009), and on the program advisory committee for the annual NeoCon® World's Trade Fair (2008, 2009).

have struggled to gain the recognition they have sought in establishing the profession's legitimacy and requiring licensure to practice across all states and provinces. To date, only 26 states and the District of Columbia and Puerto Rico have some form of legislation (Title Acts or Practice Acts) regulating the profession (American Society of Interior Designers, 2009), although all Canadian provinces have some form of regulation. In other states, wars are being waged in our courts where opponents of licensure are claiming an infringement on their First Amendment rights to freedom of speech—presumably to be able to call themselves "interior designers" as opposed to "interior decorators"—and with the mission to annihilate the idea that the work interior designers do has any measurable impact on the health, safety, and welfare of the public (Carpenter II, 2006). Add to all this the fact that interior designers essentially are divided in their allegiances to one of two professional associations—the American Society of Interior Designers (ASID) and International Interior Design Association (IIDA)—and it becomes clear why the profession of interior design needs to resolve its inner conflicts and unify its members under a common body of knowledge, with a common purpose of serving the public (not narrow self-interests), if it hopes to be taken seriously and survive the challenging years ahead. In short, the profession needs a unity of purpose and practice with a well-developed identity.

SHORT-TERM CHALLENGE

With that being said, let's take a look first at the more immediate, pressing challenge presented by the current economic recession in the United States and what design firms can do to weather the storm. As it stands today, by all indications, nonresidential construction is in a downward spiral. Reports indicate that construction activity is expected to drop by 11% in 2009 (American Institute of Architects, 2009), which means companies will have fewer seats to fill in their facilities, fewer construction and renovation projects to complete, and as a result, design firms will have fewer projects in the pipeline. As projects begin to dry up, design firms will be hard pressed to find and retain new clients for future business. In fact, nearly 50% of respondents to a recent (unscientific) online poll (*Interiors & Sources*, 2009) indicated that finding and retaining clients will be their most pressing issue in the year ahead, while budget constraints came in second.

In a deep recessionary economy, there is no magic silver bullet for insulating oneself against negative financial impacts. However, opportunities exist for those firms willing to take measured risks and capitalize on their strengths. In his article in a recent issue of *Interiors & Sources* (January/February, 2009), ASID president Bruce J. Brigham, FASID, offered anecdotal evidence suggesting how design firms can capture (or retain) business, even when business is hard to find:

> In my retail design work, I have often noticed that those clients of mine who have worked on the positioning of their brand most diligently and created the most unique and personal customer experience seem to be the ones who weather these [economic] storms the best. They seem to find some small piece of customer loyalty—hard as that is these days to find—and that loyal customer base gets them through the hard times. (p. 59)

Brigham notes this connection between the two challenges: clients who have an identity, a brand, are those most likely to weather an economic storm. The interior design profession must create an identity, a brand, for their future health. Further, Brigham cites research published in an issue of the *McKinsey Quarterly* (2008) based on past recessions to further support his claims:

While most companies tightened their belts, successful leaders, trading short-term profitability for long-term gain, refocused rather than cut spending. Indeed, these successful leaders actually spent significantly more on selling, general, and administrative costs than did companies that lost their market leadership. . . . Thus, when other companies simply battened down the hatches, seeing only risk during the recession, the more successful competitors found opportunity and pressed their advantages. (p. 59)

The underlying message here is that unless clients understand the value of the services that professional interior designers bring to the table, it will be difficult, if not impossible, to remain competitive and attract new business, especially when companies are hard-pressed to spend money.

But, perhaps the most promising factor on the economic horizon is the commitment by the Obama administration to invest significantly in the green building industry (U.S. Green Building Council, 2009). With a major investment in sustainable development domestically, the construction market should experience a rebound, particularly with government/municipal projects. In fact, a report from ZweigWhite (2009) cites healthcare, government, and green building markets as the most promising segments to watch in 2009. As the government begins reinvesting in building and infrastructure projects to green the economy, and as the market eventually begins to correct itself, things will return to normal—although that normality may not look the way it did before the recession, and it remains to be seen how the current financial crisis will have affected the profession as a whole.

With clients now looking more carefully at their spatial needs and seeking to do more with less, interior designers are working within a more conservative set of parameters that call for flexibility and a sometimes more modest approach to space design, which by some estimation is a good thing.

LONG-TERM CHALLENGE

The much larger challenge—and perhaps the greatest threat—to the profession of interior design is much more ominous than a short-term financial crisis, which predictably rebounds in a free market economy in cycles. The aforementioned identity crisis is, in my opinion, far more dangerous because it threatens the profession's legitimacy and, consequently, its survival (in its current form anyway). And, no single issue facing the profession of interior design is more polarizing than that of regulating the practice of interior design.

I got my first taste of just how bitter (and critical) this issue really is only a year ago when I published an editorial in the April 2008 issue of *Interiors & Sources*. In it, I quoted excerpts both in support and in opposition to the idea of interior design legislation. Ultimately, I sided with the evidence in favor because after examining the scope and breadth of the profession's body of knowledge, it was abundantly clear to me that interior designers do have a significant impact on the health, safety, and welfare of people.

Until then, I had only received the occasional letter from a reader who told me how much they liked (or disliked) an article we had published. This time, the letters and e-mails came in fast and furious (and I do mean furious). Readers from across the country wanted me to know exactly what they thought about the issue, and whereas almost half applauded and congratulated me for taking a position in favor, the other half were throwing rotten tomatoes (figuratively, of course). I was accused of being complicit in helping a "design cartel" (i.e., ASID) further its self-interests and presenting only the minority view on legislation—and worse.

Obviously hitting a raw nerve, I decided to probe further and posted another unscientific online reader poll (*Interiors & Sources*, 2008), asking if readers were in favor of legislation that would require interior designers to be licensed. Again, this topic generated the highest number of responses we have received to date to any of our online polls, drawing literally thousands of visitors to our site to cast their votes, which were split evenly for weeks. Ultimately, those against legislation won out with more than 60% of the total vote, but the conclusion remains the same: the industry is split nearly in half over the issue, and until it is resolved, the profession will remain in a state of limbo until it either decides to advance together or regress divided.

At the heart of the debate, I believe, is general confusion over interior design and interior decoration—i.e., how the work of these distinctly related but different practices affect the public's health, safety, and welfare. Organizations such as The Institute for Justice (IJ), the Interior Design Protection Council (IDPC), and the National Kitchen & Bath Association (NKBA) all insist that there is little to no distinction between an "interior designer" and an "interior decorator," although they do suggest that there is overlap between interior design and architecture (Carpenter II, 2006), which has historically created its own "turf war" throughout the years. In its now-famous report, *Designing Cartels: How Industry Insiders Cut Out Competition*, the IJ (Carpenter II, 2006) likens the work interior designers or interior decorators do to that of casket retailers or florists:

> Licensing some professions, such as dentists, engenders little question about the utility of government oversight, particularly in the interest of protecting public health and safety. Yet others, such as casket sellers and florists, lack any clear need for government regulation. As this report demonstrates, interior designers could be added to that list, although some leaders in that industry work to convince legislators otherwise. (p. 2)

On the flip side, in a "Key Points" summary of her "Rebuttal of the Report by the Institute for Justice Entitled *Designing Cartels: How Industry Insiders Cut Out Competition*," Caren S. Martin, PhD, of the College of Design at the University of Minnesota (and coeditor of this book), notes that "interior design has followed the steps as outlined by professionalism theory to progress from a practice to a profession, especially attendant to the three E's—formalized education, experience, and examination—for well over 35 years" (2008a, p. 1). In contrast, within the *Journal of Interior Design*'s publication of her article, Martin explains that interior decoration does not prescribe these actions (nor should it), as it "has strived for broad-based inclusion, circumventing any efforts to standardize requirements for specific qualifications to practice interior decoration" (2008b, p. 7).

Clearly, there is a difference in the way the two practices approach standards and qualifications, and they diverge further in terms of how they affect the lives of the people they serve. Martin points out that the *Designing Cartels* report challenges that interior design does not impact the public's health, safety and welfare, citing a lack of evidence; yet it is legally impossible to report violations against an unlicensed professional outside of civil court. Further, in addition to building codes, licensed interior designers are well versed in national fire and life safety codes, energy codes and standards, accessibility codes, and environmental standards (Martin, 2008).

The bottom line is that the profession of interior design needs to decide what it wants to be: interior architecture, interior decoration, or interior design, which I believe is another sphere that overlaps both professions and utilizes the best of their knowledge and skill sets to create dynamic spaces that impact the health, safety, and welfare of its occupants. The question is: how does the profession get there? For one, the infighting must come to a stop if the profession hopes to move forward. Otherwise, it will continue to be a deeply entrenched struggle to the top of a mountain that future interior designers aren't sure they understand or will want to climb. Secondly, all stakeholders need to come to the table and agree on a common body of knowledge that respects the overlap between interior design's related occupations of architecture and interior decoration, yet distinctly defines the profession as a unique practice that requires education, examination, and experience. If not, I fear we could lose a uniquely creative and practical field of professionals to a lousy political debate—and that truly would be a shame.

REFERENCES

American Institute of Architects. (2009). *American Institute of Architects' consensus construction forecast.* New York: PR Newswire for Journalists.

American Society of Interior Designers. (2009). *ASID—State licensing regulations.* Retrieved February 10, 2009, from http://www.asid.org/legislation/state/

Carpenter II, D. (2006). *Designing cartels: How industry insiders cut out competition.* Arlington, VA: The Institute for Justice.

Interiors & Sources. (2008, November). *Interiors & Sources polls.* Retrieved February 10, 2009, from http://www.interiorsandsources.com/Polls/Default.aspx

Interiors & Sources. (2009, January). *Interiors & Sources polls.* Retrieved February 20, 2009, from www.interiorsandsources.com/Polls/Default.aspx

Lees-Maffei, G. (2008). Introduction: Professionalization as a focus in interior design history. *Journal of Design History*, 1–18.

Martin, C. (2008a). *Key points: Rebuttal of the report by the Institute for Justice entitled "Designing cartels: How industry insiders cut out competition."* Retrieved February 10, 2009, from https://netfiles.umn.edu/users/cmartin/Martin%20IJ%20Rebuttal

Martin, C. (2008b). Rebuttal of the report by the Institute for Justice entitled "Designing cartels: How industry insiders cut out competition." *Journal of Interior Design, 33*(3), 1–49.

U.S. Green Building Council. (2009, January). *USGBC update.* Retrieved February 10, 2009, from http://communicate.usgbc.org/newsletters/USGBC_Update/01-09.html

ZweigWhite. (2009). *2009 AEC industry outlook: Strategy and insight for design & construction firms.* Chicago: ZweigWhite.

> Who or which entity should represent the interior design profession on an organizational level and could it move the profession forward? Is a "unified voice" dead? Should it be?

BRADFORD J. POWELL

OFF COURSE: THE UNHEARD VOICES OF INTERIOR DESIGN

As I write this in February 2009, the Institute for Justice (IJ), the National Kitchen & Bath Association (NKBA), and the Interior Design Protection Council (IDPC) are dedicating ever-increasing resources and efforts to fight proposed and existing interior design legislation in various states. Due to recent regulatory action against contract furniture dealerships and related businesses in Florida for violations of the interior design practice act, this anti-legislation coalition has gained sympathy and advocacy.

Of the two primary interior design professional organizations, only the American Society of Interior Designers (ASID) has stepped forward to push for legislation, and as a result it has been the subject of vicious attacks. The International Interior Design Association (IIDA) has kept silent, apparently feeling that incurring the political and resource costs is not prudent. The newsletter of which I am the publisher and editor, *officeinsight*, has been the only independent trade publication that has

BRADFORD J. POWELL, Esq., earned his JD with honors from Boston College Law School and a BS in psychology from the University of Wisconsin–Madison. He is the cofounder and editor in chief of *officeinsight*, a weekly newsletter created in 1995 to foster the exchange of information relating to workplace design and furnishings. Before joining the writing and publication industry, Powell was a commercial finance lawyer in New York City for 25 years, representing such clients as General Electric, Prudential Insurance Company, Bankers Trust Company, and an array of international banking organizations. In addition to private practice, he was SVP, General Counsel & Secretary, of a consortium banking organization owned by the largest banks in the Nordic countries.

strongly and consistently argued for appropriate legislation, but the basis for our advocacy has been severely undercut as a result of the recent Florida enforcement actions, whose goals seem less directed to right to practice issues and the public health, welfare, and safety than to overly broad turf protection (and necessarily, exclusion of legitimate and valuable competition).

Through it all, we see fragmentation rather than coherent and cohesive leadership, infighting rather than professional pride and support, and self-serving rhetoric rather than public service. Regulatory proposals that were intended to create a needed recognition of interior designers' right to practice and a public awareness of the knowledge and expertise of interior designers have, instead, created new levels of public ignorance or disdain. It is one thing for a libertarian organization such as the IJ to object to what it perceives as unnecessary government action; it is quite another for a noted columnist such as George Will (2007) to climb on board referring to interior designers as those who pick colors and decorative pillows.

WHO ARE PROTECTED FROM HARM?

On the sidelines of this legislation pillow fight sit the increasing numbers of people in vulnerable populations—those who have little or no say regarding their living, working, or educational habitats, who are suffering in environments that impede learning, impair health, and interfere with treatment. Consider:

> People with asthma and other respiratory illnesses whose homes, schools, and workplaces aggravate their condition instead of lessening the effects of outdoor air pollution

> The elderly and others at risk because of physical and mental challenges whose conditions could be mitigated by advanced knowledge of universal and healthcare design

> Students (i.e., everyone at work) whose learning capabilities and motivation could be strikingly improved by the proper interior environment

> The unfortunate people who were displaced by Hurricane Katrina, deprived of their homes by forces of nature, only to be cast into human-created toxic living environments compromised by formaldehyde off-gassing and unventilated trailers

Without doubt, the need for the advice of an interior designer did not cross the mind of a single person in the Federal Emergency Management Agency (FEMA), or the public in general before, during, or after the many months during which the respiratory suffering of displaced people was in the national news. Yet, qualified interior designers have the knowledge to solve these problems.

The list is endless, and while avoiding harm is a major objective of interior design legislative proposals, even our short list indicates that the need for improved environments that enhance the quality of life and the performance of students and workers is equally important. Note, for example, the recent studies (Belluck, 2009; Mehta & Zhu, 2009) that indicate that the color red enhances performance of competitive and detail-oriented activities, whereas blue promotes use of the imagination. Consider the applications of this knowledge for work and learning environments.

In sum, Rome continues to burn, so to speak, while interior design professionals fiddle. What can the interior design profession do to get back on course?

What do we mean by *a single voice*, and what can it accomplish? Presently in the United States, the interior design profession has many voices, of which the two primary, general membership organizations are the ASID and the IIDA. No one doubts that each of these organizations has brought important messages and services to its members, the profession, and to the field of study and practice. Yet, interior design continues to struggle to achieve an intelligent recognition and acceptance of its knowledge and expertise, and remains far from this goal despite the great strides that have been made in the formation and business practices of architecture and design firms, the accretion of experience, a growing body of knowledge, and an accumulation of best practices and methods.

The formation of the IIDA in 1994 was an important step forward, consolidating into a single organization the Institute of Business Designers (IBD), the International Society of Interior Designers (ISID), and the Council of Federal Interior Designers (CFID). Its mission had a decidedly international tint, and it also served to bring attention to the increased importance of interior designers whose work was primarily in business and institutional workplaces. This also had the desirable effect of laying a foundation for distinguishing the rapidly developing field of interior design from the widely held perception of interior decoration in the home. But circumstances have changed, and the time seems right for the next evolutionary step: consolidating existing professional organizations into a single entity able and willing to address, gain consensus on, and advocate for important professional issues throughout the country.

Let us be clear that this is not a move to silence the productive advocacy of different perspectives. Interior design is a multifaceted discipline of knowledge and expertise, encompassing many of the most significant and complex aspects of human existence. The exploration of each of these areas, from individual emotional reactions to interior styles to the intriguing complexities of workplace cultures, is only beginning. The goal is the development of a comprehensive understanding of what the interior environment is and what its contribution to a better and more productive quality of life might be. This will evolve only when we have vibrant and open discussions regarding the value of each of the multiplying facets of interior design in the context of a firm understanding that these facets all share the same core values and make up a more complete and brilliant whole.

What we see developing, however, are not the productive discussions leading to a cross-pollination of knowledge and the development of interrelated support structures, but rather a strident and often demeaning internecine warfare for ascendancy. And, some of this seems driven by the popular media, such as magazines and cable TV shows. Interior design doesn't even have its own hall of fame; instead this function is filled by a trade publication serving the personal interests of the editor and the commercial interests of the publisher.

The present difficulties of the existing fragmentation are well illustrated in the present state of the initiatives for interior design regulation. For over 20 years, interior designers have been trying to gain professional status for the discipline to ensure the right of interior designers to practice with the knowledge acquired through their education and experience, to ensure that the public is aware of the difference between the expertise of an interior designer and an interior decorator, and to ensure that populations that have no say in the design of their habitat will nevertheless have the benefit of qualified interior designers.

These initiatives have consistently been opposed by the American Institute of Architects (AIA) at the national level as well as by members of local chapters who believe that recognition of interior design would cause them to lose business, even though many of them have never had any education in interior design and are not aware of, nor interested in, the growth of information relating to evidence-based interior design.

The greatest problems, however, have arisen from the interior design field itself. Because professions are regulated on a state-by-state basis, professional organizations and most practitioners have deferred to local coalitions to formulate legislative proposals for legislators of the various states. Although this might seem like a reasonable, even inevitable, approach, the lack of leadership and of a common, well-thought-out approach has resulted in a mélange of regulatory forays. And where there have been examples of initial regulatory success, some of these have produced unpleasant experiences that threaten to do more harm to the profession than create the anticipated benefits, especially for the vulnerable public. These initiatives need to be addressed by a single, organized professional organization that represents the range of the profession.

Lack of unified effort is shown in recent regulatory examples. Governors in the states of New York and Massachusetts have vetoed (New York, three times) legislation passed by the respective state legislative houses that would regulate the use of the title *interior designer*. But by far, the most painful experience has been the practice act in effect in Florida. There, the legislation centers around the prohibition of anyone other than a licensed interior designer to engage in any form of space planning for any business

or institutional purpose, regardless of size. The statute is so inartfully drafted that even its interior design advocates found it necessary to petition for, and obtain, a declaratory clarification that furniture dealerships can *sell* furniture.

Without getting into the particulars of the manifest problems with the Florida interior design legislation, I note with alarm that some of the natural allies of interior designers have now switched sides and are working with the IJ, the IDPC, and the NKBA to overturn the Florida interior design practice act. Former allies of the Florida interior designers, including contract furniture manufacturers, independent representatives, dealerships, and ancillary services, had not anticipated the severe adverse consequences to their own businesses. Needless to say, the experience in Florida is unfortunate, and will be used—and is being used—as evidence of the undesirability and political unacceptability of interior design legislation, and it could not come at a worse economic time.

Sound national leadership could have provided a clearer path to interior design recognition and right to practice without creating unnecessary anti-competitive effects or alienation of natural allies. Unfortunately, only the National Council for Interior Design Qualification (NCIDQ) has provided leadership through its formulation of model legislation and a descriptive definition of the work of interior design. Unfortunately, this reflects the thinking of too narrow a constituency and falls far short of what is needed.

WE NEED A SINGLE VOICE

The aim of a single voice is to provide leadership and a sense of mission that would attract the support and contributions of the many whose sense of a common goal and purpose would elevate the profession to the prominence it deserves. Contrary to stifling differing views, a single voice serves, as one of its primary functions, the role of discerning and coalescing the

basic principles of interior design and its practice, providing guidance on regulatory initiatives (after collaboration with other affected parties), and disseminating this knowledge to the profession and the public.

Presently, much of the interesting conversation about the field seems to be in the form of ephemeral brainstorming sessions, the content of which dissipates even as the participants leave the discussion. Progress seems unlikely unless a diverse, collaborative body is charged with a continuing mandate to study the profession with a view to formulating the field's and the profession's core values, its proper scope of study and practice, and its recommended relationship with other professions in the built environment and with society at large. Part of that, of necessity, would embrace the formulation of model legislation and a code of ethics to govern the profession, to the extent that is deemed necessary or desirable. Although this approach would take years to bear fruit, the alternative appears to lead to more decades of wheel-spinning. Furthermore, if progress is to be made, it seems obvious that the profession must lift its eyes to a farther horizon. That means, among other things, that the valuable time and other resources expended in intramural discussions among the leadership of interior design professional organizations should be spent developing collaborative techniques among other members of the supply chain that ultimately serves the client.

Without overcoming the roadblocks and making progress along the lines described, the social, political, and economic heft of the interior design profession will remain negligible. This profession has not yet even been able to convince architecture of its merits, so much so that the identity *interior designer* remains anathema to many architects who helped create the field, but who cling to the prestige of the phrase *interior architect*. The most successful, relevant U.S. trade magazine, *Interior Design*, largely features and extols the work of architects and interior decorators. Even prominent practitioners seem to be more focused on winning architecture merit badges than in educating the profession and the public about the incredible potential arising out of, and the great public need for, the knowledge, experience, and skills of interior design.

A single unifying voice, one which, over time, can clearly define the core values and contributions of interior design, will surely help overcome the barriers that are, in large part, a legacy of the profession's origins. One barrier is the persistent infighting among interior designers with different areas of focus. For some, an all-important issue is one of professional pride, which has been dubbed cultural differences. The gist of this roadblock is that qualified interior designers who do commercial and institutional work believe that their experience sets them apart from, and above, interior designers with the same qualifications who choose to work in a residential setting. This seems to be another example of passing contempt downhill: as architects look down upon interior designers, commercial interior designers (many of whom are architects) look down upon residential interior designers (many of whom are, in fact, interior decorators of various talent and experience, rather than interior designers). But, again, this thinking is rather medieval, and although one might expect this to be prevalent among the general public, it approaches the bizarre to find it among interior designers, who should be well aware of matters that affect residential design, such as:

> Universal design
> Aging-in-place, especially for retiring baby boomers who are expected to remain in their own residences
> Expansion of the home office
> K–12 learning that takes place in the home
> Need for clean air in the home because some figures suggest that indoor air quality is three times worse than outdoor air quality, and asthma rates are dramatically rising
> Need for sustainability in residential construction
> Necessary transference of learning from residential design to institutional residences, and vice versa, for vulnerable populations
> Emerging trend of bringing residential design concepts and crafts to the workplace and workplace products

Another important consideration is that interior design needs the support of furnishings manufacturers and their distributors. We are now in the worst economic environment in the United States since the Great Depression. Yet, the ASID and IIDA rely greatly upon the support of manufacturers and distributors, and money is needed to support other organizations such as the Council for Interior Design Accreditation (CIDA). The simple fact is, there is much to be done and not enough money to do it.

There have been several formal discussions about merger from the early 1990s into 2002, and even informal discussions more recently. When merger talks collapsed between ASID and IIDA in the fall of 2002, one petitioning design group wrote:

> I cannot in good conscience go to our friends in the industry and ask for funds for programs when we are duplicating staffs (national as well as local), energies, programs, initiatives, salaries, time, and efforts. This latest roadblock to unification can only be seen as a refusal to get over saving an organizational structure versus what is best for the profession. I am angry and I am not going to stand for it any longer. (A random walk, 2002)

This sentiment is even stronger in the manufacturing community, a senior marketing executive wrote to me recently:

> Anytime [*officeinsight*] can try to get the Interior Design Industry to realize that they need to come together for the common good, it seems you [*officeinsight*] have tried. We all need to keep trying until the powers-to-be come to their senses. (confidential correspondence with Powell, January 19, 2009)

In the first example, it's a question of dollars, but in a greater sense, it is the frustration of sensible businesspersons as they see their contributions wasted in duplication of effort and nonproductive activities. Moreover, as previously mentioned, this same important source of support and funding is now being subjected to the penalizing effects of the enforcement of the Florida practice act for doing in business what they, and others like them throughout North America, have been doing in the normal course of business for decades without a hint of a threat to the public health, safety, or welfare. (And let me add that the arguments—i.e., code violations—advanced by some proponents of interior legislation in Florida insult the intelligence of those on both sides of the regulatory issue and show a clear lack of understanding of the role of professional regulation in United States and state law.)

The clear lack of progress in getting the general public to be aware of, let alone value, the contributions and potential of interior design can be laid, substantially, at the feet of the interior design professional organizations and their inability to create a clear and convincing voice for interior design and the need for a carefully considered regulatory scheme. Although the profession is admirably behind the movement to save the natural environment, it is sadly unfocused and ineffective in creating a movement for a better, safer, and much needed built interior environment, which, after all, is where most of us spend the majority of our time.

We understand the reasons that design firms and others have for economic protectionism, but that is not the way to a future that is far brighter than the past. Interior design is a noble profession in all aspects of the practice. A single professional voice should speak for the broad interests, talents, and contributions of its members and should build and articulate a strong and credible case for the contribution of the profession and field of study to the public health, safety, and welfare.

REFERENCES

A random walk: Putting all of the wood behind one arrowhead for the interior design profession. (2002, October 14). Unpublished correspondence cited in *officeinsight*. Retrieved May 29, 2009, from www.officeinsight.com

Belluck, P. (2009, February 5). Reinvent wheel? Blue room. Defusing a bomb? Red room. *The New York Times*. Retrieved February 5, 2009, from http://www.nytimes.com/2009/02/06/science/06color.html

Mehta, R., & Zhu, R. (2009, February 27). Blue or red? Exploring the effect of color on cognitive task performance. *Science, 323*(5918), 1226–1229.

Will, G. (2007, March 22). Wallpapering with red tape. *Washington Post*, p. A.

> Interior design is at a crossroads.
What is your "call to action" to sustain
and grow the profession of interior design?

TREVOR KRUSE

GLOBALIZATION, EDUCATION, AND REGULATION

The relatively young profession of interior design is at a crossroads. We have been diligently working on securing title and practice acts where we live and work to protect the public and advance the profession. As we move into the 21st century, there are developments both inside the profession and around the world that may require us to stop our efforts and reflect, analyze, and review exactly who we are and what we do. In this way, we can again move forward with our efforts to advance the profession.

CURRENT STANDARDS AND REGULATION

A couple of issues spring to mind with respect to recent changes in our profession that would appear at first glance to support the profession's current education and experience requirements, but in fact, could actually limit the profession's access to the legislation we seek.

First, there is currently a broadening of educational credentials and work experience, both

TREVOR KRUSE, BAAID, ARIDO, IDC, IIDA, is a principal of Hudson Kruse Design, a Toronto interior design firm. He has volunteered for ARIDO for over 20 years, also serving as president. Kruse has been the chair of IIDEX NeoCon® Canada. In 2007, he received IIDA's Leader Award and was awarded a President's Citation by IDC for his commitment to the Canadian interior design profession. He has served as an adjunct faculty for interior design education programs at various institutions. Kruse has participated in strategic planning, legislative review committees, and the body of knowledge study commissioned by ARIDO (2001). As Ontario's delegate to NCIDQ for many years, he also worked to secure permanent funding for all Canadian provinces to provide delegates to NCIDQ (2007), ensuring 100% Canadian participation. Kruse focuses his dedication, passion, and leadership efforts toward advancement of the interior design profession.

in North American design offices and from broadly experienced practitioners arriving from around the world, which is creating a new global workforce that legitimately practices interior design across international borders. Second, the rush to incorporate technology into interior design education programs over the last decade has resulted in a compression of hours available to both foster the creativity expected of graduates and time available to prepare for the increased complexity of projects, construction methods, and environmental concerns to meet the expectations of potential employers.

Unless they are reshaped and integrated into the profession, issues such as these could actually limit our efforts at expanded legislation for our profession. We should take the time now to review and readjust our vision and expectations regarding education and experience in a global context. Only then will we be able to move forward when looking to governments for expanded regulation to protect the public. Several questions come to mind:

> Do we adhere to traditional and narrow definitions of interior design education to define ourselves en route to increased legislative regulation?
> Do we embrace alternate paths of a global workforce with varied educational paradigms to support an increasingly specialized profession?
> What will strengthen our argument and position when we approach government for increased regulation?

THE STRAIN OF CURRENT EDUCATIONAL STANDARDS ON THE PROFESSION'S ABILITIES

Ironically, the graduates from our current, recognized interior design Canadian institutions, who we are putting forward to government legislators as having a preferred level of education, actually may no longer have the training and creativity that meets the needs of the profession. I currently sit on several advisory councils for interior design education programs, and the ongoing conversation is with respect to appropriateness of education and level of preparedness for the workforce. Our current educational programs may no longer be what we are telling governments they are.

Increased education requirements with an expanded knowledge base grounded in creativity, investigation, and design development with potential for further specialization are the appropriate goals for our growing profession. Yet the education guidelines campaigned for by practitioners may have actually watered down rather than bolstered the knowledge base of graduates. Increasingly, practitioners are demanding more technically competent graduates. In response to this, interior design programs have devolved into a series of technical institutions focusing too much on preparing the graduates to draw documents using technology.

One of the most important pieces of a well-rounded interior design education has always been studio time for investigation and experimentation. Many programs cannot find the curricular balance—or credit hours necessary to meet the requirements of the industry while preparing both creatively curious and technically competent graduates. At the same time, educational institutions are suffering from funding cuts as expenses increase, forcing classes to be cut while programs struggle to remain relevant. Is it possible that the education model we have been holding out as the minimum standard for the profession is actually becoming less rigorous or appropriate? If this is the case, the profession may need to revisit our education requirements. This could be a golden opportunity to broaden our view of education to include alternative paths of diverse educational programs, broadly based experience, and a stronger route to legislation.

Although there is both a desire and a need for increased education and qualification, the profession is faced with a much broader range of educational experiences and alternative paths that fall outside our current definition. Although our present standards help to set the parameters of what an interior designer is, this exclusion may be limiting our ability to achieve regulation and legislation.

It is common that interior design legislative coalitions in jurisdictions set rigid guidelines for professional qualification to demonstrate to the public, government, and allied professions that there are strict requirements to be legislated. This approach may have limiting consequences for the profession as a whole, potentially leaving behind qualified practitioners who become either silent participants in our design teams or vocal opponents to our legislative initiatives.

We understand the need for increasing minimum levels of competency, measured through rigorous education, monitored work experience, and qualifying examinations. However, there are many equally capable practitioners who work side by side with us every day, and whom our pursuits may be disenfranchising. In almost every firm, there are practitioners from different educational backgrounds with entirely different work experiences who are performing the same tasks as a professionally recognized interior designer. This is a large group of professionals practicing interior design who may be unable to meet our narrowing definition of a growing profession. Historically, they may have graduated from architectural schools, architectural technologist programs, environmental studies programs, or have engineering backgrounds.

More recently, these practitioners may have even studied online, utilizing technology to graduate from a distance-learning program, programs that certainly have little or no valid studio experience or instructor contact

as recommended by the Council for Interior Design Accreditation (CIDA). Recently, at the Issues Forum meeting—a collaboration of the American Society of Interior Designers (ASID), CIDA, the Interior Designers of Canada (IDC), the Interior Design Educators Council (IDEC), the International Interior Design Association (IIDA), and the National Council for Interior Design Qualification (NCIDQ)—it was discussed that most American jurisdictions accept these types of distance-learning programs, whereas Canadian jurisdictions do not.

Every week, jurisdictions receive applications from potential candidates who have attended schools around the world with extremely diverse educational qualifications and work experiences, which have landed them in the profession of interior design. Is it legitimate to expect that every practitioner arrive in our profession via an identical syllabus? Could this be seen as unrealistic or even protectionist?

Every regulated jurisdiction in North America has unrecognized practitioners actively working in interior design firms as interior designers. Across the United States and Canada, there are countless interior design superstars who have received wide recognition from both within the profession and the public at large, yet who have not followed traditional paths in meeting the educational guidelines or examination qualifications expected to be titled or to practice interior design. These respected practitioners work not only on residential projects but vast commercial and institutional spheres of design with international scope. As the profession does not formally acknowledge the contributions or the role of these professionals, are we implying that these individuals are not practicing interior design?

For these practitioners with their alternative education and work experience, it is likely that they would continue to find a way to practice by surrounding themselves with staff or allied consultants, even if legislation were enacted in their jurisdictions that limited their official participation in the profession.

Many of these interior designers could become valuable advocates for increased legislation if allowed a path to examination and qualification. Although it is not suggested that the bar be lowered for entry into the profession, it is possible to increase our legitimate professional ranks by developing stringent yet expanded alternative route guidelines.

ALTERNATIVE PATHS

In Canada, there are several colleges with recognized interior design programs that offer three-year diplomas. Due to governmental limitations, these highly recognized programs do not have the ability to offer a baccalaureate degree as preferred by our profession's standards. Potentially, after graduating from these post-secondary institutions, two-thirds of the candidates who try to enter the profession will not be able to participate. We have not recognized their alternative path into the profession. And yet today, many of these graduates are considered as interior designers, working in design firms or running successful firms of their own.

Throughout 2008 and into 2009, several existing laws or initiatives for legislation have been overturned or have met defeat, whereas the profession continues to strengthen its requirements for regulation. On the surface, this effort seems logical; raising the bar should demonstrate to legislators that specific education, appropriate experience, and rigorous examination have defined who we are. However, could this increased and limited definition of interior design competency leave behind thousands of legitimate interior designers with different training, education, and broad experience?

AN INTENTIONAL PAUSE

Because the profession is so young and the workforce so diverse, it is necessary that we reflect on how the interior design profession evolved, and contemplate how it should grow. Interior design as a profession is perhaps a hybrid of knowledge and abilities demonstrated by architect and decorator, artisan and craftsperson, specification writer and salesperson, engineer and detailer, and countless others. Over time, we have decided as a group that the only educational path to merit consideration is the one taught in a recognized interior design program. This automatically negates most other paths to the profession.

As the world workplace becomes more global in nature, invisible boundaries that currently separate us and define who we are by ability and scope will start to disappear. International and national trade agreements may be imposed so as not to limit trade through protectionist approaches. At the highest level of government, "buy American" or "buy Canadian" is no longer a tenable approach for flourishing trade agreements. This has recently been demonstrated in Canada with a newly enshrined law entitled Access to Internal Trade (AIT). The premiers of all the provinces and territories have agreed that all regulated professions across the country will be recognized from jurisdiction to jurisdiction. On the surface, for reciprocity, this appears to make sense.

However, it has undone advances in interior design legislation where progress has been made. Under the new law, all jurisdictions with any kind of regulation will have to observe the jurisdiction with the minimum requirements. Within the profession of interior design, this has tremendous implications. For example, in

TABLE 12.1

PROPOSAL FOR ARCHITECTURAL LICENSURE WITHOUT DEGREE (INTERN ARCHITECT INITIATIVE)

NOW

OAA Council may waive requirements and grant a license for Broadly Experienced Professionals. This is rarely done.

PROPOSED

The benchmark for admittance to the profession for these individuals is to demonstrate skills and knowledge in the areas of design, technology, legal skills, and management equivalent to licensed architects with 15 years' experience beyond graduation.

Those skills and knowledge would be demonstrated as follows:
* Show evidence of 20 years of experience employed by an architect in Ontario
* Submit two letters of reference from architects licensed in Ontario
* Submit a portfolio of architectural work, which would be the basis for the interview
* Candidate and references to be interviewed to verify experience
* Complete the ExAC or ARE

the province of Nova Scotia, where there is a practice act, they must allow professionals from other provinces access to practice there without the need to meet the requirements as outlined in their provincial practice act.

Their current practice act requires a minimum three-year interior design education and completion of the NCIDQ exam, but the AIT legislation overrides this and forces Nova Scotia to accept interior designers from Saskatchewan, a jurisdiction that currently requires only two years of interior design education and completion of the NCIDQ exam. This new legislation effectively lowers the bar for professional interior designers in Nova Scotia and undermines the qualifications achieved by professionals residing in the jurisdiction by allowing lesser-qualified designers to compete at the same level.

Prime Minister Harper released a statement on January 16, 2009, that reads "The revised Labour Mobility Chapter of AIT will provide that any worker certified for an occupation by a regulatory authority of one province or territory is to be recognized as qualified for that occupation by all other provinces and territories" (Office of the Prime Minister, 2009). This allows for reciprocity, but only by lowering the standards to the lowest common denominator across the country.

This Access to Internal Trade law has forced allied professions to consider accepting broadly experienced paths as a viable option toward licensure. The proposed language in Table 12.1 suggests architecture, for example, has already begun discussions of its effect.

Although this issue has not been seen as critical by architects in Ontario, a national discussion has begun. British Columbia has already approved a process for licensure for those without an architectural degree, which reduces reciprocity between the provinces. This initiative would recognize those individuals who achieved the necessary skill levels through experience.

Interior design is a young profession eager to be accepted perhaps to the detriment of advancing the profession. A broader, more inclusive approach could be considered as viable and yet still have the expected rigor required ensuring competency to safeguard life, health, safety, and welfare of the public. Is there an opportunity for the profession to expand the definition of interior design education and simultaneously strengthen our position on health, safety, and welfare for the public?

Increased regulation is inevitable as it is with banking, insurance, and healthcare. Consequently, traditional built-environment design professionals will have to moderate their positions. The interior design profession will have to reconsider who we are and how vastly our education differs from interior designer to interior designer. We will have to find a mechanism that allows the full spectrum of interior designers to become qualified without forcing them back to school for years to be educated about something they already practice. An increased period of monitored experience, or a measurable and quantifiable work experience, should be a realistic expectation. Not only will increased education be a necessity prior to examination and qualification for interior designers, but also the profession will have to continue to expand its body of knowledge. Globalization, education, and regulation should be able to find a recipe for coexistence under the title "interior design."

REFERENCES

Intern Architect Initiative—Improve the Process. *Intern initiative survey results.* Retrieved March 5, 2009, from http://www.internarchitect.ca

The Office of the Prime Minister of Canada. (2009, January 16). *First Ministers endorse full labour mobility across Canada.* Retrieved March 5, 2009, from http://www.pm.gc.ca/eng/media .asp?id=2384

➤ Interior design is at a crossroads. What is your "call to action" to sustain and grow the profession of interior design?

MICHAEL D. KROELINGER

INTERIOR DESIGN AT A CROSSROADS

This essay defines several key interior design education issues that impact why interior design is at a significant crossroads. These collective issues are among many that clearly do, or will, affect the development of the profession and establish its context relative to other design disciplines and their counterpart or allied professions. Educators, designers, and clients must recognize this call to action to sustain and grow the interior design profession as a distinct discipline if it is to thrive in today's rapidly changing world economy. The main issue discussed in this essay is the question of the level of the first-professional degree. Interrelated issues include standards of practice, reshaping accreditation, and revision of standard tools of practice. The final important issue is how the interior design profession is represented to its constituency and to the public through professional organizations. This latter issue clearly demonstrates, in a totally separate way, why interior design *is* at a crossroads.

MICHAEL D. KROELINGER, PhD, FIIDA, AIA, LC, is a professor and the executive dean of the newly created Herberger Institute for Design and the Arts at Arizona State University. Kroelinger has lectured extensively on various aspects of the built environment and has conducted research projects that evaluate how buildings perform and how they should be designed. He maintains relationships with universities throughout the world and is a frequent lecturer on architectural lighting and daylighting. Prior to his faculty appointments, Kroelinger practiced full time and was previously an officer in the U.S. Army. A partner in MK Design Associates in Tempe, Arizona, the firm provides daylighting, energy, and architectural lighting consultation and research. Kroelinger is a registered architect in Arizona and is also lighting certified by the National Council on Qualifications for the Lighting Professions. Kroelinger has a doctoral degree from the University of Tennessee and an MArch from the University of Arizona.

The continued evolution of the requirements of practice, legal regulation (e.g., registration), movement toward 4+2 (four years of undergraduate education plus two years of graduate education), and graduate-education-only models must be considered based on the increased complexity of the knowledge base required for practice. Additionally, any design discipline must consider the rapidly evolving characteristics of teaching, scholarship, and practice as well as resulting implications on what the nature of academic programs may need to become in the future. With an increased emphasis on cross-disciplinary work within universities and increased levels of integrated practice relying on multiple disciplines, design educators should continually assess the nature of academic programs.

This essay places its primary emphasis on consideration of the studio-based, first-professional degree (and not the research-based degree, which deserves separate discussion). *Should more interior design programs consider a shift from primarily undergraduate-based programs to studio-based master's programs?* Increasing complexity of practice is a given, as noted previously. This issue alone could define reasons for a movement to the first-professional degree at the graduate level. Changes in, and the increasing demands of, higher education require more thorough delineation.

Recently, extensive discussion has been presented in the *Journal of Interior Design* regarding graduate education, yet virtually no discussion has emerged regarding the need to consider a graduate versus undergraduate professional program model for interior design. Emerging patterns in U.S.-based universities support this need for reassessment. These items are but a small segment of current issues facing the nature of any academic institution. There has been an increasing tendency to reduce undergraduate programs to a 120-semester credit model, thus restricting the knowledge content of undergraduate professional programs. Although this approach is not yet a universal approach, it does represent an attempt by administrations to increase the percentage of students graduating in a traditional four-year time frame and, at the same time, reduces critical design credits within programs. Although much more limited in the current discussion, a similar exploration of three-year academic program models is also emerging for some disciplines in higher education.

Whereas tendencies of administrative models within universities vary, there is also a current pattern in U.S. public universities to focus closely on retention models as a method of income generation within undergraduate programs, thereby increasing access for more students. These models place more emphasis on retaining higher percentages of students rather than focusing on selectivity and excellence, which is more typical of competitive admission at the upper division level by many undergraduate interior design programs.

The movement toward an "access" model has merit, but in many settings raises questions about the pedagogical focus of undergraduate interior design programs. The one-on-one and one-on-many studio-based model is generally structured around a student-faculty ratio of approximately 15:1. Large enrollments at undergraduate levels and access-based retention models tax the traditional faculty resources found within many undergraduate programs because multiple studio sections are required to meet enrollment.

Increased retention generally means increased resources for a program, but these resources are often only adequate to hire part-time versus full-time, tenure-track faculty. Increases in facility requirements for studio space, especially at upper division levels where students are assigned a specific studio space for the semester or the year versus hot-desk models, often put natural limits on enrollment and are also problematic. Large enrollment lecture classes generally require graduate teaching assistantship support, part-time faculty support, or a significantly larger number of full-time faculty. These large enrollment classes generate tuition revenue, which is often the basis of program funding.

Enrollment growth within programs is clearly valued but can strain programs at a time when qualified interior design educators with appropriate graduate credentials entering education as a career path are limited, even if adequate resources are available. Even more limited are the programs at universities where the budget resources are simply not available to hire needed qualified faculty. Additionally, admitting large numbers of students at lower levels of interior design, and other programs, followed by very selective admission at upper program levels counters the retention and access model.

Although economic conditions tend to cycle, it generally takes universities years to catch up, resource-wise, when positions are frozen, eliminated, or not otherwise available at times when even more pressure exists to increase student retention rates. Graduate student or special fees and increasing tuition charges within many universities are creating the potential of a more realistic resource model for creating excellence and impacting professional programs, thus enhancing the viability of the first-professional degree at the graduate level. In academic settings where other design disciplines reside, interior design students often do not gain the collaborative and cross-disciplinary benefits of working with other design students if the culminating degree in the other disciplines is the master's degree. The dominant example of this later example is a setting wherein the 4+2 master of architecture or the 3+ master of architecture model is in place.

Given this context, *which may or may not apply to all interior design programs*, should undergraduate programs become less studio-focused, thus allowing the emergence of studio-based, first-professional degree at the graduate level? This would ultimately require a rethinking of the accreditation model for interior design (at least in North America), thus causing interior design education to emerge into a degree path model more similar to the 4+2 or 3+ models noted earlier. If larger undergraduate enrollments are maintained, and a studio model stays in place at the undergraduate level, more personnel resources and more studio spaces are essential—a near impossibility in the current economic climate. *Or, could this call for program evolution to allow a total rethinking of the nature of undergraduate and graduate education, thus allowing a new conceptual framework to emerge* that is more closely linked to existing models of other professions—the common examples historically cited have been medicine, pharmacy, and law.

There is not space in this essay to outline proposed degree program structures; rather, I am calling for an active and aggressive dialogue exploring these issues and their impact of the emergence of interior design education at a point in time when the profession is at a clearly identifiable crossroads.

INTERRELATED ISSUES

Three interrelated issues feed into, or from, an exploration of the nature of first-professional interior design education and, therefore, of practice:

1. There is the need for more rigorous standards for practice, including more universal professional development criteria that work with state-by-state registration or certification.
2. There is the need to reshape accreditation to accommodate first-professional, studio-based, graduate interior design programs.
3. There is the need to move to a foundation of building information modeling (BIM) as a standard tool for practice, thus allowing interior design to assume a more direct role within integrated design practice, which is now or soon will be required for large-scale projects.

The latter point has a significant impact on competency areas that are minimally required for interior design education because BIM should not be viewed as a straightforward replacement for CAD-based construction document production. Simply put, BIM requires a sound understanding of building assemblies, construction details, and materials and techniques. Many existing interior design programs introduce, but do not thoroughly address, these aspects that are so vital to designing and building complex buildings and interior spaces. These three points are cyclical, not linear, in nature. For example, increased core knowledge in how a building or space is assembled and constructed must directly impact minimum accreditation standards.

THE FINAL ISSUE: REPRESENTATION OF THE INTERIOR DESIGN PROFESSION

In the United States, the interior design profession continues to be primarily represented through two interior design organizations—the American Society of Interior Designers (ASID) and the International Interior Design Association (IIDA). Whereas each of these associations should be commended for the excellent work they do as advocates for the profession, *it is well past the time in the evolution of interior design as a profession for its representation to be served by one professional organization.* This body needs clear, distinct, and achievable goals that help nurture and develop the profession and provide advocacy with related professions through one voice. Sadly, as late as publication time for this essay, efforts to bring the two organizations together have again failed. Two large organizations with significant overlap in agenda, staffing, resource needs, and membership targeting the same audience simply cannot separately lead the discipline and profession past its current crossroads. The staff and organization of both associations are excellent. Programs and activities do vary from one to the other, but a collective single new organization combining the best of both is absolutely essential. It is time for the leadership of both organizations to set aside whatever differences or values exist and move forward. We elect our association leaders to set examples, lead the profession through challenging times, and address the future needs of the profession. The current and future members of the profession expect it!

Let the dialogue begin on this series of issues. They certainly give the opportunity for varied opinions, positions and, most importantly, actions!

CAREN S. MARTIN &
DENISE A. GUERIN

EPILOGUE:
FINAL THOUGHTS

I believe that if you don't want to do
anything, then sit there and don't do it,
but don't expect people to hand you
a corn beef sandwich and wash your socks
for you and unzip your fly for you.

—Shel Silverstein

The issues discussed in these chapters by the essay authors are interrelated and often get mixed up with one another. You undoubtedly noticed this overlap in the essay content between chapters and among issues. These relationships may not have been explicitly stated by authors, but are implicit in our understanding of the forces that affect our future.

The need to regulate interior design practice is based on our ability to protect the public's health, safety, and welfare, which is not always understood because of the perceived identity of interior designers as contributors to aesthetics only. This brings up the need to define the value proposition of interior design, which could be based in evidence from the body of knowledge (BOK). However, the need has been pointed out to further document the BOK at all stages in the career cycle from entry-level to embedded knowledge of the experienced practitioner.

Then, as our world has become more complex and the design of the built environment adds layers, the challenge to deliver first-professional degree education has come to a crisis borne of new knowledge, increased student numbers, and decreasing faculty numbers;

we have reached a crisis. Add to this the idea that practice has changed significantly by new approaches of evidence-based design, technology, and sustainability—all of which assumes that interior design brings value to built environment teams and projects. This, of course, is based on the idea of design thinking, i.e., the ability to be creative and innovative. And, our capabilities as strategic, holistic thinkers, the process being heralded by those outside of design as the holy grail of problem-solving processes, are something we have used for generations!

Globalization and diversity underpin these overt concepts—we are a globalized profession that could learn much from our worldwide counterparts but we seem to be ethnocentric, which may be based on the fact that in North America we are not a racially, ethically, or culturally diverse profession. Finally, tie this up with a look at what happens to practice, education, and research when the legal and ethical issues are brought into the conversation—are these challenges or opportunities to learn and grow?

Learning about the issues that face the interior design profession is achievable; you have a good start here, and there are a host of other resources, both publications and people, from which you can learn. What is not easy is jumping in to become involved because of difficulty in focusing on one issue. There is obvious overlap between the complexity of the interior design profession and the influences that steer us on our way.

However, it is essential that we celebrate these complexities and be prepared to do something—to not expect others to do it for you. Where will we be in 10 years as current leaders grow weary or retire if *you* do not emerge as a leader and tackle these issues in a planful, systematic way? Don't wait for others to "make your sandwich" or "wash your socks." We are *designers*—we can design our own identity. We are *creators*—we can create our own value. We are *planners*—we can plan the right strategies to meet the challenges of education. We are *thinkers*—we can promote design thinking as a way to solve society's problems.

The interior design profession is evolving and maturing. Many books about the history of the profession exist, but none of these interpret, appreciate, or critique where the profession is *today* and *where it might want to go* in the future. *The State of the Interior Design Profession* can provide ideas about where you want to focus your leadership. It will also inspire individuals to step forward as leaders.

We believe this book should be the desktop reading of every interior design industry leader, their employees, and the new generation of interior designers. It provides access to current perspectives about the state of the interior design profession to design firm owners, design managers, project managers, junior and senior-level designers, architects, business professionals, industry leaders, manufacturer representatives, academicians, legislators, and the media. This is the first and only book that brings together a majority of the interior design profession's current issues and challenges with recognized thinkers and emerging leaders who are working on these issues and opportunities for the profession's future in a comprehensive, intelligent conversation. *You*, too, need to engage in the dialogue and debate; the interior design profession needs *you*!

INDEX OF CONTRIBUTORS

INDEX